Royal Netherlands Academy of Arts and Sciences
Social Science Information- and Documentation Centre

Centre for the Study of Social Conflicts (C.O.M.T.), State University of Leiden

Alex P. Schmid

POLITICAL TERRORISM

A RESEARCH GUIDE TO CONCEPTS, THEORIES, DATA BASES AND LITERATURE

With a bibliography by the author and a world directory of
"Terrorist" organizations by A. J. Jongman

North-Holland Publishing Company – Amsterdam

Transaction Books, New Brunswick (USA), distributors for the Western Hemisphere

ISBN 0 4448 5602 1

C.O.M.T.-Publication No. 12.

For information, address

      Sociaal-Wetenschappelijk Informatie- en
      Documentatiecentrum (SWIDOC)
      Herengracht 410
      1017 BX Amsterdam, The Netherlands

      Transaction Books
      Rutgers – The State University
      New Brunswick, New Jersey 08903
      United States of America

      Centre for the Study of Social Conflicts (C.O.M.T.)
      Hooigracht 15
      2312 KM Leiden, The Netherlands

Printed by Krips Repro, Meppel, the Netherlands for the Editorial Dept. of the
Royal Netherlands Academy of Arts and Sciences

First printing, January 1984

TABLE OF CONTENTS

I. C O N C E P T S

II. T H E O R I E S

III. D A T A   B A S E S

IV. L I T E R A T U R E

LIST OF TABLES AND DIAGRAMS

OVERVIEW OF AUTHORS WHOSE DEFINITIONS ARE LISTED CHRONOLOGICALLY IN APPENDIX I (pp. 119-158)

Alexander & Finger 1977
Anonymous (n.d.)
Arendt 1951, 1970
Aron 1966
Bassiouni 1979, 1981
Bell 1978
Bite 1975
Bonanate 1979
Bouthoul 1975
Cerny 1975
Chisholm 1948
Clutterbuck 1977
Crenshaw 1972, 1978, 1981
Crozier 1960, 1974
Dallin & Breslauer 1970
Evans & Murphy 1978
Fairbairn 1974
Fallah 1981
Fearey 1976
Francis 1981
Friedlander 1980
Fromkin 1975
Funke 1977
Furlong 1981
Gaucher 1965
Greisman 1977
Gross 1972
Guenther 1972
Hacker 1973, 1980
Hamilton 1978
Hardman 1936
Hazelip 1980
Herman & Van der Laan Bouma 1978
Hess 1981
Heyman 1980
Horowitz 1973, 1977, 1977
Iviansky 1977
Jenkins 1975, 1977, 1978, 1979
Jenkins & Johnson 1975
Kaplan 1978
Karanović 1978
Laqueur 1977
Leiden & Schmitt 1968
Leiser 1977
Lodge 1981
Lösche 1978
Mallin 1971, 1977
Mickolus 1977, 1978, 1980
Milbank 1976
Miller 1980

Monday 1980
Morrison 1972
Moss 1971, 1972
Neale 1973
Paust 1974, 1977
Pierre 1976
Pontara 1979
Price 1977
Quainton 1979
Qureshi 1976
Roucek 1962
Russell, Banker & Miller 1979
Schmid & De Graaf 1978
Schreiber 1978
Schwind 1978
Sederberg 1981
Shultz 1978
Silverman & Jackson 1970
Silverstein 1977
Singh 1977
Smith 1977
Sobel 1975
Stohl 1981
Thornton 1964
Tromp 1979
United Kingdom 1974
U.S. Congress, House 1979
U.S. Government 1979
U.S. Task Force 1976
Waciorski 1939
Waldmann 1977
Walter 1964
Watson 1976
Weisband & Roguly 1976
Wilkinson 1973, 1974, 1976, 1977, 1979
Wolf 1976
Wördemann 1977
Wurth 1941
Zinam 1978

OVERVIEW OF COUNTRIES AND TERRITORIES LISTED IN APPENDIX II (pp. 284-416)

Foreword

This volume before you, POLITICAL TERRORISM by Alex P. Schmid, delivers
precisely what is promised by the subtitle: A Research Guide To Concepts,
Theories, Data Bases and Literature. Dr. Schmid has made the task of
researchers in this area both simpler and devastatingly more complex.
It is simpler in the sense that one can now simply go to the Schmid
volume for all the basic definitions, conceptual frameworks, paradig-
matic formulations, and bibliographic sources which are available. Here
then is truly a data base worthy of that much abused phrase. At the same
time, the very monumental nature of this undertaking has an intimidating
quality to all but the most intrepid scholars. It is almost as if the
volume has a sign hanging over it: "All those who enter do so at their
own risk."
It is in the nature of contemporary reality, a reality omnipresent in
its possibilities and prospects for total nuclear annihilation, that
as ordinary human beings we attempt to restore the political act to
human proportions by reducing the proportion of actions. It should not
be forgotten that in all of its infinite shadings and meanings terrorism
permits activities in proportions that can be managed by ordinary individuals. Hence, in some peculiar way the emergence of terrorism as a
major global enterprise in our times is not simply a function of the
ever-present desire for social change, but a strange back-handed recognition that the channels of social change are much harder to manipulate in
a universe of nuclear superpowers and totalitarian superstates. In this
sense, and without either the brutalization or trivialization of the
sentiment for terror, the acute problems terrorism introduces are manageable because of the individual characters and responsibilities of
the act.
As one moves through Dr. Schmid's work, in which terrorism is compared
to all manner of doctrines such as anarchism, and an equal number of
theories in which terrorism becomes the dependent variable for the further
study of imperfect regimes, surrogate warfare, and violence in general,
it becomes evident that this political growth industry of the late twentieth century has a long tradition, a history linking it to the late
nineteenth century, particularly the 1880's and 1890's in which the cry
of the individual against the state took on similar gargantuan and un-
manageable proportions. It is almost as if terrorism has as its latent

function, not so much a general political ideology but a specific re-
minder to the authorities by the anonymous, self-appointed representatives of the masses that those locked outside the political process
will be felt, if not heard.

It is a tribute to Dr. Schmid that he both confronts and yet avoids
falling prey to ideological definitions of the concept of political
terrorism. His work is thoroughly informed by a social scientific attitude, one that appreciates that no given social system has a monopoly
on the uses of political terrorism, and therefore no social system can
claim virtue in one form of terrorism over another. This is not to say
that Dr. Schmid is gratuitously relativistic or blasé. Underneath the
careful analysis and attempted balance is a painful realization on his
part of the victims, the innocents, the non-combatants, who bear the
price of terror but rarely wear the garments of victory.

It is this carefully understated presumption both of the sense of the
sociological and a sense of the humane that raises Political Terrorism
beyond a data base, into a fundamental effort at understanding in its
own right. The temptation to argue the virtues of one form of air piracy
or hijacking over another, or left-wing forms of terror over right-wing
forms of terror, or the simple-minded change of rhetoric in describing
allies vis-a-vis enemies, these convenient linguistic and ideological
failings are avoided by Dr. Schmid. In the very listing and even repetition of the major statements by the leading theorists of terrorism, we
have a subtle indication on the part of Dr. Schmid that there must be
something beyond the self-serving if we are truly to have a social
science recognition of the humanistic potential for cooperation instead
of conflict.

So many services are performed by Dr. Schmid, that one can only single
them out in a brief foreword. His volume includes the extraordinary
collection of information on major political and military movements
developed by Drs. A.J. Jongman. For example, the tendency to think of
the struggle between the Soviet Union and Afghanistan as a rather simplistic one-to-one relationship is dealt a severe blow when one examines
Jongman's tables of Afghanistan political movements: their formation,
tendencies, leaders, strengths, and numbers. The Soviet monolith may be
one, their Afghan opponents are diffuse. The word terrorism has a snappy,
singular ring to it. But when it is probed with care, the researcher
becomes painfully aware of its manifold forms, sizes and shapes. When

the reader reaches this level of understanding, he can better appreciate just how complex is the phenomena being studied and collated by Dr. Schmid. It is thus a simple act of becoming a better citizen to become aware of the materials contained in this truly encyclopedic effort. The volume also includes a bibliography containing more than 4000 separate entries that cover the world-wide literature with remarkable thoroughness.

I looked in vain for a major research grant underwriting this research. It would appear that other than a relatively small pair of grants from the Ministry of Education and Sciences and the Ministry of Home Affairs of the Netherlands, no other fiscal support was forthcoming. True enough, academic figures the world over contributed their knowhow and information to Dr. Schmid. However, ultimately this is a labor of love on a subject that hardly invites a casual use of the word love. This becomes then an even more amazing achievement in terms of the sheer volume of material covered, coupled with the relative paucity of support funds. Here again we are confronted with a curiosity: the imagination, drive and will of a single individual brought such a work into fruition. It was not the sort of team work, or collective effort, that has become customary in large, big time social science research projects that made this volume possible; but the reverse: a singular commitment to study a problem. There is almost a quality of putting together the Oxford English Dictionary in this compendium. Alex P. Schmid may well turn out to be the James A.H. Murray of this peculiar field. For like Murray, Schmid may not be the first to see the full range and nature of the subject of terrorism (or in Murray's case, language), but he is certainly the first to organize the details, arrange the old materials, and conceptualize the new in a Scriptorium that will stand for many years as a quintessential effort to gather the facts, theories and histories of terrorism as event and ideology. Schmid has done so in such a way as not to prejudge outcomes, but make possible new interpretations. This work reverses the ancient Greek maxim that a large book is a great evil. It compels a reverse modern maxim: This is a large book which is in fact a great good.

One is left at the end of this academic journey with a distinct feeling that no matter how hard Dr. Schmid tried to isolate and place terrorism under a political microscope, that the fact remains that terrorism is part and parcel of the political process as a whole. Indeed, terrorism forms a seemless web with those dedicated to the maintenance no less than those pledged to the overthrow of established authority. If this compendium does not necessarily bring us any closer to a universal theorem of violence, it does bring us much closer to a practical appreciation of terrorism as part of the political process - past and present -, for better or for worse. Before we attempt to celebrate or eradicate this tactic-turned-principle, we would be wise to understand and evaluate. Schmid's volume provides us with an opportunity to do just that.

Irving Louis Horowitz
Rutgers University

Acknowledgements

This study has been made possible by grants from the Ministry of Education and Sciences and the Ministry of Home Affairs of the Dutch government. It is unusual that a government provides grants with no strings attached for the study of a controversial subject like terrorism and especially when it is for basic conceptual work rather then for an applied study directly relevant to government policy. Though unusual it is not unwise: when not enough attention has been given to the conceptual and theoretical groundwork in a new area of study, more practical work is likely to be built on sand and suffer from the absence of an adequate framework for analysis. My first thanks therefore go to those officials of the Dutch government who shared this view and made this Research Guide to Political Terrosrism possible.

I am equally indebted to A.J.F. Köbben, director of the Centre for the Study of Social Conflicts at the State University of Leiden for supporting wy work. Thanks are also due to J.F. Brand for his organizational support and his help with the content analysis and the computer bibliography. With regard to the latter, I also wish to thank, C. Bronsveld, J.F.A. de Graaf, as well as P. de Guchteneire, J. van 't Hof and R. de Vries from the staff of the Steinmetz Archives - SWIDOC. Two persons have to be singled out, for without them the computerized bibliography would never have seen the light of white paper. At the Centre for the Study of Social Conflicts in Leiden, Maartje Wildeman's circumspect organization kept the enterprise from stranding and at the Steinmetz Archives - Amsterdam, Henk Schrik's technical expertise and singular dedication made a timely realization possible.

E. Méjan and A.C.M. van der Poel who typed out the manuscript also deserve special mentioning.

I have benefitted greatly from the collaboration of fifty social scientists active in the field of terrorism research. By answering a lengthy questionnaire they have helped me to gain a better insight into the state of the literature on terrorism than would have been possible if I only had my own judgement to follow. Some of them wish not to be named, a request I of course have to honour. Their contribution has, however, by no means been minor to the one of the other respondents whom I wish to thank herewith: C.C. Aston, A. Blok, L. Bonanate, R.L. Clutterbuck, M. Crenshaw, V. Dimitrijević, Y. Dinstein, E.S. Efrat,

S.T. Francis, J. Gleason, L.C. Green, W. Hahlweg, H. Hess, T. Hondrich, the Institute for the Study of Conflict, J. Lador-Lederer, B.M. Leiser, J. Mallin, A. Merari, M.I. Midlarsky, M. Monday, M. Morris, F.M. Ochberg, G. Pontara, U. Rosenthal, A.P. Rubin, P.C. Sederberg, M. Stohl, K. Tomasevski, V. Vasilijevic, Ch. G. Wilber, P. Wilkinson, J.B. Wolf, T.R. Young and Z. Zofka.

Special thanks go to H. Daudt, Ph. Schlesinger and H. Tromp for commenting on a draft version of this study.

While they all helped to make this a richer book, the responsibility for its shortcomings rest with me alone.

Leiden, June 1983.

"Rule by terror, a familiar process in history, has virtually escaped systematic analysis. Working for the modern state, this old scourge of human communities destroys men for the same ends it once achieved as the instrument of immemorial despots. This form of power remains at the edges of rational inquiry, but the experience of recent times, punctuated by terroristic outbreaks and burdened by regimes of terror, makes the world tremble with an awareness that seeks general explanations."
(E.V. Walter, 1969.) [1]

Introduction

The newcomer to the field of terrorism research has to find his way with little to guide him. There is no clear and generally accepted definition of what constitutes terrorism to begin with. Its relationship to other concepts like political violence, guerrilla warfare, political assassination, etc. is insufficiently clarified. The theories which attempt to explain the occurrence of state terrorism or the rise of insurgent terrorism are widely dispersed in the psychological, historical, sociological, criminological and political science literature and the newcomer to the field is likely to waste much time before he gains an overview of the state of thinking. He might get stuck with conspiracy theories or with the older frustration-aggression theories which both contribute little to the understanding of political terrorism. When the newcomer has arrived at some theoretical framework and he would like to test his hypotheses empirically he is likely to find little or no uniform and trustworthy data that are in consonance with his working definition of terrorism. Yet in many cases the data are somewhere and it is a question to locate them and to obtain access to them. Familiarity with concepts, theories and data-bases is usually resulting from a first-hand knowledge of the literature. In the case of political terrorism this literature is spread over several disciplines and also over several languages. Although the Anglo-American output dwarfs all others, some of the more interesting contributions have been made by non-English language authors.
The purpose of the present volume is to bring the main concepts, theories, data-bases and literature together in one volume so that

it can serve as a research guide to newcomers in the field. This is done in the hope that research on political terrorism can be made more cumulative when researchers have some common orientation provided to them.

J. Bowyer Bell, a maverick among the researchers of terrorism, has written some years ago:

> "The academic response to terrorism has been ahistorical, exaggerated, and closely associated with congenial political postures. There is no consensus on the bounds of terrorism: some observers define as terrorism nearly every act of disruptive violence and ignore violence by established regimes; some scholars want psychopaths and criminals to be examined and others do not; and there are those who, defending a cherished cause, deny that their patriots are terrorists. (...) No one has a definition of terrorism. In academia, the various concerned disciplines could not even define "terror" or the basic causes of the phenomenon, or the best means of approach to analyze it." 2)

This judgement is in the meantime six years old but the state of the art is not much higher now than it was then. The present study is a modest effort to take stock of the state of research. Although this writer could profit from the insights of fellow researchers in the field [3], this is, in essence, a personal effort. An exception to this forms Appendix II, which contains a directory of "terrorist" organizations and other groups, movements and parties involved in political violence. It has been compiled by A.J. Jongman from the Polemological Institute of the State University of Groningen.

Notes

1) E.V. Walter. Terror and Resistance. A Study of Political Violence. London, Oxford University Press, 1969, p. 3.

2) J.B. Bell. Trends in Terror: The Analysis of Political Violence. World Politics, Vol. 29, no. 3, April 1977, p. 447, 481.

3) A lengthy questionnaire was mailed to some 200 researchers in the field of Political Terrorism. Fifty scholars answered our questions on conceptual, theoretical and data problems. Their answers have been used both as touchstone for our own ideas as well as a source of information. While not all wanted to be quoted with attribution (hence a number of anonymous quotes in the text) and some provided background information only, the overall contribution of these scholars from eleven nations has been substantial. Their background varies from Criminology, to Political Science, Law, Philosophy, Sociology, Psychiatry, Antropology, International Law and International Relations and Decision Sciences. In terms of national origin the distribution is as follows: 21 of them are residing in the United States, three in Canada, nine in the United Kingdom. Of the remaining seventeen, four are from the Netherlands, three from Yugoslavia, the German Federal Republic and Israel respectively; Australia, South Africa, Sweden and Italy provided one respondent each.

I. CONCEPTS

On Definition in General and Terrorism in Particular

A definition is basically an equation: an new, unknown or ill-understood term (the definiendum) is described (defined) by a combination of at least two old known, understandable terms (the definiens) [1]. If the right side of the equation contains less than two terms the equation is not a definition but a synonym, a translation or a tautology. A definition says what a word is meant to mean.

For a time it was thought that words and things stood in some one-to-one relation to each other: that an object or phenomenon had some real property, characteristics or essence which could be discovered and described [2]. The opposite view we find in Lewis Carroll's Alice in Wonderland: that words mean what you claim them to mean [3]. The result of such idiosyncratic usage of words would be babylonic. In general, the meaning of a term is established either by decree (like in law) or by some less visible process. Usually users of words achieve some agreement as to a meaning of a term after some time following the introduction of a new word (this meaning, however, is not fixed for all time). In many, even in most situations, the adoption of a standard meaning is just a matter of convenience. In other cases, however, controversy arises to the true meaning since the connotations of a word involve social approval or disapproval. The word "aggression", for instance, was an uncontroversial word in international law usage up to World War I because war was considered to be an acceptable activity of nations states, deriving from the inherent rights of sovereignty. From the Versailles Conference until the 1970s when the United Nations arrived at a legal definition of international aggression the meaning of the term was disputed and the interpretation of the meaning is still a matter of controversy [4].

Berger and Luckmann have offered some suggestions why definitions are controversial. "The edifice of legitimations", they write, "is built upon language and uses language as its principle instrumentality" [5]. Language, in this view, is not a neutral vehicle between the brain and the world, it is a cultural artifact. As such it orders the structure of things for those who accept its terminology. In the words of Berger and Luckmann:

> "It locates all collective events in a cohesive unity that includes past, present and future. With regard to the past, it establishes "memory" that is shared by all individuals socialized within the collectivity." 6)

When groups or individuals have different interests in a situation, the definition of one and the same situation has - given the legitimizing function of words - implications for the situation itself and its permanence. As the Thomas theorem puts it: "If men define situations as real, they are real in their consequences" [7]. This raises the question of the "defining agency", the holder of definition power in a given situation. He who has this power can, especially if those who utilize his definitions are not aware of the origin of the definition, exercise a hegemony in the sense described by A. Gramsci:

> "An order in which a certain way of life and thought is dominant, in which one concept of reality is diffused throughout society in all its institutional and private manifestations, informing with its spirit all taste, morality, customs, religious and political principles, and all social relations, particularly in their intellectual and moral connotations." [8]

The question of definition of a term like terrorism can not be detached from the question of who is the defining agency. Three American authors have written "The ideal definition is one that both the adherents and abhorrers of terrrorism could agree upon" [9]. Yet we are not living in an ideal world but in a world where people have conflicting interests. The best we can hope for is a definition which is acceptable to social science analysts, leaving the political definition to the parties involved in terrorism and counter-terrorism. Terrorists rarely use the word terrorism at all (Carlos Marighela was exceptional in this regard) when referring to their own activities. Governments, on the other hand, have great definition powers. Chomsky and Herman claim that

> "The words "terror" and "terrorism" have become semantic tools of the powerful in the Western world. In their dictionary meaning, these words refer to "intimidation" by the "systematic use of violence" as a means of both governing and opposing existing governments. But current Western usage has restricted the sense, on purely ideological grounds, to the retail violence of those who oppose the established order. (...) In the 1970s this usage has been institutionalized as a device to facilitate an exclusive preoccupation with the lesser terror of the alienated and the dispossessed, serving virtually as a disguised form of apologetics for state terror and client fascism. Many analysts simply define "terror" as retail and unofficial terror, and will talk of nothing else. (...) This terminological decision affords endless possibilities for dredging up incidents of anti-establishment violence and for demonstrating its frequent senselessness and lack of specific connection with any injustice, while enhancing the general disregard for the wholesale terror of the established states." [10]

According to these authors the defining agents are "the powerful in the Western world". One of the targets of their analysis is Walter Laqueur, Chairman of the International Research Council of the Center of Strategic and International Studies, a think tank in Washington D.C. with close

links to the U.S. government and intelligence community. In Laqueur's view
there is no defining agency but a babylonic confusion of meanings. He
refers to

> "... the vagueness - indeed the utter carelessness - with which the
> term is used, not only in the media but also in government announce-
> ments and by academic students of the subject. Terrorism is used as
> a synonym for rebellion, street battles, civil strive, insurrection,
> rural guerrilla war, coup d'état, and a dozen other things. The indis-
> criminate use of the term not only inflates the statistics, it makes
> understanding the specific character of terrorism and how to cope with
> it more difficult." 11)

The confusion Laqueur notices, however, is a one-directional one: all synonyms he utilizes denominate anti-government forms of violence so that
it is not impossible to deduct from this statement that "the powerful in
the Western world" can label all sorts of violence against the state "terroristic". In his standard work on Terrorism Laqueur himself concentrates
almost exclusively on anti-government violence.
Another analyst of terrorism, the Italian political scientist Luigi
Bonanate, notices the existence of a labelling proces which stands as
substitute for analysis:

> "... deciding whether an action is terrorist ... is more the result
> of a verdict than the establishing of a fact; the formulating of a
> social judgement rather than the description of a set of phenomena." 12)

A third analyst of terrorism, J. Bowyer Bell is equally aware of the definition problem, although he sees less pressure from the state or from society on the users of the term:

> "The very word [terrorism] becomes a litmus test for dearly held be-
> liefs, so that a brief conversation on terrorist matters with almost
> anyone reveals a special world view, an interpretation of the nature
> of man, and a glimpse into a desired future. Some of those who write on
> terrorism seem to notice this, but many, including my academic col-
> leagues, often do not, oblivious to the fact that they are shaping
> analysis into advocacy." 13)

While Bell does not address himself to the narrower problem of definition
but rather addresses the discourse on terrorism, another scholar, a
sociologist, whose main work lies outside the field of terrorism, has
stated:

> "... I should like to argue that no commonly agreed definition can in
> principle be reached, because the very process of definition is in it-
> self part of a wider contestation over ideologies or political objec-
> tives. I do not therefore believe that cumulative research on an empi-
> ricist scientific model is possible. I do not, however, mean to argue
> that this means that the subject cannot advance through debate, nor
> that intellectual frameworks are necessarily so incompatible that every-
> one must plough his own furrow."

This response came in answer to a question in our questionnaire (see p.3, nr. 3)
("Do you find that endeavours to come to commonly agreed upon definitions
in the field of Political Violence in general and Terrorism in particular
are a) a waste of time; b) necessary precondition for cumulative research;
c) other"). Six of our fifty respondents chose the first option, 28 the
second (though four of them used some qualifiers) while thirteen chose for
the third possibility, with comments as "... it is entirely acceptable to
have different schools within the discipline which use differing definitions", "desirable but not necessary" or "helps clarify the political
character of language and social research and is therefore most useful".
From this it would seem that Walter Laqueur's view that "... disputes
about a comprehensive, detailed definition will ... make no notable contribution toward the understanding of terrorism" is not universally
shared [14].

The problem is in our view not one of comprehensiveness or degree of detail of a definition. The problem is which general framework is chosen
for definition. Laqueur himself has made a choice in this regard when he
writes "terrorism grew out of the time-honoured tradition of tyrannicide
..." [15]. In the introduction to his book on terrorism - in all probability
the most influential book written on the subject - he rejects another
framework, namely the (urban) guerrilla warfare conceptualization: "This
essay grew out of a study of guerrilla warfare, and the conclusion that
urban terrorism is not a new stage in guerrilla warfare, but differs from
it in essential respects, and that it is also heir to a different tradition." [16] Another author, J. Bowyer Bell uses a different framework in
his 1978 book wherein terror is equated with "revolutionary violence". On
closer inspection it turns out that he alludes to several frameworks since
he equates terror with "a form of political violence that falls between
war and peace and offers a model for madmen and criminals ..." [17], although the "revolutionary violence" paradigm is the dominant one for Bell.
To define, we have said earlier, is to explain something new by something
old, adding the distinctive feature. In this way the new object or phenomenon becomes embedded into a known framework of reference, is situated
into the order of things. Basing ourselves on the previous paragraph we
can already discern some common reference categories, such as:
1. terrorism = tyrannicide + something else
2. terrorism = (urban) guerrilla warfare + something else
3. terrorism = violence + revolution

4. terrorism = war + something else

5. terrorism = crime + something else

6. terrorism = madness + something else

7. terrorism = violence + politics

The problem which raises at this point is twofold: 1. which framework
(if any or any single) is the appropriate one for defintion, and 2. what
is the "correct" meaning of the known term like violence? Everybody "knows"
what "violence" is when he is a victim of it but in the social sciences
the meaning of violence is not fixed. Johan Galtung has written that
"... it has at least not happened to the present author to encounter any
pair of researchers in the field using the same definitions. There is not
even any single tradition that has crystallized as the dominant one, with
others competing for recognition...." [18]
J. van der Dennen, in a conceptual study on aggression and violence and
related terms lists no less than 48 definitions of violence. Which one,
if any, is meant in the third or 7th equation above?
In the following section we will have a closer look at the meanings of
violence. Then we shall proceed to look at some of the other reference
categories such as crime, guerrilla warfare and assassination.
This procedure, it is hoped, will help us to reduce confusion on the
concept of terrorism. The ensueing discussion is not conducted with the
tools of contemporary analytical philosophy. In retrospect I have to
admit that it could have benefitted greatly from the method applied by
Felix E. Oppenheim in his "Political Concepts. A Reconstruction" [19].
Unfortunately his work only came to my notice when this study had been
completed.

Notes

1) Helmut Seiffert. Einführung in die Wissenschaftstheorie. Vol. 1, München, Verlag C.H. Beck, 1971, p. 33-34.

2) Paul David Reynolds. A primer in theory construction. Indianapolis, 1971, p. 48.

3) Cit. Yngve Lithman. On Culture and Identity. Stockholm, EIFO, 1982, p. 1.

4) A. van Wynen Thomas and A.J. Thomas. The concept of aggression in international law. Southern Methodist University Press, Dallas, 1972; cit. J.M.G. van der Dennen. Problems in the Concept and Definition of Aggression, Violence and Some Related Terms. Groningen, Polemological Institute, 1980, p. 95.

5) P.L. Berger and Th. Luckman. The Social Construction of Reality. A Treatise in the Sociology of Knowledge. Garden City, N.Y., Doubleday, 1966, p. 64.

6) Berger and Luckman, cit., J. Veenma and L.G. Jansma. Molukkers in Nederland: beleid en onderzoek. Mens en Maatschappij, jg. 53, no. 2, 1978, p. 217.

7) W.I. Thomas. The Child in America. New York, 1928, p. 572; cit. Veenma and Jansma, op. cit., p. 221.

8) G.A. Williams. Gramsci's Concept of Egemonia. Journal of the History of Ideas. Vol. 21, no. 4, 1960, p. 487; cit. R. Miliband. State and Capitalist Society, 1972, p. 180n.

9) Charles A. Russell, Leon J. Banker, J. Bouman and H. Miller. Out-Inventing the Terrorist. In: Yonah Alexander, David Carlton and Paul Wilkinson (Eds.). Terrorism: Theory and Practice. Boulder, Colorado, Westview Press, 1979, p. 37n.

10) Noam Chomsky and Edward S. Herman. The Washington Connection and Third World Fascism. Vol. I of:The Political Economy of Human Rights. Nottingham, Spokesman, 1979, p. 85-87.

11) W. Laqueur. Terrorism - a Balance Sheet. Harper's Magazine, March and November 1976, reprinted in W. Laqueur. The Terrorism Reader, 1978, p. 262.

12) L. Bonanate. Some Unanticipated Consequences of Terrorism. Journal of Peace Research, Vol. 16, no. 3, 1979, p. 197; cit. Philip Elliott, Graham Murdock and Philip Schlesinger. Televising "Terrorism": Political Violence in Popular Culture. London, Comedia, 1983 (quoted from draft MS).

13) J.Bowyer Bell. A Time of Terror. How Democratic Societies Respond to Revolutionary Violence. New York, Basic Books, 1978, p. X.

14) W. Laqueur. Terrorism. London, Weidenfeld and Nicholson, 1977, p. 79n.

15) Ibid., p. 262.

16) Ibid., p. V.

17) J. Bowyer Bell, op. cit., p. 3.

18) J. Galtung. The Specific Contribution of Peace Research for the Study of the Causes of Violence. Typologies. Paris. UNESCO, 1975, p. 1 (Mimeo).

19) Chicago, The University of Chicago Press, 1981.

Terrorism and Violence

There is hardly a definition of terrorism wherein the definiens - the
right side of the equation - does not contain the word "violence". The
British Prevention of Terrorism Act, for instance, says: "For purposes
of the legislation, terrorism is 'the use of violence for political
ends'" [1].

In this section we will take a closer look at what is meant by "violence",
basing ourselves in part on the study of J.M.G. van der Dennen whose conceptual work deserves wider dissemination. From his discussion of the
"Problems in the Concepts and Definitions of Aggression, Violence and
Some Related Terms" [2], it becomes clear that many of the definitional
problems plagueing analysts of terrorism can be found back in the scientific and ideological discourse on violence. Van der Dennen writes:

> "Violence has been defined in terms of force, coercive power, autho-
> rity, (il)legitimacy. It has been defined in terms of behavior, mo-
> tives, intentions, antecedents and consequences. It has been defined
> in terms of violation: violation of corporal integrity, violation of
> territorial or spatial integrity, violation of moral and legal inte-
> grity, violation of rules and expectations, even violations of self-
> esteem, dignity, autonomy.
> The concepts of violence comprises phenomena as far apart as a
> drunken embroglio and an all-out nuclear holocaust; and ranges from
> the calculated and instrumental aspects to the impulsive, spasmodic
> and chaotic. The use of the term has been literal, metaphoric, des-
> criptive, explanatory, even prescriptive. The term has been used to
> blame, to indicate disapproval, to vituperate, to inflame passions,
> to mobilize support, to define the guilty party, to justify and con-
> done our own actions. Violence is mostly what others do. Violence,
> like beauty, is very much in the eye of the beholder. 'Violence' has
> more often than not been equated with 'aggression' which, in view of
> the same sorry state of affairs concerning the conceptualization and
> definition of 'aggression', has been to the detriment of both con-
> cepts.(...)
> Then there has been, moreover, a veritable avalanche of adjectives
> and epithets attempting to further delineate and specify the generic
> concept of violence: structural violence, systemic violence, institu-
> tional violence, mental violence, verbal violence, physical violence,
> indirect violence, insurgent violence, incumbent violence, counter-
> insurgency violence, etc. Instead of being instrumental in clarifica-
> tion of the overburdened concept of violence, the epithets have had
> a nasty habit of pushing the concept still further into obscurantism,
> oblivion and utter irrelevance.
> By and large, a similar dissensus haunts the concept of 'political
> violence'." [3]

The implications of this passage for defining terrorism in terms of violence are obvious. In our questionnaire authors of books and articles on
terrorism were therefore asked what their own definition of violence was

or whose definition of violence they found adequate for their purposes. The answers we received from fifty respondents diverged widely. Almost one third of the respondents offered definitions of their own. We would like to reproduce a number of them here:

CLUTTERBUCK: "The use of force to hurt, injure or kill persons or to damage property."

DINSTEIN : "Violence is the unlawful exercise of physical force."

FRANCIS : "Violence is the use or explicit threatened use of means capable of inflicting physical harm to persons or objects for the purpose of obtaining an illegal or socially forbidden goal."

X : "Merely putting one in fear of bodily injury or death would be sufficient to define violence."

LEISER : "Any act of physical destruction that is inconsistent with commonly accepted principles of law and morals."

MIDLARSKY : "An attempted or actual injury (ordinarily not sanctioned by law or custom) perpetrated on persons or property with the actual or intended consequences of effecting transformations either within structures of political authority or within economic and/or social systems."

MONDAY : "Force and/or intimidation."

OCHBERG : "Needless destructive aggression (new definition)."

PONTARA : "An act, as performed by an agent P (person or group) as part of a method of struggle M in a situation of conflict S, is an act of violence = def. 1) there is at least one human being (or more generally a sentient being) Q, such that (I) P's performance of a, in S as a part of M, causes that Q dies, suffers or is injured, and (II) it is in S against Q's will to be killed or made to suffer; and 2) P, in S, believes 1) to be the case.
Note that by "act" is here understood both a commission and an omission, and that the suffering or injury inflicted can be either physical or psychical, or both."

SEDERBERG : "Acts of coercion in violation of the boundaries that define the acceptable use of coercion in social relations."

Y : "Social interaction, characterized by unilateral physical enforcement of demands and expectations by means of direct physical confrontation."

WILKINSON : "The illegitimate use or threatened use of coercion resulting or intended to result in, the death, injury, restraint or intimidation of persons or the destruction or seizure of property ... whether by the state, by factions, or individuals. (Terrorism and the Liberal State, p. 19-23)"

WOLPIN : "Bodily injury."

ZOFKA : "Any act of compulsion, destruction and harm to persons."

Such a wide variation in definitions of violence was also encountered in response to our question "Whose definition of violence do you find adequate for your purpose? Of the 21 authors mentioned by our respondents, only three were mentioned more than once: Galtung received 14 mentionings, Arendt 13 and Gurr 2. For the reader's convenience these three definitions are reproduced here too, although it has to be said that the authors in question used various formulations at different points in time.

GALTUNG: distinguishes between physical, psychological and structural
(1969) violence. Physical violence is directed to hurt human beings
somatically, to the point of killing. Psychological violence
is violence inflicted on the human psyche. He mentions lies,
brainwashing, indoctrination of various kinds, threats, etc.
(...) Structural violence is present, according to Galtung,
"when human beings are being influenced so that their actual
somatic and mental realization are below their potential rea-
lizations ... Violence is here defined as the cause of the difference between the potential and the actual." 4)

ARENDT : "Violence ... is distinguished by its instrumental character.
(1970) Phenomenologically, it is close to strength, since the imple-
ments of violence, like all other tools, are designed and used
for the purpose of multiplying natural strength until, in the
last stage of their development, they can substitute for it.
(...) Violence can be justifiable, but it never will be legitimate. (...) No one questions the use of violence in self-defence
... (...) Power and violence, though they are distinct phenomena,
usually appear together. (...) To sum up: politically speaking,
it is insufficient to say that power and violence are not the
same. Power and violence are opposites; where the one rules absolutely, the other is absent. Violence appears where power is
in jeopardy, but left to its own course ends in power's disappearance. (...) Violence can destroy power, it is utterly incapable of creating it." 5)

GURR : "By violence I mean deliberate use of force to injure or destroy
(1973) physically, not some more general category of coercive actions
or politics, and not institutional arrangements that demean or
frustrate their members. This definition is independent of agents,
or contexts of violence ... There is an element of self-assertion
in almost all acts of violence: a desire to satisfy anger, obtain
revenge, assert pride, create fear in others." 6)

The frequent mentionings of Galtung and Arendt cannot be considered to indicate some consensus. The difficulty with Galtung's perspective is that it is much too encompassing, equating as it does structural violen-ce with "any avoidable suffering in human beings" 7). Arendt's definition on the other hand is, at best, a philosophical one, but not a social science definition. It is internal inconsistent (with regard to self-defence) and the relationship power - violence is problematical. Arendt uses terms like "power" and "violence" as symbols of her idiosyncratic political algebra rather than as conceptual tools, as Smart has pointed out 8).

Both Galtung's ultrabroad definition and Arendt's idiosyncratic definition seem te be questionable points of departure for defining terrorism. Yet at

the same time these are the definitions most often volunteered by the
authors on terrorism in our sample. Gurr's definition, which is a fairly
narrow one, has, with only two mentionings in our sample, no great claim
to acceptance by this forum on terrorism. The partial consensus on Galtung
and Arendt is therefore one of vagueness only. If, however, violence is
the key term used to define terrorism and it is so undetermined or open-
ended, there is little prospect to come to a satisfactory definition of
terrorism.

Perhaps the chief reason for this state of affairs has to be sought in
the discourse on violence. Three levels of discourse can be discerned:

1. the common parlance discourse, expressed in lexical definitions
   of violence,
2. the political discourse, where the use of the term violence has
   often a labelling, guilt-attributing (or glory-claiming) function,
   expressed in legal language and media terminology, and
3. social-sciences discourse where operational definitions are sought
   for hypothesis-testing and theory-construction.

Between these levels, but especially between the second political one and
the third scientific one, there is mutual interference in terms of questions deemed to be in need of investigation as well as in terms of finan-
cing research on some aspects of 'violence' but not on others.

J.H. Skolnik has written:

> "The kinds of acts that become classified as "violent", and, equally im-
> portant, those which do not become so classified, vary according to
> who provides the definition and who has superior resources for dis-
> seminating and enforcing his definitions. (...) The term "violence"
> is frequently employed to discredit forms of behavior considered im-
> proper, reprehensible, or threatening by specific groups which, in
> turn, mask their own violent response with the rhetoric of order or
> progress." 9)

Quite frequently a common perception and framework of reference exists
between the defining agency in the political discourse and the authoritative scholars in the social sciences whose definitions are utilized by
the majority of fellow-scientists.

In many of the definitions mentioned earlier we find, to varying degrees,
echoes of what can be seen as consonance of political and social science
definitions of violence. This is perhaps strongest with scientists with
a legal training. Dinstein, as we have seen, defines violence in terms
of unlawful force and the law also appears as yardstick, either partially
or entirely, in the definitions of Francis, Leiser, Midlarsky. This is a
common feature of many other definitions as well.

Leslie Macfarlane, for instance, says, echoing some usages of Gurr:

> "Violence is the capacity to impose, or the act of imposing, one's
> will upon another, where the imposition is held to be illegitimate.
> Force is the capacity to impose, or the act of imposing, one's will
> upon another, where the imposition is held to be legitimate." 10)

This immediately begs the question "held by whom?". Ted Hondrich who

defines the act of violence as "a use of considerable or destroying

force against people or things, a use of force that offends against a

norm" sees the law as norm for political violence but it has to be the

law of "a state which has authority" 11). Yet is this authority based

on true representation of public interests or on the (covert) threat

of "force"? And what happens if there is no authority or more than one

authority? It is a question to which Michael Stohl addressed himself:

> "We have defined domestic political violence as violence that takes
> place within the autonomous political system. However, within the
> boundaries of a single state more than one political system (a struc-
> ture of allocating goods and services) may exist, and as Nardin (1971)
> discusses in general and Rose (1971) points out in the Northern
> Ireland case, there may exist structures that compete for authority
> within the system. Violence may result from opposing forces attempting
> to impose their authority on the subjects. Thus, violence in practi-
> cal terms becomes a rational instrument in the pursuit of political
> goals." 12)

The reference to competing normative orders, however, throws us back to

the question of a 'defining agency' and 'definition power'.

In fact the problem addressed might be less one of violence per se but

of political violence. We will come back to the question of political

violence with emphasis on political in the following section. The point

to be made here is that the context is important for definition. A medi-

cal definition of violence, for instance, might be rather uncontroversial,

focusing perhaps on the "intentional rupture of human body tissues for non-

surgical purposes".

A clear awareness of the context of a definition and an explicit limita-

tion of the reach of the definition is required to proceed further.

Giuliano Pontara is one of the few in our sample who has kept this in

mind. In explaining his conceptualization of violence he states:

> "In this paper attention will be focused on 'violence' and 'nonvio-
> lence' as denoting methods of struggle, that is actions, courses of
> actions, or activities considered or performed by parties to a dis-
> pute as means of conducting the conflict and trying to achieve the
> ends disputed." 13)

Pontara's goal was to come to a definition which was "adequate in the

context of peace research" 14). Awareness of context saves the researcher

from futile attempt of constructing a universal definition for all times

and occasions. Such awareness we also encounter in the conceptualization
of Baha Abu-baban, presented aptly under the title "The Social Context of
American Sociology and the Violence of the Sixties":

> "A conceptual definition of violence includes the following elements:
> (1) violence is culturally defined (i.e. some violent acts are not
>   viewed with social disapproval),
> (2) it is institutionally sanctioned (in a family situation, parents
>   may be allowed to beat their children),
> (3) it can be covert or overt, verbal or physical (legal manipulation
>   or verbal laceration may be just as painful or injurious as phy-
>   sical assault),
> (4) neither violence nor nonviolence is an absolute (both are a matter
>   of degree), and
> (5) moral indignation regarding violence is xenophobic (violent acts
>   performed by the enemy in times of war are barbarous, identical
>   acts performed by the other side are justified).
> This definition of violence underlines the relativity of the concept.
> Violence against the individual via institutionalized means is more
> often ignored than violence against institutions by individuals." 15)

The distance between the defining social scientist and the political defining agency or the common language definitions can be a source of fric-
tions and misunderstandings. While an author might use a narrow definition
of violence to start with, the reader, belonging to either the political
defining elite or to the common language users group is likely to forget
about the "given" definition in the course of reading and introduces his
own meaning, in consonance with his own interests and experience. The
choice of a narrow or broad definition of violence can have political implications. Grundy and Weinstein refer to this in the following passage
where the problem of manipulation is also raised:

> "The most restrictive definitions tend to confine violence to those
> uses of physical force which are prohibited by a normative order pre-
> sumed to be legitimate, while the broadest definitions expand vio-
> lence to all deprivations of asserted human rights. In between these
> poles is the definition of violence as any use of physical force.
> Ideologists tend to manipulate these definitions in accordance with
> their broader public aims. The most basic pattern is for defenders
> of constituted authority to use more restrictive definitions of vio-
> lence and for opponents to constituted authority to use broader de-
> finitions of violence. (...) Manipulation of these definitions occurs
> when an ideologist or movement goes from one to another over time, or
> when two definitions are used by an ideologist simultaneously. An
> example of the first kind of manipulation is the shift from broad to
> restrictive definitions of violence by former opposition movements
> after they gain power. (...) The use of two definitions simultaneously
> by an ideologist is also widespread." 16)

Based on the above, one could postulate that the minimum distinction between the ideologist and the social scientist would be consistency in the
use of a definition, independent of the perpetrator of acts to be labelled

violent. A violent act such as rape would be rape whether performed by a
stranger or a husband and torture would be torture whether performed in
a campaign to overthrow the ruling order or in the name of law and order
(state-sanctioned torture of prisoners by the British in Northern Ireland
has been redefined as 'inhuman and degrading treatment', which "sounds"
better than torture) [17]. On this basis it would seem that from the following four schools of conceptualization of violence in the social and
political science literature which Van der Dennen identified, the third
would seem to be the most problematical:

1. Violence defined in terms of 'violation' and 'social injustice'
2. Violence defined in terms of 'physical force'
3. Violence defined in terms of 'illegitimate force'
4. Violence as a natural form of political behavior [18]

In the context of this inquiry into terrorism a more extended discussion
of violence is not possible. Our main concern was to direct the reader's
attention to the fact that the main definiens for terrorism is as controversial as the term te be defined. Some of the questions raised here, will
be discussed in the following sections. We would like to conclude this
section with an extended passage from Van der Dennen, wherein he summarizes
his reconceptualization of "aggression" and "violence":

"In my lectures, I have found it very useful
and instructive to conceptualize and visualize
the relationship between aggression and violence as a simple Venn-diagram, as follows:
(1) Adopting the term 'aggression', 'sensu
stricto', as a non-reified, non-unitary motivational construct (2) which generates,
together with other motivations, instiga-
tors, facilitators and inhibitors a (pheno-
menal) category of behaviors (or behavioral
polymorphism) to be called 'aggressive' or
'agonistic' behavior; (3) to be distinguished
from (not coinciding with) 'violence' as the
category of (instrumental) behaviors involving elimination and/or destruction; (4) the
intersection of two sets to be called 'violent aggression'. (The 'universe of discourse'
being 'conflict behavior').

Diagram I: Relation-
ship Between Aggres-
sion and Violence

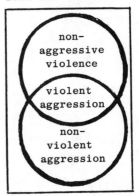

The sets of aggression and violence are to be considered 'fuzzy sets'.
In other words:
- 'Aggression' proper is a motivational construct (whether conceived
  of as 'impulse' or 'drive' or 'attitude' or whatever
- which may, together with other motivations (some synergistic, some
  antagonistic) give rise to a category of behaviors, some of which
  may be labeled 'aggressive behaviors'
- Some of the 'aggressive behaviors' may also be labeled 'violent
  behaviors'
- Most violent behaviors (especially in the political - including
  war - and criminal domains) are not aggressively motivated but are

purposely calculated, instrumental acts only remotely related to whatever motivations might have initiated them (cf. the premeditated homicide versus the 'crime passionnel').

Now focusing on the category 'violence', I found it very instructive to visualize 'violence' as a set of expanding concentric circles of diminishing restrictions, 'hard-cored' but becoming nebulous and blurred at the edges (the outer circles): I. the hard core may be considered to be direct physical violence done to human beings; II. dropping the restriction of 'physical', we may include 'mental violence', menticide, malicious manipulation, etc.; III. dropping the restriction 'direct', we may include indirect forms of violence; IV. dropping the restriction 'human beings' we may include other organisms: organismic violence, cruelty to animals; V. dropping the restriction 'organisms' we may include ecocide, violence done to the environment.

And so on, dropping more and more restrictions we may expand the conception of violence to include VI. violence done to structures, systems, ideologies, etc.; VII. violations of self-esteem, dignity, autonomy, etc.; VIII. ritualized social violence or 'social spoiling', meaning the reduction of viability or individual fitness due to traditions, customs, rites of a population; IX. institutional violence; X. structural violence." 19)

Notes

1) Prevention of Terrorism (Temporary Provisions) Act of 1974.
   cit. E.F. Mickolus, The Literature of Terrorism. Westport, Conn.,
   Greenwood Press, 1980, p. 295.

2) Groningen, Polemologisch Instituut, 1980.

3) Ibid., p. 59-60.

4) Cit. J.M.G. van der Dennen, op. cit., p. 118.

5) Hannah Arendt, On Violence. New York, Harcourt, Brace, Jovanovich,
   1970, p. 46, 52 and 56. - This is the closest thing to a definition
   I could find in her work.

6) T.R. Gurr, The revolution-social change nexus: some old theories and
   new hypotheses. Comparative Politics, Vol. 5, no. 3, 1973, p. 359-392;
   Cit. v.d. Dennen, 1980, p. 118-119.

7) J. Galtung, On Violence in General and Terrorism in Particular. Geneva,
   Unitar, 1978, p. 1 (unpublished paper).

8) I.M.H. Smart, The Power of Terror. Repr. in John D. Elliott and L.K.
   Gibson (Eds.), Contemporary Terrorism. Gaithersburg, Md., IACP, 1978,
   p. 33n.
   As a further illustration of idiosyncratic usage: On one occasion
   Arendt said "Terror is the realization of the law of movement".
   (Cit. Vincent Descombes, Maintenant tout est tranquille. In: Gilles
   Lipovetsky (Comp.), Territoires de la Terreur. Silex (Grenoble),
   no. 10, 1978, p. 24.

9) J.H. Skolnik (Ed.), The Politics of Protest. New York, Simon and
   Schuster, 1969, p. 4.

10) Leslie J. Macfarlane, Violence and the State. London, Thomas Nelson,
    1974, p. 46.

11) Ted Hondrich, Violence for Equality. Hardmondsworth, Penguin, 1980,
    p. 153, 23 and 104.

12) Michael Stohl, War and Domestic Political Violence. The American
    Capacity for Repression and Reaction. Beverly Hills, Sage, 1976, p. 22.

13) Guiliano Pontara, The Concept of Violence. Journal of Peace Research,
    Vol. 15, no. 1, 1978, p. 19.

14) Ibid.

15) Baha Abu-baban et al., The Social Context of American Sociology and
    the Violence of the Sixties. Revue Internationale de Sociologie,
    1973, nos. 1-2, April-Aug., p. 38-62, quoted from a bibliographic
    abstract.

16) K.W. Grundy and M.A. Weinstein, The Ideologies of Violence. Columbus,
    Merrill, 1974, p. 113.

17) Ph. Schlesinger, 'Terrorism', the media and the liberal-democratic
    state. Social Research, Vol. 48, No. 1, Spring 1981, p. 74-99 (quoted from draft MS)

18) Van der Dennen, op. cit., p. 62-73.

19) Ibid., p. 73-74.

What is Political Violence?

Fewer people experience violence than politics. From this one would
guess that people have a more precise notion as to what is "political".
However, the semantic range of the word politics is extremely broad. Originally it referred to common concerns of the citizens in the Greek city
states. In the late 16th century the "politiques" were those lawyers who
pleaded for a neutral and sovereign state power above the parties of the
confessional quarrels [1]. In political science "politics" is usually
defined in terms of one or several of the following concepts: policy,
power, authority, state, conflict and allocation of resources [2]. While
the terms policy, allocation of resources and authority tend to occur in
narrow definitions of what can be called political, the power and conflict dimensions appear more often in broad definitions. Given the wide
semantic field covered by both "violence" and "politics", the expression
"political violence" can mean many things.
We asked members of the research community when they labelled violence
"political violence". Some respondents speak of political violence when
either the goals of the perpetrators are political (e.g. Lodge, Tomasevski,
Green, Clutterbuck) or the motives are political (e.g. Bonanate,
Zofka). One author, a student of Clausewitz, defined political
violence as "total politics" (Hahlweg). Apart from such definitions
which are, strictly speaking, circular, a number of respondents choose
for an explication in terms of power (e.g. Morris, Dimitrijević, Wright).
An example is Youngs explanation: "...when it is used to sustain or oppose a structure of privilege and power". The dimension of authority appears in a definition of Midlarsky: "... when it is directed against
some authority structure", or in a formulation of Grabovsky where it is
used more in the sense of David Easton: "when it is undertaken for the
purpose of influencing the authoritative allocation of values". Surpri-
singly broad is Wilkinson's usage: "... whenever violence is used by
or against state agencies". This can be interpreted to cover inter-state
war as well. The conflict theme turns up in one of the meanings cited
by Lador-Lederer: "... when situated in group-to-group hostilities".
Some authors use the term political violence to refer to - among other
things - a rational motivation (Rubin) and a usage where (personal) material gain is absent (Efrat).
If we look for further guidance as to what political can mean in relation to violence in the literature rather than with the respondents in

our sample, some new themes or at least variations of already mentioned ones appear. Ekkart Zimmermann introduces three criteria which are considered useful as first delimitations, although they are not exhaustive:

1. The number of persons taking part in acts of violence. The higher the number, the more likely that their acts of violence are labelled political.
2. The intention of the actors.
3. The reaction of the relevant community or public. 3)

Another political scientist, Harold Nieburg, distinguishes between the "private violence" which is "frictional" and not likely to escalate when the police tries to handle it, and "political violence" [4]. The latter he describes as:

"... acts of disruption, destruction, injury whose purpose, choice of targets or victims, surrounding circumstances, implementation, and/or effects have political significance, that is, tend to modify the behavior of others in a bargaining situation that has consequences for the social system." 5)

Ted Gurr, one of the leading theorists in this field, uses the term "political violence" to refer to

"... all collective attacks within a political community against the political regime, its actors - including competing political groups as well as incumbents - or its policies." 6)

P. Mars, summarizing the discussion on political violence in the mid-seventies,concludes:

"The concept of political violence as distinct from violence in general has come to represent a combination of all or most of the following elements:
- activities carried out by aggregates of individuals, such as groups or collective movements;
- activities which tend to be more organized in contrast to the completely unorganized or spontaneous type of activities;
- activities which tend to challenge the legitimacy of the governing regime, thus threatening the stability of the political system as a whole;
- activities directed toward change, either of the governing regime itself or of aspects of the political system as a whole;
- activities involving a high probability of resistance and coercive reaction by the governing regime; and
- activities involving a high degree of risk of injury and economic cost to both the participants and the opponents in the political violence process." 7)

Although it does not come out strongly in the definitions cited above, the main research thrust of authors in the field of political violence has been on violence "from below" that is directed against the state authorities [8]. In addition to the anti-state bias of the term, its

usage mainly refers to various forms of domestic violence <u>within</u> polities,   leaving aside organized violence <u>between</u> polities [9] despite
the wide-spread adoption of the Clausewitzian formula of war as "a continuation of political interaction with the admixture of other means".
The few authors who apply the term to interstate violence seem to have
done this more for reasons of classification whereby war is considered
to be a subspecies of the genus political violence. For the majority
of authors the term political violence is more or less coextensive with
"internal war" (Eckstein), "mass political violence" (Hibbs), "civil
strive" (Gurr, Rosenau) or "collective violent action" (Tilly) [10].
From the above discussion we can conclude that the use of "political
violence" as definiens for terrorism poses a number of problems. Firstly,
it could imply that there is no such thing as non-political terrorism.
Secondly, the mass or collective thrust of "political violence" does
not seem to fit well in cases where there is only a very small group
of terrorists. Thirdly, the trans- or international dimension of contemporary terrorism does not come out in concept which is primarily
oriented towards domestic violence. Fourthly, and most important, political violence is as broad if not broader a concept than terrorism and
it seems pointless to define one specific phenomenon with an vague general concept. The attractiveness of using "political violence" to define terrorism stems in our view more from the anti-government thrust
and illegal nature implicit in both concepts than from more scientific
considerations.
The equation of the two concepts tends to mystify rather than to clarify
our understanding of political terrorism. Anthony Arblaster has made
some pertinent remarks on this. In his review of studies on terrorism
written or edited by Alexander, Bell, Burton, Clutterbuck, Dobson, Ellis,
Halperin, Hyams, Schaerf, Styles and Wilkinson, he notes:

> "There is an evident tendency here to equate political violence with
> a single form of such violence - terrorism; and then to imply, or
> to assume, that all terrorism is 'revolutionary' or 'aimed at the
> overthrow of governments'. Neither of these assumptions is valid.
> (...) Nor are war and terrorism the only forms of contemporary <u>poli-</u>
> <u>tical</u> violence. There has been in recent decades a world-wide revival
> in the use of torture, especially against political prisoners. (...)
> So let us be more precise about the subject-matter of the majority
> of the books and essays under discussion here. With the conspicious
> exception of Edward Hyams, and to a lesser degree J. Bowyer Bell
> and Paul Wilkinson, most of these writers are not primarily con-
> cerned with terrorism as such... They are concerned with terrorism
> as and when it is used for political ends which they do not endorse,
> and against states whose legitimacy they accept. (...) Not only do

these studies focus overwhelmingly on counterstate terrorism. There
is also a widespread assumption that terrorism is essentially a
left-wing or revolutionary phenomenon. (...) As Bell acutely notes:
'To the threatened, all revolutionaries are terrorists'. (...) Although terrorism is so clearly a political phenomenon, and one
which evokes strongly political responses, there is a curious way
in which so much writing about terrorism evades the political, pre-
ferring to concentrate on the moral, or tactical or psychological
dimensions of the subject." 11)

... and to the criminal dimension of the subject, we might add. It is

to this aspect that we turn next.

- 24 -

Notes:

1) Bart Tromp, reviewing Meinert Feddema, Ries van der Wouden (Eds.),
   Het Politicologendebat: Wat is politiek. Amsterdam, Van Gennep,
   1982. Volkskrant (Het Vervolg), 5 nov. 1982, p. 16.

2) A. Hoogerwerf, Politicologie. Begrippen en problemen. Alphen a.d.
   Rijn, Samsom, 1979, p. 39.

3) Ekkart Zimmermann, Soziologie der politischen Gewalt. Darstellung
   und Kritik vergleichender Aggregatdatenanalysen aus den USA. Stuttgart,
   F. Enke Verlag, 1975, p. 5-7.

4) H.L. Nieburg, Violence, Law and the Informal Polity. Journal of Conflict Resolution, vol. 13, no. 2, 1969, p. 192.

5) H.L. Nieburg, Political Violence: The Behavioral Process. New York,
   St. Martin's Press, 1969, p. 13.

6) Ted Gurr, Why Men Rebel. Princeton, N.J., Princeton University Press,
   1971, p. 3-4.

7) P. Mars, Nature of Political Violence. Social and Economic Studies,
   vol. 24, no. 5, June 1975, p. 221-239; quoted from abstract provided
   by the U.S. National Institute of Law Enforcement and Criminal Justice.

8) Cf. Herbert Hirsch and David C. Perry (Eds.). Violence as Politics.
   New York, Harper and Row, 1973, p. XII, and U.S. National Advisory
   Committee on Criminal Justice Standards and Goals. Disorders and
   Terrorism. Report of the Task Force on Disorders and Terrorism,
   Washington, D.C., GPO, 1976, p. 4.

9) J.M.G. van der Dennen, Problems in the Concepts and Definitions of
   Aggression, Violence, and Some Related Terms. Groningen, Polemological Institute, 1980, p. 60.

10) Das Gupta Kasturi, A Typological Analysis of Collective Political
    Violence. Ph.D. Thesis. Louisiana State University, 1979, p. 1.

11) Anthony Arblaster, Terrorism: Myths, Meaning and Morals. Political
    Studies, vol. 25, no. 3, Sept. 1977, p. 414, 416, 418 and 421.

What is a Political Crime?

Since terrorism is often labelled criminal and sometimes also defined
in terms of crime [1] it is necessary to take a closer look at political
crime.

The notion of "political offence" plays a special role in extradition
law and the granting of political asylum. While states claim a
"monopoly of violence" within their own territory and persecute the
private use of violence for private as well as public (political)
purposes, they often take a less vigorous stand when private violence
for public purposes is taking place in another state. Sometimes a
government is in fact more in sympathy with the use of violence inside
another state as it is practised by a private group than with the use
made by the official government in power. If a member of such a private
group flees to its territory, this state will not extradite him like a
common criminal who used violence for private, idiosyncratic purposes or
material gain. The fugitive is considered to be a political delinquent
or offender rather than a common criminal. Thus, while most states make
no distinction between common and political crimes for their own citizens,
they often do so for foreign citizens. A practice of granting political
asylum and protecting the rights of political fugitives evolved in the
nineteenth century, perhaps stimulated by considerations of self-interest
by rulers who were facing the prospect of becoming political fugitives
themselves one day.

What was regarded as a political crime in extradition law was generally
the violence exercised as "part of an organized attempt to overthrow
the government and seize power in its place" [2].

In the 19th century it often referred to short urban insurrections in
which the government was toppled or where the rising was squashed.

The losers of such risings had committed political crimes. An interesting
aspect of political crime is that - depending on the attitude of the
court towards the "criminals" - it could lead either to aggraveted
"exemplary" punishment or to preferential treatment (such as the
privileges enjoyed by persons banned by the Tsar to Siberia). [3]

This is probably what one of our respondents had in mind when he rejected
the notion of political crime, arguing that "... the philosophy underlying

this question is the classic approach of political crimes being in some
way redeemable through the absence of any personal interest ..."
The question is, of course, what one wishes to label a "crime". The
principle of Roman Law "nullum crimen sine lege" suggests that no
definition of crime is possible without a law as a yardstick. This "law"
can be what is termed "common" law, a traditional cultural
norm, or it can be a specific law passed on a particular occasion.
Another feature of Roman Law is the distinction between mala per se
(wrong or evil in itself) and mala prohibita (wrong merely because it
is prohibited by statute). The first category generally consists of
capital offences while the second involves misdemeanours and the like
(e.g. traffic violations). A further distinction of importance is that
a crime consists of a criminal act as well as the presence of (criminal)
intent. If the perpetrator of a criminal act is not aware of having
committed a transgression of a set norm he cannot be guilty of the
crime (that is why children and insane people are generally not
punished for criminal acts) [4].
If the "political crime" consists of a prohibited evil only it is likely
that international law does not regard it with the same severity as
national law. Indeed the "crime" might consist of nothing more than
exercising rights laid down for instance in the U.N. Declaration of
Human Rights. M. Cherif Bassiouni speaks in this context of a "purely
political offence" which he defines as

> "one whereby the conduct of the actor manifests an exercise in
> freedom of thought, expression and beliefs (by words, symbolic
> acts or writings not inciting to violence), freedom of association
> and religious practice which are in violation of law designed to
> prohibit such conduct." 5)

This is a distinction which Amnesty International maintains when referring
to respectively "political prisoners" (who have used violence or
propagated the use of it) and "prisoners of conscience"(who would fall
into the category defined by Bassiouni). A distinction between political
and criminal acts has been made by Amnesty International on the
following basis:

> "A political act can be defined as an act in as much as it is
> directed at the furthering of changes in current laws or existing
> government policy. The defence of current laws or current government
> policy is also a political act.

A criminal act is an act which is contrary to penal law in a
particular country for which there is no reason of exempting it
from punishment such as, for instance, circumstances beyond control
or self-defence, which remove the punishable character of the act.
A reason for exemption lies in circumstances which make it
justifiable or for which the perpetrator cannot be held
responsible." 6)

These distinctions, however, still leave it unclear what exactly

constitutes a "political crime". Indeed the concept of political crime

is not universally recognized. Anglo-American law, for instance, does

not recognize political crime as a distinguishable class of crime at

all [7].

Some or our respondents from these countries therefore answered the

question "When do you label an act of violence a political crime?" in

terms such as:

- "A crime is a breach of law, whatever its purpose and whatever view
  may be taken of its justification." (Clutterbuck);
- "A crime is a crime is a crime. The 'political' tag does not change
  the essential nature of the act." (Wilber);
- "Under U.S. law the crime must be dealt with separately, on its
  own merits. The fact that the perpetrator had a political motive
  is of interest only to academicians and researchers - it does not
  affect the legal elements involved."

Another scholar, not in our sample, writing about "Political Crime in

Europe" defined his subject as

"all acts which officials treat as if they were political and
criminal, regardless of their real nature and of the motivations
of their perpetrators." 8)

Such a delegation of definition power to an interested party is hardly

a satisfactory solution. The relationship between politics and crime

requires a better framework for analysis. Already St. Augustin reflected

on it when he asked: "What are states but bands of robbers ... without

justice?" and he went on saying that bands of robbers themselves

constitute a kind of state - presumably because of the difference

between low in-group violence vs. higher violence against out-group

persons. [9]

More recently Stephen Schafer has written:

"In the broadest sense, it may be argued that all crimes are
political in as much as all prohibitions with legal sanctions
represent the defence of a given value system or morality in
which the prevailing social power believes." 10)

One of our respondents also hinted at this nexus when he wrote that:
"... no clear distinction is made where violence as a political means
ends and where the political crime begins" (Hahlweg), adding that
these questions were at present not yet satisfactory solved.
The wide variations of answers provided by our respondents illustrate
this lack of consensus. The question we asked was: "When would you
label an act of violence a political crime?"
These are some of the answers:

- "Whenever it has clear political overtones, not outweighed by
  criminality-for-personal-gain aspects." (Morris)

- "An illegal act with a political motivation or purpose. It is not
  necessarily violent."(Francis)

- "It depends op the municipal or international context. The rules
  of the political game differ in each national community and in the
  international society. A crime signifies gross violation of the
  accepted rules." (Dimitrijević);

- "Whenever the applicable legal system of the place in which the act
  is committed defines the politically motivated violence as a crime
  - thus excluding police and military action to the extent
  authorized by both municipal and international law." (Rubin)

- "In cases where a regime decides to designate any form of political
  dissent or opposition a 'crime'. In Western-type rule-of-law
  democracies nobody is or should be punished for their political
  beliefs. However, it is a fact that some individuals/groups commit
  acts defined as crimes under the ordinary criminal code
  (e.g. murder) for political reasons." (Wilkinson)

- "When it hits at political figures or figures capable of significantly affecting the political process, and when it has evident or
  imputable political motivations."(Schlesinger)

- "Acts of corruption by politicians, acts of treason and espionage,
  acts of disinformation that cause havoc, acts that incite riot,
  mayhem or disorder, ... acts of torture." (Wolf)

- "When undertaken against or on behalf of government for the
  purpose of influencing the authoritative allocation of values."

- "In liberal democratic systems, certain types of violence are
  called political crimes by the authorities because non-legitimate
  groups perpetrate them against seemingly random and innocent
  targets (all of these terms and questions need qualifying!)."

- "If civilians are killed or injured in a diffuse act of terror
  such as bombing in a crowded market." (Midlarsky)

- "That's a subjective question and relates to the laws which may or
  may not be good ones. In a personal sense, whenever innocent
  people are knowingly and unnecessarily hurt, it is a crime." (Monday)

- "If it is breaking any kind of law and trying to escape from
  punishment." (Zofka)

- "When a non-violent method or alternative might have achieved the
  equivalent political change."

Searching for "political crime" one could place the emphasis not so much

on the crime but on the criminal. Alan F. Sewell, a psychologist, has

attempted to come to a criterion that would distinguish political

criminals from common criminals as well as from psychopathological ones:

1. The psychopathological offender, whose inconsistent behavior reflects
   idiosyncratic values. To the extent that political crime represents
   opposition of social value systems, this offender's behavior cannot
   be politically motivated.

2. The common criminal, whose behavior is consistent but does not imply
   values in conflict with those of his society; this offender's
   deviation from social values is in the realm of means, not ends.
   Hence, this offender's behavior also cannot be polically motivated.

3. The ideologically motivated offender is the true political criminal.
   His behavior demonstrates a consistent opposition of the values
   of another society to those of the society in which the offence
   is committed. His motivation is indeed to harm the political system
   of one society in furtherance of the political system of another
   society." 11)

While this tri-partition makes sense, the grounds on which it is based

are, in our view, questionable (e.g. Sewell's nonpluralist view that

"Patterns of inconsistent behavior cannot really reflect social values,

since social values are by definition consensual and hence, consistent"

is problematic) 12). Furthermore, this conceptualization seems to fit

only the insurgent offender, not the white-collar political criminal

in government.

A distinction of the common criminal from the politically motivated

insurgent criminal could be made on the basis of the ends sought

- personal enrichment or private revenge versus altruistic,

pro-social, "public" drives.

Stephen Schafer has proposed the term convictional criminal

(basing himself on the German expression "Uberzeugungstäter"):

"This element of 'conviction' may serve as a distinguishing
factor in discriminating the political criminal from the ordinary
offender. It is a settled belief, essentially a deep-seated
consideration in the political criminal's conscience that makes
him feel that he has a rendez-vous with destiny, that he is a
David striking at a Goliath of injustice on a world scale,
capable of imposing an order on the chaos of reality. (...)
The political criminal ... has an altruistic-communal motivation
rather than an egoistic drive." 13)

The result of such an attitude is that the insurgent "political criminal"
is prepared to risk his life for the "good" cause while the common criminal
and the political white-collar criminal usually are not. The political
criminal can be a "lone wolf" but more often he acts in unison with
like-minded people and the criminal acts are carefully planned and
organized like a military commando raid. The political criminal often
also works within an organization that shows some division of labor and
sometimes enjoys foreign government support. While this can also be the
case with international crime syndicates like the Mafia, the concern
of the political criminal is going beyond the welfare of the criminal
organization itself to a wider reference group as whose representative
or avant-guard he sees himself.

While these generalizations can claim some plausibility for the insurgent
political criminal, the one who uses criminal means for political ends,
we are still lacking a conceptualization of incumbent political crime.
If rulers amass personal wealth by political means for private goals
rather than for some social benefit they might be able to do so without technically breaking a law, especially if they control the law-making
machinery. Or there might be a law but it is only selectively enforced
according to the needs of the ruling clique. The label "crime" should
be fitted on all acts of a certain nature, just like the label "violence".
Otherwise "whether an act is a 'crime' depends on which side you are
on" as one of our respondents wrote. And he illustrated the point
by adding that "George Washington once approved a plan to kidnap a
British prince (the plan didn't work)". [14] (To be fair to this respondent
one also had to quote another remark of his, he added: "In a most
personal sense, I would label an act of violence in a democracy to be
a crime; I would not so label it if committed by partisans fighting
a dictatorship, left, right or center.")

In the literature we surveyed we found one conceptualization of political
crime which is more even-handed, originating from the German criminologist
Henner Hess. Hess views the Law neither as a pure instrument of rule,
nor as a neutral mechanism for conflict regulation. The Law, in his
perspective, is a historically grown combination of these two
functions. It protects the particular privileges of the ruling class
as well as the fundamental necessities of life of the community as a

whole. The Law reflects the compromises made in the past between the
conflicting groups in society who fought for their share in the
social product. The Law limits arbitrariness within and between
conflicting groups in the community by setting the rules of the game.
Crime, then, is a breach of this codified compromise. While the notion
of political crime usually refers only to the breaches of law from
below in the social order, Hess places "crimes of revolt" and "crimes
of repression" side by side. "Repressive crimes" are, in Hess'
definition, those "illegal acts which are committed for the maintenance,
strengthening or - above all - defence of privileged positions, especially
those of power and property." [15)]

This category of "repressive crimes" is much broader than what is
sometimes referred to as "crimes of government" (the abuse of public
position for private benefits) which is generally downplayed with a
reference to the personal weakness of character of an unworthy
office-holder. "Repressive crimes" cover a series of illegal means
utilized to influence the allocation of the social product or the
occupation of positions of power. Hess lists the following types:

1. Illegal measures of pre-industrial upper classes (such as the
   repression of negroes in the South of the United States after
   the Civil War).

2. Illegal measures of entrepreneurs (such as the hiring of gangsters
   to "solve" the firms' problems with trade unions).

3. Electoral fraud (such as the exclusion of certain classes from
   elections or gerrymandering to assure the victory of one party).

4. Illegal transgressions of the police (such as entry without
   search warrant, torture or aggravated interrogation procedures,
   excessive use of violence and barely disguised murder like
   "shot while trying to escape").

5. Acts of terror by organizations close to the police force (such
   as the off-duty death squads of the Brazilian police).

6. Governmental crime (such as the Stalinist repression).

7. Colonial crimes (such as those of Portugal in Angola and
   Mozambique) 16).

The importance of the concept of repressive crime is that it indicates
that the law cuts on both ends, that incumbents also violate the law
for their own purposes so that the category of political crime is not
to be applied unilaterally against those revolting against a political
order. Repressive crimes then are acts by the chief beneficiaries of

a political system. Another author uses the related concept of
"institutional criminality" to refer to the criminality of government
officials who break laws to strengthen or expand their own power or
prestige [17]. Hess' conceptualization, is should be noted, is not as
broad as Galtung's concept of "stuctural violence". Where social
injustice is embodied in law and sanctioned by law, it is not covered
by Hess's conceptualization. The question whether a particular law is
good or bad does not rise in this criminological conceptualization.

For social and political scientists, in contrast to lawyers and
criminologists, the notion of "crime" have another value. Some of our
respondents therefore answered that they did not use the label "political
crime" (Bonanate), that they did not find it a useful concept anymore
(Rosenthal) or only useful as a political category, not in a scholarly
sense (Stohl).
This is an acceptable position for social scientists. Crime represents
a political and cultural norm of what should be allowed or not and what
should be punished or not. One author therefore wrote that he was trying
to avoid the label "political crime" since it implies "a value judgement".

When is Violence Legitimate?

With our questions we were, however, also trying to find out what the
value judgments of writers on terrorism are. In addition
to the question on political crime we also included one that asked:
"When do you label the use of violence legitimate?"
The respondents to this question take several different positions.
There are those who, like C.C. O'Brien, hold that "the force used by
a democratic state is legitimate while the violence of the terrorist
is not legitimate". Among them are Dinstein, Francis and Leiser. In
this way the legitimacy question is in our view circumvented. After
all, there are democratic states turning autocratic or totalitarian;
on the other hand democracy sometimes only works for some classes in
society but not for others. Without a proper definition of what
constitutes "democratic" the issue is not fully addressed. Some of our
respondents attempted to determine what is democratic or when violence
by the state is justified.

One respondent thought that:

> "Violence is only legitimate as an "ultimate remedium" in the
> cases, that all other means of solving a problem have been used
> and failed. Only democratic and legitimate governments have the
> right to use proportionate violence; but never for the purpose
> of intimidation or suppression of political parties". (Wilferink)

Another author qualified the legitimate use of violence by the state

in this way:

> "Only within the realms in which the state authority maintains
> peace and order, using conventional means mediated by the mechanism
> of justice, prosecution and police. Additional degree of violence,
> especially the use of military force, cannot be accepted as legal,
> the same way it is not legal to use violence by any other group,
> no matter the aim." (Vasilijevic)

Also legitimate is, in the view of another respondent and probably

many others as well although they did not say so, "the use of minimum

necessary force to enforce the law." (Clutterbuck)

Another group of respondents stressed the aspect of majority sanction

for the use of violence. One of them held violence to be legitimate

"when it is used by the government with public support." A second,

"when society accepts it as right (Crenshaw, "uncomfortably" following

E. Walter). A third held that "sociologically this depends on the opinion

of the majority of the people involved" (Hess). There are, however,

situations when this 51 percent-or-more-answer is problematical: for

instance, when the majority in a nation condones governmental violence

against a racially or culturally different minority or when a "democratic"

state engages in hegemony wars abroad. This type of argument can, in

other words, degenerate into a "Fifty-million-Germans-can't-be-wrong"-

argument .

With this in mind some other authors put limits on the legitimate use

of violence by democratic governments. Externally violence is, in one

author's view, legitimate "when licensed by an appropriate authority

- a government, a belligerent, a party to an armed conflict, etc. and

within the legal authority of that body to license - thus excluding

war crimes, grave breaches, etc." (Rubin). Another American author held

government violence legitimate "in conditions of declared war or other

circumstances by a code of laws or conduct ..." These conditions seem

to licence only wars of national self-defence and defence of allies on

the one hand and, officially declared hostilities, which has become a

rarity, at least since the Second World War.

As to intranational violence a number of respondents hold violence in
democracies or against a democratic government to be legitimate under
certain conditions such as:

- "When basic, natural, human values are oppressed by a majority"

- "When basic rights and liberties of a minority are denied or
  a) removed by arbitrary government action, b) when a minority
  is attacked by another minority and fails to receive adequate
  protection from state", but only "when peaceful means have
  categorically failed" (ISC).

Another author held, without specifying the context, that some violence
against a democratic government might be permissible: "Violence against
things (not persons) as a form of protest, openly, without trying to
escape punishment, might be generally legitimate but politically has
to be judged from case to case, depending on the political goals
(relationship between goals and instruments) " (Zofka). Violence against
things is also conceived as a legitimate means of struggle in situation
of "military repression by external attack and also by internal
controllers" by a British author.

Many respondents go further than approving violence against things only
when it comes to non-democratic regimes. The ISC respondent holds
violence to be legitimate when peaceful means have categorically failed
in the following circumstances:

" a) when government fails or ceases to rule in perceived interests
  of citizens;

  b) when government removes basic rights and liberties as accepted
  inalienable by constitution or by individual tradition;

  c) when no other means of political expression exist."

One author specifies what sort of violence is legitimate in such
situations, by saying: "When it is directed against an authority
structure in a direct manner with little involvement of civilians and
one can demonstrate clear criminal behavior (leading to loss of life)
on the part of the government" (Midlarsky). A recurring theme of many
answers is self-defence more or less broadly interpreted:

- "Instances of self-defence to protect life or avoid starvation etc."
  (Wolf)

- "In self-defence or in defence of another for whom you are
  responsible" (Wilber)

- "When there is no other means of self-defence" (Wilkinson)

- "In 'self-defence' and 'to prevent unlawful violence against another
  person'" (Clutterbuck)

- "Defence of one's family, nation or self - in all these instances
  violence would be legitimate and legal"

The right to resist violently is also granted in an international

context by some authors:

- "I use international law criteria: self-defence, self-determination,
  protection of other fundamental human rights" (Tomasevski)

- "'Liberation movements', acting as much as possible by the additional
  protocols to the 1949 Geneva conventions of 1978 also can use means
  of violence against the suppressing government" (Wilferink)

Some of the responses do not address themselves to either violence by

a democratic government or violence against a democratic or

non-democratic government, but are independent from the (nature of)

the actor. These seem to be particularly interesting for the development

of a political morality:

- "When undertaken to minimize future violence"

- "It is a question of ends and means in which the character of the
  ends and the impact of the means on these ends must be carefully
  weighed. It should be used only as a last resort, and only then if
  it does not actually corrupt the ends for which it is used. Questions
  of proportionality are also important" (Sederberg)

- "In principle - but very roughly indeed - I would say that the use
  of violence is morally legitimate only when there are no alternative
  methods of nonviolent struggle which have better consequences" (Pontara)

Some of the respondents did not answer or said that they would "leave

the battle over legitimacy to others". One author noted, correctly, of

course, "That involves a value judgment and I don't (use value judgments)".

Yet it can be argued that when social scientists refuse to take a moral

stand they are in fact condoning, accepting or even backing a status

quo which is producing and reproducing violence. By saying as one

respondent did, that violence is "never" legitimate the question is

not solved either. In the end only one thing is certain: there are no

easy and fast answers. Indeed, if Schlesinger is correct there is no

answer possible at all: "There are no independent criteria for this

[question of legitimacy of violence] : political violence is inherently

part of a contest for legitimacy". Another author answered in the same

vein by saying somewhat jokingly: "When it is in accord with my values

(when else?)". It could be that the answer has to be sought exactly in

this "when else?"

The best answer to this question which this writer has seen so far has been formulated by Stuart Hampshire fifteen years ago:

"... the straight, clear question in the title of this series ("Does a political cause ever give us the right to kill?") deserves a straight, clear answer; or at least a fairly clear one, if the issue is too complex for complete clarity: yes, a political cause does sometimes give us the right to kill: in a war for the defence of one's country, but not in an unnecessary, unjust, undeclared, useless war, as in Vietnam. I will suggest the beginnings of a rough criterion for justified killing in very extreme situations in peacetime. Four conditions are necessary: first, that it is a response to a great injustice and oppression, as of a resistance movement against a foreign power ruling by force and terror so that the victim is the reverse of innocent; secondly, that it is certain that no lawful and non-violent means of rectifying the injustice and oppression will be given; thirdly, that the political killing will certainly cause far less suffering, and less widespread suffering than the present injustice and cruelty are causing: lastly, that it really is very probable that the killing will end the oppression, and that it will not provoke more violence and more horror; this last condition is very rarely satisfied, but sometimes it may have been. These principles give the outline of a possible morality of political violence, though of course a highly disputable one." 19)

- 37 -

Notes

1) For instance, in the massive study of the U.S. National Advisory
Committee on Criminal Justice Standards and Goals. Report of the
Task Force on Disorders and Terrorism. Washington D.C., GPO, 1976,
p.3, where it is held that "Political terrorism is characterized
by (1) its violent, criminal nature; (2) its impersonal frame of
reference; and (3) the primacy of its ulterior objective, which is
the dissemination of fear throughout the community for political
ends or purposes."

2) L.C. Green, in answer to the question: "When do you label an act
of violence a political crime?"

3) W.H. Nagel. A Social-Legal View on the Suppression of Terrorism.
International Journal of the Sociology of Law, no.8, 1980, pp.216-7.

4) William L. Marshall and William L. Clark. The Legal Definition of
Crime and Delinquency. In: Marvin E. Wolfgang et al.(Eds.)
The Sociology of Crime and Delinquency. New York, John Wiley & Sons,
1970, pp. 19-20.

5) M.Ch. Bassiouni. The Political Offence Exception in Extradition Law
and Practice. In: M.Ch. Bassiouni (Ed.). International Terrorism
and Political Crime. Springfield, Illinois, Charles C. Thomas,
1975, p.408.

6) Hebart Ruitenberg. Politiek en Misdaad. Wordt Vervolgd. Berichten
van Amnesty International, 78, 6 June 1978, p.3.

7) Nicholas N. Kittrie. In Search of Political Crime and Political
Criminals. New York University Law Review, Vol.50, No.1, April 1975,
p.202, cit. U.S. National Advisory Committe, op. cit., p.325.

8) Barton Ingraham. Political Crime in Europe: A Comparative Study of
France, Germany and England. Berkeley, University of California Press,
1979, cit. E.F. Mickolus (Comp.). The Literature of Terrorism. A
Selectively Annotated Bibliography. Westport, Connecticut, Greenwood
Press, 1980, p.294.

9) Cit. J.M. Cameron. On Violence. New York Review of Books, July 2 1970,
p.27.

10) Stephen Schafer. The Political Criminal: The Problem of Morality and
Crime. New York, The Free Press, 1974, p.19.

11) Alan F. Sewell. Political Crime: A Psychologist's Perspective.
In: M.Ch. Bassiouni (Ed.). International Terrorism and Political
Crime. Springfield, Illinois, Charles C. Thomas, 1975, pp. 20-21.

12) Ibid., p. 20.

13) Stephen Schafer. The Political Criminal. The Problem of Morality
and Crime. New York, Free Press, 1974, pp. 146-147.

14) J. Mallin.

15) Henner Hess. Repressives Verbrechen. <u>Kriminologisches Journal</u>.
8 Jg., Heft 1, 1976, p. 1.

16) Ibid., pp. 5-11.

17) G.P. Hoefnagels. Misdaad in de toekomst. Naar een maatschappij van
namen of van nummers. <u>De Gids</u>. No. 1, 1977, p. 44.

18) Conor Cruise O'Brien. Liberty and Terror: illusions of violence,
delusions of liberation. <u>Encounter</u>, Vol. 49, No. 4, Oct. 1977, p. 38.

19) Stuart Hampshire in a television talk, transcript in <u>The New Review</u>,
Vol. 2, No. 24, March 1967, cit.: Ted Honderich. Violence for
Equality. Inquiries in Political Violence. Harmondsworth, Pelican,
1980, p. 217.

Terrorism and (Urban) Guerrilla Warfare

Historically, the term 'terrorism' and the term 'guerrilla' are almost
contemporaries, the first taking shape in the France of the 1790s and
the second in the Spain of the early 19th century. When Napoleon attempted to break Great Britain with the continental blockade he had to
occupy the Iberian Peninsula for that purpose. A low-level armed resistance against the Napoleonic presence in Spain in the years 1808-1814,
fed by British arms supplies, was termed "small war" or, in Spanish,
"guerrilla". The use of light and highly mobile armed units to harrass
and exhaust an army stronger in numbers and fire power is of course
much older than that. But up till the early 19th century guerrilla warfare had more of a "commando-quality" than of a "mass quality". The introduction of civilians into regular armies was epitomized by the "levee
en masse", the recruitment of the national youth on a grand scale, for
the defence of the French revolution. Yet this development also brought
about a growing popular participation in irregular warfare with its
climax in the twentieth century in the Chinese and Indochinese experiences [1]. These happened to be mainly peasant societies so that the chief
location of the protracted struggle was the village and the countryside.
Since the 1960s however, there came into existence, first in the Latin
American context, the term "urban guerrilla". In turn this term was
adopted by a number of mainly left-wing movements in the industrialized
countries of the northern hemisphere as a label for their own brand of
political violence.

The equation "terrorism" = (urban) guerrilla warfare is one which has
not only been used for political propaganda or reversely for guilt attribution, but has been employed also by social and political scientists.
In the following pages we shall list a number of views which can be found
in the literature on guerrilla warfare and the one on terrorism on the
"differentia specifica" between the two phenomena. This will be followed
by a proposal for a two-dimensional division line.

To begin with, there are those who make no clear distinction. Werner
Hahlweg, for instance, a long-time student of Clausewitz and guerrilla
warfare, has written "Guerrilla movements and terrorism practically grow
to become one and the same thing to a large extent", and "Guerrilla move-

ments and Terror are in practice indistinguishable from one another" [2].

The near-equation of terrorism and guerrilla warfare we also find with

another German author, Gerd Langguth, who wrote:

> "There are many, often only slightly different terms for 'guerrilla warfare': small war, partisan struggle, underground struggle, nonconventional war, irregular warfare or subversive warfare. In place of guerrilleros one also speaks frequently about irregulars, bands, terrorists, commando groups, resistance fighters or rebels. (...) Many times these terms ultimately refer to the same form of war, which however, can assume the most diversified appearances. (...) The guerrilla is a weapon of the weaker. It is not a type of war but a form of conducting warfare in which the strategically weaker side at a moment of its own choice and a place of its own choice and with forms of its own choice becomes tactically offensive." [3]

Richard Clutterbuck, the British ex-military turned scholar, shares

this notion, when he writes:

> "Guerrilla warfare and terrorism, rural and urban, internal or international, has undoubtedly now become the primary form of conflict for our time. (...) Whether guerrilla warfare is judged to be legitimate or not, it almost inevitably incorporates an element of terrorism. (...) Terrorism is not precisely the same as violence. Terrorism aims, by the use of violence or the threat of violence, to coerce governments, authorities or populations by inducing fear." [4]

While one can only guess what motivates some of these authors to place

guerrilla warfare and terrorism into one basket, it seems that it is

chiefly the fact that both are instances of anti-government violence.

Yet there are also those taking an anti-establishment point of view

who dismiss the distinction between guerrilla warfare and terrorism.

E. Hyams, while noting that "... the conditions in which rural guerril-

las are fighting may make terrorism inappropriate (although there are

usually oppressive landlords to shoot and 'manors' to burn)", dismisses

a distinction between political guerrilla warfare and terrorism as "bo-

gus" on the grounds that interstate warfare has also reached a degree

of indiscrimination which blurrs the division between civilians and

combattants:

> "It is not clear why social war should be placed under restraints which no longer apply in international war: all belligerent powers, and especially the great powers, nowadays wage war by the terrorization of civilians, e.g. by the bombing of open cities, the use of napalm and the threat of nuclear strikes. Terrorism used for social or political ends is guerrilla warfare continued by other means, just as the atom-bombing of Nagasaki and Hiroshima was international warfare continued by terrorism." [5]

While Hyams seems to view terrorism as a "higher" stage of war and guerrilla warfare, other authors see terrorism as a stage of conflict preceeding guerrilla warfare. Brian Crozier, has noted in 1960:

> "The pattern of insurrection is, in fact, strangely consistent.
> Whatever the country or the circumstances, insurrection tends to
> follow a sequence of three phases: terrorism, guerrilla warfare
> and full-scale war. That is the tendency, but the pattern is not
> always completed: not all rebellions reach the second phase, and
> fewer still the third. (...) Terrorism is the natural weapon of
> men with small resources, fighting against superior strength. It
> dramatises their cause and - at least in the early days - enforces
> the loyalty of waverers. (...) The communist insurgents of Vietnam,
> Malaya or the Philippines shared this with Mau Mau, Eoka or the
> FLN - that terror was their first arm. (...) But the pattern of
> the rebellions that have been allowed to run their course suggests
> that when the opportunity comes, the rebels will drop terrorism
> in favor of guerrilla activities, or at least relegate it to se-
> cond place." 6)

Croziers line of thinking has been influential and can be found back
in, among others, the writings of Thornton and Schreiber [7]. But it
goes back at least to Mao Tse-Tung, who also believed in phases or
stages of revolutionary warfare. In the second phase, of the revolutionary process, "acts of sabotage and terrorism multiply", according to
Mao and the kidnapping of uncooperative landlords is also suggested. [8]
The implication of this seems to be that at certain stages of a struggle
terrorism as a technique might pay off and be a strategy that offers itself as the most logical one among several others. Thornton has elaborated this idea, postulating that the occurrence of terror is frequent
in the second stage of his five stages model. [9]

Table I: Thornton's Five Stages of Insurrection

Phase	Characteristics
I Preparatory	Previolent
II Initial Violence	Terror
III Expansion	Guerrilla Warfare
IV Victorious	Conventional Warfare
V Consolidation	Postviolent

Since he looks at "agitational terror" and "enforcement terror" from
both the insurgents and the incumbents, Thornton clearly views terrorism
and guerrilla warfare as two different phenomena.
What seems to be a majority of social scientists in fact perceive terrorism as more than "urban guerrilla-ism", as does, for instance Robert

Taber who viewed both guerrilla tactics and terrorist tactics as two
aspects of the "war of the flea" [10]. Walter Laqueur is a leading proponent of the view that terrorism is not a new stage of guerrilla warfare, but differs from it in essential respects ..." [11]. Urban guerrilla warfare, in his view is indeed urban, but not guerrilla [12]. Charac-
teristical are the anonymity of the participants in a terrorist campaign
and the violation of established norms, in Laqueurs view [13]. While rural
guerrilleros try to establish "liberated zones" and build up a political
organization, the terrorists cannot do such a thing according to Laqueur.[14]
Further differences noted by Laqueur are the size of operating units.
With rural guerrillas these are large, developing, if successful, into
whole armies, while the urban terrorists, for reasons of security, have
to operate in small units of three, four or five. He also sees
differences in the ability to move and hide between towns and countryside. The clandestine character of urban terrorists also makes open
propaganda and the carrying out of political and social reforms in "liberated zones" impossible [15]. While some of these distinctions are not
taken up by other authors, Laqueur makes one that is a recurring theme
with many:

> "Whereas guerrilla operations are mainly directed against the armed
> forces of the enemy and the security services, as well as installa-
> tions of strategic importance, modern urban terrorism is less dis-
> criminate in the choice of its targets. Operations such as bank
> robberies, hijackings, kidnappings, and, of course, assassinations
> are expected to create a general climate of insecurity." [16]

Paul Wilkinson shares some of Laqueur's set of distinctions. While conceding that many guerrillas have employed terrorism or have been supported by terrorists, he sees a higher rule-observance with the former,
the adherence to a code of conduct which Laqueur referred to when speaking
about the "violation of established norms". Wilkinson writes:

> "Guerrillas may fight with small numbers and often inadequate weapon-
> ry, but they can and often do fight according to conventions of war, ta-
> king and exchanging prisoners and respecting the rights of non-com-
> batants. Terrorists place no limits on means employed and frequent-
> ly resort to widespread assassination, the waging of 'general ter-
> ror' upon the indigenous civilian population, and even killing of
> innocent foreigners who may never have visited the country of the
> revolutionaries." [17]

Schreiber follows Wilkinson and Laqueur when he observes that

> "As soon as the leaders of the movement cease their attacks against
> noncombatants and focus their military strength against the army
> of the entrenched government, they have ceased technically (if not
> in the minds of their enemies) to be terrorists." [18].

Wördemann, a well-known German journalist, sees another distinction between the old land-based guerrilleros and the new "urban guerrilla": the
rural guerrillero occupies territory in order to capture mental space in
the end, while the latter occupies mental space because he cannot con-
quer territory. It is this strategic goal difference, rather than tactical differences - both use criminal deeds as means of struggle - which
separate the terrorist from the guerrillero, according to Wördemann. [19]
Gaucher, on the other hand, writing in the aftermath of the Algerian war
where the holding of territory was not in the power of the insurgents,
held:

> "Neither guerrilla nor terrorism aim - as we have already under-
> lined - at the occupation of territory or at the annihilation of
> the enemy forces, but [aim at] the capture of political objectives
> be that the assured control of a population or the dissemination
> of chaos and division with the enemy." [20]

I.L. Horowitz sees the size of the movement, its organizational efficacy
and geographic locale as important factors in dividing guerrilla from
terrorist movements, but he does not fail to note that it is hard to
establish clear distinctions [21].

Jay Mallin holds that urban guerrilla warfare is a broader term than
terrorism since it includes also actions such as "ambushes, street skirmishes, assaults on official installations, and other types of hit-and-
run urban combat" [22]. His view seems to run parallel to Burton's who
maintains:

> "Only those who utilize terror as a stage or tactic complementary
> to a campaign of strikes, riots and political front activity aimed
> to lead eventually to a 'revolutionary war' are properly described
> as 'guerrillas'. To give this name to other groups is to suggest a
> degree of planning, political sophistication and revolutionary in-
> tent which they only infrequently possess." [23]

Both Mallin and Burton seem to be influenced by Carlos Marighela, the
Brazilian theorist and practitioner of "urban guerrilla"-warfare who
lists in his "Mini-Manual do Guerrillheiro Urbano" as urban guerrilla
actions terrorism ("By terrorism I mean the use of bomb attacks" [24]) as
one among fourteen techniques of urban guerrilla warfare. (They are:
1. attack; 2. entry or break-in; 3. occupation; 4. ambush; 5. tactical
street fighting; 6. expropriation of arms, ammunition and explosives;
8. liberating prisoners; 9. execution; 10. kidnapping; 11. sabotage; 12.
terrorism; 13. armed propaganda, and 14. the war of nerves.) [25]
While Marighela wrote that "revolutionary terrorist acts ... are not
designed to kill members of the common people, or upset or intimidate

them in any way" [26], it was exactly the growing lack of discrimination
that, in the eyes of many observers, made the term "guerrilla" increasingly misplaced. Fritz René Allemann has referred to the attack aimed
deliberately at nonparticipating parties to the conflict at hand such
as attacks on airline passengers. These have produced a qualitative
change in guerrilla warfare as it moved from the country-side to the
cities. Alleman therefore suggests that it would be more appropriate,
in such cases to speak of "terroristic criminality" than "urban guerrilla warfare" [27].

David Rapoport, in a somewhat more systematic mould, differentiates
between military activity, guerrilla war and terrorism:

> "Military activity was bound by conventions entailing moral dis-
> tinctions between belligerents and neutrals, combatants and non-
> combatants, appropriate and inappropriate targets, legitimate and
> illegitimate methods.
> Guerrilla war was a special kind of military activity, in which
> hit and disappear tactics to disperse the enemy's military forces
> were employed to wear down and gradually defeat the enemy.
> The traditional distinguishing characteristic of the terrorist
> was his explicit refusal to accept the conventional moral limits
> which defined military and guerrilla action. Because a terrorist
> knew that others did think that violence should be limited, he ex-
> ploited the enemy's various responses to his outrages. The ter-
> rorist perpetrated atrocities and manipulated reactions to them." [28]

Martha Crenshaw, in her study on the Algerian FLN, also emphasizes the
"extraordinary character of terrorist violence that distinguishes it
from other forms of revolutionary activity, such as guerrilla warfare,
which is essentially irregular military activity by organized bands in
rural areas". Guerrilla warfare in her view, is more utilitarian in purpose, and terrorism is more symbolic" [29].

The extraordinariness consists, in the view of Abraham Kaplan in the
fact "that the victim is not the target - in contrast to genuine guerrilla action, which is carried out against military forces or their
supply lines and communications, and not against civilian populations" [30].

Yet another way of distinguishing terrorism from guerrilla warfare and
other forms of organized violence can be derived by looking at the degree
of popular involvement. Bard E. O'Neill has suggested a way of distinguishing insurgencies according to the scope of popular participation.
He writes:

> "In this type of scheme, one end of a continuum is represented by
> conspiracy - highly organized political violence with limited par-

ticipation, including mutinies, coups d'etats, political assassinations, small-scale terrorism and small-scale guerrilla activity, while the other end is represented by internal war - highly organized political violence, with wide-spread participation which includes large-scale terrorism and guerrilla warfare and civil war." 31)

This is a potentially useful differentiation criterion, although O'Neill blunts it by placing guerrilla and terrorism on both sides of the fence.

Conclusion

Rather than carrying on summing up different views, it is time to pull some of the threads together. There is clearly no consensus among the authors as to the specific differentiation between guerrilla and terrorism. Yet certain elements regularly recur, which at least suggests some common ground. Building on some of the ideas offered so far, we would like to suggest a two-dimension differentiation. Starting from the last-mentioned author , it seems to me that it would be useful to look at popular support for the carriers of violent acts rather than at direct popular participation in the fighting alone. The "people" can assist a violent movement by providing logistical support or hinder it by denunciating the fighters, depending on the degree of identification with the cause and the methods of struggle utilized by the fighters. While the classical guerrillero is supposed to move like a fish in the water, according to Mao's metaphor, the terrorist is generally less at home with the people although he usually claims to fight for the people. His presence near the center of regime power, with the concurring higher risk of being detected, forces him to minimal contacts with his political reference or identification group. He cannot build up a broad political support organization but has to provide for his own support by bank robberies or by accepting subsidies from foreign interested parties (this is also true for some guerrilleros). The guerrilla army grows in accordance with the grow of popular support and the revolution takes place when the time is ripe. The urban terrorist, however, basing himself on the foco theory of Guevara/Debray, thinks that the revolutionary can, by setting an example, create a revolutionary situation. 32) The mobilization of the people would be done in part through the reporting media and, through the popular reaction to the governmental repression which would force more and more vulnerable population segments (students, trade unionists, etc.) in the camp of the terrorists. Yet the mode of fighting (hit and hide) of the terrorists kept them, as noted before,

organisationally separate from the masses and the <u>manner</u> of fighting
(often cold-blooded murders and indiscriminate bombings of noncombatants)
alienated in many cases also the moral feelings of target reference groups.
In some cases, like in Algeria, it has been possible for a revolutionary-
minded and impatient elite to mobilize the masses through terrorism and
the anticipated enemy reactions to it. When the enemy was a foreign power, such as in the wars of national liberation in Africa or where the
enemy is of a different origin or religion, such as in the Basque country or in Northern Ireland, a considerable measure of popular support
has at times been available although this has rarely been enough to proceed to a guerrilla war. Some of the operational techniques employed in
guerrilla wars - such as the use of small, lightly armed units harrassing
the opponent intermittently at times and places of their own choosing
while deliberately avoiding decisive battles - can also be found among
movements using terrorism only. What seems to be different, however,
is the <u>widening of the targets considered to be legitimate objects of</u>
<u>threat and destruction</u> that more terroristically inclined movements appear
willing to accept. Furthermore, and perhaps even more important, there appears to be a <u>lower degree of protection granted to one's own reference group</u>.
While guerrilla movements tend to take an active concern with the security from enemy attacks of their followers and sympathizers and give
them as much protection as they can (which often might be little more
than a warning from impending government counter-actions), the insurgent
terrorists of the Marighela school generally utilized the added repression following their actions as a device to have additional segments of
the population driven into the arms of the revolutionary movement. The
brunt of the counter-measures (and often counter-terror) of the government does not reach primarily the clandestine cellular underground movement but the above ground mass organizations which are (supposed to be)
the recruiting field or feeding ground of the movement. It is this
two-fold widening of direct participants in the conflict, stemming in
part from a philosophy of "who-is-not-with-us-is-against-us", which,
in our view, is the main difference between the style of combat of terrorists and guerrilleros. (see Table I).

Table II:

Ideal-Type Differentiation Between Insurgent Movements Using Terrorist resp. Guerrilla Strategies

Actor	Relation to Reference Group	Main Targets of Violence
Guerrillero	I) Direct representative of reference group seeking to protect group from enemy countermeasures	II) Security forces (military and (secret) police) of the government; infrastructure of these (supply lines, communication network)
Insurgent Terrorist	III) Often self-chosen or indirect representative of reference group which has yet to be mobilized for the "cause" whereby the deliberate exposure of the reference group to government repression is a mobilization device	IV) Individual exponents in the government camp, unarmed people or armed forces not in combat situations; third parties which are neutrals, bystanders, noncombatants. Sabotage of infrastructure of whole population

This is, it has to be stressed once more, an ideal-type differentiation: it is perfectly possible that insurgent terrorists also select "guerrillero" targets or show traits of behaviour more in consonance with guerrilla warfare - and vice versa. However, which strategy prevails is generally revealed in the course of an insurgent campaign. Increases in strength of an insurgent movement can lead to more responsible targetting of violence and a higher capability in protecting the reference group which has to "legitimize" the use of violence. [33] Decreases in strength, without a corresponding moderation of goals, however, are likely to bring out the worst again in the sense that the own reference group in whose name the violence is perpetrated is disciplined by violence or allowed to be exposed to the counter-violence of the opponent. Powerlessness, in this sense, can also corrupt, just as absolute power does. This very last observation ought not to be lost sight of. Too easily it is held that terrorist movements have a low regard or even no regard for rules of combat while guerrilla movements behave more responsible (e.g. by treating prisoners according to the Geneva convention). Regular armies of civilized nations in this view, are then attributed with the highest degree of adherence to the laws of war. This is clearly untenable. A simple look at the casualty ratio between civilians and military in the course of twentieth century warfare suggests otherwise (see Table III).

Table III:

War Casualties [34]

	Military	Civilian
First World War	95%	5%
Second World War	52%	48%
Korea	16%	84%
Indochina	10%	90%

The bombardment of open cities from Coventry to Dresden to Hiroshima and Nagasaki to Beirut has been highly indiscriminate in terms of targeting. Providing sufficient and adequate protection for one's own population in times of war has, with a few exceptions such as Switzerland, had a low priority with most governments in the cold war period, as a look at the available public shelter capacity reveals [35]. The utilization of mercenaries and local revolutionaries by governments on both sides of the Iron Curtain, as well as the exploits of secret service agents performing assassinations for reasons of state are a sorry testimony to the higher morality of many governments condemning terrorists for not playing by the rules. The reason for this moral double standard probably lies in an observation which Brain Crozier made in 1960: "Often enough, the victim of terrorism are 'us', whereas the victims of bombing raids are 'them'." [36]

An aspect which also enters the terminological evaluation is whether a movement or government uses terrorism as main or as incidental strategy to influence the opponents' behaviour. Some of the radical movements in the cities of industrialized countries have used only terrorist tactics, which makes them more liable to be labelled "terrorist" than representatives of violent movements using a greater variety of tactics, including nonviolent ones. In this regard, guerrilla movements and governments are indeed less terrorist and reflecting a higher code of conduct in general. Yet paradoxically, some insurgent terrorists themselves are not so amoral (or immoral) as it is often asserted. Their initial motivation to engage in political violence was moral in the sense of being an outflow of a feeling of outrage at the injustices under which their chosen reference group had to suffer. They often wanted to help the "masses" sincerely, and were prepared to sacrifice their own lives for this goal. However, this initial moral commitment to help others often led to a blindness to the injustices committed by themselves in the process of trying to hit the enemies of their reference group. [37] Not being of the masses

but wanting to fight _for_ the masses these terrorists' alienation made
them easy victims of merciless indiscriminate violence against everybody
who stood between the "problem" and their "solution".

The abstractness of posing the problem, fed by the origin of the terrorists (often from the intelligentsia) and the separation from ordinary
life (necessitated by their chosen fighting technique) probably contributes to this growing lack of humanity towards their victims. Being ready
to sacrifice themselves for the cause, they must often have felt that
everybody else was also worth sacrificing. As one of the South Moluccan
terrorists put it in his memoirs:"The conclusion which we have to draw
from Vietnam is that the Moluccan people has but one alternative for a
genuine real independence: some millions of her people have to die so
that millions of others can live". [38] This absolutism too, in our view,
is probably stronger with the terrorist than with the guerrilla.
This is admittedly speculative. While the above reflections might offer
a further point of departure for separating guerrilla and terrorism, they
lack empirical verification.

Notes.

1) Hakon Wiberg. Are urban guerrillas possible? In: J. Niezing (Ed.).
   Urban Guerrilla. Studies on the Theory, Strategy and Practice of
   Political Violence in Modern Societies. Rotterdam, Rotterdam Uni-
   versity Press, 1974, p. 12.

2) Werner Hahlweg. Moderner Guerrillakrieg und Terrorismus. Probleme
   und Aspekte ihrer theoretischen Grundlagen als Widerspiegelung der
   Praxis, in: M. Funke (Ed.). Terrorismus. Untersuchungen zur Strategie und Struktur revolutionärer Gewaltpolitik. Bonn, Bundeszentrale
   für politische Bildung, 1977, p. 137; Werner Hahlweg. Theoretische
   Grundlagen der modernen Guerrilla und des Terrorismus. In: Rolf
   Tophoven (Ed.). Politik durch Gewalt. Guerrilla und Terrorismus
   heute. Bonn, 1976.; cit. Herfried Münkler. Guerrillakrieg und Terrorismus. Neue Politische Literatur, Jg. 25, no. 3, 1980, p. 302.

3) Gerd Langguth. Guerrilla und Terror als linksextremistische Kamp-
   mittel. Rezeption und Kritik. In: M. Funke (Ed.). Extremismus. Bonn,
   Bundeszentrale für Politische Bildung, 1978, p. 96.

4) R. Clutterbuck. Guerrillas and Terrorists. London, Faber and Faber,
   1977, p. 16, 20, 21.

5) E. Hyams. Terrorists and Terrorism. 1975, p. 164-166.

6) Brian Crozier. The Rebels. A Study of Post-War Insurrections. London,
   Chatto and Windus, 1960, p. 127-128.

7) J. Schreiber. The ultimate weapon. New York, 1978, p. 134-135.

8) Samuel B. Griffith. Mao Tse-Tung. On Guerrilla Warfare. New York,
   Praeger, 1961, p. 20-21; cit. Carol Edler Baumann. The Diplomatic
   Kidnappings. A Revolutionary Tactic of Urban Terrorism. The Hague,
   Martinus Nijhoff, 1973, p. 4-5.

9) Thomas P. Thornton. Terror as a Weapon of Political Agitation. In:
   Harry Eckstein (Ed.). Internal War. Problems and Approaches. New York,
   The Free Press of Glencoe, 1964, p. 92.

10) Robert Taber. The War of the Flea. A Study of Guerrilla Warfare.
    Theory and Practice. Frogmore, Paladin, 1974, p. 90.

11) W. Laqueur. Terrorism. London, Weidenfeld and Nicolson, 1977, p.v.

12) Ibid., p. 5.

13) Ibid., p. 3.

14) W. Laqueur. Guerrillas. Boston, Little Brown, 1976, p. 404.

15) W. Laqueur. The Futility of Terrorism. Harper's Magazine, no. 252,
    March 1976, repr. in W.P. Lineberry (Ed.). The Struggle Against
    Terrorism. New York, 1977, p. 131-132.

16) W. Laqueur. Guerrilla, op. cit., p. 403.

17) Paul Wilkinson. Terrorism. 1974, p. 80.

18) J. Schreiber. The Ultimate Weapon. New York, 1978, p. 135.

19) F. Wördemann. Terrorismus. München, Piper, 1978, p. 57-59.

20) R. Gaucher. Les Terrorists. Paris, Albin Michel, 1965, p. 354.

21) I.L. Horowitz. Political Terrorism and State Power. Journal of Po-
    litical and Military Sociology, Vol. 1, 1973, p. 148, 155.

22) Jay Mallin. Terrorism as a Military Weapon. In: Y. Alexander and
    S.M. Finger (Eds.). Terrorism: Interdisciplinary Perspectives. New
    York, John Jay Press, 1977, p. 95.

23) Anthony M. Burton. Urban Terrorism. Theory, Practice and Response.
    New York, The Free Press, 1975, p. 11.

24) C. Marighela. For the Liberation of Brazil. Harmondsworth, Penguin,
    1971, p. 89; C.E. Baumann. The Diplomatic Kidnappings. A Revolu-
    tionary Tactic of Urban Terrorism. The Hague, Martinus Nijhoff, 1973,
    p. 24.

25) Ibid., p. 80.

26) Ibid., p. 112.

27) F.R. Allemann. Stadtguerrilla in Lateinamerika - Model für Europas
    Extremisten. In: R. Tophoven (Ed.). Politik durch Gewalt. Bonn, Wehr
    und Wissen, 1976, p. 61.

28) David Rapoport. The Politics of Atrocity. In: Y. Alexander and S.M.
    Finger (Eds.). op. cit., p. 47 - Emphasis added - AS

29) M. Crenshaw Hutchinson. Revolutionary Terrorism. The FLN in Algeria,
    1954-1962. Stanford, Hoover Institution, 1978, p. 19.

30) Abraham Kaplan. The Psychodynamics of Terrorism. In: Y. Alexander
    and J.M. Gleason (Eds.). Behavioral and Quantitative Perspectives
    of Terrorism. New York, Pergamon Press, 1981, p. 44.

31) Bart E. O'Neill. The Success Criteria and Progression of Insurgency.
    In: Bart E. O'Neill et al. Political Violence and Insurgency: A Com-
    parative Approach. Arvada, Colo., Phoenix Press, 1974, p. 10.

32) Fritz R. Allemann. Terrorismus in Lateinamerika. Motive und Er-
    scheinungsformen. In: M. Funke (Ed.). op. cit., 1977, p. 174-175.

33) This observation has been made for instance by Thornton, who wrote:
    "If the insurgents are in a position of political strength to begin
    with, it is unnecessary - and even wasteful - for them to initiate
    terrorism."   Thomas P. Thornton. Terror as a Weapon of Political
    Agitation. In: H. Eckstein (Ed.). Internal War. New York, Free Press,
    1964, p. 88.

34) B.V.A. Röling. Vredeswetenschap. Inleiding tot de polemologie.
    Utrecht, Spectrum, 1981, p. 39, Table 2.2.

35) The Netherlands, for instance, have, in 1982, public shelters for
    only 322.000 people, leaving 14 millions without protection in case
    of a nuclear attack. This vulnerability, however, can be seen as
    part of the logic of deterrence in the framework of an East-West-
    balance of terror.   Peter Goodwin. Als de bom valt. Feiten en on-
    zekerheden over de kernoorlog. Haarlem, Rostrum, 1982, p. 78.

36) Brian Crozier. The Rebels. A Study of Post-War Insurrections. London,
    Chatto and Widnus, 1960, p. 158.

37) See: A.P. Schmid and J. de Graaf. Violence as Communication. London,
    Sage, 1982, p. 46. - This aspect is also stressed in the excellent
    review essay of Herfried Münckler to which we are endebted for the pre-
    sent chapter. - H. Münckler. Guerrillakrieg und Terrorismus. Neue
    Politische Literatur, Jg. 25, no. 3, 1980, p. 319.

38) Abe Sahetapy. Minne Strijd voor de R.M.S. Amsterdam, 1981, p. 77.

Terrorism and Anarchism

The linking of terror(ism) to certain political philosophies such as
communism and fascism (or encompassing both: totalitarianism) has been
frequent [1] and frequently undeserved in the crude form of an equation.
The equation TERRORISM = ANARCHISM is particularly frequent and persistent yet it is nevertheless largely undeserved [2]. Its main basis is
the coincidence of anarchism and terroristic attentats in the late 19th
century. Given the well-known opposition of anarchists to all authority
("Ni Dieu, ni Maître") and the political assassination attempts on kings ,
heads of state and other symbols of authority, the guilt attribution to
anarchists was understandable. But kings were also killed by republicans
without that the republican idea was sullied to any comparable degree.
Anarchism, as an outflow of the "fraternité" in the three catch-words
of the French revolution, was doctrinally rather less violence-linked
than Liberalism (basing itself on "liberté") or Socialism (basing itself on "égalité"), although it has at times also been described as
'libertarian socialism'.

An approach doing more justice to anarchism has to distinguish between
1. anarchism as a political philosophy (or a doctrine with more individualist and more collectivist schools)and 2. anarchism as a movement
and 3., in this context most importantly, the exploits of individual
anarchists.

Taking the basic common denominators of anarchist doctrine, three elements stand out. Peter Lösche has conveniently summarized them and we
follow his wording:

1. "Anarchists reject all forms of human organization that serve
   to apply ideological, political, economic or social coercion;
   in place of these they strive for voluntary associations of mature and emancipated human beings. Anarchists are therefore consistently anti-institutional for the very reason that institutions are means for effectuating authority. Hence the rejection
   of state, party, guilds, churches ... as well as the institutionalized law. (...)

2. Ideologies are, in the anarchist perception, expressions of
   existing and institutionalized relationships of domination and
   submission and contribute to their stabilization. Anarchism is
   a-theistic, a-religious. In its pretention it is not only international but a-national. (...)

3. The goal of anarchism is the domination-free society, that is
   anarchy, which substitutes for the rule of man over man the self-
   organization of autonomous personalities who have fully developed
   their human capacities. This future society is not "chaotic" but
   organized on the principle of federalism. Human conviviality
   should be structured through voluntary agreements of individuals
   with individuals ... from below to above. (...)" 3).

The enemy of the "Good society" is, in anarchist thinking, not (a class of) people themselves but a wrong organization of things. The goal of revolution was the destruction of an organization based chiefly on private property. The destruction of people was, in the view of the chief theorist, Michael Bakunin, not the right way to this goal since it would inevitably lead to a "reaction" in the form of "red" or "white" terror. The means utilized in the struggle to bring about the desired goal of a non-hierarchical federalistic network of communities had to reflect already the goal itself. Mass insurrection bringing about a social revolution was therefore considered to be not the only way. Bakunin also saw reforms, especially the abolition of the institution of inheritance, as a means. Another means was the setting of examples of the future society in the present one by enlighted and dedicated anarchists, whose deeds would create islands of utopia. Through such "cumulative anticipation", achieved by growing imitation, the libertarian state (state in the sense of a new organization of human relationships) could be brought about [4]. That was, in essence, the theory.

The practice of the anarchist movement was, in the beginning, strongly associated with the socialist movement and the organization of the working class. Bakunin's influence on the 1st International matched Marx' but the latter managed to get the anarchists excluded in 1872 from the 1st International, which, however, also marked the end of this First International Workers' Association. As a movement, anarchism survived until World War I only in Russia and, in the anarcho-syndicalist variant, in Spain where it eclipsed with the victory of Franco before World War II. The terrorism of the 1890s in Western and Southern Europe however was not the product of anarchist movements comparable to the terrorism of national liberation movements in the Balkans, Poland or Ireland, or to the social-revolutionary terrorism in Russia. Rather than being an anarchist conspiracy, as it was held by some in the period, it was more of a chain reaction of revenge and punishment by "lone wolf" anarchists practising political assassinations on kings, judges, chiefs of police and the like. [5] The fact that individual anarchists committed murders on figure-heads like the French president Sadi Carnot (1894), the Spanish Prime Minister Canovas del Castillo (1897), the Empress Elizabeth of Austria, (1898), the Italian King Humbert I (1900) and the U.S. President William McKinley (1901), and the fact that anarchist publications condoned in or even cheered at assassination attempts on highly placed persons in society was not accidental.

There were several elements in anarchist ideology which lent themselves
to being springboards to terrorism. There was, to begin with, the notion
of an "avant-garde" in Bakunin's thinking, revolutionary prototypes who
would inspire and carry with themselves the masses who, as Bakunin com-
plained, "could not be brought to be enthusiastic about their own liberation" [6]. Then there was, as Peter Lösche has pointed out, the notion
that revolutions were not brought about by patient organizing and party
work but that they were essentially spontaneous events. While socialist
thinkers saw social change in general and the revolution in particular
as the outflow of objective historical laws, anarchist theory put more
emphasis on individual initiative; it was voluntarist. The will to change
society, brought forward vigorously, came in the place of the working
of economic processes which Marxism postulated. Rather than waiting until the bourgeoisie had fully shaken off the last remnants of feudalism
and emancipated itself politically and economically before the next step
on the ladder of human progress could be made, anarchists believed in the
power of enlightment, education and demonstration by example. This example
could take the form of alternative production arrangements of a cooperative nature but it could also take the form of demonstrating that state
power was vulnerable by attacking key representatives of authority [7].
The theoretical formulation of the idea of "Propaganda of the Deed" occurred for the first time in 1877, one year after Bakunin's death, by
Paul Brousse and Peter Kropotkin [8]. Yet it was already foreshadowed in
the association of Bakunin in Geneva in 1869 with the Russian nihilist
Nechayev for whom he apparently edited or with whom he co-authored the
"Catechism of a Revolutionary" [9]. This Revolutionary Catechism is a
Machiavellian manual for the professional revolutionary who dedicates
his own life to the cause of destruction of the present "unnatural" order and tries to involve everybody else into his scheming through misleading blackmail and murder. It is sufficient to quote some lines from
it to indicate the absolutism of Sergei Nechayev:

> "The revolutionary is a lost man; he has no interests of his own,
> no feelings, no habits, no belongings ... Everything in him is ab-
> sorbed by a single, exclusive interest, one thought, one passion -
> the revolution. (...) For him, everything that allows the triumph
> of revolution is moral, and everything that stands in its way is
> immoral. 10)

While some apologists of Bakunin and anarchism have placed some distance
between Nechayev and Bakunin, there are enough writings of Bakunin himself which show traces of the same joy of indiscriminate destruction

which the "young fanatic" (Bakunin on Nechayev) [11] exhibited. In a way
the "disastrous relationship" which for a short time (1869-1872) linked
Bakunin to Nechayev, has continued to link anarchism to terrorism.

Yet as a critique of the social system and as a construct for a better
society, anarchism has been much more than an ideology of violence
or a theory of which terrorism was the practice. While all anarchists
denied authority only few of them fought it violently and only a very
few terroristically. The individualist trait of anarchism and its mechanism for revolution, the exemplary deed, lend themselves to terrorism
but beyond that the convergence is thin. Walter Laqueur has written the
following on the relationship of terrorism to another -ism - Marxism -,
which, in our view, also applies to its relationship with anarchism:

> "... unlike Marxism, terrorism is not an ideology but an insur-
> rectional strategy that can be used by people of very different
> political convictions. (...) And as the technology of terrorism
> can be mastered by people of all creeds, so does its philosophy
> transcend the traditional deviding lines between political doctrine. [12]

Notes

1) See for instance Jillian Becker. Hitler's Children: The Story of the Baader-Meinhof Terrorist Gang. Philadelphia, J.B. Lippincott, 1977; Karl Kautsky. Terrorismus und Kommunismus. Ein Beitrag zur Naturge- schichte der Revolution. Berlin, Verlag Neues Vaterland, 1919; Carl J. Friedrich and Zbigniew K. Brzezinski. Totalitarian Dictator- ship and Autocracy. Cambridge, Mass., Harvard University Press, 1966, p. 107-173.

2) George Woodcock. Anarchism. A History of Libertarian Ideas and Move- ments. Harmondsworth, Penguin, 1977, p. 12.

3) Peter Lösche. Terrorismus und Anarchismus. Internationale und histo- rische Aspekte. In: M. Funke (Ed.). Extremismus im demokratischen Rechtsstaat. Bonn, Bundeszentrale für politische Bildung, 1978, p. 85.

4) This passage is based on Th. Holterman. Anarchisme, recht en staat. Correcties van een stereotiep beeld. Intermediair, jg. 15, nos. 1-2, 12 januari 1979, p. 69.

5) A.L. Constanse. Anarchisme van de Daad. Den Haag, Kruseman Uitg., 1969, p. 80; Ze'ev Iviansky. Individual Terror: Concept and Typology. Journal of Contemporary History, Vol. 12, no. 1, 1977, p. 50.

6) Cit. Walter Theimer. Geschichte der politischen Ideen. Bern, Francke Verlag, 1955, p. 348.

7) P. Lösche, op. cit., p. 86-88.

8) W. Laqueur. Terrorism. London, Weidenfeld and Nicolson, 1977, p. 49.

9) Edward Hyams. Terrorists and Terrorism. London, J.M. Dent & Sons, 1975, p. 25-26; Albert Parry. Terrorism. From Robespierre to Arafat. New York, Vanguard Press, 1976, p. 78-79.

10) Cit. E. Hyams, op. cit., p. 26. - This catechism was not published at the time.

11) E. Hyams, op. cit., p. 25.

12) W. Laqueur, op. cit., p. 4-5.

I am endebted to C. Bronsveld for commenting on an earlier version of this chapter.

Terrorism and Assassination

The terms terrorism and political assassination are frequently used in
one breath [1] and there seems to be considerable overlapping in meanings.
Contrary to the term "murder" which is used in a context of crime, "assassination" is used in general in a political context (less frequently the
term is also used when a nonpolitical celebrity is killed). Terrorism, in
everyday parlance, is often seen as political crime, or political murder.
The link between the two concepts might at least in part be found in this
political dimension, rather than in the nature of the act of killing itself.

The etymology of the word "assassin" is of limited help in clarifying the
concept of assassination since the Arab word "hashsahashin" simply means
"those who use hashish". More specifically, it referred to a Shiite Isma
ili sect which was active in the 11th and 12th century in the Middle East.
Led by the "Old Man of the Mountains", a religious despot who had his political and religious opponents murdered by fanatic followers performing
their deeds under the influence of hashish, the Assassins gained widespread
notoriety. The crusaders of the time came home from the Holy Land with
tales of the murderers with golden daggers and so the word "assassin"
found its way into European languages, standing for sudden, secret murder
of public figures [2]. Beyond the fact that it is a particular form of
murder there seems to be little consensus as to what constitutes an assassination. J. B. Bell writes:

> "Despite the continuing prevalence of political murder and a concomi-
> tant popular and academic concern, there is little agreement even on
> a general definition of "assassination". Those who murder in the ser-
> vice of the state and those driven by fantasies are often humped to-
> gether with the gunmen of urban guerrilla organizations or even orga-
> nized criminals."

Bell himself concludes that "Assassination is simply a violent crime with
political implications" [3].

It is hard to argue with such an abstract and general definition. One can
question whether it is always a crime. In the literature on tyrannicide,
there are authors who hold that the tyrant had, by his oppression or by
his usurpation, violated Divine Law so that killing him was no murder but
the punishment for the guilt of treason against God [4].

The "political implication" mentioned by Bell is usually more manifest when a politician is murdered by a citizen than when a politician has a citizen executed. As the term is generally used, it has a pro-establishment bias in the sense that we are conditioned to think of political assassination when the <u>victim</u> is a politically important figure. A policy of "assassination" by politically dominant figures against those below in the social hierarchy is generally termed differently (e.g. Law and Order). A special case is when both killer and victim are of high rank. In that case, however, the killer is usually well hidden and acts through third parties. An example would be the alleged killing of Patrice Lumumba on orders from president Eisenhower [5].

Not every killing of a high-ranking politician needs to be a political assassination, although there might be political implications flowing from the murder. If the killer has no particular political motives for his deed and the victims are interchangeable to him as in the case of Arthur Bremer who first considered killing Richard Nixon but then settled for George Wallace, one might still speak of attempted assassination but not of <u>political</u> assassination. Generally speaking the political motive for a killing is likely to be present more strongly when the killer is not a "lone wolf" but part of a group or acting on behalf of others in the pursuit of a strategy to bring about political change. H.L. Nieburg has followed this line of thinking when he developed this comprehensive definition:

> "Political assassination: act of murder whose purpose, choice of victim, surrounding circumstances, implementation and/or effects have political significance, i.e. tend to modify the behavior of other actors in a bargaining situation of systematic social consequences." [6]

Ali A. Mazuri, on the other hand, does not think that "motive" is important for the labelling, writing "neither the speed of killing nor the role of the killer is crucial in defining assassination. What is crucial is that an assassination is the killing of someone politically important by an agent other than himself or the government - for reasons which are either political or unknown." [7]

Another author, Victor T. Le Vine, is more impressed by the special type of killing than the victim. He writes:

> "The difference between assassination and murder is admittedly a tenuous one; I would contend that it lies in two areas, the role of the killer, and the element of surprise. Assassins are usually hired or delegated, and they generally strike without warning to the victims." [8]

William J. Crotty offers this definition:

"Assassination of political consequence ... can be defined as the
murder of an individual, whether of public prominence or not, in an
effort to achieve political gain. The classic conception of the
assassination act is as a tactic in struggles for political power.
(...) The definition of the subject matter to be examined directs
attention to three factors: the nature of the victim; the ends to be
achieved by the murder; and the alleged motivations of the killer." 9)

Ivo K. Feierabend c.s. utilized for his quantitative cross-national study
the following definition:

"An assassination event was defined as an act that consists of a
plotted, attempted, or actual murder of a prominent political figure
(elite) by an individual (assassin) who performs this act in other
than a governmental role. This definition draws a distinction between
political execution and assassination. An execution may be regarded
as a political killing, but it is initiated by the organs of the state,
while an assassination can always be characterized as an illegal act." 10)

Enough has been cited to make clear that there is only limited consensus.
Each author probably has a set of events (murders) in mind which shape
his particular perspective on assassination. One might think of Caesar,
Lincoln, Kennedy, or alternatively of Jaurès, Marat and Trotsky. Depending
which set of victims comes to one's mind, the semantic load of "assassination" will be different.

The following elements recur in definitions of assassination:

1. Lethal violence is applied against a human being that is

2. a public figure of political prominence,

3. whereby no legal procedures establishing guilt preceed the execution
   which is

4. performed covertly outside the context of a battle, insurrection or
   coup d'état

5. whereby the victim - who is also the main tárget - is carefully selected

6. with the purpose to bring about political change favorable to

7. the murderer and/or his paymasters.

Obviously there are different types of assassinations, and it is worthwhile to look at some typologies. This will also enable us to get a clearer
picture of the links between terrorism and assassination. Feliks Gross, in
an article which is "concerned primarily with the individual, 'high-level'
assassination" (heads of state, kings, presidents, chief executives, members of government, and leading political personalities) [11] distinguishes
three types of assassination:

1. Political assassination as an isolated act, frequently accomplished by a deranged person. (...)
2. Sultanism, assassination of competitors to power. Related to the latter are assassinations to secure power for a new elite, to remove the one which controls political power.
3. Individual terror, systematic and tactical assassination directed against the representatives of the ruling groups or government with an objective toward weakening the government and the political system, destroying the existing legitimacy, and effecting ideological, political, and social change. Individual terror was thus far a tactic for achieving power; mass terror was applied in the past and present to consolidate and maintain power. 12)

Basing himself at least in part on Gross, Crotty divided assassination into five categories:

1. Anomic assassination: ... this is the murder of a political figure for essentially private reasons. The justification for the act is couched in broadly political terms, but the relationship between the act and the advancement of the political objectives specified is impossible to draw on any rational basis. The connection link then is assumed to be in the fantasies of the assassin. (...)
2. Elite substitution: The murder of a political leader in order to replace him or those he represents in power with an opposing group at essentially the same level. (...)
3. Tyrannicide: ... the murder of a despot in order to replace him with one more amendable to the people and needs of a nation. The assassination of Czar Alexander II of Russia is such a case, although the results were not as intended. (...) The struggles in Russia against the czar developed the systematic and tactical use of assassination as a broad-scale political weapon. The intention was to punish the government or its minions for specified acts, to decentralize and weaken it, and eventually to incapacitate it. This, in turn, developed into a fourth type of assassination.
4. Terroristic assassination: Terror through assassination can be employed on a mass basis to demonstrate a government's incapacity to deal with insurgents, to neutralize a populace's allegiance to a government, to enlist their support in a revolutionary movement, or, more ambitiously, to allow a minority to suppress and subjugate a population. Examples of mass terror in history are many: the era of mass terror associated with the French Revolution; the Inquisition, the Russian purges of the 1930's ... (...) Terroristic assassinations directed toward specified categories of civilians or officials represent a more limited and systematic attempt to achieve the same ends as mass-terror assassinations. The Viet Cong focused on village leaders, reportedly killing or kidnapping over 2,400 officials in the period 1957-1959 ... (...)
5. Propaganda by deed: This type of assassination is employed to direct attention to a broader problem, for example the subjugation of a people, with the hopes of bringing some alleviation. The assassination of Czar Alexander II was in part for propaganda purposes, as was the assassination attempt directed against President Truman and the explanation given for Senator Robert Kennedy's assassination. 13)

That fact that Crotty uses the activities against the Russian czar as explicit or implicit examples for three of the five types, indicates that his categories are not a definite improvement over Gross' tripartition. Both Gross and Crotty see individual terror as more than an isolated act of political assassination, namely as a theory of political struggle which gained shape in the fight against the Russian autocracy [14]. Their view is shared and further developed by others.

In the view of D.C. Rapoport, the assassin acts against "corrupt" persons, while the terrorist acts against a "corrupt" system [15]. In Rapoport's view "Terrorism implies a movement whose objective can only be achieved by repeated assassinations over relatively long periods of time, for fear dissipates when pressure is relaxed or exercised intermittently" [16]. Since terrorism, in this view, is directed against a system, any representative of that system can in principle serve as a target of the violence to be metted out. In the same vein Martha Crenshaw notes:

> "Terrorist targets represent specific groups within society rather than obstacles to be eliminated. (...) The victims of terrorism represent or "stand for" certain categories of people, so that violence against an individual member of a group is a threat to all other members of the same or a closely related group." [17]

While the assassin wants his victim dead, the terrorist has no particular interest in the fate of his immediate victim. For him the demonstration effect matters, not the elimination of a particular human being. The assassin's deed does not, as Thomas P. Thornton observed [18] put the question "Will I be next?" in every observer's mind. The target is the holder of some office, performing a risky role in society and his murder can be seen as discriminate and in some ways unique. Terrorism, on the other hand, while using assassination as a technique among others, is repetitive and less discriminate. While terrorism generates fear with the victim's reference group, this is not so with pure assassinations. L.J. Macfarlane writes:

> "Assassination is far more likely to generate anger than fear, and lead to a hardening of attitudes in the very opposite direction to that wanted by the assassin. Only when one is dealing with a personal tyrant, like Stalin or Hitler, is it possible to have confidence in the political value of assassination ..." [19]

A campaign of assassinations is likely to be considered terroristic, in contrast to a single attentat or series of attempts on one and the same person like the more than two dozen unsuccessful attempts on De Gaulle or Fidel Castro.

Turning to the respondents of our questionnaire we find that there is also
considerable consensus as to the relationship between assassination and
terrorism. It is enough to quote three authors:

- Political assassination "can have the goal just to kill that one
  man and nothing else - not so with terrorism".   (Zofka)
- "... political assassination in its pure form attempts to remove a
  personality from the political scene and not to impress others by
  causing fear in the circle of persons that identify with the victim.
  There are, however, very few 'pure' cases, since many political
  assassinations or acts of urban guerrilla can be terrorist."
  (Dimitrijević).
- "Political assassination may be satisfied with the elimination of
  a certain personality in the expectation that, even without any
  further terrorizing, its successor shall have different political
  views."   (Lador-Lederer)

Concluding from the above it would seem that the type of interaction between perpetrator and victim of violence is different for assassination and
terrorism. While the assassin wants to discontinue the direct influence of
the target on society by selecting him as victim for murder, the terrorist's
main target is not the victim. The demonstrative effect, the impact of the
murder on others than the victim is paramount. The target is the social
environment in general and certain sections of society linked to the victim in particular.

In reality, however, there are few pure cases and the borderline between
a terroristic murder and a political assassination remains fuzzy.

- 63 -

Notes

1) cf. e.g. David C. Rapoport. Assassination and Terrorism. Toronto, Canadian Broadcasting Company, 1971.

2) Brian McConnell. Assassinations - The Murders that Changed History. London, Marshall Cavendish Publ., 1975, p. 7-13; L. Bowyer Bell. Assassin. New York, St. Martin's Press, 1979, p. 22.

3) Ibid., p. 22, 24.

4) John of Salisbury. On Slaying Public Tyrants (Policraticus, written in 1159), partly repr. in W. Laqueur. The Terrorism Reader. New York, New American Library, 1978, p. 21.

5) U.S. Congress, Senate. Select Committee to Study Governmental Operations. Alleged Assassination Plots Involving Foreign Leaders. An Interim Report. 94th Cong., 1st Sess., Washington, D.C., GPO, 1975, p. 25; G. Heinz and H. Donnay (pseud.). Lumumba: The Last Five Days. New York, Grove Press, 1969.

6) H.L. Nieburg. Murder as Political Behavior. In: William J. Crotty (Ed.). Assassination and the Political Order. New York, Harper & Row, 1971, p. 434.

7) Ali A. Mazuri. Thoughts on Assassination in Africa. Political Science Quarterly, 83, March 1968, p. 40-48; cit. E.F. Mickolus. Transnational Terrorism. A Chronology of Events, 1968-1979. London, Aldwych Press, 1980, p. XXIX, no. 5.

8) Victor T. Le Vine. The Course of Political Violence. In: William H. Lewis (Ed.). French Speaking Africa: The search for Identity. New York, Appleton-Century-Crofts, 1965, p. 68; as quoted in Nieburg, op. cit., p. 433.

9) William J. Crotty. Assassinations and Their Interpretation within the American Context. In: W.J. Crotty, (Ed.), op. cit., p. 8.

10) Ivo K. Feierabend et al. Political Violence and Assassination: A Cross-National Assessment. In: W.J. Crotty (Ed.), op cit., p. 56.

11) F. Gross. Political Assassination. In: M.H. Livingston (Ed.) International Terrorism in the Contemporary World. Westport, Conn., Greenwood Press, 1978, p. 315.

12) Ibid., p. 312.

13) William J. Crotty. Assassinations and Their Interpretation within the American Context. In: W.J. Crotty (Ed.), op. cit., p. 10-13.

14) Feliks Gross. Violence in Politics. Terror and Political Assassination in Eastern Europe and Russia. The Hague, Mouton, 1972, p. 10.

15) D.C. Rapoport. Assassination and Terrorism. Toronto, Canadian Broadcasting Corporation, 1970, p. 38, as quoted by L.C. Green. Aspects of Terrorism. Terrorism, Vol. 5, no. 4, 1982, p. 395.

16) Cit. ibid.

17) Martha Crenshaw Hutchinson. Revolutionary Terrorism. The FLN in Algeria, 1954-1962. Stanford, Hoover Institution, 1978, p. 19-20.

18) Thomas Thornton. Terror as a Weapon of Political Agitation. In: Harry Eckstein (Ed.). Internal War: Problems and Approaches. New York, Free Press, 1964, p. 86.

19) L.J. Macfarlane. Violence and the State. London, Thomas Nelson & Sons, Ltd., 1974, p. 108-109.

Terrorism and Terror

In the literature on terrorism there is no consensus as to what the relationship between terror and terrorism is. The respondents to our questionnaire also showed a variety of opinions. One author held that the
terms could be used as synonyms and therefore interchangeably (Blok) and
others noted that this is indeed quite common. A number of authors reserve the word terror for state-induced violence and use terrorism for
insurgent violence (e.g. Francis, Wilkinson, Zofka). Related
to this usage is the use of terror to refer to some historical situation
such as France under Robespierre or Russia under Stalin (Bonanate). Yet
another author suggests an analogy of usage between fraud and defrauding
and terror and terrorism (Lador-Lederer). Another sees terrorism as "the
more organized form of terror" (Wilferink), following the usage of E.V.
Walter or perhaps thinking of the systematic character which is expressed
with the suffix in a number of Western languages. A number of other authors
(Hess, Merari, Ochberg, Wilber) stress that terror is a state of mind while
terrorism would refer to organized social activity. Many authors hold that
terrorism intends to create states of terror (Hondrich, Stohl,
Wolpin). One author, however, cautions: "If one felt compelled to make a distinction, one could say that terror is the sometimes
psychological consequence of terrorism." (Sederberg). He is in company of two
others, one of them saying that "terrorism is a special case and only indirectly related to terror" (Young) while the other notes that "terror
can occur without terrorism" (Ochberg). Yet another author maintains,
however, that "terror is the key to terrorism" (Dinstein).
Obviously some clarification is desirable. We will attempt to do this by
turning first to the etymology and then at the psychology of terror.

Etymology

While the word Terror is of Latin origin, similar words can be found in
other indogerman languages (Sanskrit: tras to tremble, to be afraid;
Greek: treô to flee away, dread; Russian: triasti to shake) all refering
to a field of meaning where fright, dread, dismay, consternation and alarm
are present. (Pierre Larousse, Dictionnaire Universel du XIX siècle. Vol.
14, Paris, 1875, p. 207.) The word entered current West-European vocabu-
lary via the French language where it first has been signaled in the 14th
century writings of the monk Bersuire [1]. For the English language the
Shorter Oxford Dictionary (3rd ed., 1965) gives the year 1528 for the first

known instance. Webster's International Dictionary of 1890 (London, p.
1489) lists under Terror "Extreme fear; fear that agitates body and mind;
violent dread; fright", and lists as second meaning "that which excites
dread; a cause of extreme fear". The Spanish 'Enciclopedia Universal illu-
strada' of 1928 (Madrid, vol. 40, p. 1549) says: "Miedo, espanto, pavor
de un mal que amenaza ó de un peligro que se teme". The Dictionnaire de
l'Académie Française (7th edition, Paris, 1935) describes Terreur as "émo-
tion profonde causée dans l'âme par la présence, l'annonce ou la peinture
d'un grand péril". German dictionaries   usually have no entry under
Terror since there is no such German word, the equivalent being "Schrecken".
But they usually contain a reference to the "Schreckensherrschaft" - the
Reign of Terror - in France prior and after 1800. (e.g. Meyers Lexikon,
Vol. 33, p. 652) The reference is to the Red Terror under Robespierre as well
as to the White Terror of the Restauration of the Monarchy in France in
1815. Since then there have been numerous other regimes of terror, so that
the term has been detached from a period in history and become generic. A
recent dictionary such as Webster's New Twentieth Century Dictionary (2nd
ed., New York, Simon and Schuster, 1979, p. 1884) is therefore likely to
give at least four meanings for

terror (L. terror, from terrere, to frighten.)

  1. intense fear.
  2. (a) a person or thing that causes intense fear;
     (b) the quality of causing dread; terribleness.
  3. (T-) a period characterized by political executions, as during
     the French Revolution, from May 1793 to July 1794.
  4. a program of terrorism or a party, group, etc. resorting to this.

For terrorism the same dictionary offers the following:

  1. a terrorizing; use of terror and violence to intimidate, sub-
     jugate, etc., especially as a political weapon or policy.
  2. intimidation and subjugation so produced. (ibid.)

The suffix "-ism" that is added to terror is sometimes held to refer to
the systematic character, either on the theoretical level where the suffix
refers to a political philosophy (liberal - liberalism, social - socialism,
etc.), or on a practical level, where it refers to a manner of acting or
an attitude (fanatic - fanaticism). While some attribute to terrorism a
doctrinal quality ("the philosophy of the bomb"), it is more common to
see it as a manner of acting, as a method of action [2]. However, the historical root of the suffix is referring to neither of these two possibilities.

In 1793,Revolutionary France was threatened by the upper class emigrants
who conspired with foreign rulers to invade the country and treason at

home in support of this reactionary move was a clear and present danger.
The National Convent, led by the Jacobins, therefore declared terror to
be the order of the day on 30 august 1793, thereby giving legal sanction
to a number of emergency measures. The Courier de l'Égalité wrote approvingly on the same day:

> "It is necessary that the terror caused by the guillotine spreads
> in all of France and brings to justice all the traitors. There is no
> other means to inspire this necessary terror which will consolidate
> the Revolution ... The Jacobin club has massively adopted this mea-
> sure ... An universal enthusiasm has manifested itself following this
> order, which will probably mark one of the greatest periods of our
> history." 3)

Originally conceived as an instrument against monarchist traitors the
Terror of the Committee of Public Safety (of which Robespierre was the
most prominent member) soon began to kill republicans too. The revolutionary allies on the right of the Jacobins (the Indulgents under Danton)
and on the left (the Hébertists) became victims of the unleashed terror.
Altogether at least 300,000 people were arrested during the Reign of Terror and 17,000 were officially executed while many died in prison or
without a trial. (Encyclopedia Britannica, 15th edition, Chicago,
1976, p. 904.) Those who had originally supported the draconic measures of Robespierre begun to fear for their lives and conspired to overthrow him. They could not accuse him of the Terror since they had declared
it to be the legitimate form of government, so they accused him of "Terrorism" which had an illegal and repulsive flavour. For this Robespierre
and his associates were sent to the guillotine on the 9th and 10th Ther-
midor of the year II (27th and 28th of July 1794) [4].

Under the Thermidoran reaction the agents and partisans of the revolutionary tribunals were termed "terrorists" and this name spread fast over
Europe, turning up in England in 1795. The Jacobin terrorists were also
labelled "anarchists" under the directorate and for the emigrés and their
monarchist followers the term "terrorist" was sometimes used synonymously
with "patriots" or used for all republicans and even for the soldiers who
defended the liberty of the republic. Another name with a similar charge
was "furoristes" [5].

In the late 19th century the term terrorist, originally used for violence
in the name of the revolutionary state and then the reactionary state of
the Restauration, became associated with anti-state violence under the
impact of the Russian terrorists of the 1880s and the anarchists of the
1890s. The 20th century experiences with state terror notwithstanding,
the anti-state thrust of the meaning of the term has become paramount

again in the second half of the 20th century under the impact of wars
of national liberation and revolutionary aspirations of students and
ethnic minorities in the industrialized countries.

Psychology

Textbooks on Psychology and Social Psychology usually index fear and anxiety but not terror. The literature on terrorism has also paid hardly any
attention to terror as a state of mind. With the exception of the more
recent literature on hostages, the experiences of being terrorized has
largely escaped attention. This strange absence can be explained perhaps
by the fact that terrorism does not only produce terror; that terror is
perhaps not even the main result for the majority of the audience of an
act or campaign of terror. Another explanation would be that policy-
oriented researchers in the field look preferably at more manipulable
variables in the terror process (e.g. the hardening of targets) than the
panic and shock which strikes the terrorized mind. This neglect of what
one would assume to be the central theme of terrorism, has been noted
by a physician, M.E. Silverstein:

> "In the midst of society's surprise, incredulity, and indignation
> the central theme of terror is often overlooked or even unconsciously
> denied. Terror is a state of intense fear induced by the systematic
> threat of imprisonment, mutilation, or death. It is intensified when
> the victim is helpless in the hands of another human being. We are
> all afraid of being hurt or killed. The terrorist manipulates persons
> and governments by making the threat of bodily harm manifest. The
> terrorist threatens the most fundamental human drive - the will to
> survive intact. He or she strips from the defenses of human courage
> that most important element of antifear, the real or supposed ability
> to fight back to defend one's person.
> Because the terrorist's victims are unarmed, noncombatant, and random
> and because they are totally helpless, the victim's fear is expe-
> rienced by all observers of the victim's plight, who are equally vul-
> nerable and who desire to live their lives unmolested. These secondary
> victims of terrorism, all who think by association that their lives
> are in equal danger, fear equally for their persons. Because they
> fear bodily harm, they are as manipulable as though the hand grenade
> were actually strapped to their bodies." 6)

One of the few political scientists in the field of terrorism who has paid
some attention to the emotion of terror has been Martha Crenshaw:

> "Psychologists commonly define the psychological condition of terror
> as extreme fear of anxiety. Following Freud, they conceive of normal
> fear as rational appreciation of a real danger, whereas anxiety is
> abnormal fear, an irrational response to a vaguely perceived, unfami-
> liar menace. (...) Though terrorism is a real, not an imaginary danger,
> it is a vague, incomprehensible, unpredictable, and unexpected menace
> - thus it can create a classic anxiety-producing situation. Persons who
> perceive this threat, even instinctively, may feel helpless and alone,

and thus anxious, but this feeling is often based on <u>actual</u> rather than imagined impotence. (...) Terrorism affects the social structure as well as the individual; it may upset the framework of precepts and images that members of society depend on and trust. The result of not knowing what sort of behavior to expect from others is disorientation. A formerly coherent community may as a result dissolve into a mass of anomic individuals, each concerned only with personal survival." 7)

When people are living in extreme fear, in constant dread of violence, an atmosphere of despair, confusion, paralysis and powerlessness is likely to arise. Such a chronic fear of being victimized at random and without warning can be caused by natural as well as human action. To live in the shadow of a vulcano, on the vault of an earthquake zone, behind a fragile dam against the sea, or having a tiger haunting the village at night can conceivably cause a pervasive atmosphere of anxiety - terror - in the minds of those who experience it. This one might call "natural terror". A second category of terror might be labelled "situational terror", following a proposal of Dallin and Breslauer, who use this term for the uncontrolled and undisciplined behavior by lower-level cadres, in contrast to, what they term, the "purposive terror" of communist policy-makers 8). However we would like to give "<u>situational terror</u>" a slightly different meaning. One of our questionnaire respondents cited as an example of terror "terror is having a flat tire in the fast lane of a Los Angeles freeway" (Monday). This half-joking reference emphasized the particular context, the clearly deliminated "terror zone". In the context of war, civilians coming under cross-fire between the opposing armies might experience such "situational terror". Terror might also come from the air when urban targets are bombed. This sort of terror is a by-product of war, not directly intended but also not clearly avoided by the perpetrators. The border between this situational terror and the more purposive can be fuzzy. The bombing of Hiroshima and Nagasaki, for instance, was, according to the interpretation given by Thomas Schelling, purposive, meant to make non-capitulation "terrible beyond endurance":

"These [atomic bombs] were weapons of terror and shock. They hurt, and promised more hurt, and that was their purpose. (...) The bomb that hit Hiroshima was a threat aimed at all of Japan. The political target of the bomb was not the dead of Hiroshima or the factories they worked in, but the survivors in Tokyo. (...) The effect of the bombs, and their purpose, were not mainly the military destruction they accomplished but the pain and the shock and the promise of more." 9)

Thus "natural" and "situational" terror can arise without terrorism as a deliberate policy of striking terror into the minds of a target group,

which is what "purposive terror" does. The distinction developed here is
also maintained by P. Wilkinson who uses a different terminology but essentially covers the same ground when he notices:

> "Much of our experience of terror is the unintended or epiphenomenal
> by-product of other happenings which are beyond our power to predict
> or control. Indeed inability to understand what is happening, say in
> a sudden automobile collision or a fire, is in itself a cause of more
> intense fear. And outbreaks of cataclysmic mass violence such as
> wars and revolutions inevitably bring a vast amount of epiphenomenal
> terror in their wake. This large-scale, and often sanguinary, epipheno-
> menal terror, should, of course, be clearly distinguished from the
> systematic regimes of terror which, for example, succeeded the French
> and Russian Revolutions. (...) I wish therefore to maintain the dis-
> tinction between epiphenomenal or incidental terror of the kind that
> frequently accompanies mass violence and the systematic terrorism of
> groups or regimes of terror in which the use of terror as a mode of
> psychological warfare is explicitly intended and planned." 10)

While some fear is evoked in the victim and/or the audience of almost any
act of violence, the relationship between fear and violence is dispropor-
tional in the case of terrorism. On this aspect, a study commissioned by
the U.S. Department of Justice, contains a useful elaboration:

> "Terror is a constituent of many ordinary crimes, either as a norma-
> tive element, as in robbery or, incidentally, such as in rape. In a
> robbery, the victim is threatened so that he will relinquish his pro-
> perty; his fear, however great and essential to the criminal's success,
> is not meant to be an example to others. Similarly, the fear generated
> by the crime of rape is aimed at overcoming the will of the instant
> victim, not at the minds or resistance of others. Such crimes may
> terrify, but they are not terrorism. An act of terrorism, on the other
> hand, has a purpose similar to general deterrence: the instant victim
> is less important than the overall effect on a particular group to
> whom the exemplary act is really addressed. Thus terrorism, although
> it has its individual victims, is really an onslaught upon society
> itself. (...) Terror is a natural phenomenon; terrorism is the con-
> scious exploitation of it. Terrorism is coercive, designed to manipu-
> late the will of its victims and its larger audience. The great degree
> of fear is generated by the crime's very nature, by the manner of its
> perpetration, or by its senselessness, wantonness, or callous indif-
> ference to human life. This terrible fear is the source of the terro-
> rist's power and communicates his challenge to society." 11)

Given the imbalance between violence and fear in terrorism, some authors
even hold that there can be terror without violence. Dallin and Breslauer
state that "terror in our usage does not necessarily include violence:
just as some violence involves no terror, some terror (e.g. intimidation)
requires no violence" 12). This is probably a fallacy since intimidation
is based on threat and threats have to be occasionally enforced to remain
credible. The position of E.V. Walter, that "violence may occur without
terror, but not terror without violence" seems to be more realistic 13).

Walter who wrote one of the few classic studies in the field of terrorism,
sees terrorism as organized terror:

> "Conventionally, the word "terrorism" means a type of violent action,
> such as murder, designed to make people afraid. In ordinary usage,
> however, the related word "terror" is ambiguous, often suggesting
> any kind of extreme apprehension, no matter what the cause. Moreover,
> it may mean, on the one hand, the psychic state - extreme fear - and,
> on the other hand, the thing that terrifies - the violent event that
> produces the psychic state. I shall try to avoid confusion by main-
> taining a precise usage, employing terms such as "terrorism" and "or-
> ganized terror" consistently as equivalents to process of terror, by
> which I mean a compound with three elements: the act or threat of vio-
> lence, the emotional reaction, and the social effects." 14)

The implicit assumption of many authors seems to be that the product of
terrorism is terror. But who exactly is terrorized? The immediate victim
of a terrorist bomb explosion may be dead before he gets a chance to be
filled with terror. The potential fellow victims in a hostage situation
where one hostage has been killed to show that the terrorists "mean
business" in their demands to the authorities or third parties are those
most likely to be terror-stricken. The families and friends of those immediately fearing for their lives, are, when notified of what is going
on, hardly less upset emotionally. They are in permanent fear that their
helpless loved ones will be wantonly slayed. But are they terrorized in
the narrow sense of the word, that is, that purposive terror is exercised
against them? One hesitates to answer no but analytically the answer
should be closer to no than yes. All depends on context: are they themselves likely victims in the future? Are they blackmailed or coerced?
Other segments of the audience to the act of terror are less likely to
be terrorized. They might be angry, they might feel outraged, they might
be vengeful, or they might be only impressed, or even merely recording
the event. That the behavioral outcome desired by the terrorist for his
target audience is fear and fear alone, is by no means certain. The real
audience of the terrorist might be different from the assumed audience.
To offer an example: the Red Cells in West Germany were planning to kill
two prominent members of the Jewish community in Frankfurt. They admitted
that they had no political reason to assassinate Heinz Galinski and Ignaz
Lipinski. But after the Entebbe debacle they had to prove to their Palestinian financier Abu Hani that they were still capable of conducting operations. The real audience was therefore Abu Hani, not the Jewish community in Germany or Israel. He had to be impressed, while the terrorization
was unimportant 15).

Struck by an act of terror people will ask "Why?" and "Will I be next?"
but those who ask "Why?" will be more numerous than those who have to
answer the second question affirmatively. Only the latter are likely to
be terrorized. Insufficient attention has so far been given to the various
responses induced by terror. Thornton, in what is one of the classical
analytic writings on the subject, stands almost alone. Basing himself on
a clear victim-target differentiation - in this he was one of the first
authors , together with Walter - he identified four levels of responses
induced by terror:

I. The one positive response to be achieved is <u>enthusiasm</u> among the
adherents of the insurgent movement. This response involves the
purely morale-building function ... and need not concern us
further.

II. The lowest level of negative reaction is <u>fright</u>. The frightened
person perceives a specific danger, which is not qualitatively
different from other dangers with which he is personnally or vicariously familiar. Since the perceived danger fits into the pattern of his previous experience, his response will be meaningful
in terms of familiar norms of action; it will be both subjectively
and objectively logical and reasonably predictable.

III. The middle level of response is <u>anxiety</u>, which is called forth by
fear of the unknown and the unknowable. Traditional norms of behavior show no relevance to the new situation, and the victim
becomes disoriented, casting about for guidance. The exact nature
of response is unpredictable, but it is likely to lead to activity
that is logical in terms of the new situation as perceived by
the target.

IV. The most extreme level of response is <u>despair</u>, an intensified
form of anxiety. The victim perceives the threat to be so great
and unavoidable that there is no course of action open to him
that is likely to bring relief. As a result, the victim with-
draws from the situation to the maximum possible extent. 16)

The response to an act of terror can vary greatly, depending on the danger
of repetition and the degree of identification with the victim. If the observer identification is not with the victim but with the target of terroristic coercion it is unlikely to be terror and if the identification
of the observer is with the terrorist himself it might even be euphoria.
What mechanisms underlie this <u>identification process</u> is still an untouched
field in the study of terrorism. Sympathy and identification with the
aggressor, however, do not seem to be an exeption from a usually identification with the victim. Depending on the cause for which the terror violence is said to be applied and depending on our in-group - out-group
identification with terrorist or victim, moral standards can be amazingly
flexible producing inconsistent attitudes towards victimization (for an
example, see pp. 197-198).

Notes

1) Paul Wurth, La répression internationale du terrorisme. Lausanne, La Concorde, 1941, p. 11.

2) This distinction between theoretical and practical systematic is taken from M. van Herpen, Terrorisme zonder Terreur. Een poging tot een sociologische definitie van de begrippen terrorisme en terreur. Nijmegen, Unpubl. paper, 1978, p. 7.

3) Cit. P. Wurth, op. cit., p. 11.

4) P. Wurth, op. cit., p. 13.

5) A. Aulard, Paris pendent la réaction thermidorienne et sous le directtoire. Paris, 1902, vol. II, p. 522; cit. P. Wurth, op. cit., p. 15.

6) Martin Elliot Silverstein, Emergency Medical Preparedness. Terrorism, Vol. 1, no. 1, 1977, p. 51-52.

7) Martha Crenshaw Hutchinson, Revolutionary Terrorism. Stanford, Hoover Institution, 1978, p. 25.

8) A. Dallin and G.W. Breslauer, Political Terror in Communist Systems. Stanford, Hoover Institution, 1970, p. 19n.

9) Thomas Schelling, Arms and Influence. New Haven, Conn., Yale University Press, 1966, p. 15, 16-17; cit. M. Stohl (Ed.), The Politics of Terrorism. New York, Dekker, 1979, p. 11.

10) P. Wilkinson, Terrorism and the Liberal State. London, Macmillan, 1977, p. 47-48.

11) U.S. National Advisory Committee on Criminal Justice Standards and Goals. Report of the Task Force on Disorders and Terrorism. Washington, D.C., GPO, 1976, p. 3.

12) Dallin and Breslauer, op. cit., p. 2n.

13) E.V. Walter, Terror and Resistance. A Study of Political Violence. London, Oxford University Press, 1969, p. 9.

14) E.V. Walter, op. cit., p. 5.

15) The plan did not go through. - Hans Joachim Klein, Da bin ich ausgeklinkt. Der Spiegel, No. 51, 17 Dec. 1979, p. 82.

16) Thomas Perry Thornton, Terror as a Weapon of Political Agitation. In: Harry Eckstein (Ed.), Internal War. Problems and Approaches. New York, The Free Press of Glencoe, 1964, p. 80-81.

Elements of Definitions of Terrorism

When a scientific field of investigation has achieved some maturity
there tends to be agreement about the basic definitions within the
dominant paradigm. In the case of terrorism there are only claims that
certain definitions have reached considerable support. Bassiouni, for
instance, states that "a consensus definition proposed by this author
has achieved a significant degree of international acceptance." [1]
Another author refers to "the standard definition of terrorism" of
Hutchinson, 1971, while the author in question has not published any
definition in that year. [2]
In our questionnaire we asked authors in the field of terrorism about
their opinion (see Table I). This is what our respondents offered:

Table IV : Answers to the Question: "Whose Definition of Terrorism
Do You Find Adequate for Your Purposes?"

Authors mentioned	Number of citations*
There is no adequate definition	10
My own definition is adequate	9
No answer	5
Walter	4
Thornton	3
Crenshaw (Hutchinson)	3
Wilkinson	3
Jenkins (& Johnson)	3
U.S. Nat. Advisory Committee on Criminal Justice	3
Paust	2
Others mentioned only once: Arendt; Boudovin, Fortin & Szabo; Clausewitz; Dantricourt; Fromkin; Glaser; Guillaume & Levasseur; Hacker; Kupperman; Leiden & Schmidt; Levy-Bruhl; Milbank & Mickolus; Münckler; Hardman; Ochberg; Schmid & de Graaf; Schreiber; Sun Tzu; Webster's Dictionary; Wördemann.	1

* Some of the 45 respondents mentioned more than one author.

Clearly there is no single author's definition dominating here (set I).
However, it might be that the definitions of some of the above
authors actually cover the same ground, although the wording might
be different. We therefore identified a number of elements in
definitions in order to find out whether there is a degree of
agreement as to the content of definitions. For this we looked at
the personal definitions which were volunteered by respondents of
our questionnaire (set II). Our main sample for content analysis, however,
consists of the more than hundred definitions reprinted in the
Appendix to this chapter (set III).

There is some overlap between these sets of definitions. Two of the
top authors of set I also figure in the 2nd and 3rd set and 12 of
the 29 authors in the 2nd set also figure in the 1st set. For
purposes of comparison this is problematical. However, this is not
the only methodological aspect which should be kept in mind when
interpreting Table II. The three samples are of such unequal size
(n= 109, 29, 7 respecively) that percentage figures are misleading
(One author counts less than 1 percent in one sample set, but more than
14 percent in another.) Another problem is, that in the biggest sample
no less than 11 authors are represented with more than one definition
(Jenkins with 5 - in one case together with Johnson, Wilkinson with 4,
Crenshaw (Hutchinson), Horowitz and Mickolus with 3 each; Arendt,
Bassiouni, Crozier, Hacker, Mallin , Moss with 2 each). The reason for
this is that these authors have developed several definitions at
different times and since these authors are leading authors in the
field their formulations were considered to be of special importance.
In other words, the 3rd sample is biased in favour of these authors.
There are more biases. Probably as many as 75% of the authors in the
first sample are Anglo-American authors or authors residing in the
United States. In the second sample 10 are from the USA, 6 from the U.K.,
2 from Canada, 3 from Yugoslavia and 3 from the Federal German Republic,
2 from the Netherlands and two from Israel and one is residing in Sweden.[3]
In Table I all the authors mentioned more than once are Anglo-Americans,
one of them being British and the rest being American. In other words,
the research community is overwhelmingly Anglo-American. But most of
the research on terrorism is Anglo-American too.

The nature of the samples should also be kept in mind. The second sample was based on questionnaire responses and these tend to be more summarily than the definitions in the third sample which were taken from books and articles. An indication of this can be found back in the average number of elements authors used to define terrorism. In the 3rd sample this was about eight elements, while in the second (questionnaire-based) sample, an average of about five elements used to define terrorism.*

* Many definitions are enumerations of elements without clear indications which element(s) must be present for a phenomenon to be qualified as terrorism and which elements are merely regularly accompanying features of the phenomenon. Practically none of the definitions are standing up to requirements of formal logic, as does, for instance, the definition of violence used by Pontara (see p.12). The definitions in our third sample are in fact often not definitions in the narrow sense at all, but passages of texts wherein authors analyse and describe the subject matter. Some of the passages we have chosen are quite long, others are short. If we had taken a longer passage in some cases an element or two might have been won. Thus, when we state that an author in the 1st sample defines terrorism in terms of elements x, y, z, etc. this refers to the textual passage reproduced in the Appendix only and not to other passages in the same or another work of the same author. Altogether we have identified 22 element-categories recurring in definitions (more precisely: in the definitional passages reproduced in the Appendix) and checked how frequently these were featured in the three samples. The selection of these 22 elements is not unsubjective. Sometimes we used broad categories in which elements of unequal meaning were put. For instance, violence and force which some authors distinguish from each other were put into one category. More problematical perhaps, we also put "organized action" and "systematic action" in one category, together with "purposive" and "planned action". Something can be planned without that it is systematic yet we only use one category for the two. However, using too many categories would prohibit the construction of a manageable list. While we chose some rather broad categories for aspects which we did not think were potential fundamenta divisionis, we selected some categories which cover common ground. For instance, we have a category for civilian victims, wherein noncombatants, neutrals and some others are subsumed, but we have placed "innocents" in a different category. The reason for this becomes clearer when we discuss the major elements later. Some authors mentioned elements which do not easily fit into any of our categories (e.g. unprovokedness of terrorist violence, indifference to human life, self-sacrificial element, romanticism, attempts at justification and explanation of terrorist deed) but since these elements were present only in the texts of one or a very few authors we did not include them as separate categories. We also began with a number of elements which we thought would turn up frequently enough to deserve a category of their own and it turned out that we were wrong (such as "Minority technique", "Warnings associated with Violence," "Claiming or Denying Responsibility for Violence"). In the end we decided on a list of 22 elements. The sorting of elements from particular definitions into these 22 categories is based on individual decisions. To make this exercise less subjective a second researcher was asked to repeat the content analysis. There were minor differences of interpretation between the two analyses. The percentages in Table II represent the median values found by the two analysts.

Table V : Frequencies of Definitional Elements in 3 Samples (sets)

	ELEMENTS	3rd Sample (n= 109) (= Appendix)	Rank within sample	2nd Sample (n= 29) (= Quest.)	Rank within sample	1st Sample (n= 7) (= Table I)	Rank within sample
1.	Violence, Force	83.5%	1.	97 %	1.	85.5%	1.
2.	Political	65 %	2.	65 %	2.	57 %	2.
3.	Fear, Terror Emphasized	51 %	3.	36 %	3.	57 %	2a.
4.	Threat	47 %	4.	28 %	7.	57 %	2b.
5.	(Psych.) Effects and (Anticipated) Reactions	41.5%	5.	34 %	4.	57 %	2c.
6.	Victim-Target Differentiation	37.5%	6.	29.5%	6.	57 %	2d.
7.	Purposive, Planned Systematic, Organized Action	32 %	7.	32.5%	5.	29 %	4.
8.	Method of Combat, Strategy, Tactic	30.5%	8.	24 %	9.	43 %	3.
9.	Extranormality, In Breach of Accepted Rules, Without Humanitarian Constraints	30 %	9.	26 %	8.	57 %	2e.
10.	Coercion, Extortion, Induction of Compliance	28 %	10.	19 %	10.	57 %	2f.
11.	Publicity Aspect	21.5%	11.	3.5%	17.	29 %	4a.
12.	Arbitrariness, Impersonal, Random Character, Indiscriminateness	21 %	12.	12 %	13.	43 %	3a.
13.	Civilians, Non-combatants, Non-resisting, Neutrals Outsiders as Victims.	17.5%	13.	12 %	13a.	14 %	5.

Table V : Frequencies of Definitional Elements in 3 Samples (sets)
(continued)

	ELEMENTS	3rd Sample (n= 109)	Rank within sample	2nd Sample (n= 29)	Rank within sample	1st Sample (n= 7)	Rank within sample
14.	Intimidation	17 %	14.	12 %	13b.	14 %	5a.
15.	Innocence of Victims Emphasized	15.5%	15.	15.5%	12.	14 %	5b.
16.	Group, Movement, Organization as Perpetrator	14 %	16.	18.5%	11.	0 %	6.
17.	Symbolic Aspect, Demonstration to Others	13.5%	17.	3.5%	17a.	29 %	4b.
18.	Incalculability, Unpredictability, Unexpectedness of Occurrence of Violence	9 %	18.	7 %	16.	29 %	4c.
19.	Clandestine, Covert Nature	9 %	18a.	7 %	16a.	0 %	6a.
20.	Repetitiveness, Serial or Campaign Character of Violence	7 %	19.	10 %	14	29 %	4d.
21.	Criminal	6 %	20.	12 %	13c.	14 %	5c.
22.	Demands Made on Third Parties	4 %	21.	8.5%	15.	0 %	6b.

Having said this the reader should be sufficiently cautioned to attribute too much precision and meaning to Table V. The main attention should be directed to sample 3 which reflects the elements utilized in more than 100 definitions constructed over a 45 year's span (1936-1981).

(Four of the definitions are from the period 1936-1949, one from
the 1950s, seven from the sixties, seventy-nine from the seventies
and 18 from the years 1980 and 1981.) The second sample represents
definitions from 1981 and 1982 only. What is remarkable is that in the
first two sets the frequencies of certain elements are about the
same. The ten top-scoring elements in the third sample all figure in
the ten top-scoring ones in the second sample, roughly in the same
order. They also figure in the top 12 of the 1st sample, although the
latter is highly coloured by the small number of authors in the sample.
While this coincidence is encouraging it is less clear what it
actually means. In fact all one can say with certainty, is that in
two samples where authors use an average of eight and five elements
respectively to define terrorism, these ten elements were utilized more
often than others to describe the concept.

In a definiens there are generally two kinds of elements. On the one
hand there are elements which situate a new concept in known contexts.
In the case of terrorism words like "violence", "threat" are such
properties. On the other hand there generally is at least one "differentia
specifica" or "fundamentum divisionis" which tells us the "specific
difference", the "basis for separation" between one concept and the
others. It is by no means always clear which elements an author
considers as generally situating and which he regards as specifying
elements. Many definitions are enumerations of elements without that
it becomes clear what an author sees as fundamentum divisionis.

A few examples from authors in and outside our samples illustrate
what we mean by fundamentum divisionis:

- Kupperman and Trent hold that "Terrorist violence is by its
  nature random". 4)

- Friedlander holds that "Innocence is the quintessential
  condition of terrorist victimology." 5)

- Galtung defined terror as "... the unpredictable use of violence
  in order to compel submission." 6)

While it is important for a definition that it fixes the meaning of
a term in a way which the greatest possible number of users of the
term can accept, the most popular definition is not necessarily the
best one since it might be too vague or ambiguous or valuational and
lack the crucial elements which indicate what is the specific difference.

In the preceeding chapters we have tried to distinguish terrorism from
some neighbouring concepts such as violence, guerrilla warfare, etc.
In the following pages we shall discuss some of the specific elements
which authors use as fundamenta divisionis to define terrorism. Our
discussion will concentrate on the process of terrorist victim
selection and follow various side roads from there. Our aim is to
reduce thereby, if possible, the number of elements necessary to define
terrorism.

The "Innocent" Victim of Terrorism

There is a Latin saying that one should not speak evil of the dead
("de mortuis nihil nisi bene"). Consciously or not a great many authors
seem to follow this line of thinking when it comes to the victims of
terrorism. In our samples many authors either stress or at least
refer to the innocence of the victims of terrorism (e.g. Arendt,
Bassiouni, Bouthoul, Bite, Crenshaw, Fromkin, Friedlander, Green, Gross,
Lador-Lederer, Leiser, Jenkins, Monday, Post, Sobel, Waldmann, Wilkinson).
Innocence of what? Not a single author has, to our knowledge, made an
attempt to develop criteria for establishing this innocence.
"Innocence needs no proof, only guilt has to be proven", is certainly
an excellent principle in legal practice, but it cannot be transferred
to social science. There are, of course, bona fide innocents like
children, but even that cannot always be taken for granted. If the
victims of terrorism were all innocents, one might expect that the
terrorists would apply some selection process in the choice of their
targets, excluding the "guilty". If the terrorists were serious about
hitting innocents, children, women, even innocent members of their own
group would be victimized. While it is quite true that bombs exploded
in marketplaces kill innocent people, it cannot be said that they were
killed because of their innocence. They might have been killed despite
their innocence, but more likely their innocence simply did not matter
very much. For the terrorist innocence is not essential, they tend to
deny it as they sometimes deny other criteria which might create
immunity from attack (e.g. pregnancy). This is not to deny that
innocence is completely irrelevant. In some cases the victim's

obvious personal innocence can increase the indignation of a target
audience and thereby might become a point worthwhile to be taken into
consideration by the planning terrorist. Noninvolved people who
become accidental victims of terrorism might be innocent. But the
terrorist is likely to attribute blame even to them. A tourist
going to a place like Israel who becomes a victim is not so innocent
in the eyes of a Palestinian observer. He might reason that the tourist
is supporting the Israeli economy with hard currency and thereby
indirectly strengthening his opponent. The tendency to see the world
in terms of supporters or opponents only is likely to eradicate the
category of innocence for terrorists. And while they might be willing
to concede personal innocence they are more interested in group innocence
or guilt. The statements of terrorists point in this direction. The
first is from the anarchist Léon-Jules Léauthier, who said: "I shall
not strike an innocent if I strike the first bourgeois I meet."
(which happened to be the Serbian Minister Georgewitch, whom he was
attacking on 12 November 1893 with his shoemaker's paring knife). [7]
Another terrorist, Alberto Franceschini, one of the top leaders of the
Italian Red Brigades, told the court when he was on trial in 1978:
"It is your function I want to eliminate. You're not a man; you're a
judge. No one here is innocent." [8]

The "Civilian" Victim of Terrorism

If innocence is irrelevant or at any rate not a condition for becoming
a victim, what better substitute can there be? A number of authors
opt for the civilian victim. On the surface, this looks like a good
choice. In war soldiers kill soldiers, in guerrilla warfare irregulars
in civilian clothes kill soldiers, in terrorist warfare nonuniformed
gunmen kill civilians evading the armed forces of the opponent.
However, wars in the second half of the twentieth century victimize
more civilians than military men; while this is not always intended it
is rarely avoided if at the same time military targets can also be hit.
But insurgent terrorists too do attack military bases (e.g. American
military headquarters in Europe), ambush military patrols (e.g. in
Northern Ireland). The assassination attempt on Nato Commander

Alexander Haig, in Mons (Belgium) by German terrorists on 25 June 1979
or the kidnapping of Nato General Dozier in Italy by the Red Brigades
in 1981 are illustrations that civilians might not be the only target.
Some victimized civilians are policemen or directors of prisons
where torture is practiced, counter-insurgency advisors or plain-cloth
special army teams and they are therefore less civilian than might be
thought at first sight.

It is of course always more tempting to attack a "soft" target where
success is more assured. Military targets tend to be "hardened" and in
many cases terrorists have only the capacity to penetrate, occupy or
destroy soft "civilian" targets. This choice, born out of operational
constraints, does in our view not constitute a fundamentum divisionis
for defining terrorism.

The "Noncombatant" Victim of Terrorism

Another possibility offered by authors either in combination with
civilian and innocent targets or alone is noncombatant
(e.g. Francis, Sederberg). A terrorist act lacks the symmetry of a duel
or the preparedness of both parties for the fight of a battle.
Rogier Trinquier has written, with the Algerian experience in mind:

> "What characterizes modern terrorism, and makes for its basic
> strength, is the slaughter of generally defenseless persons. The
> terrorist operates within a familiar legal framework, while avoiding
> the ordinary risks taken by the common criminal, let alone by
> soldiers on the field of battle, or even by partisans facing
> regular troops." 9)

In regular warfare the deliberate killing of noncombatants is not
permitted and considered as a "war crime". Soldiers taken prisoner
during hostilities are treated humanely according to conventions which
protect their rights. By becoming nonbelligerent through capitulation,
surrender or capture soldiers can be reasonably certain that their lives
will be saved. The prisoners of insurgent terrorist, however, either
as kidnapped individuals or as a group of trapped hostages, cannot
affect their own fate by handing in their weapons and promising non-
resistance. They generally are defenceless to begin with and having
been unprepared to fight they are also ill-prepared to resist. Equally,
the victims of state terrorism cannot with certainty avoid further

electric shocks, maiming, dismembering, etc. through cooperation with
the torturers in terms of confessions. In the hope for further
confessions the victim is likely to be tortured long after he has given
away whatever valuable information he may have had. Quite often he
ends up being murdered in cold blood without trial, without personal
guilt or even without reason. Like the hostage in insurgent terrorism
the prisoner of state terrorism cannot effectively affect his own fate
anymore through changes of attitude or behaviour. As Andreski has
perceptively noted, such is the situation of the terrorist victims
that "... no observance of commands - no matter how punctilious - on
the part of the prospective victims can ensure their safety." [10)]
Since terrorism avoids the armed confrontation, the battle, whenever
possible, the victim is practically always noncombatant, even when
he is in uniform. Soldiers having a drink at the end of the day in a
local bar who are killed by a time-bomb are noncombatants, although
they are not necessarily innocent and are no civilians. Of the three
terms utilized so far noncombatant seems to fit best to describe the
status of the terrorist victim. Two other descriptions occasionally
used are nonresisting victims or defenseless victims. These terms are
true as far as they go, but if they are meant to describe the inability
to extricate oneself from the conflict situation, referred to above,
they are not the best possible term. If they refer to a situation of
tactical surprise where the victim has not time to defend himself or
where resistance is not considered because of the hopelessness of any
effort in this direction, the terms are not saying very much.
Some other characterizations of the terrorist victim are that they are
neutrals, noninvolved or outsiders to the conflict at hand. These terms
might indeed describe the subjective feeling of the victim, but are
not very fortunate either. Neutrality has to be made known before the
outbreak of the conflict and the victim taken by surprise (such as the
passenger of a hijacked airliner) will be too late in establishing his
neutrality.'Outsiders' is, in this regard, more to the point but not
all and probably not even a majority of the victims of terrorist violence
are outsiders to the conflict, certainly not from the point of view
of the terrorist. Some of the accidental by-standers of terrorist
violence are indeed outsiders, but the main target is likely to be

related to a party to the conflict. The expression noninvolved is a
weak one for the same reason. If terrorist were simply aiming at the
noninvolved, they would not have to plot long to find a target of
violence.

The "Symbolic" Victims of Terrorism

A number of authors stress the "symbolic" nature of the victim
(e.g. Thornton, Singh, Crenshaw). Karber, taking the symbolic aspect
introduced by Thornton in 1964 as starting point, elaborates:

> "The symbolic concept of terrorism provides two crucial distinctions
> between terrorism and revolution and between terrorism and other
> forms of violence. If the objective of violence is the acquisition
> of useful objects (money, weapons, etc.) or the denial of such
> resources from the enemy, this action is robbery, assassination,
> sabotage, etc.; "if, on the other hand, the objective is symbolic
> expression, we are dealing with terror" [Thornton]. This highlights
> the distinction between terrorism and revolution, for symbolic
> violence can be used not only to propagandize the overthrow of a
> system, but also as a means of interest articulation to effect the
> system's output. When the "establishment" is unwilling to listen to
> nonviolent protest, terrorism permits the frustrated communicator,
> as stated by one terrorist, "to maximize significance and minimize
> getting caught".
> Thornton asserts that: "The relatively high efficiency of terrorism
> derives from its symbolic nature. If the terrorist comprehends
> that he is seeking a demonstration effect, he will attack targets
> with a maximum symbolic value. The symbols of the state are particularly
> important, but perhaps even more so are those referring to the
> normative structures and relationships that constitute the supporting
> framework of the society." 11)

If the victim of terrorism has a symbolic value this can mean two things.
A symbol can be denotative, that is specifically and literally referring
to an object or event, or it can be metaphorical - something that stands
for something other than what it appears to be. 12)
Some attitudes or ideas of an abstract character are converted into
visual image - e.g. a flag standing for a nation. Karber himself seems
to be referring more to this second, metaphorical meaning in which
a bomb explosion stands for a protest, rather than that it stands for
the specific destruction of the object which has been bombed. Thornton,
on the other hand sees the symbolism of terroristic attacks, if we
read him correctly, more in the denotative sense, where the victim of
a terrorist act stands for other victims. We will discuss these two
facets separately.

Nonhuman Terroristic Victimization?

While human beings such as Joan d'Arc can become symbols and very strong
symbols indeed, material things, like a statue, a flag have symbolic
value too. To blow up the Statue of Liberty in New York, or the Eiffel
Tower in Paris would be a shocking thing to many Americans and French,
independent of whether people got hurt or not. But can that be called
terrorism? Several authors also rank destruction of property and
sabotage under terrorism. Martha Crenshaw speaks about "agrarian or
economic terrorism" when she refers to the burning of a farmer's crops
or a landowner's forests. She writes:

> "The relationship between terrorist and victim distinguishes terrorism
> from simple sabotage and assassination. Sabotage and assassination
> are means of terrorism only if they are facets of a broader strategy.
> When such acts of violence accomplish in themselves the total
> objective of the assassin or the saboteur, their political significance
> is limited. They aim at the removal of a specific person or the
> damaging of material resources; they are not meant to serve as
> threats of future violence, even if the motives of their perpetrators
> are political." 13)

When the psychological effect of such material destruction rather than
the deprivation itself caused by it, is the aim of the terrorist, one
might be more inclined to label this terrorism. However, when
the object destroyed has an utilitarian character the two dimensions
are often not clearly separable.
The destruction of an electric power grit producing the blackout of a
whole city might cause anguish and situational terror when looting
occurs and law and order breaks down. But this is not what authors
generally have in mind when they rank destruction of property under
terrorism. The fact that acts of pure terrorism and acts of destruction
and robbery are committed by the same group of insurgents is for them
sufficient to label the latter terrorist too. In our view this is a
careless widening of the meaning of terrorism which should be rejected.
There are border cases difficult to situate, such as the following:

> - In 1974 the home of the English millionnaire Sir Alfred Beit
>   was raided by an armed gang that took nineteen paintings
>   valued $ 19.2 million. In a letter the destruction of these
>   paintings was announced unless four convicted IRA members were
>   transferred to jails in Ulster and unless $ 1.2 million in cash
>   was paid. 14)

- In January and February 1978 mercury-injected Israeli oranges
  were discovered in the Netherlands, West Germany and Sweden.
  The Dutch government received a letter from the Arab Revolutionary
  Army Palestinian Commando declaring its intentions "to sabotage
  the Israeli economy." Several people, including children, had to
  be hospitalized after eating such oranges. The sale of Israeli
  oranges declined sharply for a time. 15)

In our view, the second case is more appropriately labelled terroristic
than the first. The absence of chronic fear in the first case and the
ability to escape from victimization in the second (by checking whether
the visible mercury is present), make these imperfect cases of terrorism.
For such border cases the term "quasi-terrorism" might be utilized. 16)

The "Arbitrary" Victim of Terrorism

Several authors hold that terrorism is arbitary, that anyone can be
the victim, that nobody is safe (e.g. Wilkinson, Kupperman & Trent).
If this were true, innocence or a noncombatant status does not matter.
Yet if the terrorists were always completely indiscriminate in their
victimization then it would be difficult to explain how sporadic acts
of terrorism can be sufficient to create chronic fear. If the likelyhood
of becoming a victim of terrorism were truly equal we should all be
terrorized which is not the case. For such general terror a volume of
violence is necessary which presently can be found only in particular
zones of terror such as in Guatemala or El Salvador. Clearly, some run
higher risks of becoming victims of terrorism than others. While most
terrorism is not so focussed as assassination it is also not so random
as mugging. In fact it would seem that in most cases victimization is
selective and indiscriminate at the same time.
Feliks Gross distinguishes between three major types of terrorism on
the basis of relative discrimination: Mass Terror (as the French and
Bolshevik revolutions and in the Inquisition) and Random Terror (where
bombs are detonated in public places such as railroad stations,
post-offices or airline terminals), and Focussed Random Terror (such as
placing a bomb in a café frequented by the officers of an occupation
force). 17) Which type of terrorism is practise depends on the means
at one's disposal and the aims one has in mind. Insurgent terrorists
usually lack the resources for mass terror. Economy forces them to
concentrate on some targets. As a method of combat terrorism cannot be

completely blind in its victim selection: not everybody but only enemies
are to be terrorized. Only where terrorism is no longer a rational
method of action, but an idiosyncratic drive of a disturbed mind or a
perverted nihilist movement, victimization will be completely random.
In practice we find a balancing between indiscriminateness and
selectiveness in terrorist victimization.
Smith has expressed this well by saying:

> "The victim must represent a whole class of persons who are identified
> as possible targets. However, while the particular class of persons
> to be terrorized may be carefully selected, the actual identity of
> those attacked is arbitary. It is this lack of discrimination that
> is the source of terror." 18)

If this is true, this would also explain why the victimization of
terrorism is labelled symbolic. A symbol in the denotative sense is
one thing standing for the other thing. Terrorism is symbolic in the
sense of "You too might become a victim". Some witnesses to an act
of violence identify with the victim, because of some common quality,
e.g. membership of the same class, party, creed, race. It is primarily
in this sense that Thornton uses symbolism. He writes:

> "Terror must always have at least some element of indiscrimination,
> else it becomes predictable, loses its broad character, and can no
> longer be legitimately designated as terror. Also, it becomes
> relatively easy to combat. Total indiscrimination, however, is not
> reasonable, unless one is completely nihilist. (...) Discrimination
> plays an extremely important role in the creation of anxiety responses.
> Any element that tends to make terror more unknowable and therefore
> more disorientating contributes to the creation of anxiety. (...)
> ... total indiscrimination is not desirable, for the insurgents will
> wish to concentrate their attacks on specific targets of intent,
> social structures and symbols, to achieve economy of effort and
> ensure maintenance of those structures that are of potential value
> to them. (...) ... the optimum targets are clearly those that show
> the highest symbolic value and are dominated by symbols that are
> most vulnerable to attack. The terrorist must always have the
> distinction between apparent indiscrimination and actual
> indiscrimination clearly in mind, if he is to succeed. As a general
> rule, it may then be said that terror is most effective when it is
> indiscriminate in appearance but highly discriminate in fact." 19)

The realization "I could have been that victim" is evoked in a target
audience through the focussed random act of terror. A message of fear
is transmitted to this reference group.
The selected victim can also be chosen as a target, because he symbolizes
the reference group in his function as their representative. In cases
of symbolic victim selection the reference group itself is as a whole

not an earmarked target for future terrorist violence. By seeing that
its leaders become victims of sudden assassination this group is,
however, likely to become demoralized and disoriented, although it is
not terrorized in the narrow sense of the word. Those witnesses of
either random or symbolic terrorist violence who are not directly
linked to the victims of violence are neither terrorized not demoralized
but merely outraged or, if the psychological distance is big enough,
not even that: they are merely notified that something that deserves
attention - and violence always commands attention no matter how trivial
the cause - has occurred. One of the disturbing things about present-
day terrorism is that this dual effect of terrorizing prospective
victims on the one hand and notifying countless others on the other
has been made use of. Where the second dimension becomes the actual
objective of terrorism violence becomes a vehicle to create attentive
audiences. The purpose is not primarily to terrorize, but to communicate.
The violence is less of a warning to a target group than a power
generator for a general message. In such a situation the victim needs
no longer to be linked to a particular target group and the separation
between victim and target becomes complete.

The Victim-Target Differentiation

When discussing the relationship between the classical assassination
(as in tyrannicide) and terrorism (page 61) we have noted that
while a single assassination is unlikely to be terroristic, a campaign
of assassinations assumes a different character. This was a discovery
first made in modern times in the Russia of the late 1870s and
Nicolas Morozov, one of the theorists of Narodnaya Volya, was one of
the first to describe this new quality. In his work "Terroristic
Struggle", Morozov wrote in 1880:

"Every now and then a secret assassination of a public statesman
occurred. On January 24, 1878, the shot meant for Trepov, the police
prefect of St. Petersburg, was heard in his waiting room. This shot
was the starting point for the whole struggle that followed. From
this point on, the movement took a definite form, and it went
almost without deviation towards the new already clearly established
ideal. People unknown to society or government appeared out of
nowhere and started to dispose of one or another statesman. Having
accomplished the execution, they disappeared without a trace. In

this way Nikonov, Geiknig, Miezentzev, Kropotkin and a few others
were killed. Neither searches nor arrests, practised extensively
by the government, brought any success. (...)
This presents really a new form of struggle. It replaces by a
series of individual political assassinations, which always hit
their target, the massive revolutionary movements..." 20)

In 1867 dynamite had been invented and the bombs based on it could
be ignited at a distance so that they no longer had to be thrown by
hand which often enough led to the capture of the thrower of
nitroglycerine or fulminating mercury bombs. This increased distance
between terrorist and victim increased the personal safety of the
terrorist, but at the same time decreased the precision of targeting.
Casual victims who happened to be in the "wrong" company at the moment
of the explosion (e.g. when a railroad track was mined) became more
likely. The inhibition to kill which was a factor in hand-thrown
bombing or in gun-attempts was probably also decreased and the terrorist
no longer had to witness the bloodbath caused by his bomb.

While tyrannicide was essentially unique (there was only one tyrant per
social unit), the assassination of lower level ministers of the
ruler had to be a repetitive affair since they were many and they were
replaced fast. The officials also saw themselves as likely future
victims every time one official was removed. They were the target group,
and the victim was one of them, whereby it did not matter much which
one. This victim-target differentiation was still embryonic in the
1880s. With the advancement in the means of destruction, communication
and transportation it has become a crucial element in the technique
of terrorism. In our view the victim-target differentiation is one of
the fundamenta divisionis of terrorism. It is not the only one, however.
A latent differentiation between victim and target also occurs in
revolution and warfare, as Léon Trotsky has pointed out:

"Intimidation is a powerful weapon of policy, internationally and
internally. War, like revolution, is founded upon intimidation.
A victorious war, generally speaking, destroys only an insignificant
part of the conquered army, intimidating the remainder and breaking
their will. The revolution works in the same way: it kills individuals,
and intimidates thousands. In this sense, the Red Terror is not
distinguishable from the armed insurrection of which it is the
direct continuation. The State terror of a revolutionary class can
be condemned "morally" only by a man who on principle rejects (in
words) every form of violence whatsoever - consequently, every war
and every rising." 21)

Leaving aside the moral argument, the equation of intimidation with terrorism which Trotsky handles is incorrect. Terrorism does more than merely to intimidate. Hardman has elaborated the distinction between the two concepts:

> "Intimidation differs from terrorism in that the intimidator...
> merely threatens injury or material harm in order to arouse fear
> of severe punishment for non-compliance with his demands. (...)
> The terrorist does not threaten; death or destruction is part of
> his programme of action...." 22)

The intimidated victim can deflect the impending harm by compliance, while the terrorist's victim cannot because the demands are not addressed to him, but to a third party. In this regard intimidation is related to punishment although individual guilt does not have to be present with the former. In punishment and intimidation alike the relationship between the actor and the acted upon is a dyadic one, although it can border on a triadic one and thereby become terroristic as in cases of political justice, show-trials and exemplary punishment. E.V. Walter has discussed this perceptively:

> "Since violent punishments do evoke fear and are often justified
> by their putative deterrent value, it is sometimes hard to
> distinguish the administration of punishment from the process of
> terror. It is more difficult when political leaders use the violence
> involved in the acts of punishment to extent their political control.
> In such cases, the violence seems to serve the separate processes
> of punishment and terror simultaneously. (...)
> Punishment defined sociologically, I would maintain, is a penalty
> imposed for the transgression of a recognized norm established either
> by coercion or consent in the course of a social relationship. The
> features that distinguish violent legal punishment from other kinds
> of violence, including the terror process, are the fundamental
> conditions of legality. For violence to qualify as legal punishment,
> it must be imposed by duly constituted public authority for an act
> within its jurisdiction that is publicly judged to violate a legal
> rule promulgated before the act took place. (...) Violence in
> these conditions follows deviation from the rule, and no matter how
> destructive punishment might be, the individual who chooses to
> conform remains reasonably secure from official harm. In contrast,
> the terror process begins with violence itself, which is followed
> by intensive fear and irrational, reactive behaviour patterns.
> In contrast to terrorism, deterrance implies the anticipation of
> a probable evil and the ability to avoid it. The fear of punishment
> is different from the fear generated in the terror process." 23)

The view of terrorism as a triadic relationship in which the victim is the helpless object in the middle whose fate is decided upon by one or both of the conflicting parties has entered the scientific debate

with Walter and Thornton in 1964 and has been gaining more adherents
ever since. [24] But it is not yet generally recognized as one or the
most important fundamentum divisionis.

Salem Quershi, professor of political science at the University of
Alberta, for instance, holds:

> "The object of terrorism is to secure a change or modification in
> the behaviour of the intended victim himself or use him as an
> example for others. (...) The use of terrorist violence is based
> on the assumption that the intended victim is unreasonable and
> incapable of seeing the viewpoint of the terrorist, that the victim
> cannot be persuaded, but only compelled, in a manner where he has
> absolutely no choice except surrender." [25]

A position closer to ours, but still ambiguous, can be found in the
formulation, of two CIA analysts, David Milbank and Edward Micolus:

> "... is intended to influence the attitudes and behavior of a
> target group wider than its immediate victims". [26]

In our view, the word "wider" should be changed into "other than its
immediate victims." A formulation like the one of Duvall and Stohl
indicated more clearly this fundamentum divisionis: "The primary
intent (of terrorism) is to produce an effect in or by a target who
is distinct from the victim of violence..." [27]

This triadic view of terrorism we find most pronouncedly with Hacker,
Jenkins and Kaplan. More important, we find it also in statements of
terrorists.

Adolf Hitler, for instance, once said:

> "I shall spread terror through the surprising application of all my
> means. The sudden shock of a terrible fear of death is what matters.
> Why should I deal otherwise with all my political opponents?
> These so-called atrocities save me hundreds of thousands of individual
> actions against the protestors and discontents. Each one of them
> will think twice to oppose us when he learns what is expecting him
> in the (concentration) camp." [28]

In this terroristic structure the people victimized in the concentration
camp by the Nazi regime serve as warning to potential German resisters.
The camp inmates were kept as hostages for the good behaviour of the
German population. Hitler himself gave the instruction that the people
in the camps should be killed in case of a domestic insurrection against
his regime. [29] In the same way the Nazi occupiers of Europe in World
War II took hostages from the civilian population of the conquered
lands and killed them in retaliation for acts of resistance. The widespread killings of civilian hostages in the Second World War has

resulted in the Geneva Convention of 1949 which abolished the right to take hostages in wartime. [30] But the practice continues in civil wars. In Uruguay, for instance, the military junta holds trade union leaders and other representatives of "dangerous" organizations in isolation cells in order to ensure that their followers would not engage in subversive acts. [31] Torture of prisoners is today widely used by governments to create a sphere of terror with the opponents of the regimes in question and to set examples which are meant to intimidate others and thereby reduce the chance that resistance against a regime wins followers. [32] The "disappearances" of people in Latin America - some 90,000 over the last ten years - are also terroristic. Political opponents and even children were seized without arrest warrants by secret service agents never to be heard of or seen again. Sometimes mutilated bodies were found on the shores washed up by the sea, but more often the families and friends of the missing were left with the nagging feeling of despair mixed with (false) hope and fear for their own safety.

The structure of such events is basically the same as in a simple political kidnapping or assassination, a triangular relationship between perpetrator, victim and target, which we have expressed in another study with the following diagram:

Diagram II: The Triangle of Insurgent Terrorism

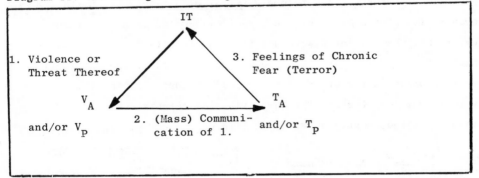

IT = Insurgent Terrorist; V_A = Victim Belonging to the Camp of the State Authorities; V_p = Victim Being Part of the Public; T_A = The Authorities as Target; T_p = The Public as Target.

In that study [33] the reference was to insurgent terrorism only, but
we believe that it applies to other types as well. To illustrate this
a more detailed look at the varieties of the terrorist-victim-target
relationship is necessary.

Varieties of Victim-Target Relationships

While little needs to be said about the term "victims" of terrorism,
the term "target" of terrorism has to specified. It is a term which
can give rise to confusion. The victim of an act of terrorism is the
target of violence, but he is not the prime target of terror. This
prime   target is the group that feels most threatened by the act of
violence, because its members are afraid that they will be the next
victims. Apart from this terrorized group there are others who witness
the act of violence either directly by being on the scene where the
deed occurred, or by being informed by the public media or otherwise
about what has happened. This general audience might or might not be
a target intended to be reached by the terrorists. If this audience -
the public opinion or an important sector thereof - is meant to be
reached (but not terrorized) it serves as target of attention. If a
secondary target is actively rather than only passively involved in
the process of terror, it can become a target of demands made by the
terrorists. It is possible that the target of demands is also a target
of terror, but that is not always so. Take the example of a skyjacking
in which a derouted airliner lands on a foreign airfield and the local
authorities become a target of demands (food, kerosine) without
being a target of terror. The three kinds of targets can be
portrayed as three, partly overlapping circles. (see Venn-Diagram).

Diagram III: Targets of Terrorism

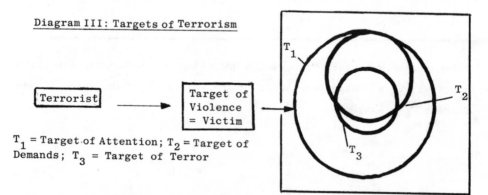

T_1 = Target of Attention; T_2 = Target of
Demands; T_3 = Target of Terror

From this multiplicity of targets it becomes clear that the victim-
target relationships can vary considerably. But the picture becomes
even more complicated when we take into account that the terrorist
and his movement or organization can also serve as target, and,
paradoxically, also serve as (pseudo-) victim.

To begin with, the terrorist himself can be a target of attention.
This is, of course, the main reason for idiosyncratic psychopathological
terrorism. This terrorist, through his act, satisfies a personal need.
The violence serves to prove to himself that he is somebody. The own
self as target also appears in the more political terrorism to which
Frantz Fanon referred. The colonial subject, by killing a white man,
can regain a sense of manhood, a sense of power, a new image of himself. [34]
Another possibility is that the terrorist movement is the target of
attention. The acts of violence can serve as an initiation rite. The
candidate to the movement has to prove to the movement what he is
"worthy" by killing somebody. Once he has been "blooded" he can join. For
the movement this is also an insurance that he will not go back into
society. He has become guilty and he can, if necessary, be blackmailed
on the basis of his initial act of violence and denounced to the police.
The terrorist movement or sectors thereof can also serve as targets of
terror. Traitors, spies or waverers are executed in the same way as
enemies of the movement and the main target of such purges are the
members of the terrorist movement or organization who are thereby
warned what the price of disloyalty is. While such violence is also
meant as punishment (in which case it is not terroristic) it is often
primarily a warning to others, a deterrent example, and as such can
become terroristic.

The terrorist as victim of a terrorist strategy would seem to be
exceptional. We are not thinking here of those examples where a terrorist
blows himself up accidentally or in the confusion of an attack is
machine-gunned by his own colleagues. An example of a "terrorist"
as "victim" would be the case of Brian Lea, the first secretary of the
British High Commission in Uganda. Lea was reported to be kidnapped on 3 May
1970. Later it turned out that he had simply gone into hiding, faking
his own kidnapping in order to dramatize the plight of the Asians in
Uganda who were threatened with expulsion. [35]

Better known are the cases of "revolutionary suicides" committed by
key members of the German Red Army Fraction. The RAF top, imprisoned
in the high-security Stammheim prison, had practised hunger-strikes
as a weapon to obtain concessions from the authorities, and to
mobilize support for themselves among the German Left. On 18 October 1977,
3 members of the RAF carried their policy of using their bodies as
"ultimate weapons" to the logical conclusion. After they learned by
radio that a coercive attempt to get them out of prison had failed, they
arranged their suicides in such a way that the blame for their death
would be placed on the "fascist" German state. Many sympathizers of the
RAF fell into this trap set up for them and even outside this immediate
target of attention suspicion about the role of the German authorities
in the deaths of Andreas Baader and his colleagues became widespread. 36)
This technique whereby the "terrorist" turns victim could be labelled
pseudo-terrorism. Another special case is the one where not the terrorist
becomes the victim but a victim becomes part of the terrorist movement,
or at least acts on its behalf. The psychological basis for this
transformation is the mechanism of "identification with the aggressor",
which was first observed on a large scale in German concentration camp
inmates who imitated their oppressors and volunteered to aid them in
their tasks. A recent case where a victim turned "terrorist" is the
one of Patty Hearst, who, transformed into "Tania" for a time, joined
the Symbionese Liberation Army.
Apart from the terrorist-victim and the victim-terrorist there is also
the victim-target that plays a role in terrorism. While it has been
said that the victim of terrorist violence cannot affect his own fate
by a change of attitude or behaviour and that the aim of the terrorist
is attitude or behaviour modification with somebody else than the
immediate victim of violence, the victims can also become objects of
terror themselves in situations where the terrorist's threat is not
acted upon immediately such as in hostage situations. Take a hijacking
situation. At the beginning when the terrorists take command of the
situation they might kill one hostage to show "that we mean business".
This "show" can be for various target-audiences: the terrorists
themselves who thereby wish to overcome their own doubts, the targets
of demands, from whom the terrorists expect compliance and the
remaining hostages who's will to resist is broken by the atrocity

committed before their eyes. They are also targets of terror for they live in constant fear of being victimized. In addition of being afraid of the terrorists they also might distrust each other, for instance, when the terrorists announce that each escape attempt will lead to the execution of half a dozen hostages.

The purest triangular situations, however, are those wherein neither the "terrorist" (organization) nor the victim (group) figure as targets. An extreme example of a pure triangular situation would be the attempted murder of U.S. President Ronald Reagan in April 1981. John W. Hinckley Jr., the 25 year old would-be assassin, wanted to impress the teenage actress Jodie Foster, with whom he had fallen in love after seeing her performance as a prostitute in the movie Taxi Driver. She was the target of attention, while the U.S. President, the victim, was the target of violence. Such a simple situation we also find in a criminal kidnapping: the terrorist seizes the victim and coerces his family - the target of demands - into paying a ransom for his release. If the kidnapping is political, the main target is not the family of the victim. It can be a government which is asked to release some prisoners in return for the victim's release or it can be the media which are asked to publish a manifesto. Quite often more than one target is addressed. A statement from the German RAF indicates this: "The bombs against the suppressive apparatus are also thrown into the consciousness of the masses." [37) Here the government is the target of terror and the "masses" are the target of attention. Members of the first are to be terrorized, members of the second are to be mobilized. Only one target group has to fear future victimization (members of the government), while the other target group is wooed by the terrorist (actually, in the case of the German terrorists the masses were destined to become victims of government counter-terror, which, in the reasoning of some RAF terrorists, would drive them into the arms of the RAF). If the victims of terrorism are clearly part of the enemy group (members of the establishment in the case of insurgent terrorism) we can speak of direct terrorism. If the victims are not part of the enemy group, but subordinates or dependents of the enemy group the victimization is often meant to bring home the message that the authorities can no longer guarantee the safety of those under their rule or jurisdiction, which presumably

destroys trust into the established power. In this case one can speak
of indirect terrorism. The second is clearly less discriminate than
the first type of terrorism. [38)]

Depending on the way the actual victim of terrorist violence is linked
to the target of terror, the target of demands or the target of
attention the purposes of terrorism will vary. By activating the
interplay between the three target groups terrorism can create multiple
secondary effects and serve a variety of purposes.

Terrorism is not "senseless" violence producing nothing more than "chaos".
Such a view, which has been widespread in certain sectors of public
opinion, is probably in consequence of a fixation on the terrorist-
victim relationship. When the victim-target relationship is looked at,
terrorism makes more sense. In our view, this differentiation should
be one of the most important elements in any definition of terrorism.

Purposes of Terrorism

If terrorism is not "senseless violence" it must have a purpose. In fact,
terrorism seems to have many purposes beyond the basic one, on which
all else depends, namely to terrorize. In Table II no less than 5
elements seem to refer to purposes or functions (elements 3, 5, 9, 11
and 14). If we look more closely at the definitions reproduced in the
Appendix and also consult other sources, no less than 20 albeit not
clearly separable purposes and functions appear (see Table III).

From this impressive list of what authors take to be the purposes and
functions of terrorism one could easily gain the idea that terrorism
is an all-powerful and an all-purpose method of action, the "ultimate
weapon", as one author put it. [39)] It would be a very useful task to
detail for each alleged purpose or function the actual mechanism of
operation of the terror process leading to the supposed result. To our
knowledge this has never been attempted.

Table VI : Purposes and Functions Attributed to Terrorism

PURPOSE and FUNCTIONS	AUTHORS (numbers refer to year and page of publication)
1. To terrorize; To put the public or sections of the public in fear.	Lenin,cit.Taber,1974:92; U.K. Prevention of Terrorism Act,1974,cit. Scorer,1976:36.
2. Provocation of (indiscriminate) countermeasures by the incumbents; Deliberately provoking repression, reprisals and counter-terrorism.	Thornton,1964:86; Stohl,1981 (Fashions...):6;Jenkins, 1975(in Carlton):17; Pike 1970:34;Bell,1975:17; Bassiouni,1979:757;Mil- bank,1978(in Elliott):54 Wolf,1976:1289-90.
3. To mobilize forces.	Thornton,1964:73-74.
4. To affect public opinion in a positive or negative way; To cause a polarization and radicalization among the public or sections thereof.	Crenshaw,1981:383; Bassiouni,1979:757.
5. To seize political power; To overthrow regimes.	Crenshaw,1972:383. Jenkins,1975:1.
6. To break down,eradicate resistance.	Chisholm,1948:11;Leiden & Schmitt,1968:30-32.
7. To obtain money to finance arms purchases and operations.	Pierre,1978:39.
8. To maintain power; To discipline, control, dissuade target groups; To enforce obedience, allegiance, conformity.	Waldmann,1977:70;Lösche, 1978:82; Crenshaw,1981:383 Bell,1975:16;Crozier, 1960:173;Thornton,1964:77.
9. Disorientation, psychological isolation of the individual from his social context, demoralization of society, causing disorder, create alarm, create an atmosphere of anxiety, insecurity; To create a climate of panic, collapse	Thornton,1964:83;Arendt (in Festschift für Jaspers) 1953:239ff;Jenkins,1975 (in Carlton):17;Gross,1972: 10;Pike,1970:34;Crenshaw, 1978:72.Milbank (in Elliott) 1978:54;Wilkinson,1976:2-3.

Table VI : Purposes and Functions Attributed to Terrorism (continued)

PURPOSE and FUNCTIONS	AUTHORS (numbers refer to year and page of publication)
10. Extermination; To damage, injure, or eliminate government property or personnel; Elimination of opposing and rivalling forces, either physically or by neutralizing their effectiveness.	Fallah,1981:13-14; Morrison,1972:130n; Thornton,1964:86;Pike,1970: 34;Crenshaw,1978:80.
11. To disrupt and discredit the processes of government; To erode democratic institutions; To destroy public confidence in government; To disrupt normal operations of society; To demonstrate the vulnerability of the government and shatter the image of strength surrounding it.	Crenshaw,1981:383; Moss,1971:1,3; Wilkinson,1976:1-3; Horowitz,1977:30; Bassiouni,1979:757; Hardman,1936:576.
12. To project an image of strength and determination (abroad).	Crenshaw,1978:136;Jenkins, 1977:1;Jenkins,1979:72.
13. Advertising the movement and/or cause; to gain publicity; to attract attention; to awaken public opinion; to force audience to take grievances seriously and to redress them; to gain recognition To acquire popular support.	Thornton,1964:82;Bell,1975: 94;Stohl,1981(Fashions and Fantasies in the Study of Political Terrorism):4;Wolf, 1975(in Police Journal):103; Jenkins,1975(in Carlton):16; Crenshaw,1981:383;Pike,1970: 34;Milbank,1978:54;Hardman, 1936:576;Chisholm,1948:21; Jenkins&Johnson,1975:3,Crenshaw,1978:136;Bassiouni,1979: 757;Russell,Banker&Miller,1979: 19;Iviansky,1977:50;Hacker, 1980:73
14. To immobilize security apparatus by typing up many of its agents for tasks of object protection; To immobilize forces.	Debray,as quoted in Fairbairn, 1974:352 Thornton,1964:77
15. To win recruits for the terrorist movement.	Crenshaw,1978:76

Table VI : Purposes and Functions Attributed to Terrorism (continued)

PURPOSE and FUNCTIONS	AUTHORS (numbers refer to year and page of publication)
16. Morale-building within the terrorist movement itself and with their sympathizers.	Thornton,1964:82;Pike,1970: 34;Crenshaw,1978:77;Milbank, (in Elliott) 1978:54.
17. To maintain discipline within the terrorist organization; To punish errant members and traitors.	Crenshaw,1978:136 Bell,1975:15
18. Winning of specific concessions through coercive bargaining (release of prisoners, publication of manifesto, etc.); Extortion; Blackmail.	Stohl(Fashions...)1981:5; Jenkins,1975:16;Bell,1975:18; U.S.Nat.Adv.Com.,1976:3; Watson,1976:1 Hannay(in Sobel)1974/75:1; Bell,1975:12;Milbank,1978(in Elliott):54 Hacker,1980:73.
19. Punishment for cooperation with enemy or for engaging in "harmful" activities, or for other "guilts"; Punishment against persons responsible for cruelties, revenges, retaliation.	Jenkins (in Carlton),1975:18; Gross,1972:10;Fairbairn,1974: 348; Fallah,1981:13-14
20. To impose domination; To subdue and paralyze; To subjugate, intimidate.	Waciorski,1939:98;Wurth,1941: 56; Bouthoul,1975:50-59 Roucek,1962:116

Motives for Terrorism

If the purpose of terrorism is a legitimate element of a definition, the motive for terrorism could likewise be a candidate element for a definition. However, motives refer to causes and causes are discussed in explanations of a phenomenon, in theories. A definition, however, is not a theory. In our view, motives do not have to be part of a definition. This view is not shared universally. A stress on motives can, for instance, be found in the wording of the mandate of the United Nations' Ad Hoc Committee which was charged to study "the underlying causes of those forms of terrorism and acts of violence which lie in misery, frustration, grievance and despair and which cause some people to sacrifice human lives, including their own, in an attempt to effect radical changes." [40)]

When the General Assembly of the United Nations discussed terrorism, representatives of the Third World nations wanted to exclude actions by National Liberation movements and violent acts of people against foreign domination from any definition of international terrorism. [41)] A salient example of this line of thinking has been offered by Yassir Arafat in his 1974 speech to the United Nations' General Assembly:

> "He who fights for a just cause, he who fights for the liberation
> of his country, he who fights against invasion and exploitation
> or singlemindedly against colonialism, can never be defined
> a terrorist." 42)

The confusion about motives seems to enter the discussion of definitions because the label terrorism is attached to certain persons who thereby become terrorists. As persons the terrorists can be motivated by a variety of inner drives ranging from pecuniary gain to revenge. But just as we can define sabotage, revolution or war without explaining the underlying motives, we can define terrorism without entering the value-ladden area of moving causes.

Duvall and Stohl appear to be correct in their view that:

> "Motives are entirely irrelevant to the concept of political
> terrorism. Most analysts fail to recognize this and, hence,
> tend to discuss certain motives as logical or necessary aspects
> of terrorism. But they are not. At best, they are empirical
> regularities associated with terrorism. More often they simply
> confuse analysis." 43)

Yet this remains a thorny area: motives and intentions, causes and goals are hard to separate.

The Acts of Terrorism

The discussions of motives for terrorism which have plagued international
bodies and prevented effective measures to be accepted to counter
terrorism has led to an alternative approach. This new approach, chosen
mainly to circumvent the thorny area of motives, was chosen by the
drafters of the European Convention on the Suppression of Terrorism.
They opted for a definitional approach which simply enumerated certain
specific threatening or violent acts which in turn were considered to
fall under the mandate of the convention. These acts included the unlawful seizure of aircrafts (hijackings), serious offences against
diplomatic agents, acts of kidnapping and hostage taking and offences
involving the use of a bomb, grenade, rocket, automatic firearm or
parcel bomb if this use endangers persons. [44]
In our view this too is a misleading approach. The nature of terrorism
is not inherent in the violent act itself. One and the same act -
e.g. a bombing - can be terroristic or not, depending on intention and
circumstances. The saying "the bomb-placer is the poor man's air force" [45]
might strike an egalitarian chord, but is ultimately misleading. [46]
We would like to illustrate this by discussing two delicts, Hijacking and
Kidnapping, which are often treated as synonyms for terrorism.*

---

* It might, at this point, be useful to recall the original meanings of these
terms: "Kidnapping" literally means the seizure (nap=snatch) of children (kids).
The term became notorious in the interwar period with the rise of gangsterism
in the United States. It then referred to the theft of children whose safe
return to their parents was made conditonal upon the payment of a ransom.
The original English word goes back to the 17th century when it referred to
the abduction of English boys aged 6 to 14 who were brought to America to work
on the tobacco fields of Maryland and Virginia (R.Clutterbuck. Kidnap &
Ransom. The Response. London,Faber & Faber,1978,p.19;C.Moorehead.Fortune's
Hostages. A Study of Kidnapping in the World Today.London,Hamish Hamilton,
1980,p.3) A modernization of the term is "diplonapping", referring to the
forceful seizure of internationally protected persons. "Hijacking" is of
American origin, a slang word becoming notorious during the prohibition area
when it referred to stealing goods in transit, especially truckloads of
illicit liquor (Edgar O'Ballace.Language of Violence.San Rafael,Presidio,
1979,p.67) The present meaning refers to the forcing of the pilot of an aircraft to fly to an unscheduled landing point. A modernization of the term is
"skyjacking". This term deserves preference over "air piracy". The pirates
of old engaged in robbery at sea. They were primarily interested in the ship
itself and its contents, not in the people on board who were a safety risk
and therefore not infrequently done away rather than their being kept as
hostages.

Take the following case of hijacking. Gunmen seize control of an airborn
jetliner and make demands. The crew and the passengers are frightened by
the gunswaying hijackers. Whether this situation is terroristic or not,
depends on the nature and the addressee of the demands. If it is only
"Fly this plane to West Berlin (or Cuba)", the pilot can, through a
change of the flight plan, accommodate the demand and thereby defuse
the threatening situation. If, however, the demands are made to a party
outside the plane (e.g. "Release the imprisoned trade unionists and end
the state of emergency") the passengers and crew in the plane can do
nothing to save their lives. In the first case the purpose of hijacking
is escape. In the second case a state of terror is created ("we are
helpless in the hands of merciless fanatics") which opens the way for
coercive bargaining for the terrorists. The underlying motives do not
matter in either situation. Whether the inner drive of the hijackers
is of a criminal, political or psychic nature is irrelevant. What matters
is to whom the demands are made.

The second example concerns kidnapping. A politician on his way to
office is intercepted in his car and forcibly taken into a secret
hiding place. Demands are made to the government, a deadline for
compliance is set and when the demanded release of imprisoned
revolutionaries is not effectuated upon the expiration of the ultimatum,
the abducted person is murdered. Clearly a terroristic kidnapping. But
not every abduction of a person that results in the subsequent death
is terroristic. Take the case of the abduction of Adolf Eichmann who
was snatched in May 1960 by Mossad agents and secretly deported from
Argentina to Israel where he was tried in public and hanged in December
of the same year. Because the former organizer of the Holocaust was
victim and enemy target at the same time, this act does not fit into
the triadic pattern of terrorism. The successful Israeli operation
might have filled other former Nazi leaders still in hiding with
chronic fear (terror) but that alone does not make it a terroristic
act. Terror might in this case have been a byproduct of the action,
but it was not the goal nor the instrument to achieve other goals. [47]
The goal was punishment for complicity in genocide.

Just as some hijackings and kidnappings are terroristic and others are
not, no act can be called terroristic in itself. There is, however, a
tendency to reify terrorism by equating it with certain acts. Carlos
Marighela, the urban guerrilla theorist, for instance, once said, "By
terrorism I mean the use of bomb attacks" [48]. That the same

tendency of attributing a concrete nature to abstractions is also
present in a document like the European Convention on the Suppression
of Terrorism is deplorable. It can place a hijacker who is attempting
to escape from a terror regime in the same category as a "real"
(i.e. triadic) terrorist.

The Actors of Terrorism

In our questionnaire we asked authors in the field of terrorism a
question which refers to the actors of terrorism (Table IV).

Table VII: Answers to the Question: "Should the Term Terrorism in
Your View Be Utilized Primarily..." - as Percentages of
Total Responses (n=50).

a) For a form of insurgent violence.	18 %
b) For a form of insurgent as well as vigilante violence.	14 %
c) For state violence as well as a).	8 %
d) For state violence as well as b).	42 %
e) Other	12 %
No Answer	6 %

In our original content analysis for Table II we also had a 23rd
category referring to the thrust of a definition in the sense whether
or not only anti-state violence was meant by terrorism. In the bigger
sample (n=109) 21 percent of the definitions were identified as being
"anti-state only". However, there were also 26% of the definitions where
state terrorism was explicitly included. In the smaller sample (n=29),
the respective figures were 19% and 10%. In the other definitions in
the two samples no specification was made as to whether or not
terroristic violence by the state was covered.
In our content-analysis there is another category (Category 16 in
Table II) which assembled references to the perpetrator of terroristic
violence, in so far as this was a group, movement or organization.

In the bigger sample (n= 109) 14 percent of the definitions contained
a reference in this sense, while in the smaller one (n = 29) the
percentage was 18.5. This category can give us another indication
of the relative weight attributed to specific actors in definitions —
at least if the state is not interpreted as an organization. A rough
conclusion which can be drawn from these figures is that those who
exclude state violence from the field of terrorism are a minority,
though a substantial minority. This conclusion somewhat surprised us
since probably more than 90 percent of the literature on terrorism is
on non-state terrorism.

An explanation for this discrepancy could be that scholars pay lip
service to the ubiquity of terrorism, but then concentrate on one type
of terrorism only, which most often is labelled "revolutionary terrorism".
This, after all, is the type of terrorism for which state funding for
research can be more easily obtained. In addition, the ideological
outlook of many authors dealing with the subject of terrorism is in all
likelihood closer to the establishment than to those forces opposing
state power.

But is it just a question of money and ideology? There are other elements
too which play a role, e.g. the problem of data availability. The violence
perpetrated by state authorities against its own citizens is likely to be
censored in the press. For instances of non-state terrorism, on the other
hand, there are professional data-assemblers in the police stations, the
secret services, the military, etc. Social scientists can get easier access
to these data than they can assemble data on the opposing force. The
relative access advantage of one type of data over the other probably
helps to steer research attention in a particular direction. Yet when
all these and other allowances are made: are there also scientific
reasons to exclude state violence from a definition of terrorism?

One can argue that the power of a state is incomparably bigger than the
one of the typically small clandestine insurgent terrorist groups who
are only capable of sporadic "needlepoint" actions. The potential for
violence of the two social units is so asymmetrical that the
quantitative difference turns into a qualitative one which makes the

subsumption of the violent activities of the two under one and the same
concept inappropriate. As a consequence terrorism should be reserved
for insurgent (and vigilante) forms of violence and the activities of
the state could then be labelled terror or repression. A second
argument for treating state violence differently can be found in the
fact that the state, in Weber's formulation (successfully) claims for
itself the legitimate monopoly of violence while the insurgent movement
does not. To this one can answer that those seeking and those holding
state power are both involved in a struggle for legitimacy. If the
insurgents win they obviously have had greater means at their disposal
than the incumbent defenders. These means need not all have been
terroristic, or violent but can also have been legal. If a revolutionary
movement like the German National Socialists in the 1920s, by a
combination of terroristic, violent and legal means manages to gain
state power and thereafter continues to wield power with a similar mix
of methods, it would be artificial, in our view, to rebaptize the
terroristic methods into something different for the period after 1933.
The (mis)use of the legal machinery of the state for political justice,
the use of show trials for teaching the public the lesson that
resistance is hopeless can assume terroristic features. When the state
does not only punish those who violate a law, but punishes some people
(guilty or not) so that others are deterred to violate repressive laws,
then we enter the field of terrorism. Where the law has become
unpredictable in its application, because individual guilt is less
important to the regime than collective obedience, we are clearly no
longer dealing with a legitimate monopoly of violence, but with state
terrorism. [49)]

While the term "state terrorism" admittedly figures as an instrument
of psychological warfare operations (as does "international terrorism"),
there is in our view enough evidence which points to structural
similarities with insurgent terrorism to warrant its maintenance.
However, a more neutral term such as "regime terrorism" might be
preferable. State refers to a territory, a people and a government,
while regime is less broad, excluding territory and most of the
population and at the same time does not have to cover the whole of
government. [50)] Analogous to such a change in nomenclature from state
terrorism to regime terrorism one might also consider to replace the

expression "revolutionary terrorism" with "insurgent terrorism".
While the aspirations of individual terrorists might be revolutionary
in the sense of desiring to bring about fundamental changes in the
socio-political and/or economic order, these rebels are, until they
have been victorious, merely revolting, i.e. engaged in revolt.
Revolutions are generally effected with mass participation. It is
exactly the lack of mass participation which is one of the deficiencies
of "revolutionary terrorism". In so far there is a contradiction in
terms in the concept "revolutionary terrorism".
If, however, the violent revolutionairies see quality rather than
quantity as criterion for their endeavours, there is also room for
scepticism: one is reminded of Bart de Ligt's remark "The more violence, the less revolution." [51)]
From the above it should be clear that, in our view, terrorism should
not be linked to a particular actor only to the exclusion of others.
Whether the perpetrator is a "lone wolf", a criminal, a vigilante,
a psychopath, an insurgent or an agent of a regime should be irrelevant
in assessing whether or not certain forms of violence should be defined
as terroristic.

Terrorism's "Extranormal" Qualities

A number of authors stress the "extranormal means" the "unacceptability"
or the "amoral and antinomian nature" (Wilkinson,1974) of terrorism
(see category 9 in Table V).
This naturally begs the question when violence is normal, acceptable
and moral. These are evaluative terms depending on history, geography,
culture and socialization. Cannibalism was normal in Central America
before the White Man came. Slavery became normal in North America when
the White Man brought black labour from Africa. Both are no longer
considered normal.
If ours is the "Age of Terrorism" as, for instance, Ray S. Cline holds [52)]
terrorism has presumably become normal so that the qualification extranormal becomes self-liquidating.
Yet, with all these reservations "extranormal" remains a handy category
for shelfing some of the peculiar features of terrorism. It can be

argued that terrorism owes its power chiefly to this quality. Normal
occurrences lead to standardized responses and coping mechanisms.
Terrorist violence breaks the pattern of normal human actions.
The extranormal qualities of terrorism, can arguably be found in
the following five elements (which have not all to be present
simultaneously).

The Weapon Utilized for the Terror-Inducing Act is Extranormal

When tanks and poison gas were used for the first time in World War I,
the unfamiliar experience created panic and terror. The psychological
effect of these new weapons produced an impact far beyond the actual
casualties lost. In contrast to the more calculated use of the
flying rockets V 1 and V 2 in the Second World War this terror was,
however, more situational than purposive.
With regard to the French Revolution it is arguable that a good deal
of terror was produced by the peculiar machine invented by docteur J.I.
Guillotin for decapitating the "enemies of the people". After the
invention of dynamite in 1867 the Russian terrorists took great
pains to work with this new and more "terrible" stuff. Chernov, the
leader of one wing of the Russian Socialist Revolutionary party, noted
in 1909:

> "Terror is a form of military combat, a form of war, and as in
> war, any state whose military tactics are outdated exposes itself
> to failure. (...) Terror will be terror in the true sense of the
> word only if it represents the revolutionary implementation of
> the achievements of the most advanced technical sciences at any
> given moment." 53)

In recent years great attention has been paid to those few instances
where terrorists used ground-to-air missiles or radioactive materials.
There is considerable concern that terrorists will go "nuclear". The
multiplicity of bomb threats at nuclear power plants can also be seen
in this light: the mystery and threat surrounding things atomic makes
them a particularly effective source of terrorist manipulation. 54)
However, one should not forget that most terrorist acts are committed
with quite common weapons so that this category might not represent a
necessary property of terrorism.

The Nature of the Terrorist Act Shows Extranormal Features

The atrocity of terrorist threats and actual practices frequently
strikes one as extranormal. Cutting of an ear to put force behind an
extortionist kidnapping, disembowling pregnant women, legshooting,
kneecapping, the shooting of a teacher in front of his students rather
than sparing the children the sight of such a deed by taking the victim
outside the classroom, the drinking of the blood of a victim - these
are some illustrations of this extranormal dimension. Jacques Soustelle,
the French Governor-General of Algeria, offers another:

> "... terror is a psychological lever of unbelievable power. Before
> the bodies of those who(se) throats have been cut and the
> grimacing faces of the mutilated, all capacity for resistance
> lapses: the spring is broken." 55)

Another military man, Colonel Neal, offers a possible explanation for
the marked cruelty of terroristic violence:

> "Terroristic violence must be totally ruthless, for moral scruples
> and terror do not mix and one or the other must be rejected. There
> can be no such thing as a weak dose of terror. The hand that
> controles the whip must be firm and implacable." 56)

The Time and Place of a Terrorist Attack are Extranormal

For tactical reasons the terrorist act is taking place without previous
announcement (although there is sometimes a warning that a bomb is about
to go off or death-lists are published). The attack occurs unexpectedly
and causes surprise. The time is generally a peacetime. The place of
the terrorist act is also unpredictable. There are no frontlines, there
is no battlefield. The sudden outbreak of violence can occur at home,
during a sportive event or in a cinema, in a barroom or on the marketplace - places which have the character of zones of peace. The contrast
between the familiar surroundings and the violent disruption enhances
the fear. There is a sporadic, irregular pattern to the violence, whereby
no one can be really certain that he is not facing imminent danger the
very next moment. The thought where and when the next attack will take
place and who will be the victim is on everybody's mind of those who
belong to the targets of terror. There is "electricity in the air".

The Clandestine, Covert Nature Makes Terrorism Extranormal

Normalcy presupposes an insight into what is going on. If things happen secretly, rather than in public, if the actors wear skicaps to hide their true identity, or people disappear without a trace and rumour is rampant some conditions are present which are a fertile ground for terror to arise. While secrecy and conspiracy are an operational necessity for weak underground movements, state terrorism also draws its strength from the anonymity of its agents, the uncertainty about their directives and the impenetrability of the organization which creates the terror. This property, and the one preceeding it referring to time and place, can, in our view, be collapsed into one.

The Deliberate Violation of Basic Human Rules of Conduct is Extranormal

Even in wartime some minimal rules of conduct are observed most of the time by the belligerents. Deliberate attacks on civilians are not considered justified in war either as an end or as a means to an end. [57] Certain basic rights are granted to the enemy in war, such as a humane treatment of prisoners and special consideration for women, children and old people. There is also respect for the neutrality of third parties who do not want to take sides in a conflict. [58] All this is absent when we speak of terrorism. With terrorism we associate a marked indifference towards basic moral codes: prisoners are killed, children are taken hostage, noncombatant civilians are slaughtered, women are tortured by terrorists. No rule of combat is respected if rule violation serves the terrorist purpose.

The adherence to social norms in human interactions makes behaviour predictable and thereby contributes to a sense of security. Whenever manmade violence occurs we look for a reason and generally find it in a breakdown of the actor-victim relationship. The terrorist, however, has generally not had such a relationship at all. The victim is often not his real opponent, he is only an object to activate a relationship with his opponent. This instrumentalization of human beings for a cause of which they are not part in a conflict in which they are often not active participants strikes many observers as extranormal. Although we all have inconsistent attitudes towards victimization, depending whether the victim is a friend or foe, most people have a minimal respect for

more or less arbitrarily victimized noncombatants who have not sought
nor provoked the confrontation with the terrorists. In such cases our
norms of justice and proportionality are violated and we tend to react
with outrage or terror depending how close to ourselves the terrorist
act has occurred.

Of the five ways terrorist violence is perceived by many observers as
extranormal this is the most profound one.

Conclusion

In the preceeding pages we have tried to come to grips with the concept
of terrorism. First, we were looking at the way authors in the field
of violence relate terrorism to neighbouring concepts such as guerrilla
warfare, assassination, political violence and the like. We have then
looked how about one hundred key authors define terrorism by
analyzing which elements they use to construct their definitions. Then
we scrutinized some of the major elements in terms of logical consistency
and adequacy for describing that part of reality which they pretend to
cover. In our search to determine what terrorism is meant to be by
users of this term we have also looked at some areas of agreement and
disagreement among users. Some of the contested areas were subjected
to more detailed analysis in the hope to solve some contradictions by
finding a new element which is able to contain two seemingly exclusive
old ones. In this we have often followed the suggestions of others who
were engaged in conceptual work.

At the end of this exercise we cannot offer a true or correct definition
of terrorism. Terrorism is an abstract phenomenon of which there can
be no real essence which can be discovered and described. Definitions
serve as agreements on the way concepts should be used. The correct
definition would be the one which is consistently used by all users.
In the field of terrorism there is no agreement about any single
definition. But there is, in our view, considerable agreement about
the main elements which definitions should contain (the top ten in the
first two samples of Table V).

There is also considerable support for seeing the victim-target
differentiation as an important if not the most important specific
feature of terrorism (next to terror, of course).

At the beginning of this chapter we expressed the hope to be able to
reduce the 22 elements of Table II to a smaller number of elements,
dropping all those which were implicit in others or not mandatory.
Based on the preceeding discussion this writer has come to the
following definition:

> "Terrorism is a method of combat in which random or symbolic
> victims serve as instrumental target of violence. These instrumental
> victims share group or class characteristics which form the basis
> for their selection for victimization. Through previous use of
> violence or the credible threat of violence other members of that
> group or class are put in a state of chronic fear (terror). This
> group or class, whose members' sense of security is purposively
> undermined, is the target of terror. The victimization of the
> target of violence is considered extranormal by most observers
> from the witnessing audience on the basis of its atrocity; the
> time (e.g. peacetime) or place (not a battlefield) of victimization
> or the disregard for rules of combat accepted in conventional war-
> fare. The norm violation creates an attentive audience beyond
> the target of terror; sectors of this audience might in turn form
> the main object of manipulation. The purpose of this indirect
> method of combat is either to immobilize the target of terror in
> order to produce disorientation and/or compliance, or to mobilize
> secondary targets of demands (e.g. a government) or targets of
> attention (e.g. public opinion) to changes of attitude or
> behaviour favouring the short or long-term interests of the users
> of this method of combat."

This definition includes 13 of the 22 elements of Table V, but it also
contains some new elements which makes it rather a long definition.
The fundamenta divisionis are the random or symbolic selection of
instrumental targets of violence and their use to manipulate either
targets of terror, targets of demands or targets of attention.
Whether this definition is really an improvement on Thornton's classic
1964 definition to which it is most indebted, or on other authors'
definitions is up to the reader to judge.

Some readers will undoubtedly find that this definition is too narrow,
excluding as it does violence against things and demanding the existence
of a target of terror. While we would concede that some violence
against symbolic things can be considered terroristic in effect, we
see this as an exception to the rule and therefore it needs not to
be included. The second objection is more serious. We would admit that

there are many triadic acts of violence where there is a target of
demands or a target of attention without that there is a clearly
distinguishable target of terror. This can be a consequence of
inconsistent victim selection or infrequency of acts of violence
to maintain a climate of terror in a particular sector in society.
A criminal kidnapping with a ransom demand also has no immediate target
of terror. However, while individual acts of triadic violence might be
unable to build up terror in a third party, individual acts by
different parties for different purposes, political and other, can,
taken together, create a climate of insecurity and terror in certain
sectors of society. They reinforce each other and waves of kidnappings,
waves of assassinations, perpetrated independently in one society,
collectively create terrorized groups. The murder of John F. Kennedy
in 1963 was not perceived as terroristic at the time; today, after many
presidential assassination attempts both in the United States and abroad,
presidents are likely to see it in terms of terrorism. Put differently:
individual actors perpetrating some forms of violence, can count on a
kind of déjà-vu effect which ties their deed in with others and thereby
gives it a meaning it would otherwise lack. Dyadic forms of violence
can also add to the apprehension of certain groups in society. However,
such spill-over effects from other forms of violence are also likely
to affect the concept of terrorism and make it less precise.

The emotive nature of the subject-matter, the term's derogatory thrust
in political discourse, are additional factors contributing to
deformations of the concept. The fact that certain human beings - the
terrorists - are seen as the carriers of the concept is particularly
harmful to the concept, since all or most of their diverse deeds are
likely to be subsumed under the heading of terrorism. Nobody would
conceptualize "war" or "love" in terms of all that warriors and lovers
do. Terrorism, however, is suffering this fate only too often. Rather
than being considered as a technique of applying violence which in
principle can be used by anyone in all sorts of conflict situations,
the concept is often linked to certain actors only for certain types
of conflicts only. The result has been that "one man's terrorist is
the other man's patriot". The concept has thereby often been subjected
to a double standard based on definition power and an in-group -

out-group distinction. Social scientists should not accept this
for the very substance of science is then endangered, its universality.
If science is sacrificed to Western, Marxist, Islamic, Jewish,
Nationalist or other ideologies, it is no longer science. The price
for corrupting the integrity of concepts is too high.
What's in a name? A lot!

Notes

1) M.Ch. Bassiouni. Prolegomenon to Terror Violence. Creighton Law Review, Vol.12, No.3, Spring 1979, p.752.

2) H. Edward Price. The Strategy and Tactics of Revolutionary Terrorism. Comparative Studies in Society and History, January 1977, p.52.
- From the pagination referred to it appears that the reference is to Martha Crenshaw Hutchinson, The Concept of Revolutionary Terrorism. Journal of Conflict Revolution, Vol. 16, September 1972, pp.383-395.

3) Three of the 29 authors of the second sample preferred not to be identified. The others were: Aston, Blok, Clutterbuck, Crenshaw, Dimitrijević, Dinstein, Efrat, Francis, Green, Hahlweg, Hess, Hondrich, ISC, Leiser, Mallin, Merari, Ochberg, Pontara, Rosenthal, Rubin, Sederberg, Tomasevski, Vasilijevic, Wilkinson, Wolf, Zofka.

4) Robert H. Kupperman and Darrell M. Trent. Terrorism, Threat, Reality, Response. Stanford, Hoover Institution Press, 1979, p.14.-Emphasis added, AS.

5) R.A. Friedlander. Terrorism and the Law: What Price Safety? Gaithersburg, Md., IACP, 1980, p.3.- Emphasis added, AS.

6) J. Galtung. Zur Strategie der nichtmilitärischen Verteidigung - Probleme und Lösungsvorschläge. In: J. Galtung. Anders verteidigen. Rowohlt, Reinbek, 1982, p.238.-Emphasis added, AS.

7) Cit. M. Fleming. Propaganda by the Deed. Terrorism and Anarchist Theory in Late Nineteenth Century Europe. Terrorism. Vol.4, Nos.1-4, p.14.

8) Cit. U.S. News & World Report, 22 May 1978. Special Report. Terror Gang. Is Anyone Safe?, p.32.

9) Rogier Trinquier. Modern Warfare: A French View of Counterinsurgency. New York, Praeger, 1964, p.17; cit. Philip A. Karber. Terrorism: Baseline Data and Conceptual Framework. Social Science Quarterly, Vol.52, December 1971, p.528n.

10) S. Andreski. "Terror" in: A Dictionary of the Social Sciences. Glencoe, Free Press, 1964; cit. P. Wilkinson. Terrorism and the Liberal State. London, Macmillan, 1977, p.53.

11) Thomas Perry Thornton. Terror as a Weapon of Political Agitation. In: Harry Eckstein (Ed.). Internal War: Problems and Approaches. New York, 1964, p.77, cit. Philip A. Karber. Urban Terrorism: Baseline Data and Conceptual Framework. Social Science Quarterly, Vol.52, Dec.1971, pp.527-528.

12) G. Lindzey et al. Psychology. New York, Worth Publ., 1976, p.323.

13) M. Crenshaw Hutchinson. Revolutionary Terrorism. The FLN in Algeria, 1954-1962. Stanford, Hoover Institution, 1978, pp. 20, 23.

14) Brian M. Jenkins and Janera Johnson. International Terrorism: A Chronology, 1968-1974. Santa Monica, Rand, 1975, p. 56.

15) Edward F. Mickolus. Transnational Terrorism. A Chronology of Events, 1968-1979. London, Aldwich Press, 1980, pp.770-771.

16) This term has been proposed by the U.S. National Advisory Committee on Criminal Justice Standards and Goals. Report of the Task Force on Disorders and Terrorism. Washington, D.C., GPO, 1976, p. 5. - The meaning attached to the term there, is different, since it refers mainly to criminal acts of "protective" hostage-taking, e.g. by bank robbers trapped on the scene who attempt to organize their escape by using human beings as shields and bargaining chips. While "true" terrorism has, in the wording of this Report, "the prime purpose of creating overwhelming fear for coercive purposes" (Ibid., p. 3), "Quasi-terrorism is a description applied in this report to those activities incidental to the commission of crimes of violence that are similar in form and method to true terrorism but which nevertheless lacks its essential ingredient." (Ibid., p. 5.)

17) Feliks Gross. Violence in Politics. The Hague, Mouton, 1972, pp. 18-19.

18) W.H. Smith. International Terrorism. A Political Analysis. In: The Yearbook of World Affairs, 1977. London, Stevens and Smith, 1977, Vol. 31, pp. 138-139.

19) T.P. Thornton, op. cit., p. 81.

20) Nicolas Morozov. Terroristic Struggle. London, 1880. Repr. fully in F. Gross, op. cit., pp. 103-104, 106. - Emphasis added, AS.

21) Leon Trotsky. Against Individual Terrorism. New York, Pathfinder Press, 1974, pp. 3-4.

22) J.B.S. Hardman. Terrorism. In: Encyclopedia of the Social Sciences. Vol. 14, New York, Macmillan, 1936, pp. 575-576.

23) E.V. Walter. Terror and Resistance. A Study of Political Violence. London, Oxford University Press, 1969, pp. 22-23, p. 25.

24) The triadic method of combat can also be encountered in nonviolent struggles. Take the example of a strike of hospital personnel for better wages. The target of the strike is the government which is put under pressure to pay higher wages. The immediate victims are the patients in the hospital whose deteriorating condition is the lever to force the government to capitulate or at least to make concessions. The outcome of the strike is generally determined by the side which public opinion takes. If patients actually die this is likely to reflect negatively on the hospital personnel - this is why some emergency facilities are kept operative.
While in this situation human beings are victimized in a dispute between two parties of which they are not part, the patients still have some room for manoeuvre (move to another hospital, call for an army doctor in government service etc.). Their situation is better than it would be in case of terrorist victimization.

25) Saleem Qureshi. Political Violence in the South Asian Subcontinent.
In: Y. Alexander (Ed.). International Terrorism. National, Regional,
and Global Perspectives. New York, Praeger, 1976, p. 151. - Emphasis
added, AS.

26) David L. Milbank. International and Transnational Terrorism. Diagnosis
and Prognosis. Repr. in: John D. Elliott & Leslie K. Gibson (Eds.).
Contemporary Terrorism. Selected Readings. Gaithersburg, Md., IACP, 1978,
p. 54; see also: Edward F. Mickolus. Transnational Terrorism. A
Chronology of Events 1968-1979. London, Aldwych Press, 1980, p. XIII.
- Emphasis added, AS.

27) Raymond D. Duvall and Michael Stohl. Governance by Terror. Chapter Six
of the forthcoming The Politics of Terrorism. Ed. by Michael Stohl,
New York, Marcel Dekker, Inc., 1983, p. 13.

28) Herman Rauschning. Gespräche mit Hitler. Wien, 1940, p. 82;
cit. Friedrich Hacker. Terror. Mythos, Realität, Analyse. Reinbek,
Rowohlt, 1975, p. 323.

29) Hitlers Tischgespräche, 14-15 Sept. 1941; cit. J. Blokker. Volkskrant,
(Het Vervolg), 4 October 1980, p. 11.

30) Das Parlament (Bonn), 21. Jan. 1978, p. 14.

31) NRC-Handelsblad, 8 March 1980, p. 5.

32) P.R. Baehr. Een campagne tegen het martelen. De Gids, no. 3, 1975, p. 187.

33) A.P. Schmid and J. de Graaf. Violence as Communication. London, Sage,
1982, p. 176.

34) P. Wilkinson. Political Terrorism. London, Macmillan, 1974, pp. 101-102.

35) E.F. Mickolus. Transnational Terrorism. A Chronology of Events, 1968-
1979. London, Aldwych Press, 1980, p. 176; B.M. Jenkins & J. Johnson.
International Terrorism: A Chronology, 1968-1974. Santa Monica, RAND,
1975, pp. 11, 21.

36) Cf. A.P. Schmid & J. de Graaf. Violence as Communication. London, Sage,
1982, pp. 49-50.

37) Cit. Der Spiegel, No. 23, 1972, p. 24.

38) This distinction has been made by Edward Hyams. Terrorists and Terrorism.
London, J.M. Dent & Sons, 1975, p. 10.

39) Jan Schreiber. The Ultimate Weapon: Terrorists and World Order. New York,
Morrow, 1978.

40) Agenda item, cit. John Dugard. International Terrorism: Problems of
Definition. International Affairs, Vol. 50, No. 1, 1974, p. 73n.

41) Rainer Lagoni. Die Vereinigten Nationen und der internationale Terrorismus. Europa-Archiv, Folge 6, 1977, p. 176.

42) Cit. L. Bonanate (Ed.). Dimensioni del Terrorismo Politico. Milano, Franco Angeli Editore, 1979, p. 101, transl. from Italian.

43) Raymond D. Duvall and Michael Stohl. Governance by Terror. (Chapter Six of the forthcoming edition of M. Stohl (Ed.). The Politics of Terrorism. New York, Marcel Decker, 1983, pp. 12-13 in the draft manuscript.)

44) Council of Europe. Explanatory Report on the European Convention on the Suppression of Terrorism. Strassbourg, 27 January 1977, pp. 20-21, Article 1.

45) Cit. J. Shaw et al. (Eds.). Ten Years of Terrorism. New York, Crane, Russak & Co., 1979, p. 15.

46) This is not to deny that there are terroristic aspects to contemporary warfare. If low degree of discrimination between combattants and civilians alone is taken to be sufficient for the qualification terrorism, the case for equating bomb-placer and airborne bomb-thrower is a stronger one. If victim-target differentiation and the purposive creation of terror are added as necessary elements for defining terrorism, the equation becomes weaker. There are many fuzzy areas in warfare. What to think, for instance, of the "demographic targeting" practised by the U.S. Airforce in Vietnam? The decision which villages were to be bombed was taken by computers on the basis of programmes and information entered by various officers. Places for which the computer predicted a certain likelyhood for the presence of enemy forces were selected as legitimate targets for bombing. - Hermann C. Flessner, reviewing Joseph Weizenbaum's Die Macht der Computer und die Ohnmacht der Vernunft. Frankfurt a.M., Suhrkamp, 1978, Der Spiegel, no. 32, 7 August 1978, p. 147.

47) The example is taken from A.P. Schmid & J. de Graaf. Violence as Communication. London, Sage, 1982, p. 58.

48) C. Marighela. For the Liberation of Brazil. Harmondsworth, Penguin, 1971, p. 89.

49) This paragraph is indebted to some ideas offered by Raymond D. Duvall and Michael Stohl, op. cit., pp. 6-7.

50) I am endebted to Henry Lobert, the Belgian chargé d'affairs in Athens, for this suggestion. - Cf. also: Centre for International Understanding. Athens Conference, 1981, Consensus Statements. St. Louis, L.A. Wallace Foundation, 1982, p. 6

51) Cit. G. Sharp. Social Power and Political Freedom. Boston, Porter Sargent, 1980, p. 332.

52) In his Foreword to Y. Alexander & John M. Gleason (Eds.). Behavioral and Quantitative Perspectives on Terrorism. New York, Pergamon Press, 1981, p. XII.

53) Cit. A. Spiridovich. Histoire du Terrorisme Russe, 1886-1917. Paris, 1930, pp. 587-588, as quoted in Z. Iviansky. Individual Terror: Concept and Typology. Journal of Contemporary History, Vol. 12, no. 1, 1977, p. 49. - Emphasis added, AS.

54) For the frequency of this type of threat, see, for instance Allan Mazur. Bomb Threats and the Mass Media: Evidence for a Theory of Suggestion. American Sociological Review, Vol. 47, June 1982, pp. 407-411.

55) Cit. B. Crozier. The Rebels: A Study of Post-War Insurrections. 1976, p. 176.

56) William D. Neal. Terror - Oldest Weapon in the Arsenal. Army, August 1973; cit. Jay Mallin. Terrorism as a Military Weapon. Air University Review, Jan.-Febr. 1977, Vol. 28, No. 2, p. 56.

57) Michael Walzer. Just and Unjust Wars. Harmondsworth, Penguin, 1980; cit. M. Randle. Ethics and Tactics in Civilian Based Defence. Unpubl. Paper, 1981, p. 7.

58) F. Hacker. Terror. Mythos, Realität, Analyse. Reinbek, Rowohlt, 1975, p. 188.

Appendix I: Definitions

HARDMAN (1936)

"Terrorism is a term used to describe the method or the theory behind
the method whereby an organized group or party seeks to achieve its
avowed aims chiefly through the systematic use of violence. Terroristic
acts are directed against persons who as individuals, agents or representatives of authority interfere with the consummation of the objectives of such a group. (...) The terrorist does not threaten; death or
destruction is part of his program of action, and if he is caught his
behavior during trials is generally directed primarily not toward winning his freedom but toward spreading a knowledge of his doctrines.
(...) Terrorism is a method of combat in the struggle between social
groups and forces rather than individuals, and it may take place in
any social order. Terrorism as a method is always characterized by the
fact that it seeks to arouse not only the reigning government or the
nation in control but also the mass of people to a realization that
constituted authority is no longer safely intrenched and unchallenged.
The publicity value of the terroristic act is a cardinal point in the
strategy of terrorism." 1)

WACIORSKI (1939)

"Terrorism is a method of action by which an agent tends to produce terror
in order to impose his domination." 2)

WURTH (1941)

"... we propose the following definition of criminal political terrorism,
that is to say, terrorism in its strict meaning, 'Terrorism is a method
of action by which the agent tends to produce terror to impose his domination on the State in order to transform or destroy it'." 3)

CHISHOLM (1948)

"Political terror is the planned use of violence or threat of violence
against an individual or social group in order to eradicate resistance
to the aims of the terrorist. Political terror differs from fear in its
organization and aims. Terror is a comparatively commonplace social
phenomenon. The lynching of a negro by a white mob is an act of terror.
However, unlike political terror it is generally an unplanned act with
limited aims. A mob convenes because of some real or imagined offense
against the white portion of the population. (...) The mob is either
successful in lynching the victim or is frustrated. In either event the
mob disperses and the same group is never reconstructed. (...) The political terrorist on the other hand engages in planned acts designed to
reduce his opponents to a plastic state of mind wherein they surrender
all opposition to the wielder of the sword, and passively agree to support his projects blindly, unquestioningly ... (...) Political terror
is a type of fear, or more accurately, a combination of fear and dread.
Dread is the awareness of an imminent, but unknown danger. It is a para-
lyzing, isolating emotion that renders impossible any constructive action. Fear either serves as a powerful inhibiting factor that deters us
from acting because of unpleasant consequences or as an energizing agent
that drives us to act in an effort to escape an unpleasant situation.
Political terrorism harnesses both of these emotions. The first task of
the mass terrorist is to destroy group solidarity. (...) A second element of political terrorism is ruthlessness. (...) Political terror is
not a secret device. Indeed, it is really a publicity campaign. The political terrorist does not desire to kill off his opponents (who may

number the vast majority of the population) but to subjugate them.
Therefore the actual instances of violence are merely examples of the
treatment given to obstructionists. (...) Through propaganda the terrorist spreads the word that violence rules the land." 4)

ARENDT (1951)
"A fundamental difference between modern dictatorships and all other
tyrannies of the past is that terror is no longer used as a means to
exterminate and frighten opponents, but as an instrument to rule masses
of people who are perfectly obedient. Terror as we know it today strikes
without any preliminary provocation, its victims are innocent even from
the point of view of the prosecutor. This was the case in Nazi Germany
when full terror was directed against Jews, i.e. against people with
certain common characteristics which were independent of their specific
behavior. (...) Russian practice, on the other hand, is even more "advanced" than the German in one respect: arbitrariness of terror is not
even limited by racial differentiation, while the old class categories
have long since been discarded, so that anybody in Russia may suddenly
become a victim of the police terror. We are not concerned here with
the ultimate consequence of rule of terror - namely, that nobody, not
even the executors, can ever be free of fear; in our context we are
dealing merely with the arbitrariness by which victims are chosen, and
for this it is decisive that they are objectively innocent, that they
are chosen regardless of what they may or may not have done. (...) Terror, however, is only in the last instance of its development a mere
form of government. In order to establish a totalitarian regime, terror
must be presented as an instrument for carrying out a specific ideology; and that ideology must have won the adherence of many, and even a
majority, before terror can be stabilized. The point for the historian
is that the Jews, before becoming the main victims of modern terror,
were the center of Nazi ideology.
(...) The pronounced activism of the totalitarian movements, their
preference for terrorism over all other forms of political activity,
attracted the intellectual elite and the mob alike, precisely because
this terrorism was so utterly different from that of the earlier revolutionary societies. It was no longer a matter of calculated policy
which saw in terrorist acts the only means to eliminate certain out-
standing personalities who, because of their policies or position, had
become the symbol of oppression. What proved so attractive was that terrorism had become a kind of philosophy through which to express frustration, resentment, and blind hatred, a kind of political expressionism
which used bombs to express oneself, which watched delightedly the publicity given to resounding deeds and was absolutely willing to pay the
price of life for having succeeded in forcing the recognition of one's
existence on the normal strata of society. It was still the same spirit
and the same game which made Goebbels, long before the eventual defeat
of Nazi Germany, announce with obvious delight that the Nazis, in case
of defeat, would know how to slam the door behind them and not to be
forgotten for centuries." 5)

CROZIER (1960)
"I define terrorism, provisionally, as the threat or the use of violence
for political ends. As a weapon, it may be wielded by rebels or by their
opponents; in the second case, however, it becomes counter-terrorism ...
It comes in several varieties: it may be indiscriminate or selective; it
may be used against the enemy or against members of one's own side. If
people in the terrorists' own camp are the victims, they are labelled
traitors. (...) The enforcement of conformity and obedience through fear:
that is one aspect of terrorism." 6)

ROUCEK (1962)

"Terror is usually defined as a period characterized by political executions, as during revolution, especially such a period (also called 'The Reign of Terror') during the French Revolution (from May 1793 to July 1794). But sociologically, it is a person or thing or practice that causes intense fear and suffering, whose aim is to intimidate, subjugate, especially as a political weapon or policy. In politics, its main function is to intimidate and disorganize the government through fear; it is the means through which political changes can be achieved. In its legalized form, terror includes physical constraints, or less conspicuous but very effective social measures - such as discriminatory economic, social, cultural, political and administrative measures." 7)

THORNTON (1964)

"... in an internal war situation, terror is a symbolic act designed to influence political behavior by extranormal means, entailing the use or threat of violence. (...) Terrorism may gain political ends in one of two ways - either by mobilizing forces or by immobilizing forces and reserves sympathetic to the cause of the insurgents or by immobilizing forces and reserves that would normally be available to the incumbents. (...) The political function of terror must also be emphasized, in contrast to the military role that is often ascribed to it. The military function of terror is negligible. (...) Definition of terror as a symbolic act does not mean that a person, say, is assassinated only symbolically and not in fact; rather, it means, that the terroristic act is intended and perceived as a symbol. (...) If the terrorist comprehends that he is seeking a demonstration effect, he will attack targets with a maximum symbolic value. (...) The symbolic concept of the terrorist act enables us to make two crucial distinctions: between terror and sabotage and between terror and assassination. (...) If the objective is primarily the removal of a specific thing (or person) with a view towards depriving the enemy of its usefulness, then the act is one of sabotage. If, on the other hand, the objective is symbolic, we are dealing with terror. (...) As a general rule, assassination and sabotage are nonsymbolic acts directed against persons and things, respectively. Terror is a symbolic act that may be directed against things or people." 8)

WALTER (1964)

"The word 'terrorism' conventionally means a type of violent action, such as murder, designed to make people afraid. In ordinary usage, however, the word 'terror' is ambiguous, often suggesting any kind of extreme apprehension, without regard to the cause. Moreover, it may mean, on the one hand, the psychic state - extreme fear - and, on the other hand, the thing that terrifies - the violent event that produces the psychic state. I shall try to avoid confusion by maintaining a precise usage, employing terms such as 'terrorism' and 'organized terror' consistently as equivalents to process of terror, by which I mean a compound with three elements: the act or threat of violence, the emotional reaction and the social effects. (...) A system of terror may be defined broadly to include certain states of war as well as certain political communities, as long as the term refers to sphere of relationships controlled by the terror process. (...) Systems of terror fall into two major categories, depending on whether they work against or coincide with the dominant power structure. (...) The [first] type may be referred to as a siege of terror and is not the subject of this paper. (...) The [second] form may be called a regime of terror and it is understood that the systems of terror discussed in this paper are of this type. (...) Violence, the principal element of the terror process, should

be distinguished from 'force', 'coercion', and 'power', for it is important to understand how terrorism differs from the ordinary political
practice of coercion. (...) The term 'violence' will be restricted to
the sense of destructive harm; hence a destructive kind of force. (...)
In contrast [to punishment], the terror process begins with violence,
which is followed by intense fear and irrational, reactive behavior
patterns. (...) In the terror process, no one can be secure, for the
category of transgression is, in reality, abolished. Anyone may be a
victim, no matter what action he chooses. Innocence is irrelevant." 9)

GAUCHER (1965)
"Le terrorisme est une méthode de lutte. (...) Il constitue un système
de lutte ouvertement déclarée, élaboré par un état-major, mis à l'épreuve
par une petite armée secrète, sélectionnée et disciplinée. Il multiplie
les coups, les ordonne, en calcule et en dose les effects, en escompte
tel ou tel résultat, en corrige l'exercice. (...) Bref, le terrorisme
est - ou veut être - une stratégie. L'exercise de la terreur, conçue
comme telle, choisie délibérément après d'âpres controverses, et métho-
diquement mise au point, commence ainsi véritablement en Russie vers
1879." 10)

ARON (1966)
"An action of violence is labelled 'terrorist' when its psychological
effects are out of proportion to its purely physical result. In this
sense, the so-called indiscriminate acts of revolutionaries are terrorist, as were the Anglo-American zone bombings. The lack of discrimination helps to spread fear, for if no one in particular is a target,
no one can be safe." 11)

LEIDEN and SCHMITT (1968)
"But terror can be conceptualized more broadly than this [Thornton de-
finition]: it is the emanation of an atmosphere of fear and despair,
generally accompanied by seemingly senseless and wanton threats to life
and property, carried out in normless ways by the plural centers of power. Terror, as conceived here, is a congeries of acts, specifically all
those contributing to such an atmosphere of despair: murder, assassination, sabotage and subversion, the destruction of public records, the
spreading of rumor, the closing of churches, the sequestration of property, the breakdown of criminal law enforcement, the prostitution of
the courts, the narcosis of the press - all these, as they contribute
to a common end, constitute terror. (...) Terror is an atmosphere of
despair. What value can such an atmosphere have? The answer lies, for
both those who agitate and those who defend, in the effects that this
atmosphere has on the mass and the elite, effects not readily attainable
by normal means of persuasion and coercion. (...) The creation of an
atmosphere of despair breaks down the resistance of those who need to
be persuaded; they are to be so shocked and numbed, so weakened and
demoralized, and so pessimistic of hope that they become amenable to
anything that promises release from tension. It is possible for agita-
tors to produce such despair in the minds of the ruling elite or in
those of the mass; it is also sometimes possible for a government to
destroy an opposition by terror rather than to mollify it by more normal
political methods." 12)

ARENDT (1970)

"Terror is not the same as violence: it is, rather, the form of government that comes into being when violence, having destroyed all power,
does not abdicate but, on the contrary, remains in full control...
Violence can destroy power; it is utterly incapable of creating it." 13)

DALLIN and BRESLAUER (1970)

"By 'political terror' we mean the arbitrary use, by organs of political
authority, of severe coercion against individuals or groups, the credible
threat of such use, or the arbitrary extermination of such individuals
or groups. (...) Our definition is broadly consistent with the prevailing
use of the term. (...) Although Walter's conclusions tend in a different
direction, his approach in many respects coincides with ours. But whereas he considers all terror to be violence designed to control (p. 14),
and Alfred Meyer speaks of terror as 'violence, applied or threatened'
(The Soviet Political System, p. 318), terror in our usage does not necessarily include violence: just as some violence involves no terror,
some terror (e.g., intimidation) requires no violence. (...) We distinguish between 'purposive terror', which is instituted and intended by
the policy-makers and 'situational terror' which is generally a product
of uncontrolled and undisciplined behavior by lower-level cadres. (...)
Purposive terror at this stage was essentially limited to the selective
elimination of active political opponents and representatives of prerevo-
lutionary elites with the 'demonstration effect' aimed at broader strata
of the population as yet distinctly subordinate. (...) Our definition
of terror stresses the element of arbitrariness both in the decision-
maker's ability to disregard any binding legal norms and in the calcu-
lability of the application of terror as perceived by the citizen. The
second characteristic must not be confused, however, with capriciousness
in the identification of victims. Whereas terror may come to affect any
member of society either as victim or as target, it appears that in Communist systems neither the entire society is the primary target of terror
campaigns, nor is terror randomly applied. And where the prophylatic
removal of entire categories is involved, such groups - though not necessarily the individual victims within them - tend to be chosen for
selective and total elimination by a rational, albeit peculiar, process." 14)

SILVERMAN and JACKSON (1970)

Terrorism as element in this process of violent change can be defined as
the use of physical violence, however indirect, for politico-psychological
effect through fear of one's own person. (...) Terrorism however is not
a distinct stage in revolutionary development, but a complementary tactic
to both guerrilla and conventional warfare. (...) In addition terrorism
differs from guerrilla in as much as its purpose is to influence the opponent and any third parties rather than to annihilate him. (...) The
purpose of the act, not the nature of the act itself is the essential
characteristic which distinguishes terrorism (...) The target, therefore,
is often someone other than the victim of a terrorist act. Consequently
the psychological consequences of the act are more important than the
act itself. (...) Whether a specific act of torture, murder, arson or
kidnapping can be defined as terrorism will depend on how that particular act is perceived by the intended audience. (...) In order for it to
be considered terrorism, the intended audience must identify with the
victim, be associated with what he represents and experience feelings
of fear and insecurity for their own well-being. The intended audience
must be aware that it is the target at which the influence or intimidation is directed." 15)

MALLIN (1971)

"A barroom brawl is violence; so is nuclear warfare.
Terror tactics occupy a portion of the overall spectrum. Obviously the
threat of a nuclear war - or the threat of a physical beating to an individual - can be viewed as forms of terror; but these lie within the
broad, semantic meaning of the word. In the context of internal political struggle, terror has two basic applications. Dictatorial regimes
often maintain themselves in power through the use of terror tactics.
These tactics characteristically include arbitrary arrests, tortures,
murders, kangaroo courts, lengthy imprisonments, and close vigilance
over the words, thoughts, and activities of citizens. This is one side
of the coin. The other side is the commission by revolutionary organizations of acts of violence whose psychological effects are expected
to further the causes pursued by those groups, the desired end result
almost invariably being the overthrow of the existing government. This
study will confine itself to the second application of terrorism: the
struggle for power.
The basis of terror tactics is the threat - threat to a government that
it must abandon power or face continued trouble and danger for its officials; threat to a population that they face constant disruption unless they help overthrow the government. (...) Terrorism is a form of
guerrilla warfare. The basic tactic for guerrilla warfare is to hit and
run and hide, hit, run, hide. Guerrillas conceal themselves in mountains
or rural areas. Terror tactics are employed in urban areas as well.(...)
... they are often aptly referred to as "urban guerrilla warfare". Like
guerrilla warfare, terrorism is a hit, run and hide form of conflict
- combat by attrition with the destruction of the prevailing authority
being hoped-for end result. (...) Terror tactics usually encompass
three basic types of activity: killings, bombings and kidnappings (including hijackings, which are a form of mass kidnapping).
Ordinarily all three methods are employed when a clandestine movement
launches a terror campaign." 16)

MOSS (1971)

"Terrorism could be defined as the systematic use of intimidation for
political ends... (...) It can be employed as a defensive or an offensive weapon, to preserve the status quo... It can be used to erode democratic institutions and clear the way for the seizure of power by an
authoritarian movement (like the Nazis) as well as to resist an abso-
lutist invader. (...) Terrorism is only one form of urban militancy.
Unlike riots, political strikes, student demonstrations and ghetto revolts, terrorism is a minority technique, and the deed to ensure security under urban conditions dictates a fairly standard form of organization: members of the terrorist group are divided into cells or
'firing groups' of from three to five men, with a link man in each." 17)

CRENSHAW (1972)

"Revolutionary terrorism is a part of insurgent strategy in the context
of internal warfare or revolution: the attempt to seize political power
from the established regime of a state, if successful causing fundamental political and social change. Violence is not revolution's unique
instrument, but it is almost always a principle one. Such internal war
is often of long duration and high intensity of violence. Certain essential elements of the definition of terrorism are thus situational
constants. It is a method or system used by a revolutionary organization
for specific political purposes. Therefore neither one isolated act nor

a series of random acts is terrorism. (...) Summarizing the basic components of a definition of the concepts of terrorism produces the following list of essential properties which empirical examination of data
must reveal:
(1) Terrorism is part of a revolutionary strategy - a method used by
    insurgents to seize political power from an existing government.
(2) Terrorism is manifested in acts of socially and politically unac-
    ceptable violence.
(3) There is a consistent pattern of symbolic or representative selec-
    tion of the victims or objects of acts of terrorism.
(4) The revolutionary movement deliberately intends these actions to
    create a psychological effect on specific groups and thereby to
    change their political behavior and attitudes.
(...) The reason for the frequence of revolutionary terrorism is that
it is an effective strategy: its benefits outweigh its costs. (...) There
is a boundary line in terrorism between too much clarification and too
much obscurity: overstepping the line in the first direction makes terrorism lose its unpredictability and thus its power to terrify. Going
too far in the second direction may cause the target to revolt. (...)
Terrorism is a form of coercion which influences behavior, but it effects attitudes as well. It causes a polarization of opinion; confronted
with terrorism, which affects the population as individuals not as a
group, it is impossible to be neutral or uninvolved. (...) When the
target is an unpopular minority, attacks on them may arouse admiration
and respect for the insurgents among the general population. (...)
Summing up, terrorism's attractiveness and significance for revolutionary organizations are due to a combination of economy, facility and
high psychological and political effectiveness. From the insurgent viewpoint there are certain foreseeable risks in employing a terrorist strategy. (1) The danger of creating hostility rather than fear in the civilian masses; (2) the possibility that the governmental response may
destroy the revolutionary organization; and (3) the risk that the use
of terrorism may emotionally harm the terrorists themselves. (...) This
concept of revolutionary terrorism is sufficiently general to permit
useful comparative analysis of several cases, but it is applicable only
to specific circumstances: violent and lengthy conflict between a revolutionary organization and an incumbent regime over the future power
distribution in the state. (...) Nor do these propositions about terrorism necessarily apply to the governmental use of violence, although
this use may be revolutionary." 18)

GROSS (1972)
"During the second half of the 19th century, a theory of individual terror developed among revolutionary Russians in their struggle against autocracy. Unlike political assassination as an isolated act, individual
terror... is a systematic, tactical course of action with political
objectives. Individual terror attacked directly, above all, key decision
makers and administrators or acted in lieu of punishment against persons
responsible for cruelties and oppression. One of its functions was redistribution and deterrence. The leaders of the organization expected
that assassination of an oppressive administrator would deter his successor form inhuman, oppressive acts. (...) The major function of individual terror was, however, weakening of the government and of the
autocratic institutions of the Tsarist Empire. (...) It did not hurt
innocent people; it was discriminating. In a sense - in their view -
it was tactics and punishment at the same time. Individual terror was

to a large extent a tool of those who were 'outs' and stormed the autocratic institutions. (...) ... mass terror is a political tactic of the
'ins', of those in the saddle, in an effort to consolidate power, and
usually to eliminate groups of innocent people defined as class, race
or nation. Thus, objectives of mass terror are broader than solely a
rule by fear. (...) The rule of mass terror was usually in the past
and still is a government of a minority which maintains its power primarily by manipulation of fear, not by consensus." 19)

GUENTHER (1972)

"If terror [dread] alone is a neutral word belonging to the natural context, the verb and the adjective terrorize and terroristic refer to
people only who bring about dread with other people. Terrorism is therefore ultimately a systematization which operates with dread as an element of action (...) The terrorism of impotence is the one which now
produces dread in the contemporary world... A war... is already placed
at some distance for the majority of the people by the spatial element.
The terrorism of impotence, on the other hand, cannot be territorially
confined. While it claims comparatively few victims, it nevertheless
resembles those mythical beasts which can at random pick out and devour
one or the other human being." 20)

MORRISON (1972)

"Terrorism is defined as events involving relatively highly organized
and planned activity, on the part of small but cohesive groups, in which
the aim of the activity is to damage, injure, or eliminate government
property or personnel. These activities include bomb plants, sabotage
of electrical and transportation facilities, assassinations (attempted
and successful), and isolated guerrilla activities." 21)

MOSS (1972)

"Terrorism might be defined as the systematic use of intimidation for
political purposes. That formula is broad enough to cover all sort of
varying situations. Terrorists can be classified according to their
beliefs, or their targets, but it is probably more useful to single out
three tactical varieties of terrorism. Repressive terror is used by a
government to keep its grip over the population or by the rebel movement
as a means of eliminating rivals, coercing popular support, or maintaining conformity inside the organization (in other words, bumping
off 'traitors' and silencing critics). Defensive terror can be used
by private groups like the American vigilantes to keep order or uphold
the status quo; by patriots against a foreign invader; or by a community defending its traditional rights. Offensive terror... is used
against a regime or a political system." 22)

HACKER (1973)

"Terror ist die Verwendung des Herschaftsinstruments der Einschüchterung
durch die Mächtigen, Terrorismus die Nachahmung und Praxis von Terror-
methoden durch die (zumindest einstweilen noch) Machtlosen,Verachteten
und Verzweifelten, die glauben, auf keine andere Weise als durch Terrorismus ernst und für voll genommen zu werden. (...) Terror und Terrorismus sind nicht dasselbe, aber zeigen deutliche Verwandtschaft in
ihrer Abhängigkeit van Propaganda und Publizität, in ihrer rücksicht-
losen, brutal vereinfachenden und vergegenständlichten Gewaltanwendung
und vor allem in ihrer betont zur Schau gestellten Gleichgültigkeit
gegenüber menschlichem Leben. Dasselbe Wort Terror bezeichnet die
Schreckensherrschaft der Mächtigen, die der Machterhaltung dient, und
die punktuelle oder organisierte Schreckensherrschaft der Ohnmächtigen,

der Möchtegern- oder noch nicht Mächtigen, die sich gegen die Mächtigen
richtet. Terror und Terrorismus ahmen einander nach und bedingen einander wechselseitig, überschneiden sich und gehen ineinander über; ihnen
gemeinsam ist die vorwiegende oder ausschliessliche Hinwendung zur vorweggenommenen Wirkung möglichst allgemeiner Verunsicherung, Schreckensherrschaft und Einschüchterung. (...)
Terroristische Akte sind Demonstrationen von Handlungsbereitschaft und
Handlungsfähigkeit, die als Drohung beabsichtigt, Einschüchterung bewir-
ken sollen. (...) Auch die Wahnsinnstaten Geistesgestörter und die Verbrechen krimineller Einzelgänger oder Cliquen können wegen der Gefahr
von Wiederholung oder Nachahmung in kopierten Anschlusshandlungen terroristische Wirkung ausüben...; um 'echten' Terror aber handelt es sich
erst, wenn Einschüchterung nicht Zufallsfolge, sondern Absicht und
Zweck der Übung ist. (...) Terrorismus in seiner reinen Form wird durch
die von ihm einberechneten und vorweggenommenen Effekte bedingt, be-
stimmt und gerechtfertigt. Terrorismus will und muss um jeden Preis
Eindruck schinden; die Wirkung auf die Allgemeinheit ist Ziel und Sinn
der terroristischen Unternehmung; demgegenüber ist das Schicksal der
willkürlich oder gar nicht ausgewählten Opfer gleichgültig, sie sind
lediglich Faustpfänder zur Erzielung von Einschüchterung. (...)
Terror ist eine soziale Erfindung, die Ausarbeitung und Anwendung von
Herrschafts- und Kontrollmethoden über Menschen durch Ausnutzung ihrer
Angst und ihrer teilweisen manipulierten, gefügigen Passivität und
willigen Verantwortungslosigkeit. Aus dem Spektrum von Möglichkeiten
erfolgt die politische Wahl, Terror zu verwenden, immer dann, wenn
andere Alternatieven angeblich oder tatsächlich versagt haben." 23)

HOROWITZ (1973)
"The definition of someone as a terrorist is a labelling device. (...)
... what is usually referred to as terrorism is unsponsored and unsanc-
tioned violence against the body or bodies of others. However, whether
or not violence performed with official sanction, against the leadership or the membership of other groups and institutions is non-terrorist
in character, it is part of a continuous process of definition and redefinition in political life. And in the current ambiguous and even
ubiquitous conditions, performing a terrorist act does not uniquely make
one a terrorist, any more than random non-violence alone defines the
pacifist." 24)

NEALE (1973)
"Symbolic act entailing the use or threat of violence and designed to
influence political behavior by producing a psychological reaction in
the recipient that is also known as terror. Terrorism is sometimes
known as 'politics by violence' and anarchist followers of Michael
Bakunin called it 'the propaganda by the deed'." 25)

WILKINSON (1973)
"It is argued here that what fundamentally distinguishes terrorism
from other of organized violence is not simply its severity but
its amorality." 26)

CROZIER (1974)
"... 'terrorism' means 'motivated violence for political ends' (a definition that distinguishes terrorism from both vandalism and non-political crime). Measures of extreme repression, including torture, used by
States to oppress the population or to repress political dissenters,
who may or may not be terrorists or guerrillas, are termed 'terror'
(the converse of terrorism)." 27)

FAIRBAIRN (1974)

"Terrorism is a mode of behavior that is not of course confined to revolutionary guerrilla wars. As a means of dissuading people from supporting the enemy and to punish those who have supported the enemy it
has been found in most traditional guerrilla wars. To give the impression that the guerrillas are more to be feared than the enemy is an old
aim in such struggles. (...)
Terrorism is a form of violence that has, at any rate until recently,
been regarded with peculiar horror by most people. It had normally seemed
to be a cowardly form of activity - the murder of an unarmed person or
persons by a man (or woman) likely to escape in the confusion - or,
where escape was unlikely, the action of someone with a deranged mind.
If explosives were used, terrorist acts were likely also to kill innocent bystanders." 28)

PAUST (1974)

"Terrorism is thus viewed as the purposive use of violence or the threat
of violence by the precipitator(s) against an instrumental target in
order to communicate to a primary target a threat of future violence
so as to coerce the primary target into behavior or attitudes through
intense fear or anxiety in connection with a demanded power (political)
outcome." 29)

UNITED KINGDOM (1974)

"For purposes of the legislation, terrorism is "the use of violence for
political ends, and includes any use of violence for the purpose of
putting the public or any section of the public in fear." 30)

WILKINSON (1974)

"Our main concern is with political terror: that is to say with the use
of coercive intimidation by revolutionary movements, regimes or individuals. (...) We have thus identified some of the key characteristics
common to all forms of political terror: indiscriminateness, unpredictability, arbitrariness, ruthless destructiveness and the implicity
amoral and antinomian nature of a terrorist's challenge. (...) Political terrorism, properly speaking, is a sustained policy involving the
waging of organized terror either on the part of the state, a movement
or faction, or by a small group of individuals. Systematic terrorism
invariably entails some organizational structure, however rudimentary,
and some kind of theory or ideology of terror." 31)

BITE (1975)

"International terrorism may be defined as politically and socially
motivated violence conducted outside the territories of parties to a
conflict or directed against the citizens or properties of a third
party. It is effective because of the fear it generates and thrives
on publicity. Forms of terrorism include aircraft hijackings, kidnappings, seizure of hostages for ransom, assassinations and bombings.
The victims of these attacks are usually civilians." 32)

BOUTHOUL (1975)

"Terror, culminating in the threat of death, is the ultima ratio of
every socio-political and hierarchical organization. Terror sanctions
that authority whose ultimate expression is: 'obey or you will die'.
(...) Terror underlies every armed conflict and every manifestation
of violence. Invariably the aim is to subdue or paralyse the enemy by
fear. (...) Certain specific qualities of terrorism thus begin to appear. They are: 1. Its clandestine nature: terrorist actions are the
work of small and very secret groups. (...) 2. Terrorist action is not

a battle: terrorists do not restrict themselves to attacks upon an overt
enemy, but also strike at the innocent in order to create fear and insecurity. (...) 3. Terrorism attempts to act in secrecy: the anonymous,
unidentifiable threat creates huge anxiety, and the terrorist tries to
spread fear by contagion, to immobilize and subjugate those living
under this threat. (...) 4. Extreme terrorism exhibits two other traits:
the first is psychological: it is a tendency towards obsession, single-
minded fanaticism, the logic of paranoia taken to its ultimate. (...)
Such acts are for the perpetrator an emotional release and, at the same
time, a thrilling expression of his personality. The second trait may
often be the manifestation of an Adlerian compensation complex, created
by deeply resented frustrations and humiliations. 5. Terrorism is much
influenced by intellectual and doctrinal fashions. In examining its motivations, one discovers the changing ranks of ideological values. One
after another, ideological trends unleash a series of terrorist out-
rages whose justification is based, according to current thinking, on
patriotism, nationalism, racism, cultural intolerance, religious fanaticism and political dogma. At the same time, it often presents itself
as a form of propaganda action, aiming to promote a certain doctrine
or set of demands, using the modern techniques of publicity. (...)
6. There is also noticeable in terrorism an element of imitation in the
techniques employed. (...) A spectacular action, especially if the
perpetrators escape with impunity, will in general inspire a series of
imitators. 7. Among terrorists there is the power of suggestion: there
are, for example, solitary men who are controlled by an idée fixe. (...)
When terrorism involves groups, romanticism predominates, its variety
reflecting the character of the struggle, hatred or fervour, a territorial demand or love of a cause. Such romanticism and the idée fixe
are sustained by constant repetition, propaganda and autosuggestion." 33)

FROMKIN (1975)

"Terrorism is violence used to create fear; but it is aimed at creating
fear in order that the fear, in turn, will lead somebody else - not the
terrorist - to embark on some quite different program of action that
will accomplish whatever it is that the terrorist really desires. (...)
Other strategies sometimes kill the innocent by mistake. Terrorism kills
the innocent deliberately; for not even the terrorist necessarily believes that the particular person who happens to become his victim
deserves to be killed or injured. (...) Terrorism is the indirect strategy that wins or loses only in terms of how you respond to it. The
decision as to how accommodating or how uncompromising you should be
in your response to it involves questions that fall primarily within
the domain of political philosophy. (...) The important point is that
the choice is yours. That is the ultimate weakness of terrorism as a
strategy. It means that, though terrorism cannot always be prevented,
it can always be defeated. You can always refuse to do what they want
you to do. (...) But the price of doing so is constantly rising, as
technology increases the range and magnitude of horrible possibilities." 34)

JENKINS (1975)

"Without attempting to define terrorism in a way that will satisfy all
lawyers and scholars, we may for the moment satisfy ourselves with the
following description: The threat of violence, individual acts of violence, or a campaign of violence designed primarily to instill fear
- to terrorize - may be called terrorism. Terrorism is violence for
effect: not only, and sometimes not at all, for the effect on the actual victims of the terrorists' cause. Terrorism is violence aimed
at the people watching. Fear is the intended effect, not the by-product

of terrorism. That, at least, distinguishes terrorist tactics form mugging and other common forms of violent crime that may terrify but are
not terrorism.
Those we call terrorists may include revolutionaries and other political
extremists, criminals professing political aims, and a few authentic
lunatics. Terrorists may operate alone or may be members of a large and
well-organized group. Terrorists may even be government agents. Their
cause may have extreme goals - the destruction of all government, in
itself not a new idea. Or their cause may be one that is comparatively
reasonable and understandable - self-rule for a particular ethnic
group. Or their motive may be purely personal - money or revenge. The
ambition of terrorists may be limited and local - the overthrow of a
particular regime - or it may be global - a simultaneous world-wide
revolution. (...)
Terrorism may properly refer to a specific set of actions the primary
intent of which is to produce fear and alarm that may serve a variety
of purposes. But terrorism in general usage frequently is also applied
to similar acts of violence - all ransom kidnappings, all hijackings,
thrill-killings - which are not intended by their perpetrators to be
primarily terror-producing. Once a group carries out a terrorist act, it
acquires the label terrorist, a label that tends to stick; and from
that point on, everything this group does, whether intended to produce
terror or not, is also henceforth called terrorism. If it robs a bank
or steals arms from an arsenal, not necessarily acts of terrorism but
common urban guerrilla tactics, these too are often described as terrorism. At some point in this expanding use of term, terrorism can
mean just what those who use the term (not the terrorists) want it
to mean - almost any violent act by any opponent." 35)

JENKINS and JOHNSON (1975)
"Common characteristics do emerge from the list of incidents included
in the chronology... (...)
These characteristics suggest the following description: International
terrorism can be a single incident or a campaign of violence waged outside the presently accepted rules and procedures of international diplomacy and war; it is often designed to attract worldwide attention
to the existence and cause of the terrorists and to inspire fear. Often
the violence is carried out for effect. The actual victim or victims
of terrorist attacks and the target audience may not be the same; the
victims may be totally unrelated to the struggle." 36)

SOBEL (1975)
"The word terrorism is employed to specify acts of violence for political coercion. But there seems to be no definition that will satisfactorily cover all uses of the term. (...) In general, the word terrorism
is used to define almost all illegal acts of violence committed for political purposes by clandestine groups.
The lawyer William A. Hannay, writing in the April 1974 issue of International Lawyer about United Nations debate on terrorism, asserted that
'recent contemporary usage tends to curb its [the term's] meaning to
either random or extortionate violence, aimed ultimately at the target
state of a guerrilla, resistance or liberation movement but which strikes at unarmed civilians, diplomats or non-combatants'." 37)

FEAREY (1976)
"What precisely is "international terrorism"? It has three characteris-
tics.
First, as with other forms of terrorism, it embodies an act which is es-

sentially criminal. It takes the form of assassination or murder, kidnapping, extortion, arson, maiming or an assortment of other acts which
are commonly regarded by all nations as criminal.
Second, international terrorism is politically motivated. An extremist
political group, convinced of the rightness of its cause, resorts to
violent means to advance that cause - means incorporating one of the
acts I have just cited. Often the violence is directed against innocents, persons having no personal connection with the grievance moti-
vating the terrorist act.
And third, international terrorism transcends national boundaries,
through the choice of a foreign victim or target, commission of the
terrorist act in a foreign country, or effort to influence the policies
of a foreign government. The international terrorist strikes abroad,
or at a diplomat or other foreigner at home, because he believes he
can thereby exert the greatest possible pressure on his own or another
government or on world opinion.
The international terrorist may or may not wish to kill his victim or
victims. In abduction or hostage-barricade cases he usually does not
wish to kill - though he often will find occasion to do so at the out-
set to enhance the credibility of his threats. In other types of attacks innocent deaths are his specific, calculated, pressure-shock
objective. Through brutality and fear he seeks to impress his existence
and his cause on the minds of those who can, through action or terror-
induced inaction, help him to achieve that cause." 38)

MILBANK (1976)
" For the purpose of this study, international and transnational terrorism are defined as follows:
Common Characteristics: The threat or use of violence for political
purposes when (1) such action is intended to influence the attitudes
and behavior of a target group wider than its immediate victims, and
(2) its ramifications transcend national boundaries (as a result, for
example, of the nationality or foreign ties of its perpetrators, its
locale, the identity of its institutional or human victims, its declared
objectives, or the mechanics of its resolution).
International Terrorism: Such action when carried out by individuals
or groups controlled by a sovereign state.
Transnational Terrorism: Such action when carried out by basically autonomous non-state actors, whether or not they enjoy some degree of
support from sympathetic states." 39)

PIERRE (1976)
"There is nothing new about terrorism per se. The term first came into
modern usage during the Reign of Terror in revolutionary France. It commonly refers to the threat of violence and the use of fear to coerce,
persuade or gain public attention. Terror has been used by ideologies
of both the Right and the Left, by the former to repress a population
and by the latter to win self-determination and independence. Terror
has been used by governments as an instrument of state as well as by
guerrillas or insurgents as an instrument of subversion.
The conception of international terrorism is more difficult to endow
with a universally accepted definition. In this analysis it will refer
to acts of violence across national boundaries, or with clear international repercussions, often within the territory or involving the citizens of a third party to a dispute. Thus it is to be distinguished from
domestic terrorism of the sort that has taken place in Ulster, the
Soviet Union or South Africa. Admittedly,the line is often thin between
terror which is essentially domestic and that possessing a clear inter-

national character.

International terrorism is usually, though not exclusively, political
in intent and carried out by nongovernmental groups, although they
may receive financial and moral support from nation-states." 40)

QURESHI (1976)

"Terrorism is the use of violence in order to induce a state of fear
and submission in the victim. The object of terrorism is to secure a
change or modification in the behavior of the intended victim himself
or to use him as an example for others. The violence of terrorism is
the ultimate of coercion, whether actually applied or merely used as
a threat. The use of terrorist violence is based on the assumption
that the intended victim is unreasonable and incapable of seeing the
viewpoint of the terrorist, that the victim cannot be persuaded, but
only compelled in a manner by which he has absolutely no choice except to surrender. It is not necessary for violence to actually be
used in order for it to be called 'terrorism'. The threat of the use
of such violence, whether explicit or implicit, if it is perceived
by the intended victim as likely to be actually carried out, also
constitutes 'terrorism'. 41)

U.S. TASK FORCE (1976)

"In fact, terrorism is a technique, a way of engaging in certain types
of criminal activity, so as to attain particular ends. For the perpetrator of terroristic crimes, terror - or the sensation of massive,
overwhelming fear induced in victims - transcends in importance the
criminal activity itself, which is merely the vehicle or instrumentality. Terror is a natural phenomenon; terrorism is the conscious
exploitation of it. Terrorism is coercive, designed to manipulate the
will of its victims and its larger audience. The great degree of fear
is generated by the crime's very nature, by the manner of its perpe-
tration, or by its senselessness, wantonness, or callous indifference
to human life. This terrible fear is the source of the terrorist's
power and communicates his challenge to society. (...)
Thus, terrorism, although it has its individual victims, is really an
onslaught upon society itself. Any definition of terrorism for the
purpose of constructing effective responses to it must bear these considerations in mind.
It is not useful, therefore, merely to enumerate a series of violent,
criminal acts or threats that would constitute terroristic behavior;
such a definition misses, altogether, the terrorist's true objective.
Any law intended to strike at terrorism must address the purpose as
well as the instrumentality. Because they have failed to do so, international attempts at definition have substantially failed: Viewed in
terms of motivation and ends, 'what is terrorism to some is heroism
to others'. [Per M. Cherif Bassiouni, cited in International Terrorism
and Political Crimes.] Although it is presently an effective bar to any
concerted response to international or transnational terrorism, this
lack of agreement about terms and criminal policy ought not to frustrate
those responsible for this society's responses to acts of terrorism.
For the purpose of the present report, no such universality of consensus is needed in order to arrive at working definitions. Terrorism is
a tactic or technique by means of which a violent act or the threat
thereof is used for the prime purpose of creating overwhelming fear
for coercive purposes. (...)
Political terrorism is characterized by: (1) its violent, criminal nature; (2) its impersonal frame of reference; and (3) the primacy of its

ulterior objective, which is the dissemination of fear throughout the
community for political ends or purposes. Political terrorism may be
defined, therefore, as violent, criminal behavior designed primarily
to generate fear in the community, or a substantial segment of it, for
political purpose. Excluded from this definition are acts or threats
of a purely personal character and those which are psychopathological
and have no intended sociopolitical significance." 42)

WATSON (1976)

"Political terrorism can be defined as a strategy, a method by which
an organized group or party tries to get attention for its aims, or
force concessions toward its goals, through the systematic use of deliberate violence. Typical terrorists are individuals trained and disciplined to carry out the violence decided upon by their organizations.
And, if caught, true terrorists can be expected to speak and act during
their trials not primarily to win personal freedom, but to try to spread
their organization's political ideas. [n])(...) n: Not a new definition.
It was based on a more detailed one in the Encyclopedia of the Social
Sciences published in 1934." 43)

WEISBAND and ROGULY (1976)

"Violence in order to be terrorism must be political. Since terrorist
violence tries to create the framework for political interactions, terrorists are forced to locate their actions in some political or moral
context. (...) Terrorism is different from criminal violence in that
its purpose is symbolic, its means psychological, and its ends political. Terrorism often serves as the cutting edge of a revolutionary movement, but, precisely because it is the vehicle of organized insurgency,
it must point the way to a political resolution. It must negate its
nihilism. (...) An act of terrorist violence uninformed by discipline
or politics stops dead without achieving its aims. For violence to have
impact, it can never be its own reward; when effective, terrorism pulls
violence out of the realm of war and into the world of politics. But
politics has rules, patterns of normative interaction, do's and don'ts
of legitimate conduct. In the beginning it is the terrorist's task to
violate norms of civilized conduct. Yet terrorism is fundamentally a
psychological strategy and must point to a way of resolving the conflict. If terrorist violence appears wanton, it threatens to lose the
support, or at least the respect, it is seeking to gain. Thus the terrorist irrevocably comes face to face with a torturous self-contradiction:
as he becomes more successful, he must become more responsible. He is
left to live with the painful tension of responsible violence, that is,
calculated, disciplined, and permeated with politics. As he wins recognition through violence, he must place limitations on the use of violence. (...) Every resistance movement struggles for recognition. Attention is the lifeblood of its existence. For the terrorist the path to
legitimacy is through one's reputation for resilience, for self-sacrifice and daring, for brutality, and, above all, for effective discipline over words and actions. The terrorist is his own torch and bomb;
he ignites the flames of national passion and, if possible of political
sympathy, and he does it by violating universal human sensibilities.
It is the credibility that violence produces whenever it appalls that
renders terrorism horrifying yet powerful and, if successful, self-
legitimating." 44)

WILKINSON (1976)

"Political terrorism may be briefly defined as a special form of clandestine, undeclared and unconventional warfare waged without any humanitarian restraints or rules. (...) It is a common but elementary mistake
to equate terrorism with guerrilla warfare in general. Political terrorism proper through the use of bombing, assassinations, massacres,
kidnaps and hijacks can and does occur without benefit of guerrilla
war. This has been so throughout history. Historically rural war was
largely waged without resort to terrorist tactics, although today
urban and rural guerrilla movements in Africa and Latin America do
employ terrorism. (...) Terrorism is employed as a weapon of psychological warfare to help create a climate of panic, or collapse, to destroy
public confidence in government and security agencies, and to coerce
communities and movement activists into obeying the terrorist leadership." 45)

WOLF (1976)

"Political terrorism may be defined as the threat or use of deliberate
violence, indiscriminately or selectively, against either enemies or
allies to achieve a political end. The intend is to register a calculated impact on a target population and on other groups for the purpose
of altering the political balance in favor of the terrorists. (...)
Phrased another way the terrorist's strategic intent is to destroy the
confidence a particular minority group has in its government by causing
that government to act outside the law. Always, terrorist strategy aims
not to defeat the forces of the incumbent regime militarily - for the
terrorist this is an impossible task - but to bring about the moral
alienation of the masses from the government until its isolation has
become total and irreversible." 46)

ALEXANDER and FINGER (1977)

"However, 'terrorism' in its public or ideological senses has a completely different meaning in terms of its nature and implications. It
is clearly illustrated by the following cases selected at random from
world-wide press-coverage in 1976 and 1977" [follows a summary by AS] :
- The pro-independence Puerto Rican group FALN start small fires in
  three Manhattan department stores;
- 14 South Moluccans in the Netherlands seize a Dutch train and a school;
- members of a movement for the independance of the Canarian Islands
  place a bomb in the florist shop at Las Palmas Airport;
- in Karlsruhe Siegfried Buback, West Germany's Chief Prosecutor is
  killed at a stoplight when fired from a motorcycle;
- members of the Zimbabwe African National Union (ZANU) in Rhodesia
  kill seven Roman Catholic missionaries;
- in Lebanon four unidentifies gunmen kill a Druze leader driving on a
  mountain road. [end of summary]
"The foregoing acts of violent behavior - characterized by a technique
of perpetrating random and brutal intimidation, coercion or destruction
of human lives and property, and used intentionally by subnational
groups, operating under varying degrees of stress, to obtain realistic
or illusory goals - are symptomatic of what we consider 'terrorism' to
be. Indeed, we seem to have entered an 'age of terrorism', the pattern
of which is unlike any other period in history when ideological and
political violence occurred." 47)

ANONYMOUS (n.d.)

"Political terrorism is a continuation of public protest by different
means." 48)

CLUTTERBUCK (1977)
"... terrorism - the attack on an individual to frighten and coerce a
large number of others - is as old as civilization itself. It is the
recourse of a minority or even of a single dissident frustrated by the
inability to make society shift in the desired direction by what that
society regards as 'legitimate' means. It is primarily an attack on
the rule of law, aimed either to destroy it or (as in more recent
times) to change it radically to conform to the terrorist's idea of
society. (...) Terrorism is not precisely the same as violence. Terrorism aims, by the use of violence or the threat of violence, to
coerce governments, authorities or populations by inducing fear. Television has enormously expanded their ability to do so." 49)

FUNKE (1977)
"Political terrorism can be generally described as systematic, planned
threatening with, or application of violence organized to strike by
surprise." 50)

GREISMAN (1977)
"(...) For the purposes of this paper, it is necessary to shortcut the
definitional debate and focus on the one quality that gives terrorism
its unique place in the catalogue of organized violence. Terrorist acts
require an audience, the target is of secondary importance, i.e. those
that see the target attacked will become terrorized and this is the
real goal of terrorism." 51)

HOROWITZ (1977)
"The definition of terrorism employed here is the selective use of
fear, subjugation, and intimidation to disrupt the normal operations of
a society." 52)

HOROWITZ (1977)
"The definition of terrorism I employ is this: the selective use of
fear, subjugation, and intimidation to disrupt the normal operations
of a society. The power to inflict such injury is a bargaining power
which in its very nature bypasses due process of law. It seeks an outcome by means other than democratic or consensus formula. The act of
terror - whoever performs it - in some sense violates civil liberties.
All the cries about redressing injustices cannot disguise this fact." 53)

IVIANSKY (1977)
"Therefore, 'individual terror' may be defined as a system of modern
revolutionary violence aimed at leading personalities in the government
or the Establishment (or any other human targets). The motivation is
not necessarily personal but rather ideological or strategic. This
method differs from traditional political conspiracy assassination, in
that it is, in essence, not directed at individuals who are considered
stumbling-blocks to the seizure of power or sworn enemies of the organization, but rather against the foreign conqueror, the social order,
or the Establishment embodied in these individuals. Infliction of personal injury is intended to weaken or destroy regimes, but, paradoxically, one of the clearest manifestations of modern 'individual terror'
is its impersonal character. It seeks to sow discord and panic, to
undermine and jeopardize the security of rulers and regimes, and to
serve as the spearhead of revolution by stirring up the masses with
exemplary deeds and the creation of revolutionary cadres trained to
further the struggle." 54)

JENKINS (1977)

"Terrorism can be described as the use of actual or threatened violence
to gain attention and to create fear and alarm, which in turn will cause
people to exaggerate the strength of the terrorists and the importance
of their cause. Since groups that use terrorist tactics are typically
small and weak, the violence they practice must be deliberately shocking.
(...) The fundamental issue is fear. Perhaps the biggest danger posed
by terrorists lies not in the physical damage they do, but in the atmosphere of alarm they create, which corrodes democracy and breeds repression." 55)

LAQUEUR (1977)

"Terrorism, interpreted here as the use of covert violence by a group
for political ends, is usually directed against a government, less frequently against another group, class or party. The ends may vary from
the redress of specific 'grievances' to the overthrow of a government
and the taking of power, or to the liberation of a country from foreign
rule. Terrorists seek to cause political, social and economic disruption,
and for this purpose frequently engage in planned or indiscriminate
murder. [n](...) n: Any definition of political terrorism venturing
beyond noting the systematic use of murder, injury and destruction or
the threats of such acts toward achieving political ends is bound to
lead to endless controversies." 56)

LEISER (1977)

"Terrorism is any organized set of acts of violence designed to create
an atmosphere of despair or fear, to shake the faith of ordinary citizens in their government and its representatives, to destroy the structure of authority which normally stands for security, or to reinforce
and perpetuate a governmental regime whose popular support is shaky. It
is a policy of seemingly senseless, irrational, and arbitrary murder,
assassination, sabotage, subversion, robbery, and other forms of violence, all committed with dedicated indifference to existing legal and
moral codes or with claims to special exemption from conventional social norms. The politics of terrorists are pursued with the conviction
that the death and suffering of innocent persons who have little or no
direct connection with the causes to which the terrorists are dedicated
are fully justified by whatever success terrorists may enjoy in achieving
their political ends. [n](...) n: See Andreski... Thornton... Leiden
and Schmitt... Burton... Pike... Fairbairn." 57)

MALLIN (1977)

"Therefore, in this article the following working definition is offered:
Political terrorism is the threat of violence or an act or series of
acts of violence effected through surreptitious means by an individual,
an organization, or a people to further his or their political goals.
Under this definition sabotage committed for political purposes is indeed a form of terrorism. (...)
Terrorism as a military arm is a weapon of psychological warfare." 58)

MICKOLUS (1977)

"Although we may disagree on definitions of terrorism, transnational
terrorism will be defined as: The use, or threatened use of anxiety-
inducing extranormal violence for political purposes by any individual
or group, whether acting for or in opposition to established governmental authority, when such action is intended to influence the attitudes and behavior of a target group wider than the immediate victims
and when, through the nationality or foreign ties of its perpetrators,

its location, the nature of its institutional or human victims, or the
mechanics of its resolution its ramifications transcend national boundaries. [n] (...) n: Compare this formulation of the problem of transnational terrorism with that of, inter alia, Brian M. Jenkins and Janera
Johnson... 1975; David L. Milbank... 1976... and Jordan J. Paust...
1974." 59)

PAUST (1977)

"... I offer a definitional approach that is objective. (...)
Much of the reasoning behind the need for this approach has already been
publicized (and published); however, in any comprehensive focus upon
the terroristic process, the following factors should be carefully considered: 1. precipitators, 2. perspectives, 3. acts involving the
threat or use of violence, 4. instrumental targets (human and non-human),
5. primary targets and secondary targets, 6. incidental or spill-over
victims, and 7. the result of such terror which coerces the primary
target into a given behavior or attitude.
Terrorism is therefore viewed as a form of violent strategy, a form of
coercion utilized to alter the freedom of choice of others. Terrorism,
thus defined, involves the intentional use of violence or the threat of
violence by the precipitator(s) against an instrumental target in order
to communicate to a primary target a threat of future violence. The
object is to use intense fear or anxiety to coerce the primary
target into behavior or to mold its attitudes in connection with a
demanded power (political) outcome. (...)
In a specific context the instrumental and primary targets could well
be the same person or group. (...) Additionally, the instrumental target need not be a person; attacks on power stations, for example, can
produce a terror outcome in the civilian population of the community
dependent upon the station for electricity.
There must be a terror outcome, or the process could hardly be labeled
as terrorism. (...) Terrorism can also be precipitated by governments,
groups, or individuals; consequently, any exclusion of one or more sets
of precipitators from the definitional framework is highly unrealistic.
Equally unrealistic are definitional criteria which refer to 'systematic' uses of violence; terrorism can occur at an instant and by one
act." 60)

PRICE (1977)

"The standard definition is that it is planned violence intended to have
psychological influence on politically relevant behavior (Hutchinson,
1971: 383-385). To clarify this, it is noted that the multiple targets
of a terrorist act include the victim of terror, who may be too dead
to be influenced psychologically, and the group who identify with the
victim, and therefore receive the implicit message, 'You may be next.'
All others aware of the act form the resonant mass, who may react emotionally in a positive or negative fashion, depending on which side
they sympathize with in the conflict (Thornton, 1964: 78-79)." 61)

SILVERSTEIN (1977)

"Terror is a state of intense fear induced by the systematic threat of
imprisonnement, mutilation or death. It is intensified when the victim
is helpless in the hands of another human being.
We are all afraid of being hurt or killed. The terrorist manipulates
persons and governments by making the threat of bodily harm dramatically
manifest. The terrorist threatens the more fundamental human drive - the
will to survive intact. He strips from the defenses of human courage the
most important element of anti-terror, the real or supposed ability to

fight back, to defend one's person. Because his victims are unarmed,
noncombatant, random and, because they are totally helpless, the victim's fear is experienced by all observers of the victim's plight, who
are equally vulnerable and who desire to live their lives unmolested.
The secondary victims of terrorism, all those who think by association
that their lives are in equal danger, fear equally for their persons.
Because they fear bodily harm, they are as manipulable as though the
hand granade were actually strapped to their bodies." 62)

SINGH (1977)

"Political terrorism comprises only one type of violent activity subsumed under the general heading of unconventional warfare.(...)
Terror incorporates two facets: 1. a state of fear or anxiety within
an individual or a group and 2. the tool that induces the state of
fear. Thus, terror entails the threat or use of symbolic violent acts
aimed at influencing political behavior." 63)

SMITH (1977)

"Terrorism involves both the use _and_ the threat of violence. The threat
of the terrorist derives not from his words but from his deeds, from a
resort to violence that conveys a threat of further violence. This initial violence must therefore be symbolic. The victim must represent a
whole class of persons who are identified as possible targets. However,
while the particular class of persons to be terrorized may be carefully
selected, the actual identity of those attacked is arbitrary. It is
this lack of discrimination that is the source of terror. (...) Resort
to terrorism - and especially reliance on terrorism - in order to promote political objectives is an indication of weakness. Lacking sufficient popular support to challenge a government through constitutional
channels or even through full-scale civil war, a dissident group may
see in terrorism the only chance of success." 64)

WALDMANN (1977)

"... since terroristic methods are employed neither in the service of
power maintenance alone nor exclusively with the aim to bring down a
system of power, they are rather in principle useful for both purposes.
The notion of terror hints less at the goal perspective than at the
mode and degree of intensity of violence. Most authors see it, following
the classical treatment of H. Arendt, as a form of power exercise which
is based on the systematic production of dread and fear. In doing this
they attribute special weight to the social-psychological element of
[its] effect. (...) Among the general features of terroristic strategy
figure incalculability and lacking prognosticability; terror, as it
were, overfloods its victims. The arbitrariness in the selection of objects of violence, which is heightened by the disregard for all juridical and humanitarian principles, is not based on a cult of spontaneity
by the terrorist actors or on their inability to plan and direct the
violence but is elevated into a principle by them. In accordance to
this principle they victimize primarily innocent people like children
and old people who are not in the slightest manner involved in the
conflict issue. (...) The measures of terrorist groups are furthermore
not exclusively directed against their real or perceived enemies, but
can be targeted with equal severity on their own members and supporters.
(...) A further generally recognizeable trait are the attempts of justification and explanation which accompany acts of terror. (...) Here
the close interrelatedness of violence and ideology or propaganda noted
earlier finds a confirmation." 65)

WILKINSON (1977)
"Political terrorism may be briefly defined as coercive intimidation.
It is the systematic use of murder and destruction, and the threat of
murder and destruction in order to terrorize individuals, groups, communities or governments into conceding to the terrorists' political
demands. It is one of the oldest techniques of psychological warfare.
A primary target for terrorisation is selected; the objective, or message to be conveyed, is determined; and credibility is established by
convincing the target that the threat can actually be carried out. The
victim or victims of the actual act of terrorist violence may or may
not be the primary target, and the effects of relatively small amounts
of violence will tend to be quite disproportionate in terms of the numbers of people terrorised: in the words of an ancient Chinese proverb.
'Kill one, frighten ten thousand.' [n] (n: cited in an unpublished talk
by Dr. Richard Clutterbuck) As a modern American analyst has put it,
the terrorist wants a lot of people watching rather than a lot of people
dead. (Brian Jenkins, 'International Terrorism: A balance sheet, Survival 17: 4, July/August 1975, p. 158)
Though this may hold for the relatively rare cases of 'pure' terrorism,
such as mass hostage situations, repressive and revolutionary terror
often result in the massacre of large numbers of people. Furthermore,
strategic theories of terror as a psychological weapon assume a logic
and symmetry in the rationale of the terrorist which is generally lacking
in the real world. Terrorists are more often than not consumed with
hatred against a perceived class or race 'enemy'. and often deliberately
attempt mass slaughter in public. Indeed this was advocated by the pio-
neer German terrorist theorist, Johannes Most, in the 1880s. It is a
great mistake to assume that political terrorists will conform to some
minimum standard of rationality and humanity. Clausewitz once remarked
that war has its own language but not its own logic. The same is true
of terrorism which is, after all, a kind of unconventional war. (...)
... political terrorism as a form of undeclared clandestine warfare...
(...) Terrorism is a special mode or process of violence which has at
least three basic elements: the terroristic aims of its perpetrators,
their modus operandi in deploying particular forms of violence to
achieve those aims, and the psychological effects of terrorist violence upon the victims and the target audience.
Terroristic violence has the following salient characteristics.
(1) It is inherently indiscriminate in its effects. (...) No one can
be certain that they will not be the next victim. (...)
(2) Terrorism is essentially arbitrary and unpredictable, both in the
minds of its victims and audience and in its effects upon individuals
and society. (...)
(3) Terrorism implicitly denies recognition of all rules and conventions
of war. It refuses to distinguish between combatants and non-combatants
and recognises no humanitarian constraints or obligations to prisoners
or to the wounded. (...) No one is innocent... (...)
(4) The terrorists' rejection of all moral constraints is also reflected
in particularly hideous and barbarous cruelties and weapons. (...)
(5) Politically motivated terrorism is generally justified by its perpetrators on one or more of the following grounds; (I) any means are
justified to realise an allegedly transcendental end (in Weber's terms,
'value-rational' grounds); (II) closely linked to (I) is the claim that
extreme violence is an intrinsically beneficial, regenerative, cathartic
and ennobling deed regardless of other consequences; (III) terrorism can
be shown to have 'worked' in the past, and is held to be either the

'sole remaining' or 'best available' method of achieving success (in Weber's terms 'instrumental-rational' grounds); (IV) the morality of the just vengeance or 'an eye for an eye and a tooth for a tooth'; and (V) the theory of the lesser evil: greater evils will befall us or our nation if we do not adopt terror against our enemies." 66)

WÖRDEMANN (1977)

"Terror, verstanden im Sinn Hannah Arendts und in diesem Versuch einer Beschreibung so verwendet, ist eine existenznotwendige Institution der etablierten totalitären Macht, auch solcher etablierter Macht, die in Zielsetzung und Entwicklungsrichtung totalitär ist, selbst wenn sie den erstrebten Zustand des total Totalitären noch nicht erreicht hat. Terror ist die zwangsläufige innere Gewalt der totalitären Macht, gelegentlich verzweifeltes und sinnloses Kampfmittel einer demokratischen Macht, immer aber Äusserung einer etablierten Macht.
Terrorismus ist die Gewaltanwendung durch die kleine und isolierte Gruppe, die nicht über die Kraft verfügt, die etablierte Macht des Terrors oder die allgemein akzeptierte Macht des Rechts und des Gesetzes auf breitere Front, durch den Aufstand der Masse oder mit konventionellen Methoden anzugreifen." 67)

BELL (1978)

"Today terror, a form of political violence that falls between war and peace and offers a model to madmen and criminals, appears all but endemic in open, liberal societies. (...) For terror, however defined, has most assuredly now become a serious Western preoccupation.
(...) Almost without exception the public's perception of the terrorist is of someone associated with a revolutionary organization. There may be state terror or criminals and madmen, vigilantes and authorized assassins; but for the many the real terrorist belongs to a revolutionary organization...
(...) At the very beginning we face the definitional problem: one man's terrorist is another man's patriot. Like love, terrorism is easy to recognize but difficult to define. (...) In the nineteenth century the word terrorism had a relatively clear meaning. People called themselves 'terrorists'... and held to a particular revolutionary strategy - personal terror, propaganda of the deed. Today the word is often used as a pejorative, so that there is no agreeable common definition of the word." 68)

CRENSHAW (1978)

"The concept of terrorism is both historically and theoretically an inexact one.(...) Since there is no commonly accepted definition of terrorism, this analysis begins by proposing one that both corresponds to the reality of the Algerian case and potentially applies to other examples of revolutionary terrorism. (...)
The essential components of a definition of revolutionary terrorism may be summarized as follows:
1. Terrorism is a systematic and purposeful method used by a revolutionary organization to seize political power from the incumbent government of a state.
2. Terrorism is manifested in a series of individual acts of extraordinary and intolerable violence.
3. Terrorism involves a consistent pattern of symbolic or representative selection of its physical victims or objects.
4. Terrorism is deliberately intended to create a psychological effect on specific groups of people (with the nature of the effect varying

according to the identity of the group) in order to change political
behavior and attitudes in a manner consonant with the achievement of
revolutionary objectives. (...)
In its most extreme form, terrorism creates 'terror', an emotional
state of extreme fear and anxiety. It differs from other instruments
of violence because it 'lies beyond the norms of violent political
agitation that are accepted by a given society. (...) Its victims
are usually civilians, although they may include the military or
the police, and the scene is normally a peaceful one - in which such
violence is surprising. The timing and nature of a specific act of
terrorism are unpredictable, and its perpetrators are most often
anonymous. In mass-casualty bombings, for example, the victims do
not know who left the bomb. Nor does the individual victim usually
have a personal acquaintance with the assassin.(...)
It is primarily this extraordinary character of terrorist violence
that distinguishes it from other forms of revolutionary activity,
such as guerrilla warfare, which is essentially irregular military
activity by organized bands in rural areas. (...) Guerrilla warfare
is more utilitarian in purpose, and terrorism is more symbolic.
Acts of terrorism combine the present use of violence with the future
threat of it. The physical act itself communicates a threat, although
it may be preceded or followed by a more explicit warning. (...)
Terrorist targets represent specific groups within society rather
than obstacles to be eliminated. Their value to the revolution [is]
symbolic. (...)
The victims of terrorism represent or 'stand for' certain categories
of people, so that violence against an individual member of a group
is a threat to all other members of the same or a closely related
group. This statement holds for nonhuman or material objects of violence as well; as long as an attack is symbolic rather than utilitarian, it may be part of a terrorist strategy, and this symbolic
function contributes to the apparent irrationality and the real unpredictability of terrorist acts. (...)
The relationship between terrorist and victim distinguishes terrorism
from simple sabotage or assassination. [n] (...)   n: T. Thornton,
Terror as a Weapon, p. 77-78."   69)

EVANS and MURPHY (1978)
"The threat or use of violence by private persons for political ends,
where the conduct itself or its political objectives, or both, are
international in scope." 70)

HAMILTON (1978)
"For the purposes of this study, the following definition will be
used: Terrorism consists of (1) planned acts of violence, employed
for (2) explicitly political purposes, ultimately directed against
(3) an established state or organizational power, and involving (4)
a relatively small number of conspirators. Additional characteristics
include a typically sporadic pattern of activity and, frequently, an
emphasis on civilian rather than purely military targets. The definition is intended to distinguish terrorism from apolitical criminal
violence, mass turmoil such as demonstrations, riots, or strikes,
and from larger political violence phenomena involving large-scale
or continuous fighting or widespread popular revolts. It would also
be desirable to make a clear distinction between terrorism and
small-scale guerrilla war, but here the line (drawn between two
types of small-scale insurgent conspiracies) becomes less clear.

A theoretical distinction based on dissimilar tactics on rural vs. urban bases will encounter a number of exceptions when put into practice. It seems better, for present purposes, to emphasize the similarities rather than force a problematic separation.

The definition above excludes conservative, progovernment violence as well, whether in the form of covertly authorized vigilantism or of undisguised police power. With this exclusion, the definition in effect corresponds to the most general Western use of the word." 71)

JENKINS (1978)

"At some point in this expanding use of the term, terrorism can mean just what those who use the term (not the terrorist) want it to mean - almost any violent act by an opponent.

The difficulty of defining terrorism has led to the cliche that one man's terrorist is another man's freedom fighter. The phrase implies that there can be no objective definition of terrorism, that there is no universal standards of conduct in peace or war. That is not true. (...) The rules of war grant civilian noncombatants at least theoretical immunity from deliberate attack. They prohibit taking civilian hostages and actions against those held captive. The rules of war recognize neutral territory. Terrorists recognize no neutral territory, no noncombatants, no bystanders. (...) One man's terrorist is everyone's terrorist. Terrorism, in the Rand chronology, is defined by the nature of the act, not by the identity of the perpetrators or the nature of their cause. All terrorist acts are crimes - murder, kidnappings, arson. Many would also be violations of the rules of war, if a state of war existed. All involve violence or the threat of violence, often coupled with specific demands. The violence is directed mainly against civilian targets. The motives are political. The actions generally are carried out in a way that will achieve maximum publicity. The perpetrators are usually members of an organized group, and unlike other criminals, they often claim credit for the act. And finally the act is intended to produce effects beyond the immediate physical damage.

The fear created by terrorists may be intended to cause people to exaggerate the strength of the terrorists and the importance of their cause, to provoke extreme reactions, to discourage dissent, or to enforce compliance.

This definition of terrorism would not limit the application of the term solely to nongovernmental groups. Governments, their armies, their secret police may also be terrorists. Certainly the threat of torture is a form of terrorism designed to inspire dread of the regime and obedience to authorities." 72)

KAPLAN (1978)

"...What is terror? The term functions as a political symbol, as well as a category of political science... (...)

I mean by terror the use of force primarily to produce a certain fearful state of mind - terror in fact. Some element of fear is evoked by every exercise of power; in terror this element looms large, whether as cause or as reason. Moreover, the fear is to be evoked in someone other then those to whom the force is applied. Terror is the use of force in a context which differentiates the <u>victim</u> of the violence employed from the <u>target</u> of the action. Since victim and target may be related in various ways, the distinction between them may be unclear or debatable. Machine-gunning school children or bombing a civilian airliner are unmistakable acts of terror, since the victims are not involved in whatever motivated the acts, and so cannot be the targets.

(...) The killing of an isolated soldier in a barroom may be an act of terror even though he is not only victim but part of the target. Related to the distinction between target and victim is that between demands made by the terrorists and the aim of his act of terror. (...) Terror appears to be lacking a moral when it is only demands that are lacking; the aim - to terrorize - may be apparent just because the victims cannot in any way be mistaken for targets." 73)

KARANOVIĆ (1978)

"In conclusion, terrorism may be defined as systematic and organized violence against nonresisting persons to create fear in them for the purpose of retaining or gaining governmental authority, or for the purpose of using that authority for exploitation or oppression or to extract political concessions." 74)

LÖSCHE (1978)

"Allgemein kann Terrorismus als eine Form der Machtausübung begriffen werden, die auf der systematischen Erzeugung von Furcht und Schrecken beruht. Diese Definition umfasst auch die Anwendung von Terror durch staatliche Institutionen zur Aufrechterhaltung der eigenen Herrschaft, wie sie uns z.B. aus faschistischen oder stalinistischen Regimen bekannt ist. Schliesst man jedoch Gewaltanwendung von seiten des Staates oder von sozialen und politischen Klassen bzw. Gruppen in einer Revolution aus, so kann Terrorismus im engeren Sinne definiert werden als die Methode, wodurch eine organisierte Gruppe versucht, ihre Ziele durch systematische Androhung bzw. Anwendung von Gewalt (zumeist als Überraschungscoup), die in der Regel gegen solche Personen und Sachen gerichtet ist, die staatliche oder öffentliche Macht repräsentieren bzw. symbolisieren, zu erreichen.
Er lassen sich drei Merkmale für diese Art des Terrorismus nennen:
1. Die direkte, unmittelbare und aktuelle Drohung mit oder Anwendung von Gewalt gegen Sachen und Personen.
2. Die organisatorische und systematische Zusammenarbeit mehrerer Täter in einer Gruppe. (...)
3. Die Berufung auf eine politische Zielsetzung..." 75)

MICKOLUS (1978)

"The use, or threat of use, of anxiety-inducing extranormal violence for political purposes by an individual or group, whether acting for or in opposition to established governmental authority, when such action is intended to influence the attitudes and behavior of a target group wider than the immediate victims and when, through the nationality or foreign ties of its perpetrators, its location, the nature of its institutional or human victims, or the mechanics of its resolution, its ramifications transcend national boundaries." 76)

SCHMID and DE GRAAF (1978)

"The basic idea of the here proposed direction in which a definition of terrorism has to be looked for is the differentiation between victim and opponent. Only in those cases can one speak of terrorism when an instrumental human target (c) is being used systematically and deliberately in a violent way without its collaboration in a conflict between two opponents (a en b), whereby the direct victim (c) cannot escape from the conflict by means of a personal change of behavior and/ or attitude." 77)

SCHREIBER (1978)

"Definitions are important, since the rhetoric of political denunciation brands with the term 'terrorist' those people whom others may call 'revolutionaries', 'freedom fighters', or 'founding fathers', and since, on the other side, small-time criminals or unhinged fanatics have dignified their images with pretended political motives. In what follows we will not go far wrong if we define terrorism as a political act, ordinarily committed by an organized group, involving death or the threat of death to noncombatants. This definition excludes private kidnappings designed to extort money, and it excludes both gangland killings prompted by revenge motives or power struggles and well-publicized but essentially nonpolitical acts of murder, even mass murder, committed by deranged individuals or fanatical groups. What makes the terrorist act political is its motive and its direction: It must be the intent of the perpetrators to harm or radically alter the state." 78)

SCHWIND (1978)

"Following former attempts to reach a definition, terrorism could perhaps be described more precisely also as
- a (primarily) politically motivated behaviour
- of a non-state group without electoral prospects in a democratic context which aims
- by means of violent acts against persons and/or property
- to coerce people (especially the political leadership of democratic states) in order to obtain its will thereby." 79)

SHULTZ (1978)

"Political terrorism may be defined as the threat and or use of extranormal forms of political violence, in varying degrees, with the objective of achieving certain political objectives/goals. Such goals constitute the long range and short-term objectives that the group or movement seeks to obtain. These will differ from group to group. Such action generally is intended to influence the behavior and attitudes of certain targeted groups much wider than its immediate victims. However, influencing behavior is not necessarily the only aim of terrorist acts. The ramifications of political terrorism may or may not extend beyond national boundaries." 80)

ZINAM (1978)

"Though it has been stated that is useless to argue about conflicting classifications, the use of terms and their definitions is not neutral. This is especially true if the term conveys a pejorative connotation, like violence. (...) Force is morally neutral like power, its source. It can be used for both good and bad ends. Violence is defined here as an illegitimate use of force. (...)
Terrorism is the apex of violence. Once violence is defined, the definition of terrorism is a comparatively easy task. It is important to note that 'violence may occur without terror, but not terror without violence'. (...) In this study, terrorism is broadly defined as the use or threat of violence by individuals or by organized groups to evoke fear and submission to attain some economic, political, sociopsychological, ideological, or other objective." 81)

BASSIOUNI (1979)

"... a consensus definition proposed by this author has achieved a significant degree of international acceptance. It generally defines 'terrorism' as: 'A strategy of unlawful violence calculated to inspire ter-

ror in the general public or a significant segment thereof in order to
achieve a power-outcome or to propagandize a particular claim or grievance.'
Using this general definition, it was possible to draft a more specific
definition of international terrorism in this manner:
International terrorism consists of acts of terrorism containing an
international element or directed against an international target. Such
conduct contains an international element when:
1) the perpetrator and victim are citizens of different states; or
2) the conduct is performed in whole or in part in more than one state.
Internationally protected targets are:
1) innocent civilians;
2) duly accredited diplomats and personnel of international organizations
   acting in their official capacities;
3) international civil aviations;
4) the mail and other means of international communications;
5) members of non-belligerent armed forces.
Under the above stated consensus definition of terrorism, it is distinguished from other forms of violence in that it employs a strategy calculated to inspire terror whereas in other acts of violence, terror is
of incidental importance. In common crimes of violence, terror (other
than the victim's) is totally unintended. Moreover, common criminals
shun publicity for obvious reasons whereas ideologically motivated offenders seek to instill terror in the general public in order to achieve
their power-outcome. Thus, whereas all acts of violence are capable of
producing some terror, 'terroristic' acts are those calculated to produce terror as part of a coercive strategy to achieve an essentially
political outcome. By an elaboration of this concept, acts of terrorism
may be more readily contrasted with other forms of violence and consequently other sub-categories of terror violence may emerge." 82)

BONANATE (1979)

"A small group is terrorist when it works under cover, with the purpose
of obtaining victory not by physical elimination of the adversary, but
by symbolic actions (hence economic ones) intended to make the opponent
surrender in panic, rather than using greater forces, as would be the
strategic tradition in any conflict (that is, a plan of action along
the line of forms of deterrence).
The reaction caused by a neutral defintion (but also an inevitably im-
precise one: To what degree are people 'panic-stricken'?), like the
above is that it places no limits on the authors of the terrorist act,
who could have been either incumbents or opponents, internal or external with respect to the state, revolutionary or counter-revolutionary,
and so forth. [n] (...)   n: Furthermore, it must be borne in mind that
of the three components of terrorist action listed before - dimensions
of the group, clandestinity, symbolic action aimed at causing panic -
the second one is not always necessary, that is its dimensions must be
specified. For example, the atomic bomb on Hiroshima can be considered
in many ways terrorist, but it cannot be technically said that it was
a clandestine action. (...) In other words, instead of clandestinity
one could perhaps speak of impredictability, or of secrecy in a general
sense, in order for the different examples to fit into the general dimension." 83)

JENKINS (1979)

"The term 'terrorism' has no precise or universally accepted definition. It has become a fad word used promiscuously and often applied
to a variety of acts of violence which are not, strictly speaking,
terrorist in nature. Terrorism is often described as mindless violence,
senseless violence, or as irrational violence, but it is none of these.
(...) ... there is a theory of terrorism, a logic behind terrorism.
Terrorism can be described as the use or the threat of violence esca-
lated to create an atmosphere of fear and alarm which in turn will
cause people to exaggerate the strength of the terrorists and the
importance of their cause. Terrorism is thus violence for effect. Not
for the physical effect on the target. Indeed, the target or the victim of a terrorist may be irrelevant to the terrorists' cause. Terrorism is aimed at the people watching. Terrorism is theater." 84)

PONTARA (1979)

"Definition: Terrorism is every method of (political) struggle that
fulfills all three of these conditions:
1. involves the extreme use of violence
2. against innocent people
3. is not legitimate method of struggle." 85)

QUAINTON (1979)

"... the threat or use of violence for political purposes when such
action is intended to influence the attitude and behavior of a target
group other than its immediate victims and its ramifications transcend
national boundaries." 86)

RUSSELL, BANKER and MILLER (1979)

"... we define terrorism as the threatened or actual use of force or
violence to attain a political goal through fear, coercion, or intimidation... (...) Beyond this abstract definition, limitations that
exclude both civil disorders and military confrontations need to be
added. 'Political' is understood in this usage to connote the entire
range of social, economic, religious, ethnic, and governmental factors
impacting on a body politic, stressing the notions of power and influence. The ideal definition is one that both the adherents and
abhorrers of terrorism could agree upon." 87)

TROMP (1979)

"Political terrorism, defined as the systematic use of violence for
political ends, directed principally against outsiders in a political
conflict, with the goal of bringing round the actual opponent in that
conflict to desirable political behaviour, can, with regard to the increase in recent decades, probably best be explained in term of four
factors, which previously either did not exist, or could hardly have
played a role. These factors are:
1. Arms. (...) 2. Mobility. (...) 3. Communication/publicity (...)
4. Money. (...)" 88)

U.S. CONGRESS, HOUSE (1979)

"No person charged with an act of terrorism shall be ordered released
pending trial as provided in subsection a if the judicial officer determines that such a release would pose a danger to any other person or
to the community.

For purposes of this subsection, an 'act of terrorism' means any act
which is violent or dangerous to human life and violates a Federal criminal statute related to assassination, murder, sabotage, or kidnaping,
and which is used as a means or technique -
a) to demonstrate approval or disapproval of governmental policies or
   practices or the lack thereof;
b) to express a view on public issues;
c) to bring to the public's attention any issue of policy;
d) to overthrow all forms of law; or
e) to advocate the duty, necessity, or propriety of the unlawful as-
   saulting or killing of any officer of officers (either of specific
   individuals or of officers generally) of the Government of the
   United States or any other organized government (including law enforcement officers) because of his or their official function." 89)

U.S. GOVERNMENT definitions of International Terrorism (1979)

"The most widely used definition in the United States Government is:
the threat or use of violence for political purposes when such action
is intended to influence the attitude or behavior of a target group
wider than its immediate victims and its ramifications trancend national boundaries. Thomas Thornton, a former State Department Policy Plan-
ner and now member of the National Security Staff, has called terror
'a symbolic act designed to influence political behavior by extranormal
means, entailing the use or threat of violence'. An even more extensive
definition is that contained in the anti-terrorist legislation currently before the Congress. The Congressional language asserts that for an
act to be terroristic it must be intended to damage or threaten the
interests of or to obtain concessions from a state or an international
organization. It must not be committed in the course of military or
para-military operations directed essentially against military forces or
military targets of a state or an organized group. These definitions have a number of features in common. They all focus on the essential fact that
terrorism is the threat or use of violence for political goals. They
recognize that extraordinary and abnormal use of violence is involved.
Obviously we are all too familiar with political violence, both foreign
and domestic, most of which is not terroristic. It is something more
than revolutionary activity to change the behavior of governments,
whether by promoting nationalist causes, international revolution or
fundamental destruction of the capitalist system. To be sure, it often
uses the same tactics - ransom, blackmail, revenge, intimidation - but
it always seeks something beyond personal gain." 90)

WILKINSON (1979)

"It is a common error to equate terrorism with guerrilla war and violence in general. Terrorism is in fact a special mode of violence,
which may be briefly defined as coercive intimidation. It involves
the threat of murder, injury, or destruction to terrorize a given
target into conceding to the terrorists' will. As a policy or process,
terrorism therefore consists of three basic elements: The decision by
perpetrators of violence to use terrorism as a systematic weapon, the
threats or acts of extranormal violence themselves, and the effects
of this violence upon the immediate victims - the 'target' group or
'audience' - and the wider national and international opinion that
the terrorists may seek to intimidate or influence.
Many have fallen into the error of identifying a single locus, agent,
or context of terrorism with terrorism per se. Some equate it with

certain criminal and psychopathological manifestations. Many assume
it to be purely a mode of urban insurrection and thereby ignore whole
aspects of the history of terrorism in rural conflicts in, for example,
the Balkans, Indochina, and Ireland.
Commoner still is the attempt to restrict the terrorist designation to
acts of movements and individuals. (...) I do not believe it is possible
to adequately understand the former [terrorist movements] without paying
some attention to the effects of the use of force and violence by states. Indeed, the latter often helps to provoke and fuel the violence
of terrorist movements. Historically, state and factional violence have
repeatedly displayed this symbiotic relationship.
Terrorism is inherently indiscriminate both in its physical and psychological effects. (...)
Another important distinction between terrorism and other forms of violence is that terrorists recognize no ethical or humanitarian limits
to their use of violence: any means are permissible and everyone (including civilians, women, children, and neutrals) is expendable in the
interests of 'revolution', 'justice', or 'liberation'. (...)
Ultimately, it must be faced that terrorism is an evaluative concept.
(...) To assert, as I do, that terrorism, like torture, is incompatible
with a humane and civilized society, is to make a value judgment. Hence,
to pretend that interpreting or theorizing about terrorism is a 'value-
free' activity is sheer obfuscation." 91)

FRIEDLANDER (1980)

"Although there is no legal agreement on definitional characteristics,
the following description is offered as the simplest, most elemental,
and most convenient. Individual or group terror-violence may be described
as the use of force or the threat of force directed against innocent
third parties for primarily ideological, financial, or psychological
purposes.(...) Innocence is the quintessential condition of terrorist
victimology, for the terrorist victim is not the ultimate target - the
latter being either government or the public at large, or both. It is
the attack upon innocence, meaning that anyone is a potential victim,
that gives to terrorism its horror and its drama." 92)

HACKER (1980)

"The model situation of aggressive or violently aggressive acts is a
diadic relationship requiring and often demanding only two parties:
the aggressor and the victim. In contrast, terror and terrorism (the
attempt to influence by intimidation) is triadic, needing, in addition
to a perpetrator and a victim, an observer, an audience for whose
benefit the terroristic action is performed in the expectation of producing behavioral consequences. Terroristic actions are demonstrative,
spectacular, and theatrical, akin to show business in trying to bring
about calculated effects on the audience, i.e., the victim's family,
friends, nations, and identity groups. (...)
The victims... are merely pawns in the terroristic game, and are
'extras' in the terrorists' dramatic production. They are used only
as instruments to help the terrorists obtain their goals which may
be to alarm, arouse, disturb, confuse, insult, horrify, or blackmail
the audience or gain sympathy and support. Terror and terrorism (...)
are predominantly instances of strategy, well-planned, deliberate,
purposeful aggression carefully timed and figured out to produce opti-
mal results, that is, maximum audience reaction and participation." 93)

HAZELIP (1980)
"Terrorism is the use of terror and violence to intimidate segments of the community or political adversaries by individuals or groups not politically incumbent for the purpose of accomplishing political change." 94)

HEYMAN (1980)
"Terrorism may be defined as the use or threat of extraordinary political violence to induce fear, anxiety, or alarm in a target audience wider than the immediate symbolic victims. Terrorism is primarily violence for political effect, as opposed to military impact. Transnational terrorism is terrorism that transcends national boundries through the location or nationality of the victims, the targets, or the perpetrators. (...)
Transnational terrorism was born of the marriage between the urban guerrilla and the student activists. The emigrant guerrilla fed on the latent violence of the student movements, exploited the students' causes and contacts, and learned new tactics." 95)

MICKOLUS (1980)
"... the use or threat of use, of anxiety-inducing extranormal violence for political purposes by any individual or group, whether acting for or in opposition to established governmental authority, when such action is intended to influence the attitudes and behavior of a target group wider than the immediate victims and when, through the nationality or foreign ties of its perpetrators, its location, the nature of its institutional or human victims, or the mechanism of its resolution, its ramifications transcend national boundaries." 96)

MILLER (1980)
"It is not that 'terrorism' is intrinsically more difficult to define than any other political concept, but 'terrorism' escapes definition when it becomes embellished with value-ladened, political meaning. From my perspective, terrorism is first and foremost an act of political violence. It is not a tactic but a strategic mode of political violence. It is generally but not exclusively, directed at targets which have symbolic value in addition to or independent of any tactical or strategic value. It is the symbolic value which usually transcends the direct significance of any specific target, and is aimed at influencing political decision making through fear and intimidation. One of the primary ingredients of political terrorism is random violence. Where all people are targets and no one is safe, fear is heightened because it is difficult to escape into safety wrought by noninvolvement in the ongoing political struggle. Political terrorism can be and often is used by those in power as well as those attempting to attain power; however I would prefer to think of the term 'political terrorism' as a means of defining the behavior of non-state actors and the term 'state terrorism' as a means of defining the actions of state actors." 97)

MONDAY (1980)
"The word is appropriately used only when the insurgents meet three criteria. First, the person or group must have the means or potential for violence. There must be an impersonal frame of reference in the attack. The attacker cannot have a particular grudge against the victim if it is to be called a true terrorist attack. The individual vic-

tim of terrorism is unlucky, not culpable or personally answerable to
the victim.* Revenge is not terrorism. Finally, the objective of the
attack must be broader than killing someone or blowing something up.
The objective must be to SPREAD FEAR AND TERROR THROUGH THE POPULA-
TION AS A WHOLE. If an attack meets these three criteria it can be
called terrorist. Significantly, if it meets the criteria it is specifically prohibited under the rules of land warfare, meaning the insurgents cannot claim prisoner of war status under the Geneva Convention." 98) * sic AS.

BASSIOUNI (1981)
"Terrorism may be described as a strategy of violence designed to inspire terror within a particular segment of a given society. Commonly
associated with acts committed by ideologically and politically motivated individuals in order to achieve power, terrorism is also committed by individuals who are not so motivated and by individuals acting on behalf of states in time of war and peace." 99)

CERNY (1981)
"If we see pure terror tactics - anonymous attacks by clandestine
groups on either symbolic or random individual targets with the intention of spreading a generalised and abstract fear and anomie
among the mass of the target population - as a core of the concept of
terrorism, then how far can we move towards the periphery of the notion
before it becomes analytically absurd?" 100)

CRENSHAW (1981)
"Terrorism occurs both in the context of violent resistance to the
state as well as in the service of state interests. If we focus on
terrorism directed against governments for purposes of political
change, we are considering the premeditated use or threat of symbolic,
low-level violence by conspiratorial organizations. Terrorist violence
communicates a political message; its ends go beyond damaging an
enemy's material resources. The victims or objects of terrorist attack
have little intrinsic value to the terrorist group but represent a
larger human audience whose reaction the terrorists seek. Violence
characterized by spontaneity, mass participation, or a primary intent
of physical destruction can therefore be excluded from our investigation." 101)

FALLAH (1981)
"The search for a viable definition of terrorism is, in fact, a search
for one or more denominators common to all terrorist activities. One
such denominator is the use of violence - actual or threatened, physical or psychological - in some extreme form to achieve certain ends.
In some cases, violence and/or threats are used as means of coercion
to get the victim(s) to agree to certain demands. In other cases, they
are used as means of extermination, retaliation, or intimidation;
to instill fear and terror in the heart of the victims and to force
them into submission. These common threads, present in all forms of
terrorism, make it possible to qualify specific acts as terroristic
regardless of the motives behind them and regardless of whether they
are committed by persons in a weak or strong position of power." 102)

FRANCIS (1981)
"A working definition of terrorism in this study is the calculated use
of violence against non-combatant or civilian targets, individual or

institutional, for political purposes.
In the West, terrorism is usually distinguished form guerrilla warfare
in that the latter term refers to paramilitary combat carried out
against regular military forces. In practice, however, the two are
seldom distinct; almost all guerrilla movements make use of terrorism
at one or another stage of their development, and some rely on it. (...)
Terrorism under the name of 'armed struggle' is a necessary part of
the classical Leninist model of revolutionary tactics. It is not - or
has not been - the whole of this model... However, there is also an
overlap and congruence between Leninism and contemporary terrorist
ideology, and this overlap points to the central purposes of Soviet
support of terrorism. The overlap consists in the general agreement
of the Soviets and the terrorists on the nature of what they identify
as their main enemy - the imperialism of the advanced capitalist
states, particularly U.S. capitalism." 103)

FURLONG (1981)

"... I intend to use the term 'terrorism' in a narrow sense, in which
the primary aim of terrorism is indeed to terrorise, that is, to induce
terror in intended subjects. Intended subjects may be entire populations, specific sectors of society or isolated individuals. Terrorism
therefore involves among other things the use of violence to induce
compliance, where the victim of violence is of symbolic value to a
wider community rather than of direct value. Political terrorism is
terrorism used for political objectives, usually either by insurgents
wishing to overthrow an existing government ('revolutionary') or by
existing governments to maintain themselves in power or to enforce
their policies ('governmental'). (...) I think the term 'terrorism'
may also apply to non-political strategies; here we are concerned
only with political terrorism. (...)
But though terrorist violence may be unacceptable and abnormal, and
indeed often does occur in environments not normally associated with
violence, nevertheless it may not be unpredictable in its general selection of targets nor is it indiscriminate. If it were indiscriminate
or arbitrary, the symbolic value or representativeness of its victims
would be undermined. (...)
Terrorism relies for its effects not so much on any general unpredictability, but rather on its specific unexpectedness, as well as on her
eruption of violence into environments normally free from it. (...) As
Hutchinson argues, terrorism may indeed be an extremely economical instrument for insurgent organizations, since the threat implicit in the
act of violence may be imagined to be to a wider area possibly beyond
the real capacities of the operators. (...) Not all the aggressive
actions of terrorists are necessarily regarded as terroristic." 104)

HERMAN and VAN DER LAAN BOUMA (1981)

"Definitions of terrorism abound. However, for the purpose of this
chapter, we define non-governmental terrorism as: The considered and
systematic use - or threatened use - of widespread, offensive violence,
murder and destruction aimed at governmental employees and the general
population, as well as public and private property, in order to force
individuals, groups, communities, economic entities and governments to
modify or change their actual proposed behaviour and policies so as to
concede to the terrorists' political demands." 105)

HESS (1981)

"By terrorism I wish to understand:
1. A series of intentional acts of direct, psychological violence, which
2. at [various] indeterminable points but nevertheless systematically
3. with the aim of psychic effect
4. are conducted within the framework of a political strategy.
A very simple and neutral definition." 106)

LODGE (1981)

"For our purposes, terrorism is seen as the resort to violence for political ends by unauthorised, non-governmental actors in breach of accepted codes of behaviour regarding the expression of dissatifaction
with, dissent from or opposition to the pursuit of political goals by
the legitimate government authorities of the state whom they regard
as unresponsive to the needs of certain groups of people. Moreover,
terrorism - even indigenous terrorism - transcends national boundaries
in its exercise, effects, ramifications and prosecution." 107)

SEDERBERG (1981)

"... terrorism may be usefully defined as severe acts of violence
directed at noncombatants by the contending sides of a political
struggle. This definition, admittedly, is not free from all ambiguity
- what constitutes a 'severe' act of violence and who has noncombatant
status remain areas of possible contention - but at least it succinctly
identifies the special motives and victims of terrorist violence. Indeed, it is the class of victims that makes an act of violence terroristic.
'Noncombatants', though not an especially felicitous term, is less
loaded than the more common 'innocents'. Innocence, like beauty, is
often in the eye of the observer. It should prove easier to establish
an ideologically transcendent agreement on just who is a noncombatant.
For example, if Provisional I.R.A. gunmen attack a British army patrol,
this would not be construed as terrorism under this definition. If
they explode a bomb in a crowded marketplace, they do engage in terror." 108)

STOHL (1981)

"I shall follow E.V. Walter (1969) in my usage of the term terrorism.
The process of terrorism may be seen as consisting of three parts: The
act or threat of violence, the emotional reactions to such an act or
threat and the social effects resultant from the acts and reactions.
The initiation of the process of political terrorism by political actors may arise from a number of specific purposes, purposes which are
dependent upon both the position of the agents and the targets of the
terror. Generally, terrorism has as its purpose the production of both
compliance and fear. This is not to say that terrorists do not want
publicity, reaction to their actions or the mobilization of the population but rather that these aspects are considered to be intrinsic to
the production of compliance and fear. It is always important to remem-
ber that while each of the component parts of the process is important,
the emotional impact and the social effects are more important than
the particular action itself for understanding the political aspects
of terrorism. In other words, the target of the terror are far more
important for the process than are the immediate victims of the action
itself." 109)

Notes

1) J.B.S. Hardman. Terrorism. In: Encyclopaedia of the Social Sciences, Vol. 14, New York, Macmillan, 1936, p. 575-576.

2) J. Waciorsky. Le terrorisme politique. Paris, A. Pedone, 1939, p. 98 as quoted in: M. Crenshaw Hutchinson. The concept of revolutionary terrorism. Journal of Conflict Resolution, Vol. 16, no. 3, 1972, p. 383.

3) P. Wurth. La répression internationale du terrorisme. Lausanne, La Concorde, 1941, p. 56. (Translation from the French.)

4) H.J. Chisholm. The function of terror and violence in revolution. Washington, D.C., Georgetown University, 1948, p. 11-12, 18-19, 21-22. (M.A. Thesis.)

5) H. Arendt. The Origins of Totalitarianism. New York, Harcourt, Brace Jovanovich, Inc., 1951, p. 6, 331-332.

6) B. Crozier. The Rebels. A Study of Post-War Insurrections. London, Chatto and Windus, 1960, p. 159-160, 173.

7) J.S. Roucek. Sociological Elements of a Theory of Terror and Violence. American Journal of Economic and Sociology, Vol. 21, no. 2, April 1962, p. 166.

8) Th.P. Thornton. Terror as a Weapon of Political Agitation. In: H. Eckstein (Ed.). Internal War. Problems and Approaches. New York, The Free Press of Glencoe, 1964, p. 73-74, 77-78.

9) E.V. Walter. Violence and the Process of Terror. American Sociological Review, Vol. 29, no. 2, Spring 1964, p. 248-250, 256.
 - In Walter's study "Terror and Resistance" (1969), the wording remains almost identical.

10) R. Gaucher. Les Terroristes. Paris, Editions Albin Michel, 1965, p. 235, 10-11.

11) R. Aron. Peace and War. London, Weidenfeld and Nicolson, 1966, p. 170; cit. R. Wilkinson. Political Terrorism. London, Macmillan, 1974, p. 13-14.

12) C. Leiden and K.M. Schmitt. The Politics of Violence. Revolution in the Modern World. Englewood Cliffs, Prentice-Hall, 1968, p. 30-32.

13) H. Arendt. On Violence. New York, Harvest Books, 1970, p. 55-56; cit. I.M.H. Smart. The Power of Terror. International Journal, Vol. 30, no. 2, 1975, p. 225.

14) A. Dallin and G.W. Breslauer. Political terror in communist systemes. Stanford, Cal., Stanford University Press, 1970, p. 1,2, 12, 19, 26.

15) J.M. Silverman and P.M. Jackson. Terror in insurgency warfare. Military Review, Vol. 50, October 1970, p. 61-63.

16) J. Mallin (Ed.). Terror and Urban Guerrillas. A Study of Tactics and Documents. Coral Gables, Florida, University of Miami Press, 1971, p. 3-5.

17) R. Moss. Urban Guerrilla Warfare. London, Institute of Strategic Studies, 1971, p. 1, 3. (Adelphi Papers, no. 79.)

18) M. Crenshaw Hutchinson. The Concept of Revolutionary Terrorism. Journal of Conflict Resolution, Vol. 16, no. 3, 1972, p. 383-396.

19) F. Gross. Violence in Politics. Terror and Political Assassination in Eastern Europe and Russia. The Hague, Mouton, 1972, p. 9-12.

20) J. Guenther. Terror und Terrorismus. Neue Deutsche Hefte, Vol. 19, no. 4, 1972, p. 33. (translated)

21) D.G. Morrison et al. Black Africa. A Comparative Handbook. New York, The Free Press, 1972, p. 130n.

22) R. Moss. Urban Guerrillas. The New Face of Political Violence. London, Temple Smith, 1972, p. 32.

23) F. Hacker. Terror. Mythos, Realität, Analyse. Reinbek, Rowohlt, 1975, (1973), p. 17, 19, 20, 183.

24) I.L. Horowitz. Political Terrorism and State Power. Journal of Political and Military Sociology, Vol. 1, 1973, p. 150.

25) W.D. Neale. Terror - Oldest Weapon in the Arsenal. Army, August 1973, p. 11.

26) P. Wilkinson. Three Questions on Terrorism. Government and Opposition, Vol. 8, no. 3, Summer 1973, p. 292.

27) B. Crozier. Aid for Terrorism. In: Annual of Power and Conflict, 1973-1974. A Survey of Political Violence and International Influence. London, Institute for the Study of Conflict, 1974, p. 4.

28) G. Fairbairn. Revolutionary Guerrilla Warfare. The Countryside Version. Harmondsworth, Penguin, 1974, p. 348-349.

29) J.J. Paust. Some Thoughts on 'Preliminary Thoughts' on Terrorism. American Journal of International Law, Vol. 68, no. 3, 1974, p. 502.

30) Prevention of Terrorism (Temporary Provisions) Act of 1974. Cit. E.F. Mickolus. The Literature of Terrorism. Westport, Conn., Greenwood Press, 1980, p. 295.

31) P. Wilkinson. Political Terrorism. London, Macmillan, 1974, p. 11, 17-18.

32) V. Bite, Foreign Affairs Division, Library of Congress. International Terrorism - Issue Brief no. IB 74042. Appendix of:
U.S. Congress, Senate. Committee on the Judiciary. Subcommittee to Investigate the Administration of the Internal Security Act and Other Internal Security Laws. Part IV, May 14 1975, 94th Cong., Ist. Sess. Washington, D.C., GPO, 1975, p. 253.

33) G. Bouthoul. Definitions of Terrorism. In: D. Carlton and C. Schaerf (Eds.). International Terrorism and World Security. London, Croom Helms, 1975, p. 50-59.

34) D. Fromkin. The Strategy of Terrorism. Foreign Affairs, Vol. 53, no. 4, 1975, p. 693, 694, 697.

35) B. Jenkins. International Terrorism. A New Mode of Conflict. California Seminar on Arms Control and Foreign Policy, January 1975, Los Angeles, Crescent Publications, 1975, p. 1-2.

36) B.M. Jenkins and J. Johnson. International Terrorism: A Chronology, 1968-1974. Santa Monica, Rand, 1975, p. 3.

37) L.A. Sobel (Ed.). Political Terrorism. Oxford, Clio Press, 1975.

38) Remarks by R.A. Fearey, U.S. Coordinator for Combatting Terrorism, 19. Febr. 1976. In: J. Wolf. Fear of Fear. A Survey of Terrorist Operations and Controls in Open Societies. New York, Plenum Press, 1981, p. 201.

39) D.L. Milbank. Research Study: International and Transnational Terrorism. Diagnosis and Prognosis. Washington, D.C., CIA Political Research Department, April 1976, p. 1.

40) A.J. Pierre. The Politics of International Terrorism. Repr. in: J.D. Elliott and K. Gibson (Eds.). Contemporary Terrorism. Gaithersburg, IACP, 1978, (orig. 1976), p. 36.

41) S. Qureshi. Political Violence in the South Asia Subcontinent. In: Y. Alexander (Ed.). Terrorism. International, National, Regional and Global Perspectives. New York, Praeger, 1976, p. 151.

42) U.S. National Advisory Committee on Criminal Justice, Standards and Goals. Report of the Task Force on Disorders and Terrorism, Washington D.C., GPO, 1976, p.3.

43) F.M. Watson. Political Terrorism: The Threat and the Response. Washington, D.C., Robert B. Luce, 1976, p. 1.

44) E. Weisband and D. Roguly. Palestinian Terrorism: Violence, Verbal Strategy, and Legitimacy. In: Y. Alexander (Ed.). International, National, Regional, and Global Perspectives. New York, Praeger, 1976, p. 258-259, 278-279.

45) P. Wilkinson. Terrorism versus Liberal Democracy: The Problem of Response. London, Institute for the Study of Conflict, 1976, p. 1-3. (Conflict Studies, no. 76.)

46) J.B. Wolf. Controlling Political Terrorism in a Free Society. Orbis - a Journal of World Affairs, Vol. 19, no. 34, 1976, p. 1289-1290.

47) Y. Alexander and S.M. Finger (Eds.). Terrorism: Interdisciplinary Perspectives. New York, John Jay Press, 1977, p. IX-XI.

48) Cit. F. McClintock. In: R.D. Crelinsten (Ed.). Research Strategies for the Study of International Political Terrorism, Montreal, International Centre for Comparative Criminology, 1977, p. 162.

49) R. Clutterbuck. Guerrillas and Terrorists. London, Faber & Faber, 1977, p. 11, 21.

50) M. Funke. Terrorismus - Ermittlungsversuch zu einer Herausforderung In: M. Funke (Ed.). Terrorismus. Untersuchungen zur Strategie und Struktur revolutionärer Gewaltpolitik. Bonn, Schriftenreihe der Bundeszentrale für politische Bildung, 1977, p. 13.

51) H.C. Greisman. Social Meanings of Terrorism: Reification, Violence and Social Control. Contemporary Crises, no. 1, July 1977, p. 305.

52) I.L. Horowitz. Transnational Terrorism, Civil Liberties, and Social Science. In: Y. Alexander and S.M. Finger (Eds.). Terrorism: Interdisciplinary Perspectives. New York, John Jay Press, 1977, p. 283.

53) I.L. Horowitz. Can Democracy Cope with Terrorism? The Civil Liberties Review, Vol. 4, no. 1, May/June 1977, p. 30.

54) Z. Iviansky. Individual Terror: Concept and Typology. Journal of Contemporary History, Vol. 12, no. 1, p. 50.

55) B.M. Jenkins. Combatting International Terrorism: The Role of Congress. Santa Monica, Rand, January 1977, p. 1, 5.

56) W. Laqueur. Terrorism. London, Weidenfeld and Nicolson. 1977, p. 79, 79n.

57) B.M. Leiser. Terrorism, Guerrilla Warfare, and International Morality. Stanford Journal of International Studies, Vol. 12, Spring 1977, p. 39, 61(n).

58) J. Mallin, Terrorism as a Military Weapon. Air University Review, Vol. 28, no. 2, 1977, p. 60.

59) E.F. Mickolus. Statistical Approaches to the Study of Terrorism. In: Y. Alexander and S.M. Finger (Eds.). Terrorism: Interdisciplinary Perspectives. New York, John Jay Press, 1977, p. 210, 246.

60) J.J. Paust. A Definitional Focus. In: Y. Alexander and S.M. Finger (Eds.). Terrorism: Interdisciplinary Perspectives. New York, John Jay Press, 1977, p. 20-21.

61) H.E. Price. The Strategy and Tactics of Revolutionary Terrorism. Comparative Studies in Society and History, January 1977, p. 52.

62) M.E. Silverstein. Medical Rescue as an Antiterrorist Measure. A Strategist's Cookbook. In: R.D. Crelinsten (Ed.). Research Strategies for the Study of International Political Terrorism. Montreal, International Centre for Comparative Criminology, 1977, p. 91.

63) B. Singh. An Overview. In: Y. Alexander and S.M. Finger (Eds.). Terrorism: Interdisciplinary Perspectives. New York, John Jay Press, 1977, p. 5-6.

64) W.H. Smith. International Terrorism. A Political Analysis. In: The Year Book of World Affairs, 1977. London, Stevens & Sons, 1977, Vol. 31, p. 138-139, 153.

65) P. Waldmann. Strategien politischer Gewalt. Stuttgart, Kohlhammer, 1977, p. 70. (translated)

66) P. Wilkinson. Terrorism and the Liberal State. London, Macmillan, 1977, p. 48, 51, 52-53.

67) F. Wördemann. Terrorismus, Motive, Strategien. München, Piper, 1977, p. 24.

68) J.B. Bell. A Time of Terror. How Democratic Societies Respond to Revolutionary Violence. New York, Basic Books, 1978, p. 3, 49, 95-96.

69) M. Crenshaw Hutchinson. Revolutionary Terrorism. The FLN in Algeria, 1945-1962. Stanford, Hoover Institution, 1978, p. 18, 21, 77-78.

70) A.E. Evans and J.F. Murphy (Eds.). Legal Aspects of International Terrorism. Lexington, 1978. As cited in: R.A. Friedlander's book-review in The American Journal of Comparative Law, Vol. 28, 1980, p. 355.

71) L.C. Hamilton. Ecology of Terrorism: A Historical and Statistical Study. Boulder, Colorado, University of Colorado, 1978, p. 23-24.

72) B.M. Jenkins. The Study of Terrorism: Definitional Problems (1978). In. Y. Alexander and J.M. Gleason (Eds.). Behavioral and Quantitative Perspectives on Terrorism. New York, Pergamon Press, 1981, p. 4-5.

73) A. Kaplan. The Psychodynamics of Terrorism. In: Y. Alexander and J.M. Gleason (Eds.). Behavioral and Quantitative Perspectives on Terrorism. New York, Pergamon Press, 1981, p. 36-37.

74) M. Karanović. Pojam Terorizma (The Concept of Terrorism). Jugoslovenska Revija za Krimilogiju i Krivicnofravo, no. 14, 1978, p. 88.

75) P. Lösche. Terrorismus und Anarchismus, Internationale und historische Aspekten. In: M. Funke (Ed.) Extremismus im demokratischen Rechtsstaat. Bonn, Bundeszentrale für politische Bildung, 1978, p. 82-83.

76) E.F. Mickolus. Trends in Transnational Terrorism. In: M. Livingston (Ed.). International Terrorism in the Contemporary World. Westport, Conn., Greenwood Press, 1978, p. 44.

77) A.P. Schmid and J. de Graaf. Internationaal terrorisme. Begripsbepaling, structuur en strategieën. In: Intermediair, Jg. 14, no. 20, 19 May 1978, p. 5. (translated)

78) J. Schreiber. The Ultimate Weapon: Terrorists and World Order. New York, William Marrow, 1978, p. 20.

79) H.-D. Schwind. Zur Entwicklung des Terrorismus. In: H.D. Schwind (Ed.). Ursachen des Terrorismus der Bundesrepublik Berlin, Walter de Gruyter, 1978, p. 26. (translated)

80) R. Shultz. Conceptualizing Political Terrorism, A Typology. Journal of International Affairs, Vol. 32, no. 1, 1978, p. 8-9.

81) O. Zinam. Terrorism and Violence in the Light of a Theory of Discontent and Frustration. In: M.H. Livingston (Ed.). International Terrorism in the Contemporary World. Westport, Conn., Greenwood Press, 1978, p. 241, 244-245.

82) M.Ch. Bassiouni. Prolegomenon to Terror Violence. Creighton Law Review, Vol. 12, no. 13, 1979, p. 752.

83) L. Bonanate. Some Unanticipated Consequences of Terrorism. Journal of Peace Research, Vol. 16, no. 3, 1979, p. 198, 209n.

84) B.M. Jenkins. Terrorists at the Threshold. (May 15, 1979) In: E. Nobles Lowe and H.D. Shargel (Eds.). Legal and Other Aspects of Terrorism. New York, Practising Law Institute, 1979, p. 94-95.

85) G. Pontara. Violenza e terrorismo. Il problema della definizione e della giustificazione. In: L. Bonanate (Ed.). Dimensioni del terrorismo politico. Milano, Franco Angeli Editore, 1979, p. 50. (translated)

86) A.C.E, Quainton. Terrorism: US Preparedness. In: The Shingle: Philadelphia Bar Association Quarterly Magazine, Vol. 42, no. 5, 1979, p. 9. Cit. in R.A. Friedlander. Terrorism and the Law, What Price Safety? Gaithersburg, IACP, 1981, p. 3.

87) Ch.A. Russell, L.J. Banker Jr. and B.H. Miller. Out-inventing the Terrorist. In: Y. Alexander, D. Carlton, and P. Wilkinson. Terrorism: Theory and Practice. Boulder, Colorado, Westview Press, 1979, p. 4, 37n.

88) H.W. Tromp. Terrorism and Political Violence. Brussels, AFK/VVK, 1979, p. 12-13. (unpublished paper)

89) Bill to Prohibit the Pretrial Release of Any Person Charged With an Act of Aggravated Terrorism, January 31, 1979: cit. R.A. Friedlander. Terrorism and the Law: What Price Safety? Gaithersburg, Md. IACP, 1981, p. 26.

90) Cit. by Ambassador A.C.E. Quainton, as quoted in E. Nobles Lowe and
H.D. Shargel. Legal and Other Aspects of Terrorism. New York, Practising Law Institute, 1979, p. 94-95.

91) P. Wilkinson. Terrorist Movements. In: Y. Alexander, D. Carlton and
P. Wilkinson. Terrorism: Theory and Practice. Boulder, Colorado,
Westview Press, 1979, p. 99-101.

92) R.A. Friedlander. Terrorism and the Law: What Price Safety? Gaithersburg, IACP, 1981, p. 3,

93) F.J. Hacker. Contagion and Attraction of Terror and Terrorism. In:
Y. Alexander and J.M. Gleason (Eds.). Behavioral and Quantitative
Perspectives on Terrorism. New York, Pergamon Press, 1981, p. 73.

94) A.C. Hazelip. Twelve Tenets of Terrorism. An Assessment of Theory
and Practice. Ph.D. Florida State University, 1980, p. 28.

95) E.S. Heyman. Monitoring the Diffusion of Transnational Terrorism.
Gaithersburg, IACP, ca. 1980, p. 2-3.

96) E.F. Mickolus. Transnational Terrorism: A Chronology of Events,
1968-1979. London, Aldwych Press, 1980, p. XIII-XIV.

97) A.H. Miller. Terrorism and Hostage Negotiations. Boulder, Colorado,
Westview Press, 1980, p. 10-11.

98) M. Monday. Insurgent War. A Backgrounder for Reporters. San Diego,
TVI, 1980, p. 5.

99) M.Ch. Bassiouni. Terrorism, Law Enforcement and the Mass Media:
Perspectives, Problems, Proposals. The Journal of Criminal Law and
Criminology, Vol. 72, no. 1, 1981, p. 1.

100) Ph.G. Cerny. France: Non-terrorism and the Politics of Repressive
Tolerance. In: J. Lodge (Ed.). Terrorism, a Challenge to the State.
Oxford, Martin Robertson, 1981, p. 104.

101) M. Crenshaw. The Causes of Terrorism. Comparative Politics, July
1981, p. 379.

102) E.A. Fallah. Terrorist Activities and Terrorist Targets: A Tentative
Typology. In: Y. Alexander and J.M. Gleason (Eds.). Behavioral and
Quantitative Perspectives on Terrorism. New York, Pergamon Press,
1981, p. 36-37.

103) S.T. Francis. The Soviet Strategy of Terror. Washington, D.C., Heritage Foundation, 1981, p. 3, 63.

104) P. Furlong. Political Terorism in Italy. Responses, Reactions and
Immobilism. In: J. Lodge (Ed.). Terrorism: A Challenge to the State.
Oxford, Martin Robertson, 1981, p. 59-60.

105) V. Herman and R. van der Laan Bouma. Nationalists Without a Nation:
South Moluccan Terrorism in the Netherlands. In: J. Lodge (Ed.).
Terrorism : A Challenge to the State. Oxford, Martin Robertson,
1981, p. 120.

106) H. Hess. Terrorismus und Terrorismus - Diskurs. Tijdschrift voor
Criminologie, no. 4, 1981, p. 174.

107) J. Lodge. Introduction. In: J. Lodge (Ed.). Terrorism: A Challenge to
the State. Oxford, Martin Robertson, 1981, p. 5.

108) P.C. Sederberg, Defining Terrorism. Unpubl. Paper, 1981, p. 3-4.

109) M. Stohl. The Three Worlds of Terror. Unpubl. Paper, 1981, p. 2.

II. THEORIES

THEORIES AND INTERPRETATIONS OF TERRORISM

Introduction

In our questionnaire we asked authors what they thought about the
state of development of theories in the field of terrorism and offered
them some possible answers (see Table VIII).

Table VIII: Answers to the Question: "How Would You Characterize the State
of Theory Development in the Field of Political Terrorism?"

Answer	Number of mentionings *
a. Poor	12
b. One-sided, focussing on left-wing terrorism	9
c. One-sided, neglecting state terrorism	7
d. More policy-oriented than scientific	11
e. Not worse than in other areas of social science research	12
f. Other	8
g. No answer, don't know	4

* Some respondents marked more than one category.

Some of the respondents used very strong language under option f) such
as "confused, garbage, irrelevant (Morris), "confused and confusing,
often intentionally" (Lador-Lederer), "hopeless" (Merari). Others noted
that "Quantitative research based theory is in its infancy" (Gleason),
that things were "coming along slowly" (Ochberg). One author thinks that
we are still in a state of pre-theory, without cumulativeness and without
historical evidence (Crenshaw). Yet another author sees the present
state of theory primarily in the sphere of propaganda rather than social
science (Young).

Theories of terrorism are, with few exceptions, the result of work done
in the last fifteen years. In the following pages an attempt will be
made to review part of this theoretical work with an emphasis on the
theories which deal with the etiology of terrorism. It has to be stressed
from the beginning that the term theory is taken more in the sense of
"current thinking" and interpretations than in terms of formal propositions
which have been operationalized and tested empirically. Theories in the
more rigorous sense of the term, with prognostic power, are inexistent,

like in many other branches of the social sciences.

Terrorism and Political Violence Theory

In the 1960s, when counter-insurgency became a government preoccupation in the United States, a sizeable literature on political, collective and civil violence emerged in answer to this demand, stimulated by a stream of governmental research grants. One of the best-known and most influential works from this period is Ted Gurr's Why Men Rebel (Princeton, New Jersey, Princeton University Press, 1970).
In our questionnaire we asked authors which of the various theories on the occurrence of political violence they found helpful for understanding (insurgent) terrorism. Gurr's work was mentioned no less than eight time, more than any other author [1].
In one form or another the Gurr model frequently raises its head in discussions on the origins of terrorism. A paper prepared by the United Nations' Secretariat on "The Origins and Fundamental Causes of International Terrorism", for instance proclaims:

> "It thus appears that the "misery, frustration, grievance and despair" which lead to terrorism have many roots in international and national political, economic and social situations affecting the terrorists, as well as in his personal circumstances. The precise chain of causation of particular acts cannot be traced with scientific exactitude." [2]

The Gurr model is based on Freudian psychoanalysis and is derived from a conceptual framework developed by a group of Yale psychologists in the 1930s. Its principal originator was Dollard, although it has been considerably modified at later stages.
Dollard and his Yale associates held:

> "... that aggression is always a consequence of frustration. More specifically the proposition is that the occurrence of aggressive behavior always presupposes the existence of frustration and, contrariwise, that the existence of frustration always leads to some form of aggression". [3]

Building on these psychological foundations the political scientist Gurr substituted Relative Deprivation (RD) for Dollard's Frustration Aggression (FA), but also used the terms deprivation, discrepancy and frustration. In place of aggression he refers to collective and political violence and the frustration-aggression nexus applies for Gurr both to individuals and collectives.

The key term "political violence" is very broad with Gurr, referring to
"all collective attacks within a political community against the political
regime its actors - including competing political groups as well as incumbents - or its policies". It not only includes riots and rebellions
but also coups d'état, guerrilla wars and revolutions.

Gurr's thesis then is:

> "Relative Deprivations" (RD) is the term used... to denote the tension
> that develops from a discrepancy between the "ought" and the "is" of
> collective value satisfaction, that disposes men to violence. (...)
> The frustration-aggression relationship provides the psychological
> dynamic for the proposed relationship between intensity of depriva-
> tion and the potential for collective violence..."

While this model is also supposed to cover (small scale) terrorism
(which Gurr subsumes under "Conspiracy"), together with mutinies,
coups d'état, political assassinations and small scale guerilla wars [7],
there is only one short direct index reference in Gurr's classic work
to terrorism [8]. In an article written in 1976 and published in 1979
under the title "Some Characteristics of Political Terrorism in the 1960s"
Gurr himself is not invoking RD or elaborating how frustration causes
terrorism. The F-A or RD thesis also lies at the basis of the work of
many other political scientists (e.g. Davies and Feierabend & Feierabend).

Lee Seechrest commented in 1971: "It is amazing how many people in
political science, sociology and anthropology have taken on the
frustration-aggression hypothesis for their own use without realizing
its still shaky status in psychology." [10]

As to the findings in the field of psychology on the reactive mechanistic
F-A thesis it has been noted by v.d. Dennen:

> "More than two decades of research have shown that frustration does
> not invariably lead to aggression, that frustration can lead to
> non-aggression, that aggression can occur without frustration, that
> in some cultures aggression is not a typical response to frustration,
> that some situations (such as threat and insult) can evoke more
> aggression than frustration, that the injustice of frustration is
> more significant than frustration itself, that frustration subsumes
> a diverse set of conditions, and that the F-A linkage need not be
> innate and could be learned. The widespread acceptance of the F-A
> notions is perhaps attributable more to its simplicity than to its
> predictive power." [11]

Given these shortcomings of the F-A model in psychology, one wonders
how much substance can be left after the switch from psychology to
sociology, from individual to collective, from aggression to violence

and from frustration to deprivation has been made. At any rate the operationalization problem of RD has never been satisfactorily solved as Lawrence C. Hamilton, who made an interesting attempt to develop a synthetic theory of terrorism based on Gurr, has admitted: "Relative deprivation itself is as elusive of measurement as the psychological state of frustration or beliefs about the effectiveness and justification of political violence." [12)

The expansion of the field on which the model purports to apply, ranging from individual bombing acts to the outbreak of the French Revolution, has also been a major problem.

With regard to terrorism, the RD model has nothing to say on the terrorism of regimes. Nor does it have much to say on the interesting phenomenon that so many insurgent terrorists are of upper and middle class origin, rather than from the more deprived sectors of society. One of our respondents (M. Crenshaw) has written that she found theories of violence, like Gurr's were not relevant to terrorism, and in a more general vein, Paul Wilkinson has remarked that: "General theories of violence are remarkably unhelpful for the study of terrorism." [13)

While this writer happens to share this view, we nevertheless would like to offer the reader a chance to become acquainted with the work of Lawrence Hamilton, who made a rare effort to test empirically a synthetic theory of (what he calls) terrorism. In his dissertation Hamilton took from Gurr's Strive Events Data Set from the period 1961-1970 the conspiracy events "assassinations","political bombing", "small scale terrorism" and "small scale guerrilla war" and declared them to be within his own conceptual definition of terrorism. [14)

With this - in our view very questionable - working definition, Hamilton set out to formalize a number of models which he labels theories of terrorism. Hamilton discusses five such theories, and finally he sets out to build a synthetic sixth one. These theories, which he labels A, B, C, D and E theories can be summarized in the following way:

A. Theory of Terrorism: misery and oppression inspire all types of civil unrest; insurgent terrorism is one of these. Once terrorism occurs, the police are provoked to counterattacks. Under the pressure of these counterattacks the terrorists cannot hold rallies, make speeches, print newspapers, or otherwise continue political agitation among the masses without exposing both themselves and their supporters

to almost certain arrest. However, this is precisely the sort of
political work which is necessary to insure that the masses will
support the rebels in their confrontations with the regime. Thus,
by increasing repression which in turn precludes political agitation,
terrorism makes a successful revolution less likely.
According to Hamilton, this is, minor disagreements notwithstanding,
the view of Mao, Lenin and Guevara on the subject of terrorism. 15)

B. Theory of Terrorism: terrorism is caused by misery and oppression.
Once it occurs, it provokes the regime to intensify oppression. The
oppression alienates public support for the regime, and increases
sympathy for the rebels, who in turn are strengthened and encouraged
to provoke the regime even further, etc. Ultimately the populace
will side with the rebels and revolution will occur. 16)
Hamilton lists Marighela as a proponent of this theory, together
with the U.S. student leader Tom Hayden.

C. Theory of Terrorism: terrorism is caused by misery and oppression.
Once it occurs, however, the government is induced to make reforms
which directly remove some of the causes of terrorism. In particular
there is a reduction in the extent of government oppression. A
lower level of oppression will, then, cause a lower level of future
terrorism, which will reduce oppression even further, etc. If for
some reason initial terrorism failed to reduce oppression, then it
might escalate until either reform occurred or the government was
overthrown.
This theory that terrorism is, in an important sense, self-reducing,
is derived from Hyams. 17)

D. Theory of Terrorism: in this view, terrorism is not typically the
work of the poor and exploited; it is the work of the idle elites,
particularly students and the intelligentsia. It arises during periods
of unparalleled affluence rather than desperate poverty. Furthermore,
it is the most open, democratic and liberal governments that are
most afflicted. Affluence and freedom encourage, allow, or somehow
produce terrorism. Once terrorism occurs, it leads to a decrease
in freedom (increase in oppression). It also increases the probability
of a military coup. Oppressive measures will eventually succeed in
suppressing terrorism, thus decreasing the probability of revolution.
Since the more oppressive society is relatively stable, prospects for
moderate reform are also damaged. 18)
Representatives of views containing elements of this chain of causation
are, according to Hamilton, Moss, Clutterbuck and Laqueur.

E. Theory of Terrorism: frustration (caused by relative deprivation),
in combination with utilitarian justifications for violence (such as
the relative strength of regime and rebel forces, degrees of external
support for each, and the historical successes of past insurgencies)
and normative justifications (violence as a learned, cultural response)
stand at the basis of insurgent violence as well as conservative
violence (vigilantism, punitive oppression by the government), the
two of which are linked, indirectly, in a positive feedback relationship.
Unlike in the B theory there is no assumption that escalating violence
will lead to revolution.
This E theory is based on some of the views expressed by Gurr, without
encampassing the whole of Gurr's intervening variables. 19)

In his attempt to test a synthetic sixth theory of terrorism based on
elements of the other five, Hamilton found that revolts were poorly
predicted with this set of variables and that their causality was distinct
from terrorism and oppression which he found were linked to each other.
Hamilton concluded on the basis of his multivariate analysis:

> "1. Is terrorism most likely under the most oppressive governments,
>   or under the least oppressive? Other things being equal, it is
>   more likely under the least oppressive.
>
> 2. Once terrorism arises, is government oppression more likely
>   to increase or decrease? It is almost certain to increase
>   either temporarily or permanently.
>
> 3. If oppression is increased, will that stimulate terrorism to
>   increase as well? It will further stimulate terrorism if the
>   terrorists survive the government countermeasures.
>
> 4. Does terrorism increase the probability of revolution?
>   It increases the probability of wider violence, but apparently
>   does not affect the likelyhood of a successful revolution."

Hamilton pointedly adds that his findings "are inconsistent with the
theoretical rationales most frequently offered to justify terrorism" [20].
In his accompanying historical study of terrorism, he admits, with so
many words, that "the causes of terrorism are obscure", adding:

> "It has risen among rich and poor, oppressive and relatively
> unoppressive societies. It has been used to promote causes with
> no popular support as well as causes endorsed by a large majority.
> And it has emerged to fight against the overwelming forces of
> foreign invaders and has been used, by other invaders, as an
> extension of interstate war." [21]

T.R. Gurr, as noted earlier, also rearranged his old civil strife data.
He took the same period as Hamilton (1961-1970) but fewer countries
(87 in stead of 115) and his working definition is narrower, excluding
small scale guerrilla war. He took political bombings, kidnappings and
assassinations to constitute "terrorist activity" and carried out a set
of bivariate analyses. His conclusions include insights such as:

> "... the typical terrorist campaign was conducted by tiny groups
> and was short-lived. Their public motives were not notably different
> from those of groups using other unconventional methods of political
> action. More specifically, the perpetrators of terrorist activities
> seemed more often motivated by hostility towards particular policies
> and political figures than by revolutionary aspirations. Their
> actions were more often a social nuisance than a serious threat to
> life and property, more often a security problem than an immanent
> revolution."

Such insights, interesting as they are, are quite detached from the
original theoretical framework, the Relative Deprivation model. Gurr
himself admitted that his findings for the 1960s did not allow
generalizations on terrorism in the 1970s [23].

One could go further and say that the political violence theories
from the 1960s and the data generated to substantiate and test
them, are often more of a hindrance than a help to understand the
current wave of insurgent terrorism.

Common Wisdom and Common Myths on Terrorism

Theories usually consist of sets on interconnected propositions.
If the interconnections are weak we are left with isolated propositions.
In a state of pre-theory there are two kind op propositions, the first
kind stating what the phenomenon to be studied is not, contrary to
widespread assumptions, and, secondly, propositions which state what
a phenomenon positively is. A number of authors have offered such
general propositions.

J.B. Bell, for instance, offers us a list of points on which the common
wisdom is polarized:

> "1. At the very beginning we face the definitional problem one man's
>   terrorist is another man's patriot. (...)
>
> 2. Besides the definitional problem there is also the historical
>   problem. Here the conclusion is that the present epidemic of
>   terrorism is either novel or not. Some trace the long roots,
>   ideological or tactical, of present day revolutionary terrorists
>   back to the Black Hand or the People's Will or the Carbonari. (...)
>   The advocates of novelty, however, point to differences in kind,
>   not just degree. For one thing, our postindustrial society
>   presents a spectrum of highly vulnerable nodes. (...) And
>   those terrorists who seek influence rather than to maim now
>   have instant communication to hundreds of millions of people.(...)
>
> 3. One of the few firm conclusions emerging from the academic
>   investigations is that terrorism is the weapon of the weak,
>   but it is a powerful weapon. (...)
>
> 4. How important is terrorism? According to the conventional
>   wisdom, terrorism is either very important or it is very
>   unimportant. On the one end of the spectrum stand many of the
>   Union Jack School, who see the terrorist threat as releasing
>   highly undesirable forces wihtin open societies; on the other
>   end are those who insist that terrorism is counterproductive,
>   ineffectual, and unimportant. (...)
>
> 5. It is a comfort to know that the common wisdom has accepted
>   the fact that, however defined, terrorism (nonstate variant)
>   kills relatively few people (but has a great impact). (...)
>
> 6. Again the specialists have concluded that the "new" terror
>   is either a transient trend or a growth industry. (...)

7. In this connection <u>terrorists are likely to be more effective or else they may not</u>. (...)

8. What kind of person is the terrorist? <u>The terrorist is either a psychotic fanatic beyond accommodation or he is a rational rebel</u>. (...)

9. Then, it is agreed that while nothing can really be done about terrorism in an open society, something must. <u>The problem is that there is no solution</u>." 24)

A different set of propositions is offered by Walter Laqueur, one of the most-cited authors in the field. He comes with a list of seven myths on terrorism:

"1. Political terror is a new and unprecedented phenomenon. (...)

2. Terrorism is left-wing and revolutionary in character. (...)

3. Terrorism appears whenever people have genuine, legitimate grievances. Remove the grievance and terror will cease. (...)

4. Terrorism is highly effective. (...)

5. The importance of terrorism will grow enormously in the years to come as the destruction power of its weapons increase. (...)

6. Political terrorists are more intelligent and less cruel than "ordinary" criminals. (...)

7. Terrorists are poor, hungry and desperate human beings." 25)

M. Stohl gives us this list of "eight pervasive myths":

"1. Political terrorism is the exclusive province of antigovernmental forces.

2. The purpose of political terrorism is the production of chaos.

3. Political terrorism is the province of the madmen.

4. Terrorism is criminal, no political, activity.

5. All insurgent violence is political violence.

6. Governments always oppose nongovernmental terrorism.

7. Terrorism is exclusively a problem relating to internal political conditions.

8. Political terrorism is a strategy of futility. 26)

A different set of hypotheses has been put forward by the Italian political scientist L. Bonanate:

"1. Terrorism is a response to the violence of institutions.

2. Terrorism is the desperate (or fanatical) choice of those who lack the patience of the revolutionary.

3. The disintegration of sociey provokes the formation of terrorist groups.

4. Each terroristic phenomenon has pecularities which make it incomparable.

5. The global diffusion of terrorism is caused by international conspiracies.

According to the author all of these hypotheses, except the fifth, could possibly form part of a tentative general interpretation of the significance of terrorism in the contemporary world. [27)]
Strange enough the last hypothesis is the one which is currently one of the most popular and influential ones in certain political circles - at least in the United States (see chapter 2.8.).

Wilkinson offers us five propositions about "terrorism in a revolutionary context", the first three are taken from B. Crozier while the last two are Wilkenson's own generalizations derived from comparative analysis of terrorist movements:

"1. Terrorism is generally "the weapon of the weak".

2. It is usually a useful auxiliary weapon rather than a decisive one.

3. Revolutionary terrorism seems to be a strategy most suited to national liberation struggles against foreign rulers used by relatively small conspiratorial movements lacking any power base.

4. Terrorism is highly unpredictable in its effects.

5. Terroristic violence can escalate until it is uncontrollable, with terrible results for society." [28)]

Such hypotheses and propositions constitute the basic wisdom in the field. As Bell points out the minds are divided on several of them and none is properly tested (if it is possible to test them). The originators probably all had certain specific cases in mind when proposing them and they might very well hold true for these cases. But these cases might just all be exceptions to the rule - if there is a rule or law.
Given the absence of a delimination of the concept of terrorism it is not amazing that theorizing is also showing deficiencies due to the fact that the instances op political violence subsumed under the label terrorism vary.

Notes

1) 28 authors received one mentioning, Laqueur and Arendt three,
Fromm, Wilkinson and Young two.

2) Study prepared by the U.N. Secretariat in accordance with the
decision taken by the Sixth Committee at its 1314th meeting on
27 September 1972, repr. in: M.Ch. Bassiouni. International
Terrorism and Political Crimes. Springfield, Illinois, Charles C.
Thomas, 1975, p.10.

3) J. Dollard, L.W. Miller, N.E. Mowrer, O.H. & R.R. Sears.
Frustration and Aggression. New Haven, Yale University Press,
1939, cit. J.M.G. v.d.Dennen. Problems in the Concepts and
Definitions of Aggression, Violence and some Related Terms.
Groningen, Polemolgical Institute, 1981, p.21.

4) Ted Robert Gurr. op.cit., 1970, p.21.

5) Ibid., p.3-4.

6) Ibid., p.23, Emphasis added, AS.

7) Ibid., p.11.

8) Ibid., pp.212-221.

9) See pp.23-45, in M. Stohl (Ed.). The Politics of Terrorism. New York,
M. Dekker, 1979.

10) cit. M. Stohl. War and Domestic Political Violence. The American
Capacity for Repression and Reaction. Beverly Hills, Sage, 1976, p.32.

11) J.M.G. v.d.Dennen. Problems in the Concepts and Definitions of
Aggression, Violence and some Related Terms. Groningen, PI, 1980, p.21,
basing himself on R.J. Rummel. Conflict in Perspective. Understanding
Conflict and War, Vol.3, Beverly Hills, Sage, 1977. Also see
Richard de Ridder. De Frustratie Voorbij. Psychologie, September 1981,
pp.23-30, for a critique of the Frustration-Aggression Model.

12) Lawrence C. Hamilton. Ecology of Terrorism: A Historical and
Statistical Study. Boulder, University of Colorado, 1978 (PhD Thesis),
pp.91-92.

13) P. Wilkinson. Terrorism and the Liberal State. London, Macmillan,
1977, p.96.

14) L.C. Hamilton, op. cit., pp. 187-188.

15) Ibid., pp.70-71.

16) Ibid., p.76.

Notes

17) Ibid., pp.78-79.

18) Ibid., p.79 and 84.

19) Ibid., p.86,89.

20) Ibid., p.180.

21) Ibid., p.62.

22) Ted Robert Gurr. Some Characteristics of Political Terrorism in
the 1960s. In: M. Stohl (Ed.). The Politics of Terrorism.
New York, Dekker, 1979, pp.24-25.

23) Ibid., p.24.

24) J.B. Bell. A Time of Terror. How Democratic Societies Respond to
Revolutionary Violence. New York, Basic Books, 1978, pp.95-104.

25) W. Laqueur. The Futility of Terrorism (1976). Repr. in J.D. Elliott
& L.K. Gibson (Eds.). Contemporary Terrorism, Selected Readings.
Gaithersburg, Md., IACP, 1978, pp.287-290.

26) Michael Stohl. Myths and Realities of Political Terrorism.
In: M. Stohl (Ed.). The Politics of Terrorism. New York,
Marcel Dekker, Inc., 1979, p.2.

27) L. Bonanate. Dimensioni del terrorismo politico. In: L. Bonante (Ed.).
Dimensioni del Terrorismo Politico. Aspetti interni e internazionali,
politici e giuridici. Milano, Franco Angeli, Editore, 1979,
pp.169-175.

28) P. Wilkinson. Political Terrorism. London, Macmillan, 1974, p.126.

Theories of Regime Terrorism

Terrorism by regimes has a longer history than insurgent terrorism
and from this one could expect that theory formation is more advanced
and that the number of available theories is greater. But that is not
so. Except for the writings on Totalitarianism, there is not much to
fall back on. Totalitarian states, which have been characterized by
the presence of a leader, the subversion of the rule of law, the control
of the private sphere, the permanent mobilization of the population and
the legitimation through massive popular support, rule not only through
terrorism exercised by the state apparatus but also through the party
and the official ideology. [1] The link between totalitarian rule and
terrorism is in all likelyhood much weaker than portrayed by
Hannah Arendt, who wrote:

> "The extraordinary bloody terror during the initial stage of
> totalitarian rule serves indeed the exclusive purpose of defeating
> the opponent and rendering all further opposition impossible; but
> total terror is launched only after this initial stage has been
> overcome and the regime no longer has anything to fear from the
> opposition. In this context it has been frequently remarked that
> in such a case the means have become the end, but this is after
> all only an admission, in paradoxical disguise, that the category
> "the end justifies the means" no longer applies that terror
> has lost its "purpose", that it is no longer the means to frighten
> people." [2]

Arendt, together with Walter and Aron, was one of the authors mentioned
more than once in response to our question "Which of the current
theories explaining the rise of (various types of) state terrorism
do you find worthwhile to be subjected to empirical testing?"
More than half of the respondents either left this question unanswered,
answered "none" or said they did not know. [3]
In the following pages we will briefly present the work of Walter,
leaving aside Arendt and Aron. In addition we will point to the studies
of Dallin and Breslauer, De Swaan and Duval and Stoll.
Eugene V. Walter's Terror and Resistance (New York, Oxford University
Press, 1969) is an exceptionally original study based on empirical
case studies of some tribal African communities. The author attempts
to find out why rulers who already have authority nevertheless choose
to rule by violence and fear. Unlike some of the authors on totalitarianism he is not identifying organized terror with systems of total
power, which, given Walter's 19th century data on successive Zulu

rulers, is a fallacy easier to avoid than would haven been the case
with 20th century subjects. While Walter claimed that his "inquiry
is the first systematic effort to develop a general theory of
terrorism" [4] he admitted that his explanations do not cover every
typical regime of terror."...revolutionary governments and totalitarian
systems, for example, introduce factors that are beyond the scope of
the first volume" [5]. Unfortunately Walter never published - at least
to our knowledge - the second volume in which he wanted to "pursue
the analysis in other social conditions and explore the intellectual
history of the idea of terror as well as its psychodynamics."
Walter's book was a pioneering effort, given that, as he put it,
"Rule by terror, a familiar process in history, has virtually escaped
systematic analysis" [6]. As such, the conclusions he reached about the
conditions necessary for the maintenance of a terroristic regime,
which he also saw as functional prerequisites for a regime of terror,
may not strike the reader as very far-reaching. But the conditions
he lists as necessary for a rule by terror at least show some inter-
dependence which other propositions of terrorism lack. They are:

> "1. A shared ideology that justifies the violence.
>
> 2. The victims in the process of terror must be expendable -
>   that is, their loss cannot affect the system of co-operation.
>
> 3. Dissociation of the agents of violence and of the victims
>   from ordinary social life.
>
> 4. Terror must be balanced by working incentives that induce
>   co-operation.
>
> 5. Co-operative relationships must survive the effect of the
>   terror. [7]

Seeing terrorism as a "social invention and a political choice within
a range of alternatives" by which a regime may overcome the threat
of resistance and secure co-operation [8]. Walter's study in
fact offers a wealth of insights and is probably the most detached
book ever written on Terrorism.

Almost simultaneously as Walter's work A. Dallin and G.W. Breslauer's
Political Terror in Communist Systems (Stanford, Stanford University
Press, 1970) was published. They studied, among other things, the Red
Terror of the Civil War period 1918-1920 and the Great Terror of the
purges in Russia. They use the term terror broader than Walter. For
Walter all terror is violence designed to control while for Dallin

and Breslauer terror does not necessarily include violence but can consist of intimidation only. They see political terror as a coercive instrument to effect political control. In their view there are three systems of sanctions: (1) "normative power", or "positive" or "symbolic power", commonly called persuasion and including socialization, education, and the offer of prestige, recognition, or love; (2) "material power", or "technical" or "utilitarian power", commonly called incentives and including such forms as wages, rewards, bonuses, bribes, and promotions, and (3) "coercive power", or "negative" or "physical power", commonly called coercion, and including such forms as fines, penalties, terror and regulatory and police power. [9] In their study they try to find an answer to the question when (communist) government resorts to terror. They postulate that a communist party which comes to power by revolution usually lacks the normative and material resources to ensure obedience from the citizens and to satisfy the followers. The turmoil of revolution has diminished the country's material output and the revolutionary ideology as a normative control instrument has yet to be implanted in the masses. With the limited availability of material and normative incentives the resort to coercion in general and terror in particular in order to eliminate or neutralize resistance becomes mandatory for the survival of the regime. Terror is in fact a sign of weakness of the regime, as can also be deducted from a remark such as the one of Dzerzhinski the head of the Checka, who was quoted as saying that "the proletariat takes up this weapon (of terror) only when it cannot do without it". [10]

The variations in the amount of terror exercised by communist regimes after the seizure of power is explained by Dallin and Breslauer with a reference to the pre-takeover conditions:

> "If, on the other hand, prior to the takeover of the central
> government the revolutionary movement is successful in gaining
> a fair measure of popular support, in penetrating the administrative-
> organizational system of the country, and in gaining the upper hand
> over alternative organizations and authorities - whether by guerrilla
> warfare against domestic or foreign enemies (China, Yugoslavia,
> Albania) or by administrative manipulation, through front
> organizations, party and police operations, or other backstage
> moves (Czechoslovakia Hungary) - then there is correspondingly
> less "need" for terror (and no civil war) after the takeover of
> the central government. The equivalent function of terror at this
> stage will have been substantially fulfilled prior to takeover." [11]

The study of Dalling and Breslauer does, however, not manage to explain
the Great Terror of the period 1936-1939 in which about seven million
Russians were said to have been arrested, including half the officers'
corps of the Red Army and in which more than two thirds of the members
of the Central Committee as well as countless others were liquidated. [12]
Yet the authors had to start almost from scratch in their investigation.
"We soon discovered", they wrote in their preface, "to our surprise,
that the theoretical literature on political terror was not nearly so
well developed as we had expected ..." [13]
Given the ubiquity of rule by terror the uneven attention given to
regime terrorism in contrast to insurgent terrorism by social scientists
is depressing. The fact that anti-communists write on terrorism in
communist regimes and leftish authors about terrorism in capitalist
societies produces some distortions such as the near-automatic linking
of socio-economic system to state terrorist practices. While Dallin and
Breslauer are aware of this danger and Walter is, due to his subject of
inquiry removed from it, much of the literature on totalitarianism is
poisoned by it. One of the studies which is not is Abram de Swaan's
Terror as a Government Service [14], which, however, is only a short,
although highly interesting theoretical sketch of regimes of terror.
De Swaan sees torture as a linchpin of such regimes. He observes:

> "... wherever torture is being practiced on a large scale and
> over a period of time, the external effects of the system turn
> out to be foremost: to spread an ever-present fear, of arrest, of
> ill-treatment, of mutilation, of betrayal, of death. The purpose
> of all this is that people will ask themselves with every action
> whether their deeds do not create risks for themselves and for
> the people around them, that they will not just abstain from what
> is forbidden, but will avoid whatever has not expressly been
> allowed. They really most continuously try to imagine what the
> rulers would want them to do, they must become vicarious rulers
> for themselves. Only then the completion of the terrorist regime
> has been achieved." [15]

De Swaan goes on noting that every regime of intimidation and deterrence
entails two fundamental contradictions: (1) the contradiction between
publicity and secrecy in the practices of intimidation and, (2) the
contradiction between predictability and uncertainty as to prosecution
and punishment.

With regard to the first contradiction De Swaan notes:

"This twilight-zone is the essential mark of terrorist regimes.
This must be so, because, if the existence and manner of operation
of the terror apparatus were the subject of public debate, then
the citizens would inevitably try the terrorist practices against
the confessed ideals of the regime. But if the methods would remain
completely unknown, then they would not achieve their intimidating
effects. Thus, the system of terror works through a steady system
of rumours, through private conversations and personal networks.
This has been conceived of as the devilish shrewdness of the
set-up: whoever mentions it, himself thereby collaborates with
the reign of terror." 16)

It is this internal contradiction, incidentally, which lies at the

basis of the success of Amnesty International.

On the second contradiction, de Swaan remarks:

"If everyone would know (for certain) what acts would lead to
arrest and torture and which would go unpunished, most people
would refrain from the first and without worrying, commit the
others. But the purpose of an intimidation apparatus is precisely
to impose so much fear in people that of their own account they
will abstain from things that otherwise would be hard for the
regime to detect or prevent. Not even a police state can always
keep under surveillance all people in all their doings. And
because the regime cannot enforce its own commands and prohibitions,
fully or even partially, it must create a negative game of chance,
which leaves it to the citizens to avoid the risks. Herein lies
the unavoidability of a system of prosecution and correction to
be unpredictable. (...) In terrorist regimes the unpredictability
concerns what may or may not be punished and in the often extreme
severity of punishment. Yet, this uncertainty cannot be without
limits: if nobody knows anymore what will lead to arrest or
ill-treatment, anxious abiding would lose all sense, subjects would
become careless or even daring. The point is, therefore, to present
the citizens with just enough indications to make them ask themselves
continuously what the intentions of the regime are, just enough
cues to reconstruct for themselves the desires of the rulers." 17)

This ambivalence has been addressed to as well by the Russian writer

Ilya Ehrenburg who wrote about Stalin's terror of the Thirties, "The

fate of men was not like a game of chess, but like a lottery." 18)

The last theory we would like to mention has been developed by R. Duvall

and M. Stohl 19). They look beyond the totalitarian state and attempt

to find a theory that fits state terrrorism in the First World (the

developed capitalist states), the Second World (the Socialist countries)

as well as the Third World (the Developing countries). To fit the

tremendous variations in extent, scope and targeting in these three

different settings (see Table IX), they had to find a very general

Table IX: Major Aspects of Contextual Variation in State Terrorism, According to Duvall and Stohl 20).

Context:	State Terrorism Used	Social Scope of State Terrorism	Characteristics of Target Population
First World	Some, but generally little.	Very limited.	Socially isolated groups, distrusted by the general population.
Second World	Previously extremely high; now relatively little.	Previously pervasive; now quite limited.	Previously non-revolutionary classes, and members of revolutionary party; now dissident intelligentsia.
Third World	Quite variable, but very high in many societies.	Pervasive where it occurs extensively.	Potential political oppositon in general, especially "the left" as amorphous category.

model of explanation. They found it in the "Expectancy X Value" [21] theory

of motivation, which uses an "expected utility" model. They write:

> "The principal feature of this type of model is the assumption
> that an actor behaves in accordance with a basic rule which
> consists of three main elements: (1) the benefits, personally
> defined, that the actor would get from some desired state of
> affairs; (2) the actor's belief about the probability with
> which the desired state of affairs would be brought about if
> the actor were to engage in a particular action; and (3) the
> actor's belief about the probable costs, or negative consequences,
> that it would have to bear as a result of its engaging in that
> action.
> A concept of expected reward, or expected utility, is defined from
> these three elements. It is $U_i = p_i B - C_i$, where U_i is expected
> utility from engaging in action i, B is the benefit gotten from
> the desired state of affairs, p_i is the believed probability with
> which action i will bring about the desired state of affairs,
> and C_i is the believed probably costs from engaging in action i.
> In its conventional form, the rule of behaviour is that an actor
> engages in that action i, for which U_i is greatest among the set
> of variables. [22]

Readapting this rule they hold that the probability that an actor will

engage in an action i, increases monotonically with increases in U_i

relative to U_j, where j are all alternative actions, including

inaction. On the basis of this they set out to determine the preconditions

or factors p_t, C_t, p_j and C_j which explain or predict the recourse to

state terrorism if the model is realistic. From this they derive the

following principle for a theory of state terrorism:

> "If terrorism is to be believed to be a relatively more effective
> means of governance, then, the government must estimate that
> terrorism will perform better than alternative means in eliminating
> or quieting some actual or perceived potential challenge or threat." [23]

Duvall and Stohl find that their model is able not only to explain why

weak governments engage in terrorism (for this the Dallin and Breslauer

explanation for the Red Terror of the period 1918-1920 is also a

satisfactory explanation), but they also managed to solve the seeming

paradox why a strong regime in a situation of confident strength, can

also find it attractive to engage in terrorism.

The thrust of their explanation for the "weak" state terrorist lies

in the believed _relative_ effectiveness of terrorism which depends less

on the preception of terror as highly efficacious but in the belief

that other available means of rule are quite _inefficacious_. [24]

Strong states, on the other hand, are likely to engage in terrorism.
according to Duvall and Stohl, when they are reclusive states with a
low vulnerability to international pressure and domestic retribution
or when they show features of either a militaristic-state or an
ideological-mission syndrome. They write:

> "This is the syndrome of the policy with highly developed
> informational and organizational networks through which the
> regime penetrates society, and in which the government perceives
> itself in actual or potential conflict with some socially marginal
> group that is poorly integrated into ... the rest of society.
> In this syndrome, one would expect state terror to be limited
> in scope and generally of fairly low intensity - sufficient only
> to "win" the conflict with the marginal social group. At the same
> time, one would expect terror in this situation to be used more
> regularly, and perhaps with greater intensity, by governments who
> have learned its utility for rule through past experience." 25)

The model which these authors sketch in which the expected relative
effectiveness, the expected costs of producing terrorism and the
expected response costs to terrorism are key variables, can in principle
also be applied to explanations of insurgent terrorism, as Duvall and
Stohl point out. 26)

That is, if terrorism remains a rational strategy with predictable
results. As to the latter it is perhaps worthwhile recalling that
Stalin in effect admitted later that the Great Terror exceeded in
scope what he had planned. 27)

This brings us to the question whether the terrrorist themselves
have a theory.

Notes

1) L. Shapiro. Totalitarianism. London, 1972, cit. B. Tromp.
   Theorie en totalitarianisme. Amsterdam Sociologisch Tijdschrift,
   6 Jg., No.2, 1979, p.333.

2) Hannah Arendt. The Origins of Totalitarianism. New York, Harcourt,
   Brace, Jovanovich, 1973, p.440.

3) Other authors mentioned only once (the three mentioned in the text
   were listed twice) were: Rubinstein (The Cunning of History), Young
   (A Theory of Underground Structures), Hess (Repressives Verbrechen),
   Taylor (Beating the Terrorists), Dallin and Breslauer (Political
   Terror in Communist Systems) and Friedrich & Brzezinski (Totalitarian
   Dictatorship and Democracy).

4) E.V. Walter. Terror and Resistance. New York, Oxford, University
   Press, 1969, p. vii.

5) Ibid., p.viii.

6) Ibid., p.3.

7) Ibid., pp.341-434.

8) Ibid., pp.340-343.

9) A. Dallin and G.W. Breslauer. Political Terror in Communist Systems.
   Stanford, Stanford University Press, 1970, p.2.

10) Cit. ibid., p.22n.

11) Ibid., p.17.

12) Ibid., p.29.

13) Ibid., p.ix.

14) In: M. Hoefnagels (Ed.). Repression and Repressive Violence. Amsterdam,
    Swets and Zeitlinger, 1977.

15) Ibid., p.44.

16) Ibid., pp.44-45.

17) Ibid., p.45.

18) Cit. Dallin and Breslauer, op.cit., p.56.

19) Raymond D. Duvall and Michael Stohl. Governance by Terror. Chapter Six
    in: The Politics of Terrorism. Ed. by M. Stohl. New York, Dekker, 1983
    - The quotes here are from the draft manuscript.

20) Ibid., p.34 (Table I)

Notes

21) Ibid., p.34.

22) Ibid., pp.36-37.

23) Ibid., p.38.

24) Ibid., p.39, emphasis in text of authors.

25) Ibid., pp.43-44.

26) Ibid., p.49.

27) Dallin and Breslauer, op.cit., p.40.

Terrorist Theories of Terrorism

Brian Jenkins has written in his article "International Terrorism: A
New Mode of Conflict": "There is a theory of terrorism, and it often
works" (...) Unless we try to think like terrorists we are liable
to miss the point...." But what this theory is Jenkins fails to make
explicit, unless we take the following chapter-head "The Purposes of
Terror" as explaining the "theory". But the point Jenkins makes, is
well-taken. The acts of violence are not standing for themselves but
form part of a strategy, however rudimentary. Take for instance
this statement of a student involved in the occupation of the U.S.
Embassy in Tehran in November 1979. The U.S. Marines guarding the
embassy did not use their weapons when the storming took place,
something which the students could not know for sure beforehand. About
the gamble they took, one of the commented: "If the Marines don't shoot,
we take over. If they do, we have our martyr. Either way, we win."
This statement is reminiscent of a dictum of the Russian terrorist
Stepniak: "The terrorist is beautiful, terrible and irresistably
fascinating because he reunites two types of human grandeur: the martyr
and the hero." [2]
One of the commanders of the so-called "Stern gang" which fought
the British in Palestine in the 1940s wrote:

> "A man who goes forth to kill another whom he does not know must
> believe only one thing- that by his act he will change the course
> of history." [3]

The Russian terrorists of the late 1870s and thereafter were the first
to develop a "theory" of terrorism. In the party program of the
Narodnaya Volya ("The People's Will") of 1879 the terrorist strategy
was outlined in this manner:

> "Terroristic activity, consisting in destroying the most harmful
> person in the government, in defending the party against espionage,
> in punishing the perpetrators of the notable cases of violence and
> arbitrariness on the part of the government and the administration,
> aims to undermine the prestige of the government's power, to
> demonstrate steadily the possibility of struggle against the
> government, to arouse in this manner the revolutionary spirit of
> the people and their confidence in the success of the cause, and
> finally, to give shape and direction to the forces fit and trained
> to carry on the fight." [4]

In the following year. Nicholas Morozov, a theorist of Narodnaya Volya,
published a "theory" of terrorism, wherein he stated:

"... terroristic struggle has exactly this advantage that it can
act unexpectedly and find means and ways which no one anticipates.
All that the terroristic struggle really needs is a small number
of people and large material means. This presents really a new
form of struggle. It replaces by a series of individual political
assassinations, which always hit their target, the massive
revolutionary movements, where people often rise against each
other because of misunderstanding and where a nation kills off
its own children, while the enemy of the people watches from a
secure shelter and sees to it that the people of the organization
are destroyed. The movement punishes only those who are really
responsible for the evil deed. Because of this the terroristic
revolution is the only just form of revolution. At the same time
it is also the most convenient form of revolution. Using insignificant
forces it had an opportunity to restrain all the efforts of
tyranny which seem to be undefeated up to this time. "Do not be
afraid of the Tsar, do not be afraid of despotic rulers, because
all of them are weak and helpless aginst secret, sudden assassination,"
it says to mankind. Never before in history were there such
convenient conditions for the existence of a revolutionary party
and for such successful methods of struggle." [5)]

Stepniak, another theorist of the Russian Underground, writing more
than a decade later, made less exaggerated claims for the new method
of combat, but nevertheless, saw it as an effective asymmetric strategy:

"In a struggle against an invisible, impalpable, omnipresent enemy,
the strong is vanquished not by arms of his own kind, but by the
continuous exhaustion of his own strength, which ultimately exhausts
him, more than he would be exhausted by defeat.... The terrorists
cannot overthrow the government, cannot drive it from St. Petersburg
and Russia; but having compelled it, for many years running, to
neglect everything and to do nothing but struggle with them...
they will render its position untenable." [6)]

While in Tsarist Russia power was concentrated in a few hands, the
diffusion of authority in West European and American societies probably
also led to a widening of the potential targets of terroristic violence.

The vanishing of discrimination in target selection becomes even more
pronounced in cases of state terrorism. Martin Latsis, a leading
Cheka official, reflects this in a statement like this:

> "Do not seek in your accusations proof whether the prisoner has
> rebelled against the soviets with guns or by word. You must ask
> him, first, what class he belongs to, what his social origin is,
> what his education was, and his profession. The answer must
> determine the fate of the accused. That is the meaning of
> Red Terror." 7)

To hold individuals responsible for the deeds of their group or class
without looking at personal involvement of the target of terroristic
violence leads to vicarious intimidation if the "punishment" metted
out against one or a few becomes known.

In a sense, the use of torture by governments also serves the same
function. While torture is connived in or defended mostly as
"a minor intensification of interrogation practices" 8) its latent
meaning often becomes the frightening and intimidation of the population
or certain sections thereof.

Amnesty International has collected many examples of evidence which
show that torture is consciously used to inculcate a climate of fear
in order to discourage dissent. One Amnesty International report writes:

> "For those who govern without the consent of the governed this
> [torture] has proved to be an effective means of maintaining
> power. To set torture as the price of dissent is to be assured
> that only a small minority will act. With the majority neutralized
> by fear, the well-equipped forces of repression can concentrate
> on an isolated minority."

The Amnesty report on torture makes reference to a victim of the
Greek Colonel's interrogators who told his victim that he should tell
people he was being tortured so that "all who entered military police
quarters would tremble." 9)

This element of meting out cruel treatment against one to produce
reverberations with others we find both in state terrorism and insurgent
terrorism. An example from the other side would be the hanging of two
British soldiers from a tree by the terrorists from Irgun, which was
demoralizing for all British soldiers in Palestine. Menachem Begin,
the Irgun leader, later commented on the effects of such needlepoint
attacks: "In the end, the nervous system of the British resembled
an old broken piano. It was sufficient to attack one camp to make all
others resound from fear, day and night." 10)

After another attack on the King David Hotel, which was blown up by
explosives smuggled into the British headquarter in milk cans, the
mere sight of a milk can could evoke suspicion and fear. [11)]
The same kind of tactics - perhaps a shade more indiscriminate - the
British also encountered in Cyprus where General Grivas started the
struggle for independence with a small group of insurgents. He
defended the primarily terroristic form of struggle in these words:

> "The truth is that our form of war, in which a few hundred fell
> in four years, was more selective than most, and I speak as one
> who has seen battlefields covered with dead. We did not strike,
> like the bomber, at random. We shot only British servicemen who
> would have killed us, if they could have fired first, and civilians
> who were traitors or intelligence agents. To shoot down your
> enemies in the street may be unprecedented, but I was looking for
> results, not precedents. How did Napoleon win his victories?
> He took his opponents in the flank or rear; and what is right
> on the grand scale is not wrong when the scale is reduced and
> the odds against you are a hundred to one." [12)]

With such strategy - which incidentally was less discriminating than
this apologetic passage makes the reader believe - the few hundred
EOKA fighters managed to tie down 30.000 British troops for four and
a half years, producing 600 killed and 1300 wounded on both sides
before independence from Britain was achieved. The second terrorist
campaign of the EOKA-B in the early 1970s - this time for enosis,
union of the island with Greece, badly backfired, producing 280.000
Cypriote refugees when the Turkish army intervened. [13)]
The practice of urban guerrilla warfare in Latin America also showed
increasingly elements of terrorism. While Ché Guevara had rejected
terrorism in all but his Bolivian writings, because he believed
that "terrorism is of negative value, that it by no means produces
the desired effects, that it can bring a loss of lives to its agents
out of proportion to what it produces," [14)]
Carlos Marighela, the Brazilian communist, thought differently. In
his Mini-Manual he states:

> "There are two main ways in which revolutionary organizations
> can grow. One is through propaganda and ideology - by convincing
> people and arguing over documents and programmes. (...) The other
> way... is not through proselytism but by unleashing revolutionary
> action, and calling for extreme violence and radical solutions. (...)
> Since our way is through violence, radicalism and terrorism (the only
> effective weapons against the dictators' violence), anyone joining
> our organization will not be deluded as to its real nature and
> will join because he has himself chosen violence. (...).

The basic principle of revolutionary strategy in a context of
permanent political crisis is to unleash, in urban and rural
areas, a volume of revolutionary activity which will oblige the
enemy to transform the country's political situation into a
military one. The discontent will spread to all social groups
and the military will be held exclusively responsible for
failures. (...)
When we use revolutionary terrorism we know that such activities
alone will not win us power. All acts of revolutionary terrorism,
punishment of spies or sabotage are tactical operations designed
to demoralize the authorities and North American imperialism,
reduce its capacity for repression, break its communication system,
and damage the government, supporter of latifúndio property.
Revolutionary terrorist acts and sabotage are not designed to
kill members of the common people, or upset or intimidate them
in any way. The tactic of revolutionary terrorism and sabotage
must be used to combat the terrorism used by the dictatorship
against the Brazilian people." 15)

The allegation that the terrorist acts were not meant to upset or

intimidate the common people, made by Marighela was hypocritical since

his strategy depended on the state reaction against common people.

He admits this in so many words in another passage: "The government

has no alternative except to intensify repression... (...) ... the

problems in the lives of people become truly catastrophic. (...) In

their vain attempt to prevent revolutionary activity through violent

laws, the enemy has become more cruel than ever, using police terror

indistinguishable from that used by the Nazis.... In such a climate

our revolution is gaining ground." 16)

The counter-terrorism of the government in this way become an

instrumental part of the terrorist strategy.

This dual function of terrorism - propaganda for the masses on the one

hand - and repression, or extra repression of the masses by the

adversary to force the masses to become participants - on the other,

we also find by the numerous imitators of the Latin American urban

guerillas. The West German Red Army Faction's theorist Horst Mahler

later admitted:

"The strategy of the terrorist nuclei was aimed at provoking
the overreaction of the state in the hope to stir the flames
of hate against the state and to channel new recruits into
the armed underground." 17)

The weaknesses of such a strategy in a non-colonial context are

evident: the overreaction of the state and the siding of the masses

with the terrorists are taken for granted. Overreaction can in fact crush the terrorist movement whether or not the masses side with the terrorists. Alternatively the government might make some concessions which satisfy the masses though not the terrorists and effectively separate the one from the other. The historical evidence does not seem to bear out the simplistic theory of Marighela, the Tupamaros and their imitators.

Trying to make a revolution with a bad theory or an outdated, or inapplicable blueprint to bring about social change is not the exclusive privilege or urban terrorists in non-colonial or industrialized societies. Chalmer Johnson has offered the suggestion that each age has its own "revolutionary paradigm" [18]. In his view the Chinese model of the "People's War" was such a new paradigm. In the Latin American context the Cuban experience produced the "foquismo" paradigm. Like the Chinese style guerrilla war it was primarily a rural model. But in contrast to it "foquismo" did not postulate a liberated territory from which action against the powerholder was to be conducted.

Urban guerrilla warfare evolved from the "foco" concept. The Guevarra experience had shown that it was more difficult to mobilize the Latin American campesinos than the Chinese peasants. The urban surrounding, on the other hand was much more familiar to the middle class revolutionaries and the growth of urbanization with a dissatisfied new proletariat, together with the proximity of the enemy in the urban centers, made the temptation to rely on a predominantly urban strategy of insurrection great. In a way it was a return to the classic insurrection strategy of the 19th century, at strategy which had failed in the Paris Commune. The increased fire-power of the urban guerrillas, together with the present communicational infrastructure and the anonymity of metropolitan life seemed to favour again this approach, the more so because the population density made the use of heavy weapons by the powerholder impracticable. At the same time the visibility of the armed actions of the insurgents is greatly increased in the cities. [19]

The urban scene imposed a number of rules on the armed men such as secrecy, structuring in small cells, hit and run operations which in effect separated them from the masses. Their contact with the population

was dependent to a large degree on the cooperation of the media. The
freedom of the press, however, was one of the first things to go in
the clash between the militants and the security forces. And with
censorship the watchdog function of the media on governmental actions
also ceased which allowed the powerholders to engage in repressive
crimes of a magnitude completely unexpected beforehand. Torture became
the order of the day and with the cell structure of the terrorist
underground far from being perfect it was relatively easy to produce
whole chain reactions of arrest following the capture of one of the
terrorists. All those suspected as potential or actual sympathizers
of the urban guerrilla had to endure governmental repression and
thousands of potential leaders from the trade unions, the universities,
the political parties were forced into exile. The masses did not rise
but either withdrew themselves into private life or went abroad.
Driven by paranoia, hate and despair the urban guerrilla often lost
sight of what they originally stood for. Abraham Guillén, one of the
fathers of the "urban guerilla" model, had heavy criticism for the
Tupamaros, saying that they were "perilously close to resembling a
political Mafia." [20] Referring to the killing of hostages he held:

> "In a country where the bourgeoisie has abolished the death
> penalty, it is self-defeating to condemn to death even the most
> hated enemies of the people. (...) The Tupamaros' "prisoners of
> the people" do more harm than benefit to the cause of national
> liberation. (...) Moreover, it is intolerable to keep anyone
> hostage for a long time. To achieve a political or propaganda
> victory through this kind of tactic, the ransom terms must be
> moderate and capable of being met; in no event should the
> guerrillas be pressed into executing a prisoner because their
> demands are excessive and accordingly rejected. A hostage may
> be usefully executed only when a government refuses to negotiate
> on any terms after popular pressure has been applied; for then
> it is evident to everyone that the government is ultimately
> responsible for the outcome." [21]

The question of responsibility. referred to in the above quotation,
is a central issue in the terrorist strategy. For some acts of
violence terrorists "claim" or "take" responsibilities and in other
cases they deny responsibility or shift responsibility to the
adversary. Take a statement like the following one from Leila Khaled,
the famous Arab skyjacker:

> "If we throw bombs, it it not our responsibility   You may care
> for the death of a child, but the whole world ignored the death
> of Palestinian children for 22 years. We are not responsible." [22]

The implication is that the apathy of the whole world is to be blamed
for their violent actions and that if the world redresses the just
grievances of the terrorists they will no longer have to face attacks
of this nature.

This transfer of responsibility to other parties which are only
indirectly or not at all involved in their conflict is a form of
blackmail. Where hostages are threatened with death and their survival
is made conditional upon the fulfillment of demands by a third
party, this party is placed before a no-win situation of either
capitulating to terrorist demands or becoming, through inaction, an
accomplice to murder.

Perhaps it was such a theory of compellance Brian Jenkins had in mind
when he wrote, as we quoted at the beginning of this chapter,
that: "There is a theory of terrorism, and it often works." At any
rate, if terrorists have a theory of blackmail, it might be worthwhile
to put some thinking into a "theory of whitemail", which would aim at
attacking their strategy rather than play the no-win role in their
strategy. 23)

- 189 -

Notes

1) In: D. Carlton & C. Schaerf (Eds). International Terrorism
and World Security. London, Croom Helm, 1975, p.15.

2) Cit. _Time_ (European Edition), 19 November 1979, p.23.

3) Cit. E.Hyams. Terrorists and Terrorism. London, J.M. Dent & Sons Ltd.,
1975, p.143.

4) Programma Ispolnitelnago Komiteta, cit. in: Encyclopaedia of the
Social Sciences, Vol.14, New York, Macmillan, 1936, p.578.

5) Nicolas Morozov. Terroristic Struggle. London, 1880. Repr. fully
in: Feliks Gross. Violence in Politics. Terror and Political
Assassination in Eastern Europe and Russia. The Hague, Mouton, 1972,
p.106. - Emphasis added, AS.

6) Stepniak. Underground Russia, New York, Scribner's Sonns, 1892,
cit. R. Moss. Urban Guerrilaas, 1972, p.39. - Emphasis added, AS

7) M. Latsis, "Zakony grazhdanskoi voiny ne pisany" cit. p.22n of
Dallin and Breslauer, 1970.

8) Abram de Swaan. Terror as a Government Service. In: M. Hoefnagels
(Ed.). Repression and Repressive Violence. Amsterdam, Swets and
Zeitlinger, 1977.

9) Cit. Carol Ackroyd, Karen Margolis, Jonathan Rosenhead, Tim Shallice.
The Technology of Political Control. Harmondsworth, Pelican, 1977,
pp.233-234.

10) M. Begin. La Révolt d'Israel. Paris, 1953, cit. R. Gaucher.
Les Terrorists, 1965, p.254.

11) Ibid., p.254.

12) The Memoirs of General Grivas. New York, Praeger, 1964, cit. Robert
Taber. The War of the Flea. Guerilla Warfare, Theory and Practice.
Frogmore, Paladin, 1974, p.106.

13) Albert Parry. Terrorism. From Robespierre to Arafat. New York,
Vanguard Press, 1976, pp.414-415.

14) Cit. Harold Jacobs (Ed.). Weatherman. San Francisco, Ramparts Press,
1970, p.438.

15) Carlos Marighela. For the Liberation of Brazil. Harmondsworth,
Penguin Books, 1971, pp.34-35, 46, 112.

16) Carlos Marighela. Mini-Manual of the Urban Guerilla. Repr. in:
Urban Guerrilla Warfare. Adelphi Papers No.79. Robert Moss.
London, International Institute for Strategic Studies, 1971, pp.40, 33-34.
- The wording in the Penguin edition (see note 15) is less sanguine.

Notes

17) Spiegel Gespräch. "Wir müssen raus aus den Schützengräben Bundesminister Gerhart Baum und Ex-Terrorist Horst Mahler über das Phenomen Terrorismus." Der Spiegel, Jg.33, No.53, 31 Dec. 1979, p.47.

18) Autopsy of People's War. Berkeley, University of California Press, 1973, cit. H.E. Price Jr. The Strategy and Tactics of Revolutionary Terrorism. Comparative Studies in Society and History, Vol.19, No.1, Jan. 1977, p.63.

19) J. Kohl & J. Litt (Eds.). Urban Guerrilla Warfare in Latin America. Cambridge, Mass., MIT Press, 1974, pp.15-19.

20) Donald C. Hodges (Ed.). Philosophy of the Urban Guerrilla. The Revolutionary Writings of Abraham Guillén. New York, Morrow, 1973, p.271.

21) Ibid., p.267.

22) Time, 2 Nov. 1970, cit. L. Sobel (Ed.). Political Terrorism. Vol.1, Oxford, Clio Press, 1975, p.3.

23) For some ideas, see H.J.N. Horsburgh. Moral Black- and Whitemail. Inquiry, Vol.18, No.1, Spring 1975, pp.23-38.

Psychological Theories

If it is assumed that nonviolent behaviour in society is normal, those
who engage in violence, criminal or other, are necessarily "abnormal",
deviating from the rules of society. An outflow of this assumption
are the many theories which regard the terrorist as a peculiar personality
with clearly identifiable character traits. An example of this approach
in the preventive field has been the construction of a behavioural
profile of the hijacker. This profile, developed by psychiatrists and
social scientist on behalf of the U.S. Federal Aviation Administration
is still classified. [1]

If we look at profiles which are not secret, they strike us by their
lack of details. Charles A. Russell and his associates, for instance,
have constructed such a profile on the basis of information on some
350 known terrorists from 18 different groups involving 11 nationalities.

> "Once can draw a general composite into which fit the great
> majority of those terrorists from the 18 urban guerrilla groups
> examined here. To this point, they have been largely single
> men aged 22 to 24, with exceptions as noted, who have some
> university education, if not a college degree. The women terrorists,
> except for the West German groups and an occasional leading figure
> in the IRA, JRA and PFLP, are preoccupied with support rather than
> operational roles. More often than not, these urban terrorists
> come from affluent, urban, middle-class families, many of whom
> enjoy considerable social prestige. Like their fathers, many of
> the older terrorists have been trained for the professions and
> may have practiced these occupations prior to their commitment
> to a terrorist life. Whether having turned to terrorism as a
> university student or later, most were provided an anarchistic or
> Marxist world view as well as recruited into terrorist operations
> while in the university. In the universities, these young products
> of an affluent society were confronted with and provided anarchistic
> or Marxist ideological underpinnings for their otherwise unstructured
> frustrations and idealism." [2]

While this is more a sociological than a psychological profile some of
the data assembled by Russell and Miller immediately raise fundamental
psychological issues. How, for instance, to explain the relatively
prominent role of women in insurgent left-wing terrorism compared to
the smaller share of women in violent crime in general? In case of the
German RAF and the June 2nd Movement the women constituted one-third
of the operational personnel. Nearly sixty percent of the known
terrorists at large from these movements were female in 1976. [3]
This high percentage has been explained as excesses of women's

liberation on the one hand and "excess of female (self) sacrifice" for a cause on the other. [4)]

An interesting profile has been offered by the sociologist I.L. Horowitz. Unlike the Russell/Miller profile it is not empirically based but takes the form of twelve propositions:

"1. A terrorist is a person engaged in politics who makes little if any distinction between strategy and tactics on one hand, and principles on the other. (...)

2. A terrorist is a person prepared to surrender his own life for a cause considered transcendent in value. (...)

3. A terrorist is a person who possesses both a self-fulfilling prophetic element and a self-destructive element. (...)

4. A terrorist is a person for whom all events are volatile and none are determined. (...)

5. A terrorist is a person who is (a) young; (b) most often of middle class family background; (c) usually male; and (d) economically marginal. (...)

6. A terrorist performs his duties as an avocation. (...)

7. The terrorist distinguishes himself from the casual homicide in several crucial respects: he murders systematically rather than at random; he is symbolic rather than passionate... and his actions are usually well planned rather than spontaneous. Terrorism is thus primarily a sociological phenomenon; whereas homicide can more easily be interpreted in psychological terms. (...)

8. The terrorist by definition is a person who does not distinguish between coercion and terrorism because he lacks access to the coercive mechanisms of the state.

9. A terrorist is a person who, through the act of violence, advertises and dramatizes a wider discontent. (...)

10. A terrorist believes that the act of violence will encourage the uncommitted public to withdraw support from a regime or institution, and hence make wider revolutionary acts possible by weakening the resolve of the opposition.

11. A terrorist may direct his activities against the leadership of the opposition by assassinating presidents and power holders... Other terrorists may direct their activities against the symbols of establishment and agencies... (...)

12. A terrorist does not have a particularly well-defined ideological persuasion." [5)]

These observations will not strike the reader as psychological in the narrow sense of the term. We will list a number of more directly psychological theories in the following enumeration which is rather summarily and only intents to indicate the main thrust of a theory.

"1. Inconsistent mothering plays a role in the making of a terrorist. (Jonas) 6)

2. Terrorists suffer from faulty vestibular functions of the middle ear, which correlates with a history of learning to walk late, dizzy spells, visual problems and general clumsiness. (Hubbard) 7)

3. Grave political violence can be found especially in those countries where fantasies of cleanliness are frequent. (Frank) 8)

4. Terrorists are zealots who seek aggressive confrontations with authority in the name of social justice. Zealotry is thereby defined as "low rule attunement, high social sensitivity and low self-awareness" and contrasted to moral realism and moral enthusiasm as the two other basic moral attitudes. (Hogan) 9)

5. The terrorists (in Quebec) generally reject the father and the values he represents, are impatient with the constitutional process and accepted morality, and combine an above-average intelligence with emotional immaturity. The affective qualities of them seem to be replaced by instincts - sexual lust, craving for notoriety and thirst for power. (Morf) 10)

6. Neither politics nor ideology make terrorists: the politics of sex are more influential in terrorism than the politics of Mao, Trotsky or Ho Chi Minh. It is just that the latter, as a rationalization, seems so much more respectable and the terrorist, above all, craves respect. (Cooper) 11)

7. Terrorism arises periodically when the persons who are predisposed to violent actions are stimulated more strongly than before. The contemporary epidemic of psychological disorders started in 1963 with the assassination of President Kennedy. Indicators of group unrest and violence as well as of mental disorders, drug addiction, criminality, etc. were rising before that time. Craze, délire, Wahn, rabbia), a cognitive disorder is noticeable in the ideas which motivate and dominate terrorism. An epidemic of terrorism occurs when increasing numbers of action groups are constituted and held together and when they are capable of executing series of operations. (Possony) 12)

8. Terrorists show three main character traits: (1) Their handling of their own emotions is disturbed, which shows itself in fear to engage in real commitments. The fear of love leads them to choose for violence. (2) Their attitude towards authority is disturbed, whereby a principally negative attitude towards the "old authorities" is combined with an uncritical subjection under the new counter-authorities. (3) A disturbed relationship with their own identity. Having failed to develop an identity of their own they try to get one by the use of violence. (Salewski) 13)

9. Terrorism is an urge to destroy oneself and others born out of radical despair, a new form of "disease unto death" which manifests itself by way of the inability to be part of the community, the loss of the capacity to understand reality and an aimlessness due to "methodological atheism". (Kasch) 14)

10. Terrorism might in part be due to a failure of the socialization process, especially resulting from a lack of felt authority or an anti-authoritarian education. Education has to restrain,

forbid and to suppress in order to adapt children to pro-social
behaviour. Education as it is presently practised often favours
the achievement of personal advantage which can result in
blindness towards the community. The failure is not only one
of the families but also of the universities and certain publishers
who spread anarchist literature in cheap editions. (Schwind) 15)

11. Characteristic for the terrorist is the need to pursue absolute
    ends. The meaning of the terrorist act is localized in the
    violence. (The victim of the act is a sacrifice, and the
    ultimate sacrifice is oneself.) The social matrix which produces
    this kind of behaviour is one in which alienation, a sense of helplessness
    and a general lack of purpose and personal worth are widespread. (Kaplan) 16)

12. The driving forces behind terrorism include these four:
    (1) the assertion of masculinity (or femininity in the case of
    women); (2) desire for depersonalization, that is, to get outside
    or away from oneself, as a result of chronic lack of self-esteem;
    (3) desire for intimacy; and (4) belief in the magic of violence
    and blood. (Harris) 17)

13. Terrorists tend to resemble each other, regardless of their
    cause. Most of them are individuals for whom terrorism provides
    profound personal satisfaction, a sense of fulfillment through
    total dedication, to the point of self-sacrifice; a sense of
    power through inflicting pain and death upon other human beings.
    (Berger) 18)

14. Almost always insecurity, risk-seeking behaviour and suicidal
    intentions linked to it are present in varying mixtures in the
    terrorist. Out of this insecurity, the need for self-realization
    and ego-inflation arises. Then interpersonal relations of
    terrorists are always disturbed, the result being an instrumental
    use of the fellow human being. This deficiency is compensated
    by the strong dedication to the idealistic cause he or she
    purports to fight for. (Mulder) 19)

The chief assumption underlying most of these "theories" is that the
terrorist is in one way or the other not normal and that the insights
from psychology and psychiatry are adequate keys to understanding.
Some terrorists are certainly psychotics but whether all criminal and
political terrorists also fall under this label is questionable.
Some authors see little prospect in the search for the terrorist
personality and question whether a profile analogous to the
"authoritarian personality" is possible at all. Walter Laqueur, for
instance, holds that the search for a "terrorist personality" is a
fruitless one [20], but a few pages earlier he notes that "Terrorists are
fanatics and fanaticism frequently makes for cruelty and sadism". [21]
Paul Wilkinson is also ambiguous. On the one hand he maintains that
"We already know enough about terrorist behaviour to discount the crude
hypothesis of a "terrorist personality" or "phenotype" [22] but at the
same time he admits that "I do not believe we really understand much

about the inner motivations of those who readily enunciated terrorist
techniques". [23]

It seems certain that with the relatively limited empirical evidence
presently available [24], caution should be observed to declare "the
terrorist" prematurely insane. There are, indeed, some intriguing pieces
of evidence to the contrary. Psychiatrists who examined the sole
surviving Japanese terrorist of the Lydda airport massacre certified
that Koza Okamoto, was absolutely sane and rational. [25]

An examination of some members of the German Rote Armee Fraktion by a
German psychiatrist led him to the conclusion that they were "intelligent",
"humorous", showing no symptoms of psychosis or neurosis and "no
particular personality type". [26]

The possible nonexistence of a "terrorist personality" does of course
not devaluate a psychological approach to the problem of terrorism.
It is a necessary complementary approach to a sociological one. Brian
Crozier has put it well when he said:

> "... men do not necessarily rebel merely because their conditions of
> life are intolerable: it takes a rebel to rebel. Look at it
> another way: some men or groups of men will tolerate more than
> others. If one describes conditions of life as intolerable, one
> begs the question: "To whom?". 27)

Materials for an Identification Theory of Insurgent Terrorism.

In the following pages we would like to offer some materials which in
the view of this writer (a layman in the field of psychology) provide
a psychological explanation for the choice of some individuals for
terrorism. The theoretical concept utilized is the one of
Identification. This term is used in social psychology to refer to
the more or less lasting influence one person can excert on the
behaviour of another. The term has a variety of meanings in the
literature.

For our purposes we take as point of departure a passage from
Karmela Liebknecht, who bases herself on the work of Weinreich:

> "Identification can mean at least two different things; a wish
> to become or remain like the other (individual or group), or a
> recognition of existing similarities, good or bad, between the
> self and the object of identification. In the first sense, the
> other (individual or group) represents highly valued qualities,
> and the issue is about the acquisition or preservation of these
> desired attributes. In the latter case, a person simply recognizes
> that the other (individual or group) shares the same desired or
> undesired qualities with his own experienced self.

Correspondingly, the contrast of the first instance would be a
negative identification, a desire to deviate as much as possible
from the other person or group, who has many undesireable features.
The contrast of the latter instance would denote only a recognition
of differences, or a lack of identification. The difference between
the two meanings of identification thus encompasses this difference between
how people perceive things to be as opposed to how they would like
them to be. The former meaning is an assessment of the present
state of affairs, while the latter is connected to future goals
and aspirations. Often enough these meanings tend, deliberately
or not, to be mixed with each other. (...)
In a definition of a person's overall identity both of these
meanings of identification have to be incorporated: "A person's
identity is defined as the totality of his self-construal, in
which how he construes himself in the present expresses the
continuity between how he construes himself as he was in the past
and as he aspires to be in the future." 28)

With this in mind we can return to the study of terrorism.

There the use of identification is generally confined to the
"identification with the aggressor " as manifesting itself in the
positive attitude some hostages show towards their captors, which has
also been referred to as "Stockholm syndrom". Yet other identification
processes are at work as well. The tremendous public interest in acts
of hostage taking seem to be due to the fact that most members of
the audience identify with the fate of the victim, share his sufferings
in an act of empathy. Yet not all members of an audience will automatically
show compassion for the victim . Some will identify with the terrorist,
because he represents for them the aweful power of one who can destroy
life at his whim. Especially if the victim is guilty in the eyes of the
spectator he may derive pleasure from humiliation and suffering.
Depending on the way the identification goes - with the victim or with
the inflictor of pain - the attitudinal outcome may be either empathy
or cruelty. The direction of the identification can be determined by
several factors but one or two key factors like class, race, nationality,
party can be decisive for the majority of the spectators.
We can illustrate this by a reference to the assassination of John F.
Kennedy and Martin Luther King and the public reaction to it. Hearing
that the (Democrat) Kennedy had been murdered in Dallas, 64 percent of
the Democrats in a sample said that they "felt as if the whole world
was caving in", while only 5 percent of the Republican voters in the
sample had the same feeling. The violent death of the Negro leader in
1968 led 96 percent of the black people in the sample to say that they

were "shocked, grieved, saddened or angry" while only 41 percent of
the White people in the sample felt the same. 59 percent of the
whites in the sample were indifferent or even had a feeling of
satisfaction, which applied to only 4 percent of the black people.
No less than 41 percent of the whites in the sample felt that King
himself was to blame for his own death (because he started riots,etc). [29)]
Such data indicate that a polarization is taking place in the audience,
depending on whether the identification is weak or strong with the
victim or perpetrator of violence. The media provide us daily with
polarizing acts which make us more or less consciously take sides
wherever conflict and violence along lines relevent to our own context
occurs. The "good guy - bad guy" dichotomy, the "in-group - out-group"
dichotomy and a number of similar cleavages play a role in this. How
strong our emotional reaction to such polarizing acts is, depends on
the psychological distance, the spatial distance and other factors
between event and one's own situation. Identification with the aggressor
can make us feel powerful vicariously, while identification with the
victim can make us feel weak or revengeful.

This process of taking sides whenever a polarizing act occurs, can stir
some members of the passive audience so deeply that they emerge as
actors of their own engaging in new polarizing acts. Leon Trotsky has
given us a description how in this way terrorists can be made:

> "Before it is elevated to the level of a method of political
> struggle terrorism makes its appearance in the form of individual
> acts of revenge. So it was in Russia, the classic land of terrorism.
> The flogging of political prisoners impelled Vera Zasulich to give
> expression to the general feeling of indignation by an assassination
> attempt on General Trepov. Her example was imitated in the circles
> of the revolutionary intelligentsia, who lacked any mass support.
> What began as an act of unthinking revenge was developed into an
> entire system in 1879-81. The outbreaks of anarchist assassination
> attempts in Western Europe and North America always come after some
> atrocity committed by the government - the shooting of strikers or
> executions of political opponents. The most important psychological
> source of terrorism is always the feeling of revenge in search of
> an outlet." 30)

The role vengeance based on identification with the victim can play in
the making of the terrorist has also been stressed by M. Crenshaw and,
with a reference to Fromm, by P. Wilkinson (what keeps them going after-
wards cannot be explained by revenge alone). [31)]

A few more examples will stress the role of revenge:

- The beating of two anarchists by the police and their subsequent
  sentencing induced Ravachol to avenge these "martyrs of Clichy"
  by bombing the homes of judges and magistrates in 1892. In
  court he declared: "It has been my intention to terrorize in
  order to force the present society to pay attention to those
  who suffer." 32)

- The execution of Ravachol made him a martyr and a cult developed
  which led to further revenge acts, including the assassination
  of the French president Sadi Carnot by the Italian anarchist,
  S. Caserio, who was also taking revenge for the execution of
  Emil Henry for throwing a bomb in the Café Terminus on Gare
  St. Lazare in Paris in 1894. 33)

- The unprovoked killing of a student demonstrator on June 2nd 1967
  by a policeman during a visit of the Shah of Iran in Berlin (for
  which the policeman was not punished) created revenge feelings
  in many participants and led to the naming of a group "2nd June
  Movement". Michael Baumann, for instance, the author of the book
  "How it all begun", sees in this episode a key experience which
  turned him into a terrorist. 34)

- Renato Curcio, the founder of the Italian Red Brigades, experienced
  his conversion to violence in all likelihood in reaction to the
  events of 2 December 1968 in Aola. Farm laborers held a procession
  and occupied the state highway leading to Siracusa. The police
  opened fire on them for 25 minutes, leaving two dead, many wounded,
  including some children. 35)

One of the most traumatic collective experiences crying for revenge in
recent times, was the slaughter of peasant people in Vietnam by the U.S.
war machine. Horst Mahler, the co-founder of the German RAF, noted
that the massacres in Vietnam and the passivity of the German government
vis-à-vis the atrocities committed by its ally, drove them to
resistance and revenge:

"It was our moralism which led us to terrorism. Many of us (in any
case Ulrike Meinhof and Gudrun Ensslin) came the same way. The
German nation again was passive. How could we escape from the...
society which once again mixed itself in a war: that of Vietnam?
We had nothing to identify with the West, so we identified with
the Third World. From that time on we identified with the Third
World. From that time on we no longer felt like Germans; we were
the fifth column of the Third World in Europe.... (...)
From now on we observed the simple antithesis: we were on this side,
the police were on the other. We did not see by which lines of
communication the people identified with the state." 36)

On another occasion Mahler said:

"He who also shows empathy with distant suffering will find
revolutionary promises more plausible and will easier become morally
exalted. The young life which is demotivated by a sense of the
absurd seeks in the commitment to a revolutionary movement - and be

it only as a Fifth Column of the militants in the Third World -
the salvation from nihilism and desperation. (...) If you think
of it, it is a terrible thing if you can not identify with your
own people. (...) However, "the heartbeat for the welfare of
humanity", to use Hegel's phrase, "turns into the fury of self-
conceit". These people have constructed their own - you might call
it private - moral. Since I was part of them I know it. The world
is bad, every day there is untold suffering, murder, killing. This
we have to change. This can only be done by violence, which also
causes victims; but all told it will cause fewer victims than
the continuation of the present state of affairs." 37)

The switch from love for mankind to destruction of human beings is
apparently facilitated by adolescents who find it difficult to identify
with their father or their nation. Mahler admitted that he was ashamed
of being a German at a very young age. 38) Arthur Koestler has offered
some useful insights for this context:

"The longing to belong left without appropriately mature outlets,
manifested itself mostly in primitive or perverted forms."

The act of identification which enables us to empathize with others is
also capable of leading to vicarious emotions, to anger and
aggressiveness towards the apparent source of misery of the person or
group we have love and compassion for.

Koestler added:

"The total identification of the individual with the group makes
him unselfish in more than one sense.... It makes him perform
comradly, altruistic, heroic actions - to the point of self-sacrifice -
and at the same time behave with ruthless cruelty towards the enemy
or victim of the group.... In other words, the self-assertive
behaviour of the group is based on the self-transcending behaviour
of its members, which often entails sacrifice of personal interests
and even of life in the interest of the group. To put it simply:
the egotism of the group feeds on the altruism of its members." 39)

These remarks written in a different context by Koestler, offer, in our
view, some insights into the dynamics of a terrorist movement. This
identification mechanism might also be helpful in explaining the high
percentage of women and intellectuals in insurgent terrorism. It might
be that women experience other people's suffering and humiliation stronger
than men, since they recognize it easier in their own existence due to
their being dominated in a male society. The sacrificial spirit which
women manifest vis-à-vis their children might reinforce this. As to
the intellectuals' role in revolutionary and terrorist movements - Lenin
called terrorism "a specific kind of struggle practised by the
intelligentsia". 40) - it might be that the middle or upper class terrorist
has become alienated from his class by the very university education

which his parents made possible. This leads him to search for a new
reference group. Unwilling to take up the cause of his own class he
chooses another class or group for which he wants to care and by which
he wants to be appreciated. His self-styled role as liberator of the
masses and leader of another class is, however, not always accepted
in gratitude by the people in need of "liberation". The experience
of Che Guevara in Bolivia is a case in point. In another case in
Istanbul members of the Turkish People's Liberation Army had kidnapped
a fourteen year old girl and were engaged in a shootout with the police.
One of the terrorists shouted to the watching crowd: "We are doing
this for you." The crowd, however, showed little sympathy and subsequently
attempted to lynch the single surviving terrorist. [41] That the crowd
identified with the victim and not with the terrorist in this particular
case was to be expected, given the age and sex of the victim.

The strategy of insurgent terrorism is to bring about identification
processes. The Brazilian urban guerrillas leader, Ladislas Dowbor,
elaborated on this theme. Speaking in 1970 he said that political
explanations did not create revolutionary consciousness of the
population, but military actions could do this. While discontent among
the population was widespread the people "have not yet reached the stage
of holding the system responsible". Terrorists therefore "attack the
targets they (the people) consciously identify", their visible enemies -
the farm overseer, or the shop foreman, or the landowner who throws
squatters off his land". This "provokes a reaction of the system....
(W)e provoke the army, the police, the press and the clergy into taking
positions against us and in support of the visible enemy. It is then
that the workers are able to identify the system as the enemy...." [42]

While the insurgent terrorist wants the people to identify with him
he also makes use of the identification mechanism to bring home the
terror to a target group by stimulating the identification between
the instrumental victim and the victims' reference group. In his
"Blueprint for Revolution", R.M. Momboisse has stressed the role this
identification process plays:

> "Thus if the victim is a peace officer or an occupying soldier,
> others belonging to that class will identify themselves as
> members of a marked group. This group will probably be both
> "terrorized" and subjected to disorientation effects." 43)

Identification, in this writers view, is a key mechanism in the process of terrorism. How identification operates in a variety of contexts, how it is utilized to generate support are questions that require attention.

The forgoing remarks should not be taken for more than they want to be, namely an invitation by a layman to psychologists to look closer at what might be a fertile area for theory building - more fertile, at any rate than the search for the "terrorist personality".

Notes

1) E.F. Mickolus. Transnational Terrorism. A Chronology of Events,
   1968-1979. London, Aldwych Press, 1980, p.xxxvii.

2) Charles A. Russell and Bowman H. Miller. Profile of a Terrorist.
   Military Review, Vol.58, No.8, Aug. 1977, p.33.

3) Ibid. p.25.

4) Susanne von Paczensky. Ohnmächtige Wut gegen Gewaltandrohung.
   In:Thesen zum Terrorismusproblem, in A. Jeschke & W. Malanowski
   (Eds.) Der Minister un der Terrorist. Reinbek, Rowohlt, 1980, p.128.
   cf. also: W. Jubelius. Frauen und Terror. Erklärungen, Scheiner-
   klärungen, Diffamierungen. Kriminalistik, June 1981, pp.247-255.

5) I.L. Horowitz. Political Terrorism and State Power. Journal of
   Political and Military Sociology, Vol.1, 1973, pp.147-157.

6) E.F. Mickolus. The Literature of Terrorism. Westport, Connecticut,
   Greenwood Press, 1980, p.361.

7) D. Hubbard and F.G. Harris. cit. Ibid., p.361.

8) R.S. Frank. The Prediction of Political Violence from Objective
   and Subjective Social Indicators. Edinburgh, IPSA Conference paper,
   1976, as quoted by Gerhard Schmidtchen. Bewaffnete Heilslehren,
   in: H. Geissler (Ed.). Der Weg in die Gewalt. München, Olzog, 1978,p.49.

9) R.T. Hogan, J.A. Johnson, N.P. Emler. A Socioanalystical Theory of
   Moral Development. New Directions for Child Development, 1978, No.2,
   pp.1-18.

10) Gustave Morf. Le terrorisme québeçois. Montreal, Editions de l'Homme,
    1970, as quoted by R. Moss. Urban Guerrillas, 1972, p.118.

11) H.H.A. Cooper. In Testimony Before the U.S. Senate on 21 July 1977,
    as quoted in L.A. Sobel. Political Terrorism. Vol.2, Oxford, Clio,
    1978, p.6.

12) Stefan T. Possony. Kaleidoscopic View on Terrorism. Terrorism: An
    International Journal, Vol.4, pp.90-93.

13) W. Salewski. Quoted in Zdenek Zofka. Denkbare Motive und mögliche
    Aktionsformen eines Nukleärterrorismus. Essen, AUGE, 1981, p.27.

14) Wilhelm Kasch. Quoted by Walter Laqueur, in: Foreword to R. Kupperman
    and D. Trent, Terrorism. Stanford, Hoover Institution Press, 1979,
    p.xvi; cf. also Wilhelm F. Kasch. Terror - Bestandteil einer
    Gesellschaft ohne Gott? In: H. Geissler (Ed.). Der Weg in die Gewalt.
    München, Olzog, 1978, pp.52-68.

Notes

15) Hans-Dieter Schwind. Meinungen zu den "Ursachen" des Terrorismus.
In: Hans-Dieter Schwind. Ursachen des Terrorismus in der Bundesrepublik
Deutschland. Berlin, Walter de Gruyter, 1978, pp.55-57.

16) Abraham Kaplan. The psycholdynamics of Terrorism. In: J. Alexander
and J.M. Gleason (Eds.). Behavioural and Quantitative Perspectives
on Terrorism, 1981, pp.41-50.

17) F. Gentry Harris. In: testimony before the U.S. Congress Committee
on Internal Security. (Letter transmitted to the House of Representatives
Hearings. Terrorism, Part 4, 93rd Congress, 2nd Session. Washington, D.C.,
GPO, 1974, p.4429, cit. M. Stohl. Myths and Realities of Political
Terrorism. Chapter one of the revised edition of The Politics of Terrorism.
New York, Marcel Dekker, 1983, as quoted from manuscript, p.12.

18) Peter L. Berger. Worldview, May 1976, cit. L.A. Sobel (Ed.). Political
Terrorism. Vol.2, Oxford, Clio, 1978, p.8.

19) D. Mulder. Terrorism. In: J. Bastiaans, D. Mulder, W.K. van Dijk,
H.M. v.d.Ploeg. Mensen bij Gijzelingen. Alphen aan de Rijn, Sijthoff,
1981, pp.124-126.

20) W. Laqueur. Terrorism. London, Weidefeld and Nicolson, 1977, p.129.

21) Ibid., p.125.

22) P. Wilkinson. Terrorism and the Liberal State, 1977, p.193.

23) Ibid., p.193.

24) F. Hacker. Crusaders, Criminals, Crazies: Terror and Terrorism in
Our Time. New York, W.W. Norton, 1976, p.105; J. Sundberg, in:
R.D. Crelinsten (Ed.) Research Strategies for the Study of
International Political Terrorism. Montreal, International Centre
for Comparative Criminology, 1977, p.177.

25) L. Paine. The Terrorists. London, Robert Hale & Co., 1975, p.142.

26) From the account on the proceedings of a conference on terrorism
held in Berlin in December 1978, Science, No.203, 5 January 1979,
p.34, as quoted in M. Crenshaw. The Causes of Terrorism. Comparative
Politics, July 1981, p.390.

27) B. Crozier. The Rebels. A Study of Post-war Insurrections. London,
Chatto & Windus, 1960, p.9.

28) Karmela Liebkind. The Social Psychology of Minority Identity. A Case
Study of Intergroup Identicication. Theoretical Refinement and
Methodological Experimentation. Helsinki, University of Helsinki,
Department of Social Psychology, 1979; P. Weinreich. Identity
Development: Extensions of Personal Construct Theory and Application
to Ethnic Identity Conflict and Redefinition of Gender Roles, 1979.

Notes

29) William J. Crotty (Ed.). Assassination and the Political Order.
New York, Harper and Row, 1971, pp.290-306.

30) Leon Trotsky. "On Terrorism". In: Der Kampf, Nov. 1911. Repr. in
L. Trotsky. Against Individual Terrorism. New York, Pathfinder
Press, 1974, p.8.

31) M. Crenshaw. The Causes of Terrorism.Comparative Politics. July 1981,
p.394; P. Wilkinson. Social Scientific Theory and Civil Violence.
In: Y. Alexander et al. Terrorism. Theory and Practice. Boulder,
1979, pp.67-68.

32) Cit. P. Wurth. La répression internationale du terrorisme. Lausanne,
Imprimerie la Concorde, 1941, p.18n.

33) M. Crenshaw, op.cit., p.394.

34) Cit. Z. Zofka. Denkbare Motive und mögliche Aktionsformen eines
Nukleärterrorismus.Essen, AUGE, 1981, p.30.

35) A. Silj. Never Again Without a Rifle. New York, Kurz, 1979, p.207.

36) Horst Mahler in interview with Luciana Catelina in the Italian
newspaper Il Manifesto, 1977; cit. W.H. Nagel. A Socio-Legal View
in the Suppression of Terrorism. International Journal of Sociology
of Law, Vol.8, 1980, pp.221-222.

37) Spiegel - Gespräch. "Wir müssen raus aus den Schützengräben".
Bundesminister Baum un Ex-Terrorist Horst Mahler über das
Phänomen Terrorismus. Der Spiegel, Jg.33, No.53, 31 Dec. 1979, p.37.

38) Ibid., p.14.

39) Arthur Koestler. The Ghost in the Machine. London, Hutchinson, 1967,
p.243 and p.251.
The fact that compassion on the one hand and cruelty on the other
can go hand in hand might seem paradox. Anatol Rapoport has suggested
in his book "Conflict in Man-made Environment" (Harmondsworth,
Penguin, 1974) that aggression and empathy are two side of the same
coin, being nearer to each other than either is to indifference.
The latter is a lack of identification while the former are positive
and negative identification with the object of suffering (Anatol
Rapoport. Confliction in sociale systemen. Utrecht, Het Spectrum,
1976, p.128). The fact that violence is done to human beings can be
rationalized away by the terrorist and those who identify with him
in several ways. Not for nothing terrorists have a need to justify
what they are doing. There are a variety of "neutralization techniques"
which terrorists can use to justify to themselves and to others that
they cannot be murderers whatever they do. Some of them are: (1) Denial
of the victim; (2) Denial of responsibility; (3) Comdemnation of the
condemner; (4) Appeal to higher loyalties; and (5) Denial of the
injury itself. (G.M. Sykes and D. Matza. Techniques of Neutralization:
A Theory of Delinquency. American Sociological Review, 22 Dec. 1957,
pp.664-670.

- 205 -

Notes

40) Cit. W. Laqueur. Terrorism. London, Weidenfeld and Nicholson,
    1977, p.66.

41) Robert Moss. Urban Guerrilla Warfare. London, International Institute
    for Strategic Studies, 1971 (Adelphi Papers No. 79), 1971, p.2.

42) In interview with Sanche de Gramont. New York Times Magazine,
    15 Nov. 1970; cit. L.A. Sobel. Political Terrorism., Vol.1, Oxford,
    Clio Press, 1975, pp.5-6.

43) R.M. Momboisse. Blueprint for Revolution. Springfield, Illinois,
    Charles C. Thomas, 1970; cit. in: E.A. Fattah. Terrorist Activities
    and Terrorist Targets. In: Y. Alexander and J.M. Gleason, op.cit.,
    p.24.

Terrorism as Surrogate Warfare

Many authors see terrorism as a form of war. In the 1960s terrorism
was generally placed into the context of internal war. Today terrorism
is often treated as a form of international war, or rather, as its
substitute. With the internationalization of national conflicts the
two often overlap. Col. Roger Trinquier noted already in 1954 in his
book on "Modern Warfare" that:

> "The goal of modern warfare is control of the population, and
> terrorism is a particularly appropriate weapon, since it aims
> directly at the inhabitant. In the street, at work, at home, the
> citizen lives continually under the threat of violent death. (...)
> The fact that public authority and the police are no longer
> capable of ensuring his security adds to his distress... He is
> more and more drawn to the side of the terrorists, who alone are
> able to protect him." 1)

Another French author, R. Gaucher, was the first to suggest that the
nuclear balance of terror which made direct war between great powers
more difficult favoured the rise of terrorism:

> "The truth is, at a time when it is difficult to mobilize great
> masses of people without provoking a global conflict with
> irreparable damage, terrorism tends to become more and more a
> substitute for war." 2)

This thought was also reiterated by the British counter-insurgency
specialist, Robert Thompson, who, however, used the term "Revolutionary
Warfare", by which he meant "A form of warfare which enables a small
ruthless minority to gain control by force over the people of a
country and thereby to seize power by violent and unconstitutional
means." 3) Thompson held:

> "The great advantage of revolutionary war as an instrument of
> policy in the nuclear age was to be that it avoided direct
> [superpower] confrontation." 4)

Brian Jenkins, a Vietnam veteran who now heads the RAND Corporations'
research on terrorism, has firmly brought the concept of terrorism as
surrogate warfare into the literature of terrorism. Speculating about
the future direction terrorism will take, he offered three scenarios:
(1) the international conspiracy whereby all terrorists in the world
are members of a single organization, (2) the move towards new weapons
and mass destruction, for instance by nuclear terrorism, and (3)
Surrogate War.

About the latter he wrote:

> "A third possible trend is that national governments will
> recognize the achievements of terrorists and begin to employ
> them or their tactics as a means of surrogate warfare against
> other nations. (...) The alternative to modern conventional war
> is low-level protracted war, debilitating military contests, in
> which staying power is more important than fire power, and
> military victory loses its traditional meaning.... (...) Terrorists,
> though now rejected as a legitimate mode of warfare by most
> conventional military establishments, could become an accepted
> form of warfare in the future. Terrorists could be employed to
> provoke international incidents, create alarm in an adversary's
> country, compel it to divert valuable resources to protect itself,
> destroy its morale, and carry out specific acts of sabotage.
> Governments could employ existing terrorist groups to attack their
> opponents, or they could create their own terrorists." 5)

What Jenkins postulated as a future possibility in 1975 became increasingly

plausible in the years since then to a number of authors. Paul Wilkinson,

now at the University of Aberdeen, noted:

> "I believe the most significant underlying causes of the recent
> upsurge in international terrorism to be political and strategic.
> As has already been emphasized, international war has increasingly
> become a less attractive option for states in the nuclear age.
> There is the grave risk that limited war might involve intervention
> by one or more nuclear powers with the inevitable consequential
> dangers of escalation to the nuclear threshold and beyond. (...)
> But the effect of these strategic constraints is likely to be...
> that violence in the international system will increasingly take
> the form of guerrilla warfare and terrorism. (...) The Soviets
> have also encouraged their client states to share in the tasks
> of training, financing and assisting terrorist activity. (...)
> One of the major underlying political causes of terrorism,
> however, cannot be placed solely at the door of the Soviet Union
> or her allies. It is the Palestinian problem. 6)

The impossibility of normal war-waging in the present age is also one

of the elements used by H.W. Tromp to explain the increase of political

terrorism. 7) He finds it difficult to distinguish political terrorism

from war on the basis of qualitative criteria:

> "Terrorism as well as war constitutes a form of use of violence
> for political purposes, directed mainly at people who cannot
> defend themselves and who often are not even a party to the
> political conflict, the aim being to force the opposing party
> in the conflict to a certain behaviour." 8)

Rather than viewing contemporary terrorism as a series of separate

incidents, Tromp is inclined to see it as "surrogate warfare",

"camouflaged war", or "war by proxy". 9)

Tromp offered the suggestion that terrorism might have already partly

taken over the place of classical warfare in the international system,
that it might express a trend towards a "global civil war":

> "It could be that it is a "Third World War" which has assumed
> the completely unexpected form of a "protracted warfare" by
> terroristic methods, but without clear front lines, without
> clear goals, and above all without two clearly distinguishable
> parties. A war which cannot be chartered on a map since the
> parties are nonterritorial and their aim is also not the conquest
> of territory." 10)

The "Third World War" perspective, first developed in the French
'guerre revolutionnaire' literature, seems an axiom of some counter-
insurgency authors working for the Institute for the Study of Conflict
in London.

Notes

1) Cit. L.A. Sobel (Ed.). Political Terrorism. Vol.1, Oxford, Clio
   Press, 1975, p.2-3.

2) R. Gaucher. Les Terroristes. Paris, 1965, p.359.

3) Robert Thompson. Revolutionary War in World Strategy 1945-1969.
   London, Seeker & Warburg, 1970, p.4.

4) Ibid., p.32.

5) Brian M. Jenkins. International Terrorism: A New Mode of Conflict.
   In: D. Carlton & C. Schaerf (Eds.). International Terrorism and
   World Security. London, Croom Helm, 1975, pp.30-31.

6) P. Wilkinson. Terrorism and the Liberal State. London, Macmillan,
   1977, pp.181-184.

7) H.W. Tromp. Politiek Terrorisme. Transaktie, Vol.7, No.1, March 1978,
   p.13.

8) Ibid., p.5.

9) Ibid., p.2.

10) Hylke Tromp. Politiek terrorisme: de derde wereldoorlog in een volstrekt
    onverwachte vorm? Universiteitskrant (Groningen), 8. Jg., No.5,
    28 September 1978, p.11.

Conspiracy Theories of Terrorism

Terrorism, characterized often by dramatic actions staged by clandestine
groups aiming at prominent targets whose connection to the professed
conflict remains obscure to many, seems to lend itself particularly
well to conspiracy theories. Already at the end of the 19th century
the press and some police chiefs spoke of the existence of a "great
international Anarchist conspiracy", which, however, did not exist.
Individual anarchists, motivated as much by personal revenge feelings
and search for the limelight as by revolutionary dreams, bombed and
assassinated with some regularity but with no instructions or
coordination from an "anarchist party". [1)]

For police chiefs it is very tempting to blame acts they cannot prevent
or solve to international forces since it will then appear that they
are in fact engaged in a fight against a well-orchestrated campaign
backed by foreign powers, which makes failure explicable and even
forgiveable. In this vein, Francesco Cossiga, at the time Italian
Minister of the Interior, claimed that both right and left-wing
terrorism in Italy was part of an international movement. [2)]

Increasingly this perspective has also been adopted by people less
in need of scapegoats. Walter Laqueur, Chairman of the Research
Council of the Center for Strategic and International Studies in
Washington D.C., one of the most influential writers on terrorism,
wrote in 1977:

> "Modern terrorism, with its ties to Moscow and Havana, with its
> connections with Libya and Algeria, bears a certain resemblance
> to the anonymous character of a multinational corporation: whenever
> multinational enterprises sponsor patriotic causes, caution is
> called for."
> "Multinational terrorism reached its climax in the early 1970s,
> involving close cooperation between small terrorist groups in
> many countries, with the Libyans, the Algerians, the North
> Koreans and the Cubans acting as paymasters, suppliers of weapons
> and other equipment as well as coordinators.... The Soviet Union
> supported a number of terrorist movements such as some Palestinians
> and African groups and the exile Croats; mostly such assistance
> would be given through intermediairies so that its origins would
> difficult to prove and any charges of complicity could be
> indignantly denied. (...) This new multinational terrorism was,
> however, for all practical purposes surrogate warfare between
> governments." 3)

Other authors, such as Beres, Demaris, Possony and Bouchey carry this
line of reasoning further. The latter, for instance, published in 1978
"International Terrorism - The Communist Connection. [4)]
There Possony and Bouchey state:

> "There is virtually no terrorist operation or guerilla movement
> anywhere in the world today, whether communist, semicommunist or
> non-communist, from the Irish Republican Army to the Palestinian
> Liberation Organization to our own Weather Underground, with which
> communists of one sort or another have not been involved. This
> includes non-communist operations and movements, for communist
> parties and governments always stand ready to exploit disorder in
> Europe, the Middle East, Latin America and elsewhere, however, and
> by whomever it is fomented. Because Moscow, Peking, Havana and
> other communist centers are linked to so many terrorist and
> guerilla groups and orgnaizations and because so many of the
> groups look to those centers not simply for support and assistance
> but also for ideological inspiration, the groups often seem to be
> connected to one another. They are certainly in cooperation with
> one another more and more, as if they constituted a Terrorist
> International controlled and directed by some central authority.
> This study does not make that claim because the facts do not
> warrant that conclusion. But it does recognize - and will show -
> that a significant degree of coordination of terrorist activities
> does exist, and that it is mainly communists who are doing the
> coordinating. Put differently, if communist governments and
> political groupings, of one ideological emphasis or another, were
> to cease terrorist activity and assistance, the present wave of
> international terrorism would be squashed." 5)

While American congressional committees had already in the first half
of the 1970s looked for the nexus between terrorism and communism,
this largely futile activity became by the early 1980s the official
view of the White House and the U.S. Department of State and was
echoed on Capitol Hill. One national security and intelligence
analyst working for a U.S. Senator, for instance, published a book
titled "The Soviet Strategy of Terror" [6)], wherein he states:

> "Some terrorism is indeed carelessly planned and executed by
> amateurs or mentally unstable elements, but the kind of terrorism
> that has become a threat to the public order of Western societies
> - the kind of terrorism that the Soviets and their allies support -
> is not. (...) The Soviets, of course do not generally call terrorism
> by that name; they refer to it as "armed struggle", "guerrilla war",
> or "liberation struggle".
> The small terrorist cadres that have existed in Western Europe
> for the last ten years are not under formal Soviet control either,
> and their ideologies are often at odds with Soviet orthodoxy
> yet ... there is considerable evidence to indicate many clandestine
> links between these terrorists and the Soviet, East German,
> Czechoslovak, or Cuban intelligence services as well as with Libyan

and Middle Eastern surrogates. (...) The European terrorist
network, then, may not be under Soviet control, but certainly
it appears to be in de facto alliance with the Soviet Union
and its satellites." 7)

Francis goes on quoting approvingly a leading figure of the

Georgetown Center for Strategic Studies, the former deputy director

of the CIA, Ray S. Clines, who held:

"What they [the Soviets] do is supply the infrastructure of terror:
the money, the guns, the training, the background information,
the communications, the propaganda that will inspire individual
terrorist groups." 8)

The breakthrough of the Soviet Conspiracy theory occurred with the

publication of Claire Sterling's book "The Terror Network: The Secret

War of International Terrorism" (New York, Holt, Rinhart and Winston,

1980), which became a bestseller in Italy (where the author worked

as U.S. foreign correspondent since the 1950s) as well as in other

countries, most notably the United States. Secretary of State,

Alexander Haig, even distributed excerpts from it to a Congressional

Committee. Haig, who blamed the USSR publicly "for training, funding

and equipping international terrorists" 9) gave her theory the aura

of legitimacy 10).

The Sterling thesis is not substantially different from what Francis

Possony and Bouchey state. Her chief thesis is that:

"The heart of the Russian's strategy is to provide the terrorist
network with the goods and services necessary to undermine the
industrialized democracies of the West." 11)

The conspiracy started, in her view, on the orders of Moscow, in 1966

at Fidel Castro's "Tricontinental Conference" in Havana, where the

"Guerrilla International" was founded. The first big success of this

conspiracy, she implies, were the revolutionary events of 1968.

Some of her main witnesses happen to be advisors of Alexander Haig,

while at other times she refers to "confidential sources" or

"police information" for other proofs. According to her the role of

the KGB is not a object of speculation, but a documented fact. The

documents she referred to were found by the Belgian police in a car

which had had an accident. These documents, purported to come from a

KGB post in the International Atomic Energy Commission in Vienna,

stated that the KGB was planning to revitalize terroristic activity

in Western Europe. For Claire Sterling there was apparently no doubt
that these were genuine documents and not black propaganda material
planted possibly by one or another secret service [12].
The fact that her work could be labelled a "plausible analysis" by
a quality paper like the Neue Zürcher Zeitung, says more about the
political climate than about the quality of the book. In this political
climate the suggestion has already been offered that those who do not
believe that the Soviet Union is behind it all (or almost all), are
brainwashed by the "disinformation" campaigns from Moscow. The fact that
they cannot see the evidence is evidence that the Soviet propaganda
has been successfully subverted the disbelievers. [13] Among the
disbelievers, however, or at least those who do not believe in the
quality of the evidence, also belong important sectors of the U.S.
Government.

While the Pentagon Intelligence Services thought that the Russians were
deeply involved in the support of international terrorism,the CIA, hard
pressed by the Reagan administration, could only find indications
but no hard evidence. [14] The evidence of the Reagan administration
that the Soviet Union was directly helping terrorists was essentially
based on the testimony of a Czechoslovak defector, Maj.Gen. Jan Sejna.
This close associate of Antonin Novotny had fled his country when
Alexander Dubçek came to power in 1968. The evidence, in other words,
was more than a decade old and since defectors generally try to sell
the best possible stories as an entry ticket into the host camp, they
often overstate their case. [15] Yet this did not stop Alexander Haig
- himself a near victim of a terrorist attack on 25 June 1979 in the
Belgian place of Obourg - to blame the Soviets for having a "conscious
policy" of "training, funding and equipping" international terrorists. [16]
Haig declared "International terrorism will take the place of human
rights in our concern because it is the ultimate abuse of human
rights" [17].

A leading researcher in the field of terrorism, Brian M. Jenkins,
director of the Rand Corp.'s Research Program on Political Violence
and Subnational Conflict, has written on the Sterling book:

> "... the author's theme that the Soviet Union is behind much of
> today's terrorism coincides with and could reinforce the attitudes
> of Reagan administration officials who are inclined to blame Moscow
> for most of the unrest in the world. A friend of mine recently

observed that at the moment there are three kinds of people in
Washington: those who have always believed the Soviet Union is
responsible for terrorism; those who want to believe that it is;
and those who, in order to maintain their influence in government,
must pretend to believe. Because the book could have major
implications for U.S. policy, its arguments merit a careful
examination. (...) Sterling suggest that the Soviet Union and
its East European, Cuban and Palestinian proxies are behind "the
"terror network". She implies forethought on the part of the
Soviet Union and its satellites. She never actually states it as
a fact. She implies. She insinuates. Like a magican she conjures
up the impression that there is a Moscow Master Plan, leaving the
audience to flesh out the illusion. (...) ... if the "Sterling
thesis" is meant to... imply - as many are taking it to imply -
a Soviet blueprint, Soviet instigation, Soviet direction or Soviet
control, then the book offers no new evidence, and what is offered
does not make its case. 17)

Another insider, working for the CIA, found the book "poorly researched"
called the "use of evidence flawed", with "quotations taken out of
context" and "biases creeping in on every page" and with "data impossible
to reproduce" 19).

Yet the simple "Sterling thesis" - the terrorists as Lenins's children
- has gained widespread currency due to forces interested in reviving
the Cold War. It has, for instance, been spread by a "strikingly
authentic thriller" written by Arnaud de Borchgrave, a veteran foreign
correspondent for Newsweek, and Robert Moss, formerly of The Economist
and known as authors of a study on Chile which, was subsidized by the
CIA 20). In their roman clé The Spike which was announced as "The
Secret History of our Times" they unveil a Red Plot in which the Kremlin
plays the terrorists and the media in a drive to gain global supremacy 21).
There is, of course, no denying that some of the "friends" of the
Soviet Union use terrorist tactics but the important point to note is
that many non-governmental friends of big powers do so and that secret
services are deeply involved. This is nothing new. The murder of archeduke
Franz Ferdinand in July 1914 at Sarajewo was masterminded by secret
services and in the interwar period Hitler and Mussolin meddled with
terrorists in the Balkan. There is also no dispute about the fact that
many terrorist movements of ideologically diverse orientations fighting
for ethnic and revolutionary causes cooperate with each other, trading

training for weapons and helping each other out with hiding places and
money. But if the KGB should stand behind it all why should, for
instance, the Red Brigades have to risk their lives in bank-robberies
and kidnappings to raise the ten million dollars a year necessary to
function? [22] Or why should it be that European terrorist have to steal
most of their weapons from U.S. army depots in Europe? In the 1970s
the U.S. depots in Miesau and Weilerback in the German Federal Republic
lost so many explosives, ammunition and weapons through theft that
"almost a whole battalion" could be equipped, as a police report
cited by a study of the Centre for Contemporary Studies on "The
International Arms Trade and the Terrorists" indicates [23].
And if it were true that the Soviet Union equips and trains terrorists
through intermediaries like Libya: why then should Colonel Gaddafi
hire ex-CIA assassins and have U.S. explosives, electronic equipment
and terrorist weapons brought to his country? With the help of two
ex-CIA agents, Edwin Wilson and Frank E. Terpil, Libya obtained all
sorts of exotic and deadly technology and materials from the United
States which in turn ended up in the German Federal Republic, Italy, Japan
and Ireland according to the testimony of another ex-CIA agent
Kevin Mulcahy before the FBI. Why should Wilson and Terpil have had
to bring in exile Cubans, formerly employed by the CIA, for assassination
missions against enemies of Colonel Gaddafi or why should several
dozens Green Berets from the "JFK Training Center" at Fort Bragg have
instructed Libyian soldiers and mercenaries, as the Mulcahy testimony
revealed, if the Russians were behind it all, as the "Sterling thesis"
suggests? [24]
The conspiracy theory also exists in the reverse form, with the CIA
rather than the KGB pulling most strings. Philip Agee, who worked for
the CIA for twelve years, has described the close collaboration of
the U.S. Intelligence Agency with right-wing regimes and vigilante
groups. His CIA Diary reconstructs agency involvement in Latin America.
On Uruguay, it says, for instance, referring to 22 March 1964 that
some of the CIA operations "were designed to take control of the streets
away from communists and other leftists, and our squads, often with
the participation of off-duty policemen , would break up their meetings
and generally terrorize them." [25] At that period, the Tupamoros were
still in their infancy and it might very well be that the CIA tactics

were co-responsible for driving young militants on the road to terrorism.
The most complete work on U.S. involvement in international terrorism
is Noam Chomsky's and Edward S. Herman's massive study "The Political
Economy of Human Rights" (Nottingham, Spokesman 1979). The first volume,
titled "The Washington Connection and Third World Fascism" lays out
the anti-thesis to Sterling et al.:

> "The military juntas of Latin America and Asia are our juntas.
> Many of them were directly installed by us or are the beneficiaries
> of our direct intervention, and most of the others came into
> existence with our tacit   support, using military equipment and
> training supplied by the United States. (...) Terror in these states
> is functional, improving the "investment climate", at least in the
> short-run, and U.S. aid to terror-prone states.... is _positively_
> _related to terror and improvement of investment climate and_
> _negatively related to human rights_....It turns out, therefore, that
> if we cut through the propaganda barrage, _Washington has become the_
> _torture and political murder capital of the world_. (...)....the
> United States is the power under whose quite calculated and
> deliberate policy and strategy choices have brought about a system
> of clients who consistently practice torture and murder on a
> terrifying scale. (...) It is convenient to pretend that Guatamala,
> South Korea and the Philippines are "independent" in contrast to
> Rumania, Poland and Hungary. In this manner U.S. responsibility
> for terror in its sphere can be dismissed, while the Soviet Union's
> imposition of tyranny and crushing of freedom in its sphere can
> sanctimoniously deplored. Given our role in creating and sustaining
> our terror-prone clients... their alleged independence and our
> posture of innocent and concerned bystander must be taken simply
> as principles of state propaganda." 26)

Which of the two conspiracy theories of terrorism one wishes to believe,
is a question of political choice. It is safe to assume that both
theories contain elements of truth. From the point of view of documented
hard evidence the Chomsky/Herman book is, however, qualitatively different and superior to Sterling's work and to that of other authors
discussed in this chapter.

Notes

1) W. Laqueur. Terrorism. London, Weidenfeld and Nicolson, 1977, p.53.

2) Cit. Volkskrant, 17 November 1977, p.5.

3) W. Laqueur, op.cit., pp.216, 115-116.

4) S.T. Possony and L.F. Bouchey. International Terrorism.The Communist
   Connection - With a Case Study of West German Terrorist Ulrike
   Meinhof. Washington D.C., American Council for World Freedom, 1978.

5) Ibid. p.1.

6) S.T. Francis. The Soviet Strategy of Terror. Washington D.C.,
   The Heritage Foundation, 1981.

7) Ibdi., pp.2-3, 41-42.

8) Cit. Ibid., p.42.

9) In a News Conference on 28 January 1981. Current Policy, No.258,
   U.S. Department of State, p.5.

10) The official Soviet attitude towards international terrorism has been
    expressed by V. Terekhov: "Marxism-Leninism rejects individual terror
    as a method of revolutionary action since it weakens the revolutionary
    movement by diverting the working people away from the mass struggle."
    "The first and chief lesson", Lenin wrote, "is that only the
    revolutionary struggle of the masses is capable of achieving any
    serious improvement in the life of the workers...". International
    terrorism is radically different from the revolutionary movement
    of the people's masses, whose aim is to effect
    changes in society and which alone is capable of so doing. The
    terrorist act, however, even if its main point is to awaken public
    opinion and force it to pay attention to a particular political
    situation, can only have limited consequences: say, lead to the
    release of a group of prisoners, increase the financial assets of
    an organization...".-V. Terekhov. "International Terrorism and the
    Struggle Against It." Novove Vremva, 15 March 1975, pp.20-22,
    in: Foreign Broadcast Information Service, USSR International Affairs,
    III, 28 March 1974, as quoted in: W. Scott Thompson. Political Violence
    and the "Correlation of Forces". Orbis, 1976, p.1284.

11) Sterling, 1980, p.54, cit. M. Stohl. Fashions and Fantasies in the
    Study of Political Terrorism. Dubrovnik, Inter-University Center,
    1981. Unpubl. Paper, p.15.

12) Michael Haller, reviewing "Das internationale Terror-Netz." München,
    Scherz Verlag, 1982, Der Spiegel, 39. Jg., No.8, 22 Febr. 1982, pp. 206-208.

13) M. Stohl, op.cit., p.14.

14) M. Stohl, op.cit., p.12, Volkskrant, 30 March 1981, p.1, "CIA rapport
    valt beleid-Haig af".

Notes

15) Leslie H.Gelb. Soviet Terror Charge Based on Old U.S. Data.
    International Herald Tribune, 19 October 1981, p.6.

16) Cit. Ibid.

17) The Guardian, 30 January 1981 and 31 January 1981, as quoted in:
    Philip Eliott, Graham Murdock and Philip Schlesinger. The State
    and "Terrorism" on British Television. Florence, Festival dei Popoli,
    6-7 December 1981, pp.56-., see also: "Moskau, Quelle allen Terrors".
    Der Spiegel, 35 Jg., No.22, 25 May 1981, p.124.

18) Review by B.M. Jenkins, Washington Post, reprinted in International
    Herald Tribune, 28 May 1981.

19) Private information.

20) More, May 1978, p.26.

21) A. de Borchgrave and R. Moss. The Spike, New York, Avon Books, 1980.

22) C. Sterling, op.cit., p.302.

23) Contemporary Affairs Briefing no. 7 London, 1981; it revealed
    that the United States were the main source of terrorist arms.
    Der Spiegel, No. 31, 27 July 1981, p.89.

24) Der Spiegel, No. 26, 22 June 1981, pp.110-114.

25) Philip Agee. Insides the Company: CIA Diary. Harmondsworth, Penguin,
    1974, p.337.

26) Ibid., op.cit., vol.I., pp. 16-17.-Emphasis added, AS.

Communication Theory of Terrorism

In discussions on the purposes of insurgent terrorism a prominent
and sometimes even paramount place is reserved by analysts of terrorism
to the communication aspect. Martha Crenshaw, for instance writes:
"The most basic reason for terrorism is to gain recognition or
attention..." [1]
J. Bowyer Bell also sees the advertising function of terrorism as the
most important one. Jenkins uses the metaphor of terrorism as theatre
to express the notion that "Terrorists want a lot op people watching
and a lot of people listening and not a lot of people dead" [2].
It is, for sure, not the only thing terrorists want nor is it always
the main thing. Otherwise Jenkins and many others would not have
engaged in all those studies where the terrorist potential for mass
murder and nuclear blackmail is analysed.
While many authors view terrorism as either a form of internal warfare
or a form of (surrogate) war, there has always been some uneasiness
about the appropriateness of the "war model" or "war paradigm" to
terrorism. The notion that there was more to terrorism than the
visible and atrocious violence is expressed by many authors. Stephen
T. Hosmer who studied "Viet Cong Repression and Its Implication for
the Future" held that terrorism was "the violent act for psychological
rather than military reasons". [3]
Paul Wilkinson contended that "the richest theoretical insights into
political terrorism are to be gained from an analysis of terrorism
as a distinctive mode of unconventional psychological warfare aimed
ultimately at bringing about a climate of fear and collapse in an
incumbent régime or target group." [4]
In the same vein Francis M. Watson holds that "terrorism must not be
defined only in terms of violence, but also in terms of propaganda.
The two are both in operation together". [5]
This is a theme which played a role in Nazi politics. One Nazi
theorist, Eugen Hadamovsky, for instance, noted in 1933 in his book
on "Propaganda and National Power" that "Propaganda and violence are
never contradictions. Use of violence can be part of the propaganda." [6]

Goebbels, the Nazi Minister of Propaganda, shifted the emphasis even
further in the direction of communication on the war - communication-
axis, when in the spring of 1942 he gave orders to slant the news:
"News is a weapon of war. Its purpose is to wage war and not to give
out information." 7)

Some theorists of terrorism have even gone further in emphasizing
the communication aspect over the war/violence aspect of terrorism.
Returning to the sources of modern insurgent terrorism in the 1870s
one finds that the concepts of the "exemplary deed" or "propaganda by
the deed" were primarily referring to communication attempt of an
intellectual elite with masses, who seemed to lack revolutionary fervour
and were therefore in need to be "educated". Peter Kropotkin, the
Anarchist prince, wrote:

> "By actions which compel general attention, the new idea seeps
> into people's minds and wins converts. One such act may, in a
> few days, make more propaganda than thousands of pamphlets. Above
> all, it awakens the spirit of revolt; it breeds daring... Soon it
> becomes apparent that the established order does not have the
> strength often supposed. One courageous act has sufficed to upset
> in a few days the entire governmental machinery, to make the
> colossus tremble... The people observe that the monster is not
> so terrible as they thought... hope is born in their hearts." 8)

Another revolutionary theorist, the German-American Johan Most, put it
more explicitly:

> "Everyone now knows, for example, that the more highly placed
> the one shot or blown up, and the more perfectly executed the
> attempt, the greater the propagandistic effect..." 9)

In the 1960s the Brazilian Carlos Marighela reinvented   the "armed
propaganda" and the symbolic use of violence as a means of communication
and recommended it in his <u>Mini-Manual of the Urban Guerrilla</u>. In an
attempt to explain the basically nonrevolutionary bombings in the
United States during the Vietnam war, Philip A. Karber, rediscovered
the communication dimension and offered it as an alternative framework
for conceptualizing terrorism. Rather than treating bombings as
urban guerrilla warfare he treated them as a form of social protest. 10)
Karber describes his conceptual framework in these terms:

> "As a symbolic act, terrorism can be analyzed much like other
> mediums of communication, consisting of four basic components:
> transmitter (terrorist), intended recipient (target), message
> (bombing, ambush) and feed-back (reaction of target). The terrorist's
> message of violence necessitates a victim, whether personal or
> institutional, but the target or intended recipient of the communication

may not be the victim. (...)
Terrorism is subject to many of the same pathologies and disruptions
suffered by more conventional means of communication. These include
lack of fidelity in the medium of transmission (the choice of
victim conveys wrong message to target), background noise (competing
events obscure the message), target distortion (recipient misinterprets
the meaning of the one signal and fails to regulate output to
changing circumstances or target feed-back). (...)
However, if terrorism is to be conceived of as "propaganda of the
deed", we must devise a content analysis of symbolic violence." 11)

Other authors have treated terrorism in terms of communication, without
directly building on Karber. Franz Wördemann, a former German editor
in chief of a newspaper, noted that "communication is not alone the
goal, but necessary part of the terrorist act." 12)
Martha Crenshaw also stresses the role of violence as communication to
various audiences, without giving up the terrorism as revolution model. 13)
She quotes for instance, one revolutionary leader, Ramdane Abane, as
saying: "We must have blood in the headlines of all the newspapers." 14)
The spread of television and the increase in audiences made possible
by the use of satellite transmission have for several authors (Clutterbuck,
Jenkins and Wördemann) been judged as permissive causes which made
terrorism an attractive strategy and contributed to its spreading to
societies where local preconditions were largely absent.
Amy Sands Redlick concludes that transnational information-flows from
mass media (but also from international travel or intellectual exchanges)
has benefitted militants in four main ways:

"1. The information flow can be a propaganda tool.

2. The flow of information may expose societies to information
   that will inspire and justify an individual's or group's use
   of violence.

3. In providing information concerning specific terrorist tactics
   and strategies, the international communication system has
   often supplied discontented groups sufficient technological
   knowledge and ideological justification to support their use
   of violence.

4. The flow of information resulting from a successful terrorist
   attack may provide the utilitarian inspiration needed to cause
   a contagion of similar events elsewhere in the world." 15)

One behavioural expert, the Austrian-American psychiatrist F. Hacker, put
the role of mass communication as a causal agent especially high, offering
the suggestion: "If one could cut out publicity, I would say you could
cut out 75% of the national and international terrorism." 16)

An attempt to assess the influence of publicity on future terroristic
incidents by means of coding the amount of publicity, has been undertaken by Ralph William Connally in his master thesis "Third Party
Involvement in International Terrorist Extortion." [17)

The role of the media as instruments of terrorism, as agents in the
spread of terroristic acts, and as tools for manipulation by both
terrorists and their adverseries has recently been analysed by Silj,
De la Haye, Clutterbuck, Schlesinger, Schmid and De Graaf.

In the latter's studies an attempt has been made to link the rise of
mass communication to the rise of insurgent terrorism and to portray
insurgent terrorism as a violent reaction to problems of access to
newsmaking in the present information order.

In our study on "South Moluccan Terrorism, the Media and Public
Opinion", an attempt is made to assess the effects of terrorism on
various audiences, including the terrorists themselves, their reference
group, the hostages and the Dutch public. [18)

The communication model lends itself particularly well to an effect
analysis, although the Lasswellian formula for communication process
analysis "Who says what, through what channel, to whom, with what
effect?" was found insufficient. The elements "with what intention?,
"by what message generator?" and "in what social context?" have to be
introduced, and the "to whom?" has to be differentiated since there
are various audiences to terrorism - the terrorist himself, his
movement, his sympathizers, the enemy, local, national and foreign
publics.

The study of public opinion changes as a result of terroristic acts,
related to an assessment of the degree of harmony or disharmony of
interest with the goals of the terrorists of particular sectors in
society, is one of the most crucial research desiderata at the time
being.

Notes

1) M. Crenshaw. The Causes of Terrorism. Comparative Politics, July 1981,
p.386.

2) Brian M. Jenkins. International Terrorism: A New Mode of Conflict.
In: D. Carlton and C. Schaerf (Eds.). International Terrorism
and World Security. London, Croom Helm, 1975, p.15.

3) St. Monica, RAND, 1970, p.8, cit. Geoffrey Fairbairn. Revolutionary
Guerrilla Warfare. The Countryside Version. Harmondsworth, Penguin,
1974, p.353.

4) P. Wilkinson. Terrorism and the Liberal State, 1977, p.110.

5) Francis M. Watson. Political Terrorism: The Threat and the Response.
Washington D.C., Robert B. Luce Co., 1976, p.15.

6) Eugen Hadamovsky. Propaganda und nationale Macht, 1933, p.22,
cit. Hannah Arendt. The Origins of Totalitarianism. New York,
Harcourt Brace Jovanovich Inc., 1971, p.341 .

7) Cit. David M. Abshire. International Broadcasting: A New Dimension
of Western Diplomacy. Beverly Hills, Sage, 1976, p.20.

8) Peter Kropotkin. "The Spirit of Revolt", in: Revolutionary Pamphlets.
New York, 1968, pp.35-43, cit. Ze'ev Iviansky. Individual Terror:
Concept and Typology. Journal of Contemporary History, Vol.12, No.1,
1977, p.45.

9) Freiheit, 13 September 1884, Repr. in W. Laqueur (Ed.). The Terrorism
Reader. New York, New American Library, 1978, p.100.

10) Cf. Philip A. Karber. Terrorism as Social Protest. Paper, 1971.

11) Philip A. Karber. Urban Terrorism. Baseline Data and a Conceptual
Framework. Social Science Quarterly, Vol.52, December 1971, pp.527-533.

12) Franz Wördemann. Terrorismus. Motive, Täter, Strategien. München,
Piper, 1977, p.141.

13) M. Crenshaw Hutchinson. Revolutionary Terrorism: The FLN in Algeria,
1954-1962. Stanford, Hoover Institution Press, 1978, especially
pp. 88-101.

14) cit. p. 94.

15) Amy Sands Redlick. The Transnational Flow of Information as a Cause
of Terrorism. In: Y. Alexander et al. Terrorism: Theory and Practice,
Boulder, Westview Press, 1979, p.91.

16) Statement of Dr. Frederick Hacker, 14 August 1974, in: U.S. Congress
House. Committee on Internal Security. Hearings, Part 4. 93rd Congress,
2nd Session. Washington D.C., GPO, 1974, p.3039, cit. R.H. Kupperman
and Darrell M. Trent. Terrorism, Stanford, Hoover Institution Press,
1979, p.42.

Notes

17) Naval Graduate School, 1976, cit. E.F. Mickolus. The Literature
    of Terrorism, 1980, p. 12.

18) Violence as Communication: Insurgent Terrorism and the Western
    News Media, London, Sage, 1982; A.P. Schmid et al. Zuidmoluks
    terrorisme, de media en de publieke opinie. Amsterdam, Intermediair,
    Bibliotheek, 1982.

Sociological Theories and Models

If terrorism is not primarily conceived as a product of a terrorist
personality the cause of terrorism must be sought in social factors.
Various authors concentrate on different environments such as:
the international environment; the national, domestic or local
environment; the sub-cultural environment, e.g. the universities.
Following a distinction of Harry Eckstein, several authors distinguish
more or less explicity between Precipitants (the almost always unique
and ephemeral phenomena which start the outbreak of violence) and
Preconditions (those circumstances which make it possible for the
precipitants to bring about the violence). [1]
The preconditions have been subdivided into permissive factors - those
elements which enable a terrorist strategy and make it attractive to
political actors, and direct situational factors which motivate
terrorists. [2]
Surveying the literature one notes again that the theories and models
pertain mainly to insurgent terrorism, not state terrorism and that
the latter's actions are often ignored or neglected in explaining the
occurrence of terrorism. Even Walter Laqueur noted that "any analysis
of terrorism is incomplete unless it considers those against whom terror
is directed." [3]
In the following pages some models and theories and theses will be
presented.

International environment theories

The strong emphasis on international terrorism has produced a number
of analyses on the international causes of insurgent terrorism.
Brian M. Jenkins, for instance, has emphasized the role of the failure
of rural guerrilla movements in Latin America which pushed the rebels
into the cities, the defeat of the Arab armies in the Six-day war in
1967, which caused the Palestinians to abandon hope for a conventional
military solution to their problem and the reactions of students in
Europe, Japan and the United States to the Vietnam war which led to
the formation of small extremist groups dedicated to armed struggle. [4]

The same theme with different accentuation can be found with
Edward Heyman whose speciality is the mapping of the diffusion of
transnational terrorism:

> "Student activism was a global phenomenon. Student leaders met at
> international conferences to discuss the problems of capitalism,
> and to debate alternative strategies for action. They believed
> that economic resurgence in the quarter century since the end of
> World War II had not closed the gap between the rich and the poor
> and that Western society had discarded human values in the search
> for economic well being. The appeal of nationalism seemed
> increasingly powerful, and as Walter Laqueur notes, "conditions
> that had been accepted for centuries became intolerable." In Latin
> America, the rural model of guerrilla warfare collapsed in Bolivia
> with the death of Che Guevara, and the guerrillas moved to the
> cities where they believed their struggles would have more impact.
> (...) The guerrillas tapped the pool of student activism and
> adopted labour unrest and urban poverty as rallying causes. But
> the move to the cities also led to radical changes in tactics.
> The range, number, and vulnerability of urban targets led to the
> adoption of terrorism, a tactic that the theorists of rural
> guerilla warfare had eschewed. (...) Transnational terrorism was
> born of the marriage between the urban guerrilla and the student
> activists. The emigrant guerrilla fed on the latent violence of the
> student movement, exploited the student's causes and contracts, and
> learned new tactics. (...) The qualitative move to transnational
> terrorism required only a determination to use tested techniques
> against new targets to exploit the weaknesses of the international
> system." 5)

Both explanations, Jenkins' and Heyman's beg many questions. Jenkins
basically explains international terrorism out of national terrorism
without searching very deep for local causes and Heyman's hidden cause
lies in the minds of the guerrillas and students who meet and "marry"
The same explanatory mechanism we also find with J.D. Elliott, a Political-
Military officer at the U.S. Army Concepts Analysis Agency in Bethesda, who
explains one terrorism by the other:

> "Terrorists have maintained the offensive role and governments
> have had to react to their innovations. During this action-reaction
> cycle, terrorists have been forced to cross new thresholds of
> violence to retain their momentum. This has resulted in three
> transitions that will be discussed here: First, the transition
> to urban guerrilla warfare in the sixties, in which guerrillas
> moved their tactics from their traditional battleground to ambush
> the government in the cities. Second, a consideration of transnational
> terrorism in the early seventies, during which political violence
> migrated via skyjacked jumbo jets to the industrialized societies.
> And, finally, the emerging transition to international terrorism
> in which terrorism will be controlled by sovereign states." 6)

Such a theory is less notable for its insights (note the enlargement
of terrorism to political violence and the reification of terrorism

hijacking a jet), than for the status and influence of those who
maintain, spread and apparently also act on the basis of such models.
A more balanced view we find in Henk Leurdijk's summary of the proceedings
of an international conference:

"The 1960s saw two kinds of revolutionary violence in particular:
first, "national liberation" movements - each of which was unique -
in every case the main target being the foreign countries which
dominated their territory or were at least seen as dominating them;
secondly, "guerrilla movements" which erupted mostly in Latin
American countries and whose main targets were originally their
oppressive domestic governments.
The distinction between the two types is sometimes difficult to
make, but it certainly is true that in recent years we have seen
a dramatic increase in international terrorism as a result of the
failure of both types of warfare to achieve their desired goals.
The unifying idea of the various types of terrorism is to put
their cause before the world audience and their means of doing
that is to engage in dramatic acts of transnational violence, mainly
directed against those whom they consider to be especially responsible
for their ill-fortune. Acts of individual physical violence are often
carried out against innocent persons; but in a broader context they
may be regarded as small-scale reprisals for the acts of some
Western governments, which, in resisting revolutionary warfare in
the Third World, have allegedly engaged in deliberate killing of
whole villages of innocent civilians - acts which Western governments
have for the most part condemned. Some participants asked how one
can persuade Third World international terrorists, who have practically
no other means at their disposal, to agree to the outlawing of acts
of small-scale terrorism while some Western governments, controlling
enormous potential for violence perpetuate acts of terrorism on a
much larger scale." 7)

The cause of terrorism in this view is twofold: it is caused on the
one hand by colonialism and neo-colonialism, and, on the other hand
by the lack of other suitable methods of struggle.

It is quite true that the international structure, with its power
blocs, its satellite and dominant states is a powerful source for
conflicts. But not all conflicts are fought out violently and not all
violence is terroristic.

The international system is subject to many tensions. Conflicts seem
to stem frequently from two main factors:

1. Conquests in some historical past and ongoing attempts to undo
   them, and
2. Modern revolutions and counterrevolutions 8).

The first complex involves not only colonialism but also old nation-
states with a contingent territory such as Spain (e.g. the Basque region),
France (e.g. Corsica) or Great Britain (e.g. Northern Ireland). Some

of the conflicts presently waged by means of terrorism have a very long
history. The Arab-Israeli conflict goes back more than two thousand
years in time and both chief opponents, the Jews and the Palestinians
were conquerors of the land they now claim as being rightfully theirs.
The terrorism in the early seventies in Quebec, in turn, can be traced
back to the year 1759 when the British conquered the Quebec Province
and begun to dominate the French-Canadian Québeois.
Both in the colonial situations in Africa and Asia and the older states
caught by the rediscovery of ethnicism, the key issue seems to be
the reconquest of one's identity, whether national or ethnic.
The second set of circumstances in which terrorism is likely to occur
is revolution. Revolutions generally have their origin in a national
context, but given the fight for markets and influence characterizing
the international system, few national conflicts are not to some degree
internationalized. An internal factor for this internationalization of
revolutionary domestic conflicts is that the parties in the civil war
attempt to maintain or improve their position by mobilizing initially
uninvolved foreign actors, both state and non-state actors. Since the
main theme of revolution is the issue of equality versus defence of
privilege, alliances of the Haves against the Have-nots are likely
across national borders. The equality and the identity motive can
coincide and reinforce each other, but they can as often clash. In
ideological terms the main expression of these dimensions have been
nationalism and socialism. Nationalism or ethnicism, however, seems
to predominate whenever the two are at cross-purposes since most
people seem to reject more that they are exploited by foreigners than
they are exploited at all.
While these forces in the international system go some way in
explaining international conflict, the choice for terrorism is not
explained. Some national liberation struggles involved a great deal
of terrorism (e.g. Algeria), in others (e.g. Indonesia) it hardly
played a role. Martha Crenshaw, who has provided an excellent account
of the Algerian independence struggle, offers this rationale for the
choice of tactic:

> "In the case of the FLN, the dominant reason for choosing
> terrorism appears to have been its expected utility in achieving
> the insurgents' goals, despite the unquestionable influences
> of psychological, social and organizational factors. (...) The
> key motivation for terrorism in a context in which the normal

means of access to government (elections, political parties, interest
groups, strikes or demonstrations) were denied was a willingness by
the FLN to accept high risks and a considerable inequality of power
between the revolutionary movement and the French regime. The absolute
determination of the revolutionary elite was based on the intrinsic
merit of the goal of independence as well as the fact that its expected
benefits were obtainable only through violence. (...) Struggles
for freedom elsewhere, particularly in neighbouring Tunisia and
Morocco, served as inspiration to the FLN and also as a challenge. (...)
Terrorism, a low-cost and easily implemented strategy, was the only
feasible alternative for the new nationalist organization because
the FLN lacked both the necessary material resources (money, arms,
soldiers) and active popular support. When a committed core of
leaders agreed that violence was the only solution to the impasse
in which they found themselves, their inability to push the mass
of the Algerian people into open opposition or to mount large-scale
guerrilla warfare encouraged them to adopt a strategy of terrorism.
It is in this sense that terrorism is the weapon of the weak, the
result of desperation and despair. Terrorism was an attempt to
acquire political power through unusual means. Its users accepted
risk and danger, because of the importance of their goal and the
absence of choice." 9)

Behind the Algerian strategy of terrorism stood the desire to manipulate

the international situation. More concretely: part of the strategy was

to alienate the French population from the French government by increasing

the price it had to pay for controlling a territory which was not worth

much for the average Frenchman and, to drive a wedge between France and

the United States which thought colonialism outdated and, as the Vietnam

legacy from France indicated, was a breeding ground for anti-capitalist

forces if not satisfied on the issue of nationalism.

In her study Crenshaw distinguished between direct and indirect audiences

to terrorism, the first consisting of potential victims and the second

of spectators. She then notes:

"The FLN's use of terrorism demonstrated that the responses of the
indirect audiences were as important to the revolutionary cause as
the reactions of the direct audiences. The need to reach indirect
audiences may be the reason for the adoption of increasingly
spectacular violence by modern terrorist groups. Present-day terrorists
rely more extensively on the tactics of pressure and manoeuvre, or
influencing third parties to compel their opponent to concede, than
the FLN did. Terrorists with such an imperative demand the attention
of the world audience, of people who are unsympathetic to, or
unaware of, their cause." 10)

An important goal of insurgent terrorist movements operating internationally

is "the projection of an image of strength and determination abroad", to

use another phrase of Crenshaw. The Palestinians, for instance, unable

to achieve much on the borders of Israel, have been masters in this;
first acquiring in this way the attention and money of the rich Arab
nations and then, the attention and votes of many non-Arab states in
the United Nations.

A precondition for such manipulations of the international environment
is the existence of a global infrastructure permitting it. Among the
permissive causes of inter- and transnational terrorism figure, as many
authors point out, urbanization (which provides anonymity, targets and
audiences for the terrorist act), transportation (which allows
kidnappings in private transport and hostage taking in public transport
as well as escape to safe havens - nations sharing the goals
of the terrorists.), and communication (allowing for threat communication
by telephone, or the public media, the delivery of letter bombs, and
the gaining of attention of mass audiences through the creation of
newsworthy events). [11)]

A further factor is the availability of weapons. The huge arsenals
assembled by big powers, the replacement of older weapons with new ones
and the dumping of the latter in the Third World or on the black market
as well as the willingness of secret services to support foreign clients
have led to a "democratization of violence" (H.W. Tromp). The weapons
of terrorists are generally not very advanced ones. The standard weapons
are the machine pistol and the plastic bomb and only in a tiny amount
of cases more sophisticated weapons like anti-tank or man-portable
guided missiles are utilized by insurgent terrorists.

A further permissive cause mentioned in the literature is the toleration
many governments show towards certain types of terrorists when it is
a question of my enemy's enemy is my friend, when goal consonance makes
for "understanding" no matter how abominable the means, or when the
host country of terrorist actors are compliant, because they are too
weak or too intimidated by the terrorists on its soil, as in the case
of Lebanon before 1982. [12)]

A further permissive cause, at least in the beginning of a terrorist
campaign, is the absence of security measures. [13)] The ease with which
skyjacking could be arranged before the screening of handbaggage and the
physical search of boarding aircraft passengers was mandatory,

illustrated this.

Most of the elements mentioned in the preceeding pages deal with situational and permissive factors in the international environment. The reason for this is that precipitants for acts of such terrorism are basically unique and not lending themselves for generalizations the way preconditions do. This is probably not such a serious deficit as one might think. After all World War I was not primarily caused by the assassination on archeduke Franz Ferdinand in 1914, but by national rivalries, alliance policies, militarism and the like.

Theories of Domestic Causation

Quételet, the Belgian philosopher, once wrote: "Society contains in herself all the crimes which will be committed, in ,a sense, its her who commits them." [14)]

Explanations along this line of thinking have been offered by Hannah Arendt who suggested that acts of extreme revolutionary violence in contemporary industrialized societies may be a revolt against the anonymity of the bureaucratic state, against the "Rule of Nobody". Bernard Crick has likewise suggested that: "in an age of bureaucrats, tyrannicide is plainly less useful than terror." [15)]

Others have denied that terrorism rises out of the domestic situation. The German political scientist, Peter Graf Kielmansegg, for instance, maintains:

> "What can be said about social-revolutionary terrorism in a society like the West German one, in a state like the German Federal Republic, is that it has - except in its effects, no relationship with reality; the terrorists are assaulting a world which exists only in their heads. The consequence is: explanations do not fall into the province of political science, but, at best, in psychology." [16)]

And slightly less far-going, Gerhard Schmidtchen observes:

> "The scandal of German terrorism consists exactly in the fact that it is situated in an absurd, paradoxical relationship to the societal development in the Federal Republic." [17)]

The problem of analyzing insurgent terrorism in industrialized societies in sociological terms is basically due to the fact that the terrorist movements are very small. It is much easier to explain the behaviour of majorities than minorities in political and social science. It is next to impossible to explain satisfactorily the doings of the

twelve people who formed the Symbionese Liberation Army (SLA) by
looking at U.S. society as a whole. Sociological explanations are
sometimes also reflecting political guilt-attributions. The terrorism
debate in West Germany illustrates this. Therefore, the two main
lines of reasoning reflect the political positions of the Social
Democrats and the Christian-Democratic party. The latter saw in the
1970s the causes of terrorism in too much civil liberties, tolerence,
democratization and freedom in almost all social spheres, while the
first party took the contrary view, putting the blame on intolerance
and resistance against social reforms, on the suppression of freedom
of expression and diffamation of nonviolent extra-parlamentarian
strategies of action at the time of the beginning student revolt. [18]
A representative of the first line of thinking is, for instance,
Hermann Lübbe, professor of political theory, who blames the politicians
for not having acted in time to stop the left from creating a crisis
of legitimacy of the state. [19]
Ernst Topitsch, professor of sociology,blames the proponents of the
permissive society in the media and the universities for preparing the
ground for the attack on the democratic order. [20]
On the other side of the German ideological divide we find causal
interpretations like those of Fetscher and Hess.
Iring Fetscher has presented some social-psychological theses to explain
the road which part of the - mainly academic youth - took from protest
to terrorism.

His five step model takes this form:

1. Point of departure is an extreme dissatisfaction with society.
   Life is experienced as absurd notwithstanding the growing wealth
   and in part even because of it.

2. For some years left-wing students in the "SDS" are looking for
   an exit through the study of marxist theorists.

3. Mental dissatisfaction and impatience found their expression in
   mass events and mass demonstrations.

4. The death of the student Benno Ohnesorg, (June 2nd 1967) and
   the assassination attempt on the student leader, Rudi Dutschke,
   raise the anger and militancy of numerous students and other
   young people.

5. It is no accident that psychologically disturbed people (like
   the patients' collective in Heidelberg) discover, as it were,
   that one can get rid of painful symptoms of one's own sickness
   temporarily by way of armed aggression. Many former members of
   this collective have since then joined the terrorist groups.

Fetscher also refers to the brutalities of the Vietnam war as a
contributing factor to the readiness to engage openly in armed
aggression. [21)

The Hess model lists ten steps on the road to terrorism and covers
both the German and the Italian rise of insurgent left-wing terrorism.
In abreviated form, these are:

1. Point of departure is a broad social protest movement. In Germany
   and Italy this was the anti-autoritarian student movement, the
   causes and contents of which in turn were extraordinarily
   multiple: the end of the post-war reconstruction period, the
   mass university, the alienation of youth from the political
   system of the parties and trade unions which are perceived as
   offering no possibilities for opposition and change (in Germany
   the great coalition, in Italy the reformist turn of the communist
   party); a categoric rejection of the achievement compulsions
   which are seen as absurd, of the mass manipulation (especially
   the Springer press imperium) and of the compulsion to consume;
   the demand for participatory democracy in the political and
   economic field; a new directness in private life; the accusation
   of fascism against the older generation; the experience of
   Vietnam war which led to the charge of imperialism against the
   own system and to the identification with the liberation
   movements of the Third World.

2. The members of the protest movement undergo key experiences
   of repressive violence during the course of conflict with their
   adversaries. In Germany these were a visit of the Shah in Berlin
   (police violence), and the assassination attempt on Dutschke
   ("violence" of the Springer press), in Italy the bomb explosion
   in the agricultural bank on the Piazza Fontana in Milan which
   formed the beginning of a strategy of tension, by which neo-fascist
   terror groups and parts of the state apparatus were preparing
   a right-wing coup d'état. Besides this are the experiences of
   everyday police violence on less important occasions. These
   experiences produce a radicalization and a discussion on
   counter-violence.

3. Due to the lack of response from those sectors of the population
   which are addressed by the movement as potential carriers for
   social change, the members of the movement experience frustration.
   The movement deteriorates. As one of the products of deterioration
   small groups are formed in which the use of violence as a tactical
   means is discussed for achieving the aspired goals despite all.

4. Factors of individual biography have to be consulted in order
   to explain what persons choose for what reasons to engage in
   counter-violence and in aggressive violence. Both in Germany and
   in Italy a high moral engagement, a product of class- and
   family-specific socialization as well as a product of isolation
   in a small group with high internal and low external contact, seem
   to play an important role.

5. Models are available for the decision to use violence. With regard to Germany these were primarily foreign groups such as the Tupamaros and the Palestinians, with regard to Italy there was in addition an autonomous tradition of revolutionary violence and above all the anti-fascist partisan movement of the period 1943-1945.

6. The first violent actions have more the character of a test in order to see how far one's own energy goes and what freedom of action is available. The arsonist attempt on a shopping centre and the liberation of Baader as first actions of what was to become the RAF as well as the conspiratorial game of Feltrinelli and the first arsonist actions of the Collettivo Politico Metropolitano, from which the Brigate rosse emerged, appear as a sort of primary deviation, which most definitively is not yet serious terrorism.

7. The further devlopment is determined through the interplay of internal dynamics and experiences of prosecution by the state, which both produce an escalation. On the one hand successful actions affirm the chosen tactic and its elaboration, on the other hand the persecution by the police forces them to live in the illegal underground, which furthers isolation and the sizeable concomitant criminality. Much of the mature terrorism is secondary, police-control-induced deviance, but nevertheless the motivation which produced the original primary deviance is not at all lost at this latter stage.

8. Existing terroristic groups function as crystallization points which attract further persons which are pre-detestined in the sense of point (4). The attraction effect occurs by means of the mass media.

9. The span of life of a social-revolutionary terrorist group is not only determined by the effectiveness of the police, but primarily by the resonance and support, which it obtains from certain sectors of society. The quantitive size as well as the qualitative element of the willingness to use violence of such sectors which on the basis of historical experiences have been receptive for anarchism, social-revolutionary theory and praxis, plays a role in this. The greater virulence of terrorism in Italy can in part be explained by the existence of a significantly larger lumpen-proletariat, a declassé petty and medium bourgeoisie, more unemployed young people, more students in a critical economic situation and a more sizeable so-called academic proletariat.

10. Certainly not to be underestimated, but difficult to pinpoint, is the role which covert provocation plays with regard to the success and life-span of the social-revolutionary terrorist groups. The agent provocateur is a well-known figure, and especially in Italy the thesis of a conspiracy between the Right and the pseudo-left is fervently discussed. 22)

Some of the elements which Hess offers, can also be found in the explanations of other authors, although the emphasis is often different. Alessandro Silj, author of books on the Red Brigades, for instance, places rather more emphasis on the strategy of tension of the neo-fascist party MSI, and the "black conspiracy" as causes for the emergence of a left reaction. Yet Silj also concludes that, on the whole "it is fairly obvious that urban guerrillas in Italy are the product of a combination of indigenous political, economic and social conditions." 23)

Franco Ferrarotti, the eminent Italian sociologist, places strong emphasis on the immobility of politics in Italy:

> "Terrorism is a response to the lack of political education in Italy.
> It is a tragic response to an overabundance of political stability.
> I know it sounds paradoxical, but you have to remember that the
> Italian government almost never changes. The Christian-Democrats
> are in power and stay in power - always the same faces, 38 years
> Andreotti, Fanfani and so on. The country is a democracy, but its
> institutions are not run according to democratic criteria. Youth
> and the new urban classes are cut off from power. Political parties
> and trade unions carry a heavy responsibility for the birth and
> growth of terrorism since they have neglected the energy and the
> demands of the young ones." 24)

A variation to the Immobility Thesis is offered by L. Bonanate:

> "A society that knows terrorism is a blocked society, incapable of
> answering the citizens' requests for change, but nevertheless capable
> of preserving and reproducing itself.... (...) A situation seems
> blocked when there seems no innovation capable of bringing about a
> new situation.... (...) When a political system is capable of
> rejecting the requests it receives without giving them any answer
> and still does not lose its stability, then a block occurs which
> in term produces a terrorist answer. (...) When a Communist party
> collaborates with a middle-class government or actually agrees to
> share government responsibilities with the latter, how much room
> is there for an autonomous mass initiative by a "revolutionary"? (...)
> This would be our final corollary: terrorism appears whenever
> and wherever the masses lose their role as protagonists of history." 25)

The Bonanate thesis resembles in some ways the "lack of alternative" thesis, which is not only a favourite argument of terrorist practitioners themselves but also is found with some authors: E. Hyams, for instance, concludes:

> "I can find no single case in which recourse to terrorism was not
> forced on the organization in question by denial of all other means
> of fighting against social injustice. Whenever I have seemed to
> come upon such a case, it has turned out that although other means
> exist in theory, they have been found useless in practice - a common
> case in the great oligarchies called parliamentary democracies,
> and the invariable case in the great bureaucracies called Communist
> or People's Republics." 26)

If this thesis would hold true, then there should be - other things being equal - a great deal of insurgent terrorists in communist societies, which is manifestly not true.

It is probably a good idea to differentiate the causation of insurgent terrorism in democratic societies from such terrorism in more autocratic societies. Feliks Gross has made such an attempt in his study of Terror and Political Assassination in Eastern Europe and Russia. Gross sees two different sets of causes at work: where domestic autocracy or foreign conquerors are the terrorist target oppression is a causal factor, where individual terrorism is directed against representatives of democracy or against members of the revolutionary organization itself, a growing anomie takes the place of oppression (see diagrams IV and V).

Diagram IV

Causation of Tactical Terrorist Acts Against Foreign Rule or Autocracy, According to Gross.

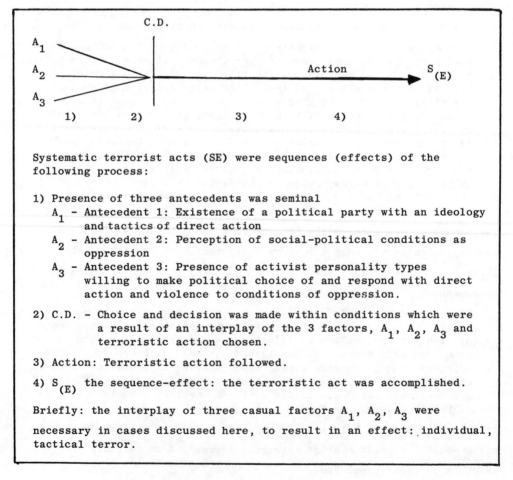

Systematic terrorist acts (SE) were sequences (effects) of the following process:

1) Presence of three antecedents was seminal
    A_1 - Antecedent 1: Existence of a political party with an ideology and tactics of direct action
    A_2 - Antecedent 2: Perception of social-political conditions as oppression
    A_3 - Antecedent 3: Presence of activist personality types willing to make political choice of and respond with direct action and violence to conditions of oppression.

2) C.D. - Choice and decision was made within conditions which were a result of an interplay of the 3 factors, A_1, A_2, A_3 and terroristic action chosen.

3) Action: Terroristic action followed.

4) $S_{(E)}$ the sequence-effect: the terroristic act was accomplished.

Briefly: the interplay of three casual factors A_1, A_2, A_3 were necessary in cases discussed here, to result in an effect: individual, tactical terror.

Diagram V

Causation of Individual Violence as Tactics Against Democratic
Institutions, According to Gross.

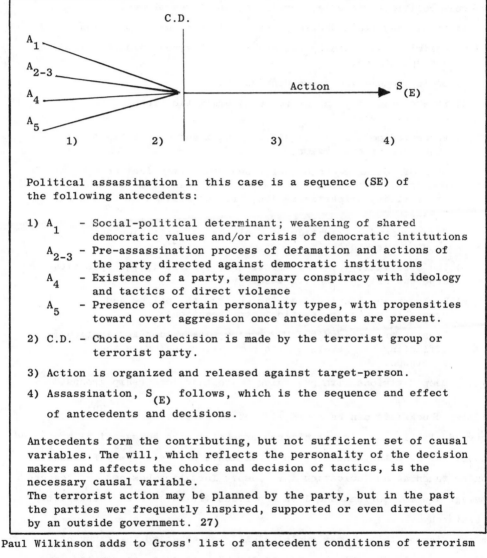

Political assassination in this case is a sequence (SE) of
the following antecedents:

1) A_1 - Social-political determinant; weakening of shared
         democratic values and/or crisis of democratic intitutions
   A_{2-3} - Pre-assassination process of defamation and actions of
         the party directed against democratic institutions
   A_4 - Existence of a party, temporary conspiracy with ideology
         and tactics of direct violence
   A_5 - Presence of certain personality types, with propensities
         toward overt aggression once antecedents are present.

2) C.D. - Choice and decision is made by the terrorist group or
      terrorist party.

3) Action is organized and released against target-person.

4) Assassination, $S_{(E)}$ follows, which is the sequence and effect
of antecedents and decisions.

Antecedents form the contributing, but not sufficient set of causal
variables. The will, which reflects the personality of the decision
makers and affects the choice and decision of tactics, is the
necessary causal variable.
The terrorist action may be planned by the party, but in the past
the parties wer frequently inspired, supported or even directed
by an outside government. 27)

Paul Wilkinson adds to Gross' list of antecedent conditions of terrorism

the following ones:

"- the diffusion of knowledge concerning terrorist "successes",
methods and technologies which facilitate emulation;

- the existence of a tradition of terrorism, and;

- the intensification of hatred and the desires for vengeance
which characterises communal violence." 28)

A recurring problem in the literature is whether the causes of
revolution, the causes of political violence in general, are also the
causes of terrorism. For Wilkinson, the latter are embedded in the
former and he therefore gives us a checklist of general causes of
internal political violence, consisting of eleven elements:

1) Ethnic conflicts, hatreds, discrimination and oppression;

2) Religious and ideological conflicts, hatreds, discriminition
   and oppression;

3) Socio-economic relative deprivation;

4) Stresses and strains of rapid modernization tending to
   accentuate 3);

5) Perceived political inequities, infringements of rights,
   injustice or oppression;

6) Lack of adequate channels for peaceful communication of
   protests, grievances and demands (e.g. denial of franchise or
   other rights of participation, representation or access to
   media);

7) Existence of a tradition of violence, disaffection and
   popular turbulence;

8) The availability of a revolutionary leadership equipped with
   a potentially attractive ideology;

9) Weakness and ineptness of the government, police and judicial
   organs (e.g. under-reaction, over-reaction);

10) Erosion of confidence in the régime, its values and institutions
    afflicting all levels of the population including the
    government;

11) Deep divisions with governing élites and leadership groups." [29]

Similar checklists can be found with other authors as well [30], but
they add little that is not already present in the enumerations presented
above. The fact that enumeration of elements are relatively frequent,
can be taken as an indication that theory formation has not yet reached
a stage where important and less important variables are grouped into
a hierarchy.

In the view of this writer sociological approaches to the study of
terrorism would probably benefit if they do not take society and its
"sick" condition as point of departure, but if they would begin by
studying the terrorist movement or organization: its internal structure,
the recruting and desertion of members, its pre-terroristic phase,
its non-terroristic activities, its internal dynamics and its external

links. Unfortunately such an approach is only possible for
movements and organizations which are no longer active and no
longer in the underground or in secrecy.
But given the short life-cycles of many movements and the high
turnover of members of many of these organizations, the problem
is perhaps less serious than would appear at first sight.
There is no shortage of study objects, as can be gathered from these
figures on the European scene:

> ".... terrorist groups tend to proliferate in certain regions
> and countries. For example, 217 terrorist groups existed in
> Europe between 1970 and 1980. In the past two years alone, 128
> groups were counted there. In Italy some 60 groups are active,
> while in Spain some 25 groups were operating in recent years. 31)

From the above quote one can deduce that 89 terrorist groups have
either changed names or ceased to exist. The latter would mean that
they are potentially accessible for social science analysis based on,
for instance, interviews with ex-members.

Conclusion

The reader might at this point rightfully ask: is that all there is?
This survey has naturally been sketchy but nevertheless it gives, in
this writers view, a fairly broad overview of what is presently
available in the open literature on the etiology of terrorism. A number
of authors are writing classified studies and there might be some
"golden eggs" there which are of a higher calibre than the "theories"
presented here. A glance of that other side can be gained from some
of the responses we received on the question: "Do you know any areas
where theoretical contributions on Terrorism have produced policy
changes?". Here are some answers:

- "Yes, but I am not at liberty to say [which]."
- "My own with regard to the ... government and its security
  authorities."
- "I must admit that my own general theory of the hardline liberal
  democratic response has been increasingly adopted in Western
  countries. This has brought cumulative policy changes over
  5-6 years."
- "Of course: everywhere in Europe, North America and South America,
  Asia... but those changes can't be identified, demonstrated by

"positivistic" research methods. The results are in the repression,
disappearance or increasing of terrorist activities."

Another respondent has soberly remarked that "Significant policy changes
are normally dictated by expediency rather than theory or even empirical
evidence. Theoreticians end up in ivory towers, not the White House"
(Monday).

The first part of this statement can be true even when the second is
not. Some theoreticians do end up at high places of policy-making.
T.P. Thornton, for instance, the author of one of the most perceptive
articles on terrorism, ended up in the White House's National Security
Council. Some areas where policy changes have become visible are
hostage negotiation techniques or screening procedures for identifying
potential hijackers. These, however, are not directly linked to the
main thrust of this survey, which was on the etiology of terrorism.

If we return from applied theories to social science theories, the
question is what ought to be done next. We put the question "Where do
you see the most fruitful areas for theory construction in the field
of Terrorism?" to our respondents. There was much pessimism emerging
from the answers. Merari, for instance, simply answered "Nowhere".
Sederberg made some very sensible remarks:

> "I find it hard to see how we can go about "constructing theories"
> when there seems so little consensus on the boundaries of the
> subject about which we are "theorizing". I see the descriptive
> studies as contributing to our understanding of past events. I see
> the typological and definitional disputes as (optimistically)
> contributing to the gradual emergence of a common sense of what we
> are talking about. The character of terroristic acts (their secrecy,
> relative infrequency, emotional nature, etc.) reinforce all the
> ambiguities that generally afflict all social sciences theorizing.
> I think the quest for "terrorist" theory, at least in the narrow
> sense of the word (as opposed to heuristic speculation, analytical
> frameworks, etc.) is otiose."

It would seem that satisfactory solutions to the definition and the
data problems would have to be found first, before much progress is
possible. On this aspect Charles Wilber placed special emphasis,
writing:

> "We need more precise and extensive data (not conjecture) on the
> various terrorist episodes plus voluminous data on practioners.
> If we could then extract some common elements we might be able to
> begin on theory construction. I suggest that the epidemiological
> approach or the natural history format might give us a preliminary
> base for hypothesis construction."

Several authors pleaded for interdisciplinary approaches or comparative
case studies, both contemporary and historical, as a means to advance
the state of thinking. An interesting avenue for theory construction
has been suggested by Mark Monday who wrote:

> "Terrorism should be studied in <u>relationship</u> to all other forms of
> social/political violence and non-violent insurgency. It is the
> intensities and the relationships of one to the other where the
> theories can be best tested."

Not infrequently terrorist groups are splinter groups from broader
political movements (like the student movement) and it might be that
the life-cycle of these movements - e.g. when such a movement stagnates
and the choice is between giving up or radicalization - can tell us
something about the decision to opt for terrorist techniques. Such an
option is often justified with the argument that there is no other
alternative than terrorism to advance one's cause. Such self-justifications
of those engaging in terrorism are in themselves worthy study objects
and a content analysis of terrorist texts can potentially reveal
much on the cosmology of the violent actors. If such texts reveal
different criteria for what constitutes a successful action or campaign
then we ourselves utilize, it is important to know their reference system.
The perceptions of terrorist actors, their justifications for what they
are doing, the validity of their strategic assumptions should not be
dismissed lightly as ideology and propaganda, but deserves serious
attention and evaluation. After all those who engage in terrorist
violence - if they are not psychopaths or mere imitators - have some
sort of theory which determines their terrorist practice. The "theories"
of the terrorist themselves are, in a sense, the most important
theories in the field and social scientists would do well to absorb
them thoroughly before proceeding to construct their own theories.

Notes

1) Harry Eckstein. On the Etiology of Internal Wars. In: Ivo K. Feierabend, Rosalind L. Feierabend, Ted Robert Gurr (Eds.). Anger, Violence & Politics. Theories and Research. Englewood Cliffs, Prentice-Hall, 1972, p.15.

2) Chalmers Johnson. Perspecives on Terrorism. Repr. in W. Laqueur (Ed.). The Terrorism Reader. New York, New American Library, 1978, p.278; M. Crenshaw. The Causes of Terrorism. Comparative Politics, July 1981, p.381.

3) W. Laqueur. Terrorism, 1977, p.80.

4) Brian M. Jenkins. Terrorists at the Threshold. In: E. Nobles Lowe Harry D. Shargel (Eds.). Legal and Other Aspects of Terrorism. New York, 1979, pp.74-75.

5) E.S. Heyman. Monitoring the Diffusion of Transnational Terrorism. Gaithersburg, Md. IACP, 1980, pp.2-3.

6) John D. Elliott and Leslie K. Gibson (Eds.) Contemporary Terrorism. Selected Readings. Gaithersburg, Md., IACP, 1978, p.1-2. See also Elliott's "Transitions of Contemporary Terrorism", Military Review, Vol.57, No.5, May 1977, p.3.

7) J. Henk Leurdijk. Summary of Proceedings: Our Violent Future. In: David Carlton & Carlo Schaerf (Eds.). International Terrorism and World Security. London, Croom Helm, 1975, p.2.

8) Imanuel Geiss. Sources of Contemporary Conflicts and Political Revolutions: A Preliminary Survey. Co-existence, Vol.14, p.11.

9) M. Crenshaw Hutchinson. Revolutionary Terrorism. Stanford, Hoover Institution Press, 1978, pp. 133-135.

10) Ibid., p.139.

11) The communication, transportation, urbanization aspects as permissive factors are stressed by Evans, Grabosky, Wördemann and Chalmers Johnson.

12) Chalmers Johnson., op.cit., p.281.

13) M. Crenshaw. The Causes of Terrorism, op.cit., pp.382-383.

14) Cit. E. Hyams. Terrorist and Terrorism. London, J.M. Dent & Sons, 1975, p.173.

15) Hannah Arendt. On Violence. In: Crisis of the Republic. Harmondsworth, Penguin, 1973, p.233. - Both quoted from P. Wilkinson. Political Terrorism, London, Macmillan, 1974, p.130.

Notes

16) Politikwissenschaft und Gewaltproblematik. In: H. Geissler (Ed.).
    Der Weg in die Gewalt. München, Olzog, 1978, p.74.

17) Bewaffnete Heilslehren, in: H. Geissler, op.cit., p.40.

18) Egbert Jahn, "Was heisst geistige Auseinandersetzung mit dem
    Terrorismus?"; zusammenfassende Thesen zum Vortrag in Groningen.
    September 1980, Mimeo, p.1.

19) Herman Lübbe. Endstation Terror. Rückblick auf lange Märsche.
    Stuttgart, 1978, p.99; cit. Hans Dieter Schwind (Ed.).
    Ursachen des Terrorismus in der Bundesrepublik Deutschland. Berlin,
    Walter de Gruyter, 1978, p.49.

20) Cit. Schwind, p.51.

21) Iring Fetscher. Terrorismus und Reaktion. Köln, Europäische
    Verlagsanstalt, 1977, pp.20-22.

22) H. Hess. Terrorismus und Terrorismus-Diskurs. Tijdschrift voor
    Criminolgie. No.4, 1981, pp.181-184.

23) A. Silj. Never Again Without a Rifle. New York, Karz, 1979, p.xii.

24) Gaither Stewart. Italië. De traditie van het terrorisme. Haagse Post,
    No.44, 31 October 1981, p.51.

25) L. Bonanate. Some Unanticipated Consequences of Terrorism.
    Journal of Peace Research, Vol.16, No. 3, 1979, pp.205-209.

26) Edward Hyams. Terrorists and Terrorism. London, J.M. Dent & Sons Ltd.,
    1975, p.170.

27) F. Gross. Violence in Politics. The Hague, Mouton, 1972, pp.89-92.

28) P. Wilkinson. Terrorism and the Liberal State. London, Macmillan,
    1977, p.96.

29) Ibid., p.37.

30) For instance in Anthony Burton. Urban Terrorism. Theory, Practise &
    Response. New York, 1975, p.248.

31) Y. Alexander and John M. Gleason (Eds.). Behavioural and Quantitative
    Perspectives on Terrorism. New York, Pergamon Press, 1981, p. xiv.

III. DATA BASES

DATA BASES
Data in the Field of Terrorism

The collection of data is dependent on theories as well as definitions.
Definitions help the data collector to focus his search on a clearly
deliminated field of facts, events or phenomena. Theories will help
him to extract from the field what is deemed important. To give an
example: people are reported to be in terror. A definition of terror
as chronic fear of impending victimization will help the analyst to
distinguish it from the shorter fright and other kinds of fears and
allow him to exclude the latter. But in addition he also needs some
theory of causation. If the data collector is interested in terrorism
he will exclude the terror caused by natural disasters and from manmade
terror he will select only purposive terror and leave out situational
terror. A data collector always works as a gate-keeper, including some
information and excluding other. The research or policy interest will,
by and large, determine the nature of the data. But the data obtained
are only as good as the source of the data is reliable. When it comes
to terrorism, the media are often the single most important source, at
least for those social scientists who are not working with classified
data.
In the following pages we will describe some data bases and some data
types and discuss, in varying depth, their utility.

Aggregate Data on Political Violence

In the 1960 aggregate data analyses on comparative political violence
in various countries became en vogue in the United States. The primary
source of information was the Index of the New York Times. However, for
the purpose of retrieving data on terrorism this particular computerized
source was silent, simply because the Index did not carry any entry
under the heading "terrorism". Only after 1969 the NYT Index started
to feature terrorism as a distinct category. [1] There were, however,
event entries under such headings as "bombings" or "assassination" in
this Index so that the researcher hunting for readily available data
could take these for terrorism, depending on his working definition.
One of the best known data sets based primarily on the New York Times

Index is Ted Gurr's <u>Strive Events Data Set</u>. It lists over 2400 strive
events in 114 countries for the years 1961 - 1970. For a description
of this data set the reader can consult T.R. Gurr, Comparative Studies
of Political Conflict and Change: Cross-National Data Sets. (Ann Arbor,
Michigan, Inter-University Consortium for Political and Social Research,
1978, Part I). There are a number of similar data sets. One of the
most comprehensive collections covering violent events for the period
1948 - 1967 can be found in the Handbook of Political and Social
Indicators, edited by Charles L. Taylor and Michael D. Hudson (New Haven,
Connecticut, Yale University Press, 1972 - a third edition is in the
making but, like its predecessor, does not list "terrorism" in a separate
category. [2]) Some other data sets which are equally useful in this
context, are the <u>Cross-polity Time Series Data</u> (A.S. Banks et. al. 1971), the
<u>Political Instability Data</u> of Feierabend and Feierabend for the period
1948 - 1962, and the data forming the basis for D.G. Morrison's et al.
Black Africa: A Comparative Handbook (1972). All of them are available
from the Inter-University Consortium for Political and Social Research
in Ann Arbor (ICPSR., P.O. Box 1248, Ann Arber, Michigan 48106, U.S.A.)
Also based in Ann Arbor and of related interest is the Correlates of
War Project of J.D. Singer et al., whose first statistical volume
The Wages of War, 1816 - 1965 (New York, Wiley & Sons, 1972), covering
only international violence has been updated and widened to include
civil wars with and without foreign intervention (J.D. Singer and
M. Small. Resort to Arms. Beverly Hills, Sage, 1982). Finally, the
<u>Conflict and Peace Data Bank</u> (COPDAB) now at the University of
Maryland, under the directorship of Edward E. Azar should be mentioned.
It records, based on over 70 sources, domestic and international events
ranging from boycotts and clashes to war for about 135 nation-states,
starting on 1 January 1948. It contains by now more than half a
million events and although it is not tailored on terrorism it is likely
to be useful in determining the context of terroristic events. For a
description, see Edward E. Azar. The Conflict and Peace Data Bank (COPDAB)
Project: <u>Journal of Conflict Resolution</u>, Vol.24, No.1, 1980.
A similar effort, though much more modest and not computer-based, to
gather data on violent events has been undertaken at the French
Polemological Institute on the initiative of the late Gaston Bouthoul.

It assembled data on macro- and microconflicts, based mainly on media
accounts. In the "Chronique de la Violence Mondiale", published from
1968 to 1970 in the journal Guerre et Paix and since then (with an
interruption from June 1976 to December 1977) in the Etudes Polémologiques,
terrorism is treated as a special category. The following manifestations
fall under the heading terrorism: (1) Political assaults against persons
and things; (2) Political assassinations and political executions;
(3) Political hostage-taking, kidnapping; and (4) Hijacking of aircrafts.
The data are, however, not very specific. Usually only the place and
date of a violent event, the type of collective violence it is part of,
the casualities and the context (religious, student protest, etc.) are
mentioned. The coverage, beginning in 1968, is uneven for many countries
and this data base is in fact mainly important because it covers France
well for which there are few other sources on terrorism (except perhaps
the Dossier de Presse issued by the Fondation Nationale de Science
Politique). The Institute Français de Polémologie is located at the
Hotel National des Invalides (Escalier M - 4e étage, pièce 10, rue de
Grenelle, 75007 Paris, France).

Chronologies of Terrorism and Violence

The most common format of data collections on terrorism are chronologies
of incidents. Sometimes these are ranged according to the type of
incidents and are global in scope such as in the case of hijacking data.
More often they concentrate on incidents of certain terrorist movements
or cover the domestic events within a nation. The national framework
for data collection is still the most widespread. In the following
sections, chronologies from four nations are presented by way of example.

Federal Republic of Germany

Various publications such as W. Althammer. Gegen den Terror. Texte und
Dokumente (Stuttgart, Bonn Aktuell, 1978) contain chronologies of terrorist
incidents. The source is almost always the Federal Criminal Office
(Bundeskriminalamt) in Wiesbaden, which has the consequence that once a
group is labelled "terroristic" all its illegal acts, such as bank
robberies and even the destruction of public transport ticket machines

are enumerated under acts of terror. The most complete "Official
Calender of Events" publicly available can be found in A. Jeschke and
W. Malanowski (Eds.). Der Minister und der Terrorist. Gespräche zwischen
Gerhart Baum und Horst Mahler. (Reinbek, Rowohlt, 1980) This chronology
of almost seventy pages covers domestic left- and right-wing terroristic
events as well as foreign events bearing on the German scene for the
period 1967 - 1980. It does, however, not include vigilante terrorism
between Yugoslavian citizens and Croatian separatists and sortlike clashes
between other foreign migrant groups. Complied by the working group
"Oeffentlichkeitsarbeit gegen Terrorismus" of the Ministry of the Interior
(which in the GFR is also responsible for the police), it lists attacks
on persons and on property as well as armed robberies by various
terroristic groups on an annual basis. For each event, the date, location,
nature of the act and the perpetrating group are listed.

Annual reports on extremist organizations are provided by the Verfassungsschutz (the office for the Protection of the Constitution). The 1972
report, for instance, lists 123 right-wing organizations (responsible
for 428 incidents - not necessarily terroristic) and 390 groups (or names)
on the Left, responsible for 515 acts of "terrorism" [3].

Such data are the public top of a bureaucratic iceberg. The terrorism
data bank of the Federal Criminal Office is held to be the best of its
kind in the world. In 1976, at a meeting of the ministers of the European
Economic Community, the German government offered the other EEC member
countries on the basis of mutuality, access to its computerized data
base which at that time included 2.1 million general files, 3.3 million
pictures and 2.8 million fingerprints [4]. According to one of our
respondents not only West Germany, but also the governments of Italy,
Great Britain and the United States have at their disposal equally
detailled data on national and international terroristic incidents.
However, as long as groups labelled terroristic are active, social
scientists are not likely to get access to this kind of data.
R.D. Crelinsten has outlined some of the problems created by this
situation.:

> "While anyone can go to newspaper archives, this is not true of
> law enforcement and government agencies. Because of the nature
> of the subject, raw data on international political terrorism is
> not easy to get. Much of the information on specific incidents is
> classified, as it is

related to intelligence operations or is considered pertinent
to "national security". This problem of secrecy creates a natural
barrier between the research community and the operations community.
The result often is, that the latter sits on the raw data and does
no research with it, while the former has the facilities and personnel
for doing research, but no access to the data." 5)

As long as the access problem is not solved, researchers have to content
themselves with often rather crude and politically biased chronologies.

Northern Ireland

The conflict in Northern Ireland is generally well-covered by the
literature on terrorism. It has also one of the finest chronologies
written on any recent conflict. The two volumes of Richard Deutsch and
Vivien Magowan. Northern Ireland, 1968 - 1973. A Chronology of Events
(Belfast, Blackstaff Press, 1973-)are in fact much more than a simple
time-table based on newspaper accounts. The authors have carefully
evaluated their sources, screened private papers and official
publications, and came up with a factual record of events which is
hard to improve on. For anybody trying to make sense of the last wave
of violence in Ireland it is mandatory background reading. It is worth
quoting the authors themselves in order to give an idea of the kind of
detachment that is still possible in a situation that invites polarized
perspectives:

> "In this Chronology we are naturally not concerned with drawing
> conclusions from events, but with the presentation of an accurate
> sequence of happenings. In order to arrive at a true picture we
> have constantly questioned and double-checked sources and have
> then questioned yet again. After determining, on a balance of
> reason and probability, what did or did not take place on a
> given day at a given time, we make no claims to be completely
> successful, but we do feel that we made a fair effort. It has been
> said that impartiality consists of doing justice to everybody: in
> the final analysis, however, one man's fact is another's falsehood
> and no human being - nor even any "official source" - can claim a
> monopoly of "absolute truth". (...) We have tried to show the life
> of the Province as it really was - not as any single person or
> individual imagined it to be ...." 6)

Less broad and more theory-orientated are the data which Steve Wright
developed for the period 1969 - 1980. Basing himself on three main
sources, The Royal Ulster Constabulary (Knock Rd., Belfast), the Army
Information Services (BFPO 824, Lisburn) and The Northern Ireland Office
(Gt. George St., London), this peace researcher built up a comprehensive

computer-based data set. It includes figures for assassinations; bomb
and shooting attacks; killings and woundings of police, army personnel
and civilians; kneecappings; internment figures; vehicle and house
searches; CS gas cartridges and grenades fired; plastic and rubber
bullets fired; convictions for acts of terrorism, etc. By presenting
these data in monthly breakdowns, the dynamics of terrorism and
governmental counter-strategies become visible and reveal "a set of
remarkably structured processes" which, according to Wright, are
sustained by "reactive rather than active processes". [7]
These data are available for secondary analyses at the Richardson
Institute for Conflict and Peace Research Department of Politics,
Fylde College, University of Lancaster, Bailrigg, Lancaster LA 1 4YF,
United Kingdom.

The Netherlands

The only overview of terroristic incidents in the Netherlands can be
found in the thesis of Joke Cuperus and Rineke Klijnsma. To Negotiate
or to Attack. The Dutch Government's Policy in Matters of Terrorism (Groningen, Polemological Instituut, 1980). The authors provide
an overview of 26 acts of "terrorism" which took place between 1970 and
1978 in the Netherlands. Fourteen of these incidents are labelled
"political" by the authors. A synopsis of each incident is given and
19 variables are listed for each incident, referring to such aspects
as age of the perpetrators, type of act, number of hostages involved
and demands made to the authorities. In their eagerness to be even-handed,
the authors also included some governmental actions, such as weapon
searches in South Moluccan neighbourhoods by the military and a shooting
incident beteen a police arrest team and terrorists form the German RAF.
Despite its limitations, this Dutch-language overview is useful.

The United States of America

One of the first chronologies in the field of terrorism was published
by Scanlan's Monthly (No. 8, January 1971). This journalistic account
covers the period 1965 - end of 1970 and lists various forms of
vandalism, sabotage and destruction as urban guerrilla activities.

The incidents are classified by targets such as government, corporations,
police and military apparatus, schools and homes. It reflects protests
against the Vietnam war and the titel of this issue "Guerrilla War in
the USA" is an overstatement of the editor of this 27 page chronology,
Warren Hinckle, the former editor of Ramparts. It has been superseded
by the very complete chronology by Marcia McKnight-Trick. Her chronology
is based mainly on newspaper accounts, supplemented by information from
the Federal Bureau of Investigation (FBI) and the Federal Aviation
Administration (FAA). Her "Chronology of Incidents of Terroristic,
Quasi-Terroristic, and Political Violence in the United States:
January 1965 - March 1976" forms Appendix 6 of the Task Force Report
on Disorders and Terrorism, issued by the U.S. National Advisory Committee
on Criminal Justice Standards and Goals (Washington, D.C., GPO, 1976).
This 80 page chronology covers incidents of a terroristic nature,
violence with political implications, hijackings and acts of hostage
taking. It is prefaced by a "Who's Who", describing 18 left-wing and
10 right-wing movements responsible for many of the incidents listed
in the chronology. A further data set covering almost the same time
span is "The BDM Corporation's Terrorism Data Base".(BDM is located in
Vienna, Virgina, U.S.A.) Using nine different sources, BDM collected
data on 4700 incidents of terrorism and other forms of violent behaviour
for the years 1965 - 1975. Three quarter of the incidents refer to
occurrences within the United States and seventy percent of the data
refer to bombings. While there is no definition of terrorism the cases
selected are based on twelve criteria. 8)

Special Data

Apart from country-based chronologies there are also a number of incident-
type-based chronologies, both national and international. There is, for
instance, a 21 page "Chronology of Transnational Terrorist Attacks upon
American Business People, 1968 - 1978", included in Y. Alexander and
Robert A. Kilmark (Eds.). Political Terrorism and Business. New York,
Praeger, 1979; For Nuclear Terrorism - so far mainly hoaxes - there is
a chronology listing more than 200 incidents for the period 1969 - 1977
under the title "Threats and Acts of Violence Against U.S. Nuclear
Facilities". It forms Appendix 2 in Augustus R. Norton and Martin H. Greenberg,

Studies in Nuclear Terrorism (Boston, G.K. Hall & Co., 1979).

For worldwide coverage of hijackings (terroristic and escape hijackings) there is a "Master List of All Hijacking Attempts, Worldwide, Air Carrier, and General Aviation", which is issued and periodically updated by the U.S. Department of Transportation, Federal Aviation Administration, Office of Aviation Medicine. This list is, however, not complete and should be consulted together with other chronologies, especially where non-American aircrafts and foiled attempts at skyjackings are involved. One such list forms Appendix A in James A. Arey. The Sky Pirates.(London, Ian Allan, 1973) This 73 pages list uses, in addition to FAA data, information provided by the International Civil Aviation Organization, the International Air Transport Association, the American Air Transport Association and news clippings.

International Chronologies

While the above mentioned chronologies covered mainly domestic violence, there are a number of broader chronologies either covering particular conflicts or international incidents. An example of the first kind would be "Palestinian Impasse: Arab Guerrillas and International Terror", edited by Lester A. Sobel. New York, Facts on File, 1977. It traces events since the Six-Day War of 1967 and chronicles not only the activities of Palestinian Arabs, but also those of the Israelis. Based on the weekly records compiled by Facts on File Inc., it gives a very detailed account going far beyond a mere incident description. Although not as thorough as the Deutsch and Magowan chronology on Northern Ireland, it gives enough context to place the terrorist incidents firmly into the political process of the Middle East. Where there are conflicting versions of an incident, the volume gives both readings which helps to make it a more balanced account than, for instance, a count assembled by the Anti-Defamation League of B'nai B'rith, which, for the period 1966 - 1977, lists Arab terrorist deeds resulting in the death of 1131 people, the wounding of 2471 and the taking of 2755 people as hostages. [9] Lester A. Sobel is also the editor of two more chronological accounts: Political Terrorism. Oxford, Clio Press, 1978. The first volume covers the period from the late 1960s on through the first half of the 1970s. The second volume carries the narrative into the early part of 1978.

Giving regional and country-by-country accounts of developments, these
well-indexed volumes form basic handbooks for anyone trying to come to
grips with the upsurge of insurgent terrorism in the last fifteen
years. The professed aim of the editor to be impartial ("Although
much that is here is highly controversial, a conscious effort was made
to set it all down without bias and to make this volume as far as
possible, a reliable and balanced reference work ") appears credible,
although the data are only as good as the wire service and newspaper
accounts which form the sources for the Facts on File compilations.

The Rand Corporation Chronology

The Rand Chronology developed by Brian M. Jenkins and his associates
has been the prototype for most other chronologies of incidents. It was
developed by the Californian Think Tank RAND for the U.S. State Department
and the Department of Defence and concentrated not on domestic U.S.
incidents, but on "International Terrorism". Jenkins describes some of
the common characteristics of the incidents he studied with these
words:

> "International terrorism can be a single incident or a campaign
> of violence waged outside the presently accepted rules and
> procedures of international diplomacy and war; it is often
> designed to attract worldwide attention to the existence and
> cause of the terrorists and to inspire fear. Often the violence
> is carried out for effect. The actual victim or victims of
> terrorist attacks and the target audience may not be the same:
> the victims may be totally unrelated to the struggle." 10)

The RAND chronology includes all incidents that had "clear international
repercussions ... - incidents in which terrorists went abroad to strike
their targets, selected victims or targets that had connections with a
foreign state (e.g. diplomats, foreign businessmen, offices of foreign
corporations), or created international incidents by attacking airline
passengers, personnel and equipment". 11) Not included were incidents
in the course of wars like Vietnam and at the border of Israel. State
Terrorism, because of its more domestic nature, was also excluded.
In their first public report, issued in March 1975, their chronology
listed 507 incidents. In the meantime more than one thousand have been
listed. The sources for the RAND data gathering effort have been press
accounts, supplemented by data from the London-based "Arab Report

and Record" (which issues a fortnightly edition) and chronologies
prepared by various U.S. government departments and Congressional
committees.

This data basis has been the foundation for many classified and open
studies. Aided by specialists with backgrounds in psychology, psychiatry,
political science, military operations, psychological operations,
intelligence, weapons technology, computer science and mathematics,
Brian Jenkins, himself a historian, has looked into such research areas
as the potential for nuclear action (See his: Attributes of Potential
Criminal Adversaries to U.S. Nuclear Programs. St. Monica, Rand, 1978
(R-1115 - SL), hostage survival chances (See his: Numbered Lives:
Some Statistical Observations from 77 International Hostage Episodes.
Conflict, Vol. 1, Nos. 1-2, 1978), the profile of a "typical hijacker"
and a "typical terrorist". Using quite simple statistical methods
these quantitative studies led to findings which apparently have had
significant influence on the U.S. governments anti-terrorist policies.
Among the findings of one of his studies, based on 90 international
hostage incidents, figured such insights as:

  -"There is almost 80 percent chance that all members of the kidnapping
   team will escape death or capture, whether or not they successfully
   seize hostages. Once they make explicit ransom demands, there is
   a close to even chance that all or some of those demands will be
   granted and virtually a 100 percent probability of achieving
   worldwide or at least national publicity." (...)

  -"In two-thirds of the cases in which explicit demands were made,
   they were directed at the local government. The release of prisoners
   was the principal demand in two-thirds of the cases in which demands
   were made."

  -"Firm no-concession policies toward individual kidnappings have
   not clearly served as deterrents to future kidnapping tactics." (...)

  -"More hostages have died during an assault by security forces than
   from cold execution by the terrorists." 13)

The Rand chronology has also been used to analyse trends of terrorism. 14)
Yet due to the flexible definition of terrorism it is questionable
whether overall assessments are possible. In the first published version,
listing slightly more than 500 incidents which occurred between
9 January 1968 and 26 April 1974, we find a congeries of acts of political
violence and destruction which stretch the concept of terrorism too
much. While it is a common thing to treat hijackings for escape as well
as hijackings for blackmail as if they belonged to the same type of

action, we also find in the chronology of terrorism incidents involving
no loss of human life or threat thereof, such as sabotage of an oil
carrying pipeline, vandalization of bank offices and theft of documents,
damaging a power line with a bomb, the firebombing of an empty car.
While such vagueness of definition of terrorism does not undermine the
value of some Rand studies dealing with particular problems (such as
examinations of the hostages own experience or the bargaining policies
and tactics with terrorists holding hostages) it casts doubt on the
usefulness of the whole data set for general trend analysis. Although
Rand's work is very policy-oriented, some of the best social science
work on terrorism has been done there. Rand studies, such as G. Bass
and B.M. Jenkins et al. Motivations and Possible Actions of Potential
Criminal Adversaries of the U.S. Nuclear Programs. Santa Monica, Rand,
February 1980, combine original   methodology with originally developed
data and have been a stimulation to other researchers in the field.
The Rand Corporation is located at 1700 Main Street, Santa Monica,
California 90406, U.S.A.

Other U.S. Non-Governmental Chronologies

A similar chronology as the one of Brian Jenkins et al. has been developed
at the University of Oklahoma (Norman, Oklahoma) at the Department of
Political Science under professor S. Sloan and his associates. Their
sources included the Rand chronology presented above, the New York Times,
Facts on File and other public sources. Starting with a data collection
on 111 incidents, Sloan later expanded his data universe to 168 cases.
These were clear-cut cases of kidnappings, armed attacks involving
hostage-taking, hijackings and assassinations. One of the key concepts
used by this group of researchers is the Non-Territorial nature of
Terrorism in their sample (abbreviated NTT). In their analysis of,
15 hijackings and 27 assassinations they found, among other things:
- "Excluding hijackings, most victims of NTT have some political
  connections [i.e. they are not outsiders to the conflict - AS].
- "Many incidents of NTT are instigated, at least in part, in
  order to free other terrorists held in custody." (...)
- "When confronted with a situation of NTT involving terrorist
  demands, few nation-states evidence a consistent   and coherent
  response strategy." (...)

- "The mass media is an intrinsic element in NTT."

- "Terrorists usually do not comply with time limits they
  have imposed on various authorities for meeting their demands." 15)

A larger effort is the one undertaken at Risks International Inc. of
Alexandria, Virginia, U.S.A., by a former member of the counter
intelligence directorate of the U.S. Air Force's Office of Special
Investigations, Dr. Charles A. Russell. This is a commercial enterprise
which caters for the protection of executives of multinational corporations
and publishes each month the Executive Risk Assessment. For an annual
fee subscribers may use the Risk data which consists of more than 5000
terrorist incidents since January 1970. This database covers incidents
within the United States as well as abroad and the information is derived
from the foreign and English-language press, U.S. and foreign government
and police reports. Actions by criminal elements are not recorded in
this data base, the definition of terrorism being "the treatened or
actual use of force and violence to attain a political goal through fear,
coercion and intimidation" by terrorist groups. The data are grouped
by type of activity, whereby the categories used consist of (1) kidnapping;
(2) hijacking; (3) assassination; (4) maiming; (5) attack against
facilities, and (6) bombing (if the damage is substantial, or the target
significant or the device involved unique or the method used to emplace
the device unusual). 16)

This data bank is probably of limited value to social scientists given
the main focus on technical variables, such as "weapons or explosives
used","ransom demanded or paid". 17)

A rather personal but interesting data-gathering effort has been made
by Mark Monday, the editor of the San Diego-based TVI Journal (the
acronym stands for Terrorism, Violence, Insurgency). In his TVI Journal
(available from Box 3830, San Diego, California 92103, U.S.A.), the
editor covers a wider range of events than terrorism alone. The
organization and attribution of the data as presented in the journal
leave much to be desired. In a special edition (Vol. 2, 1981) a 50 page
"World Directory on Dissent and Insurgency" is given. Based originally
on a public list published by the CIA, the new expanded list covers all
sorts of insurgent and dissident movements, both violent and non-violent,
indicating what sort of activities they are engaged in. Basically, it

is more a "Who's Who" in political violence and agitation than a
chronology (see also introduction to Appendix II).

Another rather personal data-gathering effort has been developed by
Dr. John B. Wolf (c/o Union College, Springfield Ave., Cranford,
New Jersey 07016, U.S.A.). Originally consisting of over 20.000 5x8 inch
cards containing information from press clippings, this card system
which was cross-indexed, has been fed into a micro-computer, according
to information provided by the author. For details, see also the
author's "Analytical Framework for the Study and Control of Agitational
Terrorism". The Police Journal, Vol. 49, July-Sept. 1976, pp. 165-171.

Also based on media-accounts, but fully computerized, is a data-
gathering effort conducted at the Artifical Intelligence Laboratory of
Yale University. At this center, directed by Roger Schauk, a programme
called IPP analyses newspaper stories on terrorism. The important
information contained in each sentence is elicited by the computer and
filed away in a way that allows the computer to make connections among
different stories. On the basis of comparative analysis the computer
comes up with generalizations such as that Italian terrorists tend to
attack businessmen, while Irish terrorist tend to shoot policemen. [18]

The CIA's ITERATE Project

The most ambitious publicly accessible data-gathering effort is probably
the one of Edward Mickolus, an Intelligence Analyst in the Office of
Policy Analysis of the U.S. Central Intelligence Agency. The first
publicly available result of this data-gathering effort surfaced in the
research study of David L. Milbank. International and Transnational
Terrorism: Diagnosis and Prognosis. Washington, D.C., CIA, April 1976.,
which was based on 913 recorded international and transnational
terrorist incidents in the period   1 January 1968 - 31 December 1975.
The pilot version of this data system (ITERATE I = International
Terrorism: Attributes of Terrorist Events) containing information on
539 terrorist incidents between January 1970 and July 1974 has been
made available to scholars via the Inter-University Consortium for
Political and Social Research, Ann Arbor, Michigan. Originally based on
two Rand chronologies and press accounts form the New York Times, the
Washington Post and other media, it now is based on more than 200 sources. [19]

148 different descriptions for each terroristic incident were sought
(ultimately 107 were used) covering a wide range of attributes such as
educational level of members of terrorist group, rank of hostages
involved, nature of demands, attitude of groups towards own death,
type of negotiator, terrorist negotiating behaviour, organizations
claiming or denying responsibility for incident, warning before
incident, etc.

The definition problem of what constitutes international terrorism was
solved by combining elements of some oft-cited definitions. The
following operational definitions were chosen:

> TERRORISM = "... the use, or threat of use, of anxiety-inducing
> extra-normal violence for political purpose by any individual
> or group, whether acting for or in opposition to established
> governmental authority, when such action is intended to influence
> the attitudes and behaviour of a target group wider than the
> immediate victims and when, through the nationality or foreign
> ties of its perpetrators, its location, the nature of its
> institutional or human victims, or the mechanics of its
> resolution, its ramifications transcend national boundaries.

> INTERNATIONAL TERRORISM = is such action when carried out by
> individuals or groups controlled by a sovereign state, whereas
> transnational terrorism is carried out by basically autonomous
> non-state actors, whether or not they enjoy some degree of support
> from sympathetic states. "Victims" are those individuals who are
> directly harmed by the terrorist incident. While a given terrorist
> action may somehow harm world stability, citizens of nations
> must feel a more direct loss than the weakening of such a
> collective good." 20)

The ITERATE II data system contains information of 3329 incidents of
transnational terrorism for the period 1 January 1968 to 31 December 1977.
A narrative description of these (and other) incidents has been published
in 1980 in a massive volume of almost one thousand pages. 21)

Given the complexity of this data system, the reader has to be referred
to the following accounts for detailed descriptions of ITERATE:

- Edward F. Mickolus. International Terrorism: Attributes of
  Terrorist Events (ITERATE). Ann Arbor, Michigan, ICPSR 1976,
  41 pp.

- Edward F. Mickolus. Statistical Approaches to the Study of
  Terrorism. In Y. Alexander and S.M. Finger. Terrorism:
  Interdisciplinary Perspectives. New York, John Jay Press,
  1977, pp. 209-269.

- Edward F. Mickolus. An Events Data Bank for Analysis of Trans-
  national Terrorism, pp.127-163, in: Richard J. Heuer (Ed.)
  Quantitiative Approaches to Political Intelligence: The CIA
  Experience. Boulder, Westview, 1978.

- Edward F. Mickolus. Transnational Terrorism. A Chronology of Events 1968-1979. London, Aldwych Press, 1980, pp. i-xxvi.

- Edward F. Mickolus and Edward Heyman. Iterate: Monitoring Transnational Terrorism. pp. 153-174, in: Y. Alexander and John McGleason (Eds.). Behavioral and Quantitative Perspectives on Terrorism. New York, Pergamon Press, 1981.

This data set has been utilized for a variety of purposes, including the following ones:

- To study global diffusion patterns of transnational terrorism over time. (Heyman)

- Terrorist trends analysis. (Milbank)

- To improve hostage negotiation techniques. (Mickolus, Miller)

- Comparison of terrorist campaigns. (CIA)

- Evaluation of policy prescriptions for crisis management. (CIA)

- Evaluation of deterrence possibilities of terrorism. (CIA)

- Evaluation of the effects of publicity on terrorist behaviour. (Researchers at the Naval Postgraduate School) 22)

Among the findings that emerge from ITERATE, these are typical:

- In 297 cases of 3329 the terrorists did not possess any real weapons. 23)

- In almost three quarter of all incidents of international terrorism persons from only two nations were involved (in 2464 out of 3329 cases).

- In most cases the terrorists have attempted to victimize only "enemy" nationals in order to avoid offending citizens of potentially supportive governements. 24)

- In 12 percent of the incidents was any one killed and in 15.7 percent of the incidents injuries were reported. 25)

Despite its explicit operational definition (at any rate more explicit than the RAND definition) the range of incidents labelled "terrorism" is wide. The total number of 3329 incidents harbours some categories which are doubtful. Out of the 22 categories listed below in declining order of frequency, categories 9, 11, 12, 13, 14, 15, 18 do, in our view, not easily fit into the operational definition.

Table X : Nature of Terrorist Incidents in the ITERATE Data Set (n=3329)

1.	Explosive bombing	1402	12. Conspiracy	30
2.	Incendiary bombing	395	13. Sabotage	16
3.	Letter bombing	321	14. Arms smuggling	16
4.	Threat	286	15. Shootout with police	12
5.	Kidnapping	242	16. Other actions	11
6.	Assassination or murder	174	17. Nonaerial takeover	9
7.	Armed attack	131	18. Occupation	8
8.	Aerial hijacking	89	19. Missile attack	6
9.	Theft or break-in	64	20. Hoax	5
10.	Barricade-hostage	56	21. Exotic pollution	1
11.	Sniping	54	22. Nuclear weapons	1
				3329 26)

Doubts about the validity of the label terrorism are not relieved if
the textual description of the chronology is consulted. Among the
incidents of international or transnational terrorism listed, the
following incidents figure:

- January 9, 1969 - Thailand - Two shots were fired at a U.S.
  Bangkok relay station vehicle during the night, causing no
  damage or injures. 0125.

- June 19, 1969 - Israel - Palestinian terrorist bombed a power
  line in Jerusalem, partially blacking out the city. 0167.

- June 12, 1970 - Uruguay - Tupamaros raided the Swiss embassy in
  Montevideo, stealing documents, typewriters and a photocopying
  machine. 0425.

- May 7, 1971 - the United States - Two well-dressed women threw
  two stink bombs into the South Vietnamese consulate in San
  Fancisco, causing no damage. "VC Will Win" was painted on the
  consulate wall. 0788.

- September 27, 1976 - Spain - A Molotov cocktail was thrown through
  the window of a Serrano store of a U.S. firm, damaging merchandize
  on display. The sprinkler heads were activated, and the fire was
  quickly contained. 2904. 27)

None of these examples - and many more could be cited - fits the
operational definition well and one begins to wonder whether policy
considerations are not playing a bigger role than scientific criteria
in   determining in- or exclusion of incidents of political protest and
violence. The Mickolus data apparently form the basis (or a basis) for
the annual terrorism count of the CIA (Central Intelligence Agency.
International Terrorism in 1976. Washington, D.C., CIA, 1977).
When the Reagan administration came to power in Washington, the
publication of the 1982 CIA report on International Terrorism in 1980
was delayed due to an intra-administration discussion about the
inclusion or exlusion of particular threats of violence and acts of
violence. The aim of the new team in the White House was, as one
official admitted, to portray the terrorism problem as the "most
serious threat to human rights around the world". Tom Wicker of the
New York Times, described the data battle in the words of an insider:

"The magic result, a state department official told reporters
would be to double - from 3336 to 7000 - the previously reported
"incidents" of world terrorism from 1968 through 1979. The
number killed or murdered, of course, would remain the same
- about 8000 - since this bookkeeping slight - of-hand merely
makes the same situation twice as bad as it did before." 28)

The battle of numbers has in the meantime apparently been won by the
Reagan-Haig hardliners who listed domestic incidents as well. In 1981
the former CIA top-official, Ray S. Cline, now Senior Associate of
the Center of Strategic and International Studies at the George Washington
University, could state:

> "From 1970 through 1980 there have been a total of 10,748 domestic
> and international terrorist operations, with a toll of 9,714
> individuals killed, 10,177 wounded and property damage of
> $ 701,839,542". 29)

To be fair, to Mr. Mickolus, we do not exactly know in how far his
ITERATE data set is co-extensive with the data referred to by Tom Wicker
and Ray S. Cline. But the fact remains that there is a strained
relationship between many of the cases cited in the textual chronology
and his operational definition. Admittedly, this could, at least in
part be the result of the incompleteness of the summary textual
descriptions. The numerical analysis describing more than one hundred
variables might yield results more commensurate with the working
definition. Because ITERATE promises to become an authoritative data
base it is worth being extra critical towards it.

Data Collections

The British Institute for the Study of Conflicts (ISC)

One of the main data-collection centers on terrorism in the 1970s
has been the London-based Institute for the Study of Conflict, which
was founded in June 1970 and directed until 1979 by Brian Crozier,
a journalist turned scholar. The scope of ISC's data collection is
broader than terrorism. The aims of the institute are, in the words
of one of its leaflets:

- "to research into the causes, manifestations and likely trends
  of political instability world-wide.

- to identify and analyse threats posed by Soviet expansionism.

- to highlight the terrorist and subversive activities of political
  extremist organizations and to trace their international links.

- to maintain a research library and reference facility unique in
  the country for the use of students and scholars."

The institute publishes a monthly monograph under the title Conflict
Studies, issues occasional Special Reports and the annual reference
work Annual of Power and Conflict. The latter, numbering some 500 pages
gives a country-by-country situation report, accompanied by a chronology

of events and regional surveys. Among its subscribers figure
universities, governments, embassies, law enforcement agencies and
industrial corporations in some 60 countries throughout the world.
The institute (presently located: 12-12a Golden Square, London W1R 3AF,
U.K.) is considered in many quarters as authoritive. Many of the
Conflict Studies, while all leaning to the political right, are indeed
scholarly products but the Annual should be treated with some caution.
An impression of its flavour can be gained from a self-description
included in the 1976-1977 edition:

> "Where applicable the articles attempt to assess whether developments
> have served or disserved the interests of NATO, the United States,
> the Soviet Union, the Warsaw Pact, China and so forth. (...)
> The country-by-country survey of conflict puts the main emphasis
> on revolutionary challenges to the internal security of States,
> but it also covers unconventional challenges, for instance, by
> ethnic or religious movements with little or no concern for social
> change, especially where these lend themselves to exploitation by
> outside powers." 30)

Brian Crozier has been,before he founded the ISC, long-time director
of an international news feature service (Forum World Features)
financed by the U.S. Central Intelligence Agency. Whether his scholarly
career has been more independent than his journalistic one can only be
guessed. Strange enough criticism on the value of the Annual has come
from another scholar whose links with the CIA have never been a secret.
In his annotation to the 1976 - 1977 issue of the ISC Annual,
E.F. Mickolus has written:

> "While still a useful survey, the author's acceptance of unsubstan-
> tiated press stories at times detracts from the volumes credibility." 31)

While this is certainly true, there might be more to it than meets the
eye. A former foreign correspondent of the Washington Post wrote in
1978: "The ISC still exists, although reliable U.S. sources say it has
no direct CIA - only British intelligence - links". 32)
Brian Crozier has left the institute in 1979, but the ISC continues to
function. It has, for instance, published a list of Embassy Occupations
in 1979-1980 in the 1980-1981 Annual of Power and Conflict and is
preparing hijacking lists and regional incidence of terrorism lists for
subsequent editions.
Besides the ISC, the International Institute for Strategic Studies (IISS)
(23 Tavistock Street, London WC7E 1NR,U.K.) also has a collection of
news clippings on terrorism.

The IACP's Clandestine Tactics and Technology Data Service

A largely U.S. source which is internationally accessible to researchers
is the Clandestine Tactics and Technology Data Service. It distributes its
documents to selected applicants at home and abroad. These consist of
analyses on terrorist groups, activities, tactics and countermeasures.
This data service is provided by the International Association of
Chiefs of Police's Bureau of Operations and Research (11 Firstfield Road,
Gaithersburg, Maryland 20760, U.S.A.). The IACP, founded in 1893, has
an international membership of some eleven thousand members. Its aim
is to exchange expertise among police executives in different countries.
In the last two decades the IACP has worked in anti-terrorist programs
and organized workshops, seminars and issued numerous publications.
John D. Elliott, the editor of a terrorism reader issued by the IACP,
has noted that: "It is now obvious that anti-terrorists are becoming
as well organized and internationally supported as the terrorist
themselves." [33] It seems that the IACP, which was working together
with the U.S. National Advisory Committee's Task Force on Disorders
and Terrorism, sees itself as fulfilling an important role in this
regard.[34] In some countries of the Western World the publications of the
IACP are available to researchers with the right credentials. For the
Netherlands the depository is: Politiestudiecentrum, Rijksstraatweg
127, 7231 AD Warnsfeld

The U.S. National Criminal Justice Reference Service

Another source of documents - such as translations of foreign language
articles on terrorism - is the National Criminal Justice Reference
Service (NCJRS), which is operated by the Law Enforcement Assistance
Administration of the U.S. Department of Justice. In many cases NCJRS
can provide microfiche copies of selected documents (a free service).
The NCJRS also operates an interlibrary loan service for U.S. users.
All documents in the NCJRS data base are available in this way, but
loans must be secured through U.S. local,public, academic or organization
libraries. The Microfiche service provides 4x6 inch sheet of film that
contain up to 98 pages text per sheet. Due to the 24 times reduction
special reading equipment is necessary. (For information write to:

NCJRS Loan Program or NCJRS Microfiche Program, P.O. Box 6000,
Rockville, Maryland 20850, U.S.A.
Various other similar institutions exist in the United States. Some
material on terrorism is, for instance, available from the U.S.
National Technical Information Service (5285 Port Royal Road,
Springfield, Virginia 22151, U.S.A.).

The U.S. Congress and the Library of Congress

The U.S. Congress is the best-informed legislative in the world and
its relative great power vis-à-vis the executive is largely due to
this fact. A variety of congressional committees has held numerous
hearings on aspects of terrorism in the last ten years for which
national and foreign experts were invited as well as representatives
of various government agencies. They usually submitted written
statements or articles in addition to their oral testimonies which
gives the outsider a glimpse of the reports and studies circulating
between various government agencies. The additional material submitted
to these committees contains numerous statistics and chronologies on
all aspects of insurgent terrorism. Many of these studies are
unfortunately out of print and are no longer available from the
Superintendent of Documents, U.S. Government Printing Office,
Washington, D.C. In such cases, however, it is possible to obtain copies
via the U.S. Library of Congress' Photoduplication Service, Washington,
D.C. 20540.
The Library of Congress, staffed by some 4000 people, is an open library
and scholars can obtain special facilities such as access to stacks.
Its computer search system SCORPIO features terrorism as a retrievable
subject and the most up-to-date bibliographic lists of the holdings of
this largest library in the world can be assembled.
The services which the Library of Congress can provide to researchers
on terrorism and in other fields surpass those of other well-equipped
libraries such as the ones of the Hoover Institution on War, Revolution
and Peace, located on the campus of Stanford University (Palo Alto,
California 94305, U.S.A.).

Institutes and Journals for the Study of Terrorism

The terroristic events at the Olympic Games in Munich in 1972 have
placed terrorism firmly on the agenda of national and international
bodies and study groups. Generally, these bodies were integrated into
existing bureaucracies. The U.S. Office of Combatting Terrorism, for
instance, was formed within the Department of State. The United Nations
formed an Ad Hoc Committee to study the question of international
terrorism. There are many such monitoring and operative agencies, which,
however, can hardly be classified as scientific institutes. But even
those institutes which see themselves as independent are often linked
to policy-making bodies in one way or another.

In the United States the State University of New York has an Institute
for Studies in International Terrorism (SUNY - Oneonta, New York 13820.
U.S.A.). Its director is Yonah Alexander, author and editor or co-editor
of more than a dozen books on terrorism. He is also the editor in chief
of Terrorism:an International Journal, a quarterly published since 1978
by Russak Inc. (347 Madison Avenue, New York, New York 10017, U.S.A.).
On the Board of Editors and on the International Advisory Board figure
the names of some of the most prominent scholars in the field of
international relations, political violence and terrorism. The general
approach of the journal is instrumental and policy-oriented, rather
than historical or behavioural. It is the most important journal in the
field and in a way still the only one dedicated exclusively to terrorism.
Y. Alexander is also editor of a new journal established in 1981,
Political Communication and Persuasion: an International Journal, which
also features articles on terrorism. A related journal, published like
the two above-mentioned ones by Russak in New York is Conflict:
an International Journal for Conflict and Policy Studies. Its editor is
George K. Tanham of the Rand Corporation's Washington base. It
concentrates on conflict situations short of war like terrorism,
subversion, economic, political and psychological warfare. Published
since 1978,it is a quarterly, almost identical in format to Alexander's
Terrorism.

Another research institution in the field is the International Terrorist
Research Center, directed by Frank W. Taggart and Gavin de Becker in
Texas (P.O.Box 26804, El Paso, Texas 79926, U.S.A.). Its first

publication was a monthly named Counterforce. According to one source
it was edited by Fred Rayne, head of an international protective agency
for corporations. [35)] Later it was named Intersearch, to be followed
by Terror Watch. These successor journals are apparently mainly
concerned with informing its executive readership with news on
techniques and actions in the field of protection and countermeasures
against terrorist attacks on business firms.

To our knowledge there are no other journals (except the TVI Journal
of Mark Monday mentioned earlier) which concentrate more or less
exclusively on terrorism. Articles on the subject are published in a
wide variety of journals. They can, however, be easily located by
consulting the Abstracts Literature (e.g. Abstracts on Criminology and
Penology, Abstracts on Police Science, Criminal Justice Periodicals
Index, Psychological Abstracts, Business Periodicals Index.)

Outside the United States there are Institutes for the Study of Terrorism in
Israel and South Africa. The independent Terrorism Research Centre in
South Africa (P.O. Box 1464 Cape Town, 8000 S.A.) is headed by M. Morris.
This "Privately-Founded Reciprocal Centre to Research Terrorism and
Security" has published a series of Special Reports on political violence
and sabotage perpetrated by the African National Congress liberation
movement and contains incident statistics and many military technicalities.
The Israeli institute was founded after the Entebbe rescue operation in
July 1976 and is named after the head of one of the rescue teams who was
killed during the operation, the Yehonathan Nethanyahu Institute.

Noteworthy are the efforts of the Terrorism Section of the Centre for
Strategic Studies at the University of Tel Aviv. Under the direction of
Dr. A. Merari an effort was made, starting in 1978, to develop a data
base on political terrorism, including not only terrorist events but also
information on groups and countries' attitudes towards them. By 1980 over
1100 events and about 200 "real groups" (not ad hoc names) were included
in this data base which covers both domestic terrorism in nation-states
and international terrorism. This project seems to be part of an emerging
international data base in which the Rand Corporation in the United States
and Paul Wilkinson from the University of Aberdeen are also participating.
According to Wilkinson, the aim of the cooperative efford is fourfold:

1. To develop precise and full incident data;

2. To produce a chronology of events;

3. To arrive at profiles of terrorist movements, and

4. To monitor the laws and measures adopted by governments
   and international bodies to deal with terrorism.

There is clearly much to be done to improve data reliability.

Data Reliability

A little test will suffice to indicate how unreliable data on terrorism can
be, even with authors who make an effort to get their facts right.
As test case we take the South Moluccan incidents in the Netherlands.
The basis for comparison is our own case study on these incidents.[36]
If we take Wilkinson's book on Terrorism and the Liberal State, we
find that he splits up the South Moluccans in two groups, the Ambonese
on the one hand and "a rather more fanatical group of Moluccans, also
exiled in Holland".[37] Ambon is the cultural centre of the South
Moluccan Islands and the terms Ambonese and South Moluccans are used
more or less interchangeably in the Netherlands. In any case they were
not two distinct groups.
Mickolus, in describing the 1975 train incident, begins his account with
the sentence "Seven members of the Free South Moluccan Youth
Organization, led by Freddy Aponno, seized a train in Beilen, killing
the engineer and a passenger later in the takeover."[38]
From this the unaware reader is likely to conclude that the leader of
the terrorist group seizing the train was Freddy Aponno. But Etty Aponno
(not Freddy), the Chairman of Pemuda Masjarakat, the Free South
Moluccan Youth, was not present at the incident and was not personally
involved in any way. The Free South Moluccan Youth is not a terrorist
organization and gave no orders for the attack. On the 1977 train
incident Mickolus' account states that the African state of "Benin said
that it would welcome the gunmen."[39] The contrary is true. These are
serious mistakes for they indict persons and countries for complicity
in incidents in which they had no part. There are also other, less
serious mistakes in Mickolus' account such as that five terrorists
boarded the train only after two terrorists had pulled the emergency

cord, while they were in fact on the train all the time. [40)]

More forgiveable are misspellings (Tan not Dan, Joop not Jup, Metiary not Metiery, Samuel not Semeul.)

Some of the misspellings seem to originate from one of the sources of Mickolus, Facts on File. Lester A. Sobel's account, based on Facts on File, in additions misspells Beilen as Beilin. On one and the same page Sobel speaks of five and seven (the latter is correct) terrorists in the consulate in Amsterdam. Sobel also suggests that the Dutch authorities were led to believe that Max Papilaya, the leader of the 1977 train terrorists, had received training from outside the country. [41)] He was a public official working in a provincial administrative centre and the authorities knew that he could not have been trained abroad. Richard Clutterbuck's account also contains a number of inaccuracies. For instance, it is not true that all of the 1977 terrorists had "probably received military training in the Dutch Army." [42)]

Nor was the seizure of the school in Bovensmilde "a private venture by South Moluccans from the neighbouring houses, who were frustrated by not being selected to take part in the train hijacking. [43)] Rather, two terrorists from the school switched in the planning stage from the school team to the train team, because they felt little for taking children as hostages.

Edgar O'Ballance, who dedicates one page to the two double incidents of South Moluccan youths, manages to get seven things wrong on one page. [44)] The reason for these and other mistakes and inaccuracies is in all likelyhood a reliance on media accounts. Newspapers and wire services work in a constant field of tension, torn between the desire to get the news out first and getting the news out right. The time pressure under which competitive journalism has to operate is very conductive to producing inaccuracies. A second factor is that both the terrorists and their adversaries are interested in getting their side of the story printed and the side that is believed by the journalist is not always the side that gives the correct version. In some cases deliberately false information is spread by interested parties in an effort to win a tactical advantage over the other side or to get public opinion on one's side. Sometimes journalists invent news when they cannot get information from the authorities on an incident. At other

times secret services plant news on terrorist incidents where there
are none. In other cases the guilt attribution is wrong. As we have
pointed out in our book Violence as Communication, news about
terrorism can be highly unreliable. [45]

Other Types of Data

Since the news media are often inaccurate sources, the prudent thing
to do is to consult several types of sources. Court proceedings, for
instance, leading to the trial of terrorists, are an underutilized, but
potentially rich source. Local newspapers (but rarely international
papers) often give ample coverage to the court proceedings sequelling
incidents. But first-hand police records and court materials are even
better source material. Interview with terrorists in prison are also
a valuable source, if the convicted terrorists are willing to talk.
Psychiatrists and psychologists have taken the lead in this field.
Gustav Morf, a psychiatrist from Montreal interviewed imprisoned
F.L.Q. members and gave an account of it in his book Terror in Quebec.
(Toronto, Clark, Irwin, 1970).
David Hubbard, from the United States, interviewed in depth a number
of skyjackers from which he drew some far-reaching general conclusions
which are highly challengeable (See his The Skyjacker : His Flight
to Fantasy, 1973, out of print). The most ambitious project in this
field was begun by J.N. Knutson. In order to come to know more about
the psychodynamic and social factors which drive people to acts of
terrorism and violence, all inmates in U.S. Federal Prisons convicted
for a politically-motivated crime were approached for an interview.
She obtained good cooperation, writing:

> "Approximately 90 percent of those inmates who have been contacted
> have been willing to be interviewed, in spite of the very natural
> suspicion that the purposes of the study might be other than as
> stated. (...) The almost universal cooperation of the inmates is
> at considerable variance with what prison authorities had predicted.
> (...) Moreover, all individuals have a need to justify their
> behavior. (...) These subjects, almost uniformly, comment on the
> frustration which they have felt that no one - judge, jury, press
> or attorney - cared to know why their terroristic act was committed;
> interest was expressed only in what was done." [46]

Judging from her account on a Croatian hijacker the outcome of this
inquiry promised to be iconoclastic, destroying some myths created
on the "terrorist personality". Unfortunately, the suicide of
Jeanne Knutson on Christmas 1981 has put an early end to this inquiry.
There are other interview materials although they are not easy to come
by for social scientists. The Israeli government has interviewed many
Fedayeen and most of them, we are told, talked quite easily. Equally,
American officials have interviewed hundreds of members of the
Vietnamese National Liberation Front. The value of such material is
hard to assess since it is not unlikely that the interview situation
was more of an interrogation, perhaps even combined with the threat of
torture in some cases. [47] Many social scientists will refuse to touch
this kind of material.

It is certainly not a full substitute for interviews in the real life
environment in which terrorists operate. A successful example of this
would be, according to J.B. Bell, the "Case Analysis of a Revolutionary",
made in Venezuela by psychologist Walter H. Slate. [48]

J. Bowyer Bell, a research associate at the Institute of War and Peace
Studies at Columbia University (New York) is himself probably the most
successful researcher in the field when it comes to interviewing active
terrorists, whether in Ireland or the Middle East. His books breath
the air of one who has been on the other side and who has absorbed the
way of thinking driving insurgents. Although his writing is at times
closer to journalism than to social science, it is far above purely
journalistic products based on interviews with terrorists in the
underground such as Gerald McKnight's The Mind of the Terrorist (London,
Michael Joseph, 1974).

Rare but extremely useful are writings of ex-terrorists who have stayed
underground and who keep equal distance from their former colleagues
and their former adversaries. Two examples of this are Bommi Bauman's
"Wie alles anfing" (München, Trikont, 1975, also in English) by one of
the few proletarian members of the German "student" terrorists and
Hans-Joachim Klein's "Rückkehr in die Menschlichkeit" (Reinbek, Rowolt,
1979). Through them some insights into the cognitive style of terrorists
can be gained, although one should be aware that there is more than
one style and more than one terrorist mind.

Here we are already dealing with another data source: memoirs of former
terrorists. While the element of self-justification as well as the
dimming of memory limit the usefulness of reminiscences, this category
of data can by no means be neglected. Terrorists were neither born as
terrorists nor condemned to stay terrorists for the rest of their lives
Some of them became adherents of nonviolence (like Alexander Berkman
whose "Prison Memoirs an an Anarchist" were published first in 1912).
Others became statesmen (like Menachem Begin, whose "The Revolt - Story
of the Irgun" became a bestseller of sorts when he became Israel's
Prime Minister a quarter of a century after its first publication).
Memoirs can also tell us something about when and why terrorists gave
up terrorism or switched to another tactic. Too much attention has so
far been given to the origins of terrorism and not enough to the end
of terrorist campaigns. For such a study a broad comparative analysis
of memoirs might provide useful insights. The study of the post-terrorist
career of terrorists might even yield policy results. If one knows what
factors cause terrorists to give up terrorism, as much if not more is
gained than when one knows what caused them to choose this course to
begin with.

An example of this type of source is Maria McGuire's To Take Arms: My
Years with IRA Provisionals (New York, Viking, 1973), the account of
a member of the IRA who left the movement when the indiscriminate bombing
campaign of 1972 begun.

It should be read in conjuction with Sean MacStiofain (real name:
John Edward Drayton Stephenson) Revolutionary in Ireland (Farnborough,
Cremonesi, 1975). This is on account of the developments in Ulster
between 1970 and 1972 - when he was chief of staff of the Provisional
IRA.

Memoirs are personal histories, often more informed but also more
biased than accounts by professional historians. Many specialsits on
terrorism have treated terrorism as if it had been invented in 1968.
Yet even modern insurgent terrorism has a tradition going back more than
a century now and regime terrorism is much older. While some features
of present-day terrorism are new, many are not and the study of past
terrorist organizations and movements can increase our understanding
of contemporary terrorism. In some cases there already exist historical

monographs on organizations and movements using terrorism and the task
is often only one of comparing them with each other and their present-
day counterparts. In other cases one has to dig up the yellowing
records in the archives, but contrary to contemporary movements'
records there are no longer restrictions to access. Historical data
are, of course, not easily quantifiable, and historical work does not
bring the researcher the same awards and recognition which up-to-date
policy-oriented studies full of incident and threat statistics do.

Data on State Terrorism and Repression

Just as most researchers in the field of terrorism shy away from the
past, most also shy away from treating in depth regime terrorism.
While insurgent terrorist and the media often seek each other, state
terrorism generally shies away from publicity and attempts to cover the
repressive activities of regimes are often dangerous to the investigating
jounalist. The imbalance of media attention to terrorism from above
and terrorism from below is not compensated by the data gathering efforts
of social scientists. There is woefully little systematic material
available on regime terrorism.
The only major source of information on state repression are the reports
and documents issued by the various offices of Amnesty International
(its international secretariat is located at 10 Southampton Street,
London WC 2E 7HF, U.K.). Amnesty International (AI) is primarily
directing its efforts to free individual prisoners of conscience, that
is, nonviolent persons who have been imprisoned by governments for
alleged crimes which basically consisted of the exercise of those human
rights guaranteed under the United Nations' Charter of Human Rights.
Indirectly, however, the reports of Amnesty International also form an
account of state terrorism and violations of human rights in more than
two thirds of all the nations forming the United Nations. [49]
Amnesty International Publications produce a wide variety of material
in many languages and countries. An overview can be found in:

- Amnesty International in Print 1962-1978. London, AI, January 1979
  (AI Index: Doc 06/01/79).

- Amnesty International Publications. 1981 Catalogue, covering major reports and documents published between 1976 and the beginning of October 1981, London, AI, Oct. 1981 (AI Index: Doc 05/01/81)

- AI in Print Update. March 1980 to July 1981. London, AI, 1981.

- AI in Print Update 1979/1980. London, March 1980.

Apart from the annual Amnesty International Report, the monthly Newsletter and the journal Chronicle of Current Events and other booklets and reports, there exists also a major collection of published and unpublished material from Amnesty International on microfiche. This collection, presently covering 105 countries, is updated annually and is available from the Inter Documentation Company, AG (Poststrasse 14, CH-6300 Zug, Switzerland).

A possible new source for monitoring state terrorism is the proposed development of a "Genocide Early Warning System", which, appropriately enough, will be set up in Israel. In the words of the driving force behind this project, prof. Israel W. Charny,: "The major function of such a system would be to collect and report to the global community information about ongoing cases of genocide and major human rights violations around the world." [50)]

While the overlap between state terrorism and genocide is only partial, it does seem that the planned effort to systematically assemble data, and to develop social warning indicators is or can be made relevant to the study of state terrorism. A description of the set-up of the project can be found in: I.W. Charny. Genocide: The Human Cancer. (Boulder, Colorado, Westview Press, 1978). For information about the present status of the project, which underwent delay due to financial problems, contact I.W. Charny, I.C.H.G., P.O. Box 29784, Tel Aviv, Israel.

Students of regime terrorism and lesser forms of repression will in many cases have to turn to special journals, often produced with shoestring budgets by concerned scholars and human rights activists. The following titles have been found useful by this writer:

1. Bulletin d'Information sur l'Intervention Clandestine, published by the Association pour le droit à l'information (ADI), rue de Vaugirard, 75005 Paris, France. The ADI also publishes a monthly supplement in English, called Parapolitics. According to its self-description, it is dedicated to the study of all forms of secret and illegitimate activity that is of national or international importance.

2. Counter Spy (P.O. Box 647, Ben Franklin Station, Washington, D.C. 20004, U.S.A.).

3. Covert Action Information Bulletin (P.O. Box 50272, Washington, D.C. 2004, U.S.A.).

4. Index on Censorship, issued six times per year, has been published since 1971 by the Writers & Scholars International Ltd. (21 Russell Street, London WC2B 5HP, U.K.). Primarily concerned with the fate of writers all over the world, the Index is also an excellent source on repressive measures by governments other than censorship.

5. Nacla's Latin America & Empire Report (formerly Nacla's Newletter), published since the late 1960s from New York (P.O. Box 57, Cathedral Park Station, New York, N.Y. 10025, U.S.A.) covers U.S. involvement in Latin America and is very well documented.

6. Pacific Research and World Empire Telegram, published by the Pacific Study Center (1963 University Avenue, East Palo Alto, California 94303, U.S.A.), focuses on the Pacific Basin and the role of the United States in the countries bordering the Pacific.

7. The Public Eye, published since 1978, is a quarterly issued by the Repression Information Project Staff, and is edited by Harvey Kahn (P.O. Box 3278, Washington, D.C. 20010, U.S.A.) It focuses on repression in the United States.

8. State Research, a bi-monthly published since 1977, monitors developments in state policy, particularly in the fields of law, policing, internal security, espionage and the military. Its main focus is on the United Kingdom (Address: 9 Poland Street, London W1, U.K.).

In our questionnaire we asked scholars whether they had themselves generated data on terrorism. Remarkably enough, only one out of the fifty respondents said that he had done so with regard to state terrorism and even this was only "a small quantity". [51]
Eighteen other respondents had generated various kinds of data on non-state terrorism. However, no less than 29 respondents listed data on state or regime terrorism and repression as being required most urgently in order to advance our knowledge on the subject of terrorism.

Data Requirements

For research on terrorism to become cumulative, the data problem has to be addressed and brought to some solution. There has to be at least some uniformity in collected data, based on acceptable working definitions. At the moment this uniformity is largely absent in the open literature. Governments have their own data banks and these are likely to be more

uniform, at least on the national level. The problem is in part one of
getting access to data collected by a variety of government agencies.
A respondent working for the U.S. government said: "There is a myriad
of data-banks within the US and other governments dealing with this
area, all have some value. However, these sources are severely
restricted." And one American academic researcher remarked: "The data
is there but is still to be effectively disseminated". This would pre-
suppose a greater degree of cooperation between the academic and the
government sector, but this raises immediately the question whether there
is a communality of purpose and data requirements. It also poses some
ethical question (see the following chapter).

Among the data which our respondents wanted to be generated or made
available, the single most often mentioned category was data on state
terrorism, as we have already said earlier. For the rest there was
great variety. One respondent asked for data relating to "The relative
frequency of terrorism in societies with different domestic situations."
Others were more interested in "The personal backgrounds of persons in
terrorism", "collective biographies of people using terror" (Midlarsky,
Blok). Another wanted data on the attitudes of former terrorists , e.g.
ten years after (Dimitrijevic). Others wanted more information on the
reasons for engaging in terrorism and the function and relevance of those
reasons (Hondrich). In the same vein another researcher would like to
see data on "Ideological pronouncements by terrorists and their
supporters, analyses of the language they use, and the compilations
of responses made to their statements of principle by governments and
scholarly leaders" (Leiser , seconded by Dimitrijevic). A number of
scholars wanted more data on the international links of terrorist
organizations (Lador-Lederer, ISC, Vasilijevic). Yet others were more
interested in "comparable data on characteristics of groups and
individuals", on "individual and group dynamics" or "profiles of
terrorist groups and their support apparatus" (Francis). Striking a
different note, one researcher would like to have data on the symbolic
use of the concept of terrorism historically contra the left (Wolpin).
Another would like to see more data on Second and Third World
Terrorism and on the commercial response to terrorism (Wright).

More suggestions for areas were data ought to be assembled can be found
in Yehezkel Dror's and R.D. Crelinsten's contributions to a volume
edited by the latter under the title "Research Strategies for the Study

of International Terrorism" (Montreal, Centre for Comparative
Criminology, 1977, pp. 161-163, and 196-209). The following
areas also seem worthwhile to this writer:

- Data of public opinion surveys for various countries over
  time, using comparable incidents in order to assess public
  attitudes and reactions whereby attention has to be paid to
  the goal-consonance/dissonance of sub-audiences with terrorists;

- Data on negotiation techniques and bargaining dynamics with
  terrorists;

- Data on terrorist demands and the target of demands' concessions
  and their relationship to nonviolent solutions of incidents and
  future demands and concession policies;

- Data on non-terroristic activities of terrorists and shifts in
  modes of action from terroristic to violent and legal methods,
  and vice versa.

- Data on terrorist victim selection patterns and threat perceptions
  in audiences sharing victim characteristics.

- Data on right-wing terrorist groups.

- Data on countermeasures taken by governments against insurgent
  terrorism and countermeasures taken by populations against regime
  terrorism.

Conclusion

The social scientist who studies terrorism faces a number of problems
when he aims at being an independent researcher rather than a policy
instrument. Ideally, he should generate his own data, by interviewing
terrorists, by participatory observation with a crisis team in a hostage
situation, etc. This poses financial problems as well as problems of
access. Therefore, the inclination to utilize data generated by others
is great. The 'others' usually are the media or the government. They
generate data for their purposes and as often as not these are at odds
with the objectivity and impartiality required from a social scientist.
The least one can do in such a situation is to spread one's sources wide
so that not a single perspective predetermines the outcome of studies
on terrorism.

At present many social scientists seem less than fully aware of the
danger of adopting the perspectives held by U.S. Government agencies.
By organizing conferences, sponsoring certain types of research but not
other, paying oversea trips to certain researchers, producing educational
kits on terrorism, etc. the prevalence of a particular paradigm has
been strongly favoured. This paradigm is in consonance with the interests
of a world power but social science on terrorism should not become a
hostage of this paradigm. This is not to say that the emerging paradigm
has been purposively developed and is pushed on both domestic and
foreign social scientists. A conspiracy theory is not necessary. There
is just such an imbalance between U.S. research on terrorism and foreign
research that the weight of the former becomes preponderant within the
research community. This is not an advocacy for rejecting the dominant U.S.
paradigm - many aspects of it are valid - but of critically assessing
it before taking over data and theories and recommendations based on
it. The fact that the CIA and RAND have pioneered in the study of
certain types of insurgent terrorism and set certain parameters and a
research agenda cannot mean that this is reason enough to reject or
accept what has been achieved. But if no caution is taken the innocent
researcher will find that he is in the end not looking at terrorism
but only at some manifestations of protest and violence which are contrary
to Western or Atlantic or U.S. interests. The availability of U.S. data

on terrorism, compared to the lesser availability of other data favours
such a development.

E.F. Mickolus and E. Heyman, working for the CIA and CACI respectively
have written:

> "While many hypotheses on terrorism have been put forward,
> depressingly little attention has been paid to the rigorous
> testing of what passes for conventional wisdom in this field. One
> of the ways to fill .this gap is to create a widely available body
> of data on the topic, subject to the critical scrutiny of
> representatives of all disciplines. One must begin this endeavour
> by tackling the thorny problem of definitions." 52)

The question is, however, whether social scientists should accept the
definition and data gathering effort which also happens to be one of
the U.S. Central Intelligence Agency. If they accept the lead given
by the CIA, will they not become unwitting assets, collecting data for
a secret agency of one particular government with interests which are
questionable to many?

I.L. Horowitz has warned:

> "Research social scientists, often responsive to a governmental or
> semi-official agency whose prime concern is political or industrial
> tranquility, can easily tailor their models to suit the needs of
> clients, thereby overlooking many alternate possibilities for
> analyzing terrorism. As the collective repository of empirical,
> even normative wisdom on the subject of both terror and liberty,
> they are charged with the task of arriving at satisfactory
> formulations of the problem, if not meaningful solutions, while
> operating within a paradigmatic framework unexamined or uncritically
> imbibed. (...)
> At this point in time, the emphasis among researchers is to
> aggregate information on letter-bombings, hijackings, assassinations,
> and consequently to blur essential distinctions between random
> terrorist movements and foreign-controlled movements. (...)
> Social science must first determine whether terrorism is a function
> of larger ambitions and aims, thereby making it a dependent variable.
> Second, social science needs to distinguish types of violence and
> injury perpetrated against persons and/or places in order to help
> establish some qualitative measures of terrorism and counterterrorism.
> Third, social science should provide empirical assistance to the
> legal efforts involved in developing international measures to
> combat terror of guerrillas and counterterror of the state.
> These three interrelated tasks will help restore a feeling of the
> independent and objective role of social science in combating
> terror and safeguarding civil liberties." 53)

The problem of data generation and collection is not only a scientific one.
The main question is what use is made by whom of these data? If social
scientists do not ask this question, others ultimately will - to their
detriment.

Notes

1) J.B. Bell. A Time of Terror. New York, Basic Books, 1978, p.38 -
   For the NYT as source see: J. Rothman. The New York Times
   Information Bank. New York, NYT Library and Information Services,n.d.

2) According to T.R. Gurr. Some Characteristics of Political Terrorism
   in the 1960s. In: M. Stohl (Ed.). The Politics of Terrorism. New York,
   Dekker, 1979,p.49.

3) Anthony M. Burton. Urban Terrorism: Theory, Practice and Response.
   London, Lee Cooper, 1975, p.112.

4) Pieter Bakker Schut, Ties Prakken, Dolf Hartkamp, Gerhard Mols.
   Kanttekeningen bij een anti-terrorisme verdrag. Nederlands Juristenblad,
   Jg.52, Aug. 1977, p.700 and p.703.

5) R.D. Crelinsten (Ed.). Research Strategies for the Study of
   International Political Terrorism. Montreal, International Centre
   for Comparative Criminology, 1977, p. 196.

6) Ibid., p. ix, vol.1.

7) Steve Wright. A Multivariate Time Series Analysis of the Northern
   Irish Conflict, 1969-1976. The Papers of the Peace Science Society
   (International), Vol.29, 1979-1980, pp.45-56.

8) E.F. Mickolus. The Literature of Terrorism,Westport, Connecticut,
   Greenwood Press, 1980, p.6.

9) Near East Report, Vol.22, No.13, 29 March 1978; cit. Y. Alexander,
   M.A. Browne & A.S. Nanes (Eds.). Control of Terrorism: International
   Documents. New York, Crane, Russak, 1979, p.xv.

10) B.M. Jenkins and Janera Johnson. International Terrorism: A
    Chronology, 1968-1974. Santa Monica, Rand, 1975, p.3.

11) Ibid., p.1.

12) Ibid., p.iii.

13) Ibid., pp.71-72.

14) See: Brian M. Jenkins. Rand's Research on Terrorism. St.Monica, Rand,
    August 1977 (P-5969), p.10.

15) Stephen Sloan & Richard Kearney. Non-Territorial Terrorism: An
    Empirical Approach to Policy Formation. Conflict, Vol.1, Nos.1-2,
    1978, pp.134 ff.; see also their report, co-authored by Ch.Wise,
    titled "Learning about terrorism: Analysis, Simulation and Future
    Directions." Terrorism: An International Journal, Vol.1, Nos.3-4,
    pp.315-329.

Notes

16) Charles A. Russell. Terrorism - An Overview, 1970-1978. In: Y. Alexander
and R.A. Kilmark (Eds.). Political Terrorism and Business, New York,
Praeger, 1979, p.296.

17) Bowman H. Miller & Charles A. Russell. The Evolution of Revolutionary
Warfare: From Mao to Marighella and Meinhof. In: Kupperman & Trent, op.
cit. 1979, p.198n.

18) Newsweek, 30 June 1980, "How Smart can Computers Get?", pp.36-37.

19) E.S. Heyman, Monitoring the Diffusion of Transnational Terrorism.
Gaithersburg, Md., IACP, 1980, p.8.

20) E.F. Mickolus. ITERATE. Ann Arbor, Michigan, ICPSR, 1976.

21) Edward F. Mickolus. Transnational Terrorism. A Chronology of Events,
1968-1979. London, Aldwych Press, 1980.

22) For a survey of various uses of ITERATE and other aggregate data see also
Appendix B "Statistical and Mathematical Approaches to the Study of
Terrorism: A Study of Current Work", in Y. Alexander and S.M. Finger,
op.cit. pp. 253-256.

23) E.F. Mickolus. Transnational Terrorism: A Chronology of Events, 1968-
1979. London, Aldwych Press, 1980, p. xxvi.

24) Ibid., p. xxv.

25) Ibid., p. xxvii.

26) Ibid., op.cit. derived from Table 3, p. xxi.

27) The 4-digit numbers refer to the record no. in Mickolus' chronology.

28) NYT, 28 April 1981, cit. M. Stohl. Fashions and Fantasies in the Study
of Political Terrorism. Dubrovnik, Inter-University Center, 1981, p.16.

29) Foreword to Y. Alexander and John M. Gleason (Ed.). Behavioural and
Quantitative Perspectives on Terrorism. New York, Pergamon Press,
1981, p. xi.

30) Brian Crozier (Ed.). Annual of Power and Conflict. A Survey of Political
Violence and International Influence. London, ISC.

31) E.F. Mickolus. The Literature of Terrorism. Westport, Connecticut,
Greenwood Press, 1980, p.14.

32) Russell Warren Howe. Asset Unwitting. Covering the World for the CIA.
More, May 1978, pp. 20, 27.

Notes

33) J.D. Elliott & L.K. Gibson (Eds.). Contemporary Terrorims. Selected Readings. Gaithersburg, Md., IACP, 1978, p.2.

34) The IACP also operates the National (U.S.) Bomb Data Center and publishes "Six Months Summary Reports". (Philip A. Karber. Urban Terrorism. Baseline Data and a Conceptual Framework. Social Science Quarterly, Vol. 52, Dec. 1971, pp. 521-522.)

35) William Steiner. Anti-Terrorism: The Making of a Bureaucracy. The Public Eye, Vol.1, No.2, April 1978, p.51.

36) A.P. Schmid et al. Zuidmoluks terrorisme, de media en de publieke opinie. Amsterdam, Intermediair, 1982.

37) P. Wilkinson. Terrorism and the Liberal State. London, Macmillan, 1977, p.112.

38) E.F. Mickolus. Transnational Terrorism. A Chronology of Events, 1968-1979, London, Aldwych Press, 1980, p.566.

39) Ibid., p.701.

40) Ibid. p. 699.

41) L.A. Sobel. Political Terrorism. Vol.2, Oxford, Robertson, 1978, p.221.

42) R. Clutterbuck. Kidnap and Ransom: The Response. London, Faber and Faber 1978, p.145.

43) Ibid.

44) E. O'Ballance. Language of Violence. The Blood Politics of Terrorism. San Rafael, Presidio Press, 1979, p.270.

45) A.P. Schmid & J. de Graaf. Violence as Communication. London, Sage, 1982, pp.57-98.

46) Jeanne N. Knutson. Social and Psychodynamic Pressures Toward a Negative Identity: The Case of an American Revolutionary Terrorist. In: Y. Alexander and J. Gleason , 1981, pp. 107-108.

47) J.B. Bell. Trends on Terror. The Analysis of Political Violence. World Politics, Vol.29, No.3, April 1977, p.482n.

48) In: Frank Bonnilla and José Silva Michelena (Eds.). A Strategy for Research on Policy. Vol.1, Cambridge, Mass., MIT Press, 1967, cit. J.B. Bell, op.cit. p.481n.

Notes

49) For general background on AI, see: Jonathan Power. Against Oblivion. Amnesty International's Fight for Human Rights. London, Fontana, 1981.

50) Israel Charney & Chanan Rapaport. A Genocide Early Warning System. The Whole Earth Papers, No.14, East Orange, New Jersey, Global Edition Associates, 1980, p.31; Emphasis added, AS.

51) Miles D. Wolpin. Militarism, Socialism and Civilian Rule in the Third World: A Comparison of Development Costs and Benefits. Instant Research on Peace and Violence, Vol.7, Nos.3-4, pp.105-133.

52) Edward Mickolus and Edward Heyman. Iterate: Monitoring Transnational Terrorism. In: Y. Alexander and J.M. Gleason, 1981, p.153.

53) I.L. Horowitz. Transnational Terrorism, Civil Liberties and Social Science. In: Y. Alexander and S.M. Finger, Terrorism, Interdisciplinary Perspectives, New York, John Jay Press, 1977, pp.284-285.

A P P E N D I X II :

A WORLD DIRECTORY OF "TERRORIST" ORGANIZATIONS AND OTHER GROUPS,
MOVEMENTS AND PARTIES INVOLVED IN POLITICAL VIOLENCE AS INITIATORS
OR TARGETS OF ARMED VIOLENCE

COMPILED BY DRS. A.J. JONGMAN, POLEMOLOGICAL INSTITUTE, GRONINGEN

Appendix II

A World Directory of "Terrorist" Organizations and Other Groups,
Movements and Parties Involved in Political Violence as Initiators
or Targets of Armed Violence
Compiled by Drs. A.J. Jongman, Polemological Institute, Groningen

Introduction

Since 1980 a data gathering effort in the broad field of political violence has been carried out at the Polemological Institute of Groningen
State University. Originally consisting of a systematic coding of all
instances of violence reported in the International Herald Tribune,
this effort has been broadened with the inclusion of another Paris-based
newspaper, Le Monde. The instances of violence coded from these two main
sources range from political suicides to inter-state wars, from terrorist acts to guerrilla operations. Attention is also given to repressive
acts of violence by government actors whether these be the armed forces,
the police or secret services. In addition, not only perpetrators of
political violence but victim groups as well are coded. Altogether the present
list of actors and "acted-upons" numbers some 1500 groups, parties,
movements or organizations without that the list can claim any complete-
ness. Nevertheless it is in all likelihood the most complete list presently available in the open literature on political violence.
The list has many limitations which the user should constantly keep in
mind. For one thing it lacks historical depth. In many cases, however,
movements of the early 1980's have already existed in the seventies and
some even in the 1960's. Where this is the case the present list provides
coverage. For many other violent actors the list is inadequate. The
reader should in these cases consult the directory recently published
by Peter Janke. (World Directory of Guerrilla and "Terrorist" Organizations: From 1945 to the Present. Hassocks, Harvester Books, 1983.) While
Janke's book could not be consulted before this Research Guide went into
print, we had the benefit of comparing and, where appropriate, supple-
menting our own data with those of Banks, Crozier, Mickolus and Monday.
Each of these authors' lists have some areas of strength and weakness.
E.M. Mickolus' "List of Organizations and Acronyms" (In: Transnational
Terrorism. A Chronology of Events, 1968-1979. London, Aldwych Press,
1980) for instance, is highly Western-oriented, underrepresenting Africa

and Asia. This 13 page list is concerned mainly with transnational actors, excluding many internally operating national groups. Given the
author's association with the U.S. Central Intelligence Agency,
it is arguably biased in its coverage in favour of anti-U.S. and leftwing manifestations of violence. A similar imbalance of emphasis can
also be found in the Annuals of Power and Conflict, issued by the London-
based Institute for the Study of Conflict. The ISC annuals concentrate
on organizations threatening the security of state power on a country-
by-country basis. While these two lists are preoccupied with insurgency
and terrorism, a third one by Mark Mónday in a Special Edition of his
TVI Journal (Vol. II, 1981) is broader. Basing himself on a CIA list
and extending it, Monday covers "insurgency and dissent" by which he
means "all acts other than voting or lobbying, aimed at the personnel,
structure or decision making process of a government with the intent
to decisively alter any of these - usually for a redistribution of advantage or power, whether political, social or economic". Insofar as
the Monday list includes nonviolent actors it is broader than the one
presented here. However the present list also contains nonviolent targets of violence which the Monday list may or may not contain depending
whether they were also actors or not. Monday's list is very extensive.
For Italy, for instance, he has many more names of "terrorist" groups
than our list has. However, most of these names appear to be cover names
of a smaller number of real organizations. The present directory limits
itself to the most important Italian groups, including, on the other
hand, in the case of Italy also the Mafia, which cannot be considered as a
purely criminal and nonpolitical organization.
Apart from checking our list against those of Monday, Mickolus and the
ISC we have also consulted Arthur S. Banks & W. Oversheet's (Eds.)
Political Handbook of the World (New York, 1981). The Handbook lists
official and illegal political parties of the countries of the world.
Our list is less broad, concentrating only on those parties which have
a military or underground wing or which were involved in election-time
violence.
The present list also contains some nonparty targets and actors, mainly
religious groups (e.g. adherents of the Bahai Faith or Pentacostalists).
In some cases special elite forces or foreign troops stationed in another
country also appear in the Jongman list reproduced here.

From the above it should be clear that this list is <u>not</u> a mere 'Directory
of "Terrorist" Movements'. Entry of a name in it can mean a number of
things: that it was engaged in violence or suffered from violence or
both, according to the sources on which this list is based. These sources
can be wrong. Some of the groups might never have existed (being cover
names) or might no longer exist. The labelling of a party to a violent
act as terrorist, guerrilla, death squad is primarily based on source
labellings and is not the result of a test of their performance against
certain criteria such as those proposed in chapter 1.6 on terrorist and
guerrilla movements. Equally, the terms movements, organizations, groups
and parties are used here in a way that is also uncritical. The term
'party' is used for political parties as well as in the sense of 'party
to a conflict'. The term 'group' refers in common parlance to a number
of people, a part, class or layer of the population. More scientific
usage attributes characteristics like "we-feeling", joint actions, common
goals and a relatively long existence in time to groups. It is questionable whether many terrorist groups would meet this last criterion. The
term group is used loosely here. In social science parlance movements
usually stand somewhere between groups and organizations in terms of
coherence, division of labour, planning and direction. In the present
list, however, the term movement like the terms groups, parties and organizations are not meant to indicate a particular structure of the
entities in question. Given the life cycles of such entities these can,
at various stages, be any of the four.

The Jongman list is structured on a country-by-country basis and the
actors or targets are enumerated alphabetically. Where a group acts
without a country of its own - like the exile Armenians and Croatians -
the country "occupying" their homeland is usually taken as category.
Exceptions to this rule (which places the Armenians under Turkey and
the Croatians under Jugoslavia) are made in a number of cases such as
Namibia, Western Sahara, Northern Ireland and Palestine. Although many
governments engage in political violence at home and abroad, these are
not listed here directly. Instead agencies of these governments engaged
in violence are listed under their official or cover names. It is worth
emphasizing that this list is much less thorough with regard to state
violence than with regard to violence directed against states. There
are many explanations for this: the deeper cover of state agencies, the
structure of media reporting and censorship are among them.

Needless to say the present list while, fairly up-to-date (up to March 1983), is far from being complete and thorough. Given the limitations, imposed by the sources, and given the nature of the subject-matter (acts of violence are sometimes committed under false names to confuse the opponents or the public or both) such a list has to be used with great caution by researchers. Errors, omissions, corrections, comments and additions should be communicated to drs. A.J. Jongman, Polemological Institute of the State University of Groningen, Heresingel 13, Groningen, The Netherlands. It is intended to improve and update the information contained in this list periodically so that it can gradually evolve into a more authoritative research instrument.

AFGHANISTAN

7151: Badakshan National Minority Front
Description: a nationalist movement.
Based in: Badakshan.

7213: Eternal Flame
(Shola-e-Jawed) Sama Tendency

7077: Eternal Flame
(Shola-e-Jawed) Raha'i tendency
Ideological position: maoist.

7093: Front of Mujahiddin Fighters
(Djebh-e-Mobarezin-e-Modjahed)
Description: an overall organization of a number of guerrilla factions;
some factions refused membership.

7214: Ghazni National Minority Front
Description: a nationalist movement.
Based in: Ghazni.

7146: Hazara National Minority Front
Description: a nationalist movement.
Based in: Hazara.
Remarks: it claims to run its own autonomous administration.

7147: Islamic Alliance for the Liberation of Afghanistan (IALA)
Description: overall organization of several guerrilla factions.
Date of establishment or first appearance: Jan.1, 1980 its formation
was reported. April 22, 1981 it was dissolved.

7004: Islamic Movement of Afghanistan
(Mahaz Melli Islami Afghanistan)
Description: one of the guerrilla factions.
Estimated strength: 8000 men.

7003: Islamic Party of Afghanistan
(Hezb-i-Islam) (Hekmatyar faction)
Description: most well armed and organized Peshawar based guerrilla
faction. It emphasizes its own variety of a strict Sunni interpretation
of Islam.
Date of establishment or first appearance: it started its armed struggle
in 1974 when it joined a clandestine effort to destabilize the Daoud
regime.
Leadership: Gulbuddin Hekmatyar.
Remarks: it stayed outside the paper federation known as the Islamic
Alliance. Hekmatyar has been accused of establishing a political
hegemony over other guerrilla factions in the style of an Islamic
warlord.

7001: Islamic Party of Afghanistan
(Hezb-i-Islam) (Younes Khales faction)
Description: a group split off from Hekmatyar's party. It is based
in Peshawar and is mainly supported by Pashtuns.

Ideological position: it is more traditionalist than fundamentalist.
Leadership: Younes Khales.
Estimated strength: 8000 men.

7006: Islamic Revolutionary Movement
(Harakat-i-Inquilabi Afghanistan)
Description: Peshawar based guerrilla faction
Ideological position: traditionalist close to fundamentalism.
Leadership: Maulvi Mohammed Nabi.
Estimated strength: 25 000 men.
Remarks: it has a certain influence on the Front of Nimruz.

7005: Islamic Society of Afghanistan
(Jamiat-i-Islami)
Description: Peshawar based guerrilla faction supported by the Tadjik.
Ideological position: fundamentalist young intellectuals.
Leadership: Prof. Burhanuddin Rabani. Field commander: Ahmed Sha
Massus.
Estimated strength: 21 000.

7148: Islamic Unity of Mujaheddin of Afghanistan
Description: a merger of six guerrilla factions.
Date of establishment or first appearance: July 7, 1981.

7118: Ittihad e Islami Mujahideen
Description: an alliance of seven guerrilla factions seeking international
recognition as the official voice of the Afghan resistance.
Leadership: rotating presidency, each party head will serve as president
for one month to overcome the sensitive leadership issue. The first
president was Prof. Abdur Rassol Sayaaf.
Estimated strength: total rebel forces number 90 000 men.

7116: KHAN
Description: the secret police of Karmal.

7149: Kunar National Minority Front
Description: a nationalist movement.
Based in: Kunar.

7117: Movement of Islamic Revolution (MIR)
Description: al alliance of two moslem extremist groups opposed to the
Taraki regime.
Date of establishment or first appearance: shortly after the 1978 coup.

7115: National Fatherland Front
Description: a movement announced by Karmal
Date of establishment or first appearance: June 16, 1981.

7119: National Front for the Islamic Revolution
Description: Peshawar based guerrilla faction.
Leadership: Pir Sayed Ahmed-al-Gailani.

7112: National Front of Militant Combatants
(Jebheye Mobarizin Mujahid-i-Afghanistan)
Description: internal based guerrilla faction. Several leftist organizations
are operating within this front which staged the Bala Hisar mutiny in

the Kabul garrison on Aug.6, 1979.

7113: Nation
(Millat)
Description: internally based guerrilla faction.
Ideological position: active element in the resistance which never
regarded itself as either pro Beiing or pro Moscow.

7002: National Liberation front
Description: Peshawar based guerrilla faction.
Leadership: Sibghatullah Mojadded.

7092: National United Front of Afghanistan
(Djebh-e-Melli)
Description: overall organization.

7150: Nuristan National Minority Front
Description: a nationalist movement which claims to run its own
autonomous administration.
Based in: Nuristan.

7111: Organisation for the Liberation of Afghanistan
(Sazman-e-Azadbaksh Mardom-e-Afghanistan)
Description: a guerrilla faction linked to a number of internal fronts.
Remarks: most active in Kabul and other urban centers.

7114: Partisans of National Liberation of Afghanistan
(Front of Nimruz)
Description: internally based guerrilla faction, mainly supported by
Baluchis.
Ideological position: purely nationalist.
Date of establishment or first appearance: Dec. 1979.
Leadership: Gol Mohammed Rahimi.
Estimated strength: 1000 men.
Remarks: liberated almost a whole province in the southwest and
developed a program to improve agriculture, education and health
situation.

7074: People's Democratic Party of Afghanistan
(Khalq faction) (Masses) (PDPA)
Description: one faction of the government party
Date of establishment or first appearance: 1965.
Leadership: Nur Mohammed Taraki.

7075: People's Democratic Party of Afghanistan
(Parcham faction) (Banner) (PDPA)
Description: the second faction of the government party. Political
withdrawal in 1973 following Khalq defiance of a Soviet directive
to support the Daoud regime.
Date of establishment or first appearance: 1965.
Leadership: Babrak Karmal was installed as president of the republic in
Dec. 1979.
Estimated strength: it had 60 000 members but by the end of 1979
membership had decreased to 20 000.
Remarks: The two factions were reunited in 1977 but most prominent
Parcham members were purged in the wake of an abortive coup on Aug.7,
1978.

Karmal has attempted to reunite the two factions within both government and party.

7110: Revolutionary Group of Afghanistan
(Grohe Inquilabi Khalqhaie Afghanistan)
Description: internally based guerrilla faction.
Remarks: extremely active in anti Soviet resistance particularly in various rural areas.

7076: Settami Melli
Description: maoist movement

7007: United Islamic Front for the Liberation of Afghanistan
(Shoura-e-Ettehad)
Description: sji'ite traditionalist movement.
Leadership: Said Behechti.

ALBANIA

3001: Anti Communist Military Council

3089: National Liberation Army
Description: a group of King Leka supporters which allegedly invaded Albania in the beginning of Oct. 1982. It was reported that the group was totally eliminated by the Albanian army.
Date of establishment or first appearance: Oct. 1982.
Leadership: King Leka.

ALGERIA

6234: Berber Tribesmen
Description: a minority movement striving for greater cultural autonomy.
Remarks: involved in riots in 1980.

6168: National Liberation Army
(Armeé de Liberation Nationale) (ALN)

169: National Liberation Front
(Front de Liberation Nationale) (FLN)

6235: Revolutionary Patriotic Anti-Fascist Front

6001: Soldier of the Algerian Opposition

6002: United Liberation Front for New Algeria

ANGOLA

5059: Joseph Stalin Group

(Nucleo Jose Stalin)

5001: Liberation Front of the Enclave Cabinda
(Frente de Libertacao do Enclave de Cabinda) (FLEC)
Description: liberation movement set up by Zaire and France to take over
the Cabinda enclave which has rich oil deposits.
Date of establishment or first appearance: Aug. 1974.
Leadership: Enrique N'Zita Tiago.
Estimated strength: 500 men.
Remarks: previously it was called the MLEC and it is mainly supported
by the local Fiote tribe. In 1977 it announced the formation of a
provisional government with Enrique N'Zita as head of state.

5080: Military Command for the Liberation of Cabinda
(Comando Militar para Libertacao de Cabinda) (CMLC)
Description: movement which split off from the FLEC in 1977 in an
attempt to restructure FLEC on a "new democratic foundation".
Date of establishment or first appearance: 1977.
Leadership: Marcelino Tumbi and Luis Matos Fernandes.

5003: National Front for the Liberation of Angola
(Frente Nacional de Libertacao de Angola) (FLNA)
Description: a liberation movement active in northern Angola.
Ideological position: the most anti-communist of active movements in
Angola.
Date of establishment or first appearance: Mar. 27, 1962 as a
cooperation between UPA and ULAZO.
Leadership: Holden Roberto (alias Jose Gilmore).
Estimated strength: between 4000 and 7000 well disciplined troops plus
the same number support troops.
Remarks: Oct. 1979 Holden Roberto was forced to leave Zaire following
an anti subversion agreement between Angola, Zaire and Zambia. In Nov.
it was reported he had also been expelled from Senegal.

5004: National Union of Total Independence of Angola
(Uniao Nacional para a Independencia Total de Angola) (UNITA)
Description: a still very active and strong liberation movement
supported by South Africa and the United States.
Ideological position: pro western.
Date of establishment or first appearance: May 13, 1966.
Leadership: Jonas Malheiro Savimbi
Estimated strength: 8000 infantry troops and about 20 000 village
militia.
Remarks: it operates mainly in the southern Ovimbundo regions. Together
with the FLNA it has tried to establish an abortive rival government at
Huambo in 1976. Since then it has been involved in guerrilla operations
against the MPLA government. It has also been involved in actions
directed at SWAPO in Namibia.

5005: Popular Liberation Movement of Angola-Labour Party
(Movimiento Popular de Libertacao de Angola-Partido de Trabacho) (MPLA)
Description: a Soviet backed liberation movement which provided the
primary resistance to Portuguese colonial rule.
Ideological position: pro Moscow.
Date of establishment or first appearance: Dec. 1956 as a cooperation
between Vamos Escobrir Angola, the PLUA and MINA.

Leadership: José Eduardo dos Santos.
Remarks: a bloodbath in Feb. 1961 which resulted in 3000 deaths was the trigger for an armed struggle. Since independence Nov. 1975 it is the official government party.

5002: Popular Movement for the Liberation of Cabinda (MPLC)
Description: set up as a "progressive" but not anti-western faction.
Date of establishment or first appearance: June 1979.
Leadership: Francisco Xavier Lubota (President)

ARGENTINA

1001: Argentine Anti Communist Alliance (AAA)
Date of establishment or first appearance: Jan. 1974.

1006: Argentine Committee for the Anti Imperialist Struggle
(Comite Argentino de Lucha Anti Imperialisto)

1002: Argentine Liberation Front
(Fuerzas Armadas de Liberacion) (FAL)
Ideological position: pro Havana
Remarks: active in 1969 and 1970.

1003: Argentine National Organization Movement
(Movimiento Argentino Nacional Organisacion) (MANO)

1004: Argentine National Social Front

1005: Argentine Youth for Sovereignty

1007: Descamisados Peronistas Montoneros

1107: Fifth of April
(Cinco del Abril)
Description: small little known leftist guerrilla group.

1173: Group of 25
Description: labour union.
Date of establishment or first appearance: 1979.

1086: Los Uturuncos
Description: one of the first urban and rural guerrilla movements in 1954 and 1960.
Remarks: nearly all members were Peronists.

1010: Maxima Mena Command

1011: Montoneros
Description: leftwing Peronist urban guerrilla group which acted from 1975 as armed branch of the PPA and seeks a "socialist revolution".
Ideological position: pro Havana.
Date of establishment or first appearance: 1970.
Leadership: Mario Eduardo Firmenich.
Estimated strength: once some 5000 with 15 000 active sympathizers but now under 350.

Remarks: by 1978 it was defeated. Fidel Castro permitted to relocate its headquarters in Cuba.

1009: National Liberation Front of South Vietnam
(Frente de Liberacion Nacional del Vietnam del Sur)

1108: New Argentine Command
Date of establishment or first appearance: June 6, 1981.
Remarks: responsible for an attack on a journalist.

1106: October 17 Montoneros
(Montoneros 17 de Octubre)
Description: a movement completely committed to insurrection.
Date of establishment or first appearance: April 1980.
Leadership: Miguel Bossano.
Remarks: named after Argentina's largest mass mobilization (1945) which started the Peronist movement.

1172: Ururo Foco
Description: guerrilla movement.

1014: People's Revolutionary Army
(Ejercito Revolucionario del Pueblo) (ERP)
Description: armed branch of the Workers Revolutionary Party (PRT).
Date of establishment or first appearance: 1969.
Remarks: a rural front in Tucaman was eradicated in 1977.

1008: People's Revolutionary Army/ August 22 (ERP)
Description: a guerrilla movement.
Ideological position: Trotskyite.

1013: Peronist Armed Forces
(Fuerzas Armadas Peronistas) (FAP)
Ideological position: mixed Peronism and Castroism.
Date of establishment or first appearance: 1950's.
Remarks: carried out bomb attacks and bankraids in 1971.

1012: Peronist Movement
(Movimiento Peronista)

1087: POR
Ideological position: Trotskyite.

1015: Revolutionary Armed Forces
(Fuerzas Armadas Revolucionario) (FAR)
Ideological position: pro Havana.
Date of establishment or first appearance: 1967.
Remarks: in 1971 it has tried to unify extremist movements into a common front.

0260: Peoples Electoral Movement
(Movimiento Electoral di Pueblo) (MEP)

AUSTRIA

3002: Justice Guerrilla

BAHREIN

6135: Islamic Front for the Liberation of Bahrein

6003: National Liberation Front Bahrein

6004: Popular liberation Front of Oman and the Arab Gulf

BANGLA DESH

7120: Awami League
Description: it was a major force in the drive for independence.
Although formally disbanded in 1975 by President Mostaque Ahmed, it
remained the best politically organized political group in the country
and served as the nucleus of the Democratic United Front, which
supported the presidential candidacy of Gen. Muhammad Ataul Ghani
Osmani at the June 1978 election.
During 1980 and 1981 there was a severe leadership struggle between a
pro Moscow faction and a pro Indian faction. In 1981 Hasine Wajed was
elected as new leader. Together with her sister they are the only
survivors of shekh Mujib's family. Wajed was a compromise candidate.
Her leadership was considered as a pro Indian lobby victory against
the stronger pro Moscow group.
Leadership: Hasine Wajed.

7123: Bangla Desh Jatiyo League (BJL)

7122: Bangla Desh Moslem League (BML)
Description: a conservative pro Pakistan group which refused to follow
other Moslem League members in joining the BNP
Leadership: Khan Abdus Sabur.

7121: Bangla Desh National Party
(Bangla Desh Jatiyabadi Dal) (BNP)
Description: a merger of a number of groups which had supported
President Zia in his election campaign.
Date of establishment or first appearance: Sep. 1978.
Leadership: Gen. Ziaur Rahman

7124: Communist Party of Bangla Desh (CPB)
Ideological position: pro Moscow.
Date of establishment or first appearance: was permitted to resume
legal existence in Nov. 1978.

7125: Gono Front

7158: Mukti Fouj (or Mukti Bahini) Liberation Forces

Description: a movement striving for greater autonomy.
Estimated strength: 30 000 (1971)
Remarks: it was based in east Pakistan now Bangla Desh and was
stiffened by defectors from the East Pakistan Rifles Regiment.

7094: Mutti Parishad

7008: National Socialist Party
(Jatiyo Samajtantrik Dal) (JSD)
Description: leftwing movement which was the principal instigator of
the 1975 army coup, which resulted in President Zia's assumption of
power.
Leadership: Mirza Sultan Raja (acting President)
Remarks: it was reinstated as a legal party Nov. 1978 after many of its
members had been arrested.

7152: Parbottya Chattyram Jana Sarghati Samity (PCJSS)
Description: buddhist ethnic minority involved in an insurgency against
the Bangla Desh government.
Based in: the Chitta Gong Hill Tracts
Remarks: it strives for a greater degree of autonomy and protection
as recognised under the constitution. By 1979 the Mizo, Tripura and
Chakma insurgencies had converged.

7095: Peace Army (Shanti Bahini)
Description: military wing of the tribal liberation movement.
Leadership: Manabendra Narayan Larma (has been living in India since
1975).
Remarks: substantial quantities of Indian arms and ammunition were sent
to tribal groups in the hill tracts in Nov. 1975 and again in Mar. 1977.
However, after the fall of mrs. Gandhi's government in the 1977
elections, Indian arms supplies to the rebels were halted.

7096: Sharbohara

7126: United People's Party (UPP)

BELGIUM

2100: Direct Action (Belgian Section)

2111: Flemish Militant Order
(Vlaamse Militanten Orde) (VMO)
Description: a militant movement calling for a Flemish republic.
Leadership: Armand "Bert" Erikson.

2118: Fouron Action
(Action Fouronnaise)
Leadership: José Happart

2001: Julien Lahaut Brigade

2193: Revenge and Freedom
(Vengenance et Liberté)

Date of establishment or first appearance: 1979.
Remarks: unsubstantiated claim of attack on Alexander Haig.

2192: Taal Aktie Komitee (TAK)
Description: non violent movement striving for secession.

2112: Tendence Dure Fouronnaise

2149: Viking Youth
(Viking Jeugd)
Description: extreme rightist movement.

BELIZE

0191: Anti Communist Society (ACS)
Description: organization suspected of engineering attacks against
leftists and of pro Guatemalan leanings.
Date of establishment or first appearance: 1980.
Leadership: Santiago Perdomo (former trade minister)

0190: Belize Action Movement
Leadership: Odinga Lumumba (arrested Aug. 1981)

BENIN

4043: Benin People's Revolutionary Party

4001: Front for the Liberation and Rehabilitation of Dahomey (FLRD)

BOLIVIA

1076: Bolivian Socialist Phalange
Description: new rightwing pro Banzer group responsible for an abortive
coup in May 1981.
Date of establishment or first appearance: 1980.

1114: Bolivian Workers' Revolutionary Party
(Partido Revolucionario de Trabajadores Bolivianos) (PRTB)
Description: political front of the ELN.
Date of establishment or first appearance: 1972.
Leadership: Paredo's brother Antonio.
Remarks: in 1978 it was decided to oppose the military government
through a wide resistance movement combining legal, semilegal and
clandestine organizations.

1184: Bridegrooms of Death

1186: Central Obrera Boliviana (COB)

1110: Death Squad

(Esquadron de la Muerte)
Description: rightwing terrorist organization.
Remarks: activity increased considerably in 1980, especially after the coup.

1111: Mitka-Tupac Katari Movement
(Movimiento Tupac Katari)
Description: an Aymara Indian national movement.
Ideological position:
Date of establishment or first appearance: 1978.
Leadership: Luciano Tapía Quisbert.
Remarks: a powerful peasant pressure group.

1083: Movement of Revolutionary Left
(Movimiento de Izquierda Revolucionaria) (MIR)
Description: predominantly a political party but responsible for some violent actions in 1979 and in 1980.
Ideological position: social democratic.
Leadership: Jose Reyes Carvajal, one of its main leaders was killed in June 1980.
Remarks: Since Meza's coup, July 17, 1980, it has been banned.

1016: Nationalist Commando

1017: National Liberation Army
(Ejercito de Liberacion Nacional) (ELN)
Description: guerrilla movement.
Ideological position: pro Havana.
Date of establishment or first appearance: 1967.
Leadership: "Coco" and "Chato" Paredo have been arrested after which activities decreased.
Remarks: inactive since 1972.

1170: National Unity Government in Hiding
Date of establishment or first appearance: 1980.

1112: Single Federation of Peasant Workers
(Federacion Unica de Trabajadores Campesinos) (FUTC)
Description: leftist peasant political pressure group active in land occupations.
Date of establishment or first appearance: 1980.
Remarks: mainly active in the Oruro department.

1109: Special Security Service (SES)
Description: paramilitary Special Security Service involved in torture and political killings; seems to operate out of Gen. Torrelio's control.

1077: Suarez Mafia

1075: Syrian Lebanese Mafia

1171: Underground Revolutionary Leftist Movement
Date of establishment or first appearance: 1981.

BRAZIL

1018: Action for National Liberation
(Acao Libertadora Nacional) (ALN)
Description: guerrilla movement, its activities decreased after the
death of its leaders in 1969 and 1970.
Ideological position: pro Havana.
Leadership: Carlos Marighela and Joachim Camara Ferreira.

1019: Armed Revolutionary Vanguard- Palmares
(Vanguardia Armada Revolucionaria) (VAR)

1020: Aurora Maria Naciamento Furtado Command

1116: Comando Delta
Description: rightwing death squad.

1117: Comando Herzog
Description: rightwing death squad.

1081: Commando of Communist Hunters
(Vanguardia do Comando de Cacu aos Comunistas) (CCC)
Description: a death squad claiming an average of 100 lives a month in
1981.
Ideological position: anti communist.

1021: Communist Party of Brazil (PCdoB)

1088: Death Squad
(Escudrao da Morte)
Description: a rightwing terrorist organization.
Leadership: Sergio Paranhos Fleury (head of police of Sao Paulo)

1120: Lieutenant Mendes
(Tenente Mendes)
Description: rightwing guerrilla group.
Remarks: operated in 1980 mainly against leftist newspapers.

1119: New Fatherland Phalange
(Falange Patria Nova) (FPN)
Description: extreme rightwing guerrilla group.
Date of establishment or first appearance: August 1980.
Remarks: carried out many bomb attacks.

1115: Operacao Bandierantes (OBAN)
Description: a death squad formed by army, navy and police officers
which operates mainly in Sao Paulo.
Date of establishment or first appearance: 1969.

1023: Popular Revolutionary Vanguard
(Vanguardia Popular Revolucionaria) (VRP)
Ideological position: pro Havana.
Leadership: Carlos Lamarca (killed by security forces in 1971).
Remarks: since the death of its leader activities have decreased.

1022: Revolutionary Movement of the Eight (MR-8)

1168: White Hand (Rio de Janeiro)
Description: death squad operating in Rio de Janeiro.

1118: Zionist Paramilitary Groups

BRUNEI

6078: Brunei People's Independence Front
(Barisan Kemerdeka'an Ra'ayat Brunei-Baker)
Description: the only current active party which is an amalgamation
of all former parties. Political parties have been largely inactive
since the 1962 rebellion.
Leadership: Zainal Abidin Puteh.

6079: Brunei People's Party
(Parti Ra'ayat Brunei) (PRB)
Description: banned organization which operates from Malaysia.
Leadership: A.M.N. Azahari.

BURMA

7009: Arakan Communist Party

7011: Burmese Communist Party (Red Flags)

7010: Burmese Communist Party (White Flags)
Description: party which supplies the SSA with Chinese arms and
training.
Ideological position: pro Bejing.
Estimated strength: 21 500 according to the Burmese defense minister.
Western sources estimate the main force of the guerrillas at 12 000.
Remarks: it operates mainly in the northeast close to the Chinese border.

7012: Federal National Democratic Front
Description: a union of the Arakan Liberation Party, the Karen National
Union, the Karenni National Program Party, the New Mon State Party
and the Shan State Program Party.

7013: Kachin Independence Army (KIA)
Description: insurgent group.
Ideological position:
Date of establishment or first appearance:
Leadership:
Estimated strength: about 2000 men although itself claimed sometimes
a strength of twice that number. The Burmese defense minister
estimated its strength at 150.
Remarks: military observers said it fragmented during 1980 with some
elements going over to the BCP and others entering into what seems to
be an accomodation with the Burmese Army.

7127: Karenni Army (KA)

7128: Karen National Union (KNU)
Description: a guerrilla movement.
Estimated strength: it fields somewhere between 2000 and 3000 soldiers
although the Burmese defense minister estimated its strength at 150.

7129: Lahu Revolutionary Army (LRA)
Description: guerrilla movement based along the border with Thailand.

7153: Nom Suk Han
Description: one of the oldest groupings under the leadership of Sao Noi.
It broke up and the nucleus of 90 men, many of them nationalistic
students, joined 140 Shan deserters from the Burmese army. Together
they were to constitute the basis of the future Shan State
Independence Army.

7130: Paluang National Liberation Organization (PNLO)
Description: guerrilla movement based in the Taunggyi area.
Estimated strength: it is thought to have 1500 armed followers.

7014: Remainder of the Kuomintang Third Army (KMT)

7132: Shan National Army (SNA)
Leadership: Duan Shiwen (a former Kuomintang general)
Estimated strength: 500 men.

7155: Shan State Independence Army (SSIA)
Description: guerrilla movement.
Date of establishment or first appearance: 1959.
Leadership: Pi Sai Luang (until 1964)
Remarks: after Pi Sai Luang's resignation and retirement the rebels
changed their name to SSA.

7131: Shan State Progress Party (SSPP)
Description: a political party supported by Shan and Paluang. The party
shapes the military organization, political officers hold positions
in the SSA and have the exclusive right to sit on committees, something
their military counterparts do not. Its central committee is based in
the district of Kyaukme.
Leadership: Hso Lane (who is also leader of the SSA)

7154: Shan State Army (SSA)
Description: born out of the Shan revolt against Rangoon in 1958.
Previously it was called the SSIA. Hso Lane assumed leadership in 1964.
It consists of four brigades and in order not to be dominated the
minorities have created their own armed groups Pa-o, Lahu and Paluang).
The Chinese weapons and ammunition come free of charge from the BCP,
a service which allows the BCP to exert a good deal of leverage over
the SSA.
Leadership: Hso Lane.
Estimated strength: 8000 but only 3-4000 are armed. The minister of
defense estimated its strength at a mere 100 men.
Remarks: it has a permanent camp at Salween. It operates in four
brigades with each three batallions.

7091: Shan State Army Eastern (SSAE)
Estimated strength: 10 000 armed insurgents with a 30 000 village militia.

7015: Shan United Army (SUA)
Description: armed group involved in the trade of opium and jade.
Leadership: Khun Sa (or Chan Shee Fu)
Estimated strength: an armed force of 3500 to 5000 men including Shan,
Wa, Lahu and Chinese.
Remarks: the force is split between Tangyang, the major transshipment
point for prized Kokang opium in the northern Shan States, and an area
east of Salween where it acts as a buffer between the BCP and SSA.

7016: Shan United Revolutionary Army (SURA)
Description: armed group involved in the trade of jade.
Leadership: Li Wen Huan (former Kuomintang general)
Estimated strength: 200 armed men.
Remarks: it remains more of an irritant to the government.

7207: The Moslem League

7156: United National Liberation Front (UNLF)
Description: a front alliance of ethnic minorities active in the
beginning of the seventies.
Leadership: U Nu.
Estimated strength: 50 000 in 1971.

7086: United Pa-o Organization
Description: guerrilla movement of the Pa-o minority operating on the
borders of the Shan and Karenni states west of Mong Mah.
Estimated strength: 300 regulars and 500 armed militia men.

BURUNDI

5070: Revolutionary Youth Rwagasore (JRR)
(Jeunesse Revolutionaire Rwagasore)
Leadership: Nanga Yivuza.

CANADA

0001: Canadian Hungarian Freedom Fighters Federation

0002: Quebec Liberation Front
(Front de Liberation du Quebec) (FLQ)
Description: urban terrorist movement responsible for more than
200 bomb attacks.
Date of establishment or first appearance: 1961.
Remarks: it operated in small autonomous groups without a central
leadership. By 1971 its main leaders were detained.

CANARY ISLANDS

2101: Canary Islands Independence Movement

2102: Canary Islands Intelligence Service

2103: Movement for Selfdetermination and Independence for the Canary Islands

CAPE VERDE ISLANDS

4002: African Party for the Independence of Guinea and Cape Verde (Partido Africano da Independencia da Guiné e Cabo Verde)

CENTRAL AFRICAN REPUBLIC

4048: Independent Group of Reflexion and Action
(Groupe Independant du Reflexion et d'Action)
(GIRA)
Leadership: Francois Pehoua (former independent presidential candidate)

4003: Movement for the Liberation of the Central African People (MPLC)
Description: opposition movement.
Leadership: Ange Patasse (former prime minister under Bokassa)
Remarks: together with other opposition leaders it announced the
Provisional Political Council in April 1981. After an abortive
coup attempt in March 1982 it was dissolved. Ange Patasse went into
political exile in Togo.

4042: Movement for the National Liberation of Central Africa
(Mouvement Centrafricain de Liberation National) (MCLN)
Leadership: dr. Idi Lala.
Remarks: it was banned by the civilian government after bomb explosions
in July 1981.

4047: Rassemblement du Peuple Centrafricain (RCP)
Leadership: Gen. Sylvestre Bangui (former ambassador to Paris)

4004: Ubangian Liberation Front
(Front de Liberation Oubanguien) (FLO)

4005: Ubangi Patriotic Front
(Front Patriotique Oubanguien) (FPO)
Date of establishment or first appearance: 1976 founded by Idi Lala.
Leadership: dr.Abel Goumba.

CHAD

4006: Armed Forces of the North (FAN)
Description: one of the guerrilla factions.

Leadership: Hissene Habre
Estimated strength: 3000 to 8000 armed men.
Remarks: withdrew from the GUNT in March 1980, following failure of
demobilization agreement under the Lagos accord of Aug. 1979. It lost
its support from the MPLT and FAO in April 1981.

4010: Armed Forces of the West (FAO)
Description: one of the guerrilla factions.
Leadership: M.M. Mahamat.

4012: Chadian Armed Forces (FAT)
Description: one of the armed factions consisting of the southern
gendarmerie and remnants of the 1979 Chadian army.
Leadership: Wadal Abdelkader Kamougue.

4007: Chadian Democratic Revolutionary Movement (MDRT)

4008: Chadian Liberation Front (FLT)

4049: Chadian National Liberation Front (fundamental) (FROLINAT)
Description: a nationalist movement opposed to a neo-colonialist policy
which split in 1972.
Date of establishment or first appearance: 1966.
Leadership: M. Hadjero Senoussi.

4009: Chadian National Liberation Front (original) (FROLINAT)
Description: a nationalist movement opposed to a neo-colonialist policy
which spilt in 1972 in a fundamental and an original faction.
Date of establishment or first appearance: 1966.
Leadership: A. Saddick.

4013: First Army (also Vulcan Army)
Description: one of the armed factions.
Leadership: M. Aboulaye Danu.

4015: Front for Joint Provisional Action (FACP)
(Front d'Action Commune)
Description: originated as the Vulcan Force, it is a union of
several armed factions.
Leadership: Acyl Ahmat (minister of foreign affairs).

4041: National Integrated Army (ANI)
Description: national army consisting of several armed factions.

4011: Popular Armed Forces (FAP)
Description: one of the armed factions consisting of the Second Army and
the FROLINAT(original). In May 1981 it announced a merger with the
FAO, CDR, and First Army to form the CNR (National Council for the
Revolution and the ANI (National Integrated Army)
Leadership: Goukouni Oueddei.
Remarks: it is backed by Libya.

4014: Popular Liberation Front (FPL)
Description: one of the armed factions.
Leadership: M.M. Abba Said.

4019: Popular Movement for the Liberation of Chad (also Third Army)
(MPLT)
Description: one of the armed factions.
Leadership: Batran Idris.

4016: Revolutionary Democratic Council (CDR) or New Vulcan.
Description: one of the armed factions.
Leadership: Acyl Ahmat, died in an accident in 1982; replaced by
Acherick Ibn Oumar.
Remarks: pro Libya.

4017: Second Army

CHILE
1025: Chilean Socialist Party

1080: Comando Carevic
Description: clandestine anti-communist association which caused
a series of deaths in June 1979.

1099: Commandos of the People's Resistance
Description: believed to be an offshoot of the MIR and has claimed a
number of bomb explosions.
Date of establishment or first appearance: 1980.

1121: Commando of Avengers of Humberto Tapia Barraza
Description: a group claiming responsibility for the killings of two
leftwing members in Santiago.
Date of establishment or first appearance: July 1981.

1079: Commando for Avenging Martyrs
(Comando Vengadores de Martires) (COVEMA)
Description: extreme rightwing informal militia consisting of members
of the Servico de Investigaciones.
Date of establishment or first appearance: Aug. 1980.

1100: Commando Salvador Allende
Description: popular militia linked with the MIR.

1102: Condor

1026: Fatherland and Liberty
(Patria y Libertad) (PL)
Description: neofascist paramilitary movement.
Date of establishment or first appearance: before the fall of Allende.
Leadership: attorney Pablo H. Rodriquez Grez.

1122: FM-7
Description: small guerrilla group linked to the MIR.

1098: Independent Armed Revolutionary Movement
(Movimiento Independista Revolucionario Armado) (MIRA)

1123: Javier Carrerera Popular Resistance Commando
(Comando de Resistencia Popular Javier Carrera) (CRP)

Description: a group believed to be an offshoot of the MIR.
Date of establishment or first appearance: April 1980.

1027: Movement of Revolutionary Left
(Movimiento de la Izquierda Revolucionaria) (MIR)
Description: mid 1979 several hundred Chilean exiles were recruited
and sent to Cuba for training. By late 1980 at least 100 MIR members
were reported to have reentered Chile and claimed responsibility for a
number of bombings and bankrobberies.
Ideological position: pro Havana.
Date of establishment or first appearance: 1965.
Leadership: Pascal Andrés Allende (returned to Chile 1979)
Estimated strength: 100 to 500 men.

1124: People's Organized Vanguard
(Vanguardia Organizada del Pueblo) (VOP)
Description: leftist guerrilla group.
Remarks: seven members were given life sentences Aug. 1979 for
the assassination of vice-president Zujevic.

1125: Popular Militias
(Milicias Populares) (MP)
Description: overall title for a number of leftist groups, predominantly
urban such as Comando Salvador Allende or Popular Resistance Militia,
which are all linked to the MIR and have been involved in a number
of killings.

1028: Proletarian Action Group (GAP)

1074: Roger Vergara Command
Description: rightist group.
Date of establishment or first appearance: named after the assassinated
director of the school of the intelligence service of the army,
Roger Vergara, July 1980.

1101: Unified Popular Action Movement
(Movimiento de Accion Popular Unitario) (MAPU)
Description: clandestine leftist group which signed declaration of unity
with the MIR in Jan. 1981.
Leadership: Anselmo Cuevas Hormazabal who was arrested April 1980.

CHINA

7204: Gang of Four, Shanghai Mafia

7079: Guards of Imperial China

7202: Petitioners

7205: Salvation Army

7203: Urban People's Militia

COLUMBIA

1084: Anti Kidnap Group
(Movimiento Anti Secuestro) (MAS)
Description: a group which was formed to bring reprisals against
guerrilla kidnappers.
Date of establishment or first appearance: Dec. 1981.

1032: April 19 Movement (M-19)
Description: leftwing guerrilla movement. Emerged in 1972 purporting
to be the armed branch of the ANAPO which however rejected the link.
Date of establishment or first appearance: 1972.
Leadership: Jaime Bateman Cayon (attended a communist cadre school in
Moscow).
Remarks: Extremely active in 1979. Announced alliance with ELN April
1979. Extremely active in 1980 and 1981, despite efficient
counterinsurgency operations. Merger was announced with FARC, MAO
and EPL to coordinate guerrilla actions. Leader announced 1982
presidential candidacy.

1126: Fatherland and Order
(Patria y Orden)
Description: extreme rightist paramilitary group.
Remarks: during 1980 it claimed several hundred lives and it continued
its activities unabated during 1981.

1029: Group of the Revolutionary Commandos

1166: Guerrillas of the Marguetalia Region

1030: Invisible Ones

1031: Military Liberation Front of Columbia

1167: Movement of Workers, Students and Peasants

1034: National Liberation Army
(Ejercito de Liberacion Nacional) (ELN)
Description: rural guerrilla group.
Ideological position: pro Havana.
Date of establishment or first appearance: 1964.
Leadership: Fr.Manuel Perez Matinez ("Poliarco")
Remarks: in 1971 it stepped up its activities by embarking on bankraids
ambushes and kidnappings. An attempt to set up an urban network was
foiled by security forces. It was active in 1980 although only a shadow
of its former strength. It cooperates closely with FARC.

1033: National Liberation Armed Forces (FALN)

1185: National Organization of Columbian Indigenes (ONIC)
Description: an overall organization of a great number of Indian
organizations.

1103: Operation Argimirio Gabaldon

1128: Patriotic Liberation Front
(Frente Patriotica de Liberacion) (FPL)
Date of establishment or first appearance: emerged in Bogota in Oct. 1979.

1127: Pedro Leon Abroleda Brigade (PLA)

1035: People's Revolutionary Army-Zero Point

1129: Popular Forces of Guerrilla action
(Fuerzas Populares de Accion Guerillera) (FPAG)
Date of establishment or first appearance: emerged in southern
Columbia in 1977.

1036: Popular Liberation Army (EPL)
Description: Columbia's third largest rural guerrilla group.
Ideological position: pro Beijing.
Date of establishment or first appearance: 1967.
Leadership: Francisco Carvello.
Estimated strength: 455 men.
Remarks: very active in 1980; and it joined the ELN.

1037: Red Flag
(Bandera Roja)

1038: Revolutionary Armed Forces of Columbia (FARC)
Description: since 1978 it formed the largest and most active guerrilla
movement in Columbia.
Ideological position: pro Moscow.
Date of establishment or first appearance: May 1966.
Leadership: Manuel Marulanda Albornoz ("Ruben")
Estimated strength: 765 men.

1039: Revolutionary Workers Party-Defense Command
(Movimiento de Autodefensa Obrera) (MAO)
Description: allegedly the urban branch of the EPL.
Date of establishment or first appearance:
Leadership: founder Armando Lopez Suarez ("Coleta") and leader Oscar
Mateus Puerto("Julian") were both arrested in May 1980.

1040: September 14 Workers Self Defense Command
(Comando de Auto Defensa Obrera 14 de Septiembre) (CAOS)
Description: Trotskyite guerrilla group.
Date of establishment or first appearance: Feb. 1978.

1041: United Front for Guerrilla Action
(Fuerzas Unidas Para la Accion Guerrillera) (FUPAG)
Description: a unified action front of several guerrilla movements.
Date of establishment or first appearance: March 1979.
Leadership: Lazaro Pineda Guerra.
Estimated strength: total strength of the four groups is estimated at
1800 men.
Remarks: it was dismantled by the police in March 1979 and since then
inactive.

1130: Workers' Independent Revolutionary Movement
(Movimiento Obrera Independiente Revolucionaria) (MOIR)
Description: leftist labour pressure group.

COMOROS

9933: Movement for a Democratic Comores Republic

COSTA RICA

0192: Carlos Aguero Echeverria Commando
Description: leftwing group based in Nicaragua responsible for two bomb
attacks in San Jose early 1981.

0168: The Family
Description: popular name of a terrorist group.
Date of establishment or first appearance: March 1981.

0193: El Gallito
Description: leftwing group backed by Cuba responsible for the killing
of policemen in June 1981.

0151: Movement for a Free Costa Rica
Description: rightwing paramilitary group.

0003: National Liberation Party (PLN)
Description: founded by former president Jose Figueres Ferrer in the
aftermath of the 1948 revolution. The PLN has traditionally been the
largest and best organized of the Costa Rican parties and is a classic
example of the democratic left in Latin America. Reformist and non
marxist, with a base in youth and liberal elements in society, it
has consistently favored progressive programs.

0169: People's Revolutionary Movement
(Movimiento Revolucionario del Pueblo) (MRP)
Description: a group suspected of terrorist activities.
Ideological position: pro Havana.
Date of establishment or first appearance: 1981.
Estimated strength: 75-100 men.

0004: People United
(Pueblo Unido) (PU)
Description: organized as a coalition of left wing groups in support
of the 1978 presidential candidacy of Rodrigo Gutierrez Saenz. Its
constituent parties are the Popular Vanguard Party, the Socialist Action
Party and the Workers Party.
Date of establishment or first appearance: 1978.
Leadership: Rodrigo Gutierrez Saenz.

0005: Popular Front
(Frente Popular)
Description: a small democratic party of the extreme left.
Leadership: Rodolfo Cerdas.

0006: Popular Vanguard Party

0007: Revolutionary Commandos of Solidarity

0008: Roberto Santucho Revolutionary Group

0287: Simon Bolivar Brigade

0009: Socialist Action Party

0194: Tupamaro
Description: Uruguayan guerrilla group believed to train students in
Costa Rica.

0010: Workers Party

CUBA

0011: Abdala

0012: Alpha 66

0013: Anti Castro Commando

0020: Cuban Anti Communist League

0170: Communist Party of Cuba (PCC)
Description: a direct decendent of Castro's Rebel Army and the 26th of
July Movement which constituted the personal political following
during the anti Batista period. The organizational revolution began
in 1961 with the formation of the Integrated Revolutionary Organizations
(ORI), which included the Popular Socialist Party, 26th of July
Movement and the Revolutionary Directorate. The ORI was transformed
into the United Party of the the Cuban Socialist Revolution in 1963
the latter being redesignated as the Communist Party of Cuba in 1965.
Leadership: Fidel Castro Ruz (first secretary).

0016: Condor

0017: Coordination of United Revolutionary Organizations (CORU)

0019: Cuba Action Commandos

0018: Cuba Action

0021: Cuban C-4 Movement

0022: Cuban Liberation Front (FLNC)

0286: Cuban National Liberation Front (FLNC)

0023: Cuban Power
(El Poder Cubano)

0024: Cuban Power 76

0025: Cuban Representation in Exile

0026: Cuban Revolutionary Directorate

0027: Cuban Revolutionary Organization

0028: Cuban Youth Group

0171: Internationalist Brigade

0029: International Secret Revolutionary Cells

0030: JNC (JNC)

0285: July 26 Revolutionary Movement

0031: Latin American Anti Communist Army

0033: Movement of the Seventh

0032: Movement for Cuban Justice

0284: National Front for the Liberation of Cuba

0034: National Integration Front (FIN)

0035: Omega Seven
Description: underground paramilitary wing of the Cuban Nationalist movement, an above ground anti Castro movement based in Miami and Union City. According to the FBI it is the most dangerous terrorist group in the USA.

0036: Pedro Luis Boitel Command

0037: Pedro Ruiz Botero Commandos

0038: Pragmatistas

0039: Scorpion
(El Acran)

0040: Second Front of Escambray

0041: Secret Anti Castro Cuban Army

0042: Secret Cuban Government

0043: Secret Hand Organization

0044: Secret Organization Zero

0045: Young Cubans

0046: Youths of the Star
Description: an anti Castro force which receives training in the USA.
Leadership: Jorge Gonzales.

CYPRUS

3004: Enosis Movement
(Ethniki Organosis Kypriakou Agoniston) (EOKA-B)
Leadership: exiled leader Nicos Sampson was ordered to return to Cyprus
to complete jail sentence Dec. 1980.

3005: National Patriotic Front (MP 14/31)

6254: Turkish Cypriot Federated State

CZECHOSLOVAKIA

3095: Charter 77

3094: Committee for the Defense of the Unjustly Persecuted (VONS)

DJIBOUTI

5040: Democratic Front for the Liberation of Djibouti (FDLD)

5037: Front for the Liberation of the Somali Coast (FLCS)

5038: National Union for Independence (UNI)

5039: Popular Movement for Liberation (MPL)
Description: a group involved in kidnappings of foreigners demanding the
release of political prisoners and better political representation for
the Afar. It was dissolved by the government Dec. 1977 after an attack
on the French military when 600 Afar youths were arrested.

DOMINICA

0195: Dominica Liberation Movement Alliance (DCLM)

0283: Dreads

DOMINICAN REPUBLIC

0122: Dominican Popular Movement
(Movimiento Popular Dominicano) (MPD)
Description: extremist group.
Ideological position: pro Beijing.
Date of establishment or first appearance: 1965.
Leadership: Maximiliano Gomez (was murdered in May 1971 in a Brussels
hotel)
Remarks: it obtained a measure of respectability as part of the coalition
that attempted to prevent President Balaguer from winning a third term
in 1974.

0172: Dominican Revolutionary Party (PRD)
Description: a party of the democratic left rejecting communism and
Castroism; has also been critical of American "imperialism".
Date of establishment or first appearance: 1939 founded by former
president Juan Bosch Gavino.
Remarks: the party boycotted both the 1970 and 1974 elections but won
the presidency and a majority in the chamber of deputies under the
relatively conservative leadership of Antonio Guzman Fernandez in 1978.

0123: January 12 Liberation Movement

0282: July 14th Movement

0290: Pedro Santa Patriotic Front

0197: Socialist Party
Description: small extremist splintergroup members of which allegedly
received military training in Cuba.

0196: Social Workers Movement
Description: small extremist splintergroup members of which allegedly
received military training in Cuba.

0124: United Anti Reelection Command

ECUADOR

1131: Liberation Front of the Poor
(Frente de Liberacion de los Pobros) (FLP)
Date of establishment or first appearance: July 1980.

1132: Revolutionary Action Movement of October 18
(Movimiento 18 de Octubre de Accion Revolucionaria Astra) (M-18-x)
Date of establishment or first appearance: April 1980.

EGYPT

6005: Al Djihad Conservative Organization

6143: Al Islamiya

6142: Al Jamiyat
Description: fundamentalist movement.

6194: Arab Egypt Liberation Front
Description: a group which claimed responsibility for an explosion of a
US jet fighter.

6130: Egyptian National Front
Description: exile movement announced by former armed forces commander
Gen. Saad El Din al-Shazli.
Date of establishment or first appearance: April 1980.

Leadership: Gen. Saad El Din al-Shazli.

6102: Gamaat Islamiya

6137: Islamic Association
Description: militant youth organization.
Ideological position:
Date of establishment or first appearance:

6138: Moslem Brotherhood
Leadership: Omar Telmessani (imprisoned chief spokesman)

6103: Repentance and Holy Flight
(Tafkir Wal Hegira)
Description: a sizable movement highly organized and spread horizontally
and vertically throughout Egyptian society. the goal is to topple Egypts
present social order and to establish an islamic order.
Estimated strength: 3000 to 5000 active members. According to the
minister of Interior some 300 odd members were professionally trained,
heavily armed and financed by a foreign country.

EL SALVADOR

0280: Andes

0199: Anti Communist Political Front
(Frente Politica Anticomunista) (FPA)
Description: rightwing militia.
Date of establishment or first appearance: May 1979.

0121: Armed Forces of National Resistance
(Fuerzas Armadas de Resistencia Nacional) (FARN)
Description: organized by a group of ERP dissidents. It is presently
the most visible of the terrorist groups, being involved in numerous
kidnappings.
Date of establishment or first appearance: 1975.
Leadership: Ernesto Jovel (was killed in Sep.1980)
Remarks: very active in 1979 and 1980.

0152: Armed Forces of the Salvadorean Revolution (FARES)

0279: Broad National Front

0278: Catholic Church

0200: Communist Party of El Salvador
(Partido Comunista de El Salvador) (PCES)
Description: a small guerrilla group which has been repudiated by most
of the currently active mass and guerrilla organizations for alleged
revisionist tendencies. The National Democratic Union has served since
1977 as its legal front.
Ideological position: pro Moscow.
Leadership: Jaime Barrios, Victor Montes and Schafik Jorge Handal.

0126: Death Squad
Description: rightist group.

0201: Eastern Anti Guerrilla Bloc
(Bloque Antiguerillero del Oriente) (BAGO)
Description: rightwing guerrilla group.
Date of establishment or first appearance: Sep. 1980.

0120: Falange
Description: a paramilitary organization with repudiated links to the
military and the "14 families".

0048: February 28 Popular Leagues (LP-28)
Description: powerful direct action leftist interest group very active
in occupations in 1979 and in 1980 moved to outright political violence.
Estimated strength: 10 000 members.

0276: Front for the Liberation of Central America

0275: Guerrilla Army of the Proletariat
(Ejercito Guerrilleros Proletario) (EGP)

0274: Marxist-Leninist Proletarian Army

0295: Maximiliano Martinez Brigade
(Comando Maximiliano Hernado Martinez)
Description: rightwing guerrilla group believed to have links with the
National Guard. It is named after the military president who crushed the
1932 Matanza uprising.
Date of establishment or first appearance: 1980.
Remarks: it killed many prominent leftist leaders.

0273: Movement for Peace and Tranquility

0125: National Democratic Organization
(Organizacion Democratica Nacional) (ORDEN)
Description: unofficial extreme rightwing militia which is very active
in killings and intimidations. It was unofficially supported by the
government until the Oct. 1979 coup after which the new government
ordered its disbanding. Some activity continued in 1980.
Date of establishment or first appearance: 1968.

0153: National Democratic Union (UDN)

0202: National Revolutionary Movement
(Movimiento Nacional Revolucionario) (MNR)
Description: a social democratic party which participated in the UNO
from 1972 to 1978.
Leadership: Guillermo Manuel Ungo (former junta member now in exile)

0203: New Death Squad
(Escuadron de la Muerte Nuevo)
Description: anti communist execution squad.
Date of establishment or first appearance: Sep. 1980.
Estimated strength: it claimed a membership of 3000.

0204: Organization for the Liberation from Communism
(Organizacion para la Liberacion del Comunismo) (OLC)
Description: a rightwing paramilitary group.
Date of establishment or first appearance: Jan. 1980.

0205: People's Armed Revolutionary Forces
(Fuerzas Revolucionarias Armadas del Pueblo) (FRAP)
Description: a terrorist arm of the ORT which split off from the ERP.
Remarks: active in 1979 and 1980, although relatively small.

0206: People's Liberation Movement
(Movimiento de Liberacion del Pueblo) (MLP)
Description: small militant leftist group.
Remarks: some activity in 1980.

0049: People's Revolutionary Army
(Ejercito Revolucionario del Pueblo) (ERP)
Description: possibly the most extreme of the guerrilla groups. It
has experienced a number of internal cleavages since its formation.
One of the most crucial (which led to the formation of the FARN) stemmed
from the murder of one of its founders, Roque Dalton Garcia, who had
criticized excesses by the group's militaristic faction. It has displayed
sympathy with the Nicaraguan FSLN and the Guatemalan EGP.
Date of establishment or first appearance: 1972.
Remarks: very active in 1979, 1980 and 1981.

0207: Popular Liberation Army
(Ejercito Popular de Liberacion) (EPL)
Description: an off shoot of the FPL.
Date of establishment or first appearance: Nov. 1979.
Leadership: Humberto Mendoza (was killed in Nov. 1980)

0047: Popular Liberation Forces Farabundo Marti (FPL-FM)
Description: guerrilla group formed after a split with the pro Moscow
PCES, by the latter's former secretary general Salvador Cayetano Carpio.
The FPL is believed to be the largest of the leftwing guerrilla movements.
In 1979 it announced a tactical alliance with the FARN. It acts more and
more as an umbrella organization consisting of the FPL, PCES, FARN,
PRTC. It is controlled by the Directorata Unifadora Revolucionaria (DRU)
under Cayetano Carpio.
Date of establishment or first appearance: 1964.
Leadership: Cayetano Carpio.
Estimated strength: a 5000 men revolutionary army plus 3000 reservists.
It can also call on a militia and self defense force which consists of
tens of thousands.
Remarks: during 1979 and 1980 it was the most active group on the
military front. It is mainly based in Chalatenango.

0050: Popular Revolutionary Bloc
(Bloque Popular Revolucionario) (BRP)
Description: leftist federation of interest groups thought to number
30 000 which favored direct but predominantly non violent action. In 1979
however it indulged in violence. Its increased militancy in the urban
sector was reflected in occupations of embassies as well as the Catholic
cathedral at San Salvador during 1979. Subsequent to the Oct. 1978 coup
it announced that it had entered into a "tactical alliance" with FAPU.

Leadership: Juan Chacon (was killed in Nov. 1980).
Estimated strength: 30 000 members.

0208: Revolutionary Action of Secondary school Students
(Accion Revolucionaria de Estudiantes Secundarios) (ARDES)
Description: direct action leftist student group

0139: Revolutionary Democratic Front
(Frente Democratico Revolucionaria) (FDR)
Description: the political arm of the FPL-FM.
Date of establishment or first appearance: Jan. 1981.
Leadership: Manuel Guillermo Ungo.
Remarks: all main leaders were killed in Nov. 1980.

0051: Revolutionary Party of Central American Workers
(Partido Revolucionario de Trabajadores de America Central) (PRTC)
Description: marxist guerrilla group.
Date of establishment or first appearance: Sep. 1979.
Remarks: operated also in Honduras and Guatemala.

0281: Revolutionary Union Coordinating Committee

0209: Salvadorean Christian Peasants Federation
(Federacion de Campesinos Cristianos Salvadorenos) (FECCAS)
Description: illegal force backed by the church.
Estimated strength: possibly 7000 members.

0210: Salvadorean Revolutionary Students Movement
(Movimiento de Estudiantes Revolucionarias Salvadorenas) (MERS)
Description: direct action leftist group active in occupations.

0156: Secret Death Commando (ESA)
Description: rightist death squad.

0203: Squadron of Death
Description: rightist death squad.
Date of establishment or first appearance: 1980.

0053: Union of White Guerrillas
(Union de Guerilleros Blancos) (UGB)
Description: rightwing paramilitary revenge squad.
Remarks: its victims are often teachers, union members and priest.

0052: Unified Popular Action Front
(Frente de Accion Popular Unificado) (FAPU)
Description: somewhat similar to the BRP but with a more distinctly
marxist orientation. It was established as a coalition of student, peasant
and trade union groups and has also participated in a number of
demonstrations at the capital, including the occupation of the Mexican
embassy in early 1979. Although neither the BRP nor the FAPU is
known to have engaged in overt guerrilla activity, the Romero
government claimed that the latter was linked to FARN.
Ideological position:
Date of establishment or first appearance: 1974.
Estimated strength: 10 000- 30 000.

0211: University Revolutionary Front
(Frente Universitario Revolucionario) (FUR 30)
Description: student offshoot of the BPR.

0212: Workers Revolutionary Organization
(Organizacion Revolucionaria de Trabajadores) (ORT)

ETHIOPIA

5112: Afar Liberation Front
Description: resistance movement which opposed the expropriation of
their grazing areas for capital intensive agriculture.
Leadership: sultan Ali Mirah.
Date of establishment or first appearance: 1977.

5071: Commission for Organizing the Party of the Working People of
Ethiopia (COPWE)
Description: a political party which remains a vehicle for Mengistu's
government. With this party he tried to give his government a civilian
appearance but it remains Amhara based and dominated by the military.
Date of establishment or first appearance: Dec. 1979.

5008: Eritrean Liberation Forces-Revolutionary Council (ELF-RC)
Description: a movement which demands autonomy for $2\frac{1}{2}$ million moslems
of the Eritrean province. In 1978 if formed a military committee with
the Marxist EPLF. In 1980 there was a rift after which it severely
depleted. In that year it also formed an alliance with the ELF-PLF.
Date of establishment or first appearance: 1958.
Leadership: Ahmad Nasser.
Estimated strength: 6500 men.

5009: Eritrean Liberation Front (ELF-PLF)
Description: emerged as a third Marxist group in Eritrea.
Date of establishment or first appearance: 1975. It is mainly based
in Sudan and Egypt. It formed a formal alliance with the ELF-RC but
resisted integration into a joint Eritrean force.
Leadership: Osman Saleh Sabbe.

5007: Eritrean Liberation Front-General Command (ELF-GC)

5010: Eritrean Peoples Liberation Forces (EPLF)
Description: Marxist guerrilla movement, set up after a split with in the
ELF.
Date of establishment or first appearance: 1970.
Leadership: Issyas Afeworki (deputy general secretary)
Estimated strength: 8000 men in the field and a 10- 15 000 militia.
Remarks: the most important and strongest group in Eritrea.

5072: Eylem Birligi Faction of the TPLF (TPLF-F)

5011: Oromo Liberation Front (OLF)

5058: Popular Liberation Forces-Revolutionary Council (PLF-RC)

5012: Popular Liberation Forces (PLF)

5073: Revolutionary Party of the Ethiopian People (EPRP)
Description: overall organization of several guerrilla organizations
which overthrew the Haile Selassi regime. Its military wing is almost
completely liquidated.

5013: Somali Abo Liberation Front (SALF)
Description: guerrilla movement active in the Ogaden desert. It has links
with the WSLF.

5114: Stranglers
Description: government liquidation squad.

5014: Tigrays People Liberation Forces (TPLF)
Description: a guerrilla movement operating in the Tigray province which
is striving for complete independence. It cooperates with the EPLF
against a common enemy. It is supported by conservative Arab
governments. It has liberated large sections of the province and
installed an effective administration.
Date of establishment or first appearance: 1974.
Estimated strength: 6000 armed men.
Remarks: has been very active in attacking government convoys.

5015: Western Somali Liberation Front (WSLF)
Description: guerrilla movement backed by Somalia.
Date of establishment or first appearance: 1975.
Leadership: Abdullah Hassan.
Estimated strength: 20 000- 30 000 men.

FARO ISLANDS

2167: Republican Party
(Tjodfeld-isflokken)

EQUATORIAL GUINEA

1152: Guianese Socialist Party (PSG)

FRANCE

2012: Action Front against Independence and Autonomy (FRANCIA)
Description: a Corsican movement.

2003: Action Front for the Liberation of the Baltic Countries

2169: Action for Renaissance of Corsica

2168: Afghan Collective

2233: Anarchist Action Group (GAA)

2004: Andreas Baader Commando

2126: Angry Farmers Movement
(Mouvement des Paysans en Colère)

2170: Anti-Nuclear Ecological Revolutionary Cell

2109: Anti Nazi Front (FAN)

2132: Armed Nuclei for Popular Autonomy
(Noyaux Armeés pour l'Autonomie Populaire) (NAPAP)
Description: group striving for workers' autonomy. Its actions are
mainly directed at firms like Citroen, Renault, Simca and Chrysler.

2171: Association of Iranian Islamic Students in France

2005: Autonomous Intervention Collective against the Zionist Presence in
France Avengers

2172: Autonome Brigades

2188: Autonomous Group for Armed Action
(Groupe Autonome pour l'Action Armee)

2173: Avengers

2133: Breton Fight
(Argaz Breizh)
Description: autonomist movement but non-violent.
Date of establishment or first appearance: Feb. 1979.
Leadership: Jean le Calvez.

2115: Breton Organization Movement
(Mouvement pour l'Organisation de la Bretagne) (MOB)
Description: autonomist movement.

2134: Breton Popular Aid
(Skoazell Vreiz)
Description: autonomist movement but non-violent.

2006: Breton Republican Army
(Front de Liberation de la Bretagne Armeé Republicaine Bretonne)
(FLB-ARB)
Description: autonomist movement.
Date of establishment or first appearance: 1966.

2174: Breton Secret Army-Brittany Liberation Front

2007: Charles Martel Group

2093: Communist Anti Nuclear Front
Remarks: group which claimed responsibility for bomb attacks in Paris
in June 1980.

2009: Committee of Coordination

2175: Committee for the Defense of Italian Workers in France

2095: Committee for the Liquidation or Deterrence of Computers (CLODO)
Description: group which has been involved in actions against computer
firms.

2008: Committee for Socialist Revolutionary Unity

2176: Coordination of Revolutionary Action
(Coordination d'Action Revolutionnaire)

2010: Corsican National Liberation Front
(Front de Liberation Nationale de Corse) (FLNC)
Description: movement striving for greater autonomy in Corsica. It has
accused the French government of colonizing the island. The Council of
National Committees is generally viewed as a legal political wing of
the front.
In the summer of 1982 it stepped up its campaign mainly against security
forces and the property of non-Corsican residents. It also introduced the
tactics of collecting a revolutionary tax. It has declared several times
that other groups are operating under the name of the FLNC. Jan. 5, 1983
it has been outlawed by the French government.
Date of establishment or first appearance: May 1976.
Estimated strength: according to the police it has 200 members and 30
active guerrillas.

2237: Corsican Revolutionary Brigades
(Brigades Révolutionaires Corses) (BRC)

2092: Direct Action
(Action Directe) (AD)
Description: an amalgamation of NAPAP and GARI with the goal to abolish
the "capitalist slave state" and to reorganize daily life with the use
of armed violence. In 1980 it had been dissolved by the police but
most members were released in an amnesty measure after the presidential
elections. When they continued their activities, the government
outlawed the organization in Aug. 1982. It has been active in attacks
on computerized information retrieval systems.
Date of establishment or first appearance: 1979.
Leadership: Jean Marc Rouillon (ex GARI member)
Estimated strength: about 100 members.

2011: Fascist Party of Revolutionary Action

2229: French Resurrection
(France Résurrection)

2124: French Revolutionary Brigade
Date of establishment or first appearance: July 1982.
Remarks: claimed responsibility for a bomb attack in Paris.

2178: Franco-Algerian Refusal Section

2177: Gazi

Date of establishment or first appearance: 1980.

2114: Group Bakunin-Gdansk-Paris-Guatemala-El Salvador
Description: anarchist movement.

2014: Group for the Defense of Europe

2113: Group for the Liberation of France
(Front de Liberation Nationale Francais) (FLNF)
Description: anti semitic organization.

2151: Hordago

2015: International Solidarity
2179: International Workers Brigades

2122: Iparretarrak
Description: French Basq organization.

2180: Jewish Brigades

2016: Jewish Self Defense Front

2190: Joris van Severen Group
Description: Flemish nationalist movement.

2110: Laser

2181: League of French Fighters against Jewish Occupation

2182: Lebanese Front

2017: Masada Action and Defense Movement

2019: Movement of Youthward Brothers in War of the Palestine People

2183: Nationalist Breton Resistance Movement
(Mouvement de Resistance Nationaliste Bretonne) (MNRB)

2129: National European Fascists
(Faisceaux Nationalistes Européens) (FNE)
Description: replaced FANE.
Leadership: Henri Robert Petit.

2091: National and European Action Federation
(Féderation d'Action Nationale et Europeénne) (FANE)
Description: propaganda organization specializing in anti semitism. It
was banned in Sep. 1980.
Leadership: Marc Frederiksen.
Estimated strength: about 200 men strong.

2184: National Islamic Union of France

2130: National Revolutionary Movement
(Mouvement Nationale Revolutionaire) (MNR)
Description: extreme rightwing movement.

Leadership: Jean Gilles Malliarkis.

2123: National Savoyard Front
Date of establishment or first appearance: 1978.
Remarks: claimed responsibility for an attack on a cable chair lift on the Mont Blanc mountain.

2020: New Order and Justice Organization
(Ordre et Justice Nouvelle)
Description: rightwing movement.

2131: Organization of Former SS Members
(Organisation der Ehemaligen SS-Angehörigen) (ODESSA)
Description: anti semitic organization.

2189: Offensive Group for the Radicalisation of the Struggle
(Groupe d'Offensive pour la Radicalisation des Luttes)

2021: Organisation Delta
Description: anti semitic organization which emanated from the OAS.

2121: Orly
Description: an Armenian organization which claimed responsibility for a bomb attack in Paris in July 1982.
Date of establishment or first appearance: 1982.

2105: Pacifist and Ecological Committee

2234: Proletarian Left
(Gauche Proletarienne)
Description: spontaneous Maoist group involved in a number of kidnappings and bomb attacks in the beginning of the 1970's.
It was banned in May 1970.
Date of establishment or first appearance: 1968.

2185: Raul Sendic International Brigade

2022: Red Army Faction of Southern France

2187: Red Brigades

2096: Revolutionary and Autonomous Brigades

2127: Revolutionary Collective

2107: Revolutionary Internationalist Action Group
(Group d'Actions Revolutionaires Internationaliste) (GARI)

2186: Revolutionary Nationalist Movement

2119: Rightist Commando Mario Tuti

2120: Rossini
Description: a group the name of which referred to a bomb attack in the rue Rossini.

2106: Secret Army Organization
(Organisation de l'Armee Secret) (OAS)

2150: Self Defense against All Powers
(Autodefense contre tous les Pouvoirs)

2023: Sixth of March Group

2024: Solidarity Resistance Front

2125: Superman
Description: anti nuclear group which has been responsible for a bomb
attack on the hydroelectric installation at Malause.

2025: Talion Law

2191: Trawlc'h

2026: Union of the Corsican People
(Unione di u Populu Corso) (UPC)
Description: legal autonomist body in Corsica.
Leadership: dr. Edmond Simeoni.

2027: WAROK

2028: We Must Do Something

2013: Youth Action group
(Groupe d'Action Jeunesse)
Description: anti semitic organization.

2128: Zionist Militant Resistance
Description: group which has been responsible for the bombing of
buildings of the Libyan embassy in Paris in May 1980.

FRENCH POLYNESIA

9928: Te Eaa Pi

9927: United Front for Internal Autonomy
(Front Uni pour l'Autonomi Interne) (FUAI)

5122: Movement of National Renovation (MORENA)

WEST GERMANY

2030: Andreas Baader Commando of the Red Army Faction

2097: Armed Secret Execution Organisation

2031: Baader Solidarity Group

2195: Battle Group East Westphalia
Description: extreme rightist movement.

2207: Communist Federation, West Germany (KWB)

2230: Comradeship of National Activists
(Kameradschaft Nationaler Aktivisten) (KNA)
Description: extreme rightist movement.

2099: Defense Sport Group
(Wehrsport Gruppe Hoffmann)
Description: extreme rightist group which was banned in Jan. 1980.
Leadership: Karl Heinz Hoffmann.
Estimated strength: 400 men.
Remarks: possibly involved in the Munich beerhall bombing.

2266: European New Order
(Europäische Neue Ordnung)
Description: extreme rightist movement.

2199: Fighting Group of German Soldiers

2205: Frankfurt University Students Association

2136: German Action Groups
(Deutschen Aktionsgruppen)
Description: extreme rightist group involved in actions against
foreigners. It is believed to have been broken by police action after
the bombing of a Vietnamese refugee hostel in Aug. 1980.

2200: German Liberation Movement

2032: German Liberation Popular Front, Andreas Baader Brigade

2033: Holger Meins Commando
Description: RAF commando.
Leadership: Siegfried Hausener.
Estimated strength: other members Hanna Krabbe and Siegfried Haag.

2035: International Anti Terror Organisation

2204: Michael Knoll-Willy Peter Stoll Commando
Description: RAF commando.

2198: National Democratic Party

2238: National Fascist Front
Description: neo nazi movement.

2135: National Socialist Action Front
(Aktionsfront Nationaler Sozialisten) (ANS)
Description: extreme rightist movement.
Leadership: Michael Kühnen.

2202: Organization of Former SS Members
(Organisation der Ehemaligen SS-Angehörigen) (ODESSA)

Description: extreme rightist movement of former SS members. It was
formed to organize escape routes. One of these routes went via Bari
in Italy.

2098: People's Socialist Movement of Germany
(Volkssozialistische Bewegung Deutschlands) (VSBD)
Description: extreme rightist movement. Previously it was called Partei
der Arbeit.
Leadership: Friedhelm Busse.
Estimated strength: 200 to 1000 members.

2240: Petra Schelm Commando
Description: RAF commando.

2036: Puig Antich-Ulrike Meinhof Commando
Description: RAF commando.

2037: Red Army Faction
(Rote Armee Fraktion) (RAF)
Description: extreme leftist terrorist organization. By the early 1980's
most of its members had died or were imprisoned. A small hardcore
of mainly women is still active. According to the police new arrests in
1982 have prevented new activities.
In the beginning of 1983 evidence was found that not the RAF or other
leftist movements were responsible for anti American attacks but rightist
organizations.

2038: Revolutionary Cells
(Revolutionaire Zellen) (RZ)
Description: a leftist organization which has been active for nearly eight
years. In its activities it tries to spread information about mark
speculation, environmental destruction and the growing militarization.
Its attacks are primarily directed against industrial property.

2039: Robert E.D. Straker Commando of the Territorial Resistance Group

2201: Rudolph Hess Restitution Commando
Description: neo nazi movement.

2040: Second of June Movement
Description: a group with common ancestry with the Baader Meinhof group.
It is named in memory of a student who was killed by the police during
a violent demonstration against the visit of the Shah of Iran. It
concentrates on spectacular kidnappings of prominent members rather
than on bankraids and on bomb and gun battles. In more recent years
its attacks are mainly directed at industrial targets. In June 1980
it has announced a merger with the RAF.
Leadership: Ralf Reinders (the Bear)
Estimated strength: hardcore of 50 members backed up by a few
thousand sympathizers and helpers.

2116: Sigurd Debus Command
Description: RAF commando.

2041: Socialists Patients Collective

2203: Spartakus
Description: extreme rightist movement.

2197: Stahlhelm
Description: extrme rightist movement.

2042: Ulrike Meinhof Commando
Description: RAF commando.

2196: Viking Youth
Description: extreme rightist movement.

GREECE

3006: Army Officers Representing the Free Greek Spirit

3043: Autonomous Resistance Group
3008: Free Greeks

3009: Greek Anti Dictatorial Youth (EAN)

3011: Greek People

3010: Greek Militant Resistance

3012: Independence Liberation Resistance (AAA)

3090: National League of Greek Regular Officers (ESEMA)

3013: National Youth Resistance Organisation

3053: New October 1980 Revolutionary Organisation
Remarks: active in 1980.

3091: New Order

3014: November 17 Revolutionary Organisation
Remarks: active in 1980.

3120: Organization for National Recovery

3015: Patriotic Front

3016: Peoples Resistance Organized Army

3007: People's Revolutionary Struggle (ELA)

3041: Popular Initiative Front
Remarks: active in 1980.

3017: Popular Liberation Organized Army

3020: Popular Resistance and Sabotage Group One (LAOS-1)

3018: Popular Resistance and Sabotage Group Eleven (LAOS-11)

3019: Popular Resistance and Sabotage Group Thirteen (LAOS-13)

3021: Popular Revolutionary Resistance Group

3054: Revolutionary Left
Remarks: active in 1980.

3022: Union of Officers Struggling for the National Idea

GRENADA

0140: Mongolian Gang
Description: secret police of deposed prime minister Gairy.

0141: New Jewel Movement
(Joint Effort for Wealth, Education and Liberty) (NJM)
Description: formed as a merger of the Joint Endeavor for Welfare
Education and Liberation with the Master assembly for the People.
Although the NJM initially called for adoption of a number of radical
programs, including nationalization of foreign owned banks, its
policies have since moderated. Prior to the 1979 coup it held three
of the People's Alliance lower-house seats.
Date of establishment or first appearance: Mar. 1973.
Leadership: Maurice Bishop.

GUADELOUPE

0150: Guadeloupe Liberation Army
(Groupe de Liberation Armée) (GLA)

GUATEMALA

0128: Anti Communist Secret Army
(Ejercito Secreto Anticomunista) (ESA)
Description: a rightwing group presumed to be an outgrowth of the
former White Hand, the ESA is reportedly linked to the more extreme
faction of the MLN. It is known to maintain a "death list" of numerous
leftwing activists and has been prominently involved in the escalation
of political assassinations that began in late 1978.

0213: Authentic Revolutionary Party
(Partido Revolucionario Autentico) (PRA)
Description: a party which joined the FUN.

0299: Church of the Word
Description: in the name of this church Gen. Rios Montt is said to pursue
a campaign to annihilate the Indian population.

0296: CUC
Description: one of the guerrilla movements.

0221: Democratic Front against Repression
(Frente Democratico contra la Repression) (FDR)

0215: Democratic Institutional Party
(Partido Institucional Democratico) (PID)
Description: a political party which was formed as a vehicle for
conservative business interests led by former president Ydigoras
Fuentes. It joined the Frente Amplio in 1978 to support the candidacy
of Gen. Romeo Lucas Garcia.
Date of establishment or first appearance: 1965.
Leadership: Donaldo Alvarez and Jorge Lamport Rodil.
Remarks: a leading PID contender for the presidency in 1982, army
Chief of Staff Gen. David Cancinos Barrios was assassinated,
reportedly by rival military officers in June 1979.

0161: Eye for an Eye
(Ojo por Ojo)
Description: rightwing movement, mainly students.
Date of establishment or first appearance: 1970.

0216: Freedom September 15
(Libertad 15 de Septiembre)

0129: Guatemalan Anti Salvadorean Liberating Acting Guerrillas (GALGAS)

0176: Guatemalan Committee of Patriotic Unity (CGUP)
Description: a political bundling of the resistance.

0173: Guatemalan Labour Party
(Partido Guatemalteco de los Trabajadores) (PGT)
Description: a communist led group which has been banned since the
CIA's overthrow of the Arbenz government in 1954. With virtual no
influence on national elections but with considerable appeal to
students and intellectuals, it endorses the strategy of the Rebel
Armed Forces while supporting its own "action arm" the FAR.
Remarks: active throughout 1981.

0130: Guatemalan Nationalist Commando

0131: Guatemalan Workers' Militia
(Milicias Obreras Guatemaltecas) (MOG)
Description: an extreme rightwing terrorist group which emerged after
the 1978 election, in opposition to the alleged "Marxist" tendencies of
vice president Villagran Kramer.
Date of establishment or first appearance: 1978.

0134: Guerrilla Army of the Poor
(Ejercito Guerrillero de los Pobres) (EGP)
Description: guerrilla movement which began operating in the Quiche
province. It stepped up its activities after the 1976 earthquake and
acknowledged responsibility for a number of terrorist activities.
It is by far the most active military group.
Date of establishment or first appearance: 1975.

Estimated strength: 700 hardcore members.

0174: Independent Armed Revolutionary Movement
(Movimiento Independista Revolucionario Armado) (MIRA)
Description: guerrilla group.
Estimated strength: 3000 to 5000 guerrillas.

0137: Movement of Organized Nationalist Action
(Movimiento de Accion Nacionalista Organizado) (MANO)
Description: rightwing paramilitary group. In 1971 it was the
principal terrorist movement.
Date of establishment or first appearance: 1966.

0217: National Authentic Central
(Central Autentica Nacionalista) (CAN)
Description: a small rightwing group formerly known as the Organized
Aranista Nacionalista (CAO). It joined with the PID and PR in endorsing
Lucas Garcia for the presidency in 1978.
Leadership: Carlos Arana Osorio, Luis Alfonso Lopez.

0132: National League for the Protection of Guatemala

0133: National Liberation Movement
(Movimiento de Liberacion Nacional) (MLN)
Description: extreme rightwing movement of which the origins date back
to the "Liberation Movement" which deposed the Arbenz government in
1954. Retaining its anti-communist orientation, it favors close ties
with the Roman Catholic Church but disclaims a reactionary philosophy.
Leadership: Mario Sandoval Alarcon (former vice president)

0219: National Renovating Party
(Partido Nacionalisto Renovador) (PNR)
Description: legally recognized party in August 1978. It was formed
by a number of MLN moderates after the parent party had endorsed the
presidential candidacy of Peralta Azurdia.
Leadership: Alejandro Maldanado Aguirre.

0162: National Revolutionary Unity of Guatemala
(Unidad Revolucionaria Nacional de Guatemala) (URGN)
Description: the military branch of an overall organization of
four guerrilla movements.
Date of establishment or first appearance: announced in Feb. 1982.

0218: National Unity Front
(Frente de Unidad Nacional) (FUN)
Description: a coalition of PDC, PRA and FPP in support of the 1978
presidential candidacy of Gen. Ricardo Peralta Mendez.

0177: New Anti Communist Organization
(Nueva Organizacion Anticomunista) (NOA)
Description: rightwing paramilitary group.
Date of establishment or first appearance: 1967.

0138: Organization of the Armed People
(Organizacion del Pueblo en Armas) (ORPA)
Description: leftwing guerrilla group which is considered non-Marxist.

It is primarily concerned with the indians. In May 1980 it signed an
agreement to cooperate with three other guerrilla groups.
Date of establishment or first appearance: Sep. 1979.

0163: Popular front
(FP'31)
Description: the political arm of the combined resistance.

0225: Popular Participation Front
(Frente de Participacion Popular) (FPP)
Description: a front which joined the FUN.

0149: Popular Resistance Committee
Description: small leftwing group which claimed responsibility
for the murder of the San Carlos University rector in Dec. 1981.
Date of establishment or first appearance: 1981.

0135: Rebel Armed Forces
(Fuerzas Armadas Rebeldes) (FAR)
Description: formed by dissidents of the extremist "13th of November
Movement". It claimed responsibility for the killing of the US ambassador
John Gordon Mein in Aug. 1968. It turned to urban action in 1969 after
which it was almost totally destroyed in counter insurgency operations.
After being relatively quiescent for a number of years it resumed
guerrilla activity in 1978. In 1981 several of its bases were destroyed.
Date of establishment or first appearance: 1963.
Leadership: Luis Augusto Turcio Lima (until his death in 1966) and then
Cesar Montes (El Chris).

0136: Revolutionary Movement of November 13
(Movimiento Revolucionario 13 de Noviembre) (MIR-13)
Description: a pro Beijing guerrilla movement which entered into a tactical
alliance with the FAR in 1971.

0220: Revolutionary Party
(Partido Revolucionario) (PR)
Description: a party which advocates land reform, administrative change
and more rapid national development. In 1966 it became government party
under president Mendez Montenegro. Its influence waned as Mendez came
increasingly under pressure from both the Right and the Left. In the
1978 elections it supported the candidacy of Lucas Garcia while a radical
faction led by Alberto Fuentes Mohr ensdorsed a Christian Democratic
nominee Gen. Ricardo Peralta Mendez. Fuentes Mohr was assassinated,
reportedly by the rightwing ESA, in Jan. 1979.
Leadership: Jorge Garcia Granados.

0175: Revolutionary Unity Front (FUR)
Description: social democratic party which went underground in 1978.
It is a successor to the former URD founded by Francisco Villagran Kramer
as a leftwing breakaway group from the PR. The party, though not
officially registered as a participant in the 1978 election, supported
the candidacy of Lucas Garcia. In March 1979, only a few days after
the FUR had joined with the PR and a large number of the moderate
groups in forming a legally recognized FDR, FUR leader Manuel Colom
Argueta was assassinated. In 1980 at least two other executives
were killed or injured in attacks.

0222: Voluntary Defense Force
(Frente Voluntario de Defensa) (FVD)
Description: small leftist guerrilla group.
Date of establishment or first appearance: July 1980.

0271: White Hand

0223: Workers Revolutionary Party of Central America
(Partido Revolucionario de Trabajadores de America Central) (PRTC)
Description: group which has been responsible for one attack in 1980.
It operates predominantly in El Salvador.

0224: Yuxa Shona Front
(Frente Yuxa Shona)
Description: Marxist group named after the murdered survivor of the
Jan. 1980 Spanish embassy siege. It sympethizes with ORPA, FAR and
EGP.
Date of establishment or first appearance: Mar. 1980.

0293: Zacapa Panthers

GUINEA

4020: Guinea Union of Senegal
(Union des Guineans au Senegal) (UGS)

4021: National Liberation Front of Guinea
(Front de Liberation Nationale de Guineé) (FLNG)
Description: liberation movement which has its headquarters in Paris.
It has also branches in Senegal and Ivory Coast.

4050: Patriotic Front (PF)
Description: an active service wing of the RGE which has been involved
in an attack on the life of president Sekou Touré.

4022: Rally of External Guineans
(Rassemblement des Guinéens a l'Exterieur) (RGE)

4023: Unified Guinea Liberation Organization
(Organisation Unifié de Libération de la Guinée) (OULG)
Description: liberation movement primary based in Ivory Coast.

4066: Union of the Guinean People
(Union des Populations de Guinée) (UPG)

GUINEA BISSAU

4002: African Party for the Independence of Guinea and Cape Verde
(Partido Africano da Independencia da Guiné Portuguesa e das Illias de
Cabo Verde) (PAIGC)
Description: Marxist liberation movement supported by the USSR and
China. After the independence of Guinea Bissau in 1974 it has

become the official government party.
Leadership: Amilcar Cabral

4024: Front for the Liberation and Independence of Guinea
(Front de Lutte pour l'Independence de la Guinee Bissau) (FLING)
Description: liberation movement which had its headquarters in Paris.

4045: Popular Revolutionary Armed Forces
(Forces Armeés Revolutionnaires du Peuple) (FARP)

GUYANA

1177: House of Israel
Description: pro government death squad and also private army of
Burnham.

1105: National Front for the Liberation of Guyana (FLNG)
Leadership: R. Charlotte.

1054: Peoples Temple
Description: religeous sect which under influence of its leader was
involved in a collective suicide.

1104: Working People's Alliance (WPA)
Description: small radical opposition group. Cuban military advisers
have provided guerrilla training outside Guyana.
Leadership: dr. W. Rodney (Black Power activist)

HAITI

0057: Coalition of National Liberation Brigades

0178: Forces of Haitian Exiles
Leadership: Bernard Sansaricq.
Estimated strength: 700 men.

0058: Haitian Coalition

0291: Hector Riobe Brigade

0267: League of Human Rights

0179: Leopard Corps
Description: an elite anti subversion unit of the army.

0143: National Security Volunteers
(Tanton Macoutes) (VSN)
Description: volunteer units involved in raiding homes and violently
breaking up public meetings.
Estimated strength: 14 000 men.

0226: United Party of Haitian Communists
(Parti Unifié des Communistes Haitiens) (PUCH)

Description: a strongly pro Moscow party which in 1978 at its first congress called for a united opposition front to bring down the Duvalier regime.
Leadership: Jacques Dorsilien.

HONDURAS

0230: Christian Democratic Party (PDC)
Description: a relatively small centrist party. In Dec. 1977 it was accorded legal recognition by the Melgar Castro government. In Nov. 1978 the action was reversed after complaints by the National Action Party that the PDC had broken the electoral law by receiving funds from abroad. In Oct. 1979 it was reported that the PN dominated National Electoral Tribunal had, on "technical" grounds, refused to register the party for the April 1980 election.
Leadership: dr. Hernan Corrales Padilla.

0180: Cinchonero Popular Liberation Movement
(Chinchonero Movimiento de la Liberacion Popular) (MLP)
Description: extreme leftwing organization which joined the URP. It is named after a long dead peasant leader. It has been involved in highjackings and bombings. One group operated under the name Comando "Lorenzo Zelaja".
Date of establishment or first appearance: Jan. 1981.

0228: Communist Party of Honduras-Marxist Leninist
(Partido Comunista de Honduras-Marxista-Leninista) (PCH-ML)

0231: Communist Party of Honduras
(Partido Comunista de Honduras) (PCH)
Description: a Moscow oriented group originally formed in 1927 and reorganized in 1954. Although formally outlawed since 1957 it has engaged in both open and clandestine activities.
Date of establishment or first appearance: 1927.
Leadership: Dionisio Ramos Bejarano.

0233: Honduran Anticommunist Movement
(Movimiento Anticomunista Hondureno) (MACHO)
Description: newly formed rightwing group.
0270: Honduras Federation of Agrarian Reform Cooperative

0232: Honduran Patriotic Front
(Frente Patriotica Hondurena) (FPH)
Description: anti government pressure group comprising 40 popular groups and four political parties.
Date of establishment or first appearance: Oct. 1979.
Leadership: Marco Orlando Iriarte.

0234: Liberal Party of Honduras
(Partido Liberal de Honduras) (PLH)
Description: a center rightwing party whose strength lies mainly in the urban areas. It favors social reform and democratic political standards and supports Central American integration.
Date of establishment or first appearance: its political ancestry traces back to 1890.

Leadership: Modesto Rodas Alvarado.

0235: Martyrs of the Talanguera
Description: new leftwing group involved in bombings.
Date of establishment or first appearance: Feb. 1981.

0157: Morazan Front for the Liberation of Honduras
(Morazanista Frente para la Liberacion de Honduras)
Description: a group which has been involved in occupations of buildings.
Date of establishment or first appearance: 1980.

0236: MR-19
Description: leftist guerrilla group claiming to consist of Salvadoreans,
Hondurans and Nicaraguans.
Date of establishment or first appearance: Nov. 1979.

0237: National Association of Honduran Peasants
(Asociacion Nacional de Campesinos Hondurenos) (ANACH)
Description: powerful leftist peasant pressure group of over 40 000
members which has been active in land occupations.
Leadership: Antonio Julian Mendez.
Estimated strength: membership increased to 80 000.

0269: National Campesino Union

0238: National Innovation and Unity Party
(Partido Innovacion Nacional y Unidad) (PINU)
Description: a small centrist party. A legal status was granted in
Dec. 1979.
Leadership: dr. Miguel Andonie Fernandez.

0181: National Party
(Partido Nacional) (PN)
Description: a party created as an expression of national unity after
a particularly chaotic period. It is a rightwing party with close
ties to the military. While dominated by rural landowning interests
it has supported modest programs of internal reform and economic and
social development and favors Central American integration.
Date of establishment or first appearance: 1923.
Leadership: Ricardo Zuniga Augustinus.

0294: Paramilitary Wing of the National Party

0239: Peasant Alliance of Honduran National Organizations
(Alianza Campesina de Organizaciones de Honduras) (ALCONH)
Description: leftist peasant pressure group which has been described
as revolutionary and belligerent.
Date of establishment or first appearance: Oct. 1980.
Leadership: Reyes Rodriquez Arevalo (former ANACH leader).

0142: People's Revolutionary Union
(Union Revolucionaria del Pueblo) (URP)
Description: a leftist guerrilla group supported by peasant groups and
unions in the north. It displayed sympathy with the Salvadorean BRP.
Date of establishment or first appearance: formed in Sep. 1979 and
announced the armed struggle in Oct. 1980.

0229: Popular Progressive Party
(Partido Popular Progresista) (PPP)
Description: not recognized as a political party.

0227: Revolutionary Party of Honduras
(Partido Revolucionario de Honduras) (PRH)
Description: not recognized as a political party.

0243: Revolutionary University Force (FUR)
Description: a group involved in training students in the use of
weapons and kidnapping techniques.

0240: University Reform Front (FRU)
Description: a group involved in training students for the use of
weapons and kidnapping techniques.

0268: United Peasant's Campesino Front

0241: White Hand
(Mano Blanco)
Description: newly formed rightwing group.

0244: Workers Revolutionary Party of Central America
(Partido Revolucionario de Trabajadores de America Central) (PRTC)
Description: a group which emerged in El Salvador but operated also in
Honduras although it remained predominantly Salvadorian.
Date of establishment or first appearance: Sep. 1979.

INDIA

7161: Akali Religious Party
(Shiromani Akali Dal) (SAD)
Description: a party whose influence is confined primarily to Punjab,
where it campaigns against excessive federal influence in Sikh affairs.
Leadership: Jathedar Jagdev Singh Talwandi.

7201: All Assam Students Group
Description: student movement campaigning against Bengali immigrants in
Assam.

7159: All India Communist Party
Description: a small section of the CPI opposed to CPI's surrender to
the CPM-M out of electoral opportunism. It regarded mrs. Ghandi as the
representative of the progressives which Moscow wanted Indian
communists to befriend. Its ideological position is in fact close
to Moscow but it is not recognized by the Soviet Union, which
still prefers the CPI.
Date of establishment or first appearance: fall of 1980.
Leadership: Roza Deshpande.

7160: All India Forward Bloc (AIFB)
Description: a leftist party confined primarily to Bengal. Its program
calls for land reform and nationalization of key sectors of the economy.
Leadership: Hemanta Kumar Bose and R.K.Haldulkar.

7017: Ananda Marg (AM)
Description: an extremist leftwing Hindu group founded by Prabhat
Ranjan Sarkar also known as Anand Murtiji ("Baba"). It wants to
establish world unity on the basis of a new social economic theory:
"Prout" (progressive utilization theory). It uses suicide as a way
of expression. There have been at least eight victims. In 1978 it
operated in Australia with largely Australian membership.

7198: Assam for the Assamese Movement
Description: movement opposed to the Bengali immigrants in Assam.

7099: Bansropar Sah
Description: naxalite movement named after its leader.

7162: Communist Party of India (CPI)
Description: though the CPI-M took with it the majority of CPI members
when it broke away in 1964, most of the party bureaucracy legislative
representatives and trade unionists remained in the CPI. Loyal to the
international goals of the Soviet Union the CPI favors large scale
urban, capital intensive industrialisation and "democratic socialism".
It is loosly allied with the INC. The party initially supported the
1975-1977 emergency. Unable to form a leftwing coalition (the CPI-M
having allied itself with Janata) some state CPI organs remained
associated with the INC at the Mar. 1977 election, and the party as a
whole suffered severe losses. After heated debate at its April 1978
convention , the CPI condemned its own support of the state of
emergency. In opposition after the 1977 election it supported the
Singh government in Aug. 1979.
Leadership: S.A.Dange, C.Rajeswara.

7163: Communist Party of India-Marxist (CPI-M)
Description: party organized in 1964 by desertion from the CPI of
"leftists" favoring a more radical line. The party supports small
scale rural oriented labor intensive development as well as
political decentralization. Allied with Janata in the Mar.1977
election primarily to insure the defeat of the INC, the CPI-M won
control over West Bengal three months later and of Tripura in
Jan. 1978. In 1969 some of its overtly pro Beijing members
had withdrawn to form India's third Communist party, the CPI-ML.
Although supporting the Desai government after the 1977 election,
it joined with the CPI in endorsing Charan Singh's efforts to
establish a parliamentary majority in 1979.
Leadership: Jyoti Basu, E.M.Sankaran Namboodiripad.

7164: Communist Party of India-Marxist Leninist
(Krishak Mukti Samiti) (CPI-ML)
Description: as a result of disagreement over operational strategy for
the spread of communism in rural India, an extreme faction within the
CPI-M organized the CPI-ML in the spring of 1969. Committed to Maoist
principles of people's liberation warfare, the party was actively
involved in the "naxalite" terrorist movement in North Bengal and
was banned during the state of emergency. Some members including
the group led by Satya Narain Singh, have since rejected revolutionary
Marxism and now support parliamentary democracy. Others retaining a
revolutionary stance, have severely criticized the present policies
of the People's Republic of China.

The party failed to secure representation in the Lok Sabha at the
1977 election.
Leadership: Satya Narain Singh and Ram Pyara Saraf. Samar
Palchouhuri, another leading member, was killed March 1980.

7102: Coolie Sanghams
Description: agricultural workers organization.

7133: Dalit Panthers
Description: an organization of young militant untouchables which took
its inspiration from the Black Panthers in the USA.
Date of establishment or first appearance: 1968.

7078: Dal Khalsa
Description: a small extremist youth group.
Leadership: Sant Jarnail Singh Bhinderanwale, who has been imprisoned.
Estimated strength: 300 members.

7101: Devendra Majhi
Description: naxalite movement named after its leader.

7164: Dravidian Progressive Federation
(Dravida Munnetra Kazha) (DMK)
Description: an anti Brahmin regional party dedicated to the promotion
of Tamil interests. It opposes the retention of Hindi as an official
language and seeks more autonomy for the states. In the 1977 election
it lost control of Tamil Nadu to the ADMK. In Sep. 1979 it formed an
alliance with the INC-I for the 1980 election.
Leadership: dr.Muthuvel Karunanidhi Era Sezhian.

7103: Harijan Samajams

7197: Indians for Democracy

7084: Indian National Congress-Indira (INC-I)
Description: calling themselves "the truly representative convention"
of the INC, Gandhi supporters met at New Delhi Jan. 1978,
to designate the former prime minister as the president of a new
national opposition party. Building from a political base in the
traditionally pro Gandhi south, the INC-I has replaced the INC as
the principal opposition force in both houses of parliament.
Mrs. Gandhi returned to the Lok Sabha with a by election victory in
Karnataka state in Nov., though in late Dec. she was stripped of her
seat and briefly imprisoned.
Leadership: Indira Gandhi.

7018: Jammu Kashmir Liberation Front
Description: a movement based in England. It has 18 branches in
Azad Kashmir, the Middle East, Europe and the USA and a good
number of sympathizers in the Indian held part of Kashmir.
Leadership: Amanullah Khan.

7104: Khetiar Kisan Mazdoor Sangh
Description: a workers organization.

7209: Kranti Ranga

7166: Maoist People's Liberation Organization (MPLA)
Description: movement which is active in manipur. It is believed to
have received training by Chinese in Tibet.
Leadership: Bisawar Singh.

7081: Mizo National Front (MNF)
Description: movement active in Mizoram.
Leadership: Lal Denga.

7200: Moslem League

7199: Nagaland Liberation Front
Description: movement active in nagaland.

7082: Nirankari Sect
Description: a Sikh sect.

7167: Peasants and Workers Party of India
(Bharatiye Krishi Kamghar Paksha) (BKKP)
Description: a Marxist party whose influence is confined primarily to
Maharashtra. In addition to nationalization of the factors of production
the party advocates redrawing of state boundaries on an exclusive
language base.
Leadership: Dajiba Desai.

7097: People's Revolutionary Government of Kungleipak

7195: People's Union for Civil Liberties and Democratic Rights

7168: Rashtriya Swayan Sewak Sangh (RSSS)
Description: a paramilitary Hindu communal group. It functions as a
secret society adjunct of the Hindu Jan Sangh sect which provoked
street violence with moslems.

7132: Research and Development Wing (RAW)
Description: Indian intelligence service.

7100: Shibu Soren
Description: naxalite movement named after its leader.

7208: Telegu Desam

7169: Tripura Sena

7134: Tripura Yuba Jati Samiti (TYJS)
Description: cultural and social organization of the hill youth. Tripura
radicals function under the cover of the TYJS. By 1978 the radicals
had formed a secret group the-Tripura National Volunteers- without
knowledge of the TYJS leadership and began sending volunteers for
guerrilla training in the Chitta Gong hill tracts where the Mizos had
regained their sanctuaries. It has links with the Mizo National Front
(weaponry, training and logistical support). By 1979 the Chakma, Mizo,
Tripura insurgencies had converged.

7170: United Liberation Army
Description: formation announced in April 1980 with the objective to

fight for the independence of the seven northern states.

7019: Universal Proutist Revolutionary Front

7210: Upajati Juba Samiti

INDONESIA

8062: Communist Party of Indonesia
(Partai Kumunis Indonesia) (PKI)
Description: a party which was banned in 1966. Since then it split in a
pro Beijing and a pro Moscow faction. The former is currently led by
Jusuf Adjitorop while Satiajaya Sudiman is frequently spokesman for the
latter. Except for new underground activists, most PKI members appear
to be in exile either in China,the Soviet Union or in Eastern Europe.

8001: Darul Islam Holy War Command
Description: members operating under this label represent at least four
seperate factions. It demands the creation of an Islamic state.

8004: Free Papua Movement
(Organisasi Papua Merdeka) (OPM)
Description: in 1971 a "Provisional Revolutionary Government of West
Papua New Guinea" was established by insurgents who by 1976 claimed
to control 15 percent of the territory in the eastern sector adjacent to
Papua New Guinea. The official Indonesian position is that the revolt is
essentially a tribal war reflecting Papuan resentment at interference
with its traditional way of life.
Leadership: Seth Rumkorem, Jacob Prai. The latter was arrested in
Sep. 1978 and subsequently convicted for illegal entry. Another leader,
Martin Tabu, surrendered April 1980.

8119: Holy War Command
(Komando Jihad)

8050: Jemaah Imran
Description: a group led by Imran Mohammed Zein which had at least
two violent confrontations with other moslems over religious issues,
one of which allegedly led to the death of a religious rival. Imran
Mohammed Zein is suspected to be behind the Mar. 28, 1981 highjacking.
Estimated strength: a total of 300 members with a hardcore of 25 to 30
followers.

8046: Melanesian Socialist Party
Description: underground political movement in Papua New Guinea
offering the USSR a foothold in the country in exchange for money
and arms. Government sources believe the new party was formed out
of an earlier one, the Christian Democratic alliance, an exile group
also based in Papua New Guinea.

8003: Muslim National Liberation Front for Acheh (NLFA)
Description: a northern sumatra group led by Hasan di Tiro which
claimed responsibility for a 1978 raid against the Arun national
gas facility. The Di Toro dynasty assumed supreme power in 1874.
Hasan di Tiro is

the present Tengku Tjhik di Tiro and the eight head of the Achenese
state from the di Tiro family. on Oct.31, 1980 his death was reported.
The majority of the leaders are doctors, lawyers and engineers.

8064: PPI
Description: Islamic vanguard which is working for the establishment
of an Islamic state. Former movements were the Darul Islam,
Muhammadiyyah, Nahdhatul Ulema and Masyumi.

8047: Red Berets
(Kopasandha)
Description: a commando unit supervised by military intelligence chief
Lt.Gen. Benny Murdani.

8005: Revolutionary Front for the Independence of East Timor
(Frente Revolucionario Timorensa de Libertacao e Independencia)
(FRETILIN)
Description: a movement which advocates independence without links to
either Portugal or Indonesia. It is believed to number 1000 effectives,
with several thousand more supporters providing the necessary back up
infrastructure. In Jan. 1980 China halted aid. Vietnam and Algeria
promised to make good the cutback in supplies.

8036: Timorese Popular Democratic Association
(Assiacao da Populaca Democratica de Timor) (APODETI)
Description: movement which campaigned for an independent western
style government with ties to Portugal. It joined the PDU in seeking
integration with Indonesia.

8037: United Democratic Party
(Partido Democratico Unido) (PDU)
Description: a party which advocated a union with Indonesia.

8048: Warman Terrorists
Description: a group which attacked a police station Aug. 1980.

IRAN

6173: Ashraf Dehghani
Description: prohibited Marxist group. Several members have been
executed.

6082: Azadegan Movement

6232: Bahai Faith

6229: Baluchi Tribesmen

6104: Black Wednesday
(Chaharshanbeh-e-Siah)
Description: an Arab rebel force that has engaged in acts of sabotage
in the southern oil province of Khuzestan.

6109: The Call (Dawa)

6199: Communist Party of Iran
(Hezb-e-Komunist-e-Iran)
Description: an extremely small group organized in early 1979 as an
alternative to the pro Soviet posture of Tudeh.
Date of establishment or first appearance: early 1979.
Leadership: Azaryun.

6008: Forghan Group
(Grouh-e-Forghan)
Description: a major Marxist underground organization which claimed
responsibility for the assassination of gen. Gharani and ayatollah
Motahari.

6084: Group of the Martyr
Description: a movement of Arab Iranians.

6230: Guardsmen of Islam

6127: Iran Liberation Army

6009: Iranian People's Strugglers, Holy Warriors
(Mujahedin-e-Khalq)
Description: a party based on the major principle of "towhid": a divinely
integrated classless society, a society with total equity. In this ideal
society there will purportedly be an end to the exploitation of man by
man. It has consistently attacked the rule of the religious leaders on the
right whom they regard as repressive, reactionary and revolutionary
dilettants. In the last month of 1981 the Mujahedin became the major
armed force fighting the extremist regime of IRP clerics. Well over
60 percent of those arrested or executed were Mujahedin members or
sympathizers. A number of its members were allegedly trained by the
PLO.
Estimated strength: 100 000 guerrillas and about 300 000 members.

6010: Iranian Students Association (ISA)

6080: Islamic Republican Party
(Hezb-e-Jomhori-e-Islami) (IRP)
Description: essentially a ruling party by late 1979. It is led by a group
of clergy men described as "fanatically loyal to ayatollah Khomeini".
A religeous rightist party supported by the masses of sji'ite believers
who compose the lower and lower middle class of society.

6239: Jangali

6200: Kurdish Democratic Party
(Hezb Democrat Kurdistan)
Description: a party supporting the interests of the Kurdish minority.
It was outlawed in 1979.
Leadership: Abdur Rahman Qassemlou.

6108: Kurdish Socialist Party (BASSOK)

6107: Majlis Ulema

6011: Moslem Liberation Front

6201: Muslim People's Republican Party
(Hezb-e-Jomhori-e-Khalq-e-Mosalman)
Description: a party established by followers of the opposition religious
leader ayatollah Shariat Madari. It favors a strong secular government
within the context of an islamic republic.
Leadership: ayatollah Sayed Kazem Shariat Madari.

6202: National Council of Resistance
Description: an organization based in Paris.
Leadership: Bani Sadr and Massoud Rajavi.

6106: National Democratic Front
(Jebhe-e-Democratic-e-Melli)
Description: an offshoot of the Union of National Front Forces formed by
heydatolloh Mateendaftari, a grandson of Mohammed Mossadeq. In June it
accused ayatollah Khomeini of attempting to establish a religious
dictatorship. In August it strongly protested the closing of the
independent newspaper Ayandegan and called for a boycott of the
constituent assembly election.
Date of establishment or first appearance: Feb. 1979.
Leadership: heydatolloh Mateendaftari.

6105: National Islamic Liberation Front

6171: National Liberation Movement of Iran
(Nehzat-e-Azadi-e-Iran)
Description: a movement established by dr.Mehdi Bazargan which
supported the opposition religious leaders during the anti shah
demonstration of 1978. Named prime minister in Feb. 1978, dr.Bazargan
resigned in the wake of the US embassy seizure the following November.
The movement has a militant affiliate known as the Holy Warriors
(Mujahedeen).
Date of establishment or first appearance: 1961.
Leadership: dr.Mehdi Bazargan.

6172: Organization of Marxist Leninists
(Sazman-e-Tudeh-e-Iran)
Description: a Maoist offshoot of the Tudeh.

6231: Organization Struggling for the Freedom of the Working Class
(Sazmane Peykar da Rahe Azadieh Tabaqe Kargar)

6233: Pan Iranist Party

6268: PARS

6013: Party of God
(Hezbollahi)
Description: a group of fanatically anti communist supporters of
ayatollah Khomeini. It is also known as the Revolutionary Guard
of the IRP.

6081: Party of the Masses
(Hezb-e-Tudeh)
Description: traditional pro Moscow communist party which was declared
illegal in 1949. It went underground in 1953. A number of its leaders

returned from exile in East Germany in 1979. The RMP and OML are
Maoist offshoots. The policy of political pragmatism worked as a
two edged sword: protecting the existence of the party in the violent
early years of the revolution   damaged its long term credibility
and recruitment potential.
Date of establishment or first appearance: 1941.
Leadership: dr.Nooreddin Kianoori and Iradj Eskandari.

6014: Party of Toilers
(Hezb-e-Kumelah)
Description: a leading kurdish party which has been popular with secular
forces in Iran because of its resistance against Khomeini.
Leadership: Sheikh Azedin Husseini.

6101: Paykar Group
Description: a small radical Marxist force with organizational strength
among both students and workers. Its position approximates that of the
minority wing of the Fedayeen.

6015: People's Sacrificers
(Fedayan-e-Khalq)
Description: nationalist Marxist group on the far left whose support is
drawn from young students and the radical wing of the intelligentsia.
Although the theoreticians of the Fedayeen differ sharply over tactics,
they all condemn what they consider capitalist and imperialist exploitation
and seek to build a radical socialist state in Iran. Its members are
intensely ideological and have a 15 year history of guerrilla warfare.
In 1980 the fedayeen splintered into three factions including the
Fedayeen Guerrillas(Cherikha), the Aqaliyyat minority and the Aksariyyat
majority. While the guerrilla and minority splinters have sought to pursue
their radical goals independently, the majority group has revealed a
willingness to compromise and to form a front with the powerful extremist
rightwing IRP.

6203: Popular Front for the Liberation of the Gulf
Description: a force trained in Iran, South Yemen and Libya. In Iran
there is a training center in the northwest. Its main task is to
destabilize conservative regimes in the Gulf area. In Iran the
training is in the hands of a high ranked ayatollah.

6140: Revolutionary Guards
(Pasdarans)
Estimated strength: 20 000 commandos confined, 200 000 commandos
unconfined and 1 000 000 commandos in training.

6016: Reza Rezai International Brigades

6176: Siakhal

6243: Pasdarans
(Ranjbaran)

6175: Tupamaros
Description: an Iraqi urban oriented terrorist movement which appeared
in Gilan province and carried out assassinations and provoked wild cat
strikes.

Estimated strength: 130 to 200 members (1971).

6012: Union of National Front Forces
(Jebhe-e-Melli)
Description: the National front was established as an essentially secular
anti regime movement in dec. 1977. One of its founders, dr.Shahpur
Bakhtiari, was formally expelled upon designation as prime minister
by the shah in late 1978. Another founder, dr.Karim Sanjabi, resigned
as foreign minister of the islamic republic in april 1979 to protest
a lack of authority accorded to prime minister Bazargan.
Leadership: dr.Karim Sanjabi, Darish Foruhar.

IRAQ

6144: Arab Baath Socialist Party
(Hizb al-Baath al-Arabi al-Ishtiraki)
Description: a long established Arab nationalist movement with branches
in Syria and other Arab countries. The principal component of the
National Front, its leadership is identical with that of the
Revolutionary Command Council.
Leadership: Saddam Hussein (president of the republic and regional
secretary general of the party), 'Izzat Ibrahim al-Duri.

6152: Arab Socialist Movement

6145: al Dawa al Islamiya

6017: Free Iraq

6148: Independent Democrats
Description: a Turcoman movement.

6018: Iraqi Communist Party
(al-Hizb al-Shy'i al-Iraqi) (ICP)
Description: a legalized party when it entered the National Front in 1973.
With its pro Moscow orientation it occasionally criticized the regime
on both domestic and foreign policy grounds, including the latter's
pro Somali posture in the Ethiopian conflict and its handling of the
kurdish insurgency, with which some elements of the party have been
associated. In May 1978 the government executed 21 communists for
engaging in political activities within the armed forces (a rights
reserved exclusively for Baath members) and by Mar.1979 several
hundred ICP members had either fled the country or relocated to
kurdish areas. With the party having withdrawn from the National Front,
then RCC vice chairman Husayn confirmed in April that communists were
in fact being purged.
Date of establishment or first appearance: 1934.
Leadership:'Aziz Muhammad (first secretary, in exile).

6204: Iraqi Islamic National Liberation Front (IINLF)
Leadership: gen. Mustafa Hasan Al-Naqib.

6205: Iraqi Vanguard Movement

6147: Islamic Revolutionary Front of Iraq
Description: consists of four smaller parties.

6206: Kurdistan Democratic Party
(al-Hizb al-Dimuqraati al-Kurd) (KDP)
Description: the original KDP was founded by mullah Mustafa al-Barzani.
It experienced a number of cleavages, both before and after the cease
fire of Mar.1975. Thus the group that joined the National front in
1974 was essentially a Marxist rump of the original party. In Sep.1978
it reaffirmed its support of the Front and of the Baath Party's
"revolutionary struggle".
Date of establishment or first appearance: 1946.
Leadership: 'Aziz Hashim Aqrawi.

6019: Kurdistan Democratic Party (Provisional Leadership) (KDP)
Description: the Provisional Leadership was formed in 1975 following the
March Algiers agreement between Iraq and Iran and the collateral
termination of aid to the Kurds by Iran and the United States. With
mullah Barzani having withdrawn from the insurgency, thereby
completing dismemberment of the original KDP, the Provisional
Leadership declared itself the legitimate successor to the mulla's
party. Having refused to cooperate with either the National Front or
communists, it undertook renewed guerrilla activity through what had
been the military wing of the old party, the Pesh Mergas.
Since then the Provisional Leadership has consistently opposed the
government efforts to resettle Kurds in southern Iraq and has engaged
in clashes with both the Iraqi army and the rival PUK. Mulla Barzani
died in Washington Mar.1979, while in mid July several hundred party
members returned to Iraq from Iran, where they had resided since 1975.
A late 1979 congress failed, however, to resolve differences between
the party's socalled "traditionalist" and "intellectual" factions.
Leadership: Massud Barzani, 'Idris Barzani (traditionalist),
'Abd al-Rahman (intellectual leader).

6207: Kurdistan Revolutionary Party (KRP)
Description: a party which originated as a secessionist offshoot of the
original KDP and in 1974 joined the National Progressive Front along with
the neo-KDP and another offshoot, the Progressive Kurdistan Movement.
At a conference in Jan.1978 KRP members remaining in
Bagdad reiterated their support of the National Front.

6146: National Democratic Patriotic Front
Description: a coalition of eight opposition parties to bring down the
government of Saddam Hussein.
Date of establishment or first appearance: Nov.12, 1980.

6151: Officers Liberation Movement

6020: Patriotic Union of Kurdistan (PUK)
Description: a Kurdish party based in Damascus. It has received
support from the Syrian Baath. It resulted from the 1977 merger of
Jalal Talabani's Kurdish National Union (KNU) with the Socialist
Movement of Kurdistan and the Association of Marxist Leninists of
Kurdistan. The KNU was formed in mid 1975 when Talabani, a leftwing
member of the original KDP, refused to accept mulla Barzani's
claim that the Kurdish rebellion had come to an end.

Supported by the Pesh Merga Units, Talabani has since attempted to unify guerrilla activity under his leadership, but the PUK suffered significant losses in june 1978 during 10 days of skirmishes in northern Iraq with the KDP Provisional Leadership, which Talabani accused of links to both the shah of Iran and the US CIA. Following the Mar.1979 withdrawal of the ICP from the National progressive front, reports surfaced that the communists and the PUK were in process of forming a united front to oppose the Husayn regime.
Leadership: Jalal Talabani.

6150: Popular Liberation Army of Iraq
Description: resulted from a split in the Communist Party in 1964.

6153: Socialist Party

6208: Those Who Face Death
(Pesh Mergas)
Description: guerrillas of the Kurdistan Democratic Party.

6149: Unified Socialist Party of Kurdistan (PSUK)
Leadership: dr.Mahmoud Osman.

IRELAND

2268: NSI-WP

ISRAEL

6179: Avengers
Description: unofficial murder brigade of the MOSSAD.

6123: Family of Jihad
Description: an Arab movement.

6169: Group 101 (or 1001)
Description: unofficial murder brigade of the MOSSAD.

6227: Gush Emunim

6248: Irgun Zevai Leumi (IZL)

6170: July Unit
Description: unofficial murder brigade of the MOSSAD.

6228: Kach Movement

6198: Massada
Description: unofficial murder brigade of the MOSSAD.

6226: Peace Now
Description: non violent movement opposing the invasion in Lebanon and the expansionist settlement policy on the West Bank.

6196: Rebirth Movement
(Tenuat Hathiya Tehiya)
Description: an organization that was organized in Oct.1979 by a number
of rightwing groups that continues to exist outside the party structure.
It advocates formal annexation of the Gaza strip, the West bank and the
Golan Heights, without their inhabitants becoming Israeli citizens.
Leadership: Yuval Ne'eman, Geula Cohen, Moshe Shamir.

6154: Terror against Terror

6249: Wrath of God
Description: unofficial murder brigade of the MOSSAD.

ITALY

3126: Alfa

3045: Alto Adige
Description: Italian speaking autonomists.

3074: Antifascist Nuclei
(Nuclei Antifascisti)

3046: Antifascist Proletarian Movement

3062: April Seven
Description: a group of autonomists.

3084: Armed Communist Cells
(Squadri Armati Comunisti)
Description: minuscule leftwing movement.

3070: Armed Nazi Squad
(Squadre Nazi Armate)

3077: Armed and Organized Proletarian Group

3060: Armed Proletarians for Communism
(Proletari Armati per il Comunismo)
Description: minuscule leftwing group.

3023: Armed Proletarian Nuclei
(Nuclei Armati Proletari) (NAP)
Description: emerged in the south in 1974 as a result of the political
indoctrination or prisoners. Police action has now reduced NAP
activities considerably.

3024: Armed Revolutionary Nucleus (NAR)
Description: neo fascist group.

3078: Assault Group for Territorial Liberation

3025: Autonomists

3122: Black Lebanon

3063: Camorro
Description: mafia group in Naples with a hardcore of 5000 men.

3130: CESIS

3066: Continued Struggle
(Lotta Continua)
Description: eclectic leftwing group, mainly involved in industrial disturbances.

3072: February Six Workers Autonomy Group

3061: First Position
(Prima Posizione)

3026: Front Line
(Prima Linea) (PL)
Description: terrorist group which emerged in 1976. It operates in alliance with the BR and is particularly active in Milan, Turin, Naples and Cosenza.
Leadership: Corrado Alunni (sentenced to 29 years of imprisonment).

3075: Group Cavallini

3064: Gruppi Armati Patigiani (GAP)

3065: Il Manifesto
Description: eclectic leftwing group. A focal point for dissident intellectuals.

3058: Italian Socialist Movement
(Movimiento Sociale Italiano) (MSI)
Description: movement which lent cover to violence committed by fringe groups in the past, but was now more anxious to distance itself from terrorism.

3092: La Catena

3123: Ludwig
Description: extreme rightwing group.

3050: March 28 Brigade
Description: a BR offshoot. All members were arrested in Sep.1980.

3121: Movement for Armed Proletarian Power.

3055: National Vanguard
(Avangardia Nazionale)
Description: fascist movement.

3082: Nuclei of Territorial Communists
(Nuclei Comunisti Territoriali)

3079: New Order
(Ordine Nuovo)
Description: neo fascist movement.

3069: Organization of Fighting Communists
(Organizzazione Comunista Combattente)

3059: Party of the Guerrilla
Description: BR offshoot. It murdered the anti terrorism expert Carlo
Alberto dalla Chiesa in Sep.1981.

3057: Popular Revolutionary Movement (MPR)

3125: Potero Operaio

3056: Proletarian Squadron
(Squadre Proletari)

3027: Red Brigades
(Brigate Rosse) (RB)
Description: terrorist movement founded by Renato Curcio and others.
The historical nucleaus consisted primarily of former catholic students
from the sociology department of the University of Trent, but also of
disillusioned PCI members. Four phases of activity: 1969-1972,
1972-1974, 1974-1976 and 1976 until now. It has a basic cellular
structure, three to five members in each cell. A series of cells
form a column in a city or a region.
It is assumed that a "second generation" of brigadists, less
intellectual but more violent and technically proficient assumed
command. The Rome column consists of about 400.
Date of establishment or first appearance: 1969.
Estimated strength: 500 members supported by a fringe group of
perhaps as many as 10 000 people.

3081: Red Squad Organized Commando

3076: Revolutionary Action
(Azione Rivoluzionaria) (AR)
Description: minuscule leftwing group.

3124: Revolutionary Fascist Squad

3068: Ronde Armate per il Comunismo

3080: Rosa Dei Venti

3129: SISDE

3128: SISMI

3067: Squadre Proletari di Combattimento

3073: Territorial Antifascist Squad
(Squadre Antifascista Territoriali)

3042: Third Position (Terza Posizione)

3044: Tyrol
Description: german speaking autonomists.

3071: Union of Communist Fighters
(Unita Combattenti Comunista)
Leadership: Antonio Campesi.

3039: Workers Autonomy Movement

JAMAICA

0059: Jamaica Defense Force

0266: Jamaican United Front Party

JAPAN

7021: Chosen Soren

7020: East Asia Anti Japan Armed Front
Description: terrorist group involved in the bombing of the Tokyo
offices of Mitsubishi heavy industries in Oct. 1974.
Leadership: Yukiko Ekita and Ayako Daidoji.

7193: Fang

7136: Hidaka Commando Unit
Description: terrorist group named after Hidaka, a comrade who had
died in prison in Jordan. It has been involved in a highjacking in
Sep. 1979.
It consisted of five men led by Osamu Maruoka (Shegenobu's husband),
others were Norio Sadaki, Kazuo Tohira, Kunio Bando and Jun
Nishikawa, all of whom had been released by the Japanese government
after the Kuala Lumpur operation in Aug. 1975.

7022: Japanese Red Army, or United Red Army, or Army of the Red
Star (Sekigunha, Rengo Sekigun or Nippon Sekigun) (JRA)
Description: a terrorist group established among disillusioned students
who saw in the Paris student riots in May 1968 their blue print for
bringing about world revolution. In March 1981 the Kyodo News service
reported that the Red Army may give up violent acts. Since 1969 80
radical leftist have been killed in internal clashes. The March report
was the first official communiqué in four years, issued from Beirut.
Date of establishment or first appearance: 1969.
Leadership: Fusako Shigenobu (original female leader)
Remarks: other known members were Takeshi Ukudari (killed in Lod),

Osamu Maruoka, Kozo Okamoto (life imprisonment in Israel) and Yasuiki Yashuda (killed in Lod).

7023: Maruseido
Description: Marxist youth league.

7024: Middle Core Faction
(Chukakuha)

7025: Okinawa Liberation League

7085: Revolutionary Marxist Faction
(Kakumaruha)

7192: Scorpion

7137: Sons of the Occupied Territory
Description: group involved in a highjacking in July 1973 which was
carried out by Osamu Maruoka (Sekigun), three arabs and a girl
(possibly a Christian Iraqi: Katie George Thomas). The action became
a disaster when the girl dropped a grenade which killed her. She
was the only one who knew the plans and the goal of the action.

7135: United Red Army
(Rengo Sekigun)
Description: formed when nine members of Sekigun joined forces
with the twenty strong Keihin Ampo Kyoto. Fourteen of its own members
were killed for dissent. After its destruction a hardcore of supporters
remained but its function was mainly to supply "soldiers" to the one
branch of the Red army which was still capable of functioning,
Fusako Shigenobu's Arab Committee working with the PFLP in Beirut.
Some known members were: Tsueno Mori, Kunio Bando and Hiroko Nagata.
Date of establishment or first appearance: 1972.

7026: VZ 58
Description: name of the Czechian assault rifle which was used by the
Red Army in the Lod massacre. Key member was Mariko Yamamoto, a
salesgirl at a Japanese department store in Paris.

7194: Wolf

JORDANIA

6021: Jordanian Free Officers Movement

6022: Jordanian National Liberation Movement

6177: People's Militia
Description: a new military force to be established by King Hussein
and charged with defense against Palestinian terrorism and Israeli
inspired acts of sabotage. It will be composed of Bedouins and
former regular Army troops whose loyalty to the king is unquestioned.

6267: Yarmak

KAMPUCHEA

8122: Black Eagle
Description: pro Sihanouk group.

8006: Communist Party of Kampuchea
(Parti Communiste du Kampuchea-PCK/ Kanapak Kumunist Kampuchea)
(PCK)
Description: began as an anti french insurgent group but split into
three factions after the 1954 Geneva agreements: a North Vietnamese
contingent called the Khmer Vietminh, the People's Party (Pracheachon)
which operated legally in Cambodia and an underground force of the
Khmer Rouges. The PCK is reported to have been formed in 1960,
although its existence was not officially acknowledged until
Sep. 1977, apparently because of its early domination by the
Vietnamese. In April 1975 Kampuchea became a one party state
which the PCK, operating through the FUNK, held a monopoly position
and directed operations of government at all levels.
The Front organized as an alliance of Kmer rouge and royalist
supporters of prince Sihanouk following the latter's ouster as
head of state by Lon Nol in 1970, held the first National Congress
in Beijing in May the same year.
In the wake of Sihanouk's resignation as head of state of
the Communist government on april 2, 1976 royalist influence within the
front diminished, and the role of the National United Front of Kampuchea
itself receded. After a border war with Vietnam and the following
occupation by Vietnam outside powers have tried to unite several
opposition groups in an attempt to unify the forces to bring down the
pro Vietnam government. This united front dominated by the Khmer
Rouge is led by Prince Sihanouk.

8054: General Association of Khmers abroad (AGKE)
Description: an organization established to coordinate activities abroad
by Son Sann. Former members of the Democratic Party of Kampuchea
joined the organization as Sim Var, Chkeam Vam and Thon Ouk.

8007: Kampuchean United Front for National Salvation
(Ranakse Samakki Sangkroh Cheat Kampuchea)
Description: a front which was organized by Khmer opponents of the
Democratic Kampuchean regime. Four of the fourteen members of its
Central Committee were included in the People's Revolutionary Council
established as a provisional government at Phnom Penh Jan. 8, 1979.
Date of establishment or first appearance: Dec. 1978.
Leadership: Heng Samrin (President Central Committee), Chea sim
(Vice President) and Ros Samay (Secretary General)

8032: Khmer People's National Liberation Front (FLNPK)
Description: guerrilla movement.
Date of establishment or first appearance: Oct. 1979.
Leadership: Son Sann (political leader), Maj. Gen. Dien Del (military
commander)
Estimated strength: 8000 armed guerrillas and 3000 recruits.
Remarks: Sokh Sann serves as its headquarters. Northern headquarters
are Nong Sumet and Nong Chan. To coordinate activities abroad the
AGKE was formed. Its forces are badly equipped using mostly captured
weapons.

8121: Khmer Rouge
Description: a faction of the PCK. In Aug. 1979 it formed the Patriotic
Democratic Front for a National United Kampuchea (FGUNPDK)
Date of establishment or first appearance: Aug. 1979.
Leadership: Pol Pot, Khieu Samphan (after Dec. 1979), since then
Pol Pot operates as commander in chief.
Estimated strength: 30 000 to 50 000 men.

8026: Khmer Serei

8126: Liberation National Government of Kampuchea (LNGK)

8057: National Armed Liberation Forces of the Khmer People
(Forces Armeés Nationales de Libération du Peuple Khmer) (FANLPK)
Description: armed branch of the FNLPK.

8033: National Liberation Movement of Kampuchea
(Mouvement de la Libération Nationale du Kampuchea) (MOULINAKA)
Description: pro Sihanouk group which is an offshoot of the organization
of Son Sann.
Date of establishment or first appearance: Aug. 1979.
Leadership: Kong Si Leah, Gen. Sek Sam Iet (commander)
Remarks: part of the Khmer Serei led by Inn Sakhan joined this force
as well.

8056: National Union for an Independent Neutral Pacifist and Cooperative
Kampuchea (FGUNPDK)
Description: a political party whose formation was announced in Mar. 1981.
Date of establishment or first appearance: Mar. 1981.
Remarks: its military wing consists of MOULINAKA and other Sihanoukist
groups.

8059: National United Front of Kampuchea
(Front Uni National du Kampuchea) (FUNK)
Description: an organization formed by Sihanouk and the Khmer Rouge
and through which the PCK operated. In the wake of Sihanouk's
resignation as head of state of the Communist government in 1976,
royalist influence within the front diminished and the role of
the front itself receded.
Date of establishment or first appearance: 1970.

8120: Organization on High, Angkar
(Angka Loeu)

8061: People's Party Faction
(Pracheachon)
Description: a faction of the PCK.

8060: People's Revolutionary Party of Kampuchea (PRPK)
Description: official government party since the occupation of Vietnam.
Leadership: Gen. Pen Sovan (Secretary General) and Heng Samrin
(President of the Revolutionary Council)

8125: Serika National Liberation Movement (SNLM)

KENYA

5074: Gikuyu, Embu, Meru Association (GEMA)

5066: Northern Frontier Liberation Front (NFLF)

5081: Shifta Bandits

KOREA

7190: Council for Freedom and Unification

7171: Korean Central Intelligence Agency (KCIA)
Description: renamed in Jan. 1981 in agency for National Security
Planning.

7189: National Congress for the Restoration of Democracy and Promotion
of the Unification of Korea

7191: National Front for the Liberation of The South

7188: New Democratic Party

LAOS

8067: Lao Front for National Reconstruction
Description: founded as successor of the Lao Patriotic Front.
Date of establishment or first appearance: 1979.
Leadership: Souphanouvong.

8066: Lao Patriotic Front
(Neo Lao Hak Xat) (NLHX)

8055: Lao People's National Liberation United Front (LPNLUF)
Description: a merger of four resistance movements in Champassak
province to fight Vietnamese domination, assimilation and
colonization of the Lao people. In July 1981 a pact was signed in
the US by exiled Lao leaders. The pact is aimed at driving the
Vietnamese out of Laos, dissolving the present government in
Vientiane and holding a general election supervised by the UN.
The front consists of functionaries of the pre 1975 government,
rightist patriots, nationalists and neutralist groups.
In the fall of 1982 an anti communist "liberation government" was
to be installed.
Date of establishment or first appearance: Sep. 1980.
Leadership: Phoumi Nosavan (former prime minister)
Estimated strength: 40 000 men.

8068: Lao People's Revolutionary Party
(Phak Pasason Pativat Lao) (LPRP)
Description: the communist core of the Lao Front for National
Reconstruction which was prior to the communist takeover known

as the People's Party of Laos (Phak Pasason Lao)
Leadership: Kaysone Phomvihan (secretary general)

8051: Laos United Liberation Front (LULF)
Description: guerrilla movement comprising the H'Mong, Lao Thung,
Lahu, Yao, Liu and Lao hill tribes. Many of the cadres are veterans
of the clandestine war waged by the US in Laos against the North
Vietnamese in the 1950's and 1960's. The ranks are now routinely
trained, armed and equipped by the People's Republic of China at
Szemao in Yunnan province. Other reports indicated that they were
trained by Thai advisers. The Meo have been hit hardest by government
counter measures. Vietnamese artillery and aircraft have destoyed
Meo villages and refugees fleeing into Thailand continue to tell
stories about the use of gas and chemical warfare.
Leadership: Kong Le, a paratroop captain who went into exile in
France in the mid sixties, dropped out of sight in 1980. Diplomatic
sources said they have confirmed reports that he went to Beijing.
Estimated strength: 2000 to 4000 men.

8118: National Salvation Party
(Pak Laos Kusa)

8053: Pathet Lao
Description: liberation movement which brought an end to the monarchy
in 1975. Since then insurgent activity within Laos has been limited by
a lack of central leadership. Several thousand Pathet Lao defectors
opposed to the influx of Vietnamese appear to be operating in small bands.
Estimated strength: 2000 to 3000 men.

LEBANON

6131: Al Amal
Description: sji'ite moslem militia. Founded by imam Moussa Sadr as the
Movement of the Disinherited. In 1976 it militarized and changed its
name. (See 6047) In 1978 Moussa Sadr disappeared during a trip to
Libya.
Date of establishment or first appearance: 1974.
Leadership: Nabih Berri.
Estimated strength: 4000 to 5000 men.

6092: Arab Liberation Front

6023: Arab Nationalist Movement
(al-Harakiyines al-Wataniyah al-'Arab)
Description: a Marxist oriented organization established by the
extremist Palestinian leader George Habash. It is also based in
Jordan and it is but one of sveral Palestinian groups operating
in Lebanon.
Date of establishment or first appearance: 1948.
Leadership: George Habash.

6024: Arab Socialist Renaissance
(al-Baath)
Description: a political party which is spilt into competing factions

as a result of the Syrian intervention in Lebanon since 1976. The two
factions were reconciled in 1978.
Leadership: 'Abd al- Majid Rafi'i (secretary general of the pro Iraqi
faction and vice president of the National Movement), Asim Qansu
(secretary general of the pro Syrian faction).

6185: Arab Democratic Party
Description: a political party comprising Alawite immigrants and
concentrated in Tripoli. It has a military wing: the Pink Panthers,
which is supported by Damascus and led by Rifaat 'Al Assad (brother
of president Hafez Al Assad)
Date of establishment or first appearance: 1981.

6025: Arab Socialist Union
Description: a small leftist party which is divided into at least three
factions.

6026: Armenian Revolutionary Federation
(Parti Dashnak)
Description: a rightwing Armenian group with a history of terrorist
activity. It was allied with Maronite groups in 1958 but, along with a
number of leftist Armenian organizations, it remained politically neutral
during the civil war. Fighting between Armenians and Falangists broke
out in Beirut in 1979, the most serious streetbattles occurring in April
May and September.
Leadership: Khatchig Babikian.

6027: Constitutional Party
(al-Dustur)
Description: a business oriented party that has long supported
Arab nationalism.
Date of establishment or first appearance: 1943.
Leadership: Michel Bechara al-Khuri.

6028: Democratic Party
(Parti Democrate)
Description: a secular group strongly supportive of private enterprise.
Leadership: Joseph Mughaizel.

6029: Falangist Party
(al Kataeb/ Phalanges Libanaises)
Description: a militant Maronite organization which was deeply involved
in provoking the 1975 civil war. A 1979 party communiqué called for
"a positive, creative, unifying diversity" within an intact Lebanon;
deployment of the Lebanese army to replace units of UNIFIL and the
Arab Deterrence Force and separation of issues of civil strife and
political reform. It forms the largest section within the Lebanese front.
Date of establishment or first appearance: 1936.
Leadership: Pierre Gemayel, Amin Gemayel, Bashir Gemayel (commander
of the Lebanese Front militia) and Joseph S'ade (secretary general).

6043: Falangist Security Group

6090: Free Lebanese Army
Description: a Christian militia trained and armed by Israel.
Leadership: Maj. S. Haddad.

Estimated strength: some 500 regulars and some 2000 part time
Falangists, National Liberals and local Sji'ites.

6129: Front for the Liberation of Lebanon of Foreigners (FLLF)
Description: choice of name and targets led many to believe that the
FLLF was part of Haddad's militia in the south or simply a cover name
for Israeli intelligence operations. Others suspected a Syrian
attempt to eliminate the Fatah leadership.

6099: The Giants
(Marada)
Description: when Syria began to support the leftists in 1978 Suleiman
Franjieh broke with the right. He reconciled himself with the traditional
Sunnite leadership in Tripoli and carved out with them a territory that
is loyal to Syria.
Leadership: Suleiman Franjieh.

6030: Imam As-Sadr Brigades

6031: Independent Nasserite Movement
(al-Murabitun) (INM)
Description: founded as a socialist party opposed to the Chamoun
government. The INM is familiarly known by the name of its military
branch, al Murabitun (the Vigilant). It forms the largest of at
least 13 extant Nasserite groups in Lebanon. It has never been
an exclusively Moslem organization, although its main support comes
from the Sunni urban poor. Reports from Beirut in September 1979
identified the INM as a participant in intra leftist fighting.
Date of establishment or first appearance: 1958.
Leadership: Ibrahim Qulaylat (vice president of the National Movement),
and Samir Sabbagh.
Estimated strength: 2000 professional fighters.

6187: Kata'eb
Description: militia of the Falangists established by Pierre Gemayel.
The Falangists have established an efficient ministate with its own
tax system, army police and intelligence service.
Leadership: Pierre Gemayel.
Estimated strength: in Aug. 1982 it was able to mobilize 25 000 men.

6098: Lebanese Arab Army

6136: Lebanese Armed Revolutionary Faction

6035: Lebanese Communist Party
(al-Hizb al-Shuyu'i al-Lubani/Parti Communiste Libanais) (LCP)
Description: a pro Moscow party which was banned in 1939 by the
French Mandate Authority but was legalized in 1970. Although
primarily Christian in the first half of the century of its
existence the party became predominantly Moslem in the wake
of the civil war.
Leadership: Niqula al-Shawi (president), George Hawi (secretary
general).

6183: Lebanese Front
Description: a coalition of rightist organizations: the Falangists,

the Free National Party, the Maronite Order of Monks, Marada and
factions of the Lebanese army.
Estimated strength: 25 000 men.

6238: Lebanese National Resistance Front

6032: Lebanese Revolutionary Guard

6033: Lebanese Revolutionary Socialist Movement

6034: Lebanse Socialist Revolutionary Organization
(Shibbu Gang)

6132: Martyr Ali Nasser Organization

6037: National Bloc
(al-Kutla al-Wataniyah/Bloc National)
Description: a long established Maronite party which has been opposed
to military involvement in politics. Its principal leader, Raymond Eddé,
has been the object of a number of assassination attempts during 1976
and subsequently he retired and went into exile in France. The bloc
has frequently been critical of other rightist groups, particularly
the Falangist Party.
Leadership: Raymond Eddé, Sa'ia Aql, Antoine Abu Zaid (secretary
general)

6250: National Liberal Party
Hizb al-Wataniyah al-Ahrar/Parti National Liberal) (NLP)
Description: a rightwing Maronite grouping which has refused to
consider any coalition with Moslem groups that would involve
Palestinians. It is the second largest party in the Lebanese Front
and has repeatedly called for the withdrawal of Syrian and other
Arab troops from Lebanon and has insisted that the federal system
is the only way to preserve the country's unity.
Leadership: Camille Chamoun (president of the party and former
president of the republic), Kazim Khalil (vice president), Dory
Chamoun (secretary general).
Remarks: it has its own militia, the Tigers' Militia.

6182: National Movement
Description: an alliance of several leftist organizations, the Murabitoun,
the Iraqi branch of the Baath party, the Lebanese Communist Party,
the Syrian Socialist Nationalist Party, the Progressive Socialist Party,
remnants of the Lebanese Army, the Palestine Liberation Ogranization
and al Amal.
Estimated strength: 5000 to 7000 men.

6038: National Syrian Socialist Party (NSSP)
Description: organized as the Syrian Nationalist Party in 1932 in
support of a "Greater Syria"embracing Iraq, Jordan, Lebanon,
Syria and Palestine. It was considered a rightist group until
1970 and was also known as the the Syrian People's Party. It was
banned in 1962 after participating in an attempted coup in 1961.
The party split into two factions in 1974, one group led by Abdallah
Saada, subsequently joining the National Movement and the other, led
by George Keneizeh and Issam Mahayri, participating in the pro Syrian

National Front. In 1978 its leadership announced that the party had
been reunited.
Date of establishment or first appearance: 1932.
Leadership: Abdallah Saada, Issam Mahayri, Mustafa Izzedine, Inam
Raad and Fa'ad Awad.

6039: Organization of Communist Action in Lebanon (OCAL)
Description: a merger of two extreme leftwing groups, the Movement of
Leftwing Socialists and Socialist Lebanon. The former had been formed
by members of the ANM, the latter by former LCP and Baath members.
Since the civil war, OCAL has closely cooperated with the LCP.
Date of establishment or first appearance: 1970.
Leadership: Muhsin Ibrahim (secretary general of OCAL and of the
National Movement), Fawwaz Trabulsi.

6040: Organization of Revolutionaries of the North
Description: a group which is believed to be linked to the Falangists
militia. It has claimed responsibility for attacks against the
Franjieh clan.

6097: Palestinian Guerrillas
Description: a great number of different groups.
Estimated strength: a total number of 10 000 to 20 000 men.

6041: Parliamentary Democratic Front
(al-Jabha al-Dimuqratiyah al-Barlamaniyah) (PDF)
Description: a front advocating the continuation of the governing model
of president Chehab, although its leader, the former prime minister,
attempted to conciliate differences between Christians and Moslems prior
to leaving office on Dec. 9, 1976.
Leadership: Rashid al-Hamid (former prime minister)

6186: People's Resistance Movement
Description: an organization which exists only in Tripoli.
Leadership: Khalil Akkawi.

6180: Pink Panthers Militia
Description: military branch of the Arab Democratic Party, supported
by Damascus. (see 6185)
Leadership: Rifaat Al Assad (brother of president Hafez Al Assad)

6096: Pro Iran Faction

6095: Pro Iraq Faction

6044: Progressive Socialist Party
(al-Hizb al-Taqaddumi al-Ishtiraki/Parti Socialiste Progressiste) (PSP)
Description: a party which advocates a socialist program with
nationalist and anti-western overtones. A rupture in relations
between former party president Kamal Jumblatt and Syrian president
Assad was followed by a Syrian intervention. On Mar. 16, 1977 Jumblatt
was assassinated, the party leadership being assumed by his son Walid.
Date of establishment or first appearance: 1948.
Leadership: Walid Jumblatt (president), Faris Jubran (vice president),
Tafiq Sultan (vice president of the National Movement).
Remarks: the party is mainly supported by the Druze.

6188: Rawwad al Islah Militia
Leadership: Saib Laam (former prime minister).

6045: Revolutionary Arab Youth Organization

6046: Socialist Labour Party

6047: Standard Bearers of Imam As Sadr Organization
Leadership: Sheikh Muhammad and Mehdi Shamseddine (both deputies for the missing Imam Moussa Sadr), (see 6131).

6184: Syrian Peace Keeping Forces
Estimated strength: 22 000 to 30 000 soldiers.

6094: Tigers Militia
Description: militia of the National Liberal Party (see 6250).
Leadership: Dory Chamoun (son of Camille Chamoun).

6178: Union of the Working People's Forces
Description: small leftist party.
Leadership: Kamal Shatila.

LESOTHO

5050: Lesotho Liberation Army (LLA)
Description: military branch of the Basutoland Congress Party which has been involved in bomb attacks on industrial installations.
Leadership: Ntsu Mokhele.
Estimated strength: 500 to 1000 men.

LIBERIA

4052: Pan African Movement for Justice in Africa (MOJA)
Leadership: Tog ba nah Tipoteh.

4070: People's Redemption Council of the Armed Forces
Description: a council which was installed after the first military coup in Liberia.
Leadership: Sgt. Doe.

4051: Progressive Alliance of Liberia (PAL)

LIBYA

6209: Front for the Liberation of Eastern Sahara
Description: a Tuareg organization supported by Libya. Kadafi began to claim they were being persecuted in many countries and declared his intentions to defend them.

6189: General People's Congress of the Socialist People's Libyan Arab Jamhitirah.

6156: Libyan Resistance Movement
Leadership: Abdel Hamil Bakusj.

6124: National Front for the Salvation of Libya
Description: anti Kadafi front.
Date of establishment or first appearance: Oct. 1981.
Leadership: Muhammad Magareef.
Estimated strength:
Remarks:

6251: World Revolutionary Committee

MADAGASCAR

5075: Congress Party for Malagasy Independence
Democratic Committee for the Malagasy Socialist Revolution
(AKFM/KDRSM)

5064: National Movement for the Independence of Madagascar
(Mouvement National pour l'Independence de Madagascar) (MONIMO)
Description: leftwing nationalist movement active in the southern
province of Tulear.
Leadership: Monji Jaona.
Estimated strength: 3000 (in 1971).

5016: Congress for the Second Republic (CSR)

MALAWI

5082: Malawi Democratic Union (MDU)
Leadership: Attati Mpakati.

5017: Malawi Freedom Movement (MAFREMO)
Description: exile grouping which claimed to have developed an
underground movement within Malawi.
Leadership: Orton Chirwa (former attorney general and minister of
justice).

5018: Socialist League of Malawi (LESOMA)
Description: exile grouping. The Malawi wing of Lesoma under Attati
Mpakati announced separation to form the MDU.

MALAYSIA

8070: Aliran Kesedaran Negara
Description: avowedly unpolitical reform movement.
Leadership: dr. Chandra Muzzafar.

8069: Asal Group
Description: communist guerrilla group working with aborigines based

in Ula Perak and Ule Kelantan.

8017: Communist Party of Malaysia (CPM)
Description: a predominantly Chinese group oriented toward Beijing.
It was officially banned in 1948. During the 1970's two rival
factions were formed, the CPM-RF and the CPM-ML. Although linkages
remain each of the three factions sponsors separate armies and front
organizations. The CPM also maintains three affiliated parties
directed towards Moslems, peasants and youths.
Leadership: Chin Peng, who sends his instructions from China.
Estimated strength: about 3000 members; intelligence sources reported
the number of 2512 guerrillas. CPM proper has about 1200 men.
Remarks: from headquarters in southern Thailand, agents have made
persistent efforts to penetrate leftwing organizations in West Malaysia
and paramilitary operations have resumed. In Nov. 1980 one of its
leaders Musa Ahmad surrendered to authorities after having spent 25
years in China. In 1974 the party went on the rampage which lasted
more than three years, costing the lives of dozens of policemen.
Some expected that Musa's call for surrender could well start another
slaughter.
The different sections of the guerrilla army operate under the
following names: 10th Regiment, 12th Regiment, 5th Assault Unit,
the 8th Assault Unit and the 10th Independent platoon. The 10th
Regiment alone has 684 members in Waeng, east of Betong salient in
Thailand.

8073: Communist Party of Malaysia-Marxist Leninist (CPM-ML)
Description: a CPM faction which broke from the 12th Regiment in
1970 and fled quietly to the north of Betong but did not become
generally known as an organization until 1974.
Date of establishment or first appearance: 1970.
Estimated strength: 550 members.

8074: Communist Party of Malaysia-Revolutionary Faction (CPM-RF)
Description: a CPM faction which first emerged in 1970.
Estimated strength: 500 members.

8072: Communist United Front (CUF)
Description: the government has identified several international
organizations which operate as welfare and professional organizations
but are actually fronts of the CUF which is Moscow oriented.

8071: Malayan Islamic Youth Organization

8077: Malayan National Liberation Front (MNLF)
Description: an underground wing of the CPM.

8076: Malayan National Liberation League (MNLL)
Description: an underground wing of the CPM.

8123: Malayan National Peking Liberation Army or
Communist Terrorist Organization (MNLA (CTO))

8052: Malayan Races Liberation Army (MRLA)

8078: North Kalimantan Communist Party (NKCP)

Description: an organization which established itself in Indonesia close to the Malay border.
Leadership: Wen Ming-Chuan.

8079: North Kalimantan People's Forces
(Pasokan Rakyat Kalimantan Utara) (PARAKU)
Description: a guerrilla force which is closely allied to the CPM. It is most active in the Sarawak first division. It operates jointly with the North Kalimantan People's Guerrilla Force.
Estimated strength: 600 to 700 guerrillas (1971).

8080: Revolutionary Malay Nationalist Party (RMNP)
Description: the government believes this is a CPM front. In a twelve point program launched June 1981 it was said that a united front had to be formed against Soviet and Vietnamese hegemonism in much the same way as the CCP and the Kuomintang had struggled against the Japanese.

8082: Sarawak People's Guerrilla Forces
(Pergerakan Guerilja Rakyat) (PGRS)
Description: a pro Beijing guerrilla force.

8081: Societies Act Coordinating Committee (SACC)
Description: militant Malayan societies have banded together in a civil disobedience campaign to resist the attempt of the government to bring them into line. It called to 14 000 clubs, societies, merchant guilds and other non political groups to defy registration and to ignore the call to be politically screened.

MARTINIQUE

0160: Groupe de Liberation de la Martinique (GLAM)

MAURETANIA

4069: Alliance for Democratic Mauretania

4064: Free Man
Description: clandestine Haratine movement.

4046: El Hor
Description: banned Haratine movement.

4025: Mauretanian Justice Party (PJM)

4026: Mauretanian Kadihines Party (PKM)

4068: Military Committee for National Redress

4027: National Democratic Movement (ADM)
Remarks: leaders are in exile in France.

MAURITIUS

5019: Independent Forward Bloc (IFB)

5020: Mauritian Democratic Union (UDM)

5021: Mauritian Militant Movement (MMM)

5022: Mauritian Socialist Progessive Movement (MMMSP)

5023: Mauritius People's Progressive Party (MPPP)

MEXICO

0060: Armed Communist League

0061: Armed Vanguard of the Proletariat

0245: Authentic Party of the Mexican Revolution
(Partido Autentico de la Revolucion Mexicana) (PARM)
Description: a splinter of the PRI which advocates a return to what it
considers the original spirit of the 1910 revolution.
Leadership: Antonia Gomez Velasco.

0246: Che Chevara Commandos
Description: previously unknown group.
Date of establishment or first appearance: 1981.
Remarks: many members were arrested in April 1981.

0247: The Falcons
(Los Halcones)
Description: a group which broke up a student demonstration in 1971
with the open connivance of the city authorities.

0062: Federation of Revolutionary Students (FER)

0248: Institutional Revolutionary Party
(Partido Revolucionario Institucional) (PRI)
Description: founded in 1929 as the National Revolutionary Party
(PRN) and redesignated in 1938 as the Mexican Revolutionary Party
(PRM), the PRI took its present name in 1946. As a union of local
and state groups with roots in the revolutionary period, it was
gradually established on a broad popular base and retains a
tripartite organization based on three distinct sectors (labor,
agrarian and "popular") although in 1970 it was officially
redesignated as a workers party. While the PRI's general outlook
may be characterized as moderately leftwing, its membership
includes a variety of factions and outlooks.
Date of establishment or first appearance: 1929.
Leadership: Jose Lopez Portillo (president of Mexico), Gustava
Carvajal Moreno and Augusto Gomez Villanueva (general secretary)

0249: Mexican Communist Party

(Partido Comunista Mexicana) (PCM)
Description: organized in 1919, recognized during the years 1936-1942,
and semi clandestine until achieving conditional recognition in 1978,
the PCM has traditionally been a relatively ineffectual group adhering to
a pro Moscow line. Since 1974, however, it has adopted an essentially
"Eurocommunist" position, finding support mainly with students,
intellectuals and independent trade unions. At the 1976 presidential
elections the PCM supported the "independent" candidacy of Valentin
Campa Salazar.
Date of establishment or first appearance: 1919.
Leadership: Valentin Campa Salazar and Arnoldo Martinez Verdugo
(secretary general).

0064: Mexican People's Revolutionary Army (MPRA)

0063: Mexican Workers' Party
(Partido Mexicano de los Trabajadores) (PMT)
Description: a rapidly growing pro Cuban leftist group which was
established in 1974.
Leadership: Heberto Castillo and Demetrio Vallejo.

0158: Movement of Revolutionary Action
(Movimiento de Accion Revolucionaria) (MAR)
Description: a pro Moscow/ North Korea group which carried out bank
raids, kidnappings and acts of sabotage in 1971.

0265: National Democratic Popular Front

0187: National Patriotic Anticommunist Front
(Frente Patriotica Anti-comunista Nacional) (FPAN)
Description: a paramilitary group.

0258: Los Negros
Description: an anti guerrilla force whose existence was reported
in Uno Mas Uno.
Date of establishment or first appearance: 1980.
Estimated strength: 2000 men.

0065: Party of the Mexican People
(Partido del Pueblo Mexicano) (PPM)
Description: a party which was organized by a faction of the PPS
following a dispute between Alejandro Gascon Mercado and PPS leader
Chruikshank that involved irregularities in connection with the
latter's election to the Senate.
Date of establishment or first appearance: 1976.
Leadership: Alejandro Gascon Mercado.

0262: Party of the Poor Assassination Brigades

0066: People's Armed Command

0263: People's Defense Command

0067: People's Liberation Army

0068: People's Revolutionary Armed Forces

(Fuerzas Revolutionarias Armadas del Pueblo) (FRAP)

0250: Popular National Democratic Front
(Frente Nacional Democratico Popular) (FNDP)

0159: Red Faction of the Workers Revolutionary Party

0185: September 16 League
Description: a paramilitary group which is possibly a section of
the FPAN (see 0187).

0069: September 23 Communist League
(Liga Comunista 23 de Septiembre)
Description: previously very active Marxist guerrilla group which is
believed to have been destroyed after the killing of its leaders.
Leadership: Carlos Jimenez Sarmiento (killed Aug. 1978), Miguel Angel
Barraza Garcia (killed Feb. 1981).

0183: Southern Liberation Army
(Ejercito de Liberacion del Sur) (ELS)

0301: Unified Socialist Party of Mexico (PSUM)

0070: United Popular Liberation Army of America

0184: Urban Zapata Front
(Frente Urbano Zapata)

0186: White Brigade
(Brigada Blanca)
Description: right wing militia with police involvement. Its existence
was revealed in Feb. 1980 but it is believed to have operated since
1976. It has been active in torture and intimidation tactics and
claimed responsibility for 500 kidnappings. Its 9th Army Brigade is
stationed in Campo Militar Numero 1 in Mexico City. It cooperates
with regular security forces and para military units in the service
of landowners and industrialists.

0264: Workers Socialist Party

0251: Workers' Revolutionary Party
(Partido Revolucionario de los Trabajadores) (PRT)
Description: a minority party which is represented in parliament.

MOROCCO

6190: Ilal Amman

6270: Istiqlal

6157: Morocco Patriotic Front

6269: Socialist Union of the Peoples Forces (USFP)

MOZAMBIQUE

5111: Dragons of Death

5076: Free Africa Movement
(Africa Livre) (FAM)
Description: guerrilla movement which operated from Malawi. Its
activities decreased after arrest of its leader and a number of
assistants. Previously it was supported by Rhodesia (now Zimbabwe).
Now it is believed that it is supported by South Africa in order to
destabilize the Mozambique goverment.
Leadership: Amos Sumane.

5024: Mozambique Liberation Front
(Frente de Libertacao de Mocambique) (FRELIMO)
Description: one of the liberation movements which succeeded in gaining
independence.
Leadership: Samora Moises Machel and Marcellino dos Santos.

5025: Mozambique Resistance Movement
(Movimiento da Resistencia Mozambiquena) (MRM)
Description: guerrilla movement which emerged in 1976 but became fully
active in late 1978/1979. It is made up of dissident Mozambicans trained
in Zimbabwe and led by ex FRELIMO guerrillas and Portuguese fighters.
It aims to overthrow the ruling FRELIMO party machine and to establish
a pro western democracy. During 1980 it carried out sabotage on
railway and power lines. In 1982 it took over the Africa Livre
connections (see 5076) in Malawi to use them for its own purposes.
It is supported by South Africa.
Date of establishment or first appearance: 1976.
Leadership: its main associates are Andreas Shimango, Miguel Murrupa,
Mateus Gwengere, Joao Mario Tudela and Afonso Dlakama.
Estimated strength: 3000 to 5000 men.

5077: Revolutionary Committe of Mozambique
(Comite Revolucionario de Mocambique) (COREMO)
Description: pro Beijing movement sporadically active, mainly in the
Tete district.
Leadership: Paulo Jose Gumane.

5026: Revolutionary Party of Mozambique (PRM)

5027: United Democratic Front of Mozambique
(Frente Unido Mocambiquena) (FUMO)
Description: an organization which was formed in the latter days of
Portuguese colonial rule. It backed the MRM and national opposition
groups such as the Zambesi Liberation Front and the Cabo Delgado
Liberation Front.
Leadership: Domingos Arouca, who had financial contacts with the
old regime.
Remarks: Jorge Jardim, banker and businessman is a prominent member
within the FUMO.

NAMIBIA

5079: Caprivi African National Union
Description: an organization which seeks independence for the Caprivi strip.
Leadership: Mishahe Muyongo.

5042: People's Liberation Army of Namibia (PLAN)
Description: the military branch of SWAPO.

5041: South West African People's Organization (SWAPO)
Description: liberation movement which consists mainly of Ovambo tribes.
In 1966 it embarked upon violence, aided by the OAU after the
International Court of Justice in the Hague had rejected a charge
that South Africa was abusing the mandate laid down by the League
of Nations. It favours a unified Namibia based upon "scientific
socialism" rejecting the ethnically based representative institutions.
Financial assistance was broadly based from East and West. Military
assistance came from the Eastern Bloc. It operates mainly in Ovambo
and aroud Tzumeh.
Leadership: Sam Nujoma.
Estimated strength: 6000 men.

5078: South West United Front (SWANUF)

NEPAL

7173: Anti Chinese Khampa Guerrillas

NETHERLANDS

2228: Autonomists
(Autonomen)
Description: name used for claiming responsibility for acts by various
elements in- and outside the squatters movement.

2231: Direct Action
(Directe Actie)

2146: Center Party
(Centrum Partij)
Description: xenophobic rightist party which gained one seat in
parliament in 1982. To avoid demonstrations it organized its closed
meetings under the cover of names of other organizations.

2226: Free South Moluccan Youth Movement
(Pemuda Masjarakat)
Description: South Moluccan youth organization not directly involved in
violence.

2225: Government of the South Moluccan Republic in Exile
Leadership: Ir.I. Manusama.

2143: Marxist Educational Collective
(Marxistisch Scholings Collectief)
Description: Moluccan organization aiming at information distribution on
the situation on the Moluccan Islands and on the militarization of
Indonesia.

2144: Militant Autonomists Front
(Militant Autonomen Front) (MAF)
Description: name used to claim responsibility for minor home-made
bombings an an arsonist attack on an underground wagon.

2145: National Autonomist Front
(Landelijk Autonomen Front) (LAF)
Description: militant group responsible for minor attacks.

2140: Red Action Front
(Rood Actie Front) (RAF)
Description: two youths which claimed responsibility for minor molotov
cocktail attacks in July 1982.

2141: Red Aid
(Rode Hulp)
Description: group sympathizing with a number of terrorist movements.
It was reported that 13 members had received training in a Palestine
commando camp in Southern Yemen in 1976.

2147: Red Resistance Front
(Rood Verzets Front) (RVF)
Description: group sympathizing with a number of terrorist
organizations and guerrilla movements. It is mainly directed at
spreading information about the goals, aims and background of these
movements. It also spreads information about the situation in
prisons in a number of Western countries and the growing militarization
and police repression.

2142: Red Youth
(Rode Jeugd)

2232: Revolutionary Front
(Revolutionair Front)

2053: Revolutionary People's Resistance of the Netherlands

2224: South Moluccan Suicide Command
Description: name assumed by three South Moluccans for their hostage
action on March 13 and 14, 1978 in Assen.

2054: South Moluccan Extremists

NEW CALEDONIA

0261: Front Indépendiste

0189: Kanak Liberation Party
(Armeé de Liberation Canaque) (PALIKA)

9932: Mana Motuhake

9931: Socialist Unity Party

NICARAGUA

0252: Anti Communist Armed Forces
(Fuerzas Armadas Anticomunistas) (FARAC)
Description: rightist militia active in 1980.

0253: Armed Democratic Forces
(Fuerzas Armadas Democraticas) (FAD)
Description: rightwing Somozist militia operating from Guatemala which
has been involved in many attacks during 1980.
Leadership: Carlos Garcia Solorzano, former head of Somoza's National
Security office.

0071: Authentic Sandinist
(Sandinist Autentica)
Description: guerrilla group which emerged after the 1978 offensive.

0289: Democratic Nicaraguan Forces
(Fuerzas Democraticas de Nicaragua) (FDN)
Description: guerrilla group operating from Costa Rica.

0188: Miskito, Sumu and Rama Indian Movement (MISURASATA)
Description: indian movement which replaced the ALPROMISU and
which has one seat in the State Council.
Ideological position: nationalist and striving for a greater autonomy
and the maintenance of the indian identity.
Date of establishment or first appearance: 1979.
Leadership: Stedman Fagoth, who was arrested, released and later
exiled in Honduras where he recruits Miskitos for guerrilla
operations in Nicaragua.
Remarks: the Sandinists are opposed to the maintenance of an indian
identity and have stressed common ancestry and the class struggle.
The Miskitos have criticized Sandinist development plans which will
incorporate the Miskito economy into the larger Nicaraguan economy
and will disturb the ecological balance and their way of life.

0165: National Army of Liberation
(Ejercito Nacional de Liberacion) (ENL)
Description: a group of ex Somoza loyalists and ex National Guards
which operate from Honduras.
Leadership: Pedro Ortega or Comandante Juan Carlos.
Estimated strength: a force of 600 men is trained in the US.

0254: Nicaraguan Armed Revolutionary Forces
(Fuerzas Armadas Revolucionarias Nicaraguenses) (FARN)
Description: rightist guerrilla group which carried out several attacks
during 1980.
Estimated strength: 280 men.

0166: Nicaraguan Democratic Union
(Unidad Democratica Nacional) (UDN)
Description: a movement of disillusioned Sandinists.
Leadership: Fernando Chamorro (el Negro).
Estimated strength: 4000 to 6000 men.

0074: Proletarian Tendency
(Tendencia Proletaria) (PT)
Description: one of the three factions within the FSLN.

0073: Protracted Popular Warfare
(Guerra Popular Prolongada) (GPP)
Description: one of the most extreme leftwing factions within the FSLN.

0288: Revolutionary Democratic Alliance
(Allianza Democratico Revolucionario) (ARDE)

0300: Revolutionary Government of Popular Unity (GRUP)

0072: Sandinist National Liberation Front
(Frente Sandinista de Liberacion Nacional) (FSLN)
Description: a liberation movement which was formed in 1961 as a
pro Havana group by Carlos Fonseca Amador. He and a number of
other leaders were killed by the government forces in Nov. 1976.
It is named after Augusto Cesar Sandino, a prominent rebel during
the US occupation in the 1920's. He was the great example for
Che Chevara and Castro. After a six year struggle with his 1000 men
force against 12 000 US marines he gave up in the end and signed
an agreement. On his way to a dinner with the president he was arrested
by the National Guard which killed him causing an international scandal.
His tactics were taken over by several other guerrilla leaders in
Latin America.
The FSLN displayed a remarkable capacity for survival, despite
numerous "eradication" campaigns during the later years of the
Somoza regime. In 1975 the Sandinists split into three factions,
the smallest of which were the Marxist Leninist GPP en TP. The
largest was the extreme Third Party or Terceristas which dropped
all ideological elements from its platform to allow the bourgeoisie
to join a common front against the Somoza regime. It succeeded in
winning a broad spectrum of support, from peasants to upper class
intellectuals.
After the abortive campaign against government forces in late 1977,
the three groups began coordinating their activities and had largely
succeeded in re-establishing operational unity by the time the Aug.
1978 offensive was launched. Subsequently unity waned and in Dec.
the two Marxist groups entered into an apparently anti-Tercerista
coalition (the MPU) while a forth faction the Authentic Sandinist
was reported to have emerged.
Although the junta installed in July 1979, appeared to be Tercerista
dominated, the three principal tendencies are equally represented in
the FSLN's Joint National Directorate.
Date of establishment or first appearance: 1961.
Leadership: Terceristas: Daniel Ortega Saavedra, Humberto Ortega
Saavedra, Victor Manuel Tirado. GPP: Bayardo Arce, Tomas Borge
Martinez, Henry Ruiz.
TP: Luis Carrion Cruz, Carlos Nunez Tellez, Jaime Wheelock Roman.

Estimated strength: after the take over it consisted of an army of
17 000 men, a police force of 5000 to 7000 men and a militia of
30 000 men. It has plans to extend the army to the strength of
50 000 men and a militia of 200 000 men.

0075: Third Party or Insurrectionists
(Terceristas or Insurreccionales)
Description: largest of the three faction within the FSLN.

0076: United People's Movement
(Movimiento del Pueblo Unidad) (MPU)
Description: a union of two Marxist groups which was formed in
Dec. 1978 as an apparently anti-tercerista coalition.

NORTHERN IRELAND

2044: Irish National Liberation Army (INLA)
Description: military wing of the Irish Republican Socialist Party.
Date of establishment or first appearance: it was formed in 1974 when
it broke away from the official party.
Estimated strength: 50 members.
Remarks: it considers itself an armed branch of a struggle which also
has to be fought in social and economic areas particularly within the
unions.

2045: Irish Republican Army (IRA)
Estimated strength: believed to be 200 strong.
Remarks: has not been involved in terrorism since 1972.

2138: National Socialist Workers' Party
Description: neo nazi organization.

2046: Provisional Irish Republican Army (PIRA)
Description: breakaway of the official IRA in 1969.
Estimated strength: a hardcore of about 350 to 400 and about ten times
as many sympathizers.

2047: Red Flag Seventy Four

2104: Red Hand Commandos

2137: Royal Ulster Constabulary (RUC)
Description: a police force which consists almost exclusively of
protestants.
Estimated strength: 7500 men.

2048: Sinn Fein

2214: Tara

2049: Ulster Defense Association (UDA)
Description: protestant paramilitary group.
Leadership: Andy Turie and John McMichael.

2139: Ulster Freedom Fighters (UFF)
Description: extreme protestant secret grouping.

2050: Ulster Volunteer Force (UVF)
Description: extreme protestant secret grouping.

2051: Young Militants

OMAN

6225: Dhofar Liberation Front

6192: National Front for the Liberation of Oman and the Persian Gulf
(NDFLOPG)
Description: pro-Beijing and Bagdad oriented organization.

6224: Peoples Liberation Army

6048: Popular Front for the Liberation of Oman (PFLO)
Description: organization which does not exist any longer according to
one of its leaders who surrendered.

6191: Popular Front for the Liberation of the Occupied Arabian Gulf
(PFLOAG)
Description: pro Beijing organization.
Estimated strength: 1500 men (1971).

6193: Zafaris
Description: a group which is involved in a guerrilla war against the
sultan for the cause of democracy.

PAKISTAN

7174: All Pakistani Jammu and Kashmir Conference
Description: founded by Ghulam Abbas as the moslem Conference and
known by its present name since the late 1960's, the Conference won
one legislative seat at the 1977 election and in Nov. 1977 announced
that it would cooperate with Tehrik-i-Istiqlal. It has long urged
that the status of Jammu and Kashmir be settled by a plebiscite.
Leadership: Sikandar Hayat Khan.

7212: Jamaat-i-Islami

7176: Jama'at-i-Islami Pakistan
Description: organized in 1941, the Jama'at-i-Islami Pakistan called for
an Islamic state based on national , rather than a purely communalistic
consensus.
Date of establishment or first appearance: 1941.
Leadership: Mian Tufail Mohammad, Qazi Hussain Ahmed (secretary
general).

7145: Jama'at-i-Ulema-i-Pakistan

Description: a popular islamic group founded in 1968. It withdrew from the PNA in July 1978. It has an armed "Thunder Squad" which has been involved in actions against leftwing student(s)(movements).

7175: Jama'at-i-Ulema-i-Islam
Description: an organization which has long urged the adoption of a constitution based on islamic principles. Its leader was the founding president of the PNA.
Leadership: Maulana Mufti Mahmud.

7139: Jiya Sindh Movement
Description: an organization which is associated with the People's Party. It has a leftwing of Hindu proto communists who advocate unity with India and a rightwing of nationalist Waderas preaching regional autonomy.

7157: Kashmir National Liberation Front
Description: organization aiming to establsih a modern independent Kashmir based on secular democratic means. It believes in guerrilla tactics to win independence. It was founded by a journalist, Maqbool Ahmed Butt who is now awaiting execution in jail.
Leadership: Amanullah Kahn.

7142: Movement for the Restoration of Democracy (MRD)
Description: a new political alliance formed Feb. 1981 comprising nine opposition parties which wants the government to resign, martial law to be lifted and elections to be held within three months.
The military tried to prevent the inaugural meeting at Lahore Feb. 27 1981 and rounded up more than 100 leaders before the meeting.

7027: National Awami Party (NAP)
Description: party which is based on peasant and labor interests and a remnant of the National Awami Party of Bangla Desh. It has endorsed a pro Beijing line. In Feb. 1975 it was officially banned after allegedly being involved in terrorist activity aimed at secession of the Baluchistan and North Western frontier Provinces.
Leadership: Abdul Wali Khan, who was released from prison in Dec. 1977.

7179: Pakistan Khaksar Party (PKP)
Description: a militant islamic party also known as Bailcha Bardar (shovel carriers) because the group's founder, Inayatullah Mashraqir, urged the use of shovels to symbolize self reliance and the glory of the armed forces.
Leadership: Mohammad Ashraf Khan.

7144: Pakistan Liberation Army
(Al Zulfikar) (PLA)
Description: a movement consisting of leftwing students, ex army officers and some from Bhutto's disbanded secret police (the Federal Security Force). In 1981 it was renamed in Al Zulfikar.

7187: Pakistan National Alliance

7178: Pakistan National Party (PNP)
Description: a moderately leftist group of Baluchi leadership that claims

nevertheless a nationwide following. It withdrew from the NDP mid 1979.
Leadership: Ghaus Bakhs Bizenjo.

7177: Pakistan People's Party (PPP)
Description: a party founded in 1967 by Zulfikar Ali Bhutto. It held a
majority of seats in the National Assembly truncated by the independence
of Bangla Desh in 1971. After 1977 its status and leadership became
uncertain. It was not clear whether a government order of Oct. 16
which banned all parties whose ideology could be construed as prejudicial
to national security, was specifically directed at the PPP. Its nominal
leader Ali Bhutto was executed in April 1979, while its secretary general
and subsequently its acting sceretary general had been arrested six
months earlier.
Date of establishment or first appearance: 1967.
Leadership: Begum Nusrat Bhutto, Benazir Bhutto, Ghulam Hussain
(secretary general).

7186: Pathan Tribesmen

7211: Plebiscite Front
Description: an active group which stands for an independent Kashmir.
It was founded in 1955 and it has a military alliance with the
national liberation front.
Leadership: A. Ansari.

PALESTINE

7028: Abdel Nasser Movement

7087: Abu Nidal Group
(Al Assifa)
Description: split in 1974 from the PLO. Its men have killed several
PLO leaders in Paris, London and Brussels and it has been involved in
repeated attacks on the European Jewish community and on Israeli
diplomats.

7029: Action Organization for the Liberation of Palestine

7140: ANSAR

7030: Arab Communist Organization

7180: Arab Nationalist Movement (ANM)
Description: a group which was previously called the Heroes of Return.
In 1969 it joined the PFLP.

7032: Arab People
(Ash-Shab al-'Arabi) (AP)

7034: Arab Revolutionary Movement

7033: Arab Revolutionary Army-Palestine Commando

7031: Arab Liberation Front (ALF)

Description: a small Iraqi backed socialist oriented movement involved in actions in Israeli occupied territory. It participates in the Rejection Front.
Leadership: Abel Wahab Kaiali.
Estimated strength: 3100 members.

7035: Arm of the Arab Revolution

7036: Black June Organization

7037: Black March Organization

7039: Black September Organization (BSO)
Description: a group formed out of the Fatah intelligence unit (Razd) centered in the Razd headquarters in Rome.
Leadership: Abu Iyad (died in the DDR), Yussuf El Nayyar (killed by the MOSSAD in April 1973).

7038: Black September June
Estimated strength: 190 members.

7040: Commando Mohammed Boudia
Description: a commando which cooperated with the June Second Movement, Black September, the Japanese Revolutionary Army and Italian and Turkish Organizations.
Leadership: Mohammed Boudia (intellectual, journalist, actor and director of the Theatre de l'Ouest in Paris) was killed in 1973 by a MOSSAD deathsquad (Wrath of God) and was replaced by Andre or Ilich Ramirez Sanchez ("Carlos").

7041: Correct Course of Fatah
(AlKhat as-Sahih Lifatah)

7042: Eagles of the Palestine Revolution or Red Eagles
(El Nisr)

7043: Al Fatah
(Falasteen Tahya Huraa)
Description: established in the winter of 1968-1969 as an Arab commando (feyadeen) group. its military arm was al-Asifa.
Leadership: Yasir Arafat (alias Abu 'Ammar).

7044: Friends of the Arabs

7045: Ghassan Kanafani Commandos

7046: Group of the Fallen Abd al Kadir Husayni
7141: Heroes of Return
Description: a group of Palestine commandos responsible for the Jerusalem "Night of Grenades" in 1964.
Leadership: Fayez Abdul Rahmin Jaber (was killed in the Entebbe raid). He was also one of the founding fathers of the PFLP (an alliance of three smaller groups which was formed in 1967). Jaber was head of the PFLP's internal security and was then appointed as commander of special operations "in the external sphere" meaning outside Israel.

7047: Mount Carmel Martyrs

7048: National Organization of Arab Youth

7049: National Youth Group for the Liberation of Palestine

7053: Organization of the Avenging Palestine Youth

7054: Organization of the Sons of Occupied Territories

7055: Organization of the Sons of Palestine

7052: Organization of the Struggle against World Imperialism (SAWIO)

7051: Organization for the Victims of Zionist Occupation

7056: Organization of Victims of Occupied Territories

7057: Palestine Liberation Army (PLA)
Description: regular army of the PLO which until the Israeli invasion
into Lebanon, consisted of a trained and well equipped conventional
force.
Estimated strength: 12 000 men.

7143: Palestine Liberation Forces (PLF)
Description: a movement which cme into existence in the end of the
1950's and was based in Syria. In 1969 a split led to the PFLP-GC.
Leadership: Ahmad Jibril (a Palestine officer in the Syrian army).

7058: Palestine Liberation Organization
(Munazamat Tahrir Falastin) (PLO)
Description: a political organization established in May 1964, led from
1969 onwards by Yasir Arafat. According to a spokesman of the
Rejectionist Front the national income of the PLO was as great as
the national income of an Arab nation such as Jordan. In Libya a
six percent deduction from the salaries of Palestine exiles was
ordered to help finance the organization. It has been estimated
that in 1974 the PLO's revenue amounted to more than £ 120 million.

7080: Palestine National Liberation Movement

7059: Palestine Popular Struggle Front (FPS)
Description: a group which joined the Rejection Front.
Leadership: dr. Samir Gosheh.
Estimated strength: 230.

7060: Palestine Rejectionist Front

7061: Palestine Revolutionary Forces

7062: Palestine Revolutionary Movement

7063: Popular Democratic Front for the Liberation of Palestine (DPLFP)
Description: a group which split from the PFLP in 1968. Previously it
was called Vengeance Youth but since 1969 DPFLP. It is more of a political
group then a military group.

Date of establishment or first appearance: 1968.
Leadership: Nayef Hawatmeh.
Estimated strength: 1100 members.

7064: Popular Front for the Liberation of Palestine
(al-Jabha al-Sha'biyyah li Tahrir Falastin) (PFLP)
Description: a group which was established in Dec. 1967 by George
Habbash and Wadi Haddad. Its military wing is lead by Naddieh Haddad.
It has been involved in operations in Paris, Vienna, Stockholm,
London and Munich. As a result of ideological differences two groups
split from the front, the PFLP-GC and the PFLP-SO.

7065: Popular Front for the Liberation of Palestine-General Command
(PFLP-GC)
Description: a group which split off from the PFLP in 1969.

7066: Popular Front for the Liberation of Palestine-Special Operations
(PFLP-SO)
Description: a group which split off from the PFLP in 1969.

7067: Punishment Squad
(al Icab)

7068: Rejectionist Front of Stateless Palestine Arabs
Description: an organization which includes the ALF, PFLP-GC and the
PSF.

7070: Seventh Suicide Squad

7071: Sons of Occupied Land

7072: Squad of the Martyr Patrick Arguello

7069: Thunderbolt
(Saiqa)
Description: a group which was established in 1968 and in a certain
sense it was led by the Syrian Baath Party. It also takes part in the
executive Committee of the PLO. Its main action area was the Golan
Heights.
Leadership: Zoher Mohsen.
Estimated strength: 1500 members.

PANAMA

0255: Revolutionary Students' Federation
(Federacion de estudiantes Revolucionarios) (FER)

PARAGUAY

1133: Agrarian Peasant League
(Liga Agraria Campesina)
Description: founded in 1961 and supported by some one million

peasants to oppose government land tenure policies. The army has been involved in major operations in Mar. 1980 against its members.
Leadership: Victor Centurion (exiled in London).

1165: May 14th Movement

1055: Political Military Organization

1056: Popular Colorado Movement (MOPOCO)
Description: a dissident faction of the Colorado party.

1164: United Front for National Liberation (FULNA)

PERU

1057: Armed Nationalist Movement Organization (MANO)

1183: Communist Party of Peru

1058: Condor

1060: Dismissed Workers Front (MTR)

1140: Leftist Revolutionary Union
(Union de Izquierda Revolucionaria) (UNIR)
Description: a coalition of three Marxist groups including the FOCEP.

1182: MOTC

1059: Movement of Revolutionary Left
(Movimiento de la Izquierda Revolucionaria) (MIR)
Description: a pro Havana movement which has been sporadically active. When its leaders were released in 1970 it began to resume its activities.

1134: National Liberation Army of Peru
(Ejercito de Liberacion Nacional) (ELN)
Description: pro Havana leftist urban guerrilla group which was dispersed by the security forces at the end of the 1960's. It reappeared in 1980.
Leadership: Juan Pablo Chang Navarro.

1179: Peasant Patrols
(Rondas Campesinas)

1061: Peruvian Anticommunist Alliance (AAP)

1163: Peruvian Left Front
(Frente Izquierdista Revolucionaria) (FIR)

1135: Popular Workers, Campesinos, Students Front
(Frente Obrero Campesino Estudiantil y Popular) (FOCEP)

1136: La Puenta Uzeda

Description: an armed guerrilla group which tried to create an uprising in Mes Pelada. It was eliminated by government forces.

1181: Puka Llacta

1138: Red Earth
(Tierra Roja)
Description: a Trotskyite movement which temporarily seized a radio station.

1062: Revolutionary Vanguard
(Vanguardia Revolucionaria)

1072: Shining Path
(Sendoro Luminoso)
Description: Maoist movement founded during a period of student unrest in the 1970's. It broke away from other leftist groups and went underground with plans to organize the peasantry. The founders were themselves sons of peasants and small traders who met each other during the study at the Huamanga university. It started with Robin Hood like actions but in a later stage the actions became more severe and more bloody. During 1981 it was very active in bombings and bank robberies. In June 1982 it claimed 2900 actions since Belaunde came to power. It is mainly active in the Ayacucho area.
Leadership: prof. Luis Kawate Makabe (arrested Feb. 1981) and prof.Abimael Guzman (arrested Oct. 1981).
Estimated strength: 400 guerrillas.

1139: Sinchis
Description: special forces of the Guardia Civil which have been trained in the US for the elimination of terrorism.

PHILIPPINES

8028: April Six Liberation Movement
Description: organization involved in an urban terror campaign which was named after the anti martial law demonstration April 6, 1978.

8090: Bangsa Moro Army (BMA)
Description: military branch of the MNLF entrenched in the Sulu archipelago. Closer cooperation with the NPA has been sought. It was once said to number 30 000 men. Defense minister Juan Ponce Enrile estimated the strength to be between 6000 to 9000 while others estimated the strength at 10 000 to 12 000 men. The government declared that 30 000 BMA soldiers have surrendered over the last years.

8091: Bangsa Moro Liberation Organization (BMLO)
Description: organization which never established a military capability. There have been charges that the movement might be a Marcos sponsored body, aiming to split the rebel camp.
Leadership: Rashid Lucman, Salipada Pendatun (two former politicians).
Remarks: In 1981 Lucman agreed to ally with Misuari under the latter leadership. Pendatun accepted the government amnesty offer and lives in Manilla, detached from political life.

8116: Black Commando

8098: Charismatic Movement of the Philippines (CMP)
Description: a movement which operates between Magpet in the north of
Cotabato province and Davao City. Its main function has been to
observe NPA movements in strategic areas where rebel bases are likely
to be set up. It also puts armed men on strategic NPA pathways
with orders to kill armed men entering their respective areas and
to confiscate arms for their own use. It tries to persuade rather
than intimidate villagers to confess what they know about their
neighbours. The CPM's converts, mostly illiterates lured with
promises of supernatural powers, have willingly -albeit suspectingly-
obliged.
Leadership: rev. Arnold Buenafe (killed Mar.1981), Maningand Kikit.

8043: Four K's Sect (KKKK)
Description: organization based in Siayan and which has been involved
in two multiple murders. It has links with the military and is said
to have much the same beliefs as those of Rock Christ (see 8045).
Leadership: Ruben Ecleo and Ptentiano Marindaque.

8083: Haring Gahum Sect
Description: a group which has affiliations with Rock Christ (see 8045).
It is formed into small groups and trained by the army.

8117: Lanao Revolutionary Command

8038: Light a Fire Movement (or Third Force)
Description: a loosely organized grouping of predominantly middle class
and in many cases, devoutly Roman Catholic radicals. It is strongly
opposed to both communism and the 15 year old authoritarian regime of
president Ferdinand Marcos. It has been involved in a wave of bombings.
Leadership: Eduardo Olaguer (chess champion, Harvard business school
graduate and IBM executive).

8100: Lost Command Group
Description: a group of military renegades loosely affiliated with the
AFP and involved in fighting with the NPA. Its tasks is to liquidate
opposition in critical areas so as to avoid direct military involvement
in operations which might bring accusations of brutality from foreign
governments. It also provides mercenaries to politicians and
business men whose interests are threatened.

8088: Maoist Communist Party of the Philippines (MCPP)
Date of establishment or first appearance: Dec. 26, 1968.
Remarks: its military wing (the NPA) was formed three months later.

8086: Mindanao Alliance Group

8092: Mindanao Independence Movement (MIM)
Description: secessionist movement in Mindanao, uncertain as to methods
by which secession was to be effected.
Date of establishment or first appearance: the late 1960's.
Leadership: Datu Udtog Matalam.

8013: Moro National Liberation Front (MNLF)
Description: an Islamic nationalist movement striving for greater
autonomy which has been involved in an armed rebellion since 1969.
It split in 1977 into a Libyan and an Egyptian backed faction after
the Tripoli agreement in 1976. The Egyptian backed Hashim Salamat
faction which is based in the Maquindanao group is opposed to the
Misuari's highly personalized left leaning leadership. Hashim
Salamat emphasizes the Islamic rather than the national character
of the struggle. Its military branch is the Bangsa Moro Army. The
guerrilla war has resulted in already 60 000 people killed.
The MNLF stopped establishing control over territory after it realized
that the army's tactic of burning down a whole village or bulldozing
a whole island dominated by the MLNF was causing the people too much
hardship. The guerrillas now attack "the enemy" in isolated incidents.
The army maintains that this is a result of reduced firepower. The
chain of command has weakened, quite often local commanders will
act on their own initiative. Also the supply lines can no longer
be maintained as a result of the government patrolling.
Nevertheless a cottage industry of weapon manufacture has developed.

8094: National Democratic Front
Description: in April 1973 the MCPP sponsored the formation of the NDF
intended to unite Communist labour and Christian groups in opposition
to the Marcos regime. Its aim is to overthrow the Marcos regime. It has
an extensive underground movement in the towns and cities among
workers, students and low income professionels. It includes the
Revolutionary Peasant Organization, the Patriotic Health
Organization and the Christians for National Liberation.

8093: National Union for Freedom (UNIDO)
Description: established Aug.30, 1980 by 70 members of different
opposition groups with the goal to end the Marcos dictatorship.

8097: National Union for Liberation (NUL)
Description: umbrella organization of anti Marcos parties formed in 1979.

8012: Nationalist Youth Organization
(Kabataang Makabayan)
Description: organization whose rioting was the immediate cause of the
declaration of martial law in 1972. It was founded by Jose Maria Sison
(CP leader) and Nur Misuari.
Remarks: it has only been successful in the north.

8014: New People's Army
(Bagong Hukbong Bayan) (NPA)
Description: military branch of the Communist party.
About 60 percent are CP members and about 80 percent appeared to be
young Kalingas. It replaced the People's Liberation Army. It is
entrenched in the northern Luzon province, Albay province, the
southern part of Quezon province, in southern Luzon, Samar island
in the eastern Visayas and in southern Mindanao's four Davao
provinces.
Date of establishment or first appearance: founded by Bernabe
Buscayo in 1969.

Estimated strength: according to CP leaders it has 10 000 guerrillas and 50 000 active sympathizers. According to the government there are no more than 2500 armed guerrillas. Intelligence estimates put the number at 3000 to 5000 guerrillas plus a support base in so-called liberated areas of 130 000 to 150 000 people.
Remarks: the struggle is organized into at least 30 strategic guerrilla fronts each with its own party structure, militia and political machinery.

8084: New Society Movement
(Kilusang Bagong Lipunan) (KBL)
Description: a movement organized from remnants of the Nacionalista Party as the personal vehicle of president Marcos prior to the Interim National Assembly election on April 7, 1978.

8101: Paramilitary force of surrendered rebels
Description: the military organized a force of surrendered NPA and BMA rebels to use it for its own purposes.

8104: People's League for Freedom
(Kabaka)
Date of establishment or first appearance: Sep. 1977.
Leadership: archbishop and cardinal of Manila Jaime Sin and ex senator Jovito Salonya.

8016: Philippine Communist Party
(Partido Komunista ng Pilipinas) (PKP)
Description: a party which was outlawed in 1948 but for some years thereafter continued to support the Hukbalahap rebellion. In recent years particularly after the Nov. 1974 surrender of PKP secretary general Felicismo Macapagal and the military leader Alejandro Briones, the party had advocated political reform rather than violent change, with Macapagal actually praising president Marcos for his leadership and his "pragmatic centrist position" in a context of "imperialist efforts to destabilize" the government. Intelligence agencies believe the PKP which has a mass base of 50 000 to 100 000 people is split into three factions and instead of taking up arms against the authorities is concentrating on infiltrating government agencies and labour unions.

8103: Presidential Assistant on National Minorities (PanaminCHDF)
Description: an organization directed at making minorities more cooperative with regard to government development programs. It uses a divide and rule tactic to split the unity of a number of minority people. In relation to the Atas it installed two new datus (chiefs) Lorenzo Gawilan and Joe Libayao, both of whom are said to control some 40 Atas. Although non-Atas they have desperately tried to secure local patronage as datus, though according to them they are merely acting as go betweens on behalf of the Atas and local and national governments. About 80 Atas have been armed.

8085: Pusyon Bisaya
Description: a small party in the Sisayas region.

8099: The Rats
(Ilaga)
Description: an armed gang which appeared in 1970 in some towns in

the southern Philippines. It is involved in a campaign of terror
against the Mindanao moslems, cutting an ear of all their victims
as a mark of their brutal work. It is an aggressive Christian
vigilante group used by the military to conduct operations which
would have brought criticism if they had been mounted by the AFP.
The activities of the Ilaga and other armed gangs in the 1968-1972
period when law enforcement agencies sided with the gangsters were
a direct motive for the moslems to step up their activities.
Leadership: Commander Toothpick (because of his skinny appearance).

8045: Rock Christ Sect
Description: a religeous fanatic movement responsible for brutal murders.
It consists of members of the Tingol clan and is based in the Osmena
town. It claims a membership of 600 of which 20 are reported to be
armed. It is basically an animistic sect with a thin overlay of
Christianity. They believe that the chiefs have healing powers and
that incantation of their special prayer, known as Orasyon,
shields them from danger. The sect's high priests are reported to be
rich landlords and farmers. It is widely believed that the army has
infiltrated the sect to form small groups and to train them.

8041: Rural Reformist Movement (RRM)
Description: movement which is involved in a terror campaign around
the town Calinan (Mar. and Apr. 1981). In February it issued a
manifesto in which it declared "to support...Marcos program for
good government". A thirty men team visits villagers to seek
recruits and to ask them about the where abouts of NPA members in
the area. Those who refuse to help are branded subversives and
become targets for liquidation. Some sources claimed that the RRM
is controlled by the National Intelligence and Security Authority
(NISA). Many of those who are forced to join the RRM are Atas who
were part of the Gawilan and Libayo tribes.
Leadership: Alitaptap (firefly).
Estimated strength: Alitaptap claimed a membership of 3000 men.

8102: Sandigan Army
Description: church guerrillas organized in 1978. The government has
encouraged it to a limited extent to undermine the NPA's link with
some church people.

8096: United Democratic Opposition
Description: a front of 45 opposition groups formed to encourage voters
to boycott the June 1981 election. For the first time traditional and
non-traditional groups came together.

8089: United Democratic Socialist Party of the Philippines
Description: party which was organized in 1978 independently of the
Communists. It has not ruled out the use of violence to attain power.

POLAND

3049: Committee for Social Self-Defense (KOS)

2222: Committee (Movement) for the Defense of Human and Civil Rights
(ROPCiO)

3132: Committee for the Defense of the Rights of Workers (KOR)

2223: Confederation for a Free Poland (KPN)

2221: Flying University

2219: Independent Self-Governing Trade Union of Farmers,
Rural Solidarity.

3126: MRKS

3086: Polish Revolutionary People's Army
Description: group involved in the occupation of the Polish embassy in
Bern Sep. 1982.

2220: Society for Educational Courses

3038: Solidarity (Solidarność)
Description: independent labour union outside the official union
structure.
Since the intervention of the military in Dec.1981 it has been severely
repressed.

2218: Student Committee for Solidarity

3133: ZOMO
Description: special riot police

PUERTO RICO

1153: Anti Communist Alliance
(Alianza Anticomunista) (AAA)
Remarks: held responsible for one attack in 1980.

1178: Armed Forces of National Liberation
(Fuerzas Armadas de Liberacion Nacional) (FALN)
Description: far left group engaged in terrorist activities.
Since 1974 it has carried out more than 100 bomb attacks; five
people were killed. It is linked to the Cuban backed Partido Socialista
Puertorriquena (PSP) and an above ground front organization, the
Puertorican Solidarity Committee.
Date of establishment or first appearance: 1972.
Leadership: Carlos Alberto Torres (arrested by the FBI in Apr. 1981)

1154: Armed Forces of Popular Resistance
Description: a terrorist group.

1155: Boricua Popular Army (or Machete Wielders)
(Ejercito Popular Boricua (or Los Macheteros) (EPB)
Description: leftist pro independence guerrilla group.
Date of establishment or first appearance: 1978.
Leadership: Manuel Mamlanda Albernoz ("Ruben").
Remarks: one action in 1979 and one in 1980. During 1981 three
bombings were recorded.

0167: Group for the Liberation of Vieques

1156: Puerto Rican Armed Resistance Movement
(Movimiento de Resistencia Armada Puertorriquena) (MRAP)
Description: leftist pro independence guerrilla group.
Date of establishment or first appearance: Jan. 1981.

1158: Puerto Rican Independence Party
(Partido Independista Puertorriqueno) (PIP)
Leadership: Ruben Barios Martinez.

1157: Puertorican Socialist Party
(Partido Socialista Puertorriquena) (PSP)
Leadership: Juan Mari Bras, Carlos Gallisa.

1159: Revolutionary Commandos of the People
(Comandos Revolucionarios del Pueblo) (CRP)
Description: leftist pro independence group.

1160: Volunteers of the Puerto Rican Revolution
(Organization de Voluntarios para la Revolucion Puertorriquena) (OVPP)
Description: leftist pro independence group which has carried out one
action in 1979 and one in 1980.

PORTUGAL

2216: Action Group for Communism

2217: Armed Forces Movement/Military Revolutionary Council

2056: Armed Revolutionary Action
(Acao Revolucionaria Armada) (ARA)
Description: eclectic leftwing clandestine urban terrorist group which
has carried out bomb attacks on national and on NATO property in 1971.

2262: Democratic Movement for the Liberation of Portugal (MDLP)

2255: International Militant Workers

2156: Liberation Front for the Azores
(Frente Libertacao dos Acores) (FLA)
Description: a movement striving for complete independence which is also
supported by emigrants in Brazil, the USA and Canada. Libya and Algeria
have asked attention for the decolonization of the Azores.
Leadership: Jose de Almeida.

2152: Liberation Front for Madeira
(Frente Libertacao Arquipelago de Madeira) (FLAMA)
Description: movement striving for independence.

2256: Luar

2257: Movement for the Reorganization of the Proletariat (MRPP)

2155: Peoples Forces of April 25 (FP-25)
Description: a movement which claimed to have links with the ETA, RB and RAF. It operates in cells and was active in 1980. It is highly selective in attacks.

2154: Popular Union Force
(Forca de Unidade Popular)
Description: ultra left movement.
Leadership: Otela Saraiva de Carvalho.

2258: Portuguese Anti-Communist Movement

2259: Portuguese Legion

2260: Portuguese Liberation Army (ELP)

2153: Revolutionary Brigades
Description: active group in 1980.

2261: Revolutionary Internationalist Solidarity

2236: Zionist Action Group

SAO TOME AND PRINCIPE

4028: Movement for the Liberation of Sao Tome and Principe

SENEGAL

4029: Moustapha Lo Command

SIERRA LEONE

5060: Resistance Movement
(Mouvement pour la Resistance)

4054: Sierra Leone Alliance Movement (SLAM)
Description: exile group based in London.
Leadership: Ambrose Ganda.

SINGAPORE

8018: Malayan National Liberation Front (MNLF)
Description: movement which advocates reintegration of Singapore with a Communist Malaysia.

8095: Singapore Malays National Organization (SMNO)
Description: an affiliate of the United Malays National Organization which

supports Malay interests and advocates reunification with Malaysia.
Leadership: Haji A. Rahman (chairman), Ibrahim Arif (secretary
general).

8035: Singapore People's Liberation Organization

8105: Socialist Front
(Barisan Sosialis)
Description: formed in 1961 by PAP militants under the leadership of
trade unionist Lim Chin Siong, the front gained a strong position in
parliament and remained the strongest opposition party until 1966, when
eleven members resigned their seats and the other two went
underground. The pro-Beijing party has had little success in
carrying its revolutionary program to the people. A number of its
leaders are now in prison.
Leadership: dr. Lee Siew Choh.

SOMALIA

5083: Democratic Front for the Salvation of Somalia (DFSS)
Description: established in 1979 in Addis Abeba as a merger of two
smaller guerrilla movements. It is mainly supported by the
Meyertein clan and by Ethiopia. Also a number of deserted army
officers joined the movement.
Estimated strength: 3000 to 5000 guerrillas (1982).

5043: Somali Abo Liberation Front (SALF)
Description: guerrilla movement operating in the Ogaden desert. Somalia
is striving for a "Great Somalia" including parts of the Ogaden desert.
Therefore it describes the inhabitants of the Ethiopian part as Somali
Abo and supports them in actions against the Ethiopian government.

5061: Somali National Movement (SNM)
Description: guerrilla movement which was established in 1981. Support
comes largely from the north. Its headquarter was first located in
London later in Addis Abeba. Actions were coordinated in cooperation
with deserted Somali officers. The Soviets have exerted pressure to
cooperate with the SDSF.

5065: Somali Salvation Front
(Front de Salut Somalien) (FOSAS)
Description: guerrilla movement operating in the Ogaden desert which
is supported by Ethiopia. It was established by some members of the
army who fled to Ethiopia. They belong to the Meyertein (1/5 of
the population) which controlled the state apparatus before 1969.
They oppose the Darob tribe which is now in power.
Estimated strength: they claim to have 10 000 members and label
themselves as nationalists.

SOUTH AFRICA

5118: Brother League of Africans
(Afrikaner Broederbond)

Description: secret while organization influential with regard to the South African government.

5029: African National Congress (ANC)
Description: oldest of the African nationalist movements. It was outlawed in 1960 after the Sharpeville massacre and turned to sabotage in 1961 with the creation of Umkhonto We Zizwe. It is supported by the multi-racial South African Communist Party which is Moscow oriented. The ANC is recognized by the OAU. It continued in 1980 to infiltrate with small groups across the border and to attack selectively mainly economic targets.

5084: Azania People's Liberation Army (APLA)
Description: armed branch of the PAC.
Leadership: until Jan. 1979 it was led by Lancel Dube (Eddie Phiri) who died in a car accident.

5052: Azanian People's Organization (AZAPO)
Description: organization which was set up in May 1978 to replace the banned Black Consciousness Organizations.
Leadership: Mkabela and Lybon Mabosa who were immediately detained.

5085: Black Consciousness Movement of South Africa (BCMSA)
Description: was founded in Botswana to unite the ANC and PAC in 1979.

5087: Black People's Convention (BPC)
Description: organization which acted as umbrella for the BCM. Associated bodies were the South African Students' Organization (SASO), and the South African Student Union (SASU). All officials of these bodies were detained in 1976.
Leadership: Nat Serache (Rand Daily Mail reporter).

5086: Black Unity Front (BUF)
Description: set up by two homeland leaders to establish "a disciplined black community and work for the emergence of a true black leadership". Date of establishment or first appearance: Nov. 1976.
Leadership: Gatsha Buthelezi of Kwazulu and dr. Cedric Phatudi of Lebowa.

5053: Inkatha ("Impis")
Description: paramilitary branch of the Inkatha movement to protect black property and to kill rioters.

5051: Koevoet
Description: criminal murder gang to kill prominent black leaders.
Estimated strength: 90 men.

5117: Labour Party

5119: Okhela
Description: radical whites in favor of cooperation with radical blacks.

5088: Ourselves (POQO)
Description: pro Beijing military wing of the PAC.

5062: Pan African Congress (PAC)

Description: formed in 1959 by the late Mangaliso Sobukwe. It operated from Dar es Salaam. It is Beijing oriented, recognized by the OAU and accorded observer status at the UN. The armed branch is called APLA. Leadership: Potlako Lebullo led Pac until he was replaced by a triumvirate in May 1979.

5120: Republican Union of Africans
(Republikeinse Afrikaner Unie)

5113: African Resistance Movement
(Afrikaner Weerstandsbeweging)
Description: extreme rightist movement.

5090: South African Black Alliance (SABA)
Description: launched Jan. 1978 by Gatsha Buthelezi who led the Kwazulu Inkatha, "a national cultural liberation movement". It included Inkatha, the Indian Reform Party and the Coloured Labour Party. It aims to lay the foundation for a possible future multi-racial national convention to map out a non-racial community and a new constitution.

5091: South African Liberation Support Committee (SALSCOM)

5089: Soweto Students' Representative Council (SSRC)
Description: set up after the Soweto riots in 1976. Its leaders fled to the UK or were arrested in 1977.

5069: Spear of the Nation
(Umkhonto We Zizwe) (SON)
Description: military wing of the ANC.
Date of establishment or first appearance: 1961.

5067: Wit Commando

SOVIET UNION

3115: Aleyeh

3113: Baptist "Initsiativniki" Movement

3112: Committee for Defense of Believers

3114: Council of Churches of Evangelical Christians-Baptists

3047: Democratic Popular Front of the Soviet Union

3104: Free Interprofessional Organization of Workers (SMOT)

3101: Free Seventh Day Adventists

3111: Georgian Rebels

3109: Helsinki Monitoring Committee, to assist the USSR
in the fulfillment of the Helsinki Accords

3131: KGB

3110: NTS

3029: October 15 Commando

3105: Pentacostalists

3103: Refuseniks

3100: Russian Liberation Army

3102: Samizdat Writers- Publishers

3099: Storozjevoi Mutineers

3108: Tartar Dissidents

3107: Trade Union for the Defense of the Workers

3106: Ukrainian Dissidents

SPAIN

2252: Anti-Communist Alliance

2059: Anticommunist Apostolic Alliance (AAA)

2057: Anti ETA Terrorism (ATE)

2070: Armed Spanish Groups (GAE)

2089: Autonomist Anticapitalist Commandos

2157: Basque Revolutionary Party
(Euskal Iraultzako Alderdia) (EIA)
Description: established by ETA-PM as political party which was
legalized by the government in 1978.

2267: CEDADE

2158: Commando Jose Garcia

2269: Party of Catalan Communists
(Partito del Comunistas de Catalunya) (PCC)

2061: Commando of Solidarity with Euzkadi

2117: Delta
Description: organization involved in the elimination of Spanish refugees
in France.

2159: Ecological Guerrillas

2251: Falangist Vanguard

2060: Freedom for the Basque Homeland
(Euskadi ta Askatasuna) (ETA)
Description: was formed as breakaway from the Basque Nationalist Party
by young activists in 1959. In 1979 ETA was split again in those
favouring terrorism (ETA-M) and those favouring a political solution
(ETA-PM).
Leadership: Domingo Iturbe-Abassol.

2160: Freedom for the Basque Homeland-Military
(Euzkadi ta Askatasuna-Militar) (ETA-M)
Description: 1979 ETA offshoot favouring terrorism. It has a cellular
structure, only one member of a cell able to communicate with a member
of another cell. It has five operational regions.

2161: Freedom for the Basque Homeland-PM
(Euzkadi ta Askatasuna-Polimilis) (ETA-PM)
Description: 1979 ETA offshoot favouring a political solution. It has,
however, continued violent actions, though on a reduced scale. It
established a political party which was legalized by the government.

2062: Free Land
(Terra Lliure)
Description: Catalan extremist group.

2254: Front d'Alliberament Catala (FAC)

2062: Hammer and Sickle Cooperative

2063: Iberian Liberation Movement
(Movimiento Iberico Liberatario) (MIL)
Description: anarchist group in Catalonia.
Leadership: Puig Antich (executed under the Franco regime in 1974).

2065: Juan Paredes Manot Internationalist Brigade

2250: Military Democratic Union

2270: Military Spanish Union (UME)

2066: Nationalist Intervention Group

2264: National Youth Front
(Frente Nacional de Juventud)

2067: New Force
(Fuerza Nueva)
Description: neo fascist movement founded in the early 1970's which has
been active in street brawls and thuggery. It was dissolved in 1982.

2058: October First Antifascist Resistance Group
(Grupo de Resistencia Antifascista Primero de Octubre)
Description: violent wing of the Maoist Reconstituted Spanish Communist
Party (PCE-R)
Date of establishment or first appearance: 1976.

Leadership: Abelardo Collazo Araujo was killed by police in Madrid
Aug. 1980. Another principal leader, Francisco Brotons Beneyto,
was arrested in Sep. 1980.

2253: "Operation Galaxy"
Description: section of the Spanish army which has been involved in an
unsuccessful coup attempt.

2244: Platform of Democratic Organizations

2068: Popular Revolutionary Armed Front (FRAP)

2242: Proletarian Armed Group

2245: Reconstructed Communist Party

2069: Revolutionary Antifascist and Patriotic Front (FRAP)

2243: Revolutionary Communist League

2064: Revolutionary Internationalist Action Groups
(Grupos de Accion Revolucionaria Internacionalista) (GARI)
Description: group which has been active in the mid seventies.

2087: Spanish Basque Batallion
(Batalon Vasco Espagnol) (BVE)
Description: small right wing terrorist group which has carried out
attacks on ETA militants.

2249: Spanish Circle of Friends of Europe
(Circulo Espanol de Amigos)

2246: Spanish Armed Groups

2071: Spanish National Organization

2072: Warriors of Christ the King
(Guerrilleros de Cristo Rey)

2247: Worker's Commissions

2248: Workers Brotherhood of Catholic Action

SRI LANKA

7181: Black Lamp
Description: pro Beijing clandestine group of the JVP responsible for
terrorist attacks and an attempt to overthrow the government in 1971.

7182: East Wind Group
Description: pro Beijing clandestine group of the JVP under a new name
to disguise their connection with an earlier uprising.

7105: Liberation Tigers

Description: young Tamil terrorist organization which took its inspiration
from the Black Panthers in the USA. A gang of about 200 insisting on
direct action to dramatize their cause and to force the government
to concede full independence. It is involved in armed robberies,
arson and assassinations.

7073: People's Liberation Front
(Janatha Vimukhti Peramuna) (JVP)
Description: a front not to be confused with the National Liberation
Front (JVP). It is a formerly outlawed Maoist organization that was
responsible for an attempt to overthrow the government in April 1971.
A variety of clandestine groups were presumed to be made up of JVP
members operating under new names to disguise their connection
with the earlier uprising. The front regained legal status
following the lifting of the state of emergency on Feb. 16, 1977.
It is active mainly in the northern central districts.
Leadership: Rohana Wijweera.

7106: Sinhalese Vigilantes Squads

7088: Tamil United Liberation Front (TULF)
Description: initially organized as the Tamil Liberation Front (TVP) in
May 1976 by a number of Tamil groups, including the Federal Party
(ITAK), the National Liberation Front (JVP), the Tamil Congress, the
Moslem United Front and the Ceylon Workers Congress. The TULF
stated in its 1977 election manifesto that its successful
candidates would serve as the constituent assembly of a proposed
Tamil state (Tamil Eelam). At the July election it became the largest
opposition group in the National Assembly.
Leadership: Appapaillai Amirthalingam (ITAK), J.R.P.Suri Yapp Ruma,
G.G.Ponnambalam (Tam,il Congress).

SUDAN

6221: Any Anya
Description: a mainly Christian negro movement of the south which
opposed northern Moslem rule. It was mainly active in the form of
sporadic skirmishes.

6158: Noba Mountain Front
Description: guerrilla movement operating from Ethiopia and trained by
Libya. Estimated strength: sveral hundred men.

6050: Sudanese National Front (SNF)

6223: Sudanese Progressive Front

6139: Sudanese Socialist Union (SSU)

SURINAM

1185: Action Committee to Restore Democracy in Surinam

(Actie Comité Herstel Democratie Suriname)
Description: organisation which has as its goal the violent overthrow of
the Bouterse regime. It represents a section Surinam people living in
the Netherlands and has a crisis center in Amsterdam-Osdorp.
Leadership: Rob Wormer.

1186: Council for the Liberation of Surinam
(Raad voor de Bevrijding van Suriname)
Description: an organisation with the aim to bring down the Bouterse
regime. The question whether armed means should be used has been
left open until now.
Date of formation: Jan.5, 1983.
Leadership: Chin a Sen (ex-President and ex-Prime-minister)

1187: League of Surinam Patriots
(Liga van Surinaamse Patriotten)

1141: Revolutionary People's Front (RPF)
Description: an amalgamation of radical army officers and several
leftwing parties launched in Nov. 1981.

1174: Surinam Liberation Platform
(Surinaams Bevrijdings Platform)

SWAZILAND

5030: Swazi Liberation Front (SWALIMO)

SWEDEN

3028: B-26

3119: KFML(R)

3087: NRP
Description: extreme rightist movement involved in intimidations of
immigrants and the destruction of their property.

3118: Nysvenska Rörelsen

3117: SKP (SKP)

3116: Slavic Mission

SWITZERLAND

2241: Armed Propaganda Union (MSPB)

2073: Les Beliers de Jura

2265: European New Order
(Ordre Nouveau Européen)
Description: extreme rightist movement.

2162: Movement of the Discontented

2074: Petra Kraus Group

2271: Rassemblement Jurassiens

SYRIA

6125: Alawite Sect of Islam

6211: Baath Party
Description: formally known as the Regional Command of the Arab Social
Renaissance Party (Hizb al-Baath al-'Arabi al-Ishtiraki). The Baath
party is the Syrian branch of an international political movement
that began in 1940 and remains active in Iraq and a number of other
Arab countries. The contemporary party dates from a 1953 merger of
the Arab Resurrectionist Party, founded in 1947 by Michel Aflak and
Salah al-Din Bitar and the Syrian socialist Party, founded in 1950
by Akram al-Hurani. The Baath philosophy stresses socialist ownership
of the means of production, redistribution of agricultural land,
political unity of the Arab World and opposition to imperialism.
Leadership: Hafiz al-Assad (president of the republic, secretary
general of the party and chairman of the Progressive Front of
National Unity), 'Abdallah alAhmar (assistent secretary general).

6210: Communist Party of Syria
(al-Hizb al-Shuyu'i al-Suriyah)
Description: the consistently pro Moscow CP is technically illegal but
is permitted to operate openly and has been represented in the cabinet
since 1966.
Leadership: Khalid Baqdash.

6083: Militia of the Syrian National Social Party (SNSP)
Estimated strength: 3000 men.

6126: Moslem Brotherhood
(Ikhwan al-Muslimin)
Leadership: Hisham Jumbaz (military chief) was killed Aug. 17, 1980 in
a battle with the government forces. Issam al Attar was killed in
Mar. 1980 in Achen (Germany).
Remarks: the organization has been the object of severe repression.
Several massacres have been reported. In Feb. 1982 the whole old
city of Hama was destroyed by government forces, following an uprising.

6266: National Alliance Charter for the Liberation of Syria

TAIWAN

7185: Formosa Movement

7184: People's Liberation Front

7183: World United Formosans for Independence

TANZANIA

5092: Revolutionary Party of Tanzania

THAILAND

8019: Committee for the Coordination of Patriotic and Democracy Loving
Forces (CCPDF)
Description: a movement formed by the CPT and dissident members of
the socialist Party and United Socialist front in support of
guerrilla operations in the north, northeast and south, where the
Thai Moslem People's Liberation Army was also established under
Communist leadership. During 1979 the conflict between Kampuchean
and Vietnamese forces had an adverse effect on the Thai insurgents
along the Kampuchean border.A number of reports indicated that
fighting had broken out between pro Beijing and pro Hanoi factions
within the CCPDF.
Date of establishment or first appearance: 1977.

8020: Communist Party of Thailand (CPT)
Description: guerrilla movement which has made efforts to expand its
base southwards into the central plains from Khao Khor, Nong Mae Na
and Khao Ya. Analysts consider that because 80 percent of the
guerrillas and their sympathizers are disaffected Hmong hill tribe
people there are ethnic barriers to their establishing a foothold
among lowland Thais. Strong rear base areas are located in the Phou
Hin Rong mountain complex.
Estimated strength: the movement is divided in several branches with
a total membership of about 3000 men. Surat Thani branch: 1040 men,
Nakon Si Thammarat branch: 820 men, Phattaung Trang Satun branch:
800 men and the Songkhla branch: 200 men.

8124: Communist Terrorist Organization (CTO)
Description: a movement which comprises activists of the Malayan CPM
driven north of the Malayan border. It is engaged in internecine feuds.
Estimated strength: 2000 to 3000 men (1982).

8063: Internal Security Operations Command (ISOC)
Description: an organization set up to plan the government's response
to the increasing activities of the CPT.Previously it was called the
Communist Operations Command (SOC). It was renamed when open
suppression of communists became unfashionable.

8065: Islamic Brotherhood Party
(Persatuan Pemuda Rakyat Islam) (PAPERI)
Description: a party set up by the CPM's 12th Regiment. It represents
an appeal to Malay and Pattani Moslems still reluctant to break with

traditional Islam. It is striving for a basic compatibility between
Marxist and islamic ideology.

8107: National Revolutionary Front
(Barisan Revolusion Nasional) (BRN)
Description: a pro Moscow movement committed to a broadly Islamic
socialist program looked at askance by both other groups (BNPP and
PULO). It seeks association of the Thai Moslem provinces with
Malaysia. It is working closely with the PULO in the jungle and
mountain ranges of Pattani and Narathiwat, close to the border
with Malaysia. Libya has recently urged PULO and BRN to merge.
Date of establishment or first appearance: 1962.
Leadership: Ustaz Abdul Karim ibn Haji Hasan, Jehku Baka (military
chief).
Estimated strength: according to intelligence sources 210 men. Other
sources reported a strength of 2300 armed men operating in Yala's
Bannang Sata district.

8108: Pattani National Liberation Front
(Barisan Nasional Pembebasan Pattani) (BNPP)
Description: a guerrilla movement operating in southern Thailand
and sometimes referred to as the National Liberation Front Pattani
(NLFP). Its objectives are to liberate the homeland of the moslem
people of Pattani from the Thai colonists. They want to re-establish
an independent and sovereign Islamic state of the Pattani, to uphold
and protect Islam as well as the Moslem race culture, traditions and
customs, to support and work closely with other Arab countries for
the advance of moslems all over the world and for world peace. They
consider themselves not separatist, since Pattani has once been
an independent kingdom, but want to regain the independence they
lost to the Thais in the early 19th century. According to the PULO
it received a fatal blow in 1976, its influence has since then been
minimal. This decline was related to the death of its former leader:
Tengku Jal Nasae. It is moving to a more radical Islamic position
influenced to some extent by the Iranian revolution.
Leadership: Tunku Sulaiman Mahmud, Por Yeh (military commander),
Bapa Idris (in charge of the army and the military council).
Estimated strength: according to Thai military intellligence 50 men.

8021: Pattani United Liberation Organization
(Petubohan Persatuan Pembebasan Pattani) (PULO)
Description: guerrilla movement operating in the southern provinces. It
stresses Islam, their Malay identity and their desire to win their own
merdeka (freedom) so as to make Islam the state religion. It maintains
a secretariat in Mecca and has good relations with the Middle East.
The Thai government considers them as bandits: poobaenggyaekpaendin
or those who split up the country. They receive political and military
support from Syria. Its founder, Tenku Biro (alias Kabir Abdul
Rahman) is also president of the unofficial government inexile of
the "Republic of Pattani". Its first armed attack was recorded on
April 3, 1976 when insurgents attacked a special duty police base in
the Yarmg district.
Date of establishment or first appearance: it was formed in 1967 in
Kelantan by Tunku Bira Kotanila, who spent many years studying in
Saudi Arabia and India.
Leadership: Hisham Abdul, a graduate of Cairo university who received

a six month guerrilla training course with the PLO in Syria. Ismail
Quazafi (military commander).
Estimated strength: it claimed a strength of 4000 armed guerrillas plus
6000 men who have received a basic training but are without arms. It
has four armies:
1. Angkatan Sri Hikmat in Naratwiwat province led by Baba Ya.
2. Angkatan Sri Negara in the Sadao Songkla region led by Nasir Ku
Hassan.
3. Angkatan Sri Pattani in Pattani province led by Quzafi Haji Ismail.
4. Angkatan Sri Takmas in Yala province led by Amri Mohammad.
According to Thai intelligence sources there are no more than 320 armed
guerrillas.

8111: Ranger Units
Description: special government units developed on the basis of
voluntary recruitment from areas where communists are active. The
men are given a crash weapon training course lasting about 45 days.
Issued with modern weapons they are sent back to the villages to mount
guerrilla operations against communist elements. In four years the
Ranger Force has grown to about 160 companies totalling 13 000 men.
They are expected to take over counter insurgency tasks from regular
army units by the end of 1982. The elite is located in Lop Buri at a
Special Warfare Center. The strategy of using guerrilla tactics to
counter a similar guerrilla warfare approach used by the CPT was
the brainchild of maj.gen. Chaowalit Yongchaiy.
Date of establishment or first appearance: 1978.
Estimated strength: 13 000 men.

8039: Red Gaur Movement
Description: extremist proto fascist organization founded to counter the
growing leftist movement in the nation's leading universities. It played
a decisive role in the bloody showdown at the Thammasat university in
Oct. 1976. Members act as guards for civilian construction crews
building roads through communist areas in Tak, Chiang Rai and Nan
province.
Date of establishment or first appearance: 1974.
Leadership: maj.gen. Sudsai Hasdin, a self-styled political policeman
now retired.

8022: Thai People's Liberation Armed Forces (TPLAF)
Description: pro Beijing guerrilla movement active in northern and
central Thailand. It is the military wing of the CPT. It has some
Chinese backing but the insurgency's indigenous infrastructure make
it partly independent of external logistic support.
Estimated strength: 8000 to 15 000 men.

TOGO

4072: Togolese Democratic Movement
(Mouvement Togolais pour la Democratie) (MTD)

TUNESIA

6213: Islamic Trend Movement (ITM)
Description: semi clandestine movement.
Date of establishment or first appearance: early 1970's.
Leadership: Rashed Ghannoushi, who has been in solitary confinement
since Sep. 1981. In July 1981 106 of its top membership were arrested.
Twentyfour served a few months in jail while 82 received prison
terms ranging between two and 19 years.

6051: Popular Unity Movement (MUP)

6264: Rassemblement Socialist Tunesien

6052: Tunesian Communist Party

6053: Tunesian Movement of Social Democrats (MTDS)

6212: Tunesian Resistance Army
Description: group which was involved in the Gafsa attack Jan. 1980,
in which 41 people were killed and 111 injured.

TURKEY

6054: Acilciler

6236: Alevis

6161: Apocular

6088: Apoists

6055: Armenian Liberation Army

6263: Armenian National Liberation Army

6056: Avengers of the Armenian Genocide

6159: Avengers for Turkish Islamic Unity
Description: extreme leftwing movement striving for an islamic
revolution.

6247: Committee for Antifascist Unity (BIRKOM)

6246: Devrimci Sol

6266: Devrimci Dogu Kültür Ocaklari (DDKO)

6214: Eagles of the Revolution

6057: Front for the Liberation of Armenia

6164: Grey Wolves

Description: fascist movement linkedto the National Action Party (MHP)
which has been involved in killing immigrant workers in European
countries. In the Netherlands its headquarter is said to be in
Rotterdam.

6241: Hizb-i-Islam

6240: Hizb-üt-Tahrir

6155: Idealist Clubs

6058: Justice Commando of the Armenian Genocide

6134: Kawa
Description: a Kurdish group.

6255: Kurdish Workers Party

6253: Leftist Liberation Army of Turkish Workers and Farmers

6166: Liberation Army of Oppressed Turks (ETKO)

6060: Marxist Leninist Armed Propaganda Squadron (MLSPB)
Description: military branch of the Party Front for the Liberation of
Turkish People. It has been involved in the killing of four Americans.
Leadership: Zeki Yumurtaci, assassinated in Istanbul Sep. 17, 1980.

6061: Mayir Cayan Suicide Group

6070: May 28 Armenian Organization

6265: Milliyctci Isciler Sendikalari Konfederasyonu (MISK)

6245: Milli Istihbarat Teskilati (MIT)
Description: Turkish intelligence.

6215: National Action Party
(Millyetci Hareket Partisi) (MHP)
Description: an ultra nationalist party known until 1969 as the
Republican Peasant National Party. The MHP was first formed in 1948
by conservative dissidents from the old Democratic Party. It was
dissolved in 1953 and reformed in 1954 when it merged with the
Turkish Peasant Party. It sustained the secession of the Nation
Party in 1962.
Leadership: col. Alparslan Turkes (president) and Nevzat Kösoglu
(secretary general).

6258: National Movement Party (HERGUN)

6062: New Armenian Resistance Group

6126: October Three Organization
Description: Armenian organisation formed to attack Swiss offices
following the arrest in Geneva of two members of the ASALA Oct.3,
1980.

6066: Party for the Liberation of the Turkish People (TPLF)

6244: Partizan

6133: People's Revolutionary Vanguard

6257: Progressive Youth Association

6242: Red Armenian Army

6087: Revolutionary Left
(Dev Sol)
Description: pro Moscow movement active in the country side.

6086: Revolutionary Path Organization
(Dev Yol)

6141: Revolutionary Trades Union Federation
(Devrimci Isci Sendikalari Konfederasyonu) (DISK)

6216: Revolutionary Youth Movement
(Devrimci Genclik Dernekleri Federasyonu)
(Dev Genc)
Description: eclectic leftwing organization. Its main leaders were
arrested   and sentenced in 1971.

6163: Rizgari
(Liberation)
Description: clandestine movement.

6260: Road Ideals Group

6217: RPP

6063: Secret Armenian Army for the Liberation of Armenia (ASALA)
Description: Armenian group held responsible for a number of terrorist
attacks directed at Turkish targets in a great number of different
countries. It probably had its headquarters in Beirut.
Leadership: Ara Yenikomoushian and Hagop Hagopian (military leader
and main spokesman). The latter probably died during the Israeli
bombardments on Beirut June 31, 1982.

6064: Slave Kortin Yanikian Group

6256: Sunni Elements

6252: Turkish Communist Party, Marxist-Leninist

6069: Turkish Communist Party
(Türkiye Komünist Partisi) (TKP)
Description: pro Moscow party proscribed since 1925. It claims a
membership of 1250 in addition to several thousand sympathizers.
Its headquarters is located in eastern Europe and is staffed by
exiles and refugees who left Turkey in the 1930's and 1940's.

6160: Turkish Communist Party-Marxist Leninist-TIKKO
(TKP-ML-TIKKO)

6089: Turkish Revolutionary Communist Union

6262: Turkish Moslem Unity

6067: Turkish Revolutionaries

6165: Turkish Revenge Brigades (TIT)

6068: Turkish Revolutionary Youth Federation (UGD)

6167: Turkish Thunder Commandos (TYK)

6261: Turkish Workers and Peasants Liberation Army

6071: Yanikian Commandos

UGANDA

5049: Democratic Party (DP)

5093: Karamojong and Turkana Cattle Raiders

5056: Movement for the Struggle for Political Rights (MSPR)

5094: National Resistance Movement (NRM)
Description: a movement created to resist the Obote government. It
was formed by a merger of PRA, UFM, UFF, UNLFIW and ULG. It is
mainly supported by the Baganda, Bayankole and Bantu tribes. Its
armed wing is called the National Resistance Army (NRA) and is
active against police and army in the north west of Uganda.
Date of establishment or first appearance: May 2, 1981.
Leadership: Lule and Museveni.
Estimated strength: 5000 men.

5045: People's Revolutionary Army (PRA)

5115: Revolutionary Youth Movement

5109: Tanzania People's Defense Forces (TPDF)
Description: Tanzanian troops which after having brought the situation
under control mainly functioned as a police force in Kampala.

5097: Uganda Freedom Fighters (UFF)
Leadership: Yusuf Lule (ex president)

5046: Uganda Freedom Movement (UFM)
Description: a movement which announced the armed struggle against
the Obote government Feb.9, 1981. Jan.7, 1982 a merger was announced
with the NRM-NRA and UNRF to cooperate within the Ugandan Popular
Front.
Date of establishment or first appearance: June 1979.
Leadership: B.K.Kirya, dr.A.K.Kayiira (ex minister of interior) and
dr.A.Bisase.

5099: Uganda Liberation Group (ULG)

5031: Uganda National Liberation Front (UNLF)
Description: a coalition of several external based opposition groups.
Date of establishment or first appearance: Mar. 1979 in Moshi
(Tanzania) during a meeting of Ugandan exiles.
Leadership: Ysufu Kironde Lule.

5047: Uganda National Liberation Army (UNLA)
Description: it represents the military arm of the revived UPC and
consists of a force loyal to Chief of Staff Lt.Col.Oyite-Ojo and
UNLA commander Col. Tito Okello. It has been able to consolidate
its hold among the Acholi and Lango tribes in the north. It is
based in the Banyankore region in the west. Some 40 percent of the
UNLA remained loyal to Yoweni Museveni the minister of regional
cooperation who was dismissed from the Defense Ministry by Binaisa
in an otherwise unsuccessful bid to reshuffle the commission
in Nov. 1979.
Estimated strength: 3000 men.

5098: Uganda National Liberation Front Internal Wing (UNLFIW)

5095: Uganda National Rescue Front (UNRF)
Description: a front which comprises three groups of remnants from
Amin's army, predominantly from the Kakwa and Aringa tribes.
Leadership: UPC secretary-general Felix Onama and former minister
of finance Brig.Moses Ali.
Estimated strength: 4000 to 5000 men.

5048: Ugandese Patriotic Movement (UPM)
Leadership: Yuweni Museveni.
Remarks: it has a program based on scientific socialism.

5116: Uganda People's Congress (UPC)
Description: a Langi based party with a program based on pragmatic
socialism.
Leadership: Milton Obote.
Remarks: it was accused of killing DP candidates and establishing an
army of northern tribes with the help of Tanzania in order to take
over power violently in case Obote would loose the elections.

5063: Uganda Popular Front (UPF)

UNITED KINGDOM

2163: Angry Brigade
Description: anarchist group involved in bomb attacks in 1971.

2263: Animal Rights Militia
Description: group which claimed responsibility for a numer of bomb
letters in 1983.

2215: Anti-Nazi League

2075: Black Liberation Army

2164: British Movement
Description: neo-fascist movement.

2090: Free Wales

2165: League of St. George
Description: rightwing group.

2235: Militant Tendency

2208: Monday Club

2212: Movement for the Defense of Wales

2084: National Front (NF)
Description: neo-fascist movement.

2108: Scottish Republican Socialist League

2210: Scottish Nationalist Party
2085: Socialist Workers Party

2209: Tartan Army

2213: Trade Union Congress

2166: Workers Army of the Republic of Wales

2211: Young Militants

UNITED STATES

0077: Black Panther Party for Self Defense (BPP)
Description: extreme left anti white movement. By 1971 it was in
disarray and in May it swore off violent tactics in order to work
"within the system".

0078: Black Revolutionary Assault Team

0302: Central Intelligence Agency (CIA)

0256: Croation Liberation Fighters
Description: an underground group which supports a free and
independent Croation state and the break up of the Yugoslavia.
Active in the USA in 1980.

0079: Hanafi Moslems

0080: Hungarian Peace and Freedom Fighters

0081: International Committee Against Nazism

0082: Jewish Action Movement

0083: Jewish Armed Resistance

0084: Jewish Armed Resistance Strike Force

0085: Jewish Armed Resistance Strike Unit

0087: Jewish Committee of Concern

0088: Jewish Defense League
Remarks: an important member is Rabbi Meir Kahane.

0089: Jewish Defense League (Wrath of God)

0090: Jewish Underground Army

0146: Ku Klux Klan (KKK)
Description: extreme rightist racist movement.

0148: May 19 Coalition
Description: a terrorist group named after the birthday of Ho Chi Minh.
An all purpose merger joining the Weathermen, BLA and FALN. It is
alleged that it had received arms, training and day to day back up
services from Cuba.

0297: Minutemen

0292: National Socialist White People's Party

0147: National Urban League

0091: New Jewish Defense League

0092: New World Liberation Front

0093: Pan Epirotic Federation of America and Canada

0298: Posse Comitatus
Description: extreme rightist vigilante group.

0094: Red Guerrilla Family

0095: Republic of New Africa

0096: Revolution Action Party

0097: Revolutionary Affinity Group Six

0098: Revolutionary Communist Party- Committee to Give a Fitting
Welcome

0099: Revolutionary Force Seven

0259: Revolutionary People's Communication Network (PPCN)
Description: pro Beijing Algiers based splinter of the BPP.
Leadership: Elridge Clevaer.

0100: Save Our Israel Land (SOIL)

0101: Student Struggle for Soviet Jewry

0257: Symbionese Liberation Army (SLA)
Description: a terrorist organization consisting of three independently
operating teams of three persons.
Leadership: teamleaders were Donald de Freeze, William Harris and Nacy
Ling Perry.

0102: United Americans

0103: United Revolutionary soldiers of the Council of Reciprocal Relief
Alliance for Peace Justice and Freedom Everywhere

0104: Weathermen
Description: a pro Beijing terrorist movement which has remained
underground   since 1970.

0105: White Panthers

URUGUAY

1176: Anti Subversive Operations Coordinating Organization (OCOA)

1063: Armed Popular Front (FAP)

1180: Defense Intelligence Service (SID)

1142: Independent Armed Revolutionary Movement
(Movimiento Independista Revolucionario Armado) (MIRA)

1143: Militant Socialist Group
(Agrupacion de Militantes Socialistas) (AMS)

1162: MMM

1064: National Liberation Movement, Tupamaros
(Movimiento de Liberacion Nacional) (MLN)
Description: movement named after the legendary Tupac Amaru. After
the failure of urban insurgency in the early 1970's several hundred
Tupamaros went to Cuba where they were provided with training in
tactics, weapons and intelligence. They have participated in
intelligence operations in Europe and Latin America and in the
Internationalist brigade.
After a final shoot out with the army in April 1972 more than 1000
members were captured. It had some popular support after a number
of spectacular actions. It also developed a sort of underground
society .
Date of establishment or first appearance: it first appeared in 1962
but stepped up its armed actions in 1969.
Leadership: Raoul Sendic.
Estimated strength: 800 to 1000 men in 1971.

1065: Organization of the Popular Revolution-33 (OPR-33)

1066: PCU

1067: Raoul Sendic International Brigade

1144: Six Point Movement
(Movimiento de Seis Puntos)
Description: alleged offshoot of the MLN said to be active in 1980.
Estimated strength: 500 members.

1146: Unifying Action Group
(Grupa de Accion Unificado) (GAU)

1145: Union of Communist Youth
(Union de la Juventud Comunista)
Description: offshoot of the pro Moscow Uruguayan CP whose leaders
have been arrested or exiled.

VANUATU

8040: Party of Our Land
(Vanuaaku Pati)

9930: Republic of Vemarana

9929: Secret Army
(l'Armee Secrete)

VENEZUELA

1147: Americo- Silva Front
Description: armed branch of the underground Bandera Roja movement.

1068: Argimirio Gabaldon Revolutionary Command

1069: Armed Forces of National Liberation
(Fuerzas Armadas de Liberacion Nacional) (FALN)
Description: pro Havana rural guerrilla group which has been
fragmented and dormant since 1977.
Leadership: Douglas Bravo, accepted presidential amnesty Nov. 1979
and returned to Caracas.

1149: M-28
Description: small leftist guerrilla group whose existence was reported
in Valencia Aug. 1980.

1078: Manuel Rojos Lusardo Commando

1070: Movement of Revolutionary Left
(Movimiento de la Izquierda Revolucionaria) (MIR)
Description: pro Havana guerrilla movement but now fragmented. It

has been sporadically active in urban areas but was weakened by desertions in 1970. In 1971 it carried out kidnappings and bankraids.

1148: Popular Revolutionary Movement
(Movimiento Popular Revolucionaria) (MPR)
Description: leftist rural guerrilla group emerging in eastern Venezuela in 1978. No activities were reported during 1979 and 1980.

1071: Red Flag
(Bandera Roja)
Description: Marxist-Leninist splinter group of the FALN. It rejected the Nov. 1979 amnesty extended by president Herrera. Minor activities and plane highjackings in December were recorded in 1981.
Leadership: brothers Carlos and Argenis Betancourt (until their capture in 1977).

1161: Revolutionary Movement for the Caribbean Area

1151: Revolutionary Party of Venezuela   .
(Partido de la Revolucion Venezolana) (PRV)
Description: former guerrilla leader Douglas Bravo ("disappeared" in Feb. 1980).

1085: Tactical Fighting Union
(Unidades Tacticas de Combate) (UTC)

1150: Zero Point
(Punto Cero)
Description: Marxist urban guerrilla group. It rejected the Nov. 1979 presidential amnesty and resurfaced in Jan. 1981.

VIETNAM

8115: Catholic Resistance

8109: Committee for National Salvation
Description: first anti government movement to be created after 1975. It is pro Beijing and the first component of a future Indochinese United front. It is open to everybody opposed to Hanoi's dictatorship, without taking into account former positions. It was formed in the USA and aims to overthrow the communist government.
Leadership: Truang Nhu Tang, minister of justice in the former Provisonal Revolutionary Government of South Vietnam who spent seven years as a guerrilla in the jungle until 1975.

8113: Hoa Hoa Self Defense Forces

8110: HX-47
Description: a resistance movement which operates in the border towns with Kampuchea. It is involved in acts of sabotage and attacks directed at the communist regime. It is led by a former major of the army under the old regime.

8114: Montagnards

8024: National Liberation Front (NLF)

8025: North Vietnam National Fatherland Front (NFF)
Description: a front which operates in Ca Mau, the extreme south of
South Vietnam.

8112: Secret Armed Group
Description: a group which operates near the northern border with China.
In 1980 it was reported that it had captured the historical Pak Bo cave,
the former headquarters of Ho Chi Minh.

8044: United Front for the Struggle of Oppressed Races
(Front Uni pour la Lutte des Races Opprimeés) (FULRO)
Description: guerrilla movement active in the South Vietnamese central
highlands. It consists mainly of pro Beijing hill tribes which have fellow
tribes in China. Yet also catholics as the Cao Dai and Hoa Hao
participate in the front. They are organizing operations along the
northern border where they have trained thousands of tribesmen
politically and militarily. Until 1975 it was supported by the USA
and since 1979 by China.
Date of establishment or first appearance: 1960's.

8023: Vietnam Communist Party
(Dang Cong san Viêtnam) (VCP)
Description: party which operated for many years as the Vietnamese
Workers' Party (VWP). This party was formed in 1954 as successor
of the Indochinese Communist Party (founded in 1930 and ostensibly
dissolved in 1954) and was the controlling party of North Vietnam's
National Fatherland Front.
In South Vietnam, the core of the Provisional Revolutionary
Government formed in 1969 was the National Liberation Front (NLF),
which was organized in 1960 by some 20 groups opposed to the
policies of president Diem. On July 6, 1976 representatives of the
NFF, the NLF and other organizations met at Hanoi to organize an all
inclusive National United Front (NUF) which was formally launched
during a congress held at Ho Chi Minh City on Jan. 31-Feb. 4, 1977.
Date of establishment or first appearance: 1954.
Leadership: Le Duan (secretary-general).

WESTERN SAHARA

4053: Anti POLISARIO (AOSARIO)
Description: a 100 men strong Moroccan special unit, led by a US
mercenary Ed Moha who worked before in Mauretania, Libya and Algeria.
With this unit he organized an attack on Tindouf, a POLISARIO
training camp in Algeria.

4077: Liberation Front of the Sahara under Spanish Domination
(Front de Liberation du Sahara sous Domination Espagnole) (FLSDE)

4075: Liberation Movement of Saquiet el-Hamra and Rio de Oro

4055: Liberation Movement for Western Sahara
Description: announced Dec. 23, 1981 in Madrid. Its secretary general,

Sidahmaed Mohammed Larosi, declared it operated already since 1975 in Sahraouis refugee camps in Tindouf.

4037: Liberation and Unity Front
(Front de Liberation et de l'Unité) (FLU)

4076: Moslem Party (NIDHAM)

4073: Movement of August 21
(Mouvement du 21 Aout)

4078: Movement for the Liberation of the Sahara
(Mouvement pour la Liberation du Sahara) (MLS)

4030: Mustafa el Wadi Bayyid Sayed International Brigade

4079: Organization for the Liberation of Saquiet el-Hamra and Oued el-Dahab (OSLHOD)

4039: Party of National Sahraouis Unity
(Partido de Unidad Nacional Sarauis) (PUNS)

4038: Popular Front for the Liberation of Saguia el Hamra and Rio de Oro (POLISARIO)

4074: Revolutionary Movement of the Blue People
(Mouvement Revolutionnaire des Hommes Bleus) (MOREHOB)

4067: Saharan Arab Democratic Front

4040: Sahraouis Popular Liberation Army
(Armée Populaire de Liberation Sahraoui) (ALPS)

YEMEN (ADEN)

6267: National Unification Army

6072: National Democratic Front (NDF)

YEMEN (SANA)

6222: Eagles of National Unity

6074: Front for the Liberation of Occupied South Yemen (FLOSY)

6220: National Grouping of Patriotic Forces
Description: opposition group announced in Bagdad Mar.26, 1980.

6073: National Liberation Front (NLF)
Description: went into exile.

6075: Popular Democratic Union

Description: communist oriented party.

6076: Popular Vanguard Party
Description: a Baath group.

6218: United National front for South Yemen
Description: Cairo based exile group which maintains opposition to the
present regime.

6077: United Political Organization National Front (UPONF)
Description: in Oct. 1975 the NLF joined with the Popular Vanguard
Party and the Popular Democratic Union in UPONF. In 1978 it was
supplanted by the Yemen Socialist Party.

6219: Yemen Socialist Party (YSP)
Description: a Marxist-Leninist vanguard party modelled on the
Communist Party of the Soviet Union. Its supreme organ is a Congress,
which meets every five years, though extraordinary sessions may be
called by the 51 member Central Committee or by one third of all
party members. The Central Committee which is elected by the Congress,
in turn elects a General Secretariat, functional committees and a
nine member Polit Bureau, where effective power resides.
Date of establishment or first appearance: Oct.11, 1978.
Leadership: 'Abd al-Fatta Isma'il.

YUGOSLAVIA

3051: Albanian Independence Movement

3098: Cominformist Congress

3097: Croatian Revolutionary Brotherhood

3031: Croatian National Liberation Forces- Fighters for a Free Croatia

3032: Croatian National Resistance

3030: Croatian Intelligence Service

3033: Freedom for the Serbian Fatherland

3127: Hrvatska Revolucja

3127: Sluzba Drzavne Bezbednosti (SDB)

3034: Trotskyite Organization

3088: USTASHE
Description: autonomist Croation movement active in emigre circles.

3035: Young Croatian Army for Freedom

3036: Young Croatian Republican Army

ZAIRE

4058: Action Movement for the Resurrection of Congo
(Mouvement d'Action pour la Resurrection du Congo) (MARC)
Description: movement founded in Brussels to "end the neo-colonialist
regime of Mobutu". It has been involved in a coup attempt Feb.1978.
Date of establishment or first appearance: 1975.
Leadership: chairman Kanyonga Mobateli died in 1978 as a result of a
bullet of unknown origin.

4033: Congolese Liberation Organization
(Organisation du Liberation du Congo) (OLC)
Description: a bundling of five smaller opposition groups.
Date of establishment or first appearance: Oct. 9, 1978.
Leadership: Mbeka Makosso, who has been former ambassador to Iran.

4044: Congolese National Liberation Front
(Front de Liberation du Congo) (FLNC)
Description: a merger of PRP and PRMC which has been involved in the
two Shaba invasions. It is predominantly Kantangese and dedicated to
the armed struggle against Mobutu. July 3, 1980 the Council for the
Liberation of Congo Kinshasa was announced as a merger of FLNC, PRP,
PSZ and MNUR was announced.
Date of establishment or first appearance: Nov. 1975.
Leadership: Nathaniel Mbumba.

4059: Council for the Liberation of Congo-Kinshasa
(Conseil pour la Liberation du Congo-Kinshasa) (CLC)
Description: a merger of FLNC, PRP, PSZ and MNUR which was
announced July 3, 1980.
Leadership: Bernardin Mungul-Diaka.

4060: Kamanyola
Description: a special elite unit of Mobutu established in 1974 after a
visit to China and North Korea. It is trained by North Korean
instructors. There have been reports that 800 soldiers deserted
after mutual killings of instructors and soldiers.

4061: Marxist Revolutionary Party of Congo Kinshasa (PRMC)
Description: party whose military arm is called the Red People's
Army which has captured large areas in the east.
Leadership: Emmanuel Kasbassu-Balenga and Kibwe Thca Malenge.

4057: Military Committee for Resistance in Angola

4063: National Congolese Movement-Lumumba
(Mouvement National du Congo-Lumumba)
Description: movement which is based in Paris.
Leadership: Paul Roger Mokedi.

4062: National Movement for Unity and Reconciliation
(Mouvement National pour l'Union et la Réconciliation) (MNUR)
Description: a movement which was launched in Brussels by Klebka
Makosso, former minister of finance. It is supported by the
MNC-Lumumba.

4036: National Revolutionary Movement (MNR)

4034: People's Army of the Oppressed in Zaire

4035: People's Revolutionary Party
(Parti Revolutionaire de Peuple Zairois) (PRP)
Description: pro Beijing Marxist-Leninist movement which operates in
the eastern mountain areas (Fizi-Baraka) since 1967. Since 1969 is
has been active as a guerrilla movement. Its army operates under
the name of the Peoples Armed Forces (FAP) and received no support
from outside until 1975. Contacts with the FLNC exist.
Leadership: Laurent Kabila, Antoine Gizenga. The latter stays abroad
(Prague and Moscow) since 1965.

4065: Zairan Socialist Party
(Parti Socialiste Zairois) (PSZ)
Leadership: Tramambu Mobu (secretary general).

ZIMBABWE

5100: African National Council-Sithole (ANC-Sithole)
Description: formed by Sithole who returned from exile to organize the
rump of ZANU followers behind an internal settlement with UANC and
ZUPO.
Date of establishment or first appearance: 1977.
Leadership: Sithole.

5055: Common Wealth Cease Fire Force
Estimated strength: 1300 soldiers.

5032: Front for the Liberation of Zimbabwe (FROLIZI)

5101: Gukurahundi
Description: a special unit for combatting internal unrest trained by
North Korean instructors.

5033: Patriotic Front (PF)
Description: set up in response to Anglo-American proposals which led
to the abortive Geneva conference. Consisted of ZAPU and ZANU. Despite
an agreement on a joint command signed in May 1979 in Ethiopia the
two movements maintained separate identities and military forces.

5102: Selous Scouts
Description: a special elite unit under the Smith regime. After the
installation of the Mugabe government almost all left to South Africa.
About 25 soldiers were of US nationality.
Estimated strength: 700 soldiers.

5103: Spear of the People
(Pfumo Revanhu)
Description: auxiliary private armies set up by black leaders as part of
the security forces.
Estimated strength: 8000 soldiers.

5105: United African National Council (UANC)
Description: a party which is accused of having an army in South Africa.
Leadership: bishop Abel Muzorewa.

5104: United National Federal Party (UNFP)
Description: tribal grouping formed in 1978 to contest the 1979 interim
elections under senator Kaysia Ndiweni in Matabele.

5035: Zimbabwe African National Liberation Army (ZANLA)
Description: military wing-of the ZANU.

5107: Zimbabwe African National Union (ZANU)
Description: founded by Ndabaningi Sithole from dissident ZAPU
members. Primarily responsible for guerrilla activity until 1976.
That year Robert Mugabe took over the leadership and found support
in Mozambique.
Date of establishment or first appearance: 1963.
Leadership: Robert Mugabe.

5106: Zimbabwe African People's Union (ZAPU)
Description: a party founded by Joshua Nkomo and based in Zambia
until about 1980. It built a disciplined guerrilla force in a later
stage but never engaged its full military strength inside Zimbabwe.
Date of establishment or first appearance: 1961.
Leadership: Joshua Nkomo.

5034: Zimbabwe's People's Revolutionary Army (ZIPRA)
Description: military wing of the ZAPU.

5036: Zimbabwe Reformed African National Council

5108: Zimbabwe United People's Organization (ZUPO)
Description: formed in 1977 by senator chief Chirau to work for an
internal settlement.

IV: LITERATURE

LITERATURE

The Literature of Terrorism

The literature of terrorism is young, most studies have been written
in the last fifteen years. Despite its volume - several thousand
titles, not counting fictional and ephemeral journalistic writings
- its substance is less than impressive. Much of the writing is im-
pressionistic, anecdotal, superficial and at the same time often also
pretentious, venturing farreaching generalizations on the basis of
episodical evidence. The subject matter is not one which invites dis-
passionateness and the eagerness to condemn has often hindered authors
to come to a deeper understanding of terrorism. Practically all authors
who write on the subject of terrorism today are opposed to terrorism
and have not practised terrorism themselves. From the point of view
of an intellectual discourse on the subject this is regrettable. Most
of us would find it strange if all books on war were written by paci-
fists and therefore welcome some books by generals. Not so with terrorism. The fact is that advocates of terrorism have gone underground
and their theoretical writings - if they produce many - are inacces-
sible. Works like Leon Trotsky's The Defence of Terrorism - Terrorism
and Communism, A Reply to Karl Kautsky (London, George Allen and
Unwin, 1935), have become rare in the last fifteen years.
The literature on terrorism is not the product of a single discipline.
Rather scholars from different fields such as psychology, criminology,
law, political science, sociology, history and the military sciences
have contributed to it. But these writers have often not taken cogni-
zance of each others work when it is from another discipline-which
might go some way to explain the lack of cumulativeness in the literature of terrorism. Rather than leaning towards each other to advance
the state of knowledge, authors from academia have leaned in one of
two directions: towards journalism, where most of their data came
from, or towards the anti-terrorist agencies of government which
sought and gave advice and guidance. The operative community has however not made much use of academic authors. They have either cultivated
their in-house researchers or hired the services of commercial
think-tanks - at least in the United States, where more than three
quarter of the literature is produced. The result has been that there
is now a classified literature on terrorism of some size. Those few
researchers sitting on the fence, with one leg in the academic and

the other in the operative sector, are having the best of both worlds
and are often leading authors.

In our questionnaire we asked our respondents to list the twenty
leading authors on the subject of terrorism in declining order of
importance. Altogether some 200 different authors were mentioned by
our respondents, whose average list contained only ten names. Because
some refused to rank them - reasonably enough for the leading authors
can be prominent or important without being both - we only counted the
mentionings (see Table XI).

Table XI: Leading Authors in the Field of Terrorism, Based on Frequency
of Being Mentioned by Fifty Authors in the Field.

20-25 mentionings	Jenkins, Wilkinson, Laqueur, Alexander
15-19 mentionings	Bell
10-14 mentionings	Gurr, Crozier, Walter, Kupperman, Mickolus, Clutterbuck, Bassiouni
5-9 mentionings	Murphy, Evans, A.E., Thornton, Chomsky, Friedlander, R.A., Crenshaw, Green, Paust, Rapoport, Sundberg, Ochberg
3-4 mentionings	Gross, Russell, Harkabi, Merari, Stohl, Ferrarotti, Arendt, Bonanate, Cooper, Sterling, Tromp, O'Brien, Moore, Miller, Lasswell, Janke, Feierabend & Feierabend, Heyman, Hobsbawn, Hacker.

+ The 50 respondents mentioned a total of 520 names, of which 199 were
different names. Within the five categories above those authors mentioned first received more mentionings than those mentioned towards
the end. Nine of our respondents belong to the "leading" authors mentioned here.

The four authors receiving the most mentionings are all to varying
extents advisors to governmental agencies. Jenkins' works for Rand,
Laqueur and Alexander are associated with the Georgetown Centre of
Strategic and International Studies and Wilkinson has also been linked to
anti-terrorist activities. Bell on the other hand is a maverick standing
closer to the insurgent terrorists. He has taken the trouble to go to
Ireland, the Middle East and Africa to talk with the terrorists which
gives his books a rare authenticity appreciated by many respondents.

The four top authors receive much praise but also much blame from our respondents. On Laqueur, for instance, one of our respondents wrote, referring to his much-quoted work "Terrorism" (1977):

> "It is, essentially, a book on an unidentified subject, so that the author can include whatever he sees fit. It is an unreliable description of selected events and other matters pertaining to terrorism but without any purpose or conclusion."

And another:

> "So historically individualist as to deny the possibility of social scientific explanation as well as blind to state repression in the West."

Wilkinson generally receives higher marks than Laqueur. One respondent wrote, for instance, "A rare combination of a thorough knowledge of the subject matter (terrorism) and historical perspective, political understanding and common sense." Another, however, judges Wilkinson's writings as "counter-insurgency masquerading as political science." Yet another writes: "immature, normative opinions unsubstantiated by facts. Frequently wrong on facts". Jenkins' work is widely acknowledged to be innovative and imaginative, even by authors who do not share his views or his events approach. Alexander, on the other hand, while being appreciated by some for creating a forum for discussion in his journal Terrorism and in his numerous books, is not getting such high marks. "One-sided, sloppy, reactionary" is one comment. Another respondent says: "Commissions others to write for his publications, does not publish his own materials. His views express the synthesis of often disparate ideas gleaned from others." From the next level Walter and Mickolus get the highest marks. A typical comment on Walter is: "It is a sophisticated theoretical discussion which is based on history and traditional philosophical argument and sensitivity..." Mickolus is appreciated for his data-gathering efforts and his bibliographic work, although many are sceptical about the events approach which takes terroristic incidents as main elements for scientific analysis.

Opinions are also divided on lesser authors. Becker and Sterling, bestselling authors of "Hitler's Children" and "The Terror Network" respectively, received some praise and more condemnation from our respondents. Becker is blamed for her lack of any scholarly detachment and Sterling is getting even more blame: "One of the poorest exercises in the whole field of terrorist literature - an example of self- and government-serving, based on a pre-determined inadequately examined thesis."

The fact that the research community we sampled is so divided in its judgement seems partly politically motivated and partly an expression of an uncertainty about the way the subject should be approached. European authors have often much criticism on the American and sometimes also the British literature. One European author writes, for instance: "Most of the American and English stuff... is one-sided and concentrated on insurgent terrorism without referring to social causes", a view echoed by one American author who sees the literature in general as "Primarily an exercise in condemnation of resistance and an apology for state repression".

One American respondent holds that "the best minds in the academic community have not addressed themselves to the issue". There seems to be some truth in this but fashionable topics attract careerists in other fields as well.

However, the subject of terrorism is also a very difficult one, due to its emotive, secretive, sporadic nature and the limits it sets to conventional data-gathering techniques. The poor data-situation has had the unfortunate consequence that the same episodes are cited again and again as evidence. Few researchers have taken the trouble to make an in-depth case study of a single organization, movement or campaign. Instead they are jumping from one episode to the other (Munich, Entebbe, Mogadishu, Tehran, etc.), without due regard to context and the different roots of terrorists, which often makes unsatisfactory reading. While other areas of research in the social sciences are also not showing much cumulativeness and maturation, despite a longer research tradition, this can be no consolation. Give the amount of money put nowadays into the study of terrorism, the literature could be more innovative and less repetitive. Too much of it is also ideological and non-rigorous, in place of scientific.

In terms of research focus, left-wing terrorism has been given almost exclusive attention and the focus has often been on questions which are more interesting to secret services and counter-terrorist agencies than to the social sciences. Why insurgents are prepared to sacrifice lives, including their own, has been less often looked into than aspects of weaponry, logistics and organization. , as one German author has correctly noted. Insufficient attention has been given to terrorism in the 2nd and 3rd World, compared to the terrorism in the industrialized Western democracies. State-terrorism and Right-wing

terrorism and vigilante terrorism have also been neglected by the
majority of authors. International terrorism by states in continuation
of the colonial gunboat diplomacy has also not received the attention
it deserves.

The most general deficiency of most of the literature of terrorism is
that the terrorist organization or movement is studied in isolation
rather than in its socío-political context. A simultaneous study of
the terrorist organizations' adversary and his (re)actions are mandatory
for a full understanding of the dynamics of terrorism. This sound trivial
but has nevertheless largely been neglected.

Among the major research desiderata figure more in-depth case studies
based on some common format which allows to compare different cases
in a following stage of research. Comparative studies are the second
step to be taken and special attention should be given to compare
right- with left-wing movements and both with vigilante movements. The
same applies to state terrorism in the First, Second and Third World
which also should be approached in an analogous manner. When this has
been done, the stage is set for comparing state and non-state terrorism.
Such analysis will benefit if the terroristic strategies of government
and non-governmental actors are compared to their nonterroristic, nonviolent and legal ones. The alternatives open to them in each case to
defend or advance their vital basic needs as well as their relative
costs and benefits, should be taken into account. Last but not least
the feeling of terror itself as well as other feelings activated by
terrorism in various sectors of witnessing audiences should be
thoroughly investigated with an eye of developing coping mechanisms.

 Some work on all these and other aspects has already been done and
a familiarity with the existing literature will prevent that new
researchers entering the field are rediscovering the wheel again and
again. The following bibliography has been assembled for this purpose
and some remarks on its characteristics are in place here.

Introduction to the Bibliography

The present bibliography on terrorism is, to our knowledge, the most
comprehensive general bibliography currently available. It has grown
to its present size as a by-product of this writers research in the
field of terrorism since 1977. A compilation by a researcher rather
than a professional bibliographer has drawbacks as well as advantages.
The advantage is a greater familiarity with the subject-matter and a
selection on the basis of qualitative criteria. The major draw-back is
that uniformity of all titles could not be achieved since the systematic
search for missing publication details for all titles would have been
too time consuming.

The character of this bibliography can perhaps be explained best by
comparing it to its five nearest rivals:

> L. Bonanate. La Violenza Politica nel Mundo Contemporaneo.
> Bibliografia internazionale sul terrorismo, i movimenti di
> ribellione, la guerrilla, le guerre di liberazione, le lotte
> anti imperialistiche. Milano, Franco Angeli, 1979, 253 pp.

> F. Mickolus. The Literature of Terrorism. A Selectively Annotated
> Bibliography. Westport, Connecticut, Greenwood Press, 1980, 553 pp.

> A.R. Norton & M.H. Greenberg. International Terrorism: An Annotated
> Bibliography. Boulder, Colorado, Westview Press, 1980, 218 pp.

> M.J. Smith Jr. The Secret Wars: A Guide to Sources in English.
> Vol. III. International Terrorism, 1968-1980. Santa Barbara,
> California, ABC-Clio, 1980, 237 pp.

> V. Tutenberg & Ch. Pollak. Terrorismus - Gestern, Heute, Morgen.
> Eine Auswahlbibliographie. München, Bernard & Graefle Verlag für
> Wehrwesen, 1978, 298 pp.

The major difference with Smith's work is that a conscious effort has
been made to cover the non-English literature as well. While journalistic
articles form the main entries in Smith's bibliography, ours generally
excludes the journalistic production except in cases where there is
no other title available covering a particular aspect. Smith's
bibliography is divided into eight major categories, namely: (1)
Reference Works, General Works; (2) Violence and Terrorism, 1968-1979;
(3) Philosophy and Psychology of Terrorism; (4) Terrorist Tactics; (5)
Terrorist Armaments; (6) Domestic and International Support For and
Countermeasures Against Terrorism; (7) International Law and Terrorism
and (8) Terrorism Around the World, 1968-1980. The present bibliography

is putting less emphasis on international terrorism than does Smith and
it goes back in time further than 1968.

The selective bibliography of Tutenberg and Pollak is divided into nine
major categories: (1) Guerrilla Warfare, Revolutionary Struggle Terrorism;
(2) Counterinsurgency and Defense against Terrorism; (3) Psychological
Warfare; (4) Espionage, Method, Countermeasures; (5) Social and Political
Backgrounds as Trigger-off Mechanisms for Revolutionary Conflicts;
(6) Theorists and Actors of Guerrilla Warfare; (7) Revolutionary Warfare -
Constitutional Problems; (8) Guerrilla Warfare and Revolutionary Struggle
in the Past and Present of Individual States and (9) International
Terrorism.

The main data bases for this bibliography were the Library for
Contemporary History in Stuttgart, the Central Library of the German
Federal Army in Düsseldorf and the Martial Library in Stuttgart.

This work is heavily coloured by the last two data bases in its military
perspective. Wartime resistance by partisans, guerrilla warfare and
terrorism and even espionage and subversion are all thrown together.
The major usefulness of this bibliography stems from its coverage of
the German and American military literature. It is superior to our
bibliography in this regard since we treat "Terrorism from a Military
Prospective" and "Military and Police Countermeasures against Terrorism"
in less depth. Our own coverage of guerrilla warfare is also limited
to items fitting under the heading "Ideologies and Doctrines of Violence
and Violent Liberation".

The bibliography of Bonanate is divided into three major parts:
(1) Politics of Terrorism; (2) Terrorism and Law; (3) Geography of
Terrorism. It covers works published between 1945 and 1977, with a very
few exceptions dating further back. The books and articles cited are
from the Italian, French, English, German and Spanish literature. This is
a sober and useful bibliography, especially strong on the article-
literature. For works on Italian terrorism and books and articles on
other terroristic activities, written in Italian and French, this
bibliography is more exhaustive than ours.

Norton and Greenberg's bibliography is selectively annotated contrary
to Smith's, Bonanate's and Tuttenberg and Pollak's works. The
annotations are generally longer than ours, but the percentage of

annotated titles - about ten percent of all titles-is approximately
the same. This bibliography also covers "Terrorism in Fiction" (so does
Mickolus' bibliography) which ours does not. It is strong on the
Middle East and on "Nuclear Terrorism and Other Macro-Terror
Possibilities" but since it contains only about one thousand titles,
it is less thorough than our bibliography even on these topics. There
is strong emphasis on the English-language literature and on
international aspects relevant to the United States. It is divided into
23 sections, seven of them representing geographic regions and terroristic
activities there. Other specific sections are titled: Philosophic,
Ideologic and Moral Foundations of Terrorism (Section C), Anarchism
and Nihilism (Section D), Biography (Section E), Legal Perspectives
(Section F), Tactics (Section G), United Nations (Section I), Terrorist
International? (Section Q), Combatting Terrorism, Macro- and Micro-
Perspectives (Sections R and S), Surveys of the Literture (Section T),
Terrorism in Fiction (Section U) and Terror Campaigns (Section V).
Mickolus' bibliography is computer-based like ours. It was published
after our own data-gathering effort had already been well on the way.
Had this writer seen this massive and solid bibliography earlier, he
would probably have desisted from starting a bibliography of his own.
It is a broad study (including titles from about a dozen languages) and
we estimate that about sixty percent of his titles can also be found
in our work and vice versa. His annotations are more frequent than ours.
Besides an author's index Mickolus' bibliography also has a title's
index which ours has not. His bibliography is stronger on the legal
literature th..n ours, as well as on the grey literature of unpublished
conference papers. In addition he also has a selection on the fictional
literature and one referring to Events Data Research. Apart from the
sections (1) General Treatments; (2) Tactics of Terrorist; (3) Terrorist
and Guerrilla Philosophies (4) Links of Terrorist Groups; (5) Terrorism
by Geographic Area; (6) State Terrorism and (7) Responses, several
miscellaneous sections are added. These include "Media and Terrorism",
"Psychological and Medical Approaches to Terrorism" and "Guerrilla Warfare"
in addition to the ones on Fiction and Events Data mentioned above.
This is an excellent bibliography, reflecting its compilers' perspective
and policy-orientation. It is, however, covering fewer titles than our

bibliography and is not quite as detailed as ours on certain aspects
(such as state terrorism).

Having compared our bibliography to some others, little needs to be added.
Our bibliography is divided into twenty major categories (plus one for
Varia and Related Studies) and 46 subcategories. Three categories have
been subdivided: Terroristic Activities, by Region and Country; Countermeasures against Terrorism, and Special Forms of Terrorism. Each title
is placed in one of the categories or subcategories only once: there are
no duplicate listings even when a title can be rightfully assigned to two
or more categories. The title is cited under the category judged to be
most appropriate by this writer. Users of the computer-file of this
bibliography can, of course, retrieve items in different ways basing
themselves on categories to be constructed with the words contained in
the cited titles themselves.

It is our intention to keep the computer-file up-to-date and to publish
periodical supplements to this bibliography. The Terror File, based on
the Remote Information Query System (RIQS) programme, is stored at the
Social Science Information and Documentation Centre (SWIDOC) in Amsterdam
(Herengracht 410, 1017 BX Amsterdam) and can be consulted upon prior
permission from the Centre for the Study of Social Conflicts (C.O.M.T.,
Hooigracht 15, 2312 KM Leiden).

A. BIBLIOGRAPHIES ON TERRORISM AND RELATED FORMS OF VIOLENCE

1. **amnesty international.** amnesty international in print, 1962-1978. london: a. i., jan. 1979. a. i. index doc. 06/01/79.

2. **bander, e. j. * ryan, m. t. * (comp.).** bibliography on disorders and terrorism. in: national advisory committee on criminal justice standards and goals. "disorders and terrorism. " report of the task force on disorders and terrorism. washington d. c.: gpo, 1976. pp. 597-634 ca. 1250 items, partly annotated.

3. **blackey, r.** modern revolutions and revolutionists: a bibliography. santa barbara, calif.: clio books, 1976.

4. **blackstock, p. w. * schaf, f.** intelligence, espionage, counterespionage, and covert operations. a guide to information sources. detroit: gala research co., 1978. 255 pp.

5. **bock, h. m.** bibliographischer versuch zur geschichte des anarchismus und anarcho-syndikalismus in deutschland. frankfurt: 1973. pp. 295-334 jahrbuch der arbeiterbewegung 1 bibliography on anarchism in germany .

6. **bonanate, l. * et. al. * (eds.).** political violence in the contemporary world. international bibliography on terrorism, movements of rebellion, guerilla warfare, antiimperialistic struggles, the map of terrorism in the contemporary world. milan: f. angeli editore, 253 pp. covers period 1945 to 1977, with some later addenda. consists of 3 major parts. i: politics of terrorism ii: terrorism and law, iii: bibliography of terrorism.

7. **bonanate, l.** la violenza politica nel mondo contemporaneo. milano: angeli, 1979. 253 pp. selected bibliography for period 1945-1978.

8. **boston, g. d. * o'brien, k. * palumbo, j.** terrorism - a selected bibliography. 2nd ed. washington d. c.: national institute of- law enforcement and criminal justice, 1976. 69 pp. 168 annotated citations of items published in the period 1969-1976.

9. **boulding, e. * passmore, j. r. * gassler, r. s.** bibliography on world conflict and peace. second edition boulder, colo.: westview press, 168 pp. one of the 26 major categories covers terrorism.

10. **bourdet, y. * brohm, j. m. * dreyfus, m. r.** que lire? bibliographie de la revolution. paris: 1975. etudes et documentations internationales.

11. **bracher, k. d. * jacobson, h. a. * funke, m. * (eds.).** bibliographie zur politik in theorie und praxis. aktualisierte neuauflage bonn: 1976. bibliography with items on notstand, widerstand, gewalt, terror.

12. **chilcote, r. h.** revolution and structural change in latin america: a bibliography on ideology, development and the radical left, 1930-1965. 2 vols. stanford: hoover institution, 1970.

13. **condit, d. m. * et. al.** a counterinsurgency bibliography. washington d. c.: soro, 1963. 269 pp. a series of 6 supplements was published until 1965.

14. **cornog, d.** unconventional warfare: a bibliography of bibliografies. washington d. c.: 1964. prepared by the information technology division of the national bureau of standards. deals with unconventional warfare including counterinsurgency, guerila warfare, special warfare, and psychological operations.

15. **cosyns-verhaegen, r.** guerres revolutionnaires et subversives: selection bibliographique. brussels: les ours, 1967.

16. **deutsch, r.** northern ireland 1921-1974: a selected bibliography. new york: garland publishing, 1975.

17. **deutscher bundestag. wissenschaftliche dienste.** bibliographien. terrorismus und gewalt. auswahlbibliographie mit annotationen. bonn: deutscher bundestag, juli 1975. 86 pp. nr. 43 38 of the ca. 1100 titles are annotated.

18. **deutscher bundestag. wissenschaftliche dienste.** bibliographien. terrorismus und gewalt, 1975-1977. auswahlbibliographie.: februar 1978. 53 pp. nr. 49 few of the ca. 600 titles are annotated.

19. **devore, r. m.** the arab-israel conflict. a historical, political, social and military bibliography. oxford: clio press, 1977. ca. 288 pp.

20. **eckert, w. g. * (ed.).** international terrorism. wichita, kansas: the milton helpern international center for the forensic sciences., 1977. 23 pp. unannotated bibliography under 27 subject headings listing 515 items, predominantly legal.

21. **fallah, s. m.** a selected bibliography on urban insurgency and urban unrest in latin america and other areas.: 1966.

22. **fbi academy.** hostages. quantico, virg.: fbi academy library, june 1980. 8 pp. a bibliography on books, periodicals, films, video cassettes and other materials on the subject.

23. **fbi academy.** kidnapping. quantico, verg.: fbi academy library, june 1980. 7 pp. lists books, periodicals, articles, governmental documents, films on the subject.

24. **fbi academy.** terrorism. mimeo. quantico, virg.: fbi academy library, june 1980. 12 pp. a bibliography on books, periodicals newspaper, movie and other material o n the subject.

25. **felsenfeld, l. * jenkins, b. m.** international terrorism: an annotated bibliography. santa monica, cal.: rand, sept. 1973. lists a great deal of

ephemeral journalism and nonenglish literature.

26. goehlert, r. anarchism: a bibliography of articles, 1900-1975.: 1976. political theory 4:113.

27. institut henry-dunant * (ed.). bibliografie selective sur la violence et les actes de terrorisme. geneve : 1975.

28. jenkins, b. m. * johnson, j. * long, l. international terrorism: an annotated bibliography. santa monica : rand corporation, 1977. concentrates on journalistic articles.

29. kelly, m. j. * mitchell, t. h. violence, internal war and revolution; a select bibliography. ottawa: the norman paterson school of international affairs, carleton university., 1976. 496 items bibliography.

30. khalidi, w. * khadduri, j. * (eds.). palestine and the arab-israeli conflict. beirut: institute for palestine studies, and kuwait university of kuwait, 1974. bibliography numbering over 4500 entries.

31. kornegay jr., f. a. a bibliographic essay on comparative guerilla warfare and social change in southern africa.: 1970. pp. 5-20 a current bibliography on african affairs. 111(new series):2 covers scholarly works published since 1966 on union of south africa, southwestangola, mozambique and rhodesia.

32. kress, l. b. selected bibliography. in: m. livingston. * et. al. * (eds.) international terrorism in the contemporary world. westport, conn.: greenwood press, 1978. pp. 469-502.

33. learning resource center of the fbi academy. hostage situations. quantico: virginia, january 1975. 11 pp. 130- items, not annotated, mostly from u. s. magazines.

34. learning resource center of the fbi academy. terroristic activities. mimeo quantico, va.: january 1975. 79 pp. ca. 1200 items, not annotated, mostly journalistic articles.

35. library of the inter-american defence college. bibliografia guerra revolucionaria y subversion en el continente. washingtond. c.: 1973. bibliography on latin american revolution and counterrevolution.

36. longolius, a. * (comp.). auswahlbibliographie zu anarchismus, radikalismus und terrorismus. berlin: bibliothek des abgeordnetenhauses von berlin, 1976. 16 pp.

37. manheim, j. b. * wallace, m. political violence in the united states, 1875-1974: a bibliography. new york: garland publishers, 1975. 116 pp.

38. mickolus, e. f. annotated bibliography on transnational and international terrorism. washington d. c.: c. i. a., december 1976. 225 pp. 1277 items, mostly in english.

39. mickolus, e. f. the literature of terrorism: a selectively annotated bibliography. westport: greenwood press, 1980. 553 pp.

40. miller, h. * lybrand, w. a. * brokheim, h. a selected bibliography on unconventional warfare. washington d. c.: american university(soro), 1961. 137 pp.

41. monroe, j. l. prisoners of war and political hostages: a selected bibliography. springfield, va.: the monroe corporation, 1973. 45 pp. not annotated, drawing from many sources.

42. n. n. annotated bibliography on transnational terrorism. 7th security assistance symposium of the foreign area officer course, u. s. army institute for military assistance. fort bragg, n. c.: u. s. army, 1975. 27 pp. with emphasis on journalistic accoun.

43. n. n. bibliographie de la revolution. paris: e. d. j. que lire?, 1975. 262 pp.

44. n. n. new modes of conflict: urban guerilla warfare and international terrorism. a bibliography of selected rand publications.: jan 1977. 4 pp. sb-1060.

45. n. n. radical militants – an annotated bibliography of empirical research oncampus unrest. lexington, mass.: heath lexington books, 1973. 241 pp. on u. s. student radicalism since 1945.

46. nettlau, m. bibliographie de l'anarchie. brussels: 1897.

47. norton, a. r. * greenberg, m. h. international terrorism: an annotated bibligraphy and research guide. boulder: westview, 1979. 200 pp.

48. norton, a. r. terror-violence. a critical commentary and selective annotated bibliography. gaithersburg, md.: iacp, 16 pp.

49. novotny, e. j. s. * whitley, j. a. g. a select bibliography on the terrorist threat to the commercial nuclear industry. draft working paper d. vienna, va.: the bdm corporation, 1975.

50. piasetzki, j. p. urban guerrilla warfare and terrorism – a selected bibliography. monticello, ill.: council of planning librarians, 1976. 16 pp. bibliography with more than 100 listings of articles, pamphlets and books.

51. roemelingh, h. e. literatuur over terroristen en verzet.: march 1977. pp. 124-133 het tijdschrift voor de politie. 39:3.

52. rose, r. ulster politics: a select bibliography of political discord.: 1972. pp. 206-212 political studies 20:2.

53. russell, ch. a. * miller, j. a. * hildner, r. e. the urban guerrilla in latin america: a selected bibliography.: 1974. pp. 37-79 latin america research review 9:1 annotated, 261 titles.

54. russell, ch. a. * schenkel, j. f. * miller, j. a. urban guerillas in argentina: a select bibliography.: 1974. pp. 53-89 latin american research review 9:3 mostly newspaper article citations.

55. sabetta, a. r. annotated bibliography on international terrorism.: 1977. pp. 157-164 stanford journal of international studies 12:1.

56. sabetta, a. r. annotated bibliography. prepared for special issue devoted to internationalterrori.: 1977. pp. 157-164 stanford journal of international studies 12.

57. schmid, a. p. * graaf, j. f. a. de. bibliography on terrorism. in: a. p. schmid and j. f. a. de graaf,a pilot-study on polical terrorism. thehague: advisory group on research into non-violent conflict resolution, 1977. 33 pp. (appendix pp 63-96).

58. sherman, j. * (ed.). the arab-israeli conflict 1945-1971: a bibliography. new york: garland, 1978. 419pp .

59. smirnoff, m. bibliographie internationale sur le probleme de la piraterie aerienne.: 1971. pp. 191-199 revue generale de l'air et de l'espace 34:2.

60. symser, w. m. * et. al. annotated bibliography on internal defense. washington, d. c.: 1968. selected books, periodicals, reports, and articles relating to internal defense. prepared by the center for research in social systems. much of the material listed deals with the problems of insurgency andurban guerilla warfare.

61. tutenberg, v. * pollak, chr. terrorismus - gestern, heute, morgen. eine auswahlbibliographie. muenchen : bernard & graefe verlag fur wehrwesen, 1978. 298 pp. unannotated bibliography, ca. 3600 titles, country by country and under headings such as espionage, psychological warfare, territorial defence, emergency law etc. since the authors do not distinguish between terrorism and guerila warfare, resistance against occupation, and revolutions, this book is of limited usefulness for research on political terrorism.

62. u. n. secretariat. international terrorism: a select bibliography. new york: united nations.,

63. u. s. air force academy library. terrorism. colorado: usafa, 1977. 47 pp. special bibliography series no. 57 ca. 600 items, many of them newspaper articles. not annotated.

64. u. s. department of justice. hostage situations. quantice va.: fbi academy, 1975. 35 pp. 426 citations, updating the 1973 bibliography.

65. u. s. department of justice. hostage situations: bibliography. quantico, va.: fbi academy, 1973. 8 pp. ca . 100 citations on ground and airhostage situations.

66. u. s. department of justice. law enforcement assistance administration. terrorism. bibliography. rockville, md.: national institute of law enforcement and criminal justice, 1978.

67. u. s. department of justice. law enforcement assistance administration. terrorism. an annotated bibliography. washington, d. c.: u. s. dept. of justice, bibliography names agency or publisher but rarely author of an item.

68. u. s. department of state. library. international terrorism and revolutionary warfare: library booklist. .: 1976. pp. 1-4 reader's advisory service 3:4.

69. u. s. department of transportation. federal aviation administration. hijacking: selected references. washington, d. c.: faa, 1969. 22 pp. bibliographical list no. 18 lists 206 items. mostly journalistic articles.

70. u. s. department of transportation. federal aviation administration. hijacking: selected references, bibliographic list no. 18. washington, d. c.: june 1969.

71. u. s. department of transportation. hijacking: selected readings. washington, d. c.: dept. of transportation, 1971. 53 pp. bibliographic list no. 5 lists 268 articles published between febr. 1969 and dec. 1970; annotated; mostly from newspapers and magazines.

72. united nations. a select bibliography on aerial piracy.: 20 nov. 1972. list no. 6.

73. united nations. a select bibliography on international terrorism.: 25 oct. 1972. list no. 5/rev. 1 .

74. united nations, secretariat. international terrorism: a selected bibliography. new york: u. n., 1973. 10 pp.

75. watson, f. m. the textbook of political violence. a selected bibliography. gaithersburg, md.: iacp, 20 pp.

76. whitehouse, j. e. a police bibliography. published and unpublished sources through 1976. new york: ams press, pp. 397-407 cover terrorism; emphasis on u. s. magazine articles.

77. wilcox, l. m. * * (comp.). bibliography on terrorism, assassination, kidnapping, bombing, guerila warfare and countermeasures against them.: 1980.

78. wilcox, l. m. bibliography on terrorism and assassination. paperb. text.: research service, 1981.

B. CONCEPTUAL, DEFINITORY AND TYPOLOGICAL ASPECTS OF TERRORISM

79. andreski, s. terror. in: j. gould and w. l. kolb * (eds.). a dictionary of the social sciences. new york : free press of glencoe, 1964. p. 179.

80. arblaster, a. terrorism: myths, meaning and morals.: sept. 1977. pp. 413-424 political studies. the journal of the political studies association of the u. k. 25:3 reviews several books on terrorism.

81. baeyer-katte, w. von * grimm, t. terror. freiburg i. br.: 1972. pp. 341 ff. sowjetsystem und demokratische gesellschaft. 6.

82. baxter, r. r. skeptical look at the concept of terrorism.: 1974. pp. 380-387 akron law review 7.

83. bell, j. b. trends on terror. the analysis of political violence.: april 1977. pp. 476-488 world politics. 29:3.

84. berger, p. l. elements of terrorism.: 1976. pp. 29-30 worldview 19:5.

85. bonanate, l. il teorema del terrorismo.: 1978. pp. 574-595 il mulino 258.

86. bonanate, l. some unanticipated consequences of terrorism.: 1979. pp. 197-211 journal of peace research 16:3.

87. bonanate, l. terrorismo, lotta politica e violenza.: 1978. pp. 23-38 biblioteca della liberta 15:68 .

88. buckley, a. d. * olson, d. d. international terrorism. current research and future directions. new york: avery publications,

89. chandler, d. b. toward a classification of violence.: 1973. pp. 63-83 sociol. symposion 9.

90. cooper, h. h. a. terrorism: the problem of the problem of definition.: march 1978. pp. 105-108 chitty's law journal 26.

91. crenshaw, m. the concept of revolutionary terrorism.: sept. 1972. 383-396 the journal of conflict resolution 16:3 a thoughtful conceptual attempt.

92. crozier, b. a theory of conflict. london: hamish hamilton, 1974.

93. crozier, b. anatomy of terrorism.: 1959. pp. 250-252 nation 188.

94. david, e. definition et repression du terrorisme.: 1973. pp. 861-864 revue de droit penal et de criminologie 52:9.

95. dennen, j. m. g., van der. problems in the concepts and definitions of aggression, violence and some related terms. groningen: polemologicalinstitu, 1980. 154 pp.

96. dimitrijevic, v. aircraft hijacking: typology and prospects of suppression. belgrade: 1972. pp. 55-64 international problems.

97. dugard, j. an ideal definition of terrorism. international terrorism: problems of definition.: january 1974. pp. 67-81 international affairs 50:1.

98. dugard, j. towards the definition of international terrorism.: 1973. pp. 94-100 american journal of international law. 67:5).

99. faleroni, a. d. what is an urban guerrilla?.: 1969. p. 94 military review 47.

100. fattah, e. a. terrorist activities and terrorist targets. a tentative typology. in: y. alexander and j. m. gleason * (eds.) behavioral and quantitative perspectives on terrorism. new york: pergamon press, 1981. pp. 11-34.

101. finer, s. e. terrorism.: 1976. pp. 168-169 new society 35:694.

102. galtung, j. on violence in general and terrorism in particular. mimeo. geneva: u. n. university, 1978. 27 pp.

103. goldaber, i. a typology of hostage terror.: june 1979. pp. 21-23 police chief.

104. govea, r. m. terrorism as a political science offering. cleveland: 1980. pp. 3-19 teaching political science 8:1.

105. greenstein, f. j. * polsby, n. w. * (eds.). handbook of political science. 8 vols. reading, mass.: 1975 . see entries "political terror"and "terrorism" in cumulativeindex, p. 80.

106. groom, a. j. r. coming to terms with terrorism.: april 1978. pp. 62-77 british journal of international studies 4:1 review abstracts on books by: burton, carlton, clutterbuck, jenkins, sobel, walter, wilkinson and others.

107. gunther, j. terror und terrorismus.: 1972. p. 32 neue deutsche hefte 19:4.

108. hardman, j. b. s. terrorism. in: e. r. seligman * (ed.). encyclopaedia of the social sciences. new york: macmillan, 1937. pp. 575-579 14 the first serious attempt of defining the subject.

109. herpen, m. van. terrorisme zonder terreur. een poging tot een sociologische definitie van de begrippen terrorisme en terreur. unpubl. paper nijmegen: studiecentrum voor vredesvraagstukken, 1978. 13 pp.

110. hess, h. repressive crime and criminal typologies.: 1977. pp. 91-108 contemporary crises 1.

111. **hess, h.** repressives verbrechen.: 1976. pp. 1-22 kriminologisches journal 8:1 repressive crime, a criminological conceptualization of lawless state acts.

112. **hess, h.** terrorismus und terrorismus-diskurs.: 1981. pp. 171-188 tijdschrift voor criminologie 4 a lucid and original conceptualization.

113. **heyman, e. s.** monitoring the diffusion of transnational terrorism. gaithersburg, md.: i. a. c. p., 1980. 36 pp.

114. **higham, r. * (ed.).** civil war, internal war, and intrasociet. al. conflict, a taxonomy and typology, in civil wars in the twentieth century. lexington: the university press of kentucky, 1972. pp. 11-26.

115. **hobsbawn, e. j.** an appraisal of terrorism.: 1972. pp. 11-14 canadian dimension 9:1.

116. **horowitz, i. l.** unicorns and terrorists. paper. conference on international terrorism, march 1976. washington, d. c.: u. s. department of state, 1976. 13pp.

117. **ivianski, z.** individual terror as a phase in revolutionary violence in the late nineteenth and the beginning of thd twentieth century. doctoral diss. jerusalem: 1973. in hebrew.

118. **ivianski, z.** individual terror. concept and typology.: 1977. pp. 44-63 journal of contemporary history 12:1.

119. **jaszi, o. * lewis, j. d.** against the tyrant; the tradition and theory of tyrannicide. glencoe, ill.: free press, 1957.

120. **jenkins, b. m.** research note: rand's research on terrorism.: 1977. pp. 85-95 terrorism 1:1.

121. **jenkins, b. m.** terrorism works - sometimes. santa monica: rand, 1974. 9 pp. rand paper p. 5217.

122. **kahn, m. w. * kirk, w. e.** the concepts of aggression. a review and reformulation.: 1969. pp. 559-573 psychological rec. 18.

123. **karanovic, m.** the concept of terrorism. washington, d. c.: u. s. department of justice. national criminal justice reference services., april 1979. pp. 219-234 jugoslovenska revija za krimologiju i krivicnopravo 3:81-88 available in international summaries: a collection of selected translations in law enforcement and criminal justice.

124. **karber, ph. a.** urban terrorism: baseline data and conceptual framework.: dec. 1971. pp. 521-533 social science quarterly 52 author stresses the symbolic quality of political terrorism and suggests that it can be analysed in much thesame fashion as other forms of communication.

125. **kasturi, d. g.** a typological analysis of collective political violence. unpubl. ph. d.: louisiana state university, 1979. 285 pp.

126. **kautsky, b. * kogon, e. * et. al.** verhandlungen der deutschen soziologentage 9. vortraege und diskussion ueber terror.: 1949. pp. 98-142 kogon's contribution is reprinted as first chapterin the author's "der ss-staat". muenchen, kindler, 1974.

127. **kessler, h.** terreur, ideologie und nomenklatur der revolutionaere gewaltanwendung in frakreich von 1770 bis 1794. muenchen: w. fink, 1973. 195 pp.

128. **laqueur, w.** coming to terms with terror.: 2 april 1976. pp. 262-263 the times literary supplement 3864.

129. **laqueur, w.** guerrillas and terrorists.: october 1974. pp. 40-48 commentary 58:4.

130. **laqueur, w.** interpretations of terrorism - fact, fiction and political science.: 1977. pp. 1-42 journal of contemporary history 12:1.

131. **leach, e. r.** custom, law and terrorist violence. edinburgh: university press, 1977. 37 pp.

132. **loesche, p.** anarchismus. versuch einer definition und historischen typologie.: 1974. politische vierteljahresschrift 1.

133. **lopez, g. a.** a scheme for the analysis of governments as terrorists. conference paper. milwaukee, wisc. : midwestpolitical science association, 1982.

134. **lopez, g. a.** terrorism and alternatives worldviews. conference paper. san antonio, texas: southwest international studies association, 1981. 19 pp.

135. **mars, p.** nature of political violence.: kingston, jamaica., june 1975. pp . 221-238 social and economic studies 24:5 activities associated with political violence are defined and arranged on a rank-orderscale to measure the intensity of political violence in a particular country. attempts definition of political violence. .

136. **mccamant, j. f.** governance without blood. social science antiseptic view of rule orthe neglect of political repression. conference paper. milwaukee, wisc.: midwest political science association, 1982. 57 pp. x

137. **merari, a.** a classification of terrorist groups.: 1978. pp. 331-346 terrorism 1.

138. **mickolus, e. f.** reflections on the study of terrorism. paper presented to the panel on violence and terror of the conference on complexity: achallenge to the adaptive capacity of american society, 1776-1976, sponsored by the society for general systems research, held at the loyola college conference center, columbia, maryland, march 24-26, 1977. 9 pp. to be published in the conference

proceedings, edited by thomas harries.

139. mickolus, e. f. reflections on the study of terrorism. in: th. harries * (ed.) complexity: a challenge to the adaptive capacity of american society. proceedings of a conference sponsored by the societyfor general systems research, columbia. md. * 24-26 march 1977.

140. mickolus, e. f. studying terrorist incidents: issues in conceptualization and data acquisition. paper presented to the annual convention of the international studies association, los angeles, march 1980.: 1980.

141. monday, m. insurgent war s backgrounder book for reporters. mimeo san diego: tvi, 1980. 34 pp.

142. muenkler, h. guerillakrieg und terrorismus.: 1980. pp . 299-326 neue politische literatur 25:3.

143. n. n. concept of terrorism. belgrade: jugoslovensko udruzenje za kriminologiju, 1976. pp. 219-234 jugoslovenska revijaza kriminologija i krivicno pravo 14:2 etymological and etiological analysis with conceptualization of elements of the terror process; in serbocroatic.

144. n. n. conflicting conceptions of political violence. in: c. p. cotter * (ed.) political science annual. indianapolis: bobb- merrill, 1973. pp. 75-126 an international review 4.

145. n. n. reflections on the definition and repression of terrorism. brussels: universite libre de bruxelles, 1973. 292 pp.

146. n. n. terror, reign of; terrorism. in: the new encyclopaedia brittanica. (micropaedia) vol. 9.: 1976. p. 904.

147. n. n. terrorismo politico. in: dizionario di politica. torino: 1976. pp. 1034 ff.

148. nagel, w. h. terrorisme.: 1975. pp. 150-156 justitiele verkenningen 4.

149. o'brien, c. c. herod: reflections on political violence. london: hutchinson, 1978.

150. o'neill, b. e. towards a typology of political terrorism: the palestinian resistance movement.: 1978. pp. 17-42 journal of international affairs 32.

151. ponsaers, p. terrorisme: aktie-reaktie-interaktie. deel 1: theoretiksch kader(poging tot algemene duiding van het begrip terrorisme). master's thesis. leuven: katholieke universiteit, 1976. 153 pp.

152. pontara, g. violenza e terrorismo. il problema della definzione e de. in: l. bonanate * (ed.) dimensioni del terrorismo politico. milano: franco angeli editore, 1979. pp. 25-98.

153. rosenthal, u. terreur: een hin derlijke analyse van stellige uitspraken.: 1978. pp. 429-438 tijdschrift v. d. politie.

154. roucek, j. s. sociological elements of a theory of terror and violence.: 1962. pp. 165-172 american journal of economics and sociology 21.

155. ruitenberg, h. politiek en misdaad.: juni 1978. p. 3 wordt vervolgd. berichten van amnesty international on the distinction between political and criminal delinquents.

156. sarhan, a. definition de terrorisme international et fixation de son contenue.: 1973. pp. 173-178 revue egyptienne de droit international 29.

157. schmid, a. p. * graaf, j. f. a. de. a pilot study on political terrorism. the hague: advisory group on research into nonviolent conflict resolution, 1977. 62 pp.

158. schmid, a. p. * graaf, j. f. a. de. internationaal terrorisme. begripsbepaling, structuur en strategieen.: , intermediair.

159. schuyt, c. j. m. denken en discussieren over terreur.: oct. 1977. pp. 529-542 delikt en delinkwent 7 :8.

160. sederberg, p. c. defining terrorism. mimeo. columbia: university of south carolina, 1981. 5 pp.

161. sloan, s. conceptualizing political terror. a typology.: 1978. journal of international affairs 32.

162. stohl, m. fashions and phantasies in the study of political terrorism. unpubl. paper dubrovnik: inter -university center, 1981. 18 pp.

163. stohl, m. three worlds of terrorism. dubrovnik: inter -university center, 1981. 20 pp. unpubl. paper.

164. tromp, h. w. politiek terrorisme.: march 1978. pp. 1-19 transaktie 7:1.

165. tromp, h. w. politiek terrorisme: de derde wereldoorlog in een volstrekt onverwachte vorm.: 28 sept. 1978. pp. 9-11 universiteitskrant groningen 8:5.

166. waciorski, j. le terrorisme politique. paris: a. pedone,

167. waldmann, p. terror. in: p. noack and th. stammen * (eds.). grundbegriffe der politischen fachsprache. muenchen: 1976. pp. 305-307.

168. walter, e. v. violence and the process of terror. in: joan v. bondurant * (ed.) conflict: violence and nonviolence. new york: aldine, atherton, 1971.

169. walter, e. v. violence and the process of terror.: april 1964. pp. 248-257 american sociological review 29:2.

170. walzer, m. * bell, j. b. * morris, r. terrorism: a debate.: 22 dec. 1975. p. 12 new republic.

171. wilkinson, p. a fatality of illusions:. paper presented at the u. s. state department conference on international terrorism in retrospect and prospect, march 1976. washington d. c.: 1976.

172. wilkinson, p. can a state be 'terrorist'?.: 1981. pp. 467-472 international affairs 57:3.

173. wilkinson, p. political terrorism. london: macmillan, 1974. 160 pp. conceptually one of the basic works on the subject.

174. wilkinson, p. three questions on terrorism.: 1973. pp . 290-312 government and opposition 8:3.

175. wolf, j. b. an analytical framework for the study and control of agitational terrorism.: july, 1976. pp. 165-171 the police journal 49:3.

176. young, r. revolutionary terrorism, crime and morality.: 1977. pp. 287-302 social theory and practice 4:3.

C. GENERAL WORKS ON TERRORRISM

177. alexander, y. * (ed.). international terrorism; national, regional and global perspectives. new york: praeger, 1976. 414 pp. contents: l. c. green. terrorism - the canadian perspective; b. k. johnpoll. perspectives on political terrorism in the u. s. ; r. e. butler. terrorism in latin america; j. bowyer bell. strategy, tactics, and terror: an irish perspective; t. e. hackey. political terrorism: the british experience; r. o. freedman. soviet policy toward international terrorism; s. qureshi. political violence in the south asian subcontinent; e. s. efrat. terrorism in south africa; y. alexander. from terrorism to war: the anatomy of the birth of israel; e. weisband and d. roguly. palestinian terrorism: violence verbal strategy and legitimacy; s. m. finger international terrorism and the united nations.

178. alexander, y. * carlton, d. * wilkinson, p. * (eds.). terrorism. theory and practice. boulder, colo.: westview press, 1978. 275 pp. analyses the use of sporadic political and ideological violence by nongovernmental groups, with a view toward understanding current challenges andimplications for the future.

179. alexander, y. * carlton, d. * wilkinson, p. * (eds.). terrorism. theory and practice. new york: praeger , 1978. westview special studies in national and international terrorism.

180. alexander, y. * carlton, d. * wilkinson, p. * (eds.). terrorism: theory and practice. boulder: westview , 1979. 280 pp.

181. alexander, y. * finger, s. m. * (eds.). terrorism: interdisciplinary perspectives. new york: the john jay press, 1977. 377 pp. contents: b. singh. an overview; j. j. paust. a definitional focus; r. a. friedlander. the origins of international terrorism; d. rapoport. the politics of atrocity; j. a. miller. political terrorism and insurgency: an interrogative approach; j. mallin. terrrorism as a military weapon; e. evans. american policy responce to international terrorism: problems of deterrence; a. p. rubin. international terrorism and international law; a. e. evans. the realities of extradition and prosecution; h. h. a. cooper. terrorism and the media; b. johnpoll. terrorism and the media in the united states; y. alexander. terrorism and the media in the middle east; e. f. mickolus. statistical approaches to the study of terrorism; j. margolin. psychological perspectives in terrorism; i. l. horowitz. transnational terrorism, civil liberties, and social science; m. crenshaw hutchinson. defining future threats: terrorists and nuclear proliferation.

182. alexander, y. super-terrorism. in: y. alexander and j. m. gleason * (eds.) terrorism: behavioral perspectives. new york: pergamon, 1980.

183. alexander, y. the role of terrorism in world power assessment. forthcoming washington, d. c.: georgetown center for strategic and international

studies,

184. argiolas, t. la guerriglia. storia e dottrina. firenze: sansoni, 1967.

185. astorg, b. d. introduction du monde de la terreur. paris: editions du seuil, 1945.

186. bassiouni, m. c. prolegomenon to terror violence.: 1979. pp. 745-779 creighton law review 12.

187. baumann, c. e. * (ed.). international terrorism. milwaukee: institute of world affairs, university of wisconsin, 1974.

188. bell, j. b. on revolt: strategies of national liberation. cambridge: harvard university press, 1976. 272 pp.

189. bell, j. b. terror: an overview. in: m. livingston * (ed.)international terrorism in the contemporary world. westport, conn.: greenwood, 1978. pp. 36-43.

190. beloff, m. terrorism and the people. in: ten years of terrorism: collected views. new york: crane-russak, 1979. pp. 109-127.

191. benewick, r. political violence and public order. harmondsworth: penguin books, 1969.

192. bennett, r. k. terrorists among us: an intelligence report. pp. 115-120 reader's digest oct. 1971.

193. bite, v. international terrorism.: library of congress, crs., 31 oct. 1975. issue brief 1 b 74042.

194. bonanate, l. * gastaldo, p. * (eds.). il terrorismo nell'eta contemporanea. firenze: le monnier, 1981.

195. bonanate, l. dimensioni del terrorismo politico. in: bobbio n. * matteucci n. * (eds.) dizionario di politica. torino: utet, 1977. pp. 76-122 comunita 177.

196. bouthoul, g. la guerra. guerriglia, guerra urbana e terrorismo. roma: armando, 1975.

197. bracher, k. d. terrorismus in der demokratischen gesellschaft. hamburg: 1978. 15pp.

198. bradshaw, j. the dream of terror.: 18 july, 1978. pp. 24-50 esquire.

199. bravo, g. m. critica dell'estremismo. milano: il saggiatore, 1977.

200. brewer, g. d. existing in a world of institutionalized danger. published in yale studies in world public order 3 <1977>. new haven, conn.: school of organization and management, yale university, march 1976. pp. 339-387 technical report 102.

201. broche, f. alexandre 1er - louis barthou. paris: balland, 1977.

202. brown, g. * wallace, m. * (eds.). terrorism. new york: thenew yorktimes arno press, 1979. 378 pp.

203. brown, l. c. transnational terrorism and foreign policy: a summary of workshop deliberation. in: proceedings of the 13th international affairs symposium of the foreign area officers course. fort bragg, n. c.: u. s. army institute for military assistance, december 1977. pp. 46-54.

204. buckman, p. the limits of protest. london: panther, 1970. 286 pp.

205. burnham, j. notes on terrorism.: 13 oct, 1972. p. 1116 national review.

206. buro buitenland der katholieke hogeschool. terrorisme als vorm van politiek geweld;. informatiemap bij de cyclus. tilburg: 1977. 242 pp. concentrating mainly on germany; containing lecture transcripts and article.

207. calvert, j. m. the pattern of guerrilla warfare.: 1966. military review 46:7.

208. camus, a. l'homme revolte. paris: gallimard, 1951.

209. carlton, d. * schaerf, c. * (eds.). violence at substate level. london: macmillan, 1978.

210. carmichael, d. j. c. terrorism: some ethical issues.: september 1976. pp. 233-239 chitty's law journal 24.

211. carrere, r. * valat-morio, p. mesure du terrorisme de 1968 a 1972.: 1973. pp. 47-58 etudes polemologiques 3:8.

212. carson, j. * (ed.). terrorism in theory and practice. proceedings of a colloquium. toronto: atlantic council of canada., 1978.

213. chairoff, p. dossier b. come barbouzes. paris: alain moreau, 1975.

214. cheason, j. m. terrorist risk exposure: a bayesian approach. paper academy of criminal justice sciences nationalmeeting, oklahoma city, oklahoma, march, 1980. oklahoma city: 1980. a less mathematical version of this paper waspresented under the title of "a bayesian framework forthe determination of terrorist risk exposure in world countries, " third annual third world conference, omaha, nebraska, october, 1979.

215. cia. international terrorism in 1976. washington, d. c.: central intelligence agency, july 1977. rp 77-10034u.

216. cia. international terrorism in 1977. washington, d. c.: cianational foreign assessmentscenter, august 1978. rp 78-10255u.

217. clutterbuck, r. l. kidnap and ransom. the response. london: faber & faber, 1978. 192 pp.

218. clutterbuck, r. l. living with terrorism. london: faber & faber, 1975. 160 pp.

219. coblentz, s. a. the militant dissenters. south brunswick: a. s. barnes & co., 1970. 291 pp.

220. connelly, r. w. third party involvement in international terrorist extortion. master's thesis: naval postgraduate school, 1976.

221. cooper, h. h. a. menace of terrorism. paper. glassboro, n. j.: international symposium on terrorism in the contemporary world, april, 1976. 6 pp.

222. cooper, h. h. a. terrorism and the intelligence function. in: m. livingston * (ed.) international terrorism in the contemporary world. westport, conn.: greenwood press, 1978. pp. 287-296.

223. d'hondt, j. terrorism and politics.: 1973. pp. 72-77 etudes internationales de psycho-sociologie criminelle 24.

224. davies, t. r. feedback processes and international terrorism. ph. d. dissertation: florida state university, 1977.

225. davies, t. r. the terrorists. san diego, cal.: grossmont press, 1978.

226. denton, f. h. * phillips, w. some patterns in the history of violence.: june 1968. pp. 182-195 journal of conflict resolution 12.

227. desjardins, t. les rebelles d'aujourd'hui. paris: presses de la cite, 1977.

228. dittrich, z. r. terrorisme. terugblikken en vooruitzien. the hague: 1979. pp. 21-24 liberaal reveil 19:4 compares russian terrorism around 1880 with present-day terrorism. article forms introduction to a series of articleson terrorism in this issue.

229. dobson, chr. * payne, r. the terrorists. their weapons, leaders, and tactics. new york: facts on file, 1979. simultaneously published as weapons of terror. london: macmillan, 1979.

230. dollinger, h. schwarzbuch der weltgeschichte. 5000 jahre der mensch des menschenfeind. munich: suedwest verlag, 1973. blackbook of world history. 5000 years of human hostility towards humans.

231. dreher, e. t. * magner, j. w. investigation of terrorist activities. gaithersburg, md.: i. a. c. p., 25 pp.

232. drew, p. domestic political violence: some problems of measurement.: 1974. pp. 5-25 sociological review 22:1.

233. elliott, j. d. * gibson, l. k. * (eds.). contemporary terrorism: selected readings. gaithersburg, md.: international association of chiefs of police, 1978. 306 pp.

234. elliott, j. d. primers on terrorism.: oct. 1976. military review,.

235. ellul, j. terrorisme et violence psychologique. in: la violence dans le monde actuel. bruxelles: desclee de brouwer, 1968. pp. 43-62.

236. erling, r. terror. skolen mobbing ei empirisk undersuknung.: 1980. 139 pp.

237. evron, y. * (ed.). international violence: terrorism, surprise and control. jerusalem: hebrew university leonarddavis institute for international relations, 1979.

238. farhi, d. the limits of dissent. facing the dilemmas posed by terrorism.

239. fearey, r. a. introduction to international terrorism. in: m. livingstone * (ed.) international terrorism in the contemporary world. westport, conn.: greenwood, 1978. pp. 25-35.

240. feierabend, i. k. * feierabend, r. l. aggressive behaviors within polities 1948-1962. a cross-national study. in: davies j. c. * (ed.) when men revolt and why. new york: the free press, 1971.

241. fishman, w. j. the insurrectionists. new york: barnes and noble, 1970.

242. friedlander, r. a. terrorism and the law. what price safety?. gaithersburg, md.: i. a. c. p., 1980. 22 pp.

243. friedlander, r. a. terrorism.: 1975. p. 10 barrister 2.

244. gallet, m. genesi del terrorismo e mito della violenza.: 1975. pp. 61-71 ladestra 1.

245. gerlach, l. p. movements of revolutionary change: some structural characteristics.: 1971. pp. 812-836 american behavioral scientist 14.

246. gleason, j. m. * lily, c. the impact of terrorism on investment decisions in the third world: a framework for analysis. paper second national conference on the third world. omaha, nebraska: 1978.

247. gleason, j. m. third world terrorism: perspectives for quantitative research. in: y. alexander and j. m. gleason * (eds.) terrorism:behavioral perspectives. new york: pergamon press, 1980. pp. 242-255.

248. gonzales-mata, l. m. terrorismo internacional: la extreme derecha la extrema izquierda, y los crimenes del estado. barcelona: libreria editorial argos, s. a., 1978.

249. goode, s. guerrilla warfare and terrorism.: 1977. juvenile literature.

250. grammens, m. enige beschouwingen over het terrorisme.: dec. 1977. pp. 195-202 tijdschrift voor diplomatie 4.

251. green, l. c. aspects of terrorism.: 1982. pp. 373-400 terrorism 5:4 review article, concentrating on books by rapoport, dobson & payne, sterling, schmid & de graaf.

252. greisman, h. c. social meanings of terrorism: reification, violence, and social control.: july 1977. pp. 308-318 contemporary crises 1.

253. gribble, l. i terroristi. milano: sugar, 1961.

254. gros, b. le terrorisme. paris: hatier, 1976. ca. 80 pp.

255. hayes, d. terrorists and freedom fighters. london: wayland, 1980. 96 pp.

256. hazelwood, l. * hayes, r. e. * harris, d. r. analyzing threats from terrorism. * hazelwood, l. * hayes, r. e. * harris d. r. in: the role of behavioralscience in physical security. special publication 480-24 washington: national bureau of standards, 1976.

257. heyman, e. s. monitoring the diffusion of transnational terrorism: a conceptual framework and methodology. master's thesis: university of north carolina, 1979. revised and published by technical notes, clandestine tactics and technology, gaithersburg, md.: international association of chiefs of police, 197.

258. hoffmann, p. widerstand, staatsstreich, attentat. muenchen: r. piper verlag, 1969.

259. holton, g. reflections on modern terrorism.: 1976. pp . 8-9 bulletin of the atomic scientists 32:9.

260. honderich, t. political violence. a philosophical analysis of terrorism. ithaca: cornell university press, 1976.

261. horner, ch. the facts about terrorism.: june 1980. pp . 40-45 commentary 69:6.

262. housman, l. terrorism by ordinance. london: the indialeague,

263. howard, b. living with terrorism.: 18 july 1976. pp. c1, c4 washington post.

264. howe, i. the return of terror.: 1975. pp. 227-237 dissent 22.

265. hyams, e. terrorists and terrorism. new york: st. martin's, 1974. 200 pp.

266. international association of chiefs of police. contemporary terrorism. gaithersburg, m. d.: iacp, 1978. 306 pp.

267. janos, a. c. the seizure of power. a study of force and popular consent. princeton: 1964, on various types of coups d'etat.

268. jenkins, b. m. * johnson, j. international terrorism: a chronology, 1974 supplement. santa monica: rand corporation, february 1976. r-1909-1-arpa.

269. jenkins, b. m. international terrorism: a new mode of conflict. in d. carlton and c. schaerf * (eds.) international terrorism and world security. london: croom helm, 1975. pp. 13-49.

270. jenkins, b. m. international terrorism: trends and potentialities: a summary.: 1978. pp. 115-124 journal of international affairs 32 orig: rand, oct. 1977.

271. jenkins, b. m. rand's research on terrorism. santa monica: rand corporation, august 1977. p-5969 reprinted in terrorism: an international journal 1, 1977, pp. 85-95.

272. johnson, ch. terror.: nov. 1977. pp. 48-52 society 15:1.

273. kaaden, j. j. van der. terrorism.: 1975. pp. 1 justitiele verkenningen 4.

274. kader, o. terrorism: comparative ideologies, strategies and tactics. ph. d. dissertation in preparation: university of southern california,

275. kelley, r. j. new political crimes and the emergency of revolutionary nationalist ideology. chicago: rand-mcnally, 1973.

276. klarin, m. terorizam. beograd: nin, 1978. 127 pp.

277. kritzer, h. m. political protest and political violence: a nonrecursive causal model.: march 1977. pp . 630-640 social forces 55.

278. kupperman, r. h. * trent, d. m. terrorism threat, reality, response. stanford, cal.: hoover institution press, 1979. 450 pp.

279. lador-lederer, j. j. on certain trivialities written on terrorism.: 1973. pp. 25-28 international problems 12:3-4.

280. lallemond, r. terrorisme et democratie. brussels: institutemile van dervelde, 1979. 74 pp.

281. laqueur, w. * (ed.). the guerrilla reader. a historical anthology. new york: new american library, 1977 . 246 pp. part 5: guerrilla doctrine today, also deals with urban guerrilla strategy.

282. laqueur, w. fehlgedeuteter terrorismus.: october 1976. pp. 567-576 schweizer monatshefte 156.

283. laqueur, w. guerrilla. a historical and critical study. boston: little, brown & co., 1976. pp. 343-352: philosophy of the urban guerrilla; pp. 321-325: on urban terrorism; pp. 352-358: theuses of

terror.

284. laqueur, w. karl heinzen: the origins of modern terrorism.: aug. 1977. pp. 23-27 encounter 49.

285. laqueur, w. terrorism. london: weidenfeld and nicolson, 1977. 277 pp. on the historical evolution of the doctrine of systematic terrorism. the author views terrorism not as a new stage of guerrilla warfare but as a development of tyrannicide.

286. laqueur, w. terrorism. new york: little, brown & co., 1977. 244 pp.

287. laqueur, w. the anatomy of terrorism. in: j. shaw, e. f. gueritz and a. e. younger * (eds.) ten years of terror. new york: crane, russak, 1979. pp. 7-21.

288. laqueur, w. the continuing failure of terrorism.: november 1976. pp. 69-74 harper's 253.

289. laqueur, w. the futility of terrorism.: march 1976. pp. 99-105 harper's 252.

290. larteguy, j. tout l'or du diable: guerre, petrole et terrorisme. paris: presses de la cite, 1974.

291. leff, a. * roos, j. v. the transformation of terrorism: three characteristics of the new terrorism.: 1977. pp. 179-184 stanford journal of international studies. 12.

292. leiden, c. * schmitt, k. m. * **(eds.).** the politics of violence. englewood cliffs, n. j.: prentice-hall, 1968. 244 pp.

293. lentner, h. h. * lewis, t. j. revolutionary terrorism in democratic society.: may 1971. pp. 3-19 freedom at issue 7.

294. leurdijk, d. a. in de ban van de terreur.: 11 april 1975. pp. 1-13 intermediair 11:5.

295. lipovetsky, g. * (comp.). territoires de la terreur. grenoble: 1978. 172 pp. silex 10 various articles dealing with both state andnonstate terrorism in the widest sense of the word.

296. lodge, j. * (ed.). terrorism a challenge to the state. oxford: martin robertson, 1981. 247 pp.

297. loman, m. train of terror. old tappan, n. j.: revell co., 1978. 63pp. memoirs of a dutch hostage in train-hijacking.

298. may, w. g. terrorism as strategy and ecstasy.: 1974. pp. 277-298 social research.

299. mcclure, b. the dynamics of terrorism. gaithersburg, md.: iacp, 31 pp.

300. meden, v. on terror.: 1975. pp. 189-190 dissent 22:2.

301. mickolus, e. f. * heyman, e. s. responding to terrorism: basic and applied research. in: s. sloan and r. shultz * (eds.) responding to the terrorist threat: prevention and control. new york: pergamon, 1980.

302. mickolus, e. f. an events data base for studying transnational terrorism. in: r. j. heuer jr * (ed.) quantitative approaches to political intelligence: the cia experience. boulder, colorado: westview press, 1978. pp. 127-163.

303. mickolus, e. f. chronology of transnational attacks upon american businessmen, 1968-1978. in: y. alexander and r. a. kilmarx * (eds.) politicalterrorism and business: the threat and response. new york: praeger, 1979. pp. 499-521.

304. mickolus, e. f. codebook: iterate(international terrorism: attributes of terrorist events. ann arbor, mich.: inter- university consortium for political and social research university of michigan, 1976. 47 pp.

305. mickolus, e. f. statistical approaches to the study of terrorism. in: s. m. finger and y alexander * (eds.) terrorism: interdisciplinary perspectives. paper presented to the ralph bunche institute's conference on international terrorism, june 9-11, 1976. new york: john jay press, 1977. pp. 209-269.

306. mickolus, e. f. transnational terrorism. in: m. stohl * (ed.) the politics of terrorism. new york: dekker, 1979. pp. 147-190.

307. mickolus, e. f. transnational terrorism: analysis of terrorists, events and environments. ph. d. dissertation in preparation: yale university,

308. moodie, m. political terrorism: a unique kind of tyranny. paper presented to the 19th annual convention of the international studies association, february 22-25, 1978, at washington, d. c.: 1978. pp. 27-38 oesterreichische zeitschrift fuer aussenpolitik 18.

309. morander, g. fnl terror eller befrielse. lund: studentlitteratur, 1972.

310. mosbey, j. c. the prison-terrorist link. cerberus, inc.: 1977. 33 pp.

311. n. n. gewalt-terrorismus. berlin: 1975. pp. 102-150 kommunitat 19:76.

312. n. n. het vraagstuk van het politiek terrorisme.: september 1978. civis mundi. tijdschrift voor burgerschapsvorming 17 whole number, pp. 193-234, on terrorism. contents: j. niezing. politiek terrorisme en oorlog; j. w. schneider. politiek terrorisme als internationaal en volkenrechtelijk vraagstuk; b. tromp. sociologie van het terrorisme; j. s. van der meulen. terrorisme en krijgsmacht; r. p. b. van der laan bouma en j. wiersma. terrorisme en burgerlijke grondrechten;c. n. peijster. politiek terrorisme en de verdediging van de demokratische rechtss; h. bianchi. politiek terrorisme en kriminaliteit; d. wijgaerts. het politiek terrorisme: een bondig literatuuroverz.

313. n. n. le terrorisme.: febr. 1979. apres-de 211 series of articles in the monthly published by the league of the rights of man.

314. n. n. proceedings of the conference on terrorism held under auspices of glassboro state college, glassboro, n. j. westport, conn.: greenwoodpress, 1978.

315. n. n. sondeo sobre terrorismo y secuestros.: octobre 1972. pp. 221-249 revista espanola de la opinion publica n. 30.

316. n. n. terrorism.: 1976. military police law enforcement journal 3 whole issue.

317. n. n. terrorism.: january 1976. skeptic 11 contains a. o. an interview with sean macbride; i. howe. the ultimate price of random terror; r. ridenour. who are the terrorists - and what do they want?; w. laqueur. can terrorism succeed; the weather underground. prarie fire; institute for the study of conflict. terrorism can be stopped.

318. n. n. terrorisme. groningen: pamflet, 1975. deas 13 whole issue of this anarcho-socialist journal.

319. n. n. the future of political substate violence. in: y. alexander, d. carlton, p. wilkinson * (eds.) terrorism: theory and practice. boulder: westview, 1979. pp. 201-230.

320. neue zuercher zeitung(redaktion der-). blutspur der gewalt. bilanz eines jahrzehnt des terrorismus. zurich: buchverlag dernzz, 1980. 185 pp.

321. nielsen, t. terror. kopenhagen: lademann, 1977. 269 pp.

322. o'brien, c. c. liberty and terror. illusions of violence, delusions of liberation.: oct. 1977. encounter 44:4.

323. osmond, r. l. transnational terrorism 1968-1974: a quantitative analysis. ph. d. dissertation: syracuse university, 1979.

324. paine, l. the terrorists. london: robert hale & co., 1975. 176 pp.

325. parry, a. terrorism: from robespierre to arafat. new york: vanguard, 1976. 624 pp.

326. paul, l. the age of terror. london: faber, 1950.

327. peifer, a. design for terror. new york: exposition press, 1962.

328. pierson-mathy, p. formes nouvelles de la lutte revolutionnaire et cooperation internationale dans le combat contre-revolutionnaire. in: reflexions sur la definition et la repression du terrorisme. brussels: editions de l'universite de bruxelles, 1974. pp. 59-94.

329. pisapia, c. v. terrorismo: delitto politico o delitto comune?.: 1975. 257-271 lagiustizia penale 80:2 .

330. plastrik, s. on terrorism.: 1974. p. 143 dissent 21.

331. quester, g. h. world tolerance for terrorisme. in: y. evron * (ed.) international violence: terrorism, surprise and control. jerusalem: hebrew university of jerusalem, leonard davis institute for international relations., 1979. pp. 166-81.

332. rapoport, d. c. * alexander, y. * (eds.). the rationalization of terrorism. frederick, md.: university publications of america, 1981.

333. rapoport, d. c. assassination and terrorism. toronto: canadian broadcasting system, 1971. 88 pp.

334. reber, j. r. threat analysis methodology. gaithersburg, md.: international association of chiefs of police, 1976.

335. rosenthal, u. terreur. een hin derlijke analyse van stellige uitspraken. unpubl. paper. rotterdam: erasmus universiteit, 20 pp.

336. russell, ch. a. * banker jr., l. j. * miller, b. h. out-inventing the terrorist. paper presented at the conference on research strategies for the study of international terrorism, may 30, 1977, at evian, france. reprinted in y. alexander, d. carlton, and p. wilkinson*(eds.) terrorism: theory and practice(new york: praeger, 1978) and u. s. senate committee on governmental affairs "report on an act to combat international terrorism, " ng. 2d sess. *may 23, 1978, pp. 372-430.

337. russell, ch. a. terrorism: an overview 1970-1978. in: y. alexander and r. a. kilmarx * (eds.) politicalterrorism and business, the threat and response. new york: praeger, 1979. pp. 491-498.

338. scherer, j. l. terrorism: an annual survey.: 1982. 224pp.

339. selzer, m. terrorist chic: an exploration of violence in the seventies. new york: hawthorne, 1979. 206 pp.

340. servier, j. le terrorisme. paris: presses universitaires, 1979. 127 pp.

341. shaffer, h. b. political terrorism.: 1970. pp. 341-360 editorial research reports 1.

342. shaw, j. * gueritz, e. f. * younger, a. e. * (eds.). ten years of terrorism: collected views. new york: crane, russak, 1979. 192 pp.

343. short jr., j. f. * wolfgang, m. e. * (eds.). collective violence. chicago: aldine, 1972.

344. shultz, r. conceptualizing political terrorism: a typology and application. paper presented to the 19th annual convention of the

international studies association, february 22-25, 1978, at washington, d. c.: 1978. pp. 7-16 journal of international affairs 32.

345. siljander, r. p. terrorist attacks.: c. c. thomas, 1980. 342 pp.

346. sloan, s. * kearney, r. non-territorial terrorism:an empirical approach to policy formation.: 1978. pp. 131-144 conflict 1.

347. snitch, t. h. political assassinations 1968-1978: a cross-national assessment. ph. d. dissertation in preparation: americanuniversity,

348. sobel, l. a. * (ed.). political terrorism. new york: facts onfile, 1975. 309 pp. gives a narrative survey of terrorist activity as reported in the world press from 1968 through 1974.

349. sobel, l. a. * (ed.). political terrorism. vol. 2. new ed. new york: facts on file, 1978.

350. stencel, s. terrorism: an idea whose time has come.: january 1976. skeptic 11.

351. stiles, d. w. sovereignty and the new violence. in: j. d. elliott and l. k. gibson * (eds.) contemporaryterroris: selected readings. gaithersburg, md.: international association of chiefs of police, 1978. pp . 261-267.

352. stohl, m. * (ed.). the politics of terror: a reader in theory and practice. new york: marcel decker, 1979. 419 pp.

353. stohl, m. myths and realities of political terrorism. in: stohl, m. * (ed.) the politics of terrorism. new york: dekker, 1979. pp. 1-19.

354. tomasevski, k. terrorism in the contemporary world. mimeographed monograph zagreb: institutefor social research, 1979. 257 pp. in croatian.

355. tomasevski, k. the challenge of terrorism. rijeka: 1981. liburnia in croatian.

356. trick, m. m. chronology of incidents of terroristic, quasi-terroristic, and political violence in the u. s.: january 1965 to march 1976. in: report of the task force on disorders and terrorism. washington d. c.: national advisory committee on criminal justice standards and goals., december 1976. pp. 507-595.

357. troncoso de castro, a. terrorismo y estado moderno. burgos: ediciones aldecoa, 1975.

358. u. s. national advisory committee on criminal justice standards and goals. disorder and terrorism. washington, d. c.: gpo, 1977. 661 pp. a study of the growth of terrorism in the united states with alist of almost 2000 incidents from 1965 to spring 1976. serves as a police manual on how to deal with terrorism and disorders.

359. villemarest, p. f. de, * faillant, d. historie secrete des organisations terroristes. 4 vols. geneva: famot, 1976. secret history of terrorist organizations.

360. wallace, m. * (ed.). terrorism. new york: arno press, 1979.

361. walter, e. v. theories of terrorism and the classical tradition. in: spitz d. * (ed.) poltical theory and social sciences. new york: atherton press, 1967. pp. 133-60.

362. watson, f. m. political terrorism: the threat and the response. washington, d. c.: robert b. luce, 1976 . 248 pp includes chronology of significant terroristic incidents, 1968-1975, and lists 97 organizations using terrorism.

363. wigne, j. s. terreur in de politiek. politieke geheime genootschappen in deze tijd. the hague: kruseman, 1967.

364. wilkinson, p. * (ed.). british perspectives on political terrorism. london: george allen and unwin, 1981.

365. wilkinson, p. "after tehran".: 1981. pp. 5-14 conflict quarterly.

366. woerdemann, f. * loeser h. j. * (mitarb.). terrorismus. motive, taeter, strategien. muenchen: piper, 1977. 394 pp.

367. wolf, j. b. economic aspects of terroristic threats. gaithersburg, md.: i. a. c. p., 1979. update report 5 :1.

368. wolf, j. b. fear of fear. a survey of terrorist operations and controls in opensocieties. new york: plenum press,

369. wolf, j. b. terrorism, the scourge of the 1980's. gaithersburg, md.: i. a. c. p., 1980. update report 6:1.

370. wright, c. d. terrorism. fayetteville, ark.: lost roads publ., 1979.

D. REGIME TERRORISM AND REPRESSION

371. accattatis, v. capitalismo e repressione. milano: 1977. discusses italian anti-terrorist legislation .

372. agee, ph. inside the company: cia diary. new york: bantam books, 1975.

373. alesevich, e. police terrorism. in: m. livingston * et. al. * (eds.) international terrorism in the contem- porary world. westport, conn.: greenwoodpress, 1978. pp. 269–275.

374. allen, f. a. the crimes of politics. cambridge, mass.: harvard university press, 1974.

375. almond, g. a. the struggle for democracy in germany. chapel hill: university of north carolinapress, 1949. on nazi-terror.

376. american committee for information on brazil. terror in brazil. a dossier. new york: april 1970.

377. amnesty international. allegations of torture in brazil. london: a. i., 1972.

378. amnesty international. report on torture. new york: farrar, strauss, and giroux, 1975. 295 pp. mainly on state terrorism.

379. amnesty international. svenska sektionen. terrorismen i soedra afrika. stockholm: amnesty international, 1974. 54 pp. south africa.

380. amnesty international. the death penalty. london: a. i ., 1979. 209 pp. chapter 4(pp. 182–198): murder committed or acquiesced by governments; deals with argentina, ethiopia, guatemala and uganda.

381. andics, h. rule of terror. new york: holt, rinehart &winston, 1969. state terror in russia until 1953. .

382. arendt, h. elemente und urspruenge totaler herrschaft. frankfurt a. m.: 1955.

383. arens, r. terrorism from above: genocide. paper presented to the conference on psychopathology and political violence. chicago: university of chicago, november 1979.

384. aron, r. frieden und krieg. eine theorie der staatengewalt. frankfurt a. m.: fischer-verlag, 1963. also contains a perceptive discussion of terrorism.

385. baldwin, r. n. * (ed.). kropotkin's revolutionary pamphlets. dover: 1970.

386. barron, j. * paul, a. murder of a gentle land. new york: reader's digest press, 1977. 240 pp. on post-1975 government terrorin cambodia.

387. barron, j. k. g. b.: the secret work of soviet secret agents. new york: reader's digest press, 1974.

388. becker, p. rule of fear: the life and times of dingane, king of the zulu. london: 1964.

389. berman, j. j. * halperin, m. h. * (eds.). the abuses of the intelligence agencies. washington d. c.: center for national security studies, 1975. 185 pp. covers fbi, nsa, irs, cia and white house activities against alleged dissidents, some of which come closeto terrorism.

390. bicudo, h. my testimony on the death squad. sao paulo, brazil: sao paulo justice and peace commission, october 1976.

391. biocca, e. strategia del terrore: il modelo brasiliano. bari: de donato, 1974. 251 pp. government terror in brazil.

392. blackstock, n. cointelpro. new york: vintage, 1976.

393. block, s. * reddaway, p. psychiatric terror. how soviet psychiatry is used to suppressdissent. new york: basic books, 1977.

394. borcke, a. von. die urspruenge des bolschewismus. die jakobinische tradition in russland und die theorie der revolutionaeren diktatur. muenchen: berchmans, 1977. 646 pp.

395. borneman, e. der staat, die herrscher, der terror. semantische notizen eines alten socialisten.: 1975. frankfurter hefte 30:10.

396. bramstedt, e. k. dictatorship and political police. the technique of control by fear. london: kegan paul, 1956. 275 pp.

397. brune, j. m. die papageienschaukel. diktatur und folter in brasilien. duesseldorf: 1971. dictatorship and torture in brazil.

398. buhrer, j. c. repression et luttes populaires en amerique centrale. le monde diplomatique repression and resistance in central america.

399. byas, h. government by assassination. london: 1943. ananti- japanese tract.

400. carmichael, j. stalin's masterpiece. the show trials and purges of the thirties, the consolidation of the bolshevist dictatorship. new york: st. martin's press, 1976. 238 pp.

401. chamberlain, w. h. beyond containment. chicago: henry regnery, 1953. 406 pp. on ussr government strategies of repression.

402. chomsky, n. * herman, e. s. the political economy of human rights. vol. 2 after the cataclysm: postwar indochina and the reconstruction of imperial ideology. nottingham: spokesman, 1979. 392 pp.

403. chomsky, n. * herman, e. s. the political economy of human rights. vol. 1 the washington connection and third world fascism. nottingham: spokesman, 1979. 441 pp. a work long suppressed in the u. s. a.

404. chossudovsky, m. capital accumulation and state violence in the third world. unpublished paper oaxtepec: ipra, 1977. 27 pp.

405. communist party of india. raise your voice against landlord-police terror in andhra pradesh. calcutta: , 1968.

406. conquest, r. the great terror. stalin's purge of the thirties. london: macmillan, 1968. 633 pp.

407. conquest, r. the soviet police system. new york: praeger, 1968.

408. crankshaw, e. gestapo - instrument of tyranny. london: putnam, 1956. 275 pp. on nazi government terrorism during world war 2.

409. da silva, r. * et. al. evidence of terror in chile. merli: 1974, transl. from the swedish.

410. dadrian, v. n. factors of anger and aggression in genocide in turkey.: 1971. pp. 394-417 journal of human relations 19.

411. dadrian, v. n. the common features of the armenian and jewish cases of genocide:a comparative victimological perspective. in : i. drapkin and e. viano * (eds.) victimology: a new focus. lexington mass.: lexington books, 1975. pp. 99-120.

412. dadrian, v. n. the structural-functional components of genocide: a victimological approach to the armenian case. in: i. drapkin and e. viano * (eds.) victimology. lexington, mass.: lexington books, 1974. pp. 123-136.

413. dehghani, a. torture and resistance in iran. london: iran committee, 1977. 153 pp.

414. denemark, r. a. * lehman, a. s. south african state terror. the costs of continuing repression. conference paper. milwaukee,wisc.: midwest political science association, 1982. 55 pp.

415. dror, y. crazy states: a counter-conventional strategic issue. lexington, mass.: d. c. heath, 1971. 118 pp.

416. duncan, p. south africa's rule of violence. london: methuen, 1964.

417. fainsod, m. how russia is ruled. rev. ed. 1964. cambridge, mass.: harvard university press, 1953.

418. fainsod, m. smolensk under soviet rule.: 1958.

419. federn, e. the terror as a system: the concentration camp.: 1948. psychiatry quarterly supplement 22.

420. fest, j. c. das gesicht des dritten reiches. muenchen: 1963. nazi germany.

421. fields, r. m. a society on the run. a psychology of northern ireland. penguin: 1973. this book was censored, than withdrawn from the british market and 10. 000 copies were shredded. an expanded version under the title 'society under siege' was published in theu. s. by temple university press in 1977.

422. frame, w. v. dialectical historicism and the terror in chinese communism. unpublished diss. university of washington: 1969. 401 pp.

423. frazier, h. * (ed.). uncloaking the c. i. a. new york: free press, 1978.

424. freed, d. * landis, f. death in washington. the murder of orlando letelier. london: zed press, 1980.

425. friedrich, c. j. * brzezinski, z. k. totalitarian dictatorship and autocracy. cambridge, mass.: harvard university press, 1956.

426. friedrich, c. j. * et. al. totalitarianism in perspective. new york: praeger, 1969.

427. friedrich, c. j. uses of terror.: november 1970. p. 46. problems of communism 19.

428. funke, m. * (ed.). terrorismus. untersuchungen zur struktur und strategie revolutionaerer gewaltpolitik. . duesseldorf: droste und athenaeum, 1977. 391 pp. deals mainly with the german scene.

429. galeano, e. guatemala: occupied country. new york: monthlyreview press, 1969. on post-1954 government terror.

430. gall, n. santo domingo: the politics of terror.: 22 july 1971. pp. 15-10 new york review of books on police terror in the dominican republic.

431. gall, n. slaughter in guatemala.: 20 may 1971. pp. 13-17 new york review of books on government terrorism via death squadrons.

432. george, a. * lall, d. * simons, w. the limits of coercive diplomacy.: 1971.

433. gliksman, j. social prophylaxis as a form of soviet terror. in: friedrich, c. j. * totalitarianism. cambridge, mass.: harvarduniversity press, 1954.

434. goldstein, r. j. political repression in modern america from 1870 to the present. boston: g. k. hall & co., 1978. 682 pp. covers red scare of the 1920s; mccarthyism and the 'dirty tricks' of the nixon administration.

435. gundersheim, a. terror and political control in communist china. unpublished paper chicago: university of chicago, center forsocial organization studies, 1966.

436. gurr, t. r. * bishop, v. f. violent nations, and others.: 1976. pp. 79-110 journal of conflict resolution 20:1.

437. gutierrez, c. m. the dominian republic: rebellion and repression. new york: monthly review press, 1972. on post-1965 government terror which claimed at least 2000 lives and drove over 150. 000 people into exile.

438. guyn, d. idi amin. death- light of africa. boston: little & brown, 1977.

439. halperin, m. * et. al. the lawless state. new york: penguin, 1976.

440. handler, b. death squad ties to brazil's regime.: 26 dec 1976. pp. a38-a39 washington post review of bicudo, h. * my testimony on the death squad sao paulo, 1976.

441. hendel, s. the price of terror in the u. s. s. r. in: m. livingston * et. al. * (eds.) international terrorism in the contem- porary world. westport, conn.: greenwoodpress, 1978. pp. 122-130.

442. henkys, r. die national-sozialistischen gewaltverbrechen. geschichte undgericht. stuttgart: 1964.

443. heynowski, w. * et. al. * (eds.). operacion silencio: chile nach salvador allende. dokumentation. berlin: verlag dernation, 1974. 237 pp.

444. hill, w. terrorismus und folter.: april 1976. merkur. deutsche zeitschrift fuer europaeisches denken 4.

445. hills, d. c. horror in uganda. amin's subjects.: 23:14, 16 sept 1976. pp. 21-23 the new york review of books.

446. hoefnagels, m. * (ed.). repression and repressive violence. amsterdam: swets & zeitlinger, 1977. 194 pp. contains a. o. an article by the editor with the title: political violence and peace research.

447. homer, f. d. government terror in the u. s. an exploration of containment policy. unpubl. paper.: 1982. 26 pp.

448. horkheimer, m. * eisenberg, e. * jacoby, r. the authoritarian state.: 1973. pp. 3-20 telos 15.

449. horowitz, i. l. genocide: state power and mass murder. new brunswick: transaction books, 1976.

450. ignotus, p. the avh. symbol of terror. problems of communism 6:5 on secret police in hungary.

451. international defence and aid fund. terror in tete: a documentary report of portuguese atrocities in tete distrit, mozambique, 1971-72. london: idaf, 1973. 48 pp.

452. jaeger, h. verbrechen unter totalitarer herrschaft. studien zur national-sozialistischen gewaltkriminalitaet.: olten, 1967.

453. johnson, k. f. guatemala - from terorism to terror. london: institute for the study of conflict, 1972. pp. 4-17 conflict studies 23 on left-wing terrorism and government 'counter'-terror.

454. kalme, a. total terror: an expose of genocide in the baltics. new york: appleton-century-croft, 1951. 310 pp. documents german and soviet state terrorism, 1940-1951.

455. kassof, a. the administered society-totalitarianism without terror.: july 1964. pp. 558-525 world politics 16.

456. kataja, s. der terror der bourgeoisie in finnland. amsterdam: verlag bef, 1920. 47 pp.

457. katsh, a. i. terror, holocaust and the will lo live(nazi germany). in: m. livingston, * et. al * (eds.) international terrorism in the contemporary world. westport, conn.: greenwood press, 1978. pp. 430-435.

458. kirchheimer, o. political justice. princeton, n. j.: princeton university press, 1961.

459. klare, m. t. * stein, n. police terrorism in latin america. secret u. s. bomb school exposed. new york: nacla, jan. 1974. pp. 19-23 nacla's latin american and empire report 8:1.

460. kogon, e. de ss-staat. het systeem der duitse concentratiekampen. amsterdam: amsterdam boek n. v., 1976 . 406 pp. orig.: derss-staat. muenchen, kindler, 1974; the first chapter, "de terreur als machtssysteem", was written in 1948 for the german sociologists' congress.

461. kogon, e. staatsterror als ordnungsfaktor.: 1976. frankfurter hefte 31:6.

462. komitee "solidaritat mit chile" * (ed.). konterrevolution in chile. analysen und dokumente zum terror. reinbek: rowohlt, 1973. 202 pp.

463. korbonski, s. terror and counter-terror in nazi occupied poland, 1939-1945. paper presented to the conference on terror: the man, the mind and the matter. new york, n. y.: john jay school of criminal justice, october 1976.

464. kren, g. m. * rapoport, l. s. s. atrocities: a psychohistorical perspective.: 1975. history of childhood quarterly 3.

465. kren, g. m. * rapoport, l. the waffen ss.: november 1976. armed forces and society.

466. kren, g. m. the ss: a social and psychohistorical analysis. in: m. livingston * et. al. * (eds.) international terrorism in the contemporary world. westport, conn.: greenwood press, 1978. pp. 436-443.

467. kropotkin, p. a. the terror in russia.: methuen, 1909.

468. labrousse, a. la terreur blanche et les chemins de l'armee.: november 1974. le monde diplomatique.

469. langguth, a. j. hidden terrors. new york: pantheon, 1978. 339 pp. u. s. aid to latin american reprssive regimes.

470. leggett, g. h. lenin, terror and the political police.: 1975. survey 21:4.

471. leonhard, w. terror in the soviet system trends and portents.: nov. 1958. p. 1-7 problems of communism 7.

472. levytsky, b. * (comp.). the stalinist terror in the thirties; documentation from the sovietpress. stanford, cal.: hoover institution press, 1974. 521 pp.

473. levytsky, b. the uses of terror: the soviet secret service, 1917-1970. london: sidgwick and jackson, 1971. 349 pp. on cheka, gpu and nkvd.

474. levytsky, b. vom roten terror zur sozialistischen gesetzlichkeit. muenchen: nymphenburger verlag, 1961 .

475. locicero, s. l. government in france during the first terror. unpublished diss.: university of washington, 1975.

476. loomis, s. paris in the terror, june 1793-1794. philadelphia: lippincott, 1964. 415 pp.

477. lorenz, r. politischer terror in der udssr wahrend der dreissiger jahre.: march 1979. pp. 224-233 das argument 21:114 stalinist terror in 1930's.

478. ludwig, g. massenmorde im weltgeschehen. stuttgart: 1951. mass murder in world history.

479. maestre alfonso, j. guatemala. unterentwicklung und gewalt. frankfurt a. m.: 1971.

480. marks, j. the c. i. a. * cuba and terrorism.: 28 june 1977. p. 31 the new york times on u. s. government use of terrorism as instrumentof foreign policy.

481. martin, d. horror in uganda. amin's butchery.: 16 sept 1976. pp 24-26 the new york review of books 23:14.

482. materne, y. au bresil, le commissaire fleury et l'escadron de la mort.: march 1978. le monde diplomatique.

483. maulnier, t. la face de meduse du communisme. paris: gallimard, 1951. 236 pp communist state terrorism.

484. maximoff, g. the guillotine at work. vol. 1: the leninist counter-revolution. sanday: over the water, 1979. 360 pp. purports that lenin was primarily concerned with holding power by means of terror.

485. medisch-juridisch comite politieke gevangenen. rechtsstaat en staatsterreur. utrecht: mjc, 1975.

486. medvedev, r. a. let history judge. new york: vintage, 1973. stalinist terrorism.

487. melady, t. * melady, m. idi amin: hitler.: febr. 1978. pp. 63-63, 66, 104, 107-108 penthouse 9 firsthand account by u. s. ambassador to uganda.

488. melgounov, s. p. the red terror in russia. london: dent, 1925.

489. merleau-ponty, m. humanism and terror: an essay on the communist problem. boston: beacon, 1969. orig. publ. in french, 1947.

490. moore jr., b. terror and progress in the u. s. s. r. cambridge, mass.: harvard university press, 1954.

491. moreira alves, m. bresil: etat terroriste et guerilla urbaine. paris: july 1971. politique aujourd'hui on state terrorism in brazil and urban guerrilla warfare.

492. n. n. a collection of reports on bolshevism in russia. cmd . 8. * russia no. 1 london: h. m. s. o., april 1919. a rather unreliable account on bolshevist atrocities.

493. n. n. a summary of interviews with former inmates of soviet labor camps. new york: international public opinion research, 1952.

494. n. n. document on terror.: march 1952. pp. 43-57 news from behind the iron curtain 1:3 purported nkvd document assessingthe various effects of stalinist terror. surfaced originally in german. theoretically interesting in dependent of autorrship question.

495. n. n. le proces du centre terroriste trotskiste-zinovieviste devant le tribunal militaire de la court supreme de l'u. r. s. s. contre: zinoviev, g. e. ; kamenev, l. b. ; evdokimov, g. e. ;. compte rendu des debats [19 aout-24 aout 1936]. milano: 1967. 183 pp. stalin' s show trials 1936, reprint of text published in moscow.

496. n. n. one year of the rule of terror in chile. documents adopted by the international commission of enquiry into the crimes of the military junta in chile at the secretariat's meeting held in stockholm, house of parliaments, sept. 7th, 1974. helsinki: 1974. 32 pp.

497. n. n. terrorist raids and fascist laws in south vietnam; documents. hanoi: foreign languages publ. house, 1959. 88 pp.

498. n. n. the treatment of armenians in the ottoman empire 1915-16. documentspresented to viscount grey of fallodon by viscount bryce. presented to both houses of parliament by command of his majesty, october 1916. london: h. m. s. o., 1916. turkey.

499. n. n. the trial of the major war criminals. nuremberg, 1947-1948. 42 vols.

500. n. n. trials of war criminals before the nurenberg military tribunals. 15 vols. washington d. c.: 1949, .

501. n. n. un ano de regimen de terror en chile. estocolmo: comisioninternaciona de la junta militar en chile, 1974. 27 pp.

502. neumann, f. the democratic and the authoritarian state. new york: free press, 1957.

503. nordlinger, e. soldiers in politics. military coups and governments. englewood cliffs: prentice-hall, 1977.

504. oppenheimer, m. * canning, j. c. the national security state. repression within capitalism.: 1978. pp. 349-365 berkeley journal of sociology 23.

505. orlov, a. the secret history of stalin's crimes. new york: random house, 1953.

506. palmer, g. god's underground in asia. new york: appleton- century-crofts, 1953. 376 pp. on red chinese policy towards the churches.

507. petras, b. * morley, m. chile: terror for capital's sake.: 1974. pp. 36-50 new politics 1.

508. pierre-charles, g. el terror como condicionante social en haiti.: 1975. revista mexicana de sociologia 37:4.

509. pierremont, e. tche-ka. materiaux et documents sur la terreur bolcheviste recueilles par le bureau central du parti socialiste revolutionnaire russe. paris: j. povalozky & cie., 1922. bolschevik terrorism 1918-1922.

510. pirkes, th. * (ed.). die moskauer schauprozesse, 1936-1938. muenchen: 1963. 295 pp. the moscow show trials, 1936-1938.

511. plaidy, j. the spanish inquisition. london: book clubassociates, 1978. 544 pp.

512. randle, m. militarism and repression.: 1980. 156 pp. 3rd world state terrorism.

513. randle, m. militarism and repression.: 1981. pp. 61-144 alternatives 7:1.

514. reifer, a. design for terror. new york: exposition press, 1962. 82 pp. analyses 1932-41 german and 1918-58 ussr governmentrepression.

515. resnick, d. p. the white terror and the political reaction after waterloo. cambridge, mass.: harvard university press, 1966. 152 pp. france

1815-1816.

516. reyes, j. g. terrorism and redemption. japanese atrocities in the philippines. manila: 1945. 91 pp. 1939- 1945.

517. roman, n. e. * o'mara, r. the juntas of chile and argentina: studies in government by terror.: 2 april 1977. pp. 12-18 saturday review.

518. rotcage, l. going for a ride with brazil's guerrilleros.: aug. 1970. atlas on government torture.

519. rubin, b. paved with good intentions. new york: penguin, 1981. repression in iran and u. s. relations with the shah.

520. runes, d. d. despotism. a pictoral history of tyranny. new york: 1963.

521. salvemini, g. la terreur fasciste. 1922-1926. paris: 1938. state terrorism in mussolini's italy.

522. sartre, j. p. * (ed.). griechenland. der weg in den faschismus. frankfurt a. m. *: melzer, 1970. 255 pp. orig.: aujourd'hui la grece.

523. schwab, p. * frangor, g. d. greece under the junta. new york: facts on file inc., 1970.

524. selznick, p. the organizational weapon: a study of bolshevik strategy and tactics. new york: the free press of glencoe, 1960. also treats use of terror.

525. six, f. a. die politische propaganda der nsdap im kampf um die macht.: 1936. on nazi's use of violence as political propaganda in germany.

526. snyder, d. theoretical and methodological problems in the analysis of government coercion and collective violence.: 1976. pp. 277-294 journal of political and military sociology 4:2.

527. solzhenitsyn, a. a world split apart. new york: harper androw, 1979.

528. solzhenitsyn, a. gulag archipelago 1918-1956: an experiment in literary investigation. new york: harper and row, 1973. 660 pp.

529. solzhenitsyn, a. the gulag archipelago, 1918-1956. london: book club associates, 1974. soviet state repression.

530. steinberg, i. n. gewalt und terror in der revolution. oktober-revolution oder bolschewismus. berlin: rowohlt, 1931. 338 pp.

531. stohl, m. national interest and state terrorism. unpubl. paper west lafayette: purdue university, march 1982. 28 pp.

532. stohl, m. war and domestic political violence. the american capacity for repression and reaction. beverly hills: sage, 1976. 153 pp.

533. swaan, a. de. terreur als overheidsdienst.: 1975. pp. 176-184 de gids 3.

534. tanin, o. * yohan, a. militarism and fascism in japan. london: 1934.

535. tavares, f. pan de arara. la violencia militar en el brazil. mexico, d. f.: siglo veintiuno, 1972.

536. taylor, e. the strategy of terror: europe's inner front. new york: houghton mifflin, 1940. on nazi germany.

537. taylor, t. * et. al. courts of terror. soviet criminal justice and jewish emigration. new york: vintage books, 1976. 187 pp.

538. terry, j. p. state terrorism. a juridical examination in terms of existing internationa law.: 1980. pp. 94-117 journal of palestine studies 10:1.

539. thompson, j. m. robespierre and the french revolution. london: english university press, 1952.

540. tiltman, h. h. the terror in europe. new york: frederick a. stokes company, 1932. 413 pp.

541. timmerman, j. prisoner without a name, cell without a number. new york: alfred a. knopf, 1981. by jewish victim of argentinian state terrorism.

542. timperley, h. j. * (comp.). what war means: the japanese terror in china. london: 1938.

543. timperley, h. j. japanese terror in china. calcutta: thacher, spink & co., 1938. 222 pp. on japanese army's treatment of the chinese civilian population in north china, 1937-38.

544. toynbee, a. j. el terrorismo aleman en belgica. londres: hayman, christly & lilly, 1917. 166 pp. german atrocities in belgium, 1914-.

545. treaster, j. b. argentina: a state of fear.: nov. 1977. pp. 16, 18, 20, 24-26 atlantic monthly 240.

546. trotsky, l. stalin. new york: harper, 1941.

547. tutino, s. la violenza di stato in america latina. l'escempio argentino.: 1978. pp. 43-49 problemi di ulisse 14:86.

548. u. s. congress, house. committee on foreign affairs. hearings. torture and oppression in brazil. washington, d. c.: gpo, 1975.

549. u. s. office of strategic services. research and analysis branch. nazi plans for dominating germany and europe; the attitude of the nsdap toward political terror. washington: 1945.

550. u. s. office of the u. s. chief of counsel for the prosecution of axis criminality. nazi conspiracy and aggression. washington, d. c.: the office, 1946.

551. vieille, p. * banisadr, a. h. * (eds.). petrole et violence: terreur blanche et resistance en iran. paris: editions anthropos, 1974. 346 pp.

552. walsh, r. terror and greed in argentina: a writer bears witness.: 1978. dissent 25:1.

553. walter, e. v. terror and resistance: a study of political violence. new york: oxford university press, 1969. a seminal work on regime terrorism.

554. wehr, p. nonviolence and nuclear terrorism. isa paper uppsala: 1978. argues that a nation's manufacture, deployment and threats to use nuclear weapons can be seen as, in effect, state terrorism.

555. weil, c. * et. al. * (eds.). the repressive state. brazilian studies documents.: toronto, 1976.

556. wise, d. the american police state. new york: random house, 1976.

557. wolin, s. * slusser, r. m. * (eds.). the soviet secret police. new york: praeger, 1957.

558. wolpin, m. militarism and social revolution in the third world. totowa, n. j.: alanheld, osmuns, oct. 1981.

559. wriggins, h. the rulers imperative. new york: columbia university, 1969. how to do it suggestions for state terrorists.

E. INSURGENT TERRORRISM

560. aaron, h. r. the anatomy of guerrilla terror.: march 1967. p. 14-18 infantry 58.

561. allemann, f. r. macht und ohnmacht der guerilla. muenchen: piper, 1974. 340 pp.

562. arendt, h. on revolution. london: faber & faber, 1963.

563. arnold, th. der revolutionaere krieg. pfaffenhofen: ilmgauverlag, 1961.

564. asprey, r. b. war in the shadows. london: macdonald and jane's, 1975. 1615 pp.

565. berger, p. l. * heuhaus, r. j. movement and revolution. garden city, n. y.: doubleday, 1970.

566. bertelsen, j. s. * (ed.). non-state nations in international politics: comparative system analyses. new york: praeger, 1977. 272 pp.

567. cappel, r. the s. w. a. t. term manual. boulder, colo.: paladin press, 159 pp.

568. casteran, c. continents dynamites par les minorites violentes. paris: denoel, 1973.

569. chaliand, g. revolution in the third world. myths and prospects. hassocks: the harvester press, 1977. 195 pp.

570. clines, th. g. the urban insurgents. new port, rhode island: naval war college, 1972.

571. clutterbuck, r. l. guerrillas and terrorists. london: faber& faber, 1977. 125 pp.

572. clutterbuck, r. l. protest and the urban guerrilla. london: abelard-schuman, 1973. 277 pp.

573. codo, e. m. the urban guerrilla.: 1971. pp. 3-10 military review 51:8.

574. crozier, b. the rebels: a study of post-war insurrections. london: chatto & windus, 1960. 256 pp.

575. dimitrijevic, v. terorizam kao sredstvo borbe antikolonija-listickih i narodnooslobodi-lackih pokreta. .: 1973. pp. 44-61 medjunarodni radnicki pokret 4.

576. dixon, c. a. * heilbrunn, d. communist guerrilla warfare. new york: praeger, 1954.

577. drinnon, r. rebels in paradise. chicago: 1961. anarchist terrorism.

578. edwards, l. p. the natural history of revolution. new york: russell & russell, 1965. 229 pp.

579. fairbairn, g. revolutionary and communist strategy. london: 1968.

580. fairbairn, g. revolutionary guerrilla warfare. the countryside version. harmondsworth: penguin, 1974. 400 pp. pp . 348-357 on terrorism. appendix 3 on the palestinians.

581. footman, d. red prelude. westport, conn.: hyperion press, 1979.

582. forster, a. violence on the fanatical left and right.: march 1966. p. 141 annals of the american academy of political and social science 364.

583. freymond, j. * (ed.). la premiere internationale. 3 vols. geneva: 1971.

584. friedmann, w. terrorist and subversive activities.: 1956. p. 475 american journal of international law 50.

585. fromkin, d. strategy of terrorism.: 1975. pp. 683-698 foreign affairs 53:4.

586. gamson, w. a. power and discontent. homewood, ill.: dorsey, 1968.

587. garin, j. l'anarchie et les anarchistes. paris: 1885.

588. garrigan, t. b. * lopez, g. d. terrorism: a problem of political violence. ohio state: consortium for international studies education, 1980.

589. gatti, a. kleines handbuch der stadtguerilla. vier stuecke. sonderreihe dtv 06 muenchen: deutscher taschenbuch verlag, 1971. 160 pp. germany.

590. gebhardt, h. guerilas: schicksalsfrage fur den westen. seewald: 1971. 168 pp.

591. gellner, j. bayonets in the streets:urban guerrilla at home and abroad. ontario: collier-macmillan canada, 1974. 196 pp.

592. gross, f. the seizure of political power in a century of revolutions. new york: philosophical library, 1958.

593. guillen, a. la rebellion del tercer mundo. montevideo: ed. andes, 1969.

594. hamilton, l. c. dynamics of insurgent violence. preliminary findings. san francisco: american sociological association, 1978. 12 pp. unpubl. conference paper on effects of terrorism.

595. heilbrunn, o. when the counterinsurgents cannot win. london: 1969. pp. 55-58 journal of the royal united service institution 114:653.

596. hodges, d. c. * shanab, r. e. a. * (eds.). national liberation fronts, 1960-1970. new york: william morrow , 1972.

597. horowitz, i. l. political terrorism and state power.: 1973. p. 147 journal of political and military sociology 1.

598. horowitz, i. l. toward a qualitative micropolitics of terror. paper conference on international terrorism, march1976. washington d. c.: u. s. department of state, 1976. 11 pp.

599. howard, a. j. urban guerrilla warfare in a democratic society.: october 1972. pp. 231-243 medicine science and the law 12:4.

600. huntington, s. p. civil violence and the process of development. london: institute for strategic studies, 1972. adelphi papers 89.

601. international association of chiefs of police. urban warfare. gaithersburg, md.: iacp, 35 pp.

602. jay, m. politics of terror.: 1971. p. 72 partisan review 38.

603. jenkins, b. m. an urban strategy for guerrillas and governments. santa monica: rand, 1972. 13 pp.

604. jenkins, b. m. the five stages of urban guerrilla warfare: challenge of the 1970's. santa monica: rand, 1971.

605. justice, b. violence in the city. fort worth, tex.: texas christian university press, 1973.

606. kautsky, k. terrorismus und kommunismus. ein beitrag zur naturgeschichte der revolution. berlin: verlag neues vaterland, 1919. 154 pp.

607. krippendorff, e. minorities, violence and peace research.: 1974. pp. 27-40 journal of peace research 16:1.

608. kuiper, r. l. theory and practice of insurgency. maxwell air force base, alabama: air force r. o. t. c. air university, sept. 1974. educational journal.

609. lamberg, r. f. la guerrilla urbana: condiciones y perspectivas de la 'segunda ola guerrilla. pp. 431-443 foro internacional 11:3.

610. laqueur, w. continuing failure of terrorism.: 1976. p . 69 harpers 253:1518.

611. leiser, b. m. terrorism, guerrilla warfare, and international morality.: 1977. pp. 39-65 stanford journal of international studies 12.

612. leites, n. * wolf, c. rebellion and authority: an analytic essay on insurgent conflicts. chicago: markham, 1970.

613. mallin, j. * (ed.). terror and urban guerrillas: a study of tactics and documents. coral gables, fla.: university of miami press, 1971.

614. mallin, j. * (ed.). terrorism as a political weapon.: 1971. pp. 45-52 air university review 22 mainly on vietnam and latin america.

615. mansback, r. w. * ferguson, y. h. * lampert, d. e. the web of world politics: nonstate actors in the global system. englewoodcliffs: prentice-hall, 1976. 326 pp.

616. mathu, m. the urban guerrilla. richmond, b. c.: lsm information center, 1974. 94 pp.

617. methvin, e. h. the riot makers: the technology of social demolition. new rochelle, n. y.: arlington house, 1970. editor of the reader's digest on terrorists.

618. mickolus, e. f. growth and prevalence of terrorism. g. s. roukis and p. j. montana. * (eds.) managing terrorism: strategies for the corporate executive. westport, conn.: greenwood press, 1982.

619. miller, j. a. terrorism and guerrilla warfare. a model for comparative analysis. ph. d. diss. washington, d. c.: american university,

620. miller, n. * aya, r. * (eds.). national liberation. revolution in the third world. new york: free press , 1971.

621. momboisse, r. m. riots, revolts and insurrections. springfield, ill.: charles c. thomas, 1967.

622. moss, r. the collapse of democracy. london: abacus, 1977.

623. moss, r. the war for the cities. new york: coward, mccann and geoghegan, 1972. 288 pp. published in the u. k. under the title: urban guerrillas: the new face of political violence. london, temple smith, 1971.

624. moss, r. urban guerilla warfare. london: international institute for strategicstudies, 1971. adelphi papers 79 in the appendix:minimanual of the urban guerilla, by carlos marighella.

625. mucchielli, r. la subversion. paris: clc, 1976.

626. mueller-borchert, h. j. guerilla im industriestaat. ziele, ansatzpunkte und erfolgsaussichten. hamburg: hoffmann undcampe, 1973. 182 pp.

627. n. n. terror as a weapon of political agitation. in: h. eckstein * (ed.) internal war. new york: free press, 1964. pp . 71-99 one of the most seminal articles.

628. n. n. terror gangs. is anyone safe?. special report: 22 may 1978. pp. 30-35 u. s. news and world report wit individual reports on italy, the middle east, japan, ireland and germany.

629. n. n. terrorisme als vorm van politiek geweld. tilburg: katholieke hogeschool tilburg, 1977. 242 pp. collection of lectures and articles.

630. n. n. trends in urban guerrilla tactics.: july 1973. pp. 3-7 fbi law enforcement bulletin 42:7.

631. nettlau, m. geschichte der anarchie. 3 vols. bremen: 1978. orig. 1925.

632. niezing, j. * (ed.). urban guerrilla: studies on the theory, strategy and practice of political violence in modern societies. rotterdam: rotterdam university press, 1974. 154 pp.

633. o'neill, b. e. * alberts, d. j. * rossetti, s. j. * (eds.). political violence and insurgency: a comparative approach. arvade, col.: phoenix press, 1974. 518 pp.

634. o'neill, b. e. * heaton, w. r. * alberts, d. j. insurgency in the modern world. boulder, colo.: westview press, 1980.

635. oppenheimer, m. the urban guerrilla. chicago: quadrangle, 1969. 188 pp.

636. paret, p. * shy, j. w. guerrillas in the 1960's. rev. ed. new york: praeger, 1962. 98 pp.

637. price jr., h. e. the strategy and tactics of revolutionary terrorism.: jan. 1977. pp. 52-66 comparative studies in society and history 19:1.

638. roberts, k. e. * munger, m. d. urban guerrillas in the americas. military issues research memo: 30 dec. 1976. 29 pp.

639. roquigny, colonel de. urban terrorism.: 1969. pp. 93-99 military review 38:11 orig. in: revue militaire d'information,fevr. '68: discusses the nature of urban terrorism as an arm of psychological warfare.

640. smart, i. m. h. the power of terror.: 1975. pp. 225-237 international journal 30:2.

641. snodgrass, t. urban insurgency: observations based on the venezuelan experience, 1960 to 1964. unpublished ma thesis austin, texas: 1972.

642. sola pool, i. de, * yates, d. j. * laqua, a. * blum, r. * weatlake, m. report on urban insurgency studies. . new york: simulmatics corp., 1966.

643. sorenson, j. l. urban insurgency cases. santa barbara: defense research corp., 1965.

644. sperber, m. uber die gewalt von unten.: 1971. merkur. zeitschrift fur europaeisches denken 25:3.

645. strother, r. s. * methvin, e. h. terrorism on the rampage.: nov. 1975. pp. 73-77 reader's digest 107 .

646. teitler, g. the urban guerrilla, as a revolutionary phenomenon and as a recruitingproblem. in: j. niezing * (ed.). urban guerilla: studies on the theory, strategy, and practice of political violence in modern societies. rotterdam: rotterdam university press, 1974.

647. veen, th. w. van. delicten plegen om de wereld te veranderen. pp. 176-181 maandblad voor berechtiging en reclassering 50: 9.

648. veen, th. w. van. het plegen van delicten uit politieke motieven.: nov. 1971. pp. 232-235 maandblad voor berechtiging en reclassering 50:11.

649. verhegge, g. bedenkingen bij een aktueel fenomeen. het verzetsterrorisme.: 18 nov. 1978. pp. 753-786 rechtskundig weekblad.

650. walzer, m. the new terrorists. 30 aug. 1975 newrepublic.

651. wilkinson, d. revolutionary civil war. palo alto, cal.: page-ficklin, 1975.

652. wohlstetter, r. terror on a grand scale.: may 1976. survival 181.

653. wolf, j. b. appraising the performance of terrorist organizations. gaithersburg, md.: lacp, 1978.

654. wolf, j. b. ethnic, religious and racial dimensions of contemporary terrorist activity :eta, ira and the kkk. gaithersburg, md.: i. a. c. p., 1979. update report 5:4.

655. wolf, j. b. terrorist manipulation of the democratic process.: april 1975. pp. 102-112 police journal(united kingdom) 48:2.

656. wolf, j. b. urban terrorist operations.: october 1976. pp. 277-284 police journal(england) 49.

F. VIGILANT TERRORISM

657. brown, r. m. legal and behavioral perspectives on american vigilantism. perspectives in america.: 1971. pp. 106-116 history 5.

658. brown, r. m. strain of violence: historical studies of american violence and vigilantism. london: oxford university press, 1975.

659. chalmers, d. m. hooded americanism. the first century of the ku klux klan 1865-1965. chicago: quadrangle books, 1968. 420 pp.

660. cutler, j. e. lynch-law an investigation into the history of lynching in the united states. westport, conn.: greenwood press, 1978. reprint of 1905 edition.

661. fortuny, j. m. guatemala: the political situation and revolutionary politics.: febr. 1967. world marxist review discusses u. s. involvement in the establishment of guatemalan death squads.

662. horn, f. s. invisible empire: the story of the ku klux klan, 1866-1871. boston: houghton mifflin, 1939. .

663. huie, w. b. die weissen ritter des ku-klux-klan. wien- hamburg: zsolnay, 1969. 226 pp. orig.: three lives for mississippi.

664. krueger, g. die brigade ehrhardt. berlin: 1932. interwar germany: free corps.

665. lipset, s. m. * rabb, e. the politics of unreason: right-wing extremism in america, 1790-1970. new york : harper & row, 1970.

666. lopes, a. l'escadron de la mort. sao paulo 1968-1971. paris: 1973,

667. madison, a. vigilantism in america. new york: seaburypress, 1973.

668. national association for the advancement of colored people. thirty years of lynching in the united states 1889-1918. reprint of 1919 edition westport, conn.: greenwood press, 1978.

669. nicolosi, a. s. the rise and fall of the new jersey vigilant societies.: 1968. new jersey history 86 .

670. rice, a. s. the ku klux klan in american politics. washington, d. c.: public affairs press, 1962.

671. rosenbaum, h. j. * et. al. * (eds.). vigilante politics. philadelphia: university of pennsylvania press, 1976.

672. rosenbaum, h. j. * sederberg, p. c. vigilantism: an analysis of establishment violence.: 1974. pp. 541-570 comparative politics 6.

673. steinmetz, s. r. selbsthilfe(private justice). in: a. vierkandt * (ed.) handwoerterbuch der soziologie. . stuttgart: ferd. enke verlag, 1931. pp. 518-522.

674. steward, g. r. committee of vigilance: revolution in san francisco, 1851. boston: hougthon mifflin co., 1964.

675. trelease, a. w. white terror: the ku klux klan conspiracy and southern reconstruction. new york: harper & row, 1971. 557pp.

G. OTHER TYPES OF TERRORISM

H. TERRORISTIC ACTIVITIES BY REGION AND COUNTRY

H.1. Western Europe, general

676. **blok, a.** the mafia of a sicilian village, 1860-1960. oxford: blackwel a, 1974. also: new york: harper & row, 1975.

677. **bugliosi, v. * gentry, c.** helter skelter. new york: bantambooks, 1975. on manson "family" atrocities in california.

678. **cohen, n.** the pursuit of the millenium. revolutionary messianism in medieval and reformation europe and its bearing on modern totalitarian movements. new york: harper, 1961.

679. **guiraud, j.** histoire de l'inquisition au moyen age. paris: 1935.

680. **holt, s.** terror in the name of god: the story of the sons of freedom doukhobors. toronto: mcclelland and steward, 1964. 312 pp. on canadian anti-authoritarian religious immigrant group.

681. **kamen, h.** die spanische inquisition. munich: 1969. the spanish inquisition.

682. **maisonneuve, h.** etude sur les origines de l'inquisition. paris: 1960.

683. **pantelone, m.** the mafia and politics. new york: 1966.

684. **sabatini, r.** torquemada and the spanish inquisition. boston: houghton mifflin, 1924.

685. **alberoni, f.** fuori e dentro l'europa.: ivi, 1978.

686. **crozier, b.** terrorism: the problem in perspective. london: institute for the study of conflict, february 1976.

687. **di biase, b. * (ed.).** terrorism today in italy and western europe. sidney: circolo g. di vittorio, 1978. .

688. **esman, m. j. * (ed.).** ethnic conflict in the western world. ithaca: cornell university press, 1977.

689. **fletcher-cooke, c.** terrorism and the european community. london: european conservative group, 1979.

690. **goodman, r. w. * et. al.** a compendium of european theater terrorist groups. alabama: maxwell air force base, 1976.

691. **grieg, i.** today's revolutionaries. a study of some prominent modern revolutionary movements and methods of sedition in europe and the united states. london: foreign affairs publ. co., 1970. 120 pp.

692. **guillaume, j. * (ed.).** l'internationale. documents et souvenirs, 1864-1887. 4 paris: 1910. anarchist terrorism.

693. **hayes, b.** the effects of terrorism in society. an analysis with particularreference to the united kingdom and the european economic community. 1979. pp. 4-10 political studies 2:3.

694. **hess, h.** entwicklung des terrorismus in italien, frankreich und den niederlanden: vergleiche zur situation in den bundesrepublik deutschland.

695. **melander, g.** terroristlagen-ett onodigt ont. stockholm: norstedts, 1975. 141 pp.

696. **salvi, s.** le nazioni proibite. guida a dieci colonie interne dell'europa occidentale. firenze: vallecchi, 1973.

697. **sjaastad, a. c.** deterrence of terrorism and attacks against off-shore oil instal- lations in northern europe. in: y. envon * (ed.) international violence: terrorism, surprise and control. jerusalem: hebrew university of jerusalem, leonard davis institute for international relations, 1979. pp. 182-202.

698. **teodori, m.** storia delle neuve sinistre in europa(1956-1976). bologna: malino, 1976. 694 pp.

699. **venohr, w. * (ed.).** europas ungeloeste fragen. die probleme nationaler und religioeser min derheiten. reinbek: rowohlt, 1971. 119 pp.

700. wilkinson, p. still working for the extinction of mankind; an assessment of the significance of the resurgence of fascist terrorism in western europe. january 1981. pp. 27-31 across the board.

701. wolf, j. b. agitational terrorism in europe: jan. 1980-febr. 1981. gaithersburg, md. i. a. c. p., 1981. update report 7:2.

702. wolf, j. b. european neo-fascist groups. gaithersburg, md. i. a. c. p., 1980. update report 6:6.

H.1.1. German Federal Republic

703. althammer, w. * rombach, b. gegen den terror. texte - dokumente. muenchen: hanns seidel-stiftung, 1978 . 213 pp. csu-publication, with chronology of terroristic acts up to nov. 1977.

704. amerongen, m. van * (comp.). de baader-meinhofgroep. een documentaire. groningen: xenos, 1975. 101 pp.

705. augstein, j. * et. al. terrorismus contra rechtsstaat. darmstadt and neuwied: 1976.

706. bartsch, g. anarchismus in deutschland. bd. 2-3: 1965-1973 hannover: 1973.

707. bauss, g. die studentenbewegung der sechziger jahre in der bundesrepublik und westberlin. handbuch. koeln: pahl-rugenstein, 1977. 353 pp. on german student movement in the 60s.

708. becker, j. hitler's children. london: panther, 1978. 415 pp. on baader-meinhof group.

709. bin der, s. terrorismus. bonn: 1978.

710. blei, h. terrorism, domestic and international: the west german experience. in: report of the task force on disorders and terrorism. washington, d. c. national advisory committee on criminal justice standards and goals, december 1976. pp. 497-506.

711. bock, h. m. geschichte des linken radikalismus in deutschland. frankfurt a. m. suhrkamp, 1976.

712. boeden, g. politisch motivierte gewaltkriminalitaet. zwischenbilanz und prognose. ein beitrag zum gegenwartigen stand des terrorismus. 1976. onterrorism in the german federal republic.

713. boehme, w. * (ed.). terrorismus und freiheit. heidelber: kriminalistik verlag, 1978. 85 pp.

714. boell, h. * gruetzbach, f. * et. al. * (comp.). freies geleit fuer ulrike meinhof. ein artikel und seine folgen. koeln: kiepenheuer & witsch, 1972. 192 pp.

715. botzat, t. * et. al. ein deutscher herbst. zustaende, berichte, kommentare. frankfurt: 1978. 205 pp. compilation of articles and analyses of media coverage of schleyer incident, 1977.

716. brudigam, h. das jahr 1933. frankfurt a. m. roderberg verlag, 1978. 136 pp.

717. brueckner, p. * sichtermann, b. gewalt und solidaritaet. zur ermordung ulrich schmueckers durchgenossen: dokumente and analysen. berlin: wagenbach, 1974. 103 pp.

718. brueckner, p. politisch-psychologische anmerkungen zur roten-armee-fraktion (raf). 1973. pp. 73-100 sozialistisches jahrbuch 5(politik):47.

719. brueckner, p. ulrike marie meinhof und die deutschen verhaeltnisse. berlin: wagenbach, 1977. 191 pp.

720. carlson, a. r. anarchism in germany. new york: 197.

721. chorus, b. als op ons geschoten wordt. gewapend verzet in de brd. groningen: pamflet, 1978. 147 pp. on raf in german federal republic.

722. conley, m. proteste, subversion und stadtguerilla. koeln: 1974. pp. 71-87 beitraege zur konfliktforschung 4.

723. corves, e. terrorism and criminal justice operations in the frg. in: r. d. crelinsten, d. laberge-altmejd and d. szabo * (eds.) terrorism and criminal justice: an international perspective. lexington, mass. lexington books, 1978.

724. crijnen, a. j. de baader-meinhof groep. utrecht: spectrum, 1975. 125 pp.

725. deppe, f. * (ed.). 2. juni 1967 und die studentenbewegung heute. beitr. von g. amendt, h. gellhardt, h. lederer, w. leferre, u. a. dortmund: weltkreis-verlag, 1977. 153 pp.

726. dokumentation der bundesregierung und des freistaates bayern. der ueberfall auf die israelische olympiamannschaft 19 sept 1974. bonn: presse-und informationsamt der bundesregierung, 63 pp.

727. eckstein, g. germany: democracy in trouble. coping with terrorism. 1978. dissent 25:1.

728. elliott, j. d. west germany's political response to contemporary terrorism. gaithersburg, md. international association of chiefs of police., 1978.

729. eucken-erdsiek, e. die macht der min derheit. eine auseinandersetzung mit dem neuen anarchismus. freiburg: herder, 1971. 123 pp.

730. fach, w. souveraenitaet und terror. leviathan, 1978. pp. 333-353 6:3 on public reaction to terrorism.

731. faina, g. * et. al. * (eds.). la guerriglia urbana nella germania federale. genova: collectivo editoriale, 1976.

732. fetscher, i. terrorismus und reaktion. frankfurt a. m. europaeische verlagsanstalt, 1977. 148 pp.

733. fetscher, i. terrorismus und rechtsstaat. 1977. neue rundschau 88:4.

734. fichter, t. * loennendonker, s. kleine geschichte der sds. von 1946 bis zur selbstaufloesung. berlin: rotbuch, 1977. history of german student movement.

735. funke, m. * (ed.). extremismus im demokratischen rechtsstaat. ausgewaehlte texte und materialien zur aktuellen diskussion. bonn: 1978. 612 pp. schriftenreihe der bundeszentrale fuer politische bildung 122.

736. funke, m. terrorismus - ermittlungsversuch zu einer herausforderung. 1977. aus politik und zeitgeschichte 41.

737. gemmer, k. problems, means and methods of police action in the federal republic of germany. in: r. crelinsten and d. szabo * (eds.) hostage-taking. lexington, mass. lexington books, 1979. pp. 119-126.

738. german federal press and information office. dokumentation zu den ereignissen und entscheidungen im zusammenhang mit der entfuehrung von hanns martin schleyer und der lufthansa machine 'landshut'. bonn: november 1977.

739. glaser, h. die diskussion ueber den terrorismus. ein dossier. 24 june 1978. aus politik und zeitgeschichte, beilage zur wochenzeitung das parlament 25.

740. goote, t. kameraden die rotfront und reaktion erschossen. berlin: 1934.

741. goyke, e. terror. bonn: bundeszentrale fuer politischebildung, zeitlupe 2.

742. grossarth-maticek, r. revolution der gestoerten? heidelberg: 1975. on german student activists' alleged pathology.

743. gruetzbach, f. * (comp.). heinrich boell: freies geleit fuer ulrike meinhof. ein artikel und seine folgen. koeln: kiepenheuer und witsch, 1972. 192 pp. documentation on reactions to boell's 10 jan. 1972 article in der spiegel dealing with bild-zeitung's coverageof german terrorists.

744. guenther, j. terror und terrorismus. 1972. pp. 32-42 neue deutsche hefte 19:4.

745. gumbel, e. j. les crimes politiques en allemagne(1919-1929). paris: 1931.

746. gumbel, e. j. vier jahre politischer mord. berlin: 1922. germany, 1918-1922.

747. habermas, j. die buehne des terrors. ein brief an kurth sontheimer. 1977. pp. 944-959 merkur 31.

748. hederberg, h. operation leo. stockholm: raben & sjogren boktorlag ab, on german raf.

749. herold, h. erscheinungsformen des terrors und anarchistischer bewegung in deutschland. deutsche ipa-sektion, 1976. ipa- zeitschrift(internat. polizei-ass.) 1.

750. herold, h. taktische wandlungen des deutschen terrorismus. dec. 1976. pp. 401-405 die polizei, zentralorgan fuer das sicherheits-und ordnungswesen 67:12.

751. hillmayer, h. roter und weisser terror in bayern nach 1818. muenchen: nasser, 1976. 224 pp.

752. horchem, h. j. die rote armee fraktion. analyse und bewertung einer extremistischen gruppe in der bundesrepublik deutschland. 1974. pp. 83-110 beitraege zur konfliktforschung 4:2.

753. horchem, h. j. extremisten in einer selbstbewussten demokratie. rote armee fraktion - rechtsextremismus - der lange marsch durch die institutionen. freiburg i. br. herder, 1975. a police officer's account.

754. horchem, h. j. right-wing extremism in western germany. london: isc, 1975. 11 pp. conflict studies 65.

755. horchem, h. j. the urban guerrilla in west germany. origins and perspectives. unpublished paper presented at the u. s. department of state conference on terrorism washington, d. c. march 1976.

756. horchem, h. j. west germany's red army anarchists. london: institute for the study of powerand conflict., 1974. conflict studies 46.

757. horchem, h. j. wurzeln des terrorismus in deutschland. 1976. die neue gesellschaft 1 roots of terrorism in the german federal republic.

758. internationales kommittee zur verteidigung politischer gefangener in westeuropa * (eds.). letzte texte von ulrike. n. p. june 1976.

759. jungsozialisten nrw. terror dient der reaktion. kritische texte. gelsenkirchen: 1977.

760. kahl, w. akteure und aktionen waehrend der formationsphase des terrorismus. bonn: 1977. p. 272 terror, schriftenreihe des bundeszentrale fuer politische bildung.

761. kaltenbrunner, g. -k. die wiederkehr der woelfe. die progression des terrors. freiburg i. br. herder, 1978.

762. kepplinger, h. m. statusdevianz und meinungsdevianz. die sympathisanten der baader-meinhof-gruppe. 1976. pp. 770-800 koelner zeitschrift fuer psychologie und sozialpsychologie 26:4.

763. kogon, e. * (ed.). terrorismus and gewaltkriminalitaet. herausforderung fuer den rechtsstaat. frankfurt a. m. aspekte, 1975. 114 pp.

764. komitees gegen folter an politischen gefangenen in der brd * (ed.). der kampf gegen die vernichtungshaft. 1975.

765. kommunistische partei deutschland. politische unterdrueckung in der brd und westberlin. koeln: verlag rote fahne, 1976. 159 pp.

766. langguth, g. die protestbewegung in der bundesrepublik deutschland 1968-1976. koeln: verlag wissenschaft und politik, 1976. 363 pp.

767. langguth, g. protestbewegung am ende. die neue linke als vorhut der dkp. mainz: 1971.

768. lasky, m. j. ulrike meinhof and the baader-meinhof-gang. june 1975. pp. 9-23 encounter 44:6.

769. luebbe, h. endstation terror. rueckblick auf lange maersche. stuttgart: 1978.

770. luebbe, h. freiheit und terror. 1977. merkur 31:9.

771. mahler, h. * et. al. bewaffneter kampf: texte der raf. auseinandersetzung und kritik. graz: verlag rote sonne, 1973.

772. mahler, h. ausbruch aus einem missverstaendnis. 1977. pp. 77-98 kursbuch 48.

773. mahler, h. erklaerungen von -. berlin: rote hilfe, 1974.

774. mahler, h. horst mahlers erklaerung zum prozessbeginn am 9. 10. 72 vor dem 1. strafsenat des westberliner kammergerichts. n. p. 1972.

775. mahler, h. interview with - on terrorism. amsterdam: febr. 1978. 't kan anders.

776. mahler, h. terrorism in west-germany: interview with horst mahler. socialist review 39.

777. mahler, h. verkehrsrechts- und verkehrsaufklaerungs-heft. die neue strassenverkehrs-ordnung mit den neuen verkehrszeichen und hinweisschildernsowi. 1971. cover title for: die luecken der revolutionaeren theorie schliessen - die rote armee aufbauen; later published as: der bewaffneter kampf in west-europa.

778. marenssin, e. * (ed.). la bande a baader ou la violence revolutionnaire. paris: edition champ libre, 1977.

779. marenssin, e. * zahl, p. p. * (eds.). die 'baader meinhof bande' oder revolutionaere gewalt. haarlem: editora oneimada, 1974. 210 pp. raf texts.

780. meinhof, u. dem volk dienen - rote armee fraktion: stadtguerilla und klassenkampf. 24 april 1972. der spiegel 18.

781. meinhof, u. dokumente einer rebellion. 10 jahre "konkret"-kolumnen. mit einem beitrag von r. riemeck und einer vorbemerkung von k. riehl. hamburg: konkret-buchverlag, 1972. 111 pp.

782. meinhof, u. pequena antologia. barcelona: anagram, 1976. 109 pp.

783. merten, k. terreur uit gevangeniscellen. 6 june 1978. pp. 305-310 het tijdschrift voor de politie 40 on raf in germany.

784. meyer, t. an ende der gewalt. der deutsche terrorismus - protokol eines jahrzehnts. frankfurt, berlin, wien: 1980.

785. mueller-borchert, h. j. grossstadtguerilla. pp. 337-340, pp. 77-79, 363-368 die polizei 61:9, 62.

786. n. n. ──. 1977. pp. 20-35 pflasterstrand . unabhaengige stadtzeitung frankfurt/m. 18 self-justification of urban guerrillas.

787. n. n. ──. revolutionaerer zorn, zeitung der revolutionaeren zellen. flugschrift ohne unterzeichnung eines presseverantwort-lichen, erschien u. a nach dem attentat auf die stockholmer botschaft im mai 1975.

788. n. n. andreas baader? er ist ein feigling! pater homann vor seiner verhaftung ueber die baader-meinhof-gruppe. 1971. pp. 47-61 der spiegel 25:48.

789. n. n. bomben in der bundesrepublik. die guerilla kaempft aus dem hinterhalt. 1972. pp. 24-34 der spiegel 26: 23.

790. n. n. buback - ein nachruf. wer sich nicht wehrt lebt verkehrt. dokumentation der auseinandersetzung um die dokumentation'buback- ein nachruf'. berlin: das politische buch, 1977.

791. n. n. der baader-meinhof-report. dokumente, analysen, zusammenhaenge. aus den akten des bundeskriminalamtes, der "sonderkommissionbonn" und dem bundesamt fuer verfassunmgsschutz. mainz: von hase und koehler verlag, 1972. 245 pp.

792. n. n. die berliner presse, die studentenschaft und die polizei. muenchen: 1968. pp. 176-182 vorgaenge 3.

793. n. n. die erschiessung des georg rauch. berlin: wagenbach, 1976. 153 pp.

794. n. n. die mescalero affaere. ein lehrstueck fuer aufklaerung undpolitische kultur. hannover: internationalismus buchladen und verlagsgesellschaft, 1977. 80 pp. on public reaction to buback murder.

795. n. n. die zeitbombe der gegenwart. terrorismus in deutschland. worms: 1977. 95 pp.

796. n. n. dokumentation der bundesregierung zur entfuehrung von hanns martinschleyer. ergebnisse und entscheidungen im zusammenhang mit der entfuehrung von h. m. schleyer und der lufthansa-maschine "landshut". muenchen: goldmann, 1977. 384 pp.

government documentation following the schleyer murder.

797. n. n. dokumentation ueber aktivitaeten anarchistischer gewalttaeter in der bundesrepublik deutschland. bonn: innenministerium, 1975. 165 pp. a compendium of confiscated baader-meinhof writings seized during raids on terrorists' cells in july 1973 and on febr. 4, 1974, publishedby the german interior ministry.

798. n. n. dokumentation zum hunger- und durststreik der politischen gefangenen. frankfurt a/m: s. lissner, aug. 1977.

799. n. n. dossier terrorisme en allemagne. 1975. pp. 29-191 documents 2-3 with extensive bibliography.

800. n. n. erklaerung der bundesregierung zum terroranschlag auf die deutschebotschaft in stockholm. abgegeben von bundeskanzler schmidt vor dem deutschen bundestag am 25. april 1975. presse - und informationsamt der bundesregierung, 1975. pp. 517-520 bulletin 55.

801. n. n. extremismus - terrorismus - kriminalitaet. bonn: 1978. schriftenreiheder bundeszentrale fuer politische bildung 38.

802. n. n. holger. der kampf geht weiter. dokumente and beitraege zum konzept stadtguerilla. gaiganz: 1975.

803. n. n. in die bank und durchgeladen! baader-meinhof-prozess gegen ruhland. horst mahler ueber stadtguerilla. d. poser antwortet heinrich boell. 1972. pp. 28-47 der spiegel 26 :5.

804. n. n. kommen sie raus. ihre chance ist gleich null. gefasst: baader. 1972. pp. 19-32 der spiegel 26 :24.

805. n. n. la morte di ulrike meinhof. rapporto commissione internazionaled'inchiestra. napels: libreria tullio pirouti, 1979. 'the death of ulrike meinhof', report of the internationalcommiss of inquiry.

806. n. n. leben gegen gewalt. 186 pp. kursbuch march1978 special issue dedicated to raf in germany.

807. n. n. nicht heimlich und nicht kuehl. entgegungen an dienst - u. a. herren. berlin: 1978. 135 pp.

808. n. n. pfarrer, die dem terror dienen? bischof scharf und der berliner kirchenstreit 1974, eine dokumentation. reinbek: rowohlt, 1975. 137 pp.

809. n. n. stadsguerilla in de brd; de revolutionaere zelle. groningen: stichting pamflet, 1977.

810. n. n. terror und gewaltkriminalitaet. herausforderung fuer den rechtsstaat. frankfurt a. m. aspekte verlag, 1975. 114 pp.

811. n. n. terror. hamburg: 1970. pp. 29-7 der monat 267.

812. n. n. terrorism and politics in west-germany. cambridge, u. k. capg, 160 pp.

813. n. n. terrorisme en allemagne. 1975. pp. 31-191 documents. revue mensuelle des questions allemandes 30:2- 3.

814. n. n. terrorismus in der demokratischen gesellschaft. bergedorfer gespraechskreis zu fragen der freien industriellen gesellschaft. hamburg: 1978. protokoll 59.

815. n. n. the west german guerilla. interviews with h. j. klein and members of the june 2nd group. orkney: cienfuegos, 1981.

816. n. n. vorbereitung der raf-prozese durch presse, polizei und justiz. berlin: 1975. 192 pp.

817. n. n. wiederkehr der woelfe. freiburg i. b. herder, 1978. 192 pp.

818. nassi, e. la banda meinhoff. milano: fabbri, 1974.

819. negt, o. * grossman, i. * (eds.). die auferstehung der gewalt. springerblockade und politische reaktion in der bundesrepublik. frankfurt a. m. eva, 1968.

820. oestreicher, p. roots of terrorism - west germany: special case. 1978. pp. 75-80 round table 269.

821. otto, k. a. vom ostenmarsch zur apo. geschichte der aussenparlementari-schen opposition in der brd 1960-1970. frankfurt: 1977.

822. philip, u. combatting terrorism in federal germany. 1979. pp. 999-1001 international defence review 12:6.

823. possony, s. t. * bouchey, l. f. international terrorism: the communist connection. with a casestudy of the west german terrorist ulrike meinhof. new york: american council for world freedom, 1978. 172 pp.

824. presse- und informationsamt der bundesregierung. der ueberfall auf die israelische olympiamannschaft. dokumentation der bundesregierung und des freistaates bayern. bonn: bundesdruckerei, 1972. 63 pp.

825. raf. raf-teksten. 280 pp.

826. raf. textes des prisonniers de la fraction armee rouge et derniereslettres d' ulrike meinhof. paris: maspero, 1977.

827. rammstedt, o. h. die instrumentalisierung des baader-meinhof gruppe. 1975. pp. 27-38 frankfurter hefte 30:3.

828. rauball, r. * (ed.). die baader-meinhof-gruppe: aktuelle dokumente de gruyter. berlin: walter de gruyter, 1973. 265 pp.

829. rinser, l. * et. al. terroristen -sympathisanten? im weltbild der rechten. eine dokumentation. sonderheft 1 muenchen: pressedienstdemokrat. initiative., 1977.

830. roehl, k. r. die genossin. muenchen: molden, 1975. 324 pp. a novel written by the ex-husband of ulrike meinhof, givingan unflattering picture of her.

831. roehl, k. r. fuenf finger sind keine faust. koeln: kiepenheuer & witsch, 1974. 456 pp. a history of konkret, by meinhof's ex-husband.

832. roemel, g. die anarchistische gewaltkriminalitaet in der brd. 1975. kriminalistiek 29:12.

833. rote armee fraktion. dem volke dienen. 1972.

834. rote armee fraktion. die aktion des schwarzen september in muenchen. 1973.

835. rote armee fraktion. r. a. f. -boek. 2 vols. groningen: stichting pamflet, 1978. ca 300 pp. 58 raf texts. .

836. rote armee fraktion. texte der r. a. f. malmoe: verlag bo cavefors, 1977.

837. rote armee fraktion. ueber den bewaffneten kampf in westeuropa. berlin: wagenbach, 1971. 70pp. rotbuch 29 "strassenverkehrs-ordnung", ascribed to horst mahler, banned in germany.

838. rote armee fraktion. zur frage des verhaeltnisses von marx zu blanqui. graz: 1973. raf texts; the title is deliberately misleading to evade censorship.

839. rupprecht, r. entwickelt sich in der bundesrepublik ein rechtsextremer terrorismus?. 1979. pp. 285ff kriminalistik 6.

840. salomon, e. von. die geaechteten. berlin: 1932. on post-world war 1 'freikorps'.

841. schaefer, g. rote armee-fraktion und baader-meinhof-gruppe. links, jan. 1972.

842. schelsky, h. die arbeit tun die anderen. klassenkampf und priesterherrschaftde intellektuellen. opladen: westdeutscher verlag, 1975. 447 pp. pp. 342-363 deal with relationship between german intellectuals(esp. h. boel and terrorism.

843. schubert, a. * (ed.). stadtguerilla. tupamaros in uruguay. rote armee fraktion in der bundesrepublik. berlin: wagenbach, 1971. 129 pp.

844. schwinge, e. terroristen und ihre verteidiger. 1975. pp. 35-49 politische meinung 20:158.

845. sochaczewski, j. "demokratischer terror" in der bundesrepublik. vorstufe oder abart des verdekten kampfes?. muenchen: 1968. pp. 187-192 wehrkunde 17:4.

846. sontheimer, k. gewalt und terror in der politik. 197. neue rundschau 88:1.

847. sperber, m. sieben fragen zur gewalt. leben in dieser zeit. deutscher taschenbuch verlag,

848. spk. aus der krankheit eine waffen machen. eine agitationsschrift des sozialistischen patientenkollektivs an der universitaet heidelberg. muenchen: trikont, 1972. 136 pp.

849. stuberger, u. g. * (ed.). in der strafsache gegen andreas baader, ulrike meinhof, jan-carl raspe, gudrun ensslin wegen mordes u. a. dokumente aus dem prozess. frankfurt: syndikat, 1972. 280 pp.

850. stumper, a. considerations a propos de l'affaire baader-meinhof. revue de droit penal et de criminologie.

851. thadden, a. von. die schreibtischtaeter. das geistige umfeld des terrorismus. hannover: greifen verlag, 1977. 148 pp.

852. tophoven, r. * (ed.). politik durch gewalt. guerilla und terrorismus heute. bonn: wehr und wissen, 1976 . 173 pp. papers on historical, political, social-psychology and military aspects and causes of subversive warfare. .

853. volck, h. rebellen um ehre. berlin: 1932.

854. volker, b. l'affaire schleyer. la guerre d'andreas baader. heure parheure. documentation de michel vey. menges, 1977. 224 pp.

855. wagenlehne, g. motivation for political terrorism in germany. in: m. livingston * et. al. * (eds.) international terrorism in the contemporary world. westport, conn. greenwood press, 1978. pp. 195-203.

856. wassermann, r. * (ed.). terrorismus contra rechtsstaat. darmstadt: luchterhand, 1976. 266 pp.

857. wassermann, r. * (ed.). terrorismus und rechtsstaat. 1978. gewerkschaftliche monatshefte 29:2.

858. wellner, a. terrorismus und gesellschaftskritik. in: j. habersmas, stichworte zur'geistigen situation derzeit'. frankfurt, 1979.

859. winn, g. f. t. terrorism, alienation and german society. in: y. alexander and j. m. gleason * (eds.) behavioral and quantitative perspectives on terrorism. new york: pergamon press, 1981. pp. 256-282.

860. wit, j. de * ponsaers, p. on facts and how to use them. 1978. pp. 363-375 terrorism 1.

861. wolff, f. * windaus, e. studentenbewegung 67-69. frankfurt a. m. roter stern, 1977. 254 pp.

H.1.2. France

862. **bruun, g.** saint-just, apostle of the terror. reissued 1966: 1932.

863. **buonarotti, p.** history of baboeuf's conspiracy for equality. london: 1836.

864. **chatelain, d. * tafani, p.** qu'est-ce qui fait courir les autonomistes?. paris: stock, 1976. 312 pp.

865. **cobb, r.** terreur et subsistances, 1793-1795. paris: librairie clavreuil, 1964.

866. **curtis, w. n.** saint-just, colleague of robespierre. 1935.

867. **daudet, e.** la terreur blanche. paris: 1978. on the excesses of the monarchist restauration in post-1815 france.

868. **deniel, a.** le mouvement breton, 1918-1945. paris: maspero, 1976. 456 pp.

869. **dispot, l.** le machine a terreur. paris: grasset, 1975. philosophical contemplation on interrelationship of 'terror'and french political history; dutch ed. de terreur machine, wereldvenster, 1980, 221 p.

870. **dubois, f.** le peril anarchiste. paris: 1894.

871. **dutcher, g. m.** the deputies on mission during the reign of terror. ph. d. thesis ithaca, n. y. cornell university, 1903. 104 pp.

872. **garraud, r.** l'anarchie et la repression. paris: 1895.

873. **gauche proletarienne.** volkskrieg in frankreich? strategie und taktik der proletarischen linken. texte zusammengest. von den genossen der gp. berlin: wagenbach, 1972. 137 pp.

874. **gershoy, l.** bertrand barere, a reluctant terrorist. 1962. french revolution.

875. **greer, d.** the incidence of the terror during the french revolution. a statistical interpretation. cambridge, mass. harvard university press, 1935. 196 pp.

876. **hanrahan, g. z. * (ed.).** chinese communist guerrilla warfare tactics. boulder: paladin press, 1974.

877. **harrington, d. b.** french historians and the terror. the origins, developments andpresent-day fate of the 'these du complot' and the 'these des circumstances'. ph. d. university of connecticut(?), 1970. 315 pp. french revolution.

878. **hentig, h. von.** terror. zur psychologie der machtergreifung. robespierre, saint-just, fouche. frankfurt a. m. ullstein, 1970.

879. **holitscher, a.** ravachol und die pariser anarchisten. berlin: 1925.

880. **ikor, r.** lettre ouverte a des gentils terroristes. paris: a. michel, 1976.

881. **jacob, j. e.** the basques and occitans of france: a comparative study in ethnic militancy. ph. d. dissertation: cornell university, 1979.

882. **jean.** vom freiheitskampf der korsen. munich: trikont, 1978. 161 pp. corsic terrorism.

883. **kerr, w. b.** the reign of terror, 1793-1794. 1927.

884. **labin, s.** la violence politique. paris: ed. france-empire, 1978. 317 pp.

885. **landorf, s.** legalisme et violence dans le mouvement autonomiste corse: l'annee1976. 1977. pp. 1270-1305 les temps modernes 23:367.

886. **laurent, f.** l'orchestre noir. paris: stock, 1978. 439 pp.

887. **lefebvre, g.** la premiere terreur. cdu, 1953. on french revolution, 1792.

888. **lefebvre, g.** the thermodorians and the directory. new york: random house, 1964.

889. **levergeois, p.** j'ai choisi la d. s. t. paris: flammarion, 1978.

890. **loomis, s.** paris in the terror, june 1793-july 1794. philadelphia: j. b. lippincott, 1964.

891. **lucas, c.** the structure of the terror: the examples of javogues and the loire. london: oxford university press, 1972.

892. **maitron, j.** histoire du mouvement anarchiste en france, 1880-1914. paris: 1955.

893. **maitron, j.** le mouvement anarchiste en france. vol. 1 des origins a 1914. 2. imp. 1978. 191 pp.

894. **maitron, j.** le mouvement anarchiste en france. vol. 2 de 1914 a nos jours. 2 imp. 1978. 440 pp.

895. **marcellin, r.** l'ordre public et les groupes revolutionnaires. paris: plon, 1969.

896. **mathiez, a.** la vie chere et le mouvement social sous la terreur. paris: 1927.

897. **mcnamara, ch. b.** the hebertists: study of french revolutionary "faction" in the reign of terror, 1793-1794. unpubl. diss. fordham university, 1974. 491 pp.

898. **n. n.** die terroristen. unsere partner, die geheimdienste. dossier b. wie barbouzes. tuebingen: initiative verlagsanstalt, 1977. 224 pp.

899. **n. n.** terrorismo y justicia en espana. madrid: centro espa de documentacion, 1975.

900. peyrefitte commission. responses a la violence. 2 vols. paris: presses-pocket, 1977. on french govt. response to political violence.

901. plumyene, j. * lassiera, r. les fascismes francais. paris: 1963.

902. scott, w. terror and repression in revolutionary marseilles. new york: barnes & noble, 1973. 385 pp. 1789-1799.

903. shapiro, g. * markoff, j. the incidence of the terror. some lessons for quantitative history. 1975 . pp. 193-218 journal of social history 9:2 reviews donald greer's work and others on late 18th century france.

904. shepard, w. f. prize control and the reign of terror: france, 1793-1795. 1953.

905. sirich jr., j. b. the revolutionary committees in the departments of france during the reign of terror(1793-1794). cambridge, mass. harvard university press, 1943.

906. stagnara, v. le sens de la revolution corse. 1976. pp. 1670-1686 les temps modernes 31:357.

907. ternaux, m. histoire de la terreur. 7 vols. paris: m. levy, 1862. on french revolution.

908. true, w. m. the dechristianizing movement during the terror, 1793-1794. ph. d. thesis. cambridge, mass. : harvard university, 1939.

909. varenne, h. de ravachol a caserio. paris: 1895.

910. wallon, h. la terreur. 2 vols. paris: hachette, 1873. on french revolution.

911. walter, g. histoire de la terreur 1793-1795. paris: michel, 1937.

H.1.3. Ireland

912. bakker, j. noord-ierland. den haag: staatsuitgeverij, nivv-reeks 24.

913. barritt, d. f. * carter, c. f. the northern ireland problem. london: oxford universitypress, 1972.

914. barry, t. b. guerrilla days in ireland: a first hand account of the black tan war, 1919-1921. new york: devin-adair, 1956.

915. bayce, d. g. englishmen and irish troubles, 1918-1922. cambridge: cambridge university press, 1972.

916. beasley, p. s. michael collins and the making of a new ireland. london: 1926.

917. beckett, j. c. northern ireland. 1971. pp. 121-134 journal of contemporary history 6:1.

918. bell, g. the protestants of ulster. london: pluto, 1976. 159 pp.

919. bell, j. b. strategy, tactics, and terror: an irish perspective, 1969-1974. in: y. alexander * (ed.) international terrorism. new york: praeger, 1976. pp. 65-89.

920. bell, j. b. the chroniclers of violence in northern ireland revisited: the analysis of tragedy. 1974. pp. 521-544 review of politics 36:4.

921. bell, j. b. the chroniclers of violence in northern ireland: a tragedy in endless acts. 1976. pp. 510-533 the review of politics 38:4.

922. bell, j. b. the chroniclers of violence in northern ireland: the first wave interpreted. october 1974. pp. 521-543 review of politics. 34.

923. bell, j. b. the escalation of insurgency: the experience of the provisional ira(1969-1971). july 1973. pp. 398-411 the review of politics 35:3.

924. bell, j. b. the secret army: the i. r. a. 1916-1974. cambridge, mass. massachusetts institute of technology press, 1974. 434 pp.

925. bennett, r. l. the black and tans. boston: houghtonmifflin, 1960.

926. blundy, d. the army's secret war in northern ireland. 13 march 1977 sunday times.

927. boulton, d. uvf(ulster volunteer force) 1966-73; an anatomy of loyalist rebellion. dublin, ireland: gill and macmillan, 1973. 188 pp.

928. bowden, t. the ira and the changing tactics of terrorism. october 1976. pp. 425-437 political quarterly(london) 47.

929. boyle, k. * et. al. law and state. the case of northern ireland. london: martin robertson, 1975.

930. breen, d. my fight for irish freedom. kerry: 1964.

931. brown, t. n. irish american nationalism. new york: 1966.

932. carlton, ch. bigotry and blood: documents on the ulster troubles. chicago, ill. nelson-hall, 1977. 160 pp.

933. charters, d. a. intelligence and psychological warfare operations in northern ireland. pp. 22-27 journalof the royal united services institute for defense studies 122.

934. clark, d. terrorism in ireland: renewal of a tradition. in: m. livingston * et. al. * (eds.) international terrorism in the con- temporary world. london: greenwood press, 1978. pp. 77-83.

935. clark, d. which way the i. r. a. ?. 1973. pp. 204-207 commonweal 13.

936. clutterbuck, r. l. britain in agony. london: faber and faber, 1978. 335 pp.

937. clutterbuck, r. l. intimidation of witnesses and juries. april 1974. pp. 285-294 army quarterly 104.

938. collins, m. the path to freedom. dublin: talbot, 1922.

939. connolly, j. revolutionary warfare. dublin: 1968.

940. coogan, t. p. the i. r. a. new york: praeger, 1970.

941. cooper, g. l. c. some aspects of conflict in ulster. sept. 1973. pp. 86-95 military review 53:9.

942. corte, t. the phoenix murders. conflict, compromise and tragedy in ireland 1879-1882. london: 1967. .

943. crozier, b. ulster: politics and terrorism. london: institute for the study of conflict., 1973. 20 pp. conflict studies 36 deals with provisional and official wing of ira as well as the ulster defense association and the ulster volunteer force.

944. crozier, f. p. ireland forever. london: jonathan cape, 1932.

945. darby, j. conflict in northern ireland: the development of a polarized community. new york: barnes & noble books, 1976. 268 pp.

946. denieffe, j. a personal narrative of the irish revolutionary brotherhood. cambridge: houghton .nifflin, 1906.

947. deutsch, r. * magowan, v. northern ireland, 1968-1973 a chronology of events. vol. 2 1972-1973. belfast : blackstaff press, 1974.

948. deutsch, r. * magowan, v. northern ireland, 1968-1973 a chronology of events. vol. 1 1968-1971. belfast : blackstaff press, 1973. an indispensable reference work.

949. devlin, b. the price of my soul?. london: andre deutsch/pan books, 1969.

950. devoy, j. recollections of an irish rebel. shannon: 1969. account of the irish nationalist movement, including description of the fenian william mackey lomasney(1841-1884).

951. dillon, m. * lehane, d. political murder in northern ireland. baltimore: penguin books, 1973. 318 pp.

952. edwards, o. d. * pyle, f. * (eds.). the easter rising. london: 1968.

953. elliott, ph. reporting northern ireland: a study of news in britain, ulsterand the irish republic. leicester: centre for masscommunication research, university of leicester, 1976. also published by unesco in a book titled ethnicity and the media.

954. enloe, c. h. police and military in ulster: peacekeeping or peace-subverting forces?. 1978. pp. 253-258 journal of peace research 15.

955. farrel, m. northern ireland. the orange state. london: pluto press, 1977.

956. fisk, r. the effect of social and political crime on the police and britisharmy in northern ireland. in : m. livingston * et. al. * (eds.) international terrorismin the contem- porary world. westport, conn. greenwood press, 1978. pp. 84-93.

957. fisk, r. the point of no return. london: deutsch, on northern ireland and media, by times correspondent.

958. fitzgibbon, c. problems of the irish revolution. can the ira meet the challenge?. new york: pathfin der, 1972.

959. fitzgibbon, c. red hand: the ulster colony. garden city: doubleday, 1972.

960. furmanski, l. s. the essence of conflict: a theoretical inquiry into conflict analysis : the case of northern ireland. ph. d. dissertation in preparation: purdue university.

961. gardiner committee. measures to deal with terrorism in northern ireland. london: hmso, 1975.

962. gleason, j. j. bloody sunday. london: davies, 1962. 212 pp.

963. goulding, l. entwicklung und ziele der irish republican army(ira). 1973. pp. 415-427 blatter fuer deutsche und internationale politik 18:4.

964. greaves, c. d. the irish crisis. london: lawrence and wishart, 1972.

965. haggerty, j. j. northern ireland. the wound that never stopped bleeding. 1979. pp. 7-14 monthly review 59:6.

966. hall, r. a. violence and its effects on the community. 1975. pp. 89-100 medical legal journal 43.

967. hamilton, i. the irish tangle. london: institute for the study of conflict, 1970. conflict studies 6.

968. harmon, m. fenians and fenianism. dublin: 1968.

969. holt, e. protest in arms. the irish troubles, 1916-1923. new york: coward-mccan, 1960.

970. houston, j. the northern ireland economy: a special case?. 16 aug. 1976. pp. 274-288 politics today 16 on impact of terrorism on economy.

971. institute for the study of conflict. spreading irish conflict. part 1: from liberalism to extremism. part 2: the security of ulster. london: isc, 1971. conflict studies 17 1049. h 1. 3.

972. irish republican army. handbook for the irish republican army. boulder, colo. paladin press, 40 pp. a manual of guerilla warfare.

973. irish republican army, official. in the 70's the ira speaks. london: s. e., 1970.

974. irish republican army, provisional. freedom struggle by the provisional ira. london: red books, 1973. .

975. janke, p. * price, d. l. ulster: consensus and coercion. london: isc, 1974. conflict studies 50.

976. kee, r. the green flag: a history of irish nationalism. new york: delacorte press, 1972.

977. kramer, g. mord und terror. britischer imperialismus: nordireland. frankfurt a. m. fischer, 1972. 286 pp.

978. lebow, r. n. civil war in ireland: a tragedy in endless acts?. 1973. pp. 247-260 journal of international affairs 26.

979. lebow, r. n. the origins of sectarian assassination: the case of belfast. 1978. pp. 43-61 journal of international affairs 32.

980. lee, a. m. insurgent and 'peacekeeping' violence in northern ireland. 1973. pp. 532-546 social problems 20.

981. lieberson, g. the irish uprising, 1916-1922. new york: hinkhouse, 1964.

982. lijphart, a. the northern ireland problem; cases, theories and solutions. 1975. pp. 83-106 british journal of political science 5:1.

983. london sunday times insight team. northern ireland: a report on the conflict. new york: vintage, 1972. .

984. manhattan, a. religious terror in ireland. london: paravision publications, 1970.

985. mcclung, l. a. insurgent and "peace keeping" violence in northern ireland. 1973. pp. 532-546 social problems 20: 4.

986. mcfee, t. ulster through a lens. 17 march 1978. new statesman.

987. mckeown, m. the first five hundred. belfast: irishnews, 1972. on the first 500 dead in northern ireland due to ethnic strife, 385 of whom were casualties of terrorism.

988. mealing, e. t. ulster, some causes and effects of low intensity operations, 1969-197. carlisle barracks, penn. army war college, 23 dec 1972.

989. middleton, r. urban guerrilla warfare and the ira. 1971. pp. 72-75 journal of the royal united services institute for defense studies. 116: 664.

990. milnor, a. politics, violence, and social change in northern ireland. ithaca, n. y. cornell university , 1976. 73 pp.

991. monday, m. a summer of sunshine. interviews with irish paramilitary leaders. phoenix: joseph davidson co., 1976.

992. moodie, m. the patriot game: the politics of violence in northern ireland. in: m. livingston * et. al. * (eds.) international terrorism in contemporary world. westport, conn. greenwood press, pp. 94-110.

993. moody, t. w. * martin, f. y. * (eds.). the course of irish history. new york: weybright & tally, 1967.

994. moss, r. * hamilton, i. the spreading irish conflict. london: isc, 1971. conflict studies 17.

995. n. n. die i. r. a. spricht: die i. r. a. in den 70-er jahren. berlin: 1972. pp. 131-142 sozialisches jahrbuch 4.

996. n. n. editorial: ulster catharsis. 2 march 1974. pp. 343-344 lancet.

997. n. n. freedom struggle by the provisional ira. london: red books, 1973. 101 pp.

998. n. n. report of the committee of privy counsellors appointed to considerauthorized procedures for the interrogation of persons suspected of terrorism. london: hmso, 1972.

999. n. n. report to the commission to consider legal procedures to deal withterrorist activities in northern ireland. london: hmso, 1972.

1000. n. n. the terror and the tears: the facts about ira brutality and the suffering of victims. belfast: government of northern ireland, information service, 1972.

1001. northern ireland, government information service. the terror and the tears: the facts about ira brutality and the sufferings of victims. belfast: government of northern ireland information service, 1972. 16 pp.

1002. o'brien, c. c. herod: reflections on political violence. london: hutchinson, 1978. 236 pp.

1003. o'brien, c. c. states of ireland. london: panther, 1974.

1004. o'brien, l. revolutionary underground: the story of the irish republican brotherhood 1858-1924. london: gill and macmillan, 1976.

1005. o'broin, l. dublin castle and the 1916 rising. new york: new york university press, 1971.

1006. o'callaghan, s. execution. london: frederick muller, 1974.

1007. o'callaghan, s. the easter lily: the story of the ira. new york: roy, 1938.

1008. o'connor, u. * (ed.). irish liberation - an anthology. new york: 1974.

1009. o'day, a. northern ireland, terrorism, and the british state. in: y. alexander, d. carlton, and p. wilkinson * (eds.) terrorism: theory and practice. boulder: westview, 1979. pp. 121-135.

1010. o'donnell, p. the irish faction fighters of the nineteenth century. dublin: 1975.

1011. o'farrell, p. ireland's english question. london: batesford, 1971.

1012. o'riordan, m. * sinclair, b. i comunisti irlandesi e il terrorismo. 1976. pp. 1287-1299 nuova rivista internazionale 10.

1013. o'sullivan, p. m. patriot graves: resistance in ireland. chicago: follett, 1972.

1014. paor, l. de. divided ulster. harmondsworth: penguin, 1970.

1015. phillips, w. a. the revolution in ireland, 1906-1923. london: longmans and green, 1927.

1016. pollard, h. b. c. the secret societies of ireland. london: philip allan, 1922.

1017. power, p. f. violence, consent and the northern ireland problem. july 1976. pp. 119-140 journal of commonwealth and comparative politics. 14.

1018. reed, d. nordirland: anatomie eines buergerkrieges. june 1975. pp. 146-191 das beste aus reader's digest(swiss ed.).

1019. rose, r. governing without consensus: an irish perspective. london: faber & faber, 1971.

1020. rose, r. northern ireland: a time of choice. london: macmillan, 1976.

1021. ryan, d. fenian memoirs. dublin: 1945.

1022. ryan, d. james connolly. dublin: 1924.

1023. ryan, d. the phoenix flame. london: 1937.

1024. ryan, d. the rising. dublin: 1957.

1025. schmitt, d. violence in northern ireland: ethnic conflict and radicaliz in an international setting. morristown, n. j. general learning press, 1974.

1026. scott, m. conflict regulation vs. mobilization: the dilemma of northern-ireland. ph. d. dissertation: columbia university, 1976.

1027. skidelsky, r. the irish problem: an historical perspective. in: y. alexander, d. carlton and p. wilkinson * (eds.) terrorism: theory and practice. boulder: westview, 1979.

1028. stewart, a. t. q. the ulster crisis. london: faber &faber, 1967.

1029. sunday times insight team. northern ireland: a report on the conflict. new york: vintage books, 1972. .

1030. tansill, c. america and the fight for irish freedom. new york: 1957.

1031. taylor, r. michael collins. london: hutchinson, 1958.

1032. tynan, p. j. f. the irish invincibles. new york: 1894.

1033. waterworth, p. northern ireland. the administration of justice in the light ofcivil disorder and sectarian violence. ba. dissertation. university of durham, 1978.

1034. williams, d. the irish struggle. london: routledgeand kegan, 1966.

1035. winchester, s. in holy terror: reporting the ulster troubles. london: faber & faber, 1975.

1036. wright, s. a multivariate time series analysis of the northern irish conflict1969-1976. in: y. alexander and j. m. gleason * (eds.) behavioral and quantitative perspectives on terrorism. new york: pergamon, 1981. pp. 283-321.

1037. younger, c. ireland's civil war. new york: tapplinger co., 1969.

H.1.4. Italy

1038. acquaviva, s. s. guerriglia e guerra rivoluzionaria in italia. milano: rizzoli editore, 1979.

1039. allum, p. l'italie de la violence. les deux vagues du terrorisme. april 1978. pp. 12 le monde diplomatique 289.

1040. allum, p. political terrorism in italy. august 1978. pp. 75-84 contemporary review 233.

1041. asor rosa, a. le due societa. ipotesi sulla crisi italiana. turin: 1977.

1042. banfi, a. terrorismo fuori e dentro lo stato. 1978. pp. 311-328 ponte 34:3-4 on 20th century terrorism, emphasis on italy.

1043. barbieri, d. agenda nera, trent'anni di neofascismo in italia. roma: coines, 1976.

1044. bell, j. b. violence and italian politics. 1978. pp. 49-69 conflict: an international journal 1:1 .

1045. bertini, b. * iranchi, p. * spagnoli, u. estremismo terrorismo ordine democratico. rome: editoririuniti, 1978.

1046. bocca, g. il terrorismo in italia. ed. rizzoli, 1978.

1047. bocca, g. il terrorismo italiano 1970-1978. milano: 1979.

1048. bocca, g. moro, une tragedia italiana. milano: casa editrice bompiani, 1978. instant history on the seven weeks between the kidnapping of aldo moro and the death of the ex-prime minister by the red brigades.

1049. bologna, s. la tribu delle talpe. milano: feltrinelli, 1978.

1050. bonanate, l. dimensioni del terrorismo politico. febr. 1977. pp. 76-122 comunita 177.

1051. bravo, g. m. zur funktion des terrorismus in der politischen entwicklung italiens. 1979. pp. 705-725 blaetter fuer deutsche und internationale politik 24:6.

1052. brigate rossi. risoluzione della direzione strategica(febr. 1978). july 1978. pp. 76-95 controinformazione 5:11-12.

1053. bufalini, p. terrorismo e democrazia. rome: editori riuniti, 1978.

1054. buonarotti, p. scritti politici. peruta, f. della * (ed.). turin: einaudi, 1976. 101 pp.

1055. campa, r. * (ed.). estremismo e radicalismo. rome, 1969.

1056. cantore, r. * rossella, c. * valentini, c. dall'interno della guerriglia. from within the guerrilla. milan: mondadori, 1978. 207pp.

1057. caserta, j. the red brigades: italy's agony. new york: manor, 1978. 240 pp.

1058. cattani, a. italiens dilemma. june 1978. schweizer monatshefte 58:6.

1059. cederna, c. pinelli. una finestra sulla strage. milan: 1971.

1060. chierici, m. i guerriglieri della speranza. milan: arnoldo mondadori, 1978.

1061. collectivo editoriale librirossi. il caso coco. milano: 1978. 99 pp.

1062. collectivo nostra assemblea. le radici di una rivolta - il movimento studentesco a roma. milano: feltrinelli, 1977.

1063. cowan, s. terrorism and the italian left. in: boggs, c. and plotke, d. * (eds.) the politics of eurocommunism, socialism in transition. london: macmillan, 1980.

1064. degli incerti, d. * (ed.). la sinistra rivoluzionaria in italia. roma: savelli, 1977.

1065. ferrarotti, f. la ypnosi della violenza. milano: 1980, on political violence in italy.

1066. fini, m. * barberi, a. valpreda - processo del processo. milano: feltrinelli, 1972. on the italian process of the alleged 1969 bomber ofa bank in milan.

1067. fini, m. la forza della tensione in italia 1969-1976. torino: einaudi, 1977.

1068. fiorillo, e. terrorism in italy: analysis of a problem. 1979. pp. 261-270 terrorism 2.

1069. galli, g. la destra italiana e la crisi internazionale. ivi, 1974.

1070. galli, g. la tigre di carta e il drago scarlatto. bologna: 1970.

1071. georgel, j. un an apres l'affaire moro. l'italie entre terrorisme et politique ou un art de survivre. . 1979. pp. 54-74 revue politique et parlemantaire 80:879.

1072. groupe anarchiste-libertaire(clandestin) "xxii mars". le complot terroriste en italie. 1970. pp. 1264-1285 les temps modernes 26:283.

1073. groupe de 22 mars. le complot terroriste en italie. 1970. pp. 1264-1285 les temps modernes 25.

1074. guiso, g. * bonomi, a. * tommei, f. * (eds.). criminalizzazione della lotta di classe. verona: . ' criminalization of class struggle' in italy.

1075. guiso, g. la condanna di aldo moro. milan: sugar c, 1979.

1076. hess, h. angriff auf das herz des staates. soziale hintergruende des terrorismus in italien. 1982 .

1077. hess, h. terrorismus in italien. 1982: .

1078. jannuzi, l. * et. al. * (eds.). la pelle del d'urso. a chi serviva, chi se l'e venduta como e stata salvata. rome: radio radicale, on italian media on urso abduction.

1079. katz, r. day of wrath. the ordeal of aldo moro, the kidnapping, the execution, the aftermath. garden city, n. y. doubleday, 1980.

1080. ledeen, m. inside the red brigades. an exclusive report. 1 may 1978. pp. 36-38 new york 11 on red brigades alleged infiltration of italian communist party.

1081. lojacono, v. alto adige suedtirol. dal pangermanismo al terrorismo. milano: mursia, 1968. 293 pp.

1082. **lojacono, v.** i dossier di septembre nero. milan: bietto, 1974.

1083. **lotta continua.** nehmen wir uns die stadt klassenanalyse, organisations paper, kampfprogramm. beitraege der lotta continua zur totalisierung der kaempfe. muenchen: trikont, 1972. 138 pp.

1084. **mariel, p.** les carbonari. idealisme et la revolution. paris: 1971.

1085. **martigoni, g. * morandini, s.** il diritto al odio. verona: bertani, 1977. on the italian autonomists.

1086. **martines, l. * (ed.).** violence and civil disorder in italian cities. berkeley: university of california press, 1972.

1087. **mchale, v.** economic development, political extremism and crime in italy. pp. 59–79 western political quarterly 31:1.

1088. **minucci, a.** terrorismo e crisi italiana. rome: ed riuniti, 1978. 'terrorism and the italian crisis'.

1089. **monicelli, m.** l'ultrasinistra in italia. the italian ultraleft. rome-bari: laterza, 1978. 237 pp.

1090. **montalera, l. r. di.** racconto di un sequestro. doss. sei: 1977, story of an italian kidnapping.

1091. **n. n.** can italy survive?. 22 may 1978. pp. 35, 36, 38. newsweek effect of moro kidnapping on italian political system.

1092. **n. n.** comitato all' automia. viberto: lerici, 1979.

1093. **n. n.** feltrinelli, il guerrigliero impotente. rome: ed. documenti,

1094. **n. n.** germania e germanizzazione. napoli: pironti, 1977.

1095. **n. n.** l'affare feltrinelli. con testimonianza di carlo ripa di meana. milan: stampa club, 1972.

1096. **n. n.** l'hypothese revolutionnaire. documents sur les luttes etudiantes a trente, turin, naples, pise, milan et roma. paris: mercure de france, 1968. 267 pp.

1097. **n. n.** le straghe di stato. roma: savelli, 1970.

1098. **n. n.** nicht heimlich und nicht kuehl. entgegnungen an dienst - u. s. herren. berlin: 1978. 135 pp.

1099. **n. n.** phenomenological and dynamic aspects of terrorism in italy. 1979. pp. 159–170 terrorism 2.

1100. **n. n.** sulla guerriglia urbana. in: formare l'armata rossa -i tupamaros d'europa?. verona: 1972. pp. 157–183.

1101. **n. n.** sulla violenze. rome: savelli, 1978. 169 pp.

1102. **natta, a.** l' uso politico de caso moro e la crisi d' oggi. intervista cona. natta. febr. 1979. rinascita 36:3.

1103. **negri, a.** il dominio e il sabotaggio. milan: feltrinelli, 1978. by alleged leader of the italian autonomists.

1104. **negri, a.** partito operaio contra il lavoro. milano: feltrinelli, 1974. negri, allegedly the leader of the italian autonomists, argues against the historical compromise of the communist party.

1105. **negri, a.** proletari e stato. milan: feltrinelli, ' proletarians and the state'.

1106. **ottolini, a.** la carboneria, dalle origini ai primi tentativi insurrezionali. modena: 1946. 18th and 19th century insurrectional movement.

1107. **padellaro, a.** il delitto moro. ivi, 1979.

1108. **panebiance, a.** italie: terrorisme et strategie non-violente. lyon: 1978. pp. 53-57 alternatives non-violentes 28.

1109. **pesenti, r. * sassano, m.** fiasconaro e allesandrino accusano. la requisatoria su la strage di piazza fontana e le bombe del '69. venice: marsilio, 1974. 287 pp.

1110. **pisano, v. s.** a survey of terrorism of the left in italy: 1970-78. 1979. pp. 171-212 terrorism 2.

1111. **pisano, v. s.** contemporary italian terrorism. washington d. c. library of congress law library, 1979. .

1112. **pisano, v. s.** the red brigades. a challenge to italian democracy. london: july 1980. 19 pp. conflict studies 120.

1113. **pisano, v. s.** the structure and dynamics of italian terrorism. gaithersburg, md. iacp, 33 pp.

1114. **possony, s. t.** giangiacomo feltrinelli. the millionaire dinamitero. 1979. pp. 213-230 terrorism 2 :3-4.

1115. **quarantotto, c.** il terrorismo in italia, 1968-1975. 1975. pp. 19-46 la destra 1.

1116. **red brigades, the.** the red brigades. new york: manor books, 1978.

1117. **ricci, a.** giovani non sono piante. milan: sugar co., 1978.

1118. **richards, v. * (ed.).** enrico malatesta. london: 196.

1119. **roggi, e. * gambescia, p. * gruppi, l. ***
(eds.). terrorismo. come opera, a che cosa mira,
come sconfiggerlo. rome: pci, 1978.

1120. **ronchey, a.** accadde in italia, 1968-1977.
milan: 1977.

1121. **ronchey, a.** guns and gray matter: terrorism
in italy. 1979. pp. 921-40 foreign affairs.

1122. **ronchey, a.** libro bianco sull' ultima
generazione. milan: garznati, 1978. 'whitebook on the
last generation'.

1123. **ronchey, a.** terror in italy, between red
and black. 1978. pp. 150-156 dissent 25:2.

1124. **rosenbaum, p.** neofaschismus in italien.
frankfurt a. m: europaeische verlagsanstalt, 1975.
117 pp.

1125. **rossanda, p. * (comp.).** il manifesto.
analyses et theses de la nouvelle
extreme-gaucheitalienne. paris : seuil, 1971. 429
pp.

1126. **rossani, o.** l'industria dei sequestri.
longanesi & co: 1978. on kidnapping industry in
italy.

1127. **rossetti, c. g.** la politica della violenza
e la crisi della legittimita razionale dello stat.
july 1980. studi de soziologia 18:3.

1128. **russell, ch. a.** terrorist incidents - italy
1978. 197. pp. 297-300 terrorism 2.

1129. **sartre, j. p.** critique de la raison
dialectique. la theorie et la practique du terrorisme
divulguees pour la premiere fois. paris: 1960. dutch
ed. wereldvenster, baarn, 1982 91)r.

1130. **scianna, f.** mafia et terrorisme. lois
d'exception en italie. febr. 1980. le monde
diplomatique.

1131. **sciascia, l.** affaire moro, verite
officielle et verite tout court. nov. 1978. le monde
diplomatique.

1132. **sciascia, l.** l'affaire moro. palermo:
sellerio ed, 1978. dutch transl. de zaak aldo moro,
1979 antwerp, lotus.

1133. **selva, g. * marucci, e.** il martirio di
moro. bologna: 1978.

1134. **sernicoli, e.** l'anarchia. 2 vols. milano:
189.

1135. **silj, a.** alle origini dei nap e delle br.
firenze: 1977. on the roots of two italian terrorist
movements.

1136. **silj, a.** brigate rosse-stato. la scontro
spettacolo nella regia della stampa quotidiana.
firenze: vallecchi, 1978. 243 pp. analyzes news
treatment of moro kidnapping in five italian
dailies.

1137. **silj, a.** never again without a rifle. new
york: karz publishers, 1979. 256 pp. reconstructs the
emergence of student protest in italy and the
escalation of violence after 1968; the italian
edition 'mai piu senza fugile' was published in
florence, vallecchi, 1977.

1138. **soccorso rosso * (ed.).** brigate rosse. che
cosa hanno fatto, che cosa hanno detto, che cosa se
ne e detto. milano: 1976.

1139. **soccorso rosso napoletano.** i nap: storia
politica dei nuclei armati proletari e requisitoria
del tribunale di napoli. the armed proletarian
nuclei. milan and naples: collettivo editoriale libri
rossi, 1976. 249 pp.

1140. **sofri, a. * mea, l. della.** zur strategie
und organisation von "lotta continua". berlin: merve
verlag, 1971. 119 pp.

1141. **sole, r.** le defi terroriste. lecons
italiennes a l'usage de l'europe. paris: le seuil,
1979. 288 pp. by le monde correspondent in rome,
placing italian terrorism against political
background.

1142. **sterling, c.** italy: the feltrinelli case.
july 1972. pp. 10-18 atlantic monthly 230.

1143. **tessandori, v.** b. r. cronaca e documenti
delle brigate rosse. milano: garzanti, 1977. on
italy's red brigades.

1144. **tessandori, v.** b. r. imputazione: banda
armata. milan: garzanti, 1977. 414 pp. b. r. =
brigate rosse, italy's red brigades.

1145. **trasatti, s.** il lago della duchessa. le
rassegna editoriale: 1978. on moro case.

1146. **weinberg, l.** patterns of neo-fascist
violence in italian politics. 1979. 231-259 terrorism
2.

1147. **whetten, l. l.** italian terrorism:record
figures and political dilemmas. 1978. pp. 377-395
terrorism 1.

1148. **wolf, j. b.** italy's year of terror.
gaithersburg, md. i. a. c. p., 1978. update report
4:6.

H.1.5. Spain

1149. **apalategui, j.** nationalisme et question
nationale au pays basque 1830-1976.

1150. **arenillas, j. m.** the basque country, the
national question and the socialist revolution.
leeds: i. l. p, square one publications, 1973.

1151. **bookchin, m.** the spanish anarchists. new
york: 1977.

1152. centro espanol de documentacion. terrorismo y justicia en espana. madrid: 1975.

1153. cuadrat, x. socialismo y anarquismo en catalunya. los origenes de la cnt. madrid: revista del trabaja , 1976. 682pp.

1154. enzensberger, h. m. der kurze sommer der anarchie. frankfurt: 1972.

1155. frank, j. a. * kelly, m. etude preliminaire sur la violence collective en ontario et auquebec, 1963 -1973. 1977. pp. 15-51 revue canadienne de science politique 10:1.

1156. frey, p. widerstand in euskadi. zuerich: 28 aug 1976. tagesanzeiger magazin on basque eta.

1157. herzog, w. * (ed.). terror in baskenland gefahr fuer spaniens demokratie?. reinbek: rowohlt, 1979. 140 pp. on eta terrorism.

1158. ibarzabal, e. 5o anos de nacionalismo vasco. san sebastian: ed. vascas, 1978.

1159. kaufmann, j. mourir au pays basque, la lutte impitoyable de l'e. t. a. plon, 1976.

1160. letemendia, f. les basques. un peuple contre les etats. paris: le seuil, 1977.

1161. lida, c. e. anarquismo y revolucion en la espana del xix. madrid: 1972.

1162. lorenz, c. m. les anarchistes espagnols et le pouvoir 1868-1969. paris: ed. du seuil, 1969. 429 pp.

1163. maura, r. terrorism in barcelona and its impact on spanish politics 1904-1919. dec. 1968. past andpresent.

1164. meaker, g. h. the revolutionary left in spain, 1914-1923. stanford: 1974.

1165. mella, r. * prat, j. la barbarie gubernamental en espana. brooklyn(in fact barcelona): 1897.

1166. nunez, l. c. la sociedad vasca actual. san sebastian: 1977.

1167. ortzi(pseud. of f. latamendia). historia de euskadi. el nacionalismo vasco y eta. paris: 1975.

1168. ortzi(pseud. of f. latamendia). historia de euskadi. barcelona: ruedo iberico, 1978. 'basque history'.

1169. padilla bolivar, a. el movimento anarquista espanol. barcelona: planeta, 1976. 358 pp.

1170. payne, s. g. el nacionalismo vasco. barcelona: 197.

1171. payne, s. g. madrid:eta- basque terrorism. 1979. pp. 109-113 washington quarterly 2:2.

1172. pertus. (pseud.). eta(71-76). san sebastian: 1978.

1173. pestana, a. el terrorismo en barcelona. seguido de principios medios yfinosdel sindicalismo communista. . barcelona: j. j. de olamela, 1978. 75 pp.

1174. pestana, a. lo que apprendi en la vida. madrid: 1933.

1175. portell, j. m. euskadi: amnistia arrancada. barcelona: dopesa, 1977.

1176. portell, j. m. los hombres de eta. barcelona: dopesa, 1976. 280 pp.

1177. tellez, a. sabate. stadtguerilla in spanien nach dem buergerkrieg, 1945-1960. muenchen: trikont, 1974. 154 pp. on francisco sabate leopart.

1178. thomas, h. the spanish civil war. new york: 1961.

1179. waldmann, p. mitgliederstruktur, sozialisationsmedien und gesellschaftlicher rueckhalt. der baskischen eta. 1981. pp. 45-66 politische vierteljahres-schriften 1.

1180. xirinacs, l. m. la sentinelle de la liberte. onbasque terrorism.

H.1.6. The Netherlands

1181. abspoel, j. j. requisitoir in de zaak van het openbaar ministerie tegen j. r. en zes anderen; bezetting indonesisch consulaat amsterdam. june 1976. pp. 304-337 delikt en delinkwent 6:6.

1182. amersfoort, j. m. m. van. de sociale positie van de molukkers in nederland. 's-gravenhage: staatsdrukkerij, 1971. 74 pp.

1183. bagley, c. the dutch plural society. a comparative study in race relations. london: oxford university press, 1973. contains material on south moluccans.

1184. barker, r. not here, but in another place. new york: st. matin's, 1979. on south moluccan terrorist acts in the netherlands;1975, 1977.

1185. begeleidings-commissie voorbereiding projekt sociaal-kultureel werk. bovensmilde, hoe verder? voorlopige voorstellen voor een nader oordeel. smilde: 1978. 59 pp. on the lifeof a dutch community after terroristic violence.

1186. bouman, p. j. vrijheidshelden en terroristen. vijf eeuwen geweld in europa. amsterdam: elsevier, 1977. 192 pp. chapter deals with 1st south moluccan train incident.

1187. commissie verwey-jonker. ambonezen in nederland. rapport 's-gravenhage: staatsdrukkerij, 1959. 111 pp.

1188. cuperus, j. * klijnsma, r. onderhandelen of bestormen. het beleid van de nederlandse overheid inzake terroristische acties. groningen: polemologisch instituut, 1980. 98 pp. negotiate or storm. the dutch government's policy during terroristic actions.

1189. decker, g. republik maluku selatan. goettingen: o schwartz and co., 1957.

1190. dittrich, z. r. terrorisme. 1978. liberaalreveil 19:4.

1191. doorne, f. van. het onafhankelijkheids-streven van de zuidmolukkers. mimeographed thesis gent: rijksuniversiteit, 1972. 164 pp. mainly dealing with the pre-1950 period.

1192. drevan, w. p. van. came the dawn: south moluccan terror in the netherlands. pp. 15-21 counterforce 1 911)september 1977.

1193. droesen, h. w. j. pleitaantekeningen in de zaak tegen j. r. en zes anderen; bezetting indonesisch consulaat amsterdam. oct. 1976. pp. 447-458 delikt en delinkwent 6:8.

1194. egter van wissekerke, f. terreur anno 1977. dec. 197. carre. maandblad voor de nederlandse officieren vereniging.

1195. ellemers, j. e. minderheden en beleid in nederland: molukkers en enkele andere categorieen allochtonen in vergelijkend perspectief. march 1978. pp. 20-40 transaktie 7:1.

1196. graaf, h. j. de. de geschiedenis van ambon en de zuid-molukken. franeker: wever, 1977.

1197. holdijk, g. terreur en terrorisme. politiek geweld in een democratische rechtsstaat. waddinxveen: . 36 pp. zicht-katernen 18.

1198. hulsman, l. h. c. juni 1976; gewelddadigheid, terrorisme en strafrechterlijke normen. june 1976. pp . 299-303 delikt en delinkwent 6:6.

1199. jong, j. p. p. de. het zuid-molukse radicalisme in nederland: een emancipatiebeweging?. pp. 413-41 sociologische gids 18:5.

1200. kaam, r. van. ambon door de eeuwen heen. baarn: inden toren, 1977.

1201. kamsteeg, a. de zuidmolukse bezetting in wassenaar. dordrecht: g. p. v., 1970.

1202. knot, g. * et. al. wat moeten ze hier? zuidmolukkers op weg naar vrijheid. groningen: de vuurbaak, 1975.

1203. knot, g. balans van 'wassenaar'. eindhoven: oct. 1970. zelfbeschikking 1:2.

1204. koebben, a. j. f. de gijzelingsakties van zuid-molukkers en hun effekten op de samenleving. groningen: , june 1979. pp. 147-154 transaktie 8:2 south moluccan hostage-taking actions and their social effects.

1205. kraker, w. a. de, * groot, f. c. v. de. analyseverslag van de gijzeling in de franse ambassade van 13 tot en met 17 september 1974. s-gravenhage: 1975. 45 pp.

1206. kranenburg, f. j. gijzeling, rechtsorde, openbare orde; een verstoorde samenleving. 10 apr. 1976. pp. 195-201 algemeen politieblad 125:8 also published in: de nederlandse gemeente 30:10, pp109-116, 1976.

1207. kruijs, p. w. van der. kanttekeningen bij een requisitoir. oct. 1976. pp. 459-462 delikt en delinkwent 6:8 on south moluccan incident in indonesian consulate in amsterdam.

1208. kuijer, k. de. de weg van de zuid molukkers. nijmegen: 1973.

1209. maarseveen, h. th. j. f. van. de verbeelding aan de macht; opmerkingen naar aanleiding van de gijzelingen. . 13 aug. 1977. pp. 697-698 nederlands juristenblad 52.

1210. manusama, j. a. om recht en vrijheid. de strijd om de onafhankelijkheid der zuid-molukken. utrecht: libertas, 85 pp.

1211. marien, m. h. actuele beschouwingen. het zuid-molukse radicalisme in nederland;nationalistische of emancipatiebeweging?. jan. 1971. 62-76 sociologische gids.

1212. marien, m. h. de zuid molukkers in nederland. migranten tegen wil en dank in de minderheidssituatie. amsterdam: 1968.

1213. meulen, e. i. van der. dossier ambon 1950 de houding van nederland ten opzichte van ambon en de rms. den haag: staatsuitgeverij, 1981. 327 pp. historical background of southmoluccanterrori.

1214. ministerie van justitie. verslag van de gebeurtenissen rond de treinkaping te beilen ende overval op het indonesische consulaat-generaal te amsterdam 12 dec. -19 dec. 1975). kamerstuk 13756 nrs. 1-3 's- gravenhage: staatsuitgeverij, 1976.

1215. n. n. de gijzelingen in bovensmilde en vries(23 mei - 11 juni 1977). kamerstuk 14610, nrs. 102 's- gravenhage: staatsuitgeverij, 1977.

1216. n. n. de molukkers. wat brengt hen tot gijzelingsakties? achtergronden, geschiedenis. rotterdam: ordeman, dec. 1975. 32 pp. short and superficial instant-history that does not deal with terrorist actions.

1217. n. n. gebeurtenissen rond de gijzeling van een aantal personen in defranse ambassade te 's-gravenhage; gebeurtenissen rond de gijzeling van 22 personen in het penitentiair centrum te 's-gravenhage; gebeurtenissen rondom dekaping van een brits vliegtuig, welke geleid heeft tot het overbrengen van tweepalestijnen naar tunis. tweede kamer der staten-generaal, zitting 1975-1976: .

1218. n. n. gijzelingen 2-19 december 1975;. persoverzicht deel a:anp-berichten 's-gravenhage: stafbureau voorlichting van het ministerie van justitie, 1975. 422 pp.

1219. n. n. maluku selatan; zuid molukken, een vergeten bevrijdingsstrijd. amsterdam: de populier, 1977. 96 pp.

1220. n. n. salawaku rms; de zuidmolukse jongeren en hun eisen. 's- gravenhage: vrije zuidmolukse jongeren, 1970.

1221. n. n. treinkaping te beilen - overval op het indonesisch consulaat-generaal te amsterdam. regeringsverslag: 1976. pp. 109-120, 140-152. algemeen politieblad 125:5-6.

1222. n. n. verslag van de gebeurtenissen rond de gijzeling van 22 personen inhet penitentiair centrum te 's-gravenhage. 21 dec. 1974. pp. 650-652 algemeen politieblad 123:26.

1223. oen, k. l. balans van 25 jaar r. m. s. -ideaal zuid-molukkers; en onvrede zuid-molukkers verklaard met het begrip "relatieve deprivatie". amsterdam: sociologisch instituut, 1975. 55 pp.

1224. organisasi wanita indonesia maluko. de molukken in de nationale strijd van indonesie. mimeo jakarta: , 1976. 23pp. a collection of translations and summaries of a book by richard z. leirissa. deals mainly with the 1945-1949 period.

1225. orie, a. m. m. * verburg, j. j. i. de koningin bedreigd. oct. 1975. pp. 475-489 delikt en delinkwent 5:8.

1226. penonton, b. de zuidmolukse republiek. schets voor een beschrijving van de nieuwste geschiedenis van het zuidmolukse volk. amsterdam: buijten & schipperheijn, 1977. 299 pp. title of the original 1970 edition: wat er gebeurde na 1950.

1227. persijn, j. (pseud.). uit de schaduw van het verleden. legende en realiteit in het molukse vraagstuk. : febr. 1976. pp. 103-110 internationale spectator 30:2.

1228. praag, c. s. van. molukse jongeren in botsing met de nederlandse maatschappij; degevolgen van een beleid. . dec. 1975. pp . 342-348 beleid en maatschappij 2:12.

1229. reijntjes, j. m. samenspanning. july 1977. pp. 418-432 delikt en delinkwent 7:7 on south moluccan terrorist incidents.

1230. rijken, a. g. l. de actie van zuidmolukkers op 31 augustus 1970 te wassenaar. 1971. pp. 153-157; 185-192; 211-215; 246-253; 272-277. algemeen politieblad 120:7-11.

1231. rijksvoorlichting/s/dienst. gijzeling assen, 13-14 maart 1978. 's-gravenhage: rijksvoorlichting/s/ dienst, 1978. 296 pp.

1232. rinsampessy, e. de mogelijke gronden van agressie onder molukse jongeren (geplaatst in het kader van de integratie-problematiek). utrecht: 1975. 76 pp. pattimura special 2.

1233. rinsampessy, e. de rms-strijd als emancipatiestrijd. 38920= madjalah pattimura 3:1, 4:1.

1234. rinsampessy, e. gewapende propaganda. jan. 1975. madjalah pattimura 1.

1235. ritzema bos, j. h. dies ater(een zwarte dag). opgedragen aan 33 zuidmolukkers. doetinchem: 1970.

1236. sahetapy, a. minnestrijd voor de r. m. s. amsterdam: j. ririmasse, 1981. 128pp. 'love struggle for the r. m. s. ', by one of the trainhijackers of 1975.

1237. schmid, a. p. * graaf, j. f. a. de, * bovenkerk, f. * bovenkerk-teerink, l. m. * brunt, l. zuidmoluks terrorisme, de media en de publieke opinie. amsterdam: pp., "south moluccan terrorism, the media and public opinion", two comtstudies.

1238. siahaya, t. mena-muria. wassenaar '70: zuid-molukkers slaan terug. amsterdam: de bezige bij, 1972. 182 pp. ona south moluccan action against the indonesian embassy in wassenaar, 1970, by a participant.

1239. utrecht, e. ambon kolonisatie, dekolonisatie en neo-kolonisatie. amsterdam: van gennep, 1972.

1240. verwey-jonker, h. * (ed.). allochtonen in nederland. beschouwingen over de: gerepatrieerden, molukkers, surinamers, antillianen, buitenlandse studentenin onze samenleving. 2nd ed. 's- gravenhage: 1973. 267 pp.

1241. wittermans, t. * gist, n. p. the ambonese nationalist movement in the netherlands. a study instatus deprivation. pp. 309-317 social forces 40.

H.1.7. Other West-European Countries

1242. botz, g. gewalt in der politik. attentate, zusammenstobe, putschversuche, unruhe in oesterreich 1918 bis 1934. muenchen: fink w., 1976.

1243. brock, g. * lusti r. * marks, l. * et. al. siege: six days at the iranian embassy. london: macmillan, 1980. on the occupation of the iranian embassy in london.

1244. carr, g. the angry brigade, a history of britain's first urban guerrilla group. london: gollancz, 1975.

1245. carvalho, j. m. o terror goncalvista. lisbon: livraria populas de f. franco, 1976. 67 pp.

1246. clissold, s. * (ed.). a short history of yugoslavia: from early times to 1966. cambridge: cambridge university press, 1966. also deals with croatian terrorists.

1247. engels, f. die bakunisten an der arbeit. in: marx/engels werke. bd 18. berlin: 1969.

1248. firth, c. e. urban guerrillas in athens. 1972. pp. 52-56 journal of the royal united service institution 117:165.

1249. goodhart, ph. the climate of collapse: the terrorist threat to britain and her allies. richmond: foreign affairs publ. co., 1975. 15 pp.

1250. haggman, b. sweden's maoist 'subversives' - a case study. london: isc, 1975. conflict studies 58.

1251. hewsen, r. h. who speaks today of the armenians?. in: m. livingston * et. al * (eds.) international terrorism in the contem- porary world. westport, conn. greenwoodpress, 1978. pp. 444-446.

1252. larsson, j. e. politisk terror i sverige. goeteborg: zinderman-solna, seelig, 1968. 82 pp.

1253. latouche, d. violence, politi0ue et crise dans la societe quebecoise. in: l. lapierre * et. al. * (eds .) essays on the left: essays in honour of t. c. douglas. toronto: mcclelland and stewart, 1971. pp. 175-199.

1254. n. n. "dossier" terrorismo. lisboa: avante, 1977. 179 pp. on portuguese right-wing terrorism 1975-1977.

1255. pinter, f. changes in the south tyrol issue. 1977. pp. 64-74 yearbook of world affairs.

1256. redlick, a. s. transnational factors affecting quebec separatist terrorism. paper, 17th. ann. convention internat. studies association toronto, canada: february 1976.

1257. reilly, d. e. urban guerrillas in turkey: causes and consequences. carlisle barracks 910)penn. army war college: .

1258. reilly, w. g. canada, quebec and theories of internal war. 1973. pp. 67-75 american review of canadian studies 3.

1259. rioux, m. quebec in question. translated by james boake. toronto: james lewis and samuel, 1971.

1260. rotstein, a * (ed.). power corrupted: the october crisis and the repression of quebec. toronto: new press, 1971.

1261. ryan, c. le devoir et la crise d'octobre 70. ottawa: lemeac, 1971.

1262. savoie, c. la veritable histoire du flq. montreal: les editions du jour, 1963.

1263. schwarz, j. e. the scottish national party: nonviolent separatism and theories ofviolence. 1970. pp. 496-517 world politics 22:4.

1264. shipley, p. revolutionaries in modern britain. london: bodley head, 1976. 255 pp.

1265. singer, h. l. institutionalization of protest: the quebec separatist movement. ph. d. dissertation: department of political science, new york university, 1976.

1266. stafford, d. anarchists in britain today. 1970. governmentand opposition 5.

1267. stafford, d. anarchists in britain today. 1971. pp. 346-353 government and opposition 6:3.

1268. torrance, j. the response of canadian governments to violence. pp. 473-496 canadian journal of political science 10.

H. TERRORISTIC ACTIVITIES BY REGION AND COUNTRY

H.2. Eastern Europe and Russia, general

1269. **gross, f.** political violence and terror in 19th and 20th century russia and eastern europe. in: j. f. kirkham, s. g. levy and w. j. crotty * (eds.). areport to the national commission on the causes and prevention of violence. vol. 8: assassination and political violence. washington, d. c. gpo, 1969. pp. 421-476.

1270. **gross, f.** violence in politics. terror and political assassination in eastern europe and russia. the hague: 1972. 139 pp.

H.2.1. Eastern Europe, excluding Russia and Balkan

1271. **lacko, m.** arrow-cross men, national socialists. budapest: 1969.

1272. **maerker, r.** angst vor dem ueberschwappen des terrorismus? die ddr und der terrorismus in der bundesrepublik. 1977. p. 1248 deutschland archiv 10.

1273. **nagorski, r.** historique du mouvement anarchiste en pologne. london: slienger, 1976. 22 pp.

1274. **pilsudski, j.** the memoirs of a polish revolutionary and soldier. london: 1931.

H.2.2. Russia

1275. **arendt, h.** the origins of totalitarianism. new york: harcourt, brace and world, 1951.

1276. **avrich, p.** the russian anarchists. new york: w. w. norton & co, 1978.

1277. **avrich, p.** the russian anarchists. princeton, n. j. princeton university press, 1967. 303 pp.

1278. **bernstein, l.** le terrorisme en russie. paris: 191.

1279. **bogucharski, v.** aktivnoe narodnichestvo. moscow: 1912.

1280. **borovoj, a.** michailu bakuninu(1876-1926): ocerk istorii anarchiceskogo dvizenija v rossii. moscow: 1926.

1281. **burtsev, v.** k oruzhyu. london: 1903.

1282. **burtsev, v.** za sto let. london: 1897. on russian terrorists, 1880's.

1283. **cannac, r.** aux sources de la revolution russe: netchaiev. du nihilisme auterrorisme. paris: 1961.

1284. **cassinelli, c. w.** total revolution. a comparative study of germany under hitler, the soviet union under stalin and china under mao. santa barbara: clio press, 1976.

1285. **chernov, v. m.** pered burei. new york: 1953.

1286. **confino, m. * (ed.).** daughter of a revolutionary, natalie herzen and the bakunin/nechayev circle. london: alcove press, 1974.

1287. **daix, p.** marxismus. die doktrin des terrors. graz- wien-koeln: verlag styria, 1976.

1288. **dragomanov, m. p.** la tyrannicide en russie et l'action de l'europe occidentale. geneva: 1883.

1289. **dragomanov, m. p.** terrorism i svobodia. geneva: 188.

1290. **figner, v.** nacht ueber russland. berlin: guhl, 1928. 590 pp. russian terrorism against the tsarist regime, 1880'sff.

1291. **five sisters.** women against the tsar. the memoirs of five revolutionaries of the 1980's. london: 1976.

1292. **gerassimoff, a.** der kampf gegen die erste russische revolution. berlin: 1933.

1293. **gorev, b.** anarchizm v rossii: ot bakunina do machno. moscow: 1930.

1294. **guerassimov, a.** tsarisme et terrorisme. paris: 1934.

1295. **hildermeier, m.** zur sozialstruktur der fuehrungsgruppen und zur terroristischen kampfsmethode der sozial-revolutionaeren partei russlands 1917. dec. 1972. jahrbuecher fuer geschichte osteuropas 20:4.

1296. **hingley, r.** nihilists. london: weidenfeld and nicolson, 1967. on russian terrorists of the 1880's.

1297. **itenberg, b. s.** dvizhenie revoliutsonnove narodnichestva. moscow: 1965. on narodnaya volya in russia, 1870's and 1880's.

1298. **knight, a.** female terrorists in the russian socialist revolutionary party. pp. 139-159 russian review 39:2.

1299. **mcdaniel, j. f.** political assassination and mass execution: terrorism in revolutionary russia, 1918-1938. unpubl. diss. university of michigan, 1976. 402 pp.

1300. **metzl, l.** communist political terror: a behaviorist interpretation. 1970. pp. 769-772 orbis 14:3 .

1301. millard, m. b. russian revolutionary emigration, terrorism and the political struggle. unpubl. diss. university of rochester, 1973. 217 pp.

1302. morozov, n. a. povest moei zhizni. moscow: 1965.

1303. n. n. literatura social 'no-revoljucionnoj partii "narodnoj voli". reprint leipzig: zentralantiquariat , 1977. 978 pp.

1304. naimark, n. m. the workers' section and the challenge of the young. narodnaiavolnia 1881-1884. july 1978. pp. 273-297 russian review 37:3.

1305. nestroev, g. iz dnevnik maksimalista. paris: 1910.

1306. nettlau, m. anarchisten und sozialrevolutionaere. berlin: 1914.

1307. payne, p. s. r. zero: the story of terrorism. new york: 1950 1950, 270 pp. on nechayev and his alleged influence on hitler and lenin.

1308. resh, r. e. the employement of terror in the soviet union and eastern europe. a changing concept. 1973. pp. 81-103 revue de droit international de sciences diplomatiques e politiques 51.

1309. savinkov, b. souvenirs d'un terroriste. paris: 1931. publ. as "memoirs of a terrorist", new york, a. & c. boni, 1931.

1310. savinkov, b. the pale horse. london: allen & unwi, 1981. publ. under pseud. v. ropsin.

1311. schmiedling, w. aufstand der toechter. russische revolutionaerinnen im 19. jahrhundert. munich: kindler, 1979. 270pp. russian 19th century terrorism and the role of women.

1312. skirda, a. les anarchistes dans la revolution russe. l. editions de la tete de feuilles, 1973.

1313. spiridovitch, a. histoire du terrorisme russe(1886-1917). paris: payot, 1930.

1314. stepniak, s. (pseud. for s. m. kravcinskij). le tsarisme et la revolution. paris: 1886.

1315. stepniak, s. (pseud. for s. m. kravcinskij). underground russia. revolutionary profiles and sketches from life. new york: scribner's, 1892.

1316. sternberg, l. politicheski terror v rossii. 1884.

1317. talmon, j. l. the origins of totalitarian democracy. london: secker and warburg, 1952. trad. it. bologna, il mulino, 1967.

1318. tarnovski, g. terrorizm i rutina. geneva: 1880. on russian terrorism; author's real name is romaneko.

1319. ulam, a. b. in the name of the people. new york: 1977. russia 1870's ff.

1320. volk, s. s. narodnaya volya. moscow: 1966.

H.2.3. Balkan, excluding Greece

1321. christowe, st. heroes and assassins. new york: holt, 1935. on de inner macedonian revolutionary organization (imro) established in the 1890s to fight the turks and achieve independence for macedonia. later it became a tool of the bulgarian government; 1890-1930.

1322. codreanu, c. z. pentru legionari. bucharest: 1936.

1323. dedijer, v. the road to serajevo. new york: 1966.

1324. doolard, d. quatre mois chez les comitadjis. paris: 1932.

1325. fatu, m. * spalatelu, i. garda de fier. bucharest: 1971.

1326. jurjevic, m. ustasha under the southern cross. melbourne: jurjevic, 1973. 71 pp.

1327. londres, a. . les comitadjis; ou, le terrorisme dans les balkans. paris: a. michel, 1932. 250 pp. in english: terror in the balkans. london, constable, 1935.

1328. papanace, c. la genesi ed il martirio del movimento legionario rumenio. n. p. 1959.

1329. sburlati, c. codreanu, il capitano. roma: 1970.

1330. tomasic, d. the ustasha movement. in: slavonic encyclopedia. new york: kennicat press, 1949. pp. 1337-1341.

1331. wuerthe, f. die spur fuehrt nach belgrad. vienna: molden verlag, 1975. on sarajewo, 1914 and serbian secret service behind the student terrorists.

1332. zwerin, m. a case for the balkanization of practically everyone. the new nationalism. london: wildwood house, 1976. 188 pp.

H. TERRORISTIC ACTIVITIES BY REGION AND COUNTRY

H.3. Middle East

1333. al-khashaf. arab terrorism, american style. gaithersburg md. international association of chiefs of police, 1974.

1334. alexander, y. terrorism in the middle east: a new phase?. 1978. pp. 115-117 washington quarterly 1.

1335. barakak, h. lebanon in strife. london: university of texas press, 1977.

1336. basker, d. grivas, portrait of a terrorist. london: 1959.

1337. bassiouni, m. c. * fisher, e. m. an arab-israeli conflict: real and apparent issues, an insight into its future from the lessons of the past. 1970. pp. 399-465 st. john's law review 44.

1338. bulloch, j. death of a country. civil war in lebanon. london: weidenfeld and nicolson, 1977.

1339. crawshaw, n. the cyprus revolt. the origins, development and aftermath of an international dispute. london: 1978.

1340. ehrlich, t. cyprus, the warlike isle: origins and elements of the current crisis. 1966. pp. 1021-1098 stanford law review 18:5.

1341. fisher, e. m. * bassiouni, m. c. storm over the arab world. chicago: follett, 1972.

1342. kazziha, w. w. revolutionary transformation in the arab world. habash and his comrades from nationalism to marxism. london: charles knight, 1975.

1343. kosut, h. cyprus, 1946-68. new york: facts on file, 1970.

1344. laffin, j. fedayeen. the arab-israeli dilemma. new york: the free press, 1974.

1345. laqueur, w. confrontation: the middle east and world politics. new york: bantam, 1974.

1346. merari, a. political terrorism and middle eastern instability. in: novik, n. and starr, j. * (eds.) challenges in the middle east. new york: praeger, 1981. pp. 101-112.

1347. miller, l. b. cyprus: the law and politics of civil strife. cambridge: harvard university press, 1968. .

1348. n. n. attentats terroristes et repression. vague d'agitation confessionelle en syrie. octobre 1979 . p. 7 le monde diplomatique terrorist assassinations and repression. wave of religious agitation in syria.

1349. n. n. terrorism in the middle east. 1974. p. 373-421 akron law review 7.

1350. n. n. the soviet attitude to the palestine problem. 1972. pp. 187-212 journal of palestine studies 2.

1351. o'ballance, e. language of violence. the blood politics of terrorism. san rafael, cal. presidio press, 1979. 365 pp. concentrating on fedayeen and zionist terrorism and their international ramifications.

1352. osmond, a. saladin!. new york: doubleday, 1976.

1353. rayfield, g. the role of terror in the middle east. ph. dissertation in preparation: city university of new york,

1354. schmidt, d. a. armageddon in the middle east. new york: john day, 1974.

1355. stephens, r. cyprus: a place of arms. london: pall mall press, 1966.

1356. wolf, j. b. middle eastern death squads. gaithersburg, md. i. a. c. p., 1980. update report 6:4.

1357. yodfat, a. the soviet union and the palestine guerrillas. febr. 1969. pp. 8-17 mizan.

H.3.1. Israel

1358. aines, r. c. the jewish underground against the british mandate in palestine. thesis schenectady, n. y. : union college, 1973.

1359. bauer, y. from diplomacy to resistance: a history of jewish palestine, 1939-1945. philadelphia: jewish publication society, 1970.

1360. begin, m. the revolt - story of the irgun. new york: henry schuman, 1951.

1361. bell, j. b. the long war: israel and the arabs since 1946. englewood cliffs, n. j. prentice-hall, 1969 .

1362. chomsky, n. a proposito di entebbe. il terrorismo civilizzato. 1976. pp. 731-734 il ponte 32:7- 8.

1363. cohen, g. women of violence: memoirs of a young terrorist, 1943-1948. london: hart-davis, 1966. on lehi.

1364. davis, m. jews fight too!. new york: jordan, 1945.

1365. dekel, e. (pseud. krasner). shai: historical exploits of haganah intelligence. new york: yoseloff, 1959.

1366. dinstein, y. terrorism and wars of liberation: an israeli perspective of the arab-israeli conflict. springfield, ill. thomas, 1975. pp. 155-172.

1367. frank, g. le groupe stern attaque. paris: laffont, 1963.

1368. frank, g. the deed: the assassination in cairo during world war ii of lord moyne. new york: simon and schuster, 1963. 319 pp.

1369. frank, g. the moyne case: a tragic history. dec. 194. pp. 64-71 commentary.

1370. goldberg, y. haganah or terror. new york: hechalutz, 1947.

1371. groussard, s. the blood of israel: the massacre of the israeli athletes, the olympics, 197 transl. by harord j. salemson. new york: morrow, 1975.

1372. hirst, d. the gun and the olive branch: the roots of violence in the middle east. new york: harcourt brace jovanovich, 1979. 357 pp. traces events from 1921 onwards.

1373. horowitz, i. l. israeli ecstasies/jewish agonies. new york: oxford university press, 1974. 272 pp.

1374. howe, i. * gershma, c. israel, the arabs and the middle east. new york: quadrangle, 1972.

1375. katz, d. the lady was a terrorist: during israel's war of liberation. new york: shiloni, 1953. 192 pp. on irgun.

1376. katz, s. days of fire: the secret history of the irgun zvai leumi. garden city, n. y. doubleday, 1968 . 317pp. memoirs of a member of the irgun.

1377. khalidi, w. from haven to conquest. beirut: institute for palestine studies, 1971. anthology of readings on the history of zionism 1897-1948.

1378. langer, f. la repressione di israele contro i palestinesi. milano: teti, 1976.

1379. lorch, n. israel's war of independence. 1947-1949. g. p. putman's sons: new york, 1961.

1380. lorch, n. the edge of the sword: israel's war of independence 1947-1949. new york: putnam, 1961. 475 pp.

1381. mardor, m. haganah. new york: new american librar, 1966.

1382. meridor, y. long road to freedom. new york: unitedzionists revisionists, 1961.

1383. monteil, v. secret dossier on israeli terrorism. pari: guy authier, 1978. 450 pp.

1384. mor, n. y. lokame herut israel. 2 vols. telaviv: 1974. on jewish terrorism in palestine, 1940s.

1385. n. n. chronology of zionist and israeli terrorism. pp . 3-8 palestine digest 2.

1386. n. n. dir yassin. 1969. pp. 27-30 west asia affairs.

1387. n. n. israeli terror, 1967-72. 1973. pp. 6-22 arab palestinian resistance 5:1.

1388. n. n. who are the terrorists? aspects of zionist and israeli terrorism. beirut: institute for palestine studies and the arab women's information committee, 1972. monograph series 33.

1389. niv, d. ma'arakhot ha'irgun hazvai halevmi. 5 vols. telaviv: 1977.

1390. nolin, t. la haganah: l'armee secrete d'israel. paris: ballard, 1971.

1391. o'neill, b. e. israel's counter-insurgency and the fedayeen. july 1973. pp. 452-460 army quarterly 53.

1392. o'neill, b. e. revolutionary warfare in the middle east: the israelis versus the fedayeen. boulder, colo. paladin,

1393. palestine arab refugees institution. tension, terror and blood in the holy land. damascus: 1955.

1394. palestine liberation organization. the "activities" of the hagana. irgun and stern bands. new york: plo,

1395. paust, j. j. selected terroristic claims arising from the arab-israeli context. 1974. akron law review 7.

1396. peeke, j. l. jewish-zionist terrorism and the establishment of israel. master's thesis: naval postgraduate school, 1977.

1397. rapoport, d. c. terrorism: the jew as perpetrator and victim in the great revolt against rome. 1979. compares zealot and sicarii strategy and tactics with that of modern groups.

1398. sacher, h. the pledge. new york: simon & schuster, 1970. 343pp. on haganah, irgun.

1399. stern, a. bedamai lead tikhi. telaviv: 1976.

1400. united nations. zionist terrorism. united nations doc. a/c. 6/c. 876 new york: un, 22 nov. 1972.

H.3.2. Palestine

1401. abul lughod, i. the palestinians since 1967. 1973. international journal.

1402. al-azm, s. j. dirasa naqdiya li fikr al-muqawama al-filastiniya. [a critical study of the thought of the palestinian resistance]. beirut: dar al-auda, 1973.

1403. alexander, y. * kittrie, n. n. crescent and star: arab-israeli perspectives on the middle east conflict. . new york: ams press, 1972.

1404. alexander, y. the legacy of palestinian terrorism. telaviv: 1976. pp. 57-64 international problems 15:3-4.

1405. alon, h. countering palestinian terrorism in israel. toward a policy analysis of countermeasures. santa monic, cal. rand, 1980.

1406. ashab, n. to overcome the crisis of the palestinian resistance. 1972. pp. 71-78 world marxist review 15:5.

1407. avineri, s. * (ed.). israel and the palestinians: reflections on the clash of two national movements. new york: st. martin's, 1971.

1408. belack, c. n. transnational terrorism and world politics: a case study of the pales tine arab resistance movement. ph. d. dissertation in preparation: columbia university,

1409. bell, j. b. arafat's man in the mirror: the myth of the fedayeen. london: april 1970. pp. 19-24 new middle east 19.

1410. bell, j. b. bab el mandeb, strategic troublespot. 1973. pp. 975-989 orbis 16.

1411. bell, j. b. terror out of zion: irgun, lehi, and the palestine underground, 1929- 1949. new york: st. martin's press, 1977. 359 pp.

1412. ben amon, s. be-akvot ha-chavlanim. telaviv: madim, 1970. 198 pp. following the arab terrorist.

1413. ben-dor, g. the strategy of terrorism in the arab-israel conflict: the case of the palestinian guerrillas. in: y. evron * (ed.)international violenc: terrorism, surprise and control. jerusalem: hebrew univ. of jerusalem. 1. davis institute for international relations, 1979. pp. 126-165.

1414. ben-dor, g. the strategy of terrorism in the arab-israeli conflict. the case of the palestinian guerillas. mimeo. haifa: university of haifa, 1976. 52 pp. appendix: arab cross-national terrorism, 1968-1974.

1415. bishop, v. f. the role of political terrorism in the palestinian resistance move- ment: june 1967-october 1973. in: m. stohl * (ed.) the politics of terrorism. new york: dekker, 1979. pp . 323-350.

1416. cetiner, y. el-fatah. istanbul: may yazinlari, 1970.

1417. chailand, g. the palestinian resistance. baltimore: penguin, 1972.

1418. churba, j. fedayeen and the middle east crisis. maxwell, ala. air university, 1969.

1419. colebrook, j. israel with terrorists. july 1974. p. 30 commentary 58:1.

1420. cooley, j. k. china and the palestinians. 1972. p . 19-34 journal of palestinian studies 1:2.

1421. cooley, j. k. green march, black september: the story of the palestinian arabs. london: frank cass, 1973. 263 pp. author is correspondent for the christian science monitor and abc in beirut.

1422. cooley, j. k. moscow faces a palestinian dilemma. 197. pp 32-35 mideast 11:3.

1423. crozier, b. * (ed.). since jordan: the palestinian fedayeen. london: institute for the study of conflict, conflict studies 38.

1424. curtis, m. * neyer, j. * waxman, c. i. * pollack, a. the palestinians: people, history, politics. new brunswick, n. j. transaction, 1975. 277 pp. contains a chronology of arab terrorist acts.

1425. darcourt, p. 5 septembre 1972. drame a munich. in: mirror de l'histoire. 1973. 275 pp.

1426. davis, u. * mack, a. * javal davis, n. * (eds.). israel and the palestinians. london: 1975.

1427. denoyan, g. el-fatah parle: les palestiniens contre israel. paris: albin michel, 1970.

1428. dethoor, n. le reveil de la palestine. 1969. pp. 13-16 croissance de jeunes nations.

1429. dhaher, a. the plo. ph. d. dissertation forthcoming: university of west virginia,

1430. dobson, chr. black september: its short, violent history. new york: macmillan, 1974.

1431. dyad, a. my home, my land. a narrative of the palestinian struggle rouleau, e. new york: 1981.

1432. el fath. la revolution palestinienne et les juifs. paris: editions de minuit, 1970.

1433. el-rayyes, r. * (ed.) * nahas, d. guerrillas for palestine. london: croom helm, 1976. trad. it. * milano, episteme, 1976.

1434. ellenberg, e. s. the plo and its place in violence and terror. n. p. 1976.

1435. francos, a. les palestiniens. paris: juillard, 1970.

1436. franjieh, s. how revolutionary is the palestinian resistance? a marxist interpretation. 1972. pp. 52-60 journal of palestine studies 1.

1437. ganahl, j. time, trial, and terror: an analysis of the palestinian guerrilla revolution. air war college professional study, 1975. 87 pp.

1438. harkabi, y. palestinians and israel. jerusalem: keter publishing house, 1974.

1439. heradstveit, d. a profile of the palestine guerrillas. 1972. pp. 13-36 cooperation and conflict 7.

1440. heradstveit, d. nahost-guerillas. eine politikologische studie. berlin: verlag arno spitz, 1973. 261 pp.

1441. howley, d. c. the u. n. and the palestinians. new york: exposition press, 1975. 168 pp.

1442. hudson, m. c. developments and setbacks in the palestinian resistance movement. 1972. pp. 64-84 journal of palestine studies 1.

1443. hudson, m. c. the palestinian arab resistance movement: its significance in the middle east crisis. , 1969. pp. 291-301 middle east journal 23.

1444. hurewitz, j. c. the struggle for palestine. new york: greenwood, 1968.

1445. hurni, f. terrorism and the struggle for palestine. febr. 1979. pp. 14-23 swiss review of world affairs 28.

1446. hussain, m. the palestine liberation organization: a study in ideology and tactics. new york: international publications service, 1975. 156 pp.

1447. hussaini, h. i. * e-boghdady, f. * (eds.). the palestinians. selected essays. washington d. c. arab information centre, 1976.

1448. ibrahim, s. zur genesis des palestinensischen widerstandes 1882-1972. 1973. pp. 517-537 blaetter fuer deutsche und internationale politik 18:5.

1449. ijad, a. heimat oder tod. der freiheitskampf der palastinenser. econ: 1978. 320 pp. by the chief of intelligence of the p. l. o.

1450. isc. since jordan: the palestinian fedayeen. london: isc, pp. 3-18 conflict studies 38.

1451. issa, m. je suis un fedayin. paris: stock, 1976.

1452. ittayem, m. the palestine national struggle: the pflp and the transformation of ideology. ph. d. dissertation: american university, 1977.

1453. jaari, e. strike terror, the story of fatah. jerusale: 1970.

1454. jabber, f. the arab regimes and the palestinian revolution, 1967-71. 1973. pp. 79-101 journal of palestinian studies 2:2.

1455. jureidini, p. a. * et. al. the palestinian movement in politics. lexington, mass. lexington books, 1976.

1456. jureidini, p. a. the palestinian revolution: its organization, ideologies, and dynamics. washington, d. c. american institutesfor research, 1972.

1457. jureidini, p. a. the relationship of the palestinian guerrilla movement with the government of jordan: 1967-70. ph. d. dissertation: american university, 1975.

1458. kadi, l. s. * (ed.). basic political documents: documents of the armed palestinian resistance movement. . beirut: palestine liberation organization research center, 1969.

1459. kelidar, a. the palestine guerrilla movement. oct. 1976. pp. 412-420 world today 29.

1460. khader, b. * khader, n. * (eds.). textes de la revolution palestinienne, 1968-1974:presentes et traduits par bichara et naim khader. paris: sindbad, 1975. 350 pp.

1461. kiernan, t. arafat: the man and the myth. new york: norton, 1976. 281 pp.

1462. koestler, a. promise and fulfilment. palestine 1917-1949. london: macmillan, 1949.

1463. krosney, h. the plo's moscow connection. 24 september 1979. pp. 64-72 new york.

1464. kuroda, y. young palestinian commandos in political socialization perspective. 1972. pp. 253-270 middle east journal 26.

1465. kurtzer, d. c. palestine guerrilla and israeli counter-guerrilla warfare: the radicalization of the palestine community to violence. ph. d. dissertation in preparation: columbia university,

1466. l'heureux, r. j. syria and the palestinian resistance movement 1965-1975. wright-patterson air force base, ohio: air force institute of technology, 11 may 1976.

1467. lagerwist, f. a. israel and the politics of terrorism in the middle east. 1981. 143 pp.

1468. leibstone, m. palestine terror. past present and future: some observations. gaithersburg, md. iacp, . 27 pp.

1469. lesch, m. the politics of palestinian nationalism. los angeles, cal. university of california press, 1973.

1470. lewis, b. the palestinians and the plo: a historical approach. january 1975. pp. 32-48 commentary.

1471. little, t. the nature of the palestinian resistance movement. 1970. pp. 157-169 asian affairs 57 .

1472. **little, t.** the new arab extremists: a view from the arab world. london: institute for the study of power and conflict, may 1970. conflict studies 4.

1473. **ma'oz, m.** soviet and chinese relations with the palestinian guerilla organization. jeruzalem: the hebrew university, 1974. jerusalem paper on peace problems.

1474. **mark, c. f.** the palestine resistance movement. report washington, d. c. legislative reference service to the library of congress, 17 june 1970.

1475. **matekolo, i.** droit vers la mort: septembre noir. 197. pp. 121-131 historama 270.

1476. **moore, j. n.** * (ed.). the arab-israeli conflict. 2 vols. princeton, n. j. princeton university press, 1974.

1477. **moshe, b.** * (ed.). issues and analysis. arab terror vs. pioneering. jerusalem: world zionist organization,

1478. **mury, g.** schwarzer september. analysen, aktionen und dokumente. berlin: wagenbach, 1974. 127 pp.

1479. **n. n.** accessories to terror. the responsibility of arab governments for the organization of terrorist activities. jerusalem: ministry of foreign affairs, 1973. 47 pp.

1480. **n. n.** arab terrorism. 1969. pp. 13-16 jewish frontier 36.

1481. **n. n.** israeli policy towards the palestinians: 25 years of terrorism. january, 1975. pp. 23-32 arab palestinian resistence 1.

1482. **n. n.** nasser terror gangs: the story of the fedayeen. jerusalem: ministry for foreign affairs, 1956.

1483. **n. n.** schwarzer september. dokumente, kommuniques. frankfurt a. m. verlag roter stern, 1973. 60 pp.

1484. **n. n.** scope and limit of a fedayeen consensus. 1970. pp. 1-8 wiener library bulletin.

1485. **n. n.** since jordan: the palestinian fedayeen. london: institute for the study of conflict, 1973. 18 pp. conflict studies 38.

1486. **n. n.** the savage kinship: a chronology of the use of violence for political ends in arab countries. jerusalem: carta, 1973.

1487. **n. n.** zwarte september. het relaas van de mysterieuze organisatie diebloedige terreuracties ondertekent met de naam zwarte september. baarn: meulenhoff, 1974. on black september.

1488. **nakleh, e. a.** the anatomy of violence: theoretical reflections of palestinian resistance. 1971. pp . 180-200 middle east journal 25.

1489. **nassar, j.** the palestine liberation organization. ph. . dissertation in preparation: university of cincinnati,

1490. **norton, a. r.** moscow and the palestinians. miami: center for advanced international studies, university of miami, 1974.

1491. **o'ballance, e.** arab guerrilla power, 1967-1972. london: faber, 1972.

1492. **o'neill, b. e.** armed struggle in palestine. an analysis of the palestinian guerrilla movement. boulder , colo. westview press, 1978. 320 pp.

1493. **pachter, h.** who are the palestinians?. 1975. pp 387-395 dissent 22:4.

1494. **porath, y.** revolution and terror in the palestinian communist party (p. c. p.) 1929-1939. 1968. pp. 246-269 hamizrah hehadash 18:3-4.

1495. **porath, y.** the palestinian arab national movement. 1929-1939. frank cass, 1977.

1496. **poupar, o.** la revolution palestinienne et l'etat palestinien. 1975. pp. 475-492 politique etrangere. 40:5.

1497. **pryce-jones, d.** the face of defeat: palestinian refugees and guerrillas. london: weidenfeld & nicholson, 1972.

1498. **quandt, w. b.** * **jabber, f.** * **leach, a. m.** the politics of palestinian nationalism. berkeley: university of california press, 1973. 234 pp.

1499. **ribet, s.** il nodo del conflitto libanese. tra resistenza palestinese e destra maronita. torino: claudiana, 1977.

1500. **rouleau, e.** abou iyad: palestinien sans patrie. entretiens avec eric rouleau. paris: fayolle, 1978. 360 pp.

1501. **said, e. w.** the question of palestine. new york: 1979.

1502. **sayegh, a.** palestine and arab nationalism. beirut: palestine liberation organization research center, .

1503. **sayigh, r.** palestinians, from peasants to revolutionaries. a people'shistory recorded from interviews with camp palestinians in lebanon. london: zed, 1979. 206 pp.

1504. **schiff, z.** * **rothstein, r.** fedayeen: guerrillas against israel. new york: david mckay, 1972. 246 pp.

1505. **sharabi, h.** palestinian guerrillas: their credibility and effectiveness. supplementary papers washington, d. c. georgetown university center for strategic and internal studies, 1970. ca. 55 pp.

1506. **sobel, l. a.** * (ed.). palestinian impasse: arab guerrillas and international terror. new york: facts on file, 1977.

1507. stetler, r. * (ed.). palestine: the arab-israeli conflict. palo alto, calif. ramparts press, 1974.

1508. syrkin, m. political terrorism - or plain murder?. nov. 1972. pp. 3-11 midstream. a monthly jewish review 18:9.

1509. tophoven, r. fedayin - guerilla ohne grenzen. geschichte, soziale struktur und politische ziele der palestinensischen widerstands-organisationen. die israelische konter-guerilla. muenchen: bernard & graefe, 1975. 159 pp.

1510. tophoven, r. guerillas in nahost. aufstieg und schicksal der palaestinensischen widerstands-organisationen. 1972. pp. 3-45 aus politik und zeitgeschichte 8.

1511. wilson, b. a. conflict in the middle east: the challenge of the palestinian movement. washington, d. c. : center for research insocial systems, jan. 1969.

1512. wilson, b. a. palestinian guerrilla movements. washington, d. c. american university, center for research in social systems, 1969.

1513. wilson, r. d. cordon and search. aldershot: gale and polden, 1949.

1514. wolf, j. b. a mideast profile: the cycle of terror and counterterror. nov. 1972. international perspectives.

1515. wolf, j. b. black september. a description of an international terrorist organization and an assessment of its implications for urban law enforcement agencies of the united states. master's thesis no. 395. new york: john jaycollege of criminal justice, 1974.

1516. wolf, j. b. black september: militant palestinianism. 1973. pp. 8-37 current history 64:377.

1517. yaari, e. strike terror: the story of fatah. new york: sabra books, 1970.

1518. yaari, e. the decline of al-fatah. may 1971. pp. 3-12 midstream.

1519. yahalom, d. fire on arab terrorism. jerusalem: carta, 1973.

1520. yahalom, y. arab terror. telaviv: world labour zionist movement, 1969.

1521. yaniv, a. p. l. o. a profile. jerusalem: israel universities study group for middle east affairs, 1974 .

1522. yedlin, r. the manifesto of the popular democratic front of the liberation ofpalestine. 1971. pp. 30-37 hamizrah hehadash 21:1.

H.3.3. Middle East, other countries

1523. alastos, d. cyprus guerillas: grivas, makarios, and the british doros alastos. london: heinemann, 1960.

1524. byford-jones, w. grivas and the story of eoka. london: robert hayle, 1959.

1525. crouzet, f. le conflict de cypre, 1946-1959. 2 vols. bruxelles: brylant, 1973. 1187 pp. etudes de cas de conflicts internationaux 4.

1526. desjardins, t. le martyre du liban. paris: librairie plon-sas production, 1976.

1527. durrell, l. bitter lemons. london: 1959. cyprus, 1950's eoka.

1528. foley, ch. * scobie, w. i. the struggle for cyprus. stanford, calif. hoover institution press, 1975. 193 pp. journalistic narrative of the grivas campaign, 1955-1960, and aftermath.

1529. foley, ch. island in revolt. london: longmans, 1962. 248 pp. cyprus 1955-1959.

1530. foley, ch. legacy of strife. cyprus from rebellion to civil war. harmondsworth: penguin, 1964.

1531. franzius, e. history of the order of assassins. new york: funk & wagnalls, 1969. on 11th century terrorist movement of hasan sabba in northwest persia.

1532. gavin, r. j. aden under british rule, 1839-1967. london: c. hurst and co., 1975. 472pp.

1533. gourlay, b. i. s. terror in cyprus. 1959. marine corps gazette 8/9.

1534. hodgson, m. g. s. the order of assassins. the hague: 1955. on 11th century islamic sect.

1535. ismail, a. f. how we liberated aden. april 1976. gulfstudies.

1536. jazani, b. armed struggle in iran. london: iran committee, 1977. 143 pp. by a member of the marxist-leninist siahkal killed in 1975.

1537. johnson, h. o. recent opposition movements in iran. unpubl. master's thesis. salt lake city: university of utah, 1975.

1538. kelidar, a. * burrell, m. lebanon: the collapse of a state. regional dimensions of the struggle. 1976. conflict studies 74.

1539. lewis, b. the assassins. a radical sect in islam. london: weidenfeld & nicolson, 1967. on the 11th century order of assassins.

1540. markides, k. the rise and fall of the cyprus republic. newhaven, conn. yale university press, 1977. .

1541. n. n. griechenland und der terrorismus auf zypern. 1957. pp. 1-7 british information 351.

1542. n. n. terrorism in cyprus: the captured documents. transcribed extracts issued by authority of the secretary of state for the colonies. london: hmso, 1956.

1543. nalbadian, l. the armenian revolutionary movement. berkeley: 1963.

1544. owen, r. * (ed.). essays on the crisis in lebanon. london: ithaka press, 1976.

1545. paget, j. last post aden, 1964-67. london: faber, 1969. on terrorist campaign which forced great britain out of south jemen.

1546. trelford, d. * (ed.). siege: six days at the iranian embassy. london: macmillan, 1980.

1547. vallaud, p. le liban au bout du fusil. paris: hachette, 1976.

1548. vocke, h. the lebanese civil war. london: c. hurst and co., 1978. 100 pp. on 1975-1976 civil war.

H. TERRORISTIC ACTIVITIES BY REGION AND COUNTRY

H.4. Asia

1549. al-kubeissi, b. storia del movimento dei nazionalisti arabi. milan: jaca, 1977.

1550. alexander, y. * nanes, a. * (eds.). the united states and iran. a documentary history. frederick, md. university publications of america, 1980.

1551. landau, j. m. radical politics in modern turkey. leiden: e. j. brill, 1974.

1552. salinger j. america held hostage. the secret negotiations. garden city, n. y. doubleday, 1981. iran 1978-1981.

1553. toynbee, a. j. armenian atrocities. the murder of a nation. london: 1915. 119 pp.

H.4.1. Indian subcontinent

1554. anand, v. s. dhananjay keer veer savarkar. london: 1967. indian terrorism.

1555. baylay, d. h. violent protests in india: 1900-1960. july 1963. the indian journal of political science.

1556. chanda, b. the revolutionary terrorists in northern india in the 1920's. in: b. r. nanda * (ed.). socialism in india. dehli: 1972.

1557. chatterji, j. c. indian revolutionaries in conference. calcutta: mukkopadhyay,

1558. chopra, p. three waves of indian terrorism: a first-hand report on the naxalite movement. 1970. pp. 433-438 dissent 17:5.

1559. dasgupta, b. the naxalite movement. new delhi: allied publishers, 1974.

1560. gopal, r. how india struggled for freedom. bombay: 1967.

1561. gordon, l. a. bengal: the nationalist movement, 1876-1940. new york: columbia university press, 1974. .

1562. hale, h. w. political trouble in india, 1917-1937. allahabad: chugh publ., 1974. 285 pp.

1563. hale, h. w. terrorism in india 1917-1936. columbus, ohio: southern asia, 1974. reprint of 1937 ed.

1564. indira devi, m. g. terrorist movement in south india. trivandrum: kercila historical society, 1977.

1565. keer, d. veer savarkar. bombay: 1966. india.

1566. khaleque, a. terrorism's menace: how to combat it. jalpaiguri: a. wadubat: jalpaiguri kohinoor printing works, 1932.

1567. kini, n. g. s. terrorist world-outlook in the 19th century western india. 1972. pp. 68 ff. political science review)11:1.

1568. lambrick, h. t. the terrorist. transl. and ed. from the sindhi mss. london: benn, 1972. 246 pp. india; hurrebellion 1942-1947.

1569. laushey, d. m. bengal terrorism and the marxist left. calcutta: firma k. l. mukhopadhyay, 1975.

1570. laushey, d. m. the bengal terrorists and their conversion to marxism: aspects of regional nationalism in india, 1905-1942. unpubl. diss. university of virginia, 1969. 276 pp.

1571. manoranjan, m. revolutionary violence: a study of the maoist movement in india. new dehli: sterling, 1977.

1572. mitchell, k. l. india without fable. new york: alfred a. knopf, 1942. on 1919ff. gandhi's satyagraha and terrorism.

1573. n. n. political violence and terrorism in benegal. in: m. stohl * (ed.) the politics of terrorism. new york: dekker, 1979. pp. 351-372.

1574. n. n. terror in east pakistan. karachi publications, 1971.

1575. n. n. terrorism in india 1917-1936. deep publications reprint 1974 simla: government of india press, 1937.

1576. nath, s. terrorism in india. new delhi: national publ. house, 1980. 350 pp.

1577. nayar, b. r. violence and crime in india: a quantitative study. delhi: macmillan co of india, 1975.

1578. ram, m. shift in naxalite tactics. 21 aug. 1971. economic and political weekly.

1579. ram, m. the urban guerrilla movement in calcutta. jan. 1972. institute for defence studies and analyses journal.

1580. roy, s. bharatera baiplabika samgramera itihasa. karachi: 1955. india. in bengali.

1581. sedition committee. report. calcutta: superintendent government printing office, 1918. gives a narrative of the major terroristic events in bengal, 1906-1916.

1582. sen, n. bengal's forgotten warriors. bombay: 1945.

1583. sleeman, j. l. la secte secrete des thugs. paris: ed. payot, 1934.

1584. tapaua, g. the gandhi murder trial. london: 1973. 336 pp.

1585. vajpeyi, j. n. the extremist movement in india. allahabad: 1974.

1586. weiner, m. violence and politics in calcutta. may 1961. pp. 275-281 journal of asian studies 20.

1587. wickramanayake, d. harijan terror in india. plural societies 6:3.

H.4.2. South-East Asia and China

1588. aerker, s. r. * krause, j. r. communist terrorist campaign: thailand-malaysian frontier. 1966. pp. 39-46 military review 4:6.

1589. brass, p. * franda, m. * (eds.). radical politics in south asia. cambridge, mass. m. i. t. press, 1973 .

1590. caldwell, m. * (ed.). ten years' military terror in indonesia. nottingham: spokesman books, 1975.

1591. chesneaux, j. * (ed.). popular movements and secret societies in china, 1840-1950. stanford: 1972.

1592. chomsky, n. * herman, e. s. counterrevolutionary violence: blood bath in fact and propaganda. trad. it. milano: il formichiere, 1975.

1593. clutterbuck, r. l. riots and revolution in singapore and malaya 1945-1963. london: faber and faber, 1973.

1594. davison, w. ph. some observations on viet cong operations in the villages. p. 2 rand abstracts rm 5367.

1595. dentan, r. k. the semai. a nonviolent people of malaya. new york: rinehart and winston, 1968.

1596. duke, w. d. h. operation metcalff. the story of a raid on a terrorist camp inmalaya. 1953. pp. 28-32 army quarterly 67:1.

1597. fall, b. b. street without joy. insurgency in indo-china 1946-1963. london: pall mall, 1964.

1598. fall, b. b. the two vietnams: a political and military analysis. new york: praeger, 1964.

1599. joiner, c. a. the politics of massacre. political processes in south vietnam. philadelphia: temple university press, 1974.

1600. jones, a. * et. al. study of threats and terror. washington, d. c. american university, cress, 1966. vietnam.

1601. kerkvliet, j. b. the huk rebellion: a study of peasant revolt in the philippines. berkeley: university of californiapress, 1977.

1602. komer, r. w. impact of pacification on insurgency in south vietnam. 1971. pp. 48-69 journal of international affairs 25:1.

1603. mallin, j. * (ed.). terror in viet nam. princeton, n. j. d. van nostrand, 1966.

1604. muros, r. l. communist terrorism in malaya. 1961. pp. 51-57 united states naval institute proceedings 87:10.

1605. n. n. a viet cong directive on "repression". in: mallin, j. *(ed.) terror and urban guerrillas. coral gables: university of miami press, 1971.

1606. n. n. la terreur, instrument de pouvoir revolutionaire. april 1971. pp. 1-124 l'ordre francais.

1607. noble, l. g. the moro national liberation front in the philippines. 1976. pp. 405-424 pacific affairs 49.

1608. o'ballance, e. malaya; the communist insurgent war, 1948-1960. london: faber & faber, 1966.

1609. pike, d. the kind of war that is vietnam: people's war with terror as the tool. june 1970. air forceand space digest.

1610. pike, d. viet cong: the organization and techniques of the national liberation front of south vietnam. . cambridge, mass. m . i. t. press, 1966.

1611. pye, l. guerrilla communism in malaya. princeton, n. j: princeton university press, 1956.

1612. rees, d. north korea's growth as a subversive center. london: institute for the study of conflict, conflict studies 28.

1613. renick, r. o. the emergency regulations of malaya. cause and effect. pp. 1-39 journal af southeast asian history 6:2.

1614. reynolds, j. a. c. terrorist activity in malaya. november 1961. marine corps gazette.

1615. schultz, r. the limits of terrorism in insurgency warfare. the case of the viet cong. 1978. pp. 67-91 polity 11:1.

1616. seymour, w. n. terrorism in malaya. april 1949. army quarterly.

1617. short, a. the communist insurrection in malaya, 1948-1960. london: frederick muller limited, 1975.

1618. shuja, s. m. political violence in southeast asia: a critical analysis of some models. 1977. pp. 48-64 pakistan horizon.

1619. shultz, r. the limits of terrorism in insurgency warfare: the case of the vietcong. 1978. pp. 67-91 polity 11.

1620. thompson, r. defeating communist insurgency. new york: praeger, 1970.

1621. u. s. government. agency for international development. mission in vietnam. viet cong use of terror; a study by united states mission in vietnam. saigon: 1967. 84 pp.

1622. zasloff, j. j. origins of the insurgency in south vietnam 1954-1960. the role of the southern vietminh cadres. santa monica: rand, 1967.

H.4.3. Japan

1623. beraud, b. la gauche revolutionnaire au japon. paris: seuil, 1970. 157 pp.

1624. boyd jr., j. a. the japanese red army. air command andstaff college, air university, april 1978. research report 0200-78 available as far 29106-n ad b028 1371.

1625. duvila, j. au japon la violence sert le pouvoir. july 1972. pp. 1069-1084 revue de defense nationale 28.

1626. iwakawa, t. making of a terrorist: suicidal fanaticism of the japanese red army. jan. 1976. p. 33 atlas 23.

1627. kuriyama, y. terrorism at telaviv airport and a "new left" group in japan. march 1973. pp. 336-346 asian survey 13:3 on united red army, japan.

1628. murofushi, t. nihon no terorisuto. 1962. assassination and coup d'etats in japan.

1629. n. n. de gijzeling in de franse ambassade. 9 nov. 1974. pp. 582-588 algemeen politieblad 123:10 occupation of french embassy in the hague by japanese terrorists.

1630. n. n. hijackings by japan's red army. january 1978. pp. 8-11 japan quarterly.

1631. n. n. terror behind the red army. 26 nov. 197. pp . 26-31 asia week a summary article on the japanese red army.

1632. n. n. tokushu: rengo sekigun jiken no imi suru mono-ningen, kakumei, skukusei. 14 april 1972. pp. 4-17 asahi journal special: te meaning of the u. r. a. incident - man, revolution, and purge.

1633. n. n. uchi geba no rouri. tokyo: 1974. symposium on united red army terrorists.

1634. **nishio, h. k.** extraparliamentory activities and political unrest in japan. toronto: 1968. pp. 122-137 international journal 24:1.

1635. **otsuka, b.** rengo sekigun: sono seiritsu kara hokai made. tokyo: may 1972. theshokun 4:5 on the founding and disintegration of the united red army.

1636. **sasho henshu committee.** sekigun. tokyo: 1975. pp. 361-484 contain a detailed bibliography on the japanese united red army.

1637. **seiffert, j. e.** zengakuren. universitaet und widerstand in japan. muenchen: trikont, 1969. 149 pp.

1638. **tachibara, t.** chukaku us kakumaru. 2 vols. tokyo: 1975. on united red army and other japanese terrorist groups.

1639. **takagi, m.** rengo sekigun to shin sayoku undo. tokyo: 14 april 1972. asahi journal on the united red army and the 'new left'.

1640. **taylor, r. w. * kim, b. -s.** violence and change in postindustrial societies: student protest in america and japan in the 1960's. in: m. livingston * et. al. * (eds.) international terrorism in the contemporary world. westport, conn. greenwood press, 1978. pp. 204-222.

H.4.4. Australia

1641. **davies, d.** the ustasha in australia. sidney: communistparty of australia, april 1972.

H. TERRORISTIC ACTIVITIES BY REGION AND COUNTRY

H.5. Africa, general

1642. **cohen, jacopetti.** africa addio. munich: 1966. accounts of violence in africa, based on documentary movie.

1643. **gibson, r.** african liberation movements. contemporary struggles against white minority rule. london: oxford university press, 1972.

1644. **grundy, k. w.** guerrilla struggle in africa. an analysis and preview. new york: grossmann publ., 1971. 204 pp.

1645. **jenkins, b. m.** urban violence in africa. 1968. p. 37 american behavioral scientist 2:4.

1646. **oruka, h. o.** punishment and terrorism in africa. kampala: east african literature bureau, 1976.

H.5.1. Northern Africa

1647. **abbas, f.** guerre et revolution d'algerie. paris: juilliard, 1962.

1648. **bayssade, p.** la guerre d'algerie 1954-1962. paris: editions planete, 1968. 263 pp.

1649. **bell, j. b.** endemic insurgency and international order. the eritrean experience. 1974. pp 427-450 orbis 17.

1650. **boutang, p.** la terreur en question. paris: fasquelle, 1958.

1651. **boyce, f.** the internationalizing of internal war: ethiopia, the arabs, and the case de eritrea. 1972. pp. 51-73 journal of international and comparative studies 5.

1652. **bromberger, s.** les rebelles algeriens. paris: 195.

1653. **buchard, r.** organisation armee secrete. paris: michel, 1963. 203 pp.

1654. **campbell, j. f.** rumblings along the red sea: the eritrean question. april 1970. pp. 537-548 foreign affairs 48.

1655. **clark, m. k.** algeria in turmoil. a history of the rebellion, 1954-58. new york: praeger, 1959. 466 pp. .

1656. **coerriere, y.** la guerre d'algerie. 4 vols. paris: fayard, 1968.

1657. **crenshaw, m.** revolutionary terrorism. the fln in algeria, 1954-1962. stanford: hoover institution press, 1978. 178 pp.

1658. duchemin, j. histoire du fln. paris: la table ronde, 1962. 331 pp.

1659. dumas, a. der krieg in algerien. zollikon: evang. verl., 1958. 148 pp.

1660. elsenhans, h. frankreichs algerienkrieg, 1954-1962. entkolonisierungs- versuch einer kapitalistischen metropole. zum zusammenbruch der kolonialreiche. muenchen: hanser, 1974. 908 pp.

1661. fanon, f. aspekte der algerischen revolution. frankfurt a. m. suhrkamp, 1969. 150 pp. orig. sociologie d'une revolution.

1662. fanon, f. sociologie d' une revolution. l'an v de la revolution algerienne. paris: maspero, 1978. orig. published in 1959.

1663. favrod, c. h. la revolution algerienne. paris: 195.

1664. gorce, p. -m. de la. histoire de l'o. a. s. en algerie. oct. 1962. la nef.

1665. heggoy, a. a. insurgency and counterinsurgency in algeria. bloomington: indiana university press, 1972 . 327 pp.

1666. henissart, p. wolves in the city. new york: simon & schuster, 1970. 508 pp. detailed history of the o. a. s.

1667. isc. libya's foreign adventures. london: institute for the study of conflict, conflict studies 41.

1668. joesten, j. the red hand; the sinister account of the terrorist arm of the french right-wing "ultras" - in algeria and on the continent. new york: abelard-schuman, 1962. 200pp.

1669. julien, ch. a. l'afrique du nord en marche. nationalismes musulmans et souverainite francaise. third edition paris: julliard, 1972.

1670. jureidini, p. a. case studies in insurgency and revolutionary warfare: algeria 1954-1962. washington: american university, 1963.

1671. keramane, h. schwarzbuch algerien. hamburg: 1961. on atrocities in algeria 1954-1960.

1672. kessel, p. * pirelli, g. le peuple algerien et la guerre. lettres et temoignages d'algeriens, 1954-1962. paris: maspero, 1962. 757 pp.

1673. khelifa, l. manuel du militant algerien. vol. i. lausanne: la cite editeur, 1962.

1674. lebjaoui, m. bataille d'alger ou bataille d'algerie?. paris: gallimard, 1972. 303 pp.

1675. lebjaoui, m. verites sur la revolution algerienne. paris: gallimard, 1970.

1676. loesch, a. la valise et le cercueil. paris: plon, 1963. 267 pp. on o. a. s.

1677. massu, j. la vraie bataille d'alger. paris: 1971.

1678. morlaud, b, * morlaud, m. histoire de l'organisation de l'armee secrete. paris: juillard, 1964. 605 pp.

1679. n. n. oas parle. paris: juillard, 1964. 353 pp.

1680. nassu, j. la vraie bataille d'algier. paris: plon, 1971.

1681. nicol, a. la bataille de l'o. a. s. paris: ed. des septcouleurs., 1963. 224 pp.

1682. o'ballance, e. the algerian insurrection, 1954-1962. hamden: shoestring, 1967.

1683. ouzagane, a. le meilleure combat. paris: juillard, 1962. 307 pp. f. l. n. ; the revolutionary movement in algeria.

1684. plumyene, j. o. a. s. et guerre d'algerie. in: j. plumyene. les fascismes francais. paris: 1963. pp. 261-298.

1685. quandt, w. b. revolution and political leadership: algeria, 1954-1968. cambridge, mass. m. i. t. press , 1969. 313 pp.

1686. roy, j. la guerre d'algerie. paris: juillard, 1960. 215 pp. engl. ed. the war in algeria. new york, grove press, 1961.

1687. solinas, p. gillo pontecorvos' the battle of algiers. new york: 1973. script of movie with same name.

1688. soustelle, j. aimee et souffrante algerie. paris: plon, 1956. by the french governor-general of algeria.

1689. tillion, g. les ennemis complementaires. paris: minuit, 1960. on terrorism and counterterrorism in algeria 1954 ff.

1690. tournoux, j. r. l'histoire secrete. paris: plon, 1962. algeria, oas.

1691. wales, g. e. algerian terrorism. october 1961. pp 26-42 naval war college review.

1692. yacef, s. souvenirs de la bataille d'alger. paris: 1962.

H.5.2. Sub-Saharan Africa

1693. barnett, d. karari njama: mau mau from within. macgibbon and kee, 1966.

1694. brom, k. l. blutnacht ueber afrika. frankfurt a. m. ammelburg, 1957. 198 pp.

1695. buijtenhuijs, r. le mouvement mau-mau, une revolte paysanne et anticoloniale en afrique noire. paris- den haag: mouton, 1971.

1696. buijtenhuijs, r. mau-mau twenty years after. the myth and the survivors. paris-den haag: mouton, 1973 .

1697. cabral, a. die revolution der verdammten. der befreiungskampf in guinea-bissao. berlin: rotbuch verlag, 1974. 142 pp.

1698. centre de recherche et d'information socio-politiques. repression, violence et terreur. rebellions au congo. bruxelles: institut d'etudes africaines, 1969.

1699. corfield, f. d. historical survey of the origin and growth of mau mau. new york: british information service-london, h. m. s. o., 1960.

1700. efrat, e. s. * (ed.). introduction to sub-saharan africa. lexington-toronto: xerox college publishing, 1973.

1701. hempstone, i. rebels, mercenaries, and dividends: the katanga story. new york: praeger, 1962.

1702. henderson, i. * goos, ph. man hunt in kenya. new york: doubleday, 1958. on hunt for the mau mau leader kinathi in kenya.

1703. holman, d. menschenjagd. der mau-mau-aufstand in kenia. muenchen: bechtle, 1966. 246 pp.

1704. horne, n. s. on patrol against mau mau terrorists. 1955. forces magazine 3.

1705. itote, w. mau mau general. nairobi: east african publ. house, 1967. 297 pp.

1706. johnson, j. t. the mau mau insurgency(1953-55). a guerrilla and counter-guerrilla study. 1967. pp. 193-222 columbia essays in international affairs 2.

1707. kariuku, j. 'mau mau' detainee. london: oxford university press, 1963.

1708. kenya, general headquarters. a handbook of anti mau mau operations. nairobi: government printer, 1954 .

1709. kenyatta, j. suffering without bitterness. the founding of the kenya nation. nairobi: east african publ. house, 1968. 348 pp.

1710. krug, w. g. terror und gegenterror in british-ostafrika. 1953. pp. 589-594 aussenpolitik 4:9.

1711. leakey, l. s. m. mau mau and the kikuyu. london: methuen, 1954.

1712. leigh, i. in the shadows of mau mau. london: 1954.

1713. maier, f. x. revolution and terrorism in mozambique. new york: american african affairs association, 1974. 60 pp.

1714. majdalany, f. state of emergency: the full story of mau mau. boston: houghton mifflin, 1963.

1715. mojekwu, chr. c. from protest to terror-violence: the african experience. in: m. livingston * et. al. * (eds.) international terrorism in the contemporary world. westport, conn. greenwood press, 1978. pp. 177-181.

1716. muehlmann, w. e. die mau-mau-bewegung in kenya. 1961. pp. 56-87 politische vierteljahresschrift 2 :1.

1717. n. n. repression, violence et terreur: rebellions au congo. brussels: centre de recherche et d'information socio-politiques-, 1969.

1718. reed, d. 111 tage stanleyville. der aufstand der simbas. vienna: 1965. violence in the congo, 1964.

1719. rosberg, c. g. * nottingham, j. the myth of "mau mau": nationalism in kenya. new york: praeger, 1966. 427 pp.

1720. sherman, r. eritrea in revolution. p-. d. dissertation in preparation: brandeis university,

1721. sundiata, i. k. integrative and disintegrative terror: the case of equatorial guinea. in: m. livingston * et. al. * (eds.) international terrorism in the contemporary world. westport, conn. greenwood press, 1978. pp. 182-194.

1722. thompson, b. ethiopia, the country that cut off its head. a diary of the revolution. london: robson, 1975.

1723. wagoner, f. e. dragon rouge. the rescue of hostages in the congo. washington: national defence university, 1980.

1724. welfling, m. b. terrorism in sub-sahara africa. in: m. stohl * (ed.) the politics of terrorism. new tork: dekker, 1979. pp. 259-300.

H.5.3. Southern Africa

1725. brigham, d. t. blueprint for conflict. new york: american-african affairs association, 1969. 34 pp. on terrorism in south africa - rhodesia, south africa, mozambique, angola.

1726. davidson b. * slovo, j. * wilkinson, a. r. southern africa: the new politics of revolution. harmondsworth: penguin, 1976.

1727. dorabji, e. v. south african national congress: change from non-violence to sabotage between 1952 and 1964. ph. d. dissertation: university of california, 1979.

1728. feld, e. urban revolt in south africa 1960-1964: a case study. evanston, ill. northwestern university press, 1971.

1729. felgas, h. a. e. os movimentos terroristas de angola, guine, mocambique. influencia externa. lisboa: 1966. 93 pp.

1730. gibson, r. african liberation movements: contemporary struggles against whiteminority rule. new york: oxford, 1972. 350 pp.

1731. horrell, m. terrorism in south africa. johannesburg: south african institute of race relations, 1968. .

1732. humbaraci, a. * mucknik, n. portugal's african wars: angola, guinea bissao, mozambique. london: macmillan, 1974.

1733. jacobs, w. d. terrorism in southern africa. portents and prospects. new york: american african affairs association, 1973.

1734. legum, c. * modges, t. after angola: the war over southern africa. london: rex collings, 1976.

1735. lejeune, a. * (comp.). the case for south west africa. london: tom stacey, 1971.

1736. mathews, a. s. terrors of terrorism. aug. 1974. p 381 south african law journal 91.

1737. metrowich, f. r. communism and terrorism in southern africa. pretoria: 1969. occasional papers of the african institute of south africa 25.

1738. metrowich, f. r. terrorism in southern africa. pretoria: african institute of south africa, 1973.

1739. mondlane, e. the struggle for mozambique. baltimore: penguin, 1969.

1740. morris, m. armed conflict in southern africa: a survey of regional terrorism from their beginnings to the present, with a comprehensive examination of the portuguese position. cape town: jeremy spence, 1974. 371 pp. .

1741. morris, m. terrorism; the first full account in detail of terrorism and insurgency in southern africa. . cape town: h. timmins, 1971. 249 pp.

1742. neves, a. razes do terrorismo em angola e mocambique, 1969. lisboa: 1970.

1743. rhodesia. ministry of information. a harvest of fear. diary of terrorist atrocities in rhodesia. salisbury: rgpo, 1976.

1744. south africa, dept. of foreign affairs. south west africa. measures taken to combat terrorism. cape town: 1968.

1745. teixeira, b. the fabric of terror: three days in angola. new york: devin-adair, 1965.

1746. terrorism research centre. armed conflict in southern africa. a survey of regional terrorisms from their beginnings to the present, a comprehensive examination ofthe portuguese position. cape town: trc, 1975.

1747. terrorism research centre. south african political violence & sabotage, 1 july 1979-30 june 1981. incident list, table and commentary. cape town: trc, 1981.

1748. venter, a. j. africa at war. old greenwich, conn. devin-adair, 1974.

1749. venter, a. j. the terror fighters. capetown- johannesburg: purnell, 1969.

H. TERRORISTIC ACTIVITIES BY REGION AND COUNTRY

H.6. Latin America, general

1750. adler, h. g. revolutionaeres lateinamerika. eine dokumentation. paderborn: schoeningh, 1970. 216 pp.

1751. anderson, t. p. political violence and cultural patterns in central america. in: m. livingston * et. al . * (eds.) international terrorism in the contem porary world. westport, conn. greenwood press, 1978. pp. 153-159 .

1752. bambirra, v. * (ed.). diez anos de insurreccion. 2 vols. santiago: prensa latino-americana, 1971. documents of struggle and analysis on guerrilla warfare in various latin american nations by participants.

1753. baudouin l. r. la guerra de guerrillas en america latina entre 1960 y 1969: el refuerzo de una ideologia y el debilitamento de un movimiento. febr. 1972. pp. 105-126 boletin uruguayano de sociologia 19-20.

1754. blackburn, r. * (ed.). strategy for revolution: essays on latin america by regis debray. new york: monthly review, 1970.

1755. butler, r. e. terrorism in latin america. in: y. alexander * (ed.) international terrorism: national, regional and global perspectives. new york: ams, 1976. pp. 46-61.

1756. charles, r. * hildner, r. e. urban insurgency in latin america. its implications for the future. pp. 54-64 air university review 22.

1757. chilcote, r. h. the radical left and revolutions in latin america. stanford: hoover institution press, 1970.

1758. craig, a. urban guerrilla in latin america. 1971. pp. 112-128 survey 17:3.

1759. deas, m. guerrillas in latin america. 1968. pp. 72- 78 worldtoday 24:2.

1760. debray, r. evolution in the revolution? armed struggle and political struggle in latin america. new york: grove press, 1967. 126 pp. an influential book on guerrilla warfare and revolution.

1761. dubois, j. freedom is my beat. new york: bobbs- merrill, 1959. a. o. on 1958 kidnapping*(ed. by raul castro).

1762. duff, e. a. * mccamant, j. f. * morales, w. q. violence and repression in latin america: a quantitative and historical analysis. new york: free press, 1976.

1763. einaudi, l. * (ed.). prospects for violence. in: latin americain the 1970s. santa monica: rand, 1972.

1764. francis, s. t. latin american terrorism: the cuban connection. heritage foundation: washington d. c., 9 nov 1979. 23 pp. backgrounder series.

1765. gerassi, f. * (ed.). venceremos!. new york: simon & schuster, 1968.

1766. gerhardt, h. p. guerillas: schicksalsfrage fuer den westen. die latein-amerikanische revolutionsbewegung. stuttgart- degerloch: seewald, 1971. 168 pp.

1767. goldenberg, b. the cuban revolution and latin america. new york: praeger, 1965.

1768. gonzales, c. p. la violence latino-americaine dans les enquetes empiriques nord-americaines. janvier 1970. pp. 159-181 l'homme et la societe 15.

1769. goodsell, j. n. terrorism in latin america. march 1966. commentator 9.

1770. gott, r. guerrilla movements in latin america. garden city, n. y. doubleday, 1971. 629pp.

1771. halperin, e. terrorism in latin america. beverly hills: sage, 1975. the washington papers 33.

1772. hennessy, a. the new radicalism in latin america. january 1972. pp. 1-26 journal of contemporary history 7.

1773. herreros, a. y. el anarquismo como doctrina y movimiento. 1978. pp. 99-114 rivista de estudios politicos 1.

1774. hoagland, j. h. changing patterns of insurgency and american response. 1971. pp. 120-141 journal of international affairs 25.

1775. hodges, d. c. the latin american revolution: politics and strategy from apro-marxism to guevarism. new york: morrow, 1974.

1776. horowitz, i. l. * castro, j. de * gerassi, j. * (eds.). latin american radicalism 1969. london: jonathan cape, 1969. 656 pp.

1777. huberman, l. * sweezy, p. m. * (eds.). regis debray and the latin american revolution; a collection of essays. new york: monthlyreviewpress, 1968. 138 pp. washington papers 33.

1778. huizer, g. peasant rebellion in latin america: the origins. forms of expression and potential of latin american peasant unrest. harmondsworth: penguin books, 1973.

1779. jaquett, j. s. women in revolutionary movements in latin america. may 1973. pp. 344-354 journal of marriage and the family 35.

1780. kohl, j. * litt, j. urban guerrilla warfare in latin america. cambridge, mass. m. i. t. press, 1974. 425 pp. a collection of texts with introductory comments.

1781. lamberg, r. f. die castristische guerilla in lateinamerika. theorie und praxis eines revolutionaires modells. hannover: verlag fuer literatur und zeitgeschehen, 1971. 173 pp. vierteljahres-berichte des forschungsinstituts der friedrich-ebert-stiftung 7.

1782. lamberg, r. f. die guerilla in lateinamerika. stuttgart: deutscher taschenbuch verlag, 1972. 250 pp.

1783. lamberg, v. b. de. la guerrilla castrista en america latina; bibliografia selecta, 1960-1970. 1970. pp. 95-111 foro internacional 21:1.

1784. landazabal, r. f. politica y tactica de la guerra revolucionaria. bogota: 1966.

1785. larteguy, j. les guerilleros. paris: r. solar, 1967. 443 pp.

1786. larteguy, j. the guerrillas; new patterns in revolution in latin america. new york: signet, 1972.

1787. lora, g. revolucion y foquismo; balance de la discusion sobre la desviacion "guerrillerista". buenos aires: el yunque editorial, 1975.

1788. martinez codo, e. the urban guerrilla. 1971. pp. 3-10 military review 51:8.

1789. max, a. guerrillas in latin america. the hague: international documentation and information centre, 1971.

1790. mcdonald, l. terrorism and subversion in latin america. in extension of remarks of larry mcdonald. , 13 july 1977. pp. e 4425-e4437 congressional record(daily ed.) 123.

1791. mercier vega, l. * (ed.). guerrillas in latin america. new york: praeger, 1969.

1792. mercier vega, l. bilancio della guerriglia in america latina. 1970. pp. 481-494 annali della fondazione luigi einaudi 4.

1793. moreno, f. j. * mitrani, b. * (eds.). conflict and violence in latin american politics. new york: thomas y. cromwell & co., 1971.

1794. moss, r. urban guerrillas in latin america. london: institute for the study of conflict, oct. 1970. pp. 4-15 conflict studies 8.

1795. n. n. les guerrillas d'amerique latine. revolutionnaires des maquis et des villes. lausanne: editions rencontre, 1971.

1796. n. n. movimientos revolucionarios de america latina. documentacion propia, 1. haverlee-louvain: informacion documental de america latina, 1972.

1797. ribeiro, d. il dilemma dell' america latina. strutture di potere e forze insorgenti. milano: il saggiatore, 1976. trad. it.

1798. sloan, j. w. political terrorism in latin america: a critical analysis. in: m. stohl * (ed.) the politics of terrorism. new york: dekker, 1979. pp. 301-322.

1799. tarabocchia, a. cuba. the technology of subversion. gaithersburg, md. iacp, 1976.

1800. uschner, m. lateinamerika: schauplatz revolutionaerer kaempfe. berlin: staatsverlag der ddr, 1975. 345 pp.

1801. warth, h. sterb fuer die indios-literaturbericht zur lateinamerikanischen revolutions bewegung. may 1973. pp. 297-309 politische studien 209.

H.6.1. Argentina

1802. barcia, p. a. las guerrillas en argentina. june 1975. pp. 30-60 interrogations 3.

1803. belloni, a. del anarquismo. historia del movimiento obrero argentino. buenos aires. a. pena lillo, 1960. 72 pp coleccion "la siringa".

1804. cooke, j. w. la lucha por la liberacion nacional. buenos aires: 1973.

1805. craig, a. urban guerrilla in argentina. 1975. pp 19-27 canadian defence quarterly 4.

1806. david, p. r. profile of violence in argentina: 1955 to 1976. in: report of the task force on disorders and terrorism. washington, d. c. national advisory committee on criminal justicestandards and goals, december 1976. pp. 474-478.

1807. geze, f. * labrousse, a. argentine, revolution et contrarevolution. paris: 1975.

1808. heyman, e. s. background to human rights violations in argentina. washington, d. c. library of congress, congressional research service, foreign affairs and national defense division, 29 july 1977.

1809. janke, p. terrorism in argentina. journal of the royal united services institute.

1810. johnson, k. f. guerrilla politics in argentina. london: institute for the study of conflict, 1975. 21 pp. conflict studies 63.

1811. montoneros. per la rivoluzione in argentina. trad it. roma: samona & savelli, 1975.

1812. muenster, a. argentinien: guerilla und konterrevolution; arbeiterkaempfe gegen oligarchische diktatur und gewerkschafts-buerokratie. muenchen: trikont, 1977. 246 pp.

1813. n. n. argentine: organizations revolutionaires armees. 1971. pp. 18-43 tricontinental 6:59.

1814. piacentini, p. terror in argentina. march 1977. pp. 3-7 index on censorship 6.

1815. rock, d. revolt and repression in argentina. june 1977. pp. 215-222 world today 33.

1816. sofer, e. f. terror in argentina: jews face new dangers. 1977. pp. 19-25 present tense 5.

1817. waldmann, p. terror-organisationen in argentinien. marz, 1977. pp. 10-22 berichte zur entwicklung spanien, portugal und lateinamerika 2:10.

H.6.2. Brazil

1818. ferreira, j. c. carlos marighella. havana: tricontinental, 1970.

1819. gramont, s. de. how a pleasant, scholarly young man from brazil became a kidnapping, gun-toting, bombing revolutionary. 15 nov, 1970. new york times magazine.

1820. marighella, c. teoria y accion revolucionarias. 2nd. ed. mexico: diogenes, 1972. 135 pp.

1821. moreira alves, m. a grain of mustard seed. the awakening of the brazilian revolution. garden city, n. y. doubleday anchor press, 1973. 194 pp.

1822. n. n. focus und freiraum: debray, brasilien, linke in den metropolen. berlin: wagenbach, 1970. 138 pp. .

1823. n. n. l'activite terroriste au brasil. paris: 26 octobre 1969. pp. 3-24 america latina.

1824. n. n. la lutte armee au bresil. 1969. pp. 590-635 les temps modernes 25:280.

1825. n. n. strategy of terror - the brazilian model. bari: de donato editore, 1974. 252 pp. in italian.

1826. quartim, j. dictatorship and armed struggle in brazil. london: new left review, 1971.

1827. quartim, j. la guerrilla urbaine au brasil. les temps modernes 27:292.

1828. quartim, j. regis debray and the brazilian revolution. jan. 1970. pp. 61-82 new left review.

1829. truskier, a. the politics of violence: the urban guerrillas in brazil. 1970. pp. 30-34, 39 ramparts 9.

1830. wedge, b. the case study of student political violence: brazil, 1964 and dominican republic, 1965. , 1969. pp. 183-206 world politics 21:2.

H.6.3. Uruguay

1831. alsina, g. the war and the tupamaros. aug. 1972. pp. 29-42 bulletin tricontinental.

1832. aznares, c. a. * canar, j. e. los tupamaros: fracaso del che?. buenos aires: orbe, 1969.

1833. biedma, f. * minello, f. experiencias de la crisis y de la guerra urbana en el uruguay. april 1972 . pp. 180-226 cuadernos de la realidad nacional 12.

1834. cardillo, l. m. the tupamaros: a case of power duality in uruguayan politics. unpublished manuscript: fletcher schoolof law and diplomacy, 1975.

1835. clutterbuck, r. l. two typical guerrilla movements: the ira and the tupamaros. 1972. pp. 17-29 canadian defense quarterly 24.

1836. connolly, s. * druehl, g. the tupamaros: the new focus in latin america. 1971. pp. 59-68 journal of contemporary revolutions 3.

1837. connolly, s. * druehl, g. the tupamaros: the new focus in latin america. pp. 95-68 journal of contemporary revolutions 3:3.

1838. costa-gavras, c. * solinas, f. state of siege. screenplay transl. by brooke leveque; documents transl. by raymond rosenthal. new york: ballantine, 1973. movie based on tupamaros and dan mitrioneincident.

1839. d'oliveira, s. l. uruguay and the tupamaro myth. april 1973. pp. 25-36 military review 53:4.

1840. debray, r. apprendre d'eux. milano: feltrinelli, 1972. italian transl.

1841. debray, r. les epreuves du feu. la critique des armes. paris: 1974. on tupamaros*et. al.

1842. debray, r. was wir von den tupamaros lernen koennen. 1972. pp. 144-175 sozialistisches jahrbuch 4.

1843. duenas ruiz, o. * rugnon de duenas, m. tupamaros. libertad o muerte. bogota: ediciones mundo andino, 1971.

1844. faraone, r. el uruguay en que vivimos. montevideo: 1969.

1845. gerassi, m. n. guerilla urbaine en uruguay. 1970. pp. 665-677 les temps modernes 27:291.

1846. gerassi, m. n. uruguay's urban guerrillas. 1969. pp. 306-310 nation 209:10.

1847. gilio, m. e. the tupamaros guerrillas. new york: ballantine, 1970. 242 pp.

1848. ginneken, j. van. de tupamaros. bevrijdingsbeweging in uraquay. odijk: sjaloom, 1977.

1849. gutierrez, c. m. tupamaros. neue methoden. stadtsguerilla. in: cuba. kursbuch 18. beilage. 1969.
.

1850. jackson, g. "halte uns nicht fuer dumm, amigo!" bericht aus der gefangenschaft bei den tupamaros in uruguay. 1973. der spiegel 27:nrs. 48-50.

1851. labrousse, a. les tupamaros. la guerilla urbaine en uruguay. paris: 1971. 206 pp.

1852. labrousse, a. the tupamaros: urban guerrillas in uruguay. harmondsworth: penguin, 1973. 168 pp.

1853. lapeyre, e. g. aspectos juridicos del terrorismo. montevideo: amalio m. fernandez, 1972. 125 pp.

1854. madruga, l. interview with a tupamaros using the pseudonym "urbane". havana: 8 oct. 1970. granma.

1855. martinez anzorena, g. los tupamaros. mendoza: editorial la tecla,

1856. max, a. tupamaros: a pattern for urban guerrilla warfare in latin america. the hague: international documentation and information centre, 1970.

1857. mayans, e. * (ed.). tupamaros: antologia documental. cuernavaca: centro intercultural dedocumentacion, 1971. the best reference work on the tupamaros with a 250 titles bibliography.

1858. mercader, a. * vega, j. de. tupamaros: estrategia y accion. montevideo: editorial alfa, 1971.

1859. miller, j. a. the tupamaro insurgents of uruguay. in: bard e. o'neill, d. j. alberts and stephen j. rossetti * (eds.). political violence and insurgency: a comparative approach. arvada, colo. phoenix, 1974. pp. 199-283.

1860. moss, r. uruguay: terrorism versus democracy. london: institute for the study of conflict, 1971. conflict studies 14.

1861. movimiento de liberacion nacional. actas tupamaros. buenos aires: schapire, 1971. 248 pp. a participant's account on past actions.

1862. n. n. ——. havana: dec. 1970. revolucion y cultura 26 special issue devoted to the tupamaros.

1863. n. n. generals and tupamaros. the struggle for power in uruguay, 1969-1973. london: latin america review of books, 1974. 77 pp.

1864. n. n. la guerrilla urbaine en uruguay. les tupamaros. 1970. pp. 20-24 est & ouest 22:439.

1865. n. n. la subversion: las fuerzas armadas al pueblo oriental. montevideo: junta de commandantes en jefe, republica oriental del uruguay, 1977. 777 pp.

1866. n. n. the tupamaros. urban guerrilla warfare in uruguay. new york: liberated guardian, 1970. a paperback pamphlet containing articles reprinted from tricontinental.

1867. n. n. tupamaros in azione. testimonianze dirette dei guerriglieri. trad. it. milano: feltrinelli, 1971.

1868. n. n. wir die tupamaros. von den tupamaros selbst verfasste berichte und analysen ueber ihre aktionen mit aktuellen dokumenten. frankfurt a. m. roter stern, 1974. 155 pp.

1869. nunez, c. los tupamaros: vanguardia armada en el uruguay. montevideo: ediciones provincias unidas, 1969. engl. the tupamaros:urban guerrillas of uruguay. new york, times change press, 1970.

1870. porzecanski, a. c. uruguay's tupamaros: the urban guerrilla. new york: praeger, 1973.

1871. rizowy, ch. the effects of support withdrawal on uruguay's political system: the tuparos urban guerrilla warfare: 1969-1973. ph. d. dissertation in preparation chicago: university of chicago,

1872. suarez, c. * sarmiento, r. a. los tupamaros. mexico, d. f. editorial extemporaneas, 1971. 247 pp.

1873. vorwerck, e. tupamaros. entstehung und entwicklung der stadtsguerillas. 1971. pp. 403-409 wehrkunde 20:8.

1874. wilson, c. the tupamaros: the unmentionables. boston: branden, 1973.

H.6.4. Other Latin American countries

1875. aguilera peralta, g. el proceso del terror en guatemala. april 1972. pp. 116-138 aportes 24.

1876. anderson, t. p. the ambiguities of political terrorism in central america. 1980. pp. 267-276 terrorism 4:1-4.

1877. bastos, r. r. el paraguay, entre el terror y la revolucion. 1970. cuadernos americanos 3.

1878. bejar, h. peru 1965:notes on a guerrilla experience. transl. by rose, w. new york: modern reader., 1971. span. las guerrillas de 1965: balance yperspectiva. lima, ediciones peisa, 1973.

1879. blanco munoz, a. modelos de violencia en venezuela. caracas: ediciones desorden, 1974.

1880. bravo, d. la guerriglia nel venezuela. milano: feltrinelli, 1967.

1881. callahan, e. f. terror in venezuela, 1960-64. febr. 1969. pp. 49-56 military review 49:2.

1882. campbell, l. g. the historiography of the peruvian guerrilla movement 1960-65. 1973. pp. 45-70 latin american research review 8:1.

1883. chanatry, f. i. a study of insurgency in venezuela. maxwell air force base, ala. air war college, 1967. 94 pp. post-1959 insurgency.

1884. correa, l. faln, brigada uno. s. c. editorial fuentes, 1973. trad. it. * venezia, marsilio, 1976.

1885. dios marin, j. de. inside a castro 'terror school'. dec. 1964. pp. 119-123 reader's digest.

1886. garcia, a. m. paraguay: il paternalismo terrorista in: levi, g. *(ed.)il fascismodipendente in america latina. bari: de donato, 1976.

1887. gude, e. w. political violence in venezuela: 1958-1964. in: davies, j. c. *(ed.) when men revolt and why. . new york: the free press, 1971. pp. 259-273.

1888. guevara, e. (che). boliviaans dagboek. amsterdam: polak & van gennep, 1968. guevara, in his last phase, unable to winoverthe peasants, tried to neutralize them through terrorizing bolivian campesinos.

1889. guevara, e. (che). episodes of the revolutionary war. new york: international publishers, 1968. 144 pp.

1890. harding, t. f. * landau, s. terrorism, guerrilla warfare and the democratic left in venezuela. 1964. pp. 118-128 student left 4:4.

1891. johnson, k. f. guatemala: from terrorism to terror. may 1972. pp. 4-17 conflict studies 23.

1892. johnson, k. f. guatemala: from terrorism to terror. london: institute for the study of powerand conflict, 1973. conflict studies 23.

1893. lacey, t. violence and politics in jamaica 1960-70. manchester: manchester university press, 1976.

1894. lamberg, r. f. die guerrilla in guatemala. 1969. pp. 57-174 vierteljahres-berichte.

1895. maullin, r. soldiers, guerrillas and politics in columbia. lexington mass. lexington books, 1973. 168 pp.

1896. medina ruiz, f. el terror en mexico. mexico: editores asociades, 1974. 159 pp.

1897. morley, m. * petras, b. chile: terror for capital's sake. 1974. pp. 36-50 new politics 11.

1898. roberts, k. e. * munger, m. d. urban guerrillas in the americas. carisle barracks, penn. army war college strategic studies institute, 30 dec. 1976.

1899. rodriguez, e. la crise du mouvement revolutionnaire latino-americain et l'experience du venezuela. , 1970. pp. 74-99 les temps modernes

27:288.

1900. stevens, e. p. protest and response in mexico. cambridge, mass. m. i. t. press, 1974.

1901. valsalice, l. guerriglia e politica. l'esemplo del venezuela. florence: 1973. on first latin america urban guerrilla movement.

1902. williamson, r. c. toward a theory of political violence: the case of rural colombia. 1965. pp. 35-44 western political quarterly 18:1.

H. TERRORISTIC ACTIVITIES BY REGION AND COUNTRY

H.7. North America

H.7.1. Canada

1903. baril, m. l'image de la violence au quebec. recherche exploratoire qualitative. montreal: centre international de criminologie comparee, 1977.

1904. beaton, l. crisis in quebec. 1971. pp. 147-152 round table 241.

1905. bergeron, l. the history of quebec: a patriot's handbook. translated by baila marcus. toronto: new canada press, 1971.

1906. breton, r. the socio-political dynamics of the october events. in: d. c. thompson * (ed.), quebec society and politics: views from the inside. toronto: mclelland and stewart, 1973. pp. 213-238.

1907. cameron, d. self-determination and the quebec question. ontario: macmillan of canada, 1974.

1908. chodos, r. * auf der maur, n. quebec. a chronicle 1968-1972. toronto: canadian journalism foundation, 1972.

1909. daniels, d. quebec, canada and the october crisis. montreal: black rose, 1973.

1910. drache, d. * (ed.). quebec - only the beginning: the manifestos of the common front. toronto: new press, 1972.

1911. frank, j. a. * kelly, m. etude preliminaire sur la violence collective en ontario et auquebec, 1963-1973. 1977. pp. 145-57 revue canadienne de science politique 10:1.

1912. golden, a. * haggart, r. rumours of war. toronto: new press, 1971. on terrorism in quebec.

1913. green, l. c. terrorism: the canadian perspective. in: y. alexander * (ed.), international terrorism: national, regional, and global perspectives. new york: ams press, 1976. pp. 3-29.

1914. haggart, r. * golden, a. e. rumors of war. canada and the kidnap crisis. chicago: follett, 1971.

1915. holt, s. terror in the name of god: the story of the sons of freedom doukhobors. toronto: mclelland & stewart, 1964.

1916. laurendeau, m. les quebecois violents.

1917. manzer, r. canada: a social-political report. new york: mcgraw-hill, 1974. also deals with the 6 deaths resulting from flq terrorism.

1918. mckinsey, l. s. dimensions of national political integration and disintegration: the case of quebec separatism, 1960-1975. october 1976. pp. 335-360 comparative political studies 9.

1919. milner, s. m. * miller, h. the decolonization of quebec: an analysis of left wing nationalism. toronto : mcclelland and stewart, 1973.

1920. moore, b. the revolution script. new york: holt, rinehart & winston, 1971. 261 pp. semi-fictionalized account of the james cross' kidnapping by the flq.

1921. n. n. dissent and disorder in canada. in: report on the task force on disorders and terrorism. washington d. c. national advisory committee on criminal justice standards and goals, december 1976. pp. 479-496.

1922. n. n. quebec separatists: the first twelve years. in: n. sheffe * (ed.), issues for the seventies. toronto: mcgraw-hill, 1971.

1923. n. n. terrorism and justice - between freedom and order - the political crime. montreal: editions du jour, 1970. 175 pp. in french. - on the historical evolution of political crime in canada and its repression.

1924. pellentier, g. the october crisis. toronto: mcclelland& stewart, 1971.

1925. radwanski, g. * windeyer, k. no mandate but terror. richmond hill, ontario: simon and schuster, 1970. .

1926. regush, n. m. pierre vallieres: the revolutionary process in quebec. new york: dial, 1973.

1927. reid, m. the shouting signpainters. a literary and political account of quebec revolutionary nationalism. new york-london: 1972.

1928. saywell, j. t. quebec 70: a documentary narrative. toronto: university of toronto press, 1971.

1929. smith, d. bleedings hearts. bleeding country: canada and the quebec crisis. edmonton: hurtig, 1971 .

1930. stewart, j. the flq:seven years of terrorism. special report by the montreal star. richmond hill, ont. simon & schuster, 1970.

1931. trait, j. c. flq 70: offensive d'automne. ottawa: les editions de l'homme, 1970. 230 pp. on cross and laporte kidnappings.

1932. vallieres, p. negres lancs d'amerique. montreal: editions parti pris, 1969. chief terrorist of flq, radical journalist. the book is an attempt to justify political terrorism(a la fanon). - an english edition, 'white nigger of america', was published in 1968 in new york.

1933. vallieres, p. the assassination of pierre laporte: behind the october '70 scenario. toronto: james lorimer, 1977.

1934. woodcock, g. * avakunovec, j. the doukhobors. toronto: oxford university press, 1968.

H.7.2. United States

1935. adamic, l. dynamite: the story of class violence in america. new york: viking, 1934.

1936. adelson, a. s. d. s. a profile. new york: scribner s, 1972. u. s. student violence, weather movement.

1937. amendt, g. * (ed.). black power. dokumente und analysen. frankfurt a. m. suhrkamp, 1970. 234 pp.

1938. avrich, p. the modern school movement. anarchism and education in the united states. princeton, n. j. , 1980. uncovers preparations for assassination attempts by a. berkman and others on john d. rockefeller in 1913-14.

1939. bacciocco, e. j. the new left in america. reform to revolution, 1956 to 1970. stanford, calif. hoover institution, 1974. 300 pp.

1940. baker, m. * brompton, s. exclusive! the inside story of patty hearst and the sla. new york: macmillan , 1974.

1941. belcher, j. * west, d. patty - tania. new york: pyramid books, 1975.

1942. broehl, w. g. the molly maguires. cambridge: harvard university press, 1964. u. s. labor struggles, 19th century.

1943. brown, r. m. the american vigilante tradition. in: h. d. graham and t. r. gurr * (eds.). violence in america. new york: signet books, 1969.

1944. burrows, w. e. vigilante. new york: harcourt brace jovanovich, 1976.

1945. cohen, m. * hale, d. the new student left. boston: beacon press, 1967.

1946. conant, r. the prospects for revolution: a study of riots, civil disobedienceand insurrection in contemporary america. new york: harper's magazine press, 1971.

1947. courtright, j. a. rhetoric of the gun: an analysis of the rhetorical modifications of the black panther party. 1974. pp. 249-268 journal of black studies 4:3.

1948. daigon, a. violence - u. s. a. new york: bantam, 1975.

1949. daley, r. target blue. new york: delacorte press, 1973. on black liberation army's attacks on the blue-uniformed new york city police.

1950. daniels, s. the weathermen. 1974. pp. 430-459 government and opposition. 9:1.

1951. david, h. the history of the haymarket affair. a study of the american social-revolutionary and labor movements. new york: 1936.

1952. davis, a. an autobiography. new york: random hous, 1974.

1953. dawson, h. b. the sons of liberty. new york: 1859. on the sons of liberty who struck at tory sympathizers during the 18thcentury american war of independence.

1954. deakin, t. j. legacy of carlos marighella. oct. 1974. pp. 19-25 fbi law enforcement bulletin 43: 10.

1955. fainstein, n. i. * fainstein, s. s. urban political movements: the search for power by minority groupsin american cities. englewood cliffs, nj: prentice hall, 1974.

1956. farren, m. * barker, e. * et. al. watch our kids. london: open gate books, 1972.

1957. fbi. ———. fbi domestic terroristdigest. originally called the summary of extremist activities; classified until 1972, recently released under the freedom of information act.

1958. fbi. legacy of carlos marighella. oct. 1974. pp. 19-25 fbi law enforcement bulletin 43:10 on u. s. disciples ·of marighella: weatherman, blackpanthers, and the sla.

1959. fbi. terrorism: its tactics and techniques. washington, d. c. gpo, 1973.

1960. foner, p. s. black panthers speak. philadelphia: j b. lippincott, 1970.

1961. forman, j. the making of black revolutionaries. new york: macmillan, 1972.

1962. foster, j. * long, d. protest: student activism in america. new york: william morrow, 1970.

1963. francis, s. t. * poole, w. t. terrorism in america: the developing internal security crisis. washington, d. c. heritagefoundation, 2 june 1978. 23 pp. backgrounder 59.

1964. gerassi, j. lutte armee aux etats-unis. 1970. pp 1779-1810 les temps modernes 26:286.

1965. gilman, i. philsophy of terrorism. oct. 1918. pp 294-305 unpopular review 6.

1966. gleason, j. m. a poisson model of incidents of international terrorism in the united states. 1980. pp. 259-265 terrorism 4.

1967. goode, s. affluent revolutionaries: a portrait of the new left. new york: new viewpoints, 1974.

1968. grathwohl, l. bringing down america. a fbi informer with the weathermen. larrygrathwohl as told to frank reagan. new rochelle, n. y. arlington house, 1976. 191 pp.

1969. greisman, h. c. terrorism in the u. s. a social impact projection. paper presented at the annual meeting of the american sociological association. new york: august 1976.

1970. gurr, t. r. * graham, h. d. violence in america: historical and comparative perspectives. areport. 2 vols. washington, d. c. 1969.

1971. hayden, t. rebellion and repression. new york-cleveland: 1969.

1972. heath, g. l. vandals in the bomb factory; the history and literature of the students for a democratic society. metuchen, n. j. scarecrow press, 1976.

1973. hinckle, w. * et. al. guerrilla-verzet in de vs. een documentaire. amsterdam: van gennep, 1971. 204 pp.

1974. hofstadter, r. * wallace, m. * (eds.). american violence: a documentary history. new york: knopf, 1970 .

1975. homer, f. d. terror in the united states: three perspectives. in: m. stohl * (ed.), the pol'tics of terrorism. new york: dekke 1979, pp. 373-405.

1976. hoover, j. e. the revolutionary-guerilla attacks law enforcement and democratic society. analysis of the destructive power of the fanatical few. albany law review 35:4.

1977. hopkins, ch. w. the deradicalization of the black panther party: 1967-1973. ph. d. dissertation: university of north carolina, 1978.

1978. horowitz, i. l. the struggle is the message. the organization and ideology of the anti-war movement. berkeley: the glendessary press, 1970.

1979. house, a. the carasso tragedy. eleven days of terror in the huntsville prison. waco, texas: texian press, 1975. on hostage episode.

1980. howell, a. ch. kidnapping in america. ph. d. temple university. ann arbor: xerox university microfilm, 1975.

1981. institute for the study of conflict. american extreme left - a decade of conflict. london: institutefor the study of conflict, dec. 1972. 19 pp.)conflict studies 29 on 1962-1972 period, analysing various leftist groups, both 'orthodox' and newleft.

1982. international association of chiefs of police. arab terrorism, american style. gaithersburg, md. iacp, 1974.

1983. jackson, g. blood in my eye. london: 1975.

1984. jacobs, h. * (ed.). weatherman. berkeley: ramparts press, 1970. 519 pp.

1985. johnpoll, b. k. perspectives on political terrorism in the united states. in: y. alexander * (ed.), international terrorism: national, regional and global perspectives. new york: ams, 1976. pp. 30-45.

1986. jones, j. h. the minutemen. garden city: doubleday, 1968.

1987. karasek, h. * (ed.). 1886 haymarket. die deutschen anarchisten von chicago. reden und lebenslaeufe. berlin: wagenbach, 1977. 190pp.

1988. karber, ph. a. * novotny, e. j. radical bombings in the united states: what happened to the revolution?. . jan. 1973. bomb incident bulletin.

1989. kedward, r. the anarchists: the man who shocked an era. new york: american heritage, 1971. reprint 1975; dutch ed. leiden, sijthoff, 1970, 125 pp.

1990. keniston, k. the young radicals. notes on committed youth. new york: harcourt, brace and world, 1968. .

1991. lasch, chr. the agony of the american left. harmondsworth: pelican, 1973.

1992. leamer, l. the paper revolutionaries. on theus underground and alternative press.

1993. lens, s. radicalism in america. new york: thomas y. cromwell, 1966.

1994. lerner, m. anarchism and the american counter-culture. 1970. pp. 430-455 government and opposition 5.

1995. lewis, g. k. notes on the puerto rican revolution: an essay on american dominance and caribbean resistance. new york: monthly review, 1975. 288 pp.

1996. los angeles board of police commissioners. the symbionese liberation army in los angeles. a report by the los angeles board of police commissioners to mayor tom bradley. los angeles: los angeles police department, 1974.

1997. luce, ph. a. the new left today. washington, d. c. capitol hill press, 1972.

1998. luce, ph. a. the new left. new york: david mckay, 1965.

1999. lum, d. d. a concise history of the great trial of the chicago anarchists. chicago: socialistic publishing co., 1887.

2000. **marine, g.** the black panthers. new york: new american library, 1969.

2001. **martin, j. j.** men against the state. the expositors of individualist anarchism in america 1827-1908. 2nd ed. colorado springs: col. ralph myles, 1970. 332 pp.

2002. **martinelli, a. * cavalli, a. * (eds.).** il black panther party. turin: 1971.

2003. **masotti, l. h. * corsi, j. r.** shoot-out in cleveland, black militants and the police. washington, d. c. gpo, 1969.

2004. **matekolo, i.** mysteries of international terrorism. paris: julliard, 1973. 221 pp.

2005. **maurer, m.** the ku klux klan and the national liberation front: terrorism applied to achieve diverse goals. in: m. livingston et al * (eds.), international terrorism in the contemporary world. westport, conn. greenwood press, 1978. pp. 131-152.

2006. **mccartney, j.** black power: past present, and future. st louis: forum press, 1973.

2007. **mcdonald, l. p.** explosion from the left: political terrorism in america. new ed. febr. 1978.

2008. **mcdonald, l. p.** trotskyisme and terror: the strategy of revolution. washington, d. c. acu education and research institute, 1977. 109 pp. on the u. s. socialist workers party and the fourth international involvement with terrorism.

2009. **mclellan, v. * avery, p.** the voices of guns: the definitive and dramatic story of the 22-month career of the symbionese lberation army. new york: putnam, 1976. 544 pp.

2010. **muhammad, a.** civil war in islamic america; behind the washington siege. 11 june 1977. pp. 721-724 nation 224 on march 1977 takeover of three buildings in washington, d. c. * by hanafis.

2011. **n. n.** ——. jan. 1971. scanlon's magazine 8 lists 1404 incidents of "guerrilla warfare and terrorism" covering the period 12 febr. 1965 to 7 sept. 1970.

2012. **n. n.** anti-soviet zionist terrorism in the u. s. 1971. pp. 6-8 current digest of the soviet press 23.

2013. **n. n.** cuban extremists in u. s. - a growing terror threat. dec. 1976. pp. 29-32 u. s. news and world report 81:23 on anti-castro cubans.

2014. **n. n.** manifeste des weathermen. 1970. pp. 1811-1836 les temps modernes 26:286.

2015. **n. n.** meir kahane: a candid conversation with the militant leader of thejewish defense league. oct. 1972. p. 69. playboy.

2016. **n. n.** outlaws of america. communiques from the weather underground. new york: 1971.

2017. **n. n.** search and destroy: a report by the commission of inquiry into theblack panthers. new york: metropolitan applied research center, 1973.

2018. **n. n.** terrorism in california. july 1974. pp. 1-8 criminal justice digest 2.

2019. **n. n.** the interrelationship of terrorism and the politics of hispanic groups in the united states 1978-1979. gaithersburg, md. i. a. c. p., 1979. update report 5:3.

2020. **n. n.** the symbionese liberation army in los angeles: a report by police commission to mayor tom bradley. . los angeles: los angeles police department, 1974.

2021. **n. n.** the weather underground. washington, d. c: gpo, 1975. the history and political theory plus a chronology of events involving the weathermen to june 1974 are discussed.

2022. **newton, h. p.** revolutionary suicide. london: wildwood house, 1974.

2023. **newton, h. p.** to die for the people: the writings of huey p. newton. new york: random house, 1972. 232 pp. black power.

2024. **novack, g.** marxism versus neo-anarchist terrorism. july, 1970. pp. 14-19 international socialist review 31:4.

2025. **overstreet, h. * overstreet, b.** the strange tactics of extremism. new york: norton, 1964. 315 pp.

2026. **parker, t. f. * (ed.).** violence in the united states. new york: facts on file, 1974. 248 pp.

2027. **payne, l. * findley, t.** the life and death of the sla. new york: ballantine books, 1976.

2028. **pearsall, r. b. * (ed.).** the symbionese liberation army. documents and communications. atlantic highlands, n. j. humanities press, 1974.

2029. **pinkney, a.** the american way of violence. new york: random house, 1972.

2030. **popov, m. i.** the american extreme left: a decade of conflict. december 1972. 19 pp. conflict studies 29.

2031. **powers, t.** diana: the making of a terrorist. boston: houghton-mifflin, 1971. 225 pp.

2032. **powers, t.** the war at home. new york: grossman, 1973. 348 pp.

2033. **randel, w. p.** the ku klux klan. a century of infamy. philadelphia: chilton books, 1965.

2034. reeves, k. j. the trial of patty hearst. san francisco: great fidelity press, 1976.

2035. reisz, j. b. a theory on terrorist activity in america and its effect on the united states army. master's thesis: u. s. armycommand and general staff college, 1979.

2036. ritz, r. the lady and the laywers. san francisco: anthelion press, 1976. on patty hearst.

2037. rose, g. f. the terrorists are coming. july 1978. pp. 22-54 politics today 5.

2038. rose, t. * (ed.). violence in america: a historical and contemporary reader. new york: vintage, 1970. 381 pp.

2039. rubenstein, r. e. rebels in eden: mass political violence in the united states. boston: little brown, 1970.

2040. russell, d. little havana's reign of terror. new york: 29 oct. 1976. pp. 36-37, 40-45 new times 7 on terrorism among the 450. 000 cuban exiles in the miami area.

2041. sale, k. s. d. s. new york: random house, 1973.

2042. sanders, e. the family: the story of charles manson's dune buggy attack battalion. new york: e. p. dutton, 1971. 383pp.

2043. schang, g. * rosenbaum, r. from the capitol's bombers. nov. 1976. more 6:11 on weather underground.

2044. seale, b. seize the time. the story of the black panther party, and h. p. newton. new york: random house, 1970. 429 pp.

2045. sederberg, p. c. the phenomenology of vigilantism in contemporary america: an interpretation. 1978 . pp. 287-305 terrorism.

2046. spichal, d. politics of violence: the new urban blacks and the watts riot. osnabrueck: biblio verlag, 1974. 268pp.

2047. stanford, m. black guerrilla warfare: strategy and tactics. san francisco: nov. 1970. the black scholar.

2048. stein, d. l. living the revolution: the yippies in chicago. new york: bobbs-merrill, 1969.

2049. stern, s. with the weathermen. new york: .

2050. thayer, g. the farther shores of politics: the american political fringe today. new york: simon and schuster, 1967. 616 pp.

2051. tierney jr., j. j. terror at home: the american revolution and irregular warfare. 1977. pp. 1-20 stanford journal of international studies 12.

2052. trautman, f. the voice of terrorism. a biography of johann most. westport, conn. greenwood press, 1980.

2053. u. s. congress, house. committee on internal security. "terrorism". hearings. 93rd congr. * 2nd sess. * 27 febr. -20 aug. 1974 washington, d. c. gpo, 1974.

2054. u. s. congress, senate. committee on the judiciary. hearings. "terroristic activity". part 2. inside the weathermen movement. 93rd congr. * 2nd sess. * 18 oct. 1974 washington, d. c. gpo, 1975.

2055. u. s. congress, senate. committee on the judiciary. hearings. "terroristic activity". part 3. testimony of dr. frederick c. schwarz. 93rd congr. * 2nd sess. * 5 july, 1974 washington, d. c. gpo, 1975.

2056. u. s. congress, senate. committee on the judiciary. hearings. "terroristic activity". part 8. terrorism in the miami area. 94th congr. * 2nd sess. * 6 may, 1976 washington, d. c. gpo, 1976.

2057. u. s. congress, senate. committee on the judiciary. hearings. state department bombing by weathermen underground. washington, d. c. gpo, 1975.

2058. u. s. congress, senate. committee on the judiciary. hearings. terroristic activity, part 1. 93rd congr. * 2nd sess. * 2 sept. 1974 washington, d. c. gpo, 1974. 96 pp.

2059. u. s. congress, senate. committee on the judiciary. report: the weather underground. 94th congr. * 1st sess. * jan. 1975 washington, d. c. gpo, 1975. 169 pp.

2060. u. s. national commission on the causes and prevention of violence. ——. new york: award books, 1969. .

2061. u. s. national governors' association. domestic terrorism. superintendent of documents. 1979,

2062. vestermark, s. d. extremist groups in the u. s. gaithersburg: international association of chief of police, 1975.

2063. walton, p. the case of the weathermen: social reaction and radical commitment. in: i. taylor and l. taylor * (eds.). politics and deviance. harmondsworth: penguin, 1973. pp. 157-181.

2064. wicker, t. a time to die. 1975. on1971 prison uprising at attica, new york where hostages were taken.

2065. williams, r. f. * rigg, r. f. grossstadtguerilla. berli: voltaire, 1969. 35 pp.

2066. wolf, j. b. * zoffer, g. r. the menace of terrorism in the united states. 3 january 1981. pp. 10-15 human events: the national conservative weekly 41:3.

2067. wolf, j. b. domestic terrorist movements. in: y. alexander and r. a. kilmarx * (eds.), political terrorism and business threat and response. new york: praeger, 1979. pp. 18-63.

2068. wolf, j. b. terrorist death squad activity in the united states. gaithersburg, md. i. a. c. p., 1980. update report 6:5.

I. INTER- AND TRANSNATIONAL TERRORISM

2069. alexander, y. * kilmarx, r. a. international network of terrorist movements. in: political terrorism and business: the threat and response. new york: praeger, 1979. pp. 64-105.

2070. alexander, y. network of international terrorism. in: y. alexander, d. * d. carlton and p. wilkinson * (eds.) terrorism: theory and practice. boulder: westview, 1978.

2071. alexander, y. some perspectives on international terrorism. telaviv: 1975. pp. 24-29 international problems 14: 3-4 overview of worldwide manifestations of terrorism and attempts to counter them.

2072. anable, d. terrorism: loose net links diverse groups: no central plot. in: j. d. elliott and l. k. gibson * (eds.), contemporary terrorism: selected readings. gaithersburg, m. d. international association of chiefs of police, 1978. pp. 247-259.

2073. bell, j. b. transnational terror and world order. 1975. pp. 404-417 south atlantic quarterly 74.

2074. bell, j. b. transnational terror. washington, d. c. american enterprise institute for public policy research, 1975. 91 pp.

2075. beres, l. r. guerillas, terrorists, and polarity: new structural models of world politics. dec. 1974. pp. 624-636 western political quarterly 27:4.

2076. bergier, j. la troisieme guerre mondiale est commencee. paris: albin michel, 1976. 183 pp. on rise of terrorism, with focus on western europe and north-south conflict.

2077. bergquist, m. surrogatkrigets uppsving: s. k. terroristgrupper som aktoerer i internationell politik. . oct. 1977. internasjonal politik 3 the increase of surrogate wars: so-called terrorist groups as actors in international politics.

2078. bouthoul, g. international terrorism in its historical depth and present dimension,1968-1975. washington, d. c. u. s. department of state, 1976. 36 pp.

2079. briant, e. het internationale terrorisme en zijn bestrijding. june 1976. pp. 413-428 kultuurleven 5.

2080. canadian council on international law. international terrorism. proceedings of the 3rd annual conference of the canadian council on international law, oct. 18-19, 1974. reviewed by a. beichman in: canadian journalof politicalscience 9:3, pp. 521-522. 1976.

2081. carlton, d. * schaerf, c. * (eds.). international terrorism and world security. london: croom helm, 1975. 332 pp. volume contains papers presented at the urbino(italy) 1974 conference of the international school on disarmamentand research on conflicts. articles on terrorism by b. jenkins, g. bouthoul,s. j. rosen, r. frank, g. sliwowski, j. bowyer bell and d. heradstveit.

2082. cia. international and transnational terrorism: diagnosis and prognosis. washington, d. c. c. i. a ., 1976. 58 pp. includes surveys of terrorist organizations and a breakdown of different types of terrorism.

2083. cia. international terrorism in 1976. washington, d. c. c. i. a., 1977. 19 pp. unlike the author's previous study, this one no longer distinguishes between international terrorism(government-backed) and transnational terrorism without direct government support).

2084. cia. international terrorism in 1978. washington, d. c. cianational foreign assessment center, march 1979. rp 79-10149.

2085. cleveland, r. h. * et. al. a global perspective on transnational terrorism; a case study of libya. maxwell air force base, ala. air war college, 1977. 66 pp. u. s. air war college research report 25.

2086. clutterbuck, r. l. terrorist international. london: january 1974. pp. 154-159 the army quarterly and defense journal.

2087. copeland, m. beyond cloak and dagger: inside the cia. new york: pinnacle books, 1975.

2088. crenshaw, m. transnational terrorism and world politics. 1975. pp. 109-129 jerusalem journal of international relations. 1.

2089. crozier, b. * (ed.). annual of power and conflict. london: institute for the study ofconflict, this yearbook provides annual overviews of terroristic trends and events.

2090. crozier, b. aid for terrorism. in: b. crozier * (ed.). annual of power and conflict. vol. 1973-1974. a survey of political violence and international influence. london: institute for the study of conflict, 1974. pp. 2-11.

2091. crozier, b. libya's foreign adventures. london: isc, 1973. conflict studies 41.

2092. crozier, b. the surrogate forces of the soviet union. london: isc, 1978. conflict studies 92.

2093. crozier, b. transnational terrorism. gaithersburg, md. international association of chiefs of police(i. a. c. p.), 98 pp.

2094. demaris, o. brothers in blood. the international terrorist network. new york: charles scribner's sons , 1977. 441 pp. the last section includes a discussion of the threat of nuclear terrorism.

2095. dobson, chr. * payne, r. the carlos complex: a pattern of violence. london: hodder & stoughton, 1977. 254 pp.

2096. dobson, chr. the carlos complex. a study in terror. fully rev. and ext, version of 1977 ed. seven oaks,: coronet, 1978. 304 pp.

2097. dugard, j. international terrorism and the just war. 1977. pp. 21-38 stanford journal of international studies 12 :1.

2098. dunn, a. m. international terrorism. targets, responses and the role of law. charlotteville, va. john bassellmoore society of international law, 1977. 195 pp.

2099. eisenberg, d. * landau, e. carlos: terror international. london: corgi, 1976. 285 pp.

2100. elliott, j. d. transitions of contemporary terrorism. may 1977. pp. 3-15 military review 57.

2101. fearey, r. a. international terrorism. march 1976. pp. 394-403 department of state bulletin 74: 1918.

2102. francis, s. t. the soviet strategy of terror. washington d. c. the heritage foundation, 1981. 78 pp. sees the soviet union supporting international terrorist movements.

2103. francis, s. t. the terrorist international and western europe. washington, d. c. heritage foundation, 21 dec. 1977. 18 pp. backgrounder series, 47.

2104. friedlander, r. a. reflections on terrorist havens. pp. 59-67 naval war college review 32.

2105. friedlander, r. a. the origins of international terrorism: a micro legal-historical perspective. 1976. pp. 49-61 israel yearbook of human rights 6.

2106. glaser, s. le terrorisme international et ses divers aspects. 1973. pp. 825-850 revue internationale de droit compare 25:4.

2107. goren, r. soviet attitude and policy to international terrorism, 1967-1977. ph. d. dissertation in preparation university of london:

2108. green, l. c. the nature and control of international terrorism. occasional paper 1 atlanta: university of atlanta, department of political science., 1974.

2109. hannay, w. a. international terrorism: the need for a fresh perspective. 1974. pp. 268-284 international lawyer 8:2.

2110. heradstveit, d. the role of international terrorism in the middle east conflict and its implication for conflict resolution. in: david carlton and carlo schaerf * (eds.). international terrorism and world security. london: croom helm, 1975.

2111. holton, g. reflections on modern terrorism. 1977. pp . 96-104 the jerusalem journal of international relations. 3:1.

2112. hunter, j. d. the terror alliance. london: seven house, 1981. 318 pp.

2113. hutchinson, m. c. transnational terrorism and world politics. 1975. pp. 109-129 jerusalem journal of international relations 1.

2114. institute for the study of conflict. china, israel and the arabs. london: i. s. c., 1971. 18 pp. conflict studies 12.

2115. institute for the study of conflict. libya's foreign adventures. london: institutefor the study of power and conflict, 1973. conflict studies 41.

2116. institute for the study of conflict. the surrogate forces of the soviet union. february 1978. conflict studies security report 92.

2117. international institute for strategic studies. civil violence and the international system. 2 vols london: i. i. s. s., 1971.

2118. irish, j. terrorismo internacional. barcelona: producciones editoriales, 1975. 226 pp.

2119. jarach, a. terrorismo internazionale. firenze: vallecchi, 1979.

2120. javits, j. k. international terrorism: apathy exacerbates the problem. 1978. pp. 111-117 terrorism 1:2.

2121. jenkins, b. m. * johnson, j. international terrorism: a chronology, 1968-1974. santa monica, calif. randcorporation, 1975. 65 pp.

2122. jenkins, b. m. international terrorism. santa monica: rand, 1975. 58 pp.

2123. jenkins, b. m. international terrorism: a balance sheet. july 1975. pp. 158-164 survival 17:4.

2124. kaufmann, j. l'internationale terroriste. paris: plon, 1977. 231 pp.

2125. kemp, a. a computer model of international violence. 1977. pp. 51-62 international interactions 3:1.

2126. kemp, a. a path analytical model of international violence. 1978. pp. 63-85 international interactions 4:1.

2127. ketelsen, d. moskaus haltung zum internationalen terrorismus. november 1978. pp. 965-977 osteuropa 28 moscow and international terrorism.

2128. kreis, k. m. der internationale terrorismus. ein unbewaeltigtes problem der statengemeinschaft. 1976. pp. 367-375 europa archiv folge 11.

2129. kreis, k. m. international terrorism - unsolved problem of international community. 1976. pp. 367-375 europa archiv 31:11.

2130. kupperman, r. h. * smith, h. a. waiting for terror. 1978. pp. 50-61 the washington review of strategic and international studies 1:2.

2131. laffin, j. murder incorporated. 30 aug 1975. spectator on libyian and other support for palestinian terrorists.

2132. lagoni, r. united nations and international terrorism. 1977. pp. 171-189 europa archiv 32:6.

2133. landau, e. * eisenberg, d. carlos: terror international. ottawa: stanke, 1976.

2134. leichter, o. die vereinigten nationen und der internationale terrorismus. febr. 1973. vereinigte nationen 21:1.

2135. leonard, l. * (ed.). global terrorism confronts the nations. 1982.

2136. lillich, r. b. * paxman, j. m. state responsibility for injuries to aliens occasioned by terrorist activities. 1977. pp. 217-313 american university law review.

2137. livingston, m. h. * (ed.). international terrorism in the contemporary world. westport, conn. greenwood press, 1978. 522 pp.

2138. matekolo, i. les dessous du terrorisme international. paris: julliard, 1973.

2139. medzini, r. china and the palestinians. 1971. pp. 34-40 the new middle east 32.

2140. merari, a. a data base on international terrorism in 1979. terrorist groups terrorist activities and countries: attitudes to terrorism. telaviv: center for strategic studies, 1980. 198 pp. in hebrew, limited distribution.

2141. mickolus, e. f. * heyman, e. s. iterate: monitoring transnational terrorism. in: y. alexander & j. m. gleason * (eds.) behavioral and quantitative perspectives on terrorism. new york: pergamon press, 1981. pp. 153-174.

2142. mickolus, e. f. * heyman, e. s. iterate: monitoring transnational terrorism. paper presented to the joint national meeting of the operations research society of america and the institute for management sciences. new york city: may 1978. the iterate data were developed by edward mickolus;theyare available through the inter-university consortium for political and social research, university of michigan.

2143. mickolus, e. f. chronology of transnational terrorist attacks upon american business people, 1968-1976. . 1978. pp. 217-235 terrorism 1:2.

2144. mickolus, e. f. international terrorism in 1979. paper presented to the annual convention of the academy of criminal justice sciences, oklahoma city, oklahoma, march 1980. 1980.

2145. mickolus, e. f. international terrorism. attributes of terrorist events (iterate). ann arbor: inter- university consortium for political and social research, 1976. 41 pp. codebook for data on 539 transnational terrorist events from january 1970 to july 1973.

2146. mickolus, e. f. project iterate: quantitative studies of transnational terrorism. paper presented to the annual convention of the northeast political science association, november 1976, at the jug end, south egremont, massachusetts: 1976. 49 pp. reprinted by the us department of state, inr/xr as far 26105-n.

2147. mickolus, e. f. transnational terrorism. a chronology of events 1968-1979. london: aldwych press, 1980 . 967 pp. the material in this volume forms the data that comprises the 'international terrorism: attributes of terrorist events'(iterate) computer system.

2148. mickolus, e. f. trends in transnational terrorism. in: m. livingston. * (ed.) terrorism in the contemporary world. westport: connecticut: greenwood press, 1978. pp. 44-73.

2149. momtaz, d. rapport de monsieur d. m. sur le terrorisme internationale. 1974. pp. 172-190 revue egyptienne de droit international 30.

2150. n. n. civil violence and the international system. 2 vols. london: the international institute for strategic studies., 1971. adelphi papers 82-83.

2151. n. n. international terrorism. 1977. whole issue stanford journal of international studies 12 contains a. o. j. tierney, jr. terror at home: the american revolution and irregular warfare; j. paust. responses to terrorism: a prologue to decisions concerning private measures of sanction; j. dugard. international terrorism and the just war.

2152. n. n. international terrorism. 1978. whole issue journalof international affairs(columbia university) 32:1 on international terrorism with articles by y. alexander, b. m. jenkins, r. n. lebow, r. k. mullen, b. e. o'neill, r. shultz, s. sloan and p. a. thorp jr.

2153. n. n. international terrorism. proceedings of an intensive panel at the 15th annual convention of the international studies association, march 23, 1974. milwaukee: institute of world affairs, 1974. 96 pp.

2154. n. n. latin america's terrorist international. 23 march 1977. pp. 1-4 economist foreign report.

2155. n. n. mysteries of international terrorism. paris: julliard, 1973. 221 pp. in french.

2156. n. n. report on international terrorism. strasbourg: council of europe, 1972.

2157. n. n. significant non-fadayeen international terrorist incidents, january 1970-march 1974. available from the london international institute for strategic studies.

2158. n. n. symposium: international terrorism in the middle east. 1974. akron law review 7.

2159. n. n. terror international. in: remarks of thomas f. eagleton. congressional record daily 124. 26 april 1978. pp. s6423-s 6427 transcript of the bbc documentary "terror international".

2160. n. n. the boss of the terrorist support networks. paris: 21 june 1976. pp. 7-13 le point on the alleged curiel apparatus.

2161. peterson, r. w. * willard, g. international terrorism threat analysis. master's thesis. montery, cal. naval post-graduateschool, 1977. 96 pp.

2162. pierre, a. j. the politics of international terrorism. 1976. pp. 1251-1269 orbis 19.

2163. prevost, j. -f. les aspects nouveaux du terrorisme international. 1973. pp. 579-600 annuaire francais de droit international 19.

2164. radovanovic, l. the problem of international terrorism. oct. 1972. p. 5 review of international affairs 23.

2165. reisman, w. m. private armies in a global war system: prologue to decision. 1973. p. 1 virginia journal of international law 14.

2166. revesz, l. christian peace conference: church funds for terrorists. london: institute for the study of conflict., 1978.

2167. romaniecki, l. the soviet union and international terrorism. july 1974. pp. 417-440 soviet studies 26:3.

2168. rosenau, j. n. internal war as an international event. in: james n. rosenau * (ed.). international aspects of civil strife. princeton, n. j. princeton university press, 1964.

2169. russell, ch. a. transnational terrorism. jan. 1976. pp. 26-35 air university review 27:2.

2170. shultz jr., r. h. international terrorism. operations and r&d measurements. gaithersburg, md. iacp, 22 pp.

2171. skolnick jr, j. m. an appraisal of studies of the linkage between domestic and international conflict. . 1974. comparative political studies 6:485.

2172. sloan, s. * wise, ch. international terrorism. nov. 1977. adl bulletin 34:9.

2173. sloan, s. the anatomy of non-territorial terrorism. in: ch. t. whittier and s. sloan * (eds.) the conduct of businessmen overseas, an oklahoma perspective. 1978. for the clandestine tactics and technology series of theiacp.

2174. smith, w. h. international terrorism. a political analysis. in: the year book of world affairs 1977. london institute world affairs. london:

stevens & sons, 1977. pp. 138-157.

2175. sottile, a. le terrorisme international. 1938. pp. 87-184 recueil des cours de l'academie de droit international de la haye. 3.

2176. stencel, s. international terrorism. 1977. pp. 911-932 washington editorial research reports 2: 21.

2177. sterling, c. the terror network. the secret war of international terrorism. new york: holt, rinehart & winston/ reader's digest, 1980. 357 pp.

2178. sterling, c. the terrorist network. november 1978. pp. 37-47 atlantic 242.

2179. styles, g. terrorism: the global war of the seventies. aug. 1976. pp. 594-596 international defense review 9.

2180. symposium on international terrorism. international terrorism. charlotteville, va. 1979. 194 pp. the society.

2181. thompson, j. rejsende i terror. en dokumentarbog om carlos, pflp, japans rode haer, baader-meinhof gruppen og andre. lynge: bogan, 1977. 136 pp.

2182. thompson, w. s. political violence and the correlation of forces. 1976. pp. 1270-1288 orbis 19:34 .

2183. tinnin, d. b. terror, inc. 1977. pp. 152-154, 158, 166, 170, 173, 175-178, 180-181 playboy 24.

2184. tobon, n. carlos: terrorist or guerrilla?. barcelona: ediciones grijalbo, 1978. 217 pp.

2185. u. s. congress, house. committee on foreign affairs. hearings. international terrorism. 93rd cong. * 2nd sess. * 11, 18, 19 and 24 june 1974. washington, d. c. gpo, 1974. 219 pp.

2186. u. s. congress, house. committee on internal security. terrorism. a staff study. 93rdcong. * 2nd sess. * 1 aug. 1974 washington, d. c. gpo, 1974. 246pp.

2187. u. s. congress, house. committee on public works and transportation. d. c. international terrorism. gpo, 1978. 392 pp.

2188. u. s. congress, house. committee on the judiciary. international terrorism. washington, d. c. gpo, 1978. 201 pp.

2189. u. s. congress, senate. committee on foreign relations. hearings. international terrorism. 95th congr. * 1st sess. * 14 sept. 1977 washington, d. c. gpo, 1977. 90 pp.

2190. u. s. congress, senate. committee on the judiciary. hearings. "terrorist activity". part 6. the cuban connection in puerto rico; castro's hand in puerto rican and u. s. terrorism. 94th cong. * 1st sess. * 30 july, 1975. washington, d. c. gpo, 1975.

2191. u. s. congress, senate. committee on the judiciary. hearings. "terroristic activity". part 9. interlocks between communism and terrorism. 94th cong. * 2nd sess. * 7 may 1976. washington, d. c. gpo, 1976. pp. 663-749 pp. 720-747 are a reprint of scanlan's vol. 1, no. 8, jan. 1971 list of guerrilla acts of sabotage and terrorism in the united states, 1965-1970.

2192. u. s. congress, senate. committee on the judiciary. hearings. "trotskyite terrorist international". 94th cong. * 1st sess. * 24 july 1975 washington, d. c. gpo, 1975.

2193. u. s. congress, senate. committee on the judiciary. hearings. terroristic activity. part 4. international terrorism. 94th cong. * 1st sess. * 14 may 1975. washington, d. c. gpo, 1975. pp. 177-260.

2194. u. s. department of state. chronology of attacks upon non-official american citizens, 1971-1975. washington d. c. 20 january 1976,

2195. u. s. department of state. chronology of significant terrorist incidents involving u. s. diplomatic official personnel, 1963-1975. washington, d. c. 20 january, 1976.

2196. u. s. department of state. international terrorism. 29 march 1976. pp. 394-403 department of state bulletin 74:1918.

2197. u. s. department of state. office to combat terrorism. the disposition of persons involved in international terrorism. washington, d. c. department of state, 1976. on release of political international terrorists by governments.

2198. united nations, general assembly. ad hoc committee on international terrorism. observations of states submitted in accordance with general assembly resolution 3034(xxvii). analytic study prepared by the secretary-general. united nations, 22 june 1973. 22 pp.

2199. united nations, general assembly. ad hoc committee on international terrorism. report. new york: united nations, 1977. 51 pp. united nations. general assembly. official records. 32nd. sess. suppl. no 37 united nations document a/32/37.

2200. walker, w. the bear at the back door. richmond, surrey: foreign affairs publ. co., 1978. 246 pp.

2201. wilkinson, p. terrorism - international dimensions. london: institute for the study of conflict, 1979 .

2202. williams, s. g. the transnational impact of insurgency terrorism: a quantitative approach. ph. d. dissertation: city university of new york, queens college, department of political science,

2203. wolf, j. b. global terrorist coalition: its incipient stage. october 1977. pp. 328-339 police journal(england) 50.

2204. wolf, j. b. the cuban connections and involvements. gaithersburg. md. i. a. c. p., 1979. update report 5:5.

2205. yonay, e. the plo underground in california. 26 february 1979. pp. 22-31 new west.

2206. zlataric, b. history of international terrorism and its legal control. in: m. cherif bassiouni * (ed.). international terrorism and political crimes. springfield, ill. 1975. pp. 474-484 discusses league of nations attemps to come to an antiterrorist convention.

J. THE TERRORIST PERSONALITY AND ORGANIZATION

2207. abel, th. the nazi movement: why hitler came into power. new york: 1966. see peter h. merkl's book for a secondary analysis.

2208. allerbeck, k. r. soziologie radikaler studentenbewegungen. eine vergleichende untersuchung in der brd und den vereinigten staaten. muenchen-wien: oldenbourg, 1973. 272 pp.

2209. american university, soro. 1966. human factors considerations of undergrounds in insurgencies. 291 pp.

2210. avner. (pseud.). memoirs of an assasin. new york: yoseloff, 1959. description by a former member of lehi of some of the organization's activities.

2211. avrich, p. bakunin and nechaev. london: 1974.

2212. bakounine, m. oeuvres completes. vol. v. michel bakounine et ses relations avecserge netchaieff. 1870-1872. a. lehning(introd. et annot.). paris: editions champ libre, 1977. 576 pp.

2213. barker, d. grivas. portrait of a terrorist. new york: harcourt, brace, 1960. 202 pp. cyprus.

2214. barrue, j. bakounine et nechaiev. paris: 1971.

2215. bartoldi. memoirs of the secret societies of the south of italy. london: 1821. on carbonari.

2216. begin, m. the revolt. revised ed. dell publishing co., 1977.

2217. bell, j. b. contemporary revolutionary organizations. in: robert o. keokane and joseph s. nye jr., * (eds.). transnational relations and world politics. cambridge, mass. harvard university press, 1973. pp. 153-168 notes the national character of the majority of revolutionary groups professinginternatio.

2218. bell, j. b. the myth of the guerrilla: revolutionary theory and malpractice. new york: alfred a. knopf, 1971.

2219. bell, j. b. the profile of a terrorist. new york: columbia institute of war and peace studies,

2220. berkman, a. prison memoirs of an anarchist. new york: schocken, 1970. orig. published in 1912.

2221. broido, v. apostles into terrorists. women in the revolutionary movement in the russia of alexander ii. . new york: viking press, 1977. 238 pp.

2222. **bryan, j.** this soldier still at war. new york: harcourt, brace, jovanovich, 1975. 341 pp. on joseph michael remiro, sla.

2223. **caso, a. * (ed.).** los subversivos. havana: 1973. onl. a. (urban) guerrilleros.

2224. **cooper, h. h. a.** what is a terrorist: a psychological perspective. 1977. legal medical quarterly 1: 1.

2225. **crozier, b.** the rebels. a study of post-war insurrections. london: chatto & windus, 1960. 256 pp.

2226. **danto, a. c.** logical portrait of the assassin. august 1974. pp. 426-438 social research 41.

2227. **delarne, j.** geschichte der gestapo. duesseldorf: 1964.

2228. **deutscher, i.** stalin. eine politische biographie. stuttgart: kohlhammer, 1962. 648 pp.

2229. **dicks, h. v.** licensed mass murder. a socio-psychological study of some ss killers. london: chatto/ heidemann, 1972. 283 pp.

2230. **donovan, w. j. * roucek, j. s.** secret movements. new york: cromwell, 1958.

2231. **downton, j. v.** rebel leadership; commitment and charisma in the revolutionary process. new york: free press, 1973. 306 pp. socio-psychological study of four movements; among them the nazi and bolsheviks.

2232. **drif, z.** la mort de mes freres. paris: maspero, 1960. memoirs of an algerian woman terrorist.

2233. **el-rayyes, r. * nahas, d. * (eds.).** guerrillas for palestine: a study of the palestinian commando organization. beirut: an- nahar press services, 1974.

2234. **falcionelli, a.** les societes secretes italiennes. paris: 1969.

2235. **falk, c.** psychologie der guerillas. 1970. allgemeine schweizeri militaerzeitschrift 7.

2236. **fallaci, o.** a leader of fedayeen: 'we want a war like the vietnam war'. interview with georg habash. : 12 june 1970. pp. 32-34 life.

2237. **figner, v.** memoirs of a revolutionist. new york: 1927. by a member of the russian "people's will".

2238. **foley, ch. * (ed.).** the memoirs of general grivas. london: longmans, 1964. 226 pp. on cyprus and eoka. .

2239. **gall, s. n.** teodoro petkoff. the crisis of the professional revolutionary. part 1: years of insurrection. hannover, n. h. american university, field staff, 1972. field staff reports 1.

2240. **geschwender, j. a.** explorations in the theory of social movements and revolutions. dec. 1968. p. 67 social forces.

2241. **giacomoni, p. d.** j'ai tue pour rien. un commando delta a alger. paris: fayard, 1974. 313 pp. on oas 1961-62 in algeria, personal observations.

2242. **godfrey, j. r.** revolutionary justice. a study of the organization, personnel, and procedure of the paris tribunal, 1793-1795. 1951.

2243. **goldman, e.** living my life. new york: 1931.

2244. **greene, t. h.** comparative revolutionary movements. englewood cliffs: prentice-hall, 1974. 172 pp.

2245. **gross, f.** the revolutionary party. essays in the sociology of politics. westport, conn. greenwood press, 1974. 280 pp.

2246. **hamon, a.** psychologie de l'anarchist-socialiste. paris: 1895.

2247. **hampden-turner, c.** radical man: the process of psycho-social development. cambridge: schenkman, 1970. .

2248. **hildermeier, m.** sozialstruktur und kampfmethode der sozial-revolutionaeren partei. in: jahrbuecher fuer geschichte osteuropas. dec. 1972. russia before 1914.

2249. **hills, d. c.** rebel people. new york: africana publ., 1978. 248 pp.

2250. **hobsbawn, e. j.** bandits. london: 1969. 128 pp.

2251. **hobsbawn, e. j.** revolutionaries. new york: pantheon books, 1973. 278 pp.

2252. **hodde, l. de la.** histoire de societes secretes. paris: 1850. reprinted new york, 1964, as history of secret societies. -the author, a french police spy, lists what sort of people joined revolutionary movements in the 1830s and 1840s.

2253. **hoess, r.** commandant of auschwitz. new york: 1960.

2254. **hoffner, e.** der fanatiker. eine pathologie des parteigaengers. reinbek: rowohlt, 1965. orig. the true believer. thoughts on the nature of mass movements.

2255. **hollstein, w.** der untergrund. zur soziologie jugendlicher protestbewegungen. neuwied: luchterhand, 1969. 180 pp.

2256. **hopper, r. d.** the revolutionary process: a frame of reference for the study of revolutionary movements. . march 1950. p. 28 social forces.

2257. **ijad, a.** un palestien sans patrie. paris: afrique biblio club, 1978. reminicenses of a co-founder of el fatah and chief of intelligence of the plo, compiled by eric rouleau, the near-east specialist of le monde.

2258. international association of chiefs of police. on organizing urban guerilla units. gaithersburg, md. iacp, 36 pp.

2259. iskenderow, a. a. die nationale befreiungsbewegung. probleme, gesetzmaessigkeiten, perspektiven. (east -)berlin: staatsverlag der deutschen demokratischen republik, 1972. 414 pp.

2260. keller, k. terrorists what are they like? how some terrorists describe their world and actions. santa monica: rand, 1979.

2261. kelly, c. m. terrorism. a phenomenon of sick men. clarmont, cal. clarmont men's college, 1974. res- publica 2 :3.

2262. khaled, l. my people shall live: the autobiography of a revolutionary. london: hodder and stoughton, 1973. memoirs of aplo terrorist.

2263. kiernan, t. jasser arafat. london: abacus books, 1976.

2264. killinger, m. von. ernstes und heiteres aus dem putschleben. munich: 1934.

2265. klein, h. j. rueckkehr in die menschlichkeit. appell eines ausgestiegenen terroristen. reinbek: rowohlt, 1979. 331 pp. return to humanity appeal of a drop-out terrorist.

2266. kreml, w. p. the vigilante personality. in: h. j. rosenbaum & p. c. sederberg * (eds.), vigilantepolitics. philadelphia: university of philadelphia press, 1976. pp. 45-63.

2267. lombroso, c. die anarchisten. eine kriminal-psychologische und soziologische studie. hamburg: richter , 1895. 139 pp.

2268. mac stiofain, s. (pseud. for j. e. d. stephenson). revolutionary in ireland. farnborough: gordon cremonesi, 1975. 372 pp. autobiography of the chief of staff of the ira provisionals.

2269. macbride, s. interview with -. jan 1976. pp. 8-11, 54-57 skeptic 11.

2270. manzini, g. indagino su un brigatista rosso. la storia di walter alasisia. torino: 1978. einaudi investigations on a member of the red brigades(italy).

2271. maser, w. studien zum typus revolutionaerer organisation. darmstadt: wittmann, 1976. 100 pp.

2272. mathiez, a. robespierre. l'histoire et la legende. 1977. pp. 3-31 ann. hist. de la revolution francaise 49:1 robespierre: history and legend.

2273. mazlish, b. the revolutionary ascetic. evolution of a political type. new york: basic books, 1976.

2274. mcguire, m. to take arms: my years with the ira provisionals. new york: viking, 1973. 159 pp. memoirs of an ex-ira-member wholeft the movement when

the indiscriminate bombing campaign began in 1972.

2275. mcknight, g. the mind of the terrorist. london: michael joseph, 1974. 182 pp. based on interviews with terrorists.

2276. melucci, a. * (ed.). movimenti di rivolta. milan: 1976. 'revolting movements'.

2277. merkl, p. h. political violence under the swastica. 581 early nazis. princeton, n. j. princeton university press, 1975. 735 pp. based on sample of 581 "altekaempfer", first analysed in 1934 by theodore abel.

2278. mickolus, e. f. * heyman, e. s. who's who in terrorism: a directory of the world's revolutionaries. in preparation.

2279. middendorff, w. die persoenlichkeit des terroristen. insbesondere die frau als terroristin. 1976. pp. 289-296 kriminalistik 30.

2280. middendorff, w. neue erscheinungsformen der gewaltkriminalitaet - zugleich versuch einer taetertypologie. nov. 1973. pp. 481-493 kriminalistik 27:11.

2281. miksche, f. o. secret forces the technique of underground movements. 3rd impr. london: faber & faber, 1951. 181 pp.

2282. molnar, a. r. * et. al. undergrounds in insurgent, revolutionary, and resistance warfare. washington, d. c. the american universityspecial operations research office, 1963.

2283. momboisse, r. m. blueprint for revolution - the rebel, the party, the techniques of revolt. springfield, ill. charles c. thomas, 1970. 336 pp.

2284. morf, g. terror in quebec. toronto-vancouver: clark, irwin, 1970. the french edition "le terrorisme quebecois" was published in montreal, editions de l'homme, 1970. - the author, a psychiatristpractici inmontreal, interviewed captured members of the f. l. q.

2285. mukerjee, d. the terrorist. new york: vintage, 1980.

2286. munger, m. d. growing utility of political terrorism. springfield, virg. national technical information service, 1977. counts approximately 300 identifiable terrorist groups.

2287. n. n. bakounine et les autres: esquisses et portraits contemporains d'un revolutionnaire. paris: union generale d'editions, 1976. 432pp.

2288. n. n. diario de un guerrillero colombiano. buenos aires: freeland, 1968. also published as: diario de un guerrillero latinoamericano. montevideo, sandoni, 1968; a series of vignettes.

2289. n. n. portrait of a terrorist. june 1974. p. 70 sciencedigest 75.

2290. n. n. revolutionary terrorist - a character analysis. 1976. pp. 38-43 militarypolice law enforcement journal 3:3.

2291. n. n. spiegel-interview mit andreas baader, ulrike meinhof, gudrun ensslin, jan-carl raspe. 20 jan. 1975. der spiegel 29:4.

2292. n. n. what makes a skyjacker?. 1972. pp. 21-22 science digest 71.

2293. nass, g. anarcho-terroristen in untersuchungs- und strafhaft. 1973. pp. 36-41 zeitschrift fuer strafvollzug 22:1.

2294. o'flaherty, l. the terrorist. london: archer, 1926.

2295. paczensky, s. von * (ed.). frauen und terror. versuche, die beteiligung von frauen an gewalttaten zu erklaeren. reinbek: rowohlt, 1978.

2296. paine, l. the assassins' world. new york: taplinger, 1975. case studies of assassins.

2297. palmer, r. r. twelve who ruled: the committee of public safety during the terror. princeton, n. j. princeton university press, 1941. reissued 1970. france 1792-3.

2298. pellicani, l. i revoluzionari di proffessioni. firenze: vallechi, 1975. 'the professional revolutionaries'.

2299. ronfeldt, d. * sater, w. the mind sets of high technology terrorists. future implications from a historical analogue. santa monica: rand, 1981.

2300. russell, ch. a. * et. al. profile of a terrorist. nov. 1977. pp. 17-34 terrorism: an international journal 1:1 based on information on some 350 known terrorists from 18 different groups involving 11 nationalities.

2301. salert, b. revolutions and revolutionaries. four theories. new york: 1976. 160 pp.

2302. scott, s. * schultz d. o. the subversive. springfield, ill. thomas, 1973. 107 pp.

2303. silbersky, l. portraett av terrorister: intervjuer med terrorister i israeliskafaengelser. stockholm: aldus/bonniers, 1977. 124 pp. transcripts of interviews with terrorists in israel.

2304. smith, c. l. carlos: portrait of a terrorist. london: deutsch, 1976. 304 pp.

2305. standing, p. d. guerrilla leaders of the world. london: cassell,

2306. steinhoff, p. g. portrait of a terrorist: an interview with kozo okamoto. pp. 830-845 asian survey 1.

2307. stepniak, s. (pseud. for s. m. kravcinskij). the career of a nihilist. kozkukhov, a. london: 1889. .

2308. stern, s. with the weathermen: a personal journal of a revolutionary woman. new york: doubleday, 1975 .

2309. stratton, j. g. the terrorist act of hostage-taking: a view of violence and the perpetrators. march 1978. pp. 1-9 journal of police science and administration 6:1 2nd part of article in june issue. - a personal etiology of violence.

2310. struyker boudier, c. e. m. * et. al. politieke dissidenten. bilthoven: 1974. 141 pp.

2311. thompson, j. m. robespierre. reissued 1968. 2 vols. 1936.

2312. tromp, b. sociologie van het terrorisme. civis mundi 5.

2313. trotsky, l. my life. gloucester, mass. p. smith, 1970.

2314. truby, j. d. women as terrorists. gaithersburg, md. iacp, 47 pp.

2315. u. s. congress, senate. committee on the judiciary. subcommittee on criminallaw and procedures. hearing . testimony of h. h. a. cooper: the terrorist and his victim. 95th cong. * 1st sess. * july 21, 1977 washington, d. c. gpo, 1977. 33 pp. includes reprint of cooper's article: what is a terrorist: a psychological perspective.

2316. wijne, j. s. terreur in de politiek. politieke geheime genootschappen in deze tijd. den haag: kruseman , 1967. 157 pp. on:mafia, oas, ku klux klan, john birch society, black moslims.

2317. wilkinson, p. the new fascists. london: grant macintyre, 1981. 179pp.

2318. wilson, c. order of assassins: the psychology of murder. london: rupert hart-davis, 1972. 242 pp. concentrates on psychological motivations of assassins.

2319. wolf, j. b. appraising the performance of terrorist organizations. selected european separatist groups, fall 1978 to summer 1979. gaithersburg, md. iacp, 25 pp.

2320. wolf, j. b. organization and management practices of urban terrorist groups. 1978. pp. 169-186 terrorism 1:2.

2321. wolf, j. b. organizational and operational aspects of contemporary terrorist groups. gaithersburg, md. : i. a. c. p., 1980. update report 6:3.

2322. worthy, w. bombs blast a message of hate: an interview with an admitted bomber. 27 march 1970. pp . 24-32 life 68.

2323. yablonski, l. the violent gang. middlesex: pelican books, 1967.

2324. zawodny, j. k. internal organizational problems and the sources of tensions of terrorist movements as catalysts of violence. 1978. pp. 277-286

K. VICTIMOLOGICAL ASPECTS

2325. **appley, m. h. * trumbull, r.** psychological stress. new york: appleton–century–crofts, 1967. hostage and victim aspects.

2326. **bakels, f.** nacht und nebel. mijn verhaal uit duitse gevangenissen en concentratiekampen. amsterdam: elsevier, 1977. 344 pp. on concentration camp experience.

2327. **baker, g. w. * chapman, d. w. * (eds.).** man and society in disaster. new york: basic books, 1962.

2328. **barton, a. h.** communities in disaster. a social analysis of collective stress situations. garden city, n. y. doubleday, 1970.

2329. **bastiaans, j. * et. al.** rapport psychologisch onderzoek naar de gevolgen van gijzelingen in nederland(1974–1977). den haag: staatsuitgeverij, 1979. 359 pp. psychological research on the effects of hostage experiences in the netherlands 1974–1977.

2330. **bastiaans, j. * mulder, d. * dijk, w. k. van * ploeg, h. m. van der.** mensen bij gijzelingen. alphen aan den rijn: sijthoff, 1981. 304 pp. four accounts of psychiatrists involved with the aftercare of dutch victims of acts of hostage taking.

2331. **bastiaans, j.** guidance and treatment of victims of terrorism. paper presented to world congress of psychiatry, honolulu, 1977. 1979.

2332. **bastiaans, j.** het kz-syndroom en de menselijke vrijheid. 1974. nederlands tijdschrift voor geneeskunde 118:31 on concentration camp experience.

2333. **bastiaans, j.** psychosomatische gevolgen van onderdrukking en verzet. amsterdam: noord-hollandse uitgevers mij., 1957.

2334. **batigne, j.** nous sommes tous des hotages. paris: plon, 1973. 253 pp.

2335. **belz, m. * et. al.** is there a treatment for terror?. oct. 1977. pp. 54–56, 61,108, 111–112, 115–116 psychology today 11 description of group therapy sessions provided to 50 hostages of the washington–march 1977-hanafi incident.

2336. **berkowitz, l. * cottingham, d. r.** the interest value and relevance of fear-arousing communications. , 1960. pp. 37–43 journalof abnormal and social psychology 60.

2337. **bettelheim, b.** individual and mass behavior in extreme situations. 1943. pp. 417–452 journal of abnormal and social psychology 38.

2338. **bloch, h. a.** the personality of inmates of concentration camps. 1946. pp. 335–341 american journal of sociology 52.

2339. **bluhm, h. o.** how did they survive? mechanisms of defense in nazi concentration camps. in: b. rosenberg * et. al. mass society in crisis. new york: macmillan, 1964.

2340. **bowlby, j.** separation, anxiety and anger. london: hogarth press, 1973. on hostage experience.

2341. **bristow, a. p.** police disaster operations. springfield, ill. thomas, 1973. 240 pp.

2342. **brockman, r.** notes while being hijacked; croation terrorists. dec. 1976. pp. 68–75 atlantic 238.

2343. **brooks, m.** hostage survival. paper presented to the conference organization by glanboro state college on 'terrorism in the contemporary world'. april 1976.

2344. **cohen, e. a.** human behavior in the concentration camp. new york: 1953. medical and psychological aspects.

2345. **cooper, h. h. a.** the terrorist and his victims. june 1976. victimology 1:2.

2346. **cressy, d. l. * krassowski, w.** inmate organization and anomie in american prisons and soviet labor camps. 1958. pp. 217–230 social problems 5.

2347. **dortzbach, k, * dortzbach, d.** kidnapped. new york: harper & row, 1975. 177 pp. on kidnapping experience in eritrea.

2348. **drapkin, i. * viano, e. * (eds.).** victimology: a new focus. 5 parts. lexington, mass. d. c. heath, 1975. material from the first international symposium on victimology, jerusalem 1973.

2349. **eggers, w.** terrorism: the slaughter of innocents. chatsworth, calif. major books, 1975.

2350. **eitinger, l.** concentration camp survivors in norway and israel. london: allen and unwin, 1964.

2351. **eitinger, l.** the stress of captivity. in: r. d. crelinsten * (ed.), dimensions of victimization in the context of terroristic acts. montreal: international center for comparative criminology, 1977. pp. 71–85.

2352. **elbrinck, ch. b.** the diplomatic kidnapping: a case study. in: international terrorism: proceedings of an intensive panel at the 15th annual convention of the isa. milwaukee: institute of world affairs, 1974. pp. 45–56 u. s. ambassador's account of his being kidnapped in sept. 1969 in brazil.

2353. **fenyvesi, ch.** living with a fearful memory. october 1977. pp. 61 ff. psychology today.

2354. **fields, r. m.** psychological sequelae of terrorization. in: y. alexander & j. m. gleason * (eds.), behavioral and quantitative perspectives on terrorism. new york: pergamon press, 1981. pp. 51–72 summary of findings on hostage experience, hanafi incident <1977> and northern ireland prisons.

2355. fields, r. m. victims of terrorism. the effects of prolonged stress. 1980. pp. 76-83 eval. and change special issue based on research conducted in northernireland and the united states.

2356. figley, ch. r. mobilization i: the iranian crisis. final report of the task forceon families of catastrophe. west lafayette: purdue university, 1980. the experience families of hostage victims.

2357. fly, c. l. no hope but god. new york: hawthorne books inc., 1973. 220 pp. author, an american agronomist, was held for 208 days as hostage by tupamaros in 1971; relates his experience.

2358. fromm-reichmann, f. psychiatric aspects of anxiety. in: m. r. stein * (ed.), identity and anxiety. new york: free press, 1960.

2359. fuentes mohr, s. a. sequestro y prison. dos caras de la violencia en guatemala. san jose(costa rica): , 1971. recollections of the foreign minister of guatemala who was kidnapped in 1970.

2360. grey, a. hostage in peking. 1970. a foreign correspondent's account of his two years imprisonment in china.

2361. grosser, g. h. * wechsler, h. * greenblatt, m. * (eds.). the threat of impending disaster: contributions to the psychology of stress. cambridge, mass. mit press, 1964. 335 pp.

2362. hirshleifer, j. some thoughts on the social structure after a bombing disaster. 1956. pp. 206-227 world politics 8.

2363. holkers, a. * bijlsma, j. nazorg gegijzelden. 1978. on dutch ex-hostage treatment and experiences.

2364. hulsman, l. h. c. terrorism and victims. in: r. d. crelinsten * (ed.), dimensions of victimization in the context of terroristic acts. montreal: international center for comparative criminology, 1977. pp. 149-163.

2365. israel, ch. e. the hostages. toronto: macmillan of canada, 1966. 319 pp.

2366. istha, d. * smit, n. w. de. crisisinterventie: therapie of strategie. alphen a/d rijn: samson, 1977.

2367. jackson, g. surviving the long nights: an autobiographical account of a political kidnapping. new york: vanguard, 1974. 222 pp. hostage experience in a "people's prison" of the tupamaros by a british diplomat.

2368. jacobson, s. leadership patterns and stress adaptations among hostages in three terrorists-captured planes. telaviv: jan. 1975. paper presented at the international conference on psychological stress and adjustment in time of war and peace.

2369. jost, w. rufzeichen: haifa. ein passagier erlebt die entfuehrung des swissair dc-8 "nidwalden" u. als geisel den krieg der fedayin. zuerich: schweizer verl. -haus, 1972. 317 pp. hostage account of the 1970 multiple-hijacking ending on dawson field, jordan.

2370. kelman, h. c. violence without moral restraint. reflections on the dehumanizationof victims and victimizers. 1964. pp. 25-62 journal of social issues 29.

2371. kent, g. the effects of threats. columbus: ohio stateuniversity press, 1967.

2372. kho-so, chr. naar een diagnose van het gijzelingssyndroom en psychotherapie van gegijzelden. 1977 . pp. 206-213 tijdschrift voor psychotherapie 3:5 on experiences of the 36 hostagesin the siege at the indonesian consulat amsterdam, 4-19 dec. 1979.

2373. kits, t. p. de opvang van de familieleden van de gegijzelden in de trein bij de punt. 1977. pp. 683-687 maandblad geestelijke volksgezondheid 32.

2374. lador-lederer, j. j. 'victims'law, jus cogens and national law. telaviv: 1978. pp. 267-295 israel yearbook on human rights 1978.

2375. lang, d. a reporter at large: the bank drama. 25 nov. 1974. pp. 56-126 new yorker magazine on the hostage-terrorist interaction during an incident in a swedish bank resulting in the victim's identification with theaggressor - "the stockholm synrome".

2376. lazarus, r. psychological stress and the coping process. new york: mcgraw-hill, 1966. victim aspects in hostage situations.

2377. leventhal, h. * et. al. effects of fear and specificity of recommendation upon attitudes and behavior. . 1965. pp. 20-29 journal of personality and social psychology 2.

2378. lindroth, k. het bankdrama in norrmalmstorg(stockholm). may 1974. pp. 153-165 tijdschrift voor de politie 36:5 on "stockholm syndrome".

2379. lyons, h. a. violence in belfast: a review of the psychological effects. nov. 1973. pp. 163-168 community health bristol 5:3.

2380. middendorff, w. viktimologie der geiselnahme. april 1974. pp. 145-148 kriminalistik 28:4.

2381. milgram, s. research on victimization. in: r. d. crelinsten * (ed.), dimensions of victimizationin the context of terroristic acts. montreal: international center for comparative criminology, 1977. pp. 177-180.

2382. mills, r. t. nazorg gegijzelden verslag van het projekt nazorg gegijzelden van de treinen bij wijster en de punt. assen: 1979, unpublished account on aftercare of 1975 and 1977 dutch train hostages.

2383. murphy, j. r. political terrorism: means to an end?. sept. 1974. encore author was kidnapped by the "american revolutionary army" in anincident modelled after the patty hearst kidnapping.

2384. n. n. kidnapping victims: tragic aftermaths. april 1976. pp. 62-65, 106-107, 113, 116. saturday evening post 248.

2385. n. n. nazorg gegijzelden. verslag van het projekt nazorg gegijzelden van de treinen bij wijster en de punt. assen: drents centrum voor geestelijke gezondheidszorg, 1979. 81 pp. on aftercare of dutch train hostages, 1975 and 1977.

2386. nagel, w. h. het viktimologisch aspekt in de penologische benadering van terrorisme. 1976. pp. 26-53 ars aequi libri the victimological aspect in the penological approach to terrorism.

2387. ochberg, f. m. * (ed.). victims of terrorism. boulder, colo. westview, 1979. 200pp.

2388. ochberg, f. m. * et. al. * (eds.). the victim of terrorism. boulder, colo. westview, 1982.

2389. ochberg, f. m. hostages in teheran. may 1980. psych. annals 10:5.

2390. ochberg, f. m. preparing for terrorist victimization. in: y. alexander and r. a. kilmarx * (eds.), politicalterrorism and business: the threat and response. new york: preager, 1979. pp. 201-218.

2391. ochberg, f. m. the victim of terrorism - psychiatric considerations. in: u. s. congress, senate. committee on governmental af "an act to combat international terrorism". report to accompany s. 2236. 95th cong. * 2nd. sess. washington, d. c. gpo, 1978. pp. 335-371 includes an account of g. vaders's hostage experience in beilen.

2392. ochberg, f. m. the victim of terrorism. psychiatric considerations. 1978. terrorism 1:2.

2393. ochberg, f. m. victims of terrorism. march 1980. journal for clinical psychiatry 41:3.

2394. oren, u. 99 days in damascus: the story of professor shlomo samueloff and the hijack of twa flight 848. . london: weidenfeld and nicolson, 1970. victim's experience of skyjacking.

2395. pascal, f. * pascal, j. the strange case of patty hearst. new york: american library, 1974.

2396. pepitone, a. * kleiner, r. the effects of threat and frustration on group cohesiveness. 1957. pp. 192-199 journal of abnormal and social psychology 54.

2397. pepper, c. b. kidnapped. 20 nov. 1977. pp. 42-46, 126, 128, 131-132, 134, 136, 138-152. new york times magazine factual account of the kidnapping victim paolo lazzaroni, italy.

2398. pereira, o. g. effects of violence on military personnel in the portugese colonies. paper presented to the symposium on the effects of institutional coercion by law, government, and violence, of the 94th annual convention of the psychological association. washington, d. c.

2399. pres, t. des. an anatomy of life in the death camps. new york: oxford university press, 1976.

2400. rauter, e. a. folter-lexikon. die kunst der verzoegerten humanschlachtung vom nero bis westmoreland. hamburg: konkret verlag, 1969.

2401. rossi di montelera, l. racconto di un sequestro. torino: societa editrice internazionale, 1977. account of the heir of themartini and rossi vermouth business on his kidnapping experience.

2402. rueckerl, a. * (ed.). national-sozialistische vernichtungslager im spiegel deutscher strafprozesse. deutscher taschenbuch verlag, 1977.

2403. salewski, w. luftpiraterie. muenchen: 1976. by a munich psychologist commissioned by lufthansa to interview passengers and crew members involved in various skyjacking incidents. his report "luftpiraterie" was the basis for a training film made by lufthansa to prepare crew members on how to cope with hijack situations.

2404. schultz, d. p. panic behavior. new york: random house, 1964.

2405. sebastian, r. j. immediate and delayed effects of victums suffering on the attacker's aggression. . pp. 312-328 journal of research on personality 12:3.

2406. segal, j. * hunter, e. j. * segal, z. universal consequences of captivity: stress reactions among divergent populations of prisoners of war and their families. 1976. international social science journal 28:3 .

2407. silverstein, m. e. the medical survival of victims of terrorism. in: r. h. kupperman and d. m. trent * (eds.), terrorism. stanford: hoover, 1979. pp. 349-392.

2408. szabo, d. * (ed.). dimensions of victimization in the context of terroristic acts. montreal: international centre for comparative criminology, 1977.

2409. thompson, c. identification with the enemy and loss of the sense of the self. 1940. pp. 15-21 psychoanalytic quarterly 8.

2410. u. s. arms control and disarmament agency. the medical survival of the victims of terrorism. prepared for the office of the chief scientist: 1976.

2411. vaders, g. strangers on a train: the diary of a hostage. 1976.

2412. van voris, w. h. violence in ulster: an oral documentary. amherst: univ. of massachusetts press, 1975 . 326 pp. based on hundreds of interviews with ulstermen.

2413. wallace, a. f. c. human behavior in extreme situations. washington, d. c. national academy of sciences, national research council, 1956. publ. no. 390.

2414. weed, s. * swanton, s. my search for patty hearst. london: secker & warburg, 1976. 343 pp. by her ex-fiancee.

2415. wolfenstein, m. disaster: a psychological essay. glencoe, ill. free press, 1957.

L. TERRORISM FROM A PSYCHOLOGICAL PERSPECTIVE

2416. batselier, s. de. sadomasochisme: antropologisch interpretatiemodel van de terreur van minderheden als secundair aktiepatroon op het strukturele geweld. in: l. g. h. gunther moor * (ed.). terreur. criminologische en juridische aspecten van terrorisme. utrecht: arsaequi, 1976. pp. 12-25.

2417. bossle, l. soziologie und psychologie des radikalismus-phaenomens in der politik. -. muenchen: 1975. politische studien 220.

2418. brueckner, p. politisch-psychologische anmerkungen zur roten-armee-fraktion. in: w. dressen * (ed.). socialistisches jahrbuch, 5. berlin: 1973. pp. 73-100.

2419. committee on violence of the dept. of psychiatry. * gigula, m. f. * ochberg, f. m. * (eds.). violence and the struggle for existence. boston: stanford university school of medicine, 1970. 451 pp.

2420. crawford, t. j. * naditch, m. relative deprivation, powerlessness, and militancy: the psychology of social protest. may 1970. pp. 208-223 psychiatry 33.

2421. dowling, j. a. prolegomena to a psychohistorical study of terrorism. in: livingston, m. h. * (ed.) with kress, l. b. and wanek, m. g. international terrorism in the contemporary world. westport, conn. greenwood press, 1978. pp. 223-230.

2422. duster, t. conditions for guilt-free massacre. in: n. sanford * et. al. * (eds.), sanctions for evil. san francisco: 1971. pp. 25-36.

2423. fields, r. m. psychological genocide: the children of northern ireland. 915)historyof childhood quarterly. 1975. pp. 201-224 3.

2424. freedman, l. z. why does terrorism terrorize. a psychiatric perspective. conferencepaper chicago: uiversity of chicago, november 1979.

2425. fromm, e. the anatomy of human destructiveness. new york: rinehart & winston, 1973.

2426. geen, r. g. * stoner, d. context effects in observed violence. january 1973. pp. 145-150 journal of personal and social psychology 25.

2427. glaser, h. radikalitaet und scheinradikalitaet - spielraum. zur sozialpsychologie und sozialpathologie des protests. 1969. pp. 1-32 auspolitik und zeitgeschichte 12.

2428. goldman, e. anarchism and other essays. new york: 1910. includes an essay on: the psychology of political violence.

2429. guggenberger, b. kulturkritik und guerilla-mythos. die dritte welt als identifikations-objekt. koeln: , pp. 91-108 beitraege zur konfliktforschung 3:4.

2430. guiness, o. violence - crisis or catharsis?. rev. ed. downers grove, ill. intervarsity, 1974.

2431. gurr, t. r. psychological factors in civil violence. 1968. pp. 245-278 world politics 20:2.

2432. hacker, f. j. aggression. die brutalisierung der moderne welt. wien: 1971.

2433. hacker, f. j. contagion and attraction of terror and terrorism. in: y. alexander & j. m. gleason * (eds.) behavioral and quantitative perspectives on terrorism. new york: pergamon press, 1981. pp. 73-85.

2434. hacker, f. j. crusaders, criminals, crazies. terror and terrorism in our time. new york: norton, 1976. 371 pp.

2435. hassel, c. v. political assassin. december 1974. pp. 399-403 journal of police science and administration 2.

2436. hebb, d. o. on the nature of fear. 1946. pp. 259-276 psychological review 53.

2437. heilman, m. e. threats and promises: reputational consequences and transfer of credibility. 1974. pp. 310-324 journal of experimental social psychology 10.

2438. hubbard, d. g. a glimmer of hope: a psychiatric perspective. in: m. c. bassiouni * (ed.), international terrorism and political crimes. springfield, ill. thomas, 1975. pp. 27-32.

2439. hubbard, d. g. a story of inadequacy: hierarchical authority vs. the terrorist. in: y. alexander and r. a. kilmarx * (eds.), politicalterrorism and business: the threat and response. new york: praeger, 1979. pp. 187-200.

2440. hubbard, d. g. extortion threats: the possibility of analysis. 1975. pp. 17-19 assets protection 1.

2441. hubbard, d. g. organic factors underlying the psychology of terror. in: y. alexander and j. gleason * (eds.), terrorism: behavioral perspe. new york: pergamon, 1980.

2442. hubbard, d. g. the skyjacker: his flight of fantasy. new york: macmillan, 1971. 262 pp. on pathological elements interrorism;the author, a psychologist, concludes that a majority of the skyjackers were motivated not bypolitics but by personal frustrations.

2443. hubbard, d. g. the terrorist mind. april 1971. pp. 12-13 counterforce.

2444. janis, i. effects of fear arousal on attitude change. in: l. berkowitz * (ed.), advances in social psychology. new york: 1961.

2445. janis, i. l. air war and emotional stress. new york: mcgraw-hill, 1957.

2446. janis, i. l. psychological effects of warnings. in: baker and d. w. chapman * (eds.), man and society in disaster. new york: basic books, 1962.

2447. jaspers, j. p. c. gijzelingen in nederland. een onderzoek naar de psychiatrische, psychologische en andragologische aspecten. lisse: swets & zeitlinger, 1980. 475 pp. largely identical with j. bastiaans*et. al. * 1979.

2448. kaplan, a. the psychodynamics of terrorism. in: y. alexander and j. gleason * (eds.), terrorism: behavioral perspectives. new york: pergamon, 1980. pp. 237-254 terrorism. revised version.

2449. karber, ph. a. some psychological effects of terrorism as protest. paper presented before the annual convention of theamerican psychological association. august 1973.

2450. karber, ph. a. the psychological dimensions of bombing motivations. gaithersburg, md. international association of chiefs of police, research division, june 1973. pp. 24-32 bomb incident bulletins tab 02: targets and tactics.

2451. leloup, j. j. h. vliegtuigkapingen, terreurdaden, gijzelingen: een psychiatrische visie. 20 juni 1975. pp. 11-3 intermediair.

2452. lichter, s. r. psychopolitical models of student radicals. a methodological critique and west german case study. ph. d. dissertation: harvard university, 1977.

2453. lichter, s. r. young rebels. a psychological study of west german male radical students. oct. 1979 . pp. 29-48 comparative politics 12:1.

2454. liebert, r. radical and militant youth: a psychiatrist's report. new york: praeger, 1971.

2455. lowenthal, l. crisis of the individual: terror's atomization of man. 1946. pp. 1-8 commentary.

2456. macdonald, j. m. * whittacker, l. psychiatry and the criminal. springfield, ill. charles c. thomas, 1969.

2457. milte, k. l. * bartholomew, a. a. * ohearn, d. j. * campbell, a. terrorism - political and psychological considerations. 1976. pp. 89-94 australian and new zealand journal of criminology 9:2.

2458. miron, m. s. psycholinguistic analysis of the sla. 1976. assets protection 1.

2459. n. n. aggression, violence, revolution and war. in: knutson, n. * (ed.), handbook of political psychology. san francisco: jossey-bass, 1973.

2460. n. n. belfast syndrome: irish violence damages psyches. pp. 26-27 science digest 74.

2461. n. n. terror: psychologie der taeter und der opfer. 1978. psychologie heute 1.

2462. pepitone, a. the social psychology of violence. 1972. international journal of group tensions 2: 19.

2463. riezeler, k. the social psychology of fear. 1944. pp . 489-498 american journal of sociology 49.

2464. roth, w. psychosomatic implications of confinement by terrorists. in: r. d. crelinsten * (ed.), dimensions of victimization inthe context of terroristic acts. montreal: international center for comparativecriminolo, 1977. pp. 41-60 journalof consulting clinical psychology 41.

2465. scharff, w. h. * schlottman, r. s. the effects of verbal reports of violence on aggression. july 1973. pp. 283-290 journal of psychology 84.

2466. sewell, a. f. political crime: a psychologist's perspective. in: m. c. bassiouni * (ed.), international terrorism andpolitical crimes. springfield, ill. thomas, 1975. pp. 11-26.

2467. silverman, s. m. a symbolic element in the pflp hijackings. international journal of social psychiatry 1973.

2468. slomich, s. j. * kantor, r. e. social psychopathology of political assassination. march 1969. pp. 9- 12 bulletin of the atomic scientists 25.

2469. sperber, m. the psychology of terror. 1969. pp. 91-107 survey 15:72.

2470. storr, a. sadism and paranoia. in: m. livingston * (ed.), international terrorism in the contemporary world. westport, conn. greenwood press, 1978. pp. 231-239.

2471. strentz, th. the terrorist organizational profile: a psychological evaluation. in: y. alexander and j. gleason * (eds.), terrorism: behavioral perspectives. new york: pergamon, 1980.

2472. weinstein, e. a. * lyerly, o. g. symbolic aspects of presidential assassination. february 1969. pp. 1-11 psychiatry. journal for the study of interpersonal processes 32:1.

2473. wiesbrock, h. * (ed.). die politische und gesellschaftliche rolle der angst. frankfurt a. m. europaeische verlagsanstalt, 1967. 297pp.

2474. wilkins, j. l. * scharff, w. h. * schlottman, r. s. personality type, reports of violence, and aggressive behavior. august 1973. pp . 243-247 journal of personality and social psychology 30.

2475. wykert, j. psychiatry and terrorism. 2 febr. 1979. pp. 1, 12-14 psychiatric news 14.

M. TERRORISM FROM A CRIMINOLOGICAL PERSPECTIVE

2476. baudouin, j. l. * fortin, j. * szabo, d. terrorisme et justice; entre la liberte et l'ordre: le crime politique. montreal: editions du jour, 1970. 175 pp.

2477. beristain, a. terrorism and hijacking. nov. 1974. pp . 347-389 international journal of criminology and penology 2:4.

2478. bianchi, h. politiek terrorisme en kriminaliteit. sept 1978. pp. 227-231 civis mundi 17:5.

2479. clinard, m. b. * abbott, d. j. crime in developing countries. new york: john wiley and sons, 1973.

2480. crelinsten, r. d. * (ed.). research strategies for the study of international political terrorism. montreal: international centre for comparative criminology, 1977. 218 pp. final report of a conference held in evian from may 30- june 1, 1977.

2481. crelinsten, r. d. * laberge-altmejd, d. * szabo, d. terrorism and criminal justice. lexington, mass. lexington books, 1978. 131 pp.

2482. crelinsten, r. d. * szabo, d. dimension of victimization in the context of terroristic acts. montreal: centre international de criminologie comparee, 1977. 218 pp.

2483. cullinan, m. j. terrorism - a new era of criminality. 1978. pp. 119-124 terrorism 1:2.

2484. davidson, e. the nuremberg fallacy. wars and war crimes since world war ii. new york: 1973. 331 pp. .

2485. dessaur, c. i. foundations of theory-formation in criminology. the hague: mouton & co., 1971.

2486. dessaur, c. i. golven van terreur. febr. 1978. delikten delinkwent.

2487. dietrich, p. terroristische und erpresserische gewaltkriminalitaet. 1973. pp. 190-201 kriminalistik 5:4.

2488. fishman, g. criminological aspects of international terrorism: the dynamics of thepalestinian movement. . in: marc riedel and terence p. thornberry * (eds.). crime and delinquency: dimensions of deviance. new york: praeger, 1974. pp. 103-113.

2489. gallois, p. balance of terror. new york: 1978. on nuclear strategy in the east-west conflict.

2490. gurr, t. r. * et. al. rogues, rebels, and reformers. a political history of urban crime and conflict. beverly hills: sage publ., 1976. 192 pp.

2491. hassel, c. v. terror: the crime of the privileged - an examination and prognosis. 1977. pp. 1-16 terrorism 1: 1.

2492. kelley, r. j. new political crimes and the emergence of revolutionary nationalist ideology. chicago: rand-mcnally, 1973. includes treatment of terroristic activities of palestinian nationalist groups.

2493. kelly, c. m. statement on terrorism. washington, d. c. n. c. j. r. s. microfiche program, 31 may 1974. by fbi director.

2494. kittrie, n. n. in search of political crime and political criminals. april 1975. pp. 202-209 new york university law review 50.

2495. langemann, h. das attentat. eine kriminalwissenschaft-liche studie zum politischen kapitalverbrechen. . hamburg: 1956.

2496. leaute, j. notre violence. paris: editions denoel, 1977.

2497. lombroso, c. * laschi, r. le delitto politico e rivoluzionari. torino: bocca, 1890. the german edition "der politische verbrecher und die revolution in anthropologischer, juridischer und staatswissenschaft-licher beziehung" was published in two volumes in hamburg, 1891-1892.

2498. mednick, s. a. * shoham, s. g. * (eds.). new paths in criminology. lexington: lexington books, 1979.

2499. middendorff, w. das kleine uebel oder: das ansehen des staates; historisch-kriminologische betrachtung zu geiselnahme und kidnapping. 1973. pp. 71-82 kriminalistik 5:2.

2500. middendorff, w. die gewaltkriminalitaet unserer zeit. geschichte, erscheinungsformen, lehren. stuttgart: 1976, polizei aktuell 19.

2501. milte, k. l. terrorism and international order. june 1975. pp. 101-111 the australian and new zealand journal of criminology 8:2.

2502. most, j. science of revolutionary war: manual for instructions in the use and preparation of nitro-glycerne, dynamite, gun-cotton, fulminating mercury bombs and poisons, etc. new york: international zeitung verein, 1884.

2503. n. n. terrorisme. 's-gravenhage: ministerie van justitie, 1975. pp. 150-156 justitiele verkenningen 4 conceptual analysis of the phenomenon of terrorism from a criminological point of view.

2504. nagel, w. h. devil's advocate on the question of terrorism. 1971. pp. 15-17 etudes internationales de psycho-sociologie criminelle. 20-23.

2505. nagel, w. h. terrorisme. jan. 1978. pp. 17-25 tijdschrift voor criminologie 20:1.

2506. schafer, s. the political criminal. the problem of morality and crime. 1974. 179 pp. new york free press.

2507. sousa santos, b. de, * scheerer, s. * schwinghammer, t. * et. al. terrorism and the violence of the state. hamburg: european groupfor the study of deviance and social control, 1979. working papers in european criminology 1.

2508. springer, w. kriminalitaets-theorien und ihr realitaetsgehalt. stuttgart: ferd. enke verlag, 1973.

2509. stanciu, v. v. macrocriminologie psychologie des terroristes. 1973. pp. 189-198 revue internationale de criminologie et de police technique 26:2.

2510. stanciu, v. v. terrorisme et crime politique. 1972. pp. 28-37 revue politique et parlementaire 74 :832.

2511. stinson, j. l. * heyman, e. s. analytic approaches for investigating terrorist crimes. gaithersburg, md. iacp, 43 pp.

2512. szabo, m. o. political crimes. a historical perspective. 1972. denver journal of international law and politics 2:7.

2513. taylor, d. l. terrorism and criminology: the application of a perspective. west lafayette, ind. purdue university institute for the study of social change, 1978.

2514. taylor, i. * taylor, l. * (eds.). politics and deviance. harmondsworth: penguin, 1973.

2515. taylor, i. * walton, p. * young, j. the new criminology. for a social theory of deviance. london: routledge & kegan paul, 1973.

2516. turk, a. t. political criminality. the defiance and defense of authority. london: sage, 1982. 232 pp.

2517. united nations. fifth congress on prevention of crime and the treatment of offenders. changes in forms and dimensions of criminality - transnational and national. working paper geneva: u. n., 1975.

2518. wilson, j. q. thinking about crime. new york: basic books, 1975.

N. TERRORISM FROM A MILITARY PERSPECTIVE

2519. allemann, f. r. wie wirksam ist terrorismus?. 25 juni 1978. pp. 343-358 europa-archiv 33:12 discusses effectiveness of urban guerrillas in latin america, europe and israel.

2520. aron, r. peace and war. london: weidenfeld and nicolson, 1966.

2521. asprey, r. b. war in the shadows. 2 vols. new york: doubleday & co., 1975.

2522. avery, w. p. terrorism and the international transfer of conventional armaments. in: y. alexander & j. m. gleason * (eds.) behavioral andquantitative perspectives on terrorism. new york: pergamon press, 1981. pp. 329-342.

2523. bayo, a. 150 questions to a guerrilla. transl. by r. i. madigan and a. de lumus medina montgomery, ala. air university, a spanishcivil war veteran general who trained castro gives his experience on howto wagea guerrilla.

2524. beaufre, a. la guerre revolutionnaire. paris: 1972. also deals with terrorism.

2525. bigney, r. e. * crancer, j. w. * hamlin, t. m. * hetrick, b. w. * munger, m. d. exploration of the nature of future warfare. 3 june 1974. 106 pp.

2526. black, r. j. change in tactics? the urban insurgent. jan. 1972. pp. 50-58 air university review 23.

2527. blaufarb, d. s. the counter-insurgency era. new york: free press, 1977.

2528. bottome, e. m. the balance of terror. boston: 1971.

2529. bouthoul, g. * carrere, r. le defi de la guerre(1740-1974). deux siecles de guerres et de revolutions. . paris: presses universitaires, 1976.

2530. bouthoul, g. le terrorisme. april 1973. pp. 37-46 etudes polemologiques 3.

2531. browne, m. w. the new face of war. indianapolis: bobbs -merrill co., 1965.

2532. cabral, a. la practique revolutionnaire. paris: maspero, 1975. 309 pp.

2533. caine, p. d. urban guerrilla warfare. 1970. pp. 73-78 military review 50:2.

2534. center for contemporary studies * (eds.). the international arms trade and the terrorist. london: ccs , 1981. contemporary affairs briefing 7 shows u. s. armed forces in germany to be chief supply source by thefts.

2535. chisholm, h. j. the function of terror and violence in revolution. unpubl. m. a. thesis, georgetown university washington, d. c. 1948. 202 pp.

2536. cobb, r. les armees revolutionnaires. instrument de la terreur dans les departements. 2 vols. mouton , 1964.

2537. dach, h. von. total resistance. boulder, colo. panther, 1965.

2538. dalen, h. van. terror as a political weapon. 1975. pp. 21-26 military police law enforcement journal 2:1.

2539. dror, y. crazy states: a counterconventional strategic problem. telaviv: department of defense, 1973. .

2540. elliott-bateman, m. * (ed.). the fourth dimension of warfare. manchester: 1970.

2541. elliott-bateman, m. revolt to revolution. studies in the 19th and 20tn century europeanexperience. vol. 2: manchester univ. press, 1974. 373 pp. the fourth dimension of warfare.

2542. ellis, j. a short history of guerrilla warfare. london: ian allen, 1975.

2543. esson, d. m. r. the secret weapon - terrorism. 1959. p . 167 army quarterly 78.

2544. gablonski, e. terror from the sky: airwar. garden city, n. y. doubleday, 1971.

2545. gann, l. h. guerrillas in history. stanford: hoover institution press, 1971. 99 pp.

2546. giap, v. n. big victory, great task. london: pall mallpress, 1968.

2547. giap, v. n. la guerre de liberation et l'armee populaire. hanoi: 1950.

2548. giap, v. n. people's war, people's army: the viet-cong insurrection manual for underdeveloped countries. . new yoek: praeger, 1962. 217 pp.

2549. giap, v. n. recits de la resistance vietnamienne 1925-1945. textes reunies par l. puiseux. paris: 1966.

2550. giap, v. n. the military art of people's war. selected writings, ed. and with an introd. by r. stetler. new york-london: monthly review press, 1970. 332 pp.

2551. giap, v. n. the south vietnam people will win. hanoi: foreign languages publishing house, 1966.

2552. grivas-dighenis, g. guerrilla warfare and eoka's struggle. a politico-military study. london: longmans, green, 1964.

2553. guevara, e. (che). obra revolucionaria. 4th ed. mexico: ediciones era, 1971.

2554. haggman, b. terrorism: var tids krigfoering. malmoe: bergh, 1978. 236 pp.

2555. hahlweg, w. guerilla - krieg ohne fronten. stuttgart: 1968.

2556. hahlweg, w. theoretische grundlagen der modernen guerilla und des terrorismus. in: r. tophoven * (ed.). politik durch gewalt. guerilla und terrorismus heute. bonn: 1976.

2557. hahlweg, w. typologie des modernen kleinkrieges. wiesbaden: steiner, 1967. 74 pp.

2558. heilbrunn, o. partisan warfare. new york: praeger, 1962.

2559. heilbrunn, o. warfare in the enemy's rear. new york: praeger, 1963.

2560. institute for the study of conflict. annual of power and conflict 1979-1980. london: isc, 1980.

2561. jacobs, w. d. urban guerilla warfare. 1971. pp. 62-70 nato's fifteen nations 16:6.

2562. janos, a. c. unconventional warfare: framework and analysis. 1963. pp. 636-646 world politics 15.

2563. jender, d. urban guerrilla warfare in western countries. 1971. pp. 12-20 army journal 260.

2564. jenkins, b. m. international terrorism: a new kind of warfare. santa monica: rand, june 1974. rand paper p-5261.

2565. johnson, charles. autopsy on people's war. berkeley: univ. of california press, 1973.

2566. kern, j. w. terrorism and gunrunning. gaithersburg, md. iacp, 15 pp.

2567. knorr, k. unconventional warfare: strategy and tactics in internal political strife. may 1962. p. 346 the annals of the american academy of political and social science.

2568. laqueur, w. guerrillas and terrorists. oct. 1974. pp . 40-48 commentary 54:4.

2569. mallin, j. terrorism as a military weapon. january 1977. pp. 54-64 air university review revised version in m. livingston*et. al. *(eds.), international terrorism in the contemporary world, pp. 389-401. westport, greenwood press, 1978.

2570. mallin, j. terrorism is revolutionary warfare. 1974. pp. 48-55 strategic review 2.

2571. mao tse-tung. basic tactics. new york: praeger, 1966.

2572. mao tse-tung. on guerilla warfare. new york: praeger, 1961.

2573. mao tse-tung. theorie des guerillakrieges oder strategie der dritten welt. reinbek: rowohlt, 1966. 203 pp. selected military writings.

2574. marighella, c. urban guerrilla minimanual. vancouver: pulb press, 37 pp.

2575. miller, d. m. o. insurgency. the theory and practice of contemporary insurgencies. 1966. pp. 33-46 army quarterly and defence 91:1-2.

2576. minnery, j. * truby, j. d. improvised modified firearms. boulder, colo. paladin press, 1975.

2577. moss, r. urban guerrilla war. in: richard g. head and ervin j. rokke * (eds.). americandefence policy. 3rd ed. baltimore: johns hopkins press, 1973. pp. 242-259.

2578. most, j. revolutionaere kriegswissenschaft. ein handbuechlein zur anleitungbetreffend gebrauches und herstellung von nitroglycerin, dynamit, schiessbaumwolle, knallquecksilber, bomben, brandsaetzen, giften, usw. 3. aufl. reprint london: slienger, 1976. 74 pp. bibliotheca historico militaris 3 the orig. edition in english was titled: science of revolutionary war; ma nual for instruction in theuse and preparation of nitro-glycerine, dynamite, guncotton, fulminating mercury, bombs, fuses, and poisons, etc. new york, international. zeitung verein, 1884.

2579. munger, m. d. the growing utility of political terrorism. 7 march 1977. 23 pp. military issues research memo.

2580. n. n. terrorist explosive handbook. vol. 1: the irish republican army. boulder, colo. paladin press, 31 pp. described as aconcise up-to-date intelligence report on ira bombings.

2581. nasution, a. h. fundamentals of guerrilla warfare. new york: praeger, 1965.

2582. neale, w. d. oldest weapon in the arsenal: terror. aug. 1973. p. 10 army.

2583. ney, v. guerrilla warfare and propaganda. unpubl. m. a. thesis, georgetown university washington, d. c. 1958. 106 pp.

2584. niezing, j. politiek terrorisme en oorlog. pp. 193-196 civis mundi 5.

2585. nkrumah, k. * (ed.). handbook of revolutionary warfare. a guide to the armed phase of the african revolution. 2nd ed. new york: international publishers, 1969. 122 pp.

2586. osanka, f. m. modern guerilla warfare. glencoe, ill. the free press, 1962.

2587. peters, c. c. m. urban guerrillas. 1975. pp. 21-48 army journal 311.

2588. peterson, h. c. urban guerrilla warfare. 1972. pp. 82-89 military review 52:3.

2589. qualter, t. h. propaganda and psychological warfare. new york: random house, 1962.

2590. quintero morente, f. empleo de la violencia urbana por la subversion(i-iv). pp. 23-28, pp. 28-33, pp. 7-16, pp. 57-66 ejercito 33:394, 33:395, 34:398,34:399.

2591. quintero morente, f. terrorism. 1965. p. 55 military review 45.

2592. robinson, d. * (ed.). the dirty wars. guerilla actions and other forms of unconventional warfare. new york: delacorte, 1968.

2593. roetter, ch. psychological warfare. london: faber, 1974.

2594. ruiz molina, j. de la guerrilla urbana(i-ii). 1973. pp. 35-42, 27-35 ejercito 34:404-405.

2595. ryter, s. l. terror as a psychological weapon. may 1966. pp. 21, 145-146, 149-150 the review.

2596. schamis, g. war and terrorism in international affairs. new brunswick: transaction books, 1980. 100 pp.

2597. schmitt, c. theorie der partisanen. berlin: 1963.

2598. schreiber, j. the ultimate weapon: terrorists and world order. new york: morrow, 1978. 218 pp.

2599. scott, a. m. * hill, c. insurgency. university of north carolina press, 1970. 139 pp.

2600. short, k. the dynamite war. atlantic highlands, n. j. humanities press, 1979.

2601. silverman, j. m. * jackson, p. m. terror in insurgency warfare. 1970. pp. 61-70 military review 50 :10.

2602. singh, b. theory and practice of modern guerrilla warfare. new york: asia publishing house, 1971.

2603. spengele, r. terrorism in unconventional warfare. unpublished m. a. thesis: university of california, 1964.

2604. taber, r. the war of the flea. a study of guerrilla warfare. theory and practice. frogmore: paladin, 1970.

2605. thompson, r. * fuchs, n. l. * kloppenberg, r. e. * stokreef, j. * wegener, u. terrorism and security force requirements. in: ten years of terrorism. new york: crane, russak, 1979. pp. 128-146.

2606. thompson, r. revolutionary war in world strategy, 1945-1969. london: seeker & warburg, 1970.

2607. trinquier, r. modern warfare. a french view of counterinsurgency. new york: praeger, 1964.

2608. truby, j. d. improvised/modified small arms used by terrorists. gaithersburg, md. iacp, 16 pp.

2609. walter, h. terror by satellite. london: faber, 1980.

2610. weisl, w. von. terror als methode moderner kriegsfuehrung. 1969. pp. 437-447 allgemeine schweizerische militaerzeitschrift 135:8.

2611. wilkinson, p. terrorism - weapon of the weak. 1979. pp. 128-137 encyclopaedia britannica book of the year 1979.

2612. wohlstetter, a. the delicate balance of terror. jan. 1959. foreign affairs 38 on east-west conflict.

2613. zawodny, j. k. guerrilla and sabotage: organization, operations, motivations, escalation. may 1962 . annals of the american academy of political and social science 341 special edition on "unconventional warfare".

2614. zawodny, j. k. guerrilla warfare and subversion as a means of political change. stanford: stanford university, 1961.

O. JURIDICAL ASPECTS OF TERRORISM

2615. adu-lugha, i. unconventional violence and international politics. nov. 1973. pp. 100-104 american journal of international law 67.

2616. agrawala, s. k. aircraft hijacking and international law. dobbs ferry, 1973.

2617. akehurst, m. arab-israeli conflict and international law. 1973. p. 231 newzealand universities law review 5.

2618. argoustis, a. hijacking and the controller. 1978. pp . 91-95 air law 111:2 legal, representing a position of a member of the international federation of air traffic controllers' association(ifatca).).

2619. atala, ch. * groffier, e. terrorisme et guerilla: la revolte armee devant les nations. ottawa: dossiers interlex, les editions lemeac, 1973. 181 pp.

2620. bailey, s. d. prohibitions and restraints in war. london: oxford university press, 1972. 194 pp.

2621. bakker-schut, p. h. * prakken, t. * hartkamp, d. * mols, g. kanttekeningen bij een anti-terrorismeverdrag. 13 aug. 1977 nederlands juristenblad 52 77/28.

2622. barrie, g. n. crimes committed aboard aircraft. 1968. pp. 203-208 south african law journal 83.

2623. bassiouni, m. c. * mann, c. * paust, j. j. legal aspects of international terrorism. american society of international terrorism, 1978.

2624. bassiouni, m. c. methodological options for international legal control of terrorism. 1974. pp. 388-396 akron law review 7.

2625. bauer, e. f. die voelkerrechtswidrige entfuehrung. berlin: 1968. 208 pp.

2626. bemmelen, j. m. van. terrorisme. pp. 945-949 nederlands juristenblad no. 33.

2627. bloomfield, l. m. * fitzgerald, g. f. crimes against internationally protected persons: prevention and punishment: an analysis of the u. n. convention. new york: praeger, 1975. 273 pp.

2628. bolle, p. h. le droit et la repression du terrorisme. april 1977. pp. 121-128 revue internationale de criminologie et de police technique 30:2.

2629. bond, j. e. application of the law of war to internal conflicts. 1973. p. 345 georgia journal of international and comparative law 3.

2630. bond, j. e. the rules of riot: internal conflict and the law of war. princeton, n. j. princeton university press, 1974. 280 pp.

2631. bradford, a. l. legal ramifications of hijacking airplanes. 1962. pp. 1034-1039 american nab association journal 48.

2632. bravo, n. m. apoderamiento ilicito de aeronaves en vuelo. 1969. pp. 788-809 revista espanola de deerecho internacional 22.

2633. breton, j. m. piraterie aerienne et droit international public. 1971. pp. 392-445 revue generale de droit international public 75.

2634. buchheit, l. c. secession. the legacy of self-determination. new haven, conn. yale university press, 1978.

2635. cautrell, ch. l. political offence exemption in international extradiction. a comparison of the united states, great britain and the republic of ireland. 1977. pp. 777-824 marquette law review)60:3.

2636. chandam, k. s. le terrorisme devant la s. d. n. paris: publications contemporaines, 1935.

2637. chaturvedi, s. c. hijacking and the law. 1971. pp. 89-105 indian journal of international law 11.

2638. chung, d. y. some legal aspects of aircraft hijacking in international law. ph. d. dissertation: university of tennessee, 1976.

2639. crelinsten, r. d. * laberge-altmejd, d. * (eds.). the impact of terrorism and skyjacking on the operations of the criminal justice system. montreal: international centre for comparative criminology, 1976. 348 pp. final report on basic issue seminar.

2640. david, e. le terrorisme en droit international. in: reflexions sur la definition et la reprssion du terrorisme; actes du colloque sous la presidence d'honneur de henri rolin, 19 et 20 mars 1973. bruxelles: editions de l'universite de bruxelles, 1974. pp. 103-173.

2641. denaro, j. m. in-flight crimes, the tokyo convention and federal judicial jurisdiction. 1969. pp. 171-203 journal of air law and commerce 35.

2642. dimitrijevic, v. aktuelna pitanja medjunarodnog terorizma. 1974. pp. 55-63 jugoslovenska revija za medjunarodno pravo.

2643. dimitrijevic, v. internationaler terrorismus und auslieferungsrecht. in: t. berberich, w. holl, k. j. maass * (eds.): neue entwicklungen im offentlichen recht. stuttgart: w. kohlhammer, 1979. pp. 63-83.

2644. dimitrijevic, v. terorizam i saobracaj. in: razmatranja o pravnom regulisanju saobracaja, beograd: jugosloven- sko udruzenje za medjunaroono pravo, 1976, pp. 49-55.

2645. dinstein, y. criminal jurisdiction over aircraft hijacking. 1972. pp. 195-206 israel law review 7.

2646. draper, th. the ethical and juridical status of constraints in war. 1972. p. 169 military law review 55.

2647. emanuelli, c. legal aspects of aerial terrorism. the piecemeal vs. the comprehensive approach. 1975. pp. 503-518 annual of international law and economics 10.

2648. enzensberger, h. m. * (ed.). freisprueche. revolutionaere vor gericht. frankfurt a/m: 1970.

2649. evans, a. e. * murphy, j. f. * (eds.). legal aspects of international terrorism. lexington, mass. lexington books, 1978. 696 pp. also contains a compilation of hijacking incidents between 1. 1. 1960 and 31. 7. 1977.

2650. evans, a. e. terrorism and political crimes in international law. in: proceedings, 67th annual meeting of the american society of international law, 12-14 april 1973. pp. 87-110.

2651. falk, r. a. * (ed.). the international law of civil war. baltimore: 1971. 452 pp.

2652. falk, r. a. terror, liberation movements, and the process of social change. 1969. pp. 423-427 american journal of international law 63.

2653. faller, e. w. gewaltsame flugzeug-entfuehrungen aus voelkerrechtlicher sicht. berlin: dunker & humbolt , 1972. 212pp.

2654. feller, s. z. comment on criminal jurisdiction over aircraft hijacking. 1972. pp. 207-214 israel law review 7.

2655. fenwick, c. g. "piracy" in the caribbean. 1961. pp. 426-428 american journal of international law 55.

2656. fitzgerald, g. f. development of international rules concerning offences and certain other acts committed on board aircraft. 1963. pp. 230-251 canadian yearbook of international law 1.

2657. flores castro altomirano, e. el delito de terrorismo. mexico: 1963. 110pp.

2658. francke, h. flugzeug-entfuehrungen als weltverbrechen. zum haager abkommen vom 16. 12. 1970. goettingen : 1973. pp. 301-327 jahrbuch fuer internationales recht 16.

2659. friedlander, r. a. terrorism and international law: what is being done?. 1977. pp. 383-392 rutgers camden law journal 8.

2660. galyean, t. e. acts of terrorism and combat by irregular forces: an insurance 'war risk'. 1974. p. 314 california western international law journal 4.

2661. garcia-mora, m. r. international responsibility for hostile acts of private persons against foreign states. the hague: martinus nijhoff, 1962.

2662. garcia-mora, m. r. the nature of political offenses: a knotty problem of extraditionlaw. 1962. p. 122 virginia law review 48.

2663. gjidara, m. la "piraterie aerienne" en droit international et en droit compare. 1972. pp. 791-844 revue internationale en droit compare 24:4.

2664. gonzales lapeyre, e. aspectos juridicas del terrorismo. montevideo: fernandez, 1972. 125 pp.

2665. green, l. c. double standards in the united nations. the legislation of terrorism. 1979. archiv der voelkerrechts 18: 2.

2666. green, l. c. international terrorism and its legal control. 1973. pp. 389-301 chitty's law journal 21.

2667. heilbronner, k. luftpiraterie in rechtlicher sicht. hannover: 1972.

2668. hennings, a. die unabhangigkeit der strafverteidigung im spannungsfeld von rechtsstaatlichkeit und terroristen-bekaempfung. 1978. pp. 31-42 gegenwartskunde 27:1.

2669. hewitt, w. e. respect for human rights in armed conflict. 1971. p. 41 new york university journal of international law and politics 4.

2670. horlick, g. n. the developing law of air hijacking. 1971. pp. 33-70 harvard international law journal 12.

2671. jenkins, b. m. should corporations be prevented from paying ransom?. santa monica: rand, 1974.

2672. joyner, n. d. aerial hijacking as an international crime. dobbsferry, n. y. oceana publ., 1974. 352 pp.

2673. khan, r. guerrilla warfare and international law. new dehli: 9 oct. 1967. international studies.

2674. khan, r. hijacking and international law. 1971. pp. 398-403 africa quarterly 10.

2675. kossoy, e. living with guerrilla. guerrilla as a legal problem and a politicalfact. geneva: librairie droz, 1976. 405pp.

2676. krieken, p. j. van. hijacking and asylum. leiden: 1975. pp. 3-30 netherlands international law review 22:1.

2677. kwiatkowska-czechowska, b. the problem of terrorism in the light of international law. warsaw: polish institute ofinternational affairs, 1977. pp. 119-138 studies on international relations 9.

2678. laan-bouma, r. van der, * wiersma, j. terrorisme en burgerlijke grondrechten. 1978. pp. 210-215 civis mundi 17:5.

2679. lador-lederer, j. j. a legal approach to international terrorism. april 1974. pp. 194-220 israel law review 9:2.

2680. lauterpacht, h. revolutionary activities by private persons against foreign states. 1928. p. 105 american journal of international law 22.

2681. malawer, s. s. united states foreign policy and international law: the jordanian civil war and air piracy. 1971. pp. 31-40 international problems 10.

2682. malik, s. legal aspects of the problem of unlawful seizure of aircraft. 1969. pp. 61-71 indian journal of international law 9.

2683. mallison jr., w. t. * mallison, s. v. concept of public purpose terror in international law, doctrines and sanctions to reduce the destruction of human and material values. 1973. p. 12 howard law journal 18.

2684. marcuse, h. ethics and revolution. in: e. kent * (ed.), revolution and the role of law. englewood cliffs, n. j. prentice hall, 1971.

2685. mayer-tasch, p. c. guerillakrieg und voelkerrecht. nomos, 1972. 221 pp.

2686. mcwhinney, e. w. * et. al. aerial piracy and international law. leiden: sijthoff-oceana, n. y., 1971. 213 pp. also: dobbs ferry, 1971.

2687. mcwhinney, e. w. the illegal diversion of aircraft and international law. leiden: sijthoff, 1975. 123 pp.

2688. mcwhinney, e. w. the illegal diversion of aircraft and international law. the hague: academy of international law, 1973. hague recueil.

2689. mendelsohn, a. i. in-flight crime: the international and domestic picture under the tokyo convention. : 1967. pp. 509-563 virginia law review 53.

2690. meron, th. some legal aspects of arab terrorists' claim to privileged combatancy. 1970. pp. 47-85 nordisk tidaskrift for international ret 40:1-4 also published in new york, sabra, 1970.

2691. meyrowitz, h. status des guerrilleros dans le droit international. oct. 1973. pp. 875-923 journal du droit international 100.

2692. moore, j. n. terrorism and political crimes in international law. 1973. p. 87 american journal of international law 67.

2693. n. n. airport security searches and the fourth amendment. 1971. pp. 1039-1058 columbia law review 71.

2694. n. n. approaches to the problem of international terrorism. 1975. pp. 483-538 journal of international law and economics 10:2-3.

2695. n. n. bestraffing gewapende overvallen en gijzelingen verzwaard. may 1975. p. 177 tijdschrift voor de politie 37: 5.

2696. n. n. the abu daoud affair. 1977. pp. 539-582 journal of international law and economics 2:3 background information and documentation for analysis.

2697. nagel, w. h. terrorisme. 1972. pp. 135-156 tijdschrift voor sociale wetenschappen 17:2.

2698. paust, j. j. terrorism and the international law of war. 1974. pp. 1-36 military law review 64.

2699. peterson, e. a. jurisdiction-construction of statute-aircraft piracy. 1964. pp. 292-295 journal of air law and commerce 30.

2700. poulantzas, n. m. hijacking or air piracy?. 1970. pp. 566-574 nederlands juristenblad 20.

2701. poulantzas, n. m. hijacking v. piracy: a substantial misunderstanding, not a quarrel over semantics. : 1970. pp. 80-90 revue hellenique de droit international 23:1-4.

2702. poulantzas, n. m. some problems of international law connected with urban guerrilla warfare: the kidnapping of members of diplomatic missions, consular offices andother foreign personnel. 1972. pp. 137- 167 annales d'etudes internationales 3.

2703. richard, ph. la convention de tokyo. etude de la convention de tokyo relative aux infractions et a certaines autres actes survenant a bord des aeronefs. lausanne: 1971. 240 pp.

2704. rouw, a. c. j. de. vliegtuigkaping en luchtvaartsabotage. studentenscriptie volkenrecht 3, interuniversitairins voor internationaal recht t. m. c. asser instituut 's-gravenhage. haarlem etc: 1973. 62 pp.

2705. rozakis, c. l. terrorism and internationally protected persons in the light of the i. l. c. 's draft articles. 1974. pp. 32-72 the international and comparative law quarterly 23, 4th series:1.

2706. saldana, i. le terrorisme. 1936. pp. 26-37 revue internationale de droit penal 13.

2707. schornhorst, f. th. the lawyer and the terrorist: another ethical dilemma. 1978. pp. 679-702 indiana lwa journal 53:4.

2708. schwarzenberger, g. terrorists, hijackers, guerrileros and mercenaries. 1971. pp. 257-282 current legal problems. 24.

2709. seidl-hohenveldern, i. kombattantenstatus fuer terroristen?. berlin: 1973. pp. 81-88 neue zeitschrift fuer wehrrecht 15:3.

2710. shubber, s. aircraft hijacking under the hague convention 1970 - a new regime?. oct. 1973. pp. 687-726 international and comparative law quarterly 22.

2711. shubber, s. is hijacking of aircraft piracy in international law?. 1968. pp. 193-204 british yearbook of international law 43.

2712. stevenson, j. r. international law and the export of terrorism. 1972. p. 716 record of the association of the bar of the city of new york 27.

2713. tate, d. law agencies braced for possible years of terror. 25 jan. 1976. rocky mountain news.

2714. tomasevski, k. some thoughts on constraints upon the approach of international law tointernational terrorism. 1980. pp. 100-109 yugoslav review of international law 27:1.

2715. united nations. report of the ad hoc committee on international terrorism. 1970. a/9028.

2716. vasilijeric, v. a. essai de determination du terrorisme en tant que crime international. 1973. p. 169 jugoslavenska revija za medunarodno praro 20.

2717. vucinic, m. the responsibility of states for acts of international terrorism. 1972. pp. 11-12 review of international affairs 23:536-537.

2718. wille, j. die verfolgung strafbarer handlungen an bord von schiffen und luftfahrzeugen. berlin: 1974 . 288 pp.

2719. zivic, j. die blockfreien laender und das problem des internationalen terrorismus. 1973. pp. 7-9 internationale politik 24:547.

P. MASS COMMUNICATION ASPECTS OF TERRORISM

2720. alexander, y. communications aspects of international terrorism. telaviv: 1977. pp. 55-60 international problems 16:1-2.

2721. alexander, y. terrorism and the media in the middle east. in: y. alexander, s. m. finger * (eds.), terrorism: interdiciplinary perspectives. nwe york: the john jay press, 1977.

2722. alexander, y. terrorism and the media: some considerations. in: y. alexander, d. carlton, and p. wilkinson * (eds.), terrorism: theory and practice. boulder: westview, 1979. pp. 159-174.

2723. alexander, y. terrorism, the media and the police. 1978. pp. 101-113 journal of international affairs 32.

2724. alexander, y. the role of communications in the middle east conflict: ideological and religious aspects. new york: praeger, 1973.

2725. andel, w. m. van. media en gijzeling. 2 aug. 1975. pp . 384-386 algemeen politieblad 124:16.

2726. arieff, i. tv terrorists. the news media under siege. pp. 44-46 videography may 1977.

2727. arlen, m. j. reflections on terrorism and the media. june 1977. pp. 12-21 more 7.

2728. bandura, a. * ross, d. * ross, s. a. transmission of aggression through imitation of aggressive models. . 1961. journal of abnormal and social psychology 63.

2729. barnett, m. rich news, poor news. new york: th. y. crowell, 1978. 244 pp. pp. 98-113 are on terrorism and the media.

2730. bassiouni, m. c. terrorism, law enforcement and the mass media. perspectives, problems, proposals. 1981. pp. 1-51 the journal of criminal law and criminology 72:1.

2731. bazalgette, c. * paterson, r. real entertainment. the iranian embassy siege. 1980. pp. 55-67 screen education 37 on british media and the siege in the iranian embassy in london, 31 a 1980.

2732. bechelloni, g. il colpo di stato indiretta. problemi dell' informazione. jan. 1978: . on italian media and moro kidnapping; reprinted in a. silj, brigate rosse firenze, 1978 pp. 217-228.

2733. bechelloni, g. terrorismo, giovani, mass media. i limiti del modello liberale. 1977. pp. 303-309 problemi dell' informazione 3 on italian media, terrorism and youthful dissidents.

2734. bell, j. b. terrorist scripts and live-action spectaculars. may 1978. pp. 47-50 columbia journalism review on terrorism and the media.

2735. berkowitz, l. * macaubry, j. the contagion of criminal violence. 1971. pp. 238-260 sociometry 34

2736. blumler, j. g. ulster on the small screen. 23 dec 1971 new society.

2737. bramstedt, e. k. goebbels and national socialist propaganda 1925-1945. east lansing: michigan state university press, 1965.

2738. brousse, p. * kropotkin, p. a. la propaganda par le fait. bulletin de la federation jurasienne. 5 august 1877.

2739. brunnen, a. die rolle des mediums fernsehen in krisenzeiten. zusammenfassung aktueller ueberlegungen und beschluesse. march 1975. pp. 110-112 fernseh-informationen 6 onlorenz kidnapping.

2740. brustein, r. revolution and social change: revolution as theatre. 1970. pp. 3-9 current 118.

2741. brustein, r. revolution as theatre: notes in the new radical style. new york: liveright, 1971.

2742. cantor, n. the age of protest. london: allen and unwin, 1970.

2743. catton jr., w. r. militants and the media: partners in terrorism?. 1978. pp. 703-715 indiana law journal 53:4.

2744. chibnall, s. law-and-order news. an analysis of crime reporting in the british press. london: tavistock publ., 1977. 288 pp. also deals with news treatment of "angry brigade".

2745. chicago sun-times and chicago daily news. the media and terrorism. a seminar. chicago: field enterprises, 1977. 38 pp.

2746. clutterbuck, r. l. the media and political violence. macmillan: 1981. 191 pp. (sale temporarily suspended due to libel suit.

2747. commer, k. nicht mehr heiter, aber: weiter. versuch einer subjektiven bilanz nach der fernseh-olympiade. 14 sept 1972. pp . 13-17 funk-korrespondenz 37 on munich olympic games 1972 and palestinian attack on israeli athletes.

2748. cooper, h. h. a. terrorism and the media. in: y. alexander and s. m. finger * (eds.), terrorism: interdisciplinary perspectives. new york: john jay press, 1977. pp. 141-156.

2749. cooper, h. h. a. terrorism and the media. chitty's lawjournal 24:7.

2750. cumberbatch, g. the mass media and northern ireland.

2751. debord, g. la societe du spectacle. paris: ed. champlibre, 1971. orig. 1967.

2752. dimbleby, j. the bbc and northern ireland. new statesman 31 december 1971 article unsigned.

2753. doktoraalwerkgroep van het frans en occitaans instituut, utrecht. de haagse gijzeling in de franse en in de nederlandse pers. 72 pp. a comparison of french and dutch newspaper reporting of the embassy occupation in 1974 by the japanesered army.

2754. doyle, e. j. propaganda by deed. the media's response to terrorism. june 1979. pp. 40-41 police chief.

2755. drummond, w. j. * zycher, a. arafat's press agents. march 1976. pp. 24, 26, 27, 30 harper's magazine on role of international press in palestinian terrorist campaign.

2756. duve, f. * boell, h. * staeck, k. * (eds.). briefe zur verteidigung der republik. reinbek: rowohlt- verlag, 1977.

2757. ellinghaus, g. * rager, g. arbeitsmaterialien zu einer vergleichenden untersuchubg der presseberichter-stattung ueber die entfuehrung des berliner cdu-vorsitzenden peter lorenz., 1-18: may 1975. pp . 1-10 funk report 11:7-8.

2758. epstein, e. c. the uses of terrorism: a study in media bias. 1977. pp. 67-78 stanford journal of international studies 12.

2759. ertl, e. geisel-dramen. ueber den unterhaltungswert der gewalt. frankfurt a. m. 1975. pp. 4-6 medium 5:6.

2760. faber-de heer, t. * leeuwen, w. van. voorlichting bij gijzelingen zo eerlijk en zo snel mogelijk. 1 dec. * 1976. pp. 10-11 de journalist 27:23.

2761. fleming, m. propaganda by the deed. terrorism and anarchist theory in late nineteenth-century europe. . pp. 1-23 terrorism 4:1-4.

2762. francis, r. broadcasting to a community in conflict - the experience in northern ireland. london: bbc, 1977. 16 pp. a lecture given by the bbc controller, northern ireland.

2763. francis, r. the bbc in northern ireland. 3 march 1977. listener.

2764. franck, th. m. * weisband, e. word politics. verbal strategy among the superpowers. london: oxford universitypress, 1971.

2765. friedlander, r. a. terrorism and the media a contemporary assessment. gaithersburg, md. i. a. c. p., 1981. 22 pp.

2766. gallasch, p. f. informatoren oder komplizen in den funkhaeusern? terrorismus und elektronische medien - modellfall geiselnahme beilen. 14 jan. *

1976. pp. 1-4 funk-korrespondenz 3 on dec. 1975 south moluccan train incident.

2767. gamson, w. a. the strategy of social protest. homewood, ill. dorsey, 1975. 217 pp.

2768. gill, g. n. press viewpoints in civil disorders and riots. april 1969. policechief 36.

2769. gladis, s. d. the hostage/ terrorist situation and the media. fbi law enforcement bulletin 48:9.

2770. grave, j. quarante ans de propaganda anarchiste. paris: 1973.

2771. greenberg, b. s. * parker, e. b. * (eds.). the kennedy assassination and the american public. social communication in crisis. stanford, calif. 1965. 392 pp.

2772. greenberg, b. s. diffusion of news of the kennedy assassination. 1964. pp. 225-232 public opinion quarterly 28.

2773. gruen, g. e. public opinion and terrorism. paper presented to the conference on international terrorism, sponsored by the ralph bunche institute. new york city: june 1976.

2774. gunther moor, l. g. h. gijzelingen in de media. 1976. pp. 182-183 delikt en delinkwent 3.

2775. gutman d. killers and consumers: the terrorist and his audience. mimeographed northwestern university medical school: .

2776. hall, p. c. nachrichtensperre als publizistische mitschuld. 1977. p. 2 medium 7:14 brd government, press and schleyer kidnapping.

2777. halloran, j. d. mass communication. symptom or cause of violence?. 1978. international social science journal 30: 4.

2778. hartland, p. terror and the press. politics and greed when lives are at stake, where is the difference? . nov 1977. pp. 5-7 ipi report 26:10.

2779. haye, y. de la. petit traite des media en usages terroristes. in: g. lipovetsky * (comp.), territoires de la terreur. grenoble: 1978. pp. 117-125 silex 10 analyzes news treatment of the moro case based in 'le monde' .

2780. herman, v. * laan-bouma, r. van der. martyrs, murderers or something else? terrorism in the netherlands,the united kingdom and the federal republic of germany. unpubl. manuscript rotterdam: erasmus university, 1979. a comparative analysis of public opinion towards terrorist groups.

2781. heron, p. television's role in reporting ulster violence. belfast: 1974. harrangue: a political and social review 2.

2782. hickey, n. terrorism and television, part i. 31 july 1976. pp. 2-6 tv-guide.

2783. hickey, n. terrorism and television, part ii. 7 aug. 1976. pp. 10-13 tv-guide.

2784. hoar, w. p. the human cost of betrayal. pp. 5-6, 9-10, 77, 79, 81, 83,85, 87-88 american opinion 20 the terror in indochina andthe silence of the news media in the west.

2785. hofmann, g. bemerkungen eines bonner journalisten zur nachrichtenlenkung. 1977. pp. 3-5 medium 7 :11 brd government, press, and schleyer kidnapping.

2786. huebner, h. w. wdr-fernsehdirektor huebner zur "nachrichtensperre". 1977. pp. 7-14 hoerfunk, fernsehen, film 27:10 on press, government, and schleyer kidnapping.

2787. institute for the study of conflict. television and conflict. london: isc, 1978.

2788. international association of chiefs of police. newspaper coverage of domestic bombings: reporting pattern of americanviolence. i . a. c. p., march 1973. bomb incident bulletin.

2789. international press institute, affari esteri * (eds.). terrorism and the media. 1980. conference contributions.

2790. isaac, d. entebbe televised. june 1977. pp. 69-73 midstream 23:6.

2791. jaehnig, w. b. journalists and terrorism: captives of the libertarian tradition. 1978. pp. 717-744 indiana law journal 53:4.

2792. jenkins, b. m. the psychological implications of media-covered terrorism. santa monica: rand, june 1981. rand paper series 6627.

2793. johnpoll, b. k. terrorism and the media in the u. s. in: y. alexander and s. m. finger * (eds.). terrorism:interdisciplinary perspectives. new york: the john jay press, 1977.

2794. jones, j. b. * miller, a. h. terrorism and the media. resolving the first amendment dilemma. 1979. pp. 70-71 ohio northern university law review 6:1.

2795. kelly, m. j. * mitchell, t. h. transnational terrorism and the western elite press. paper presented to the annual meeting of the canadian political science assciation saskatoon, saskatchewan: 30 may 1979.

2796. kopkind, a. publish and perish. april 1978. pp. 12-21 more 8 discusses the increase in incidents of violence against journalists by the police and political extremists. includes a list, by country, of journalists, publishers and news organizations which have been targets of "extra-legal" political violence since jan. 1, 1977. (pp. 16-21).

2797. kracauer, s. hollywood's terror films: do they reflect an american state of mind?. 1946. pp. 132-136 commentary 2.

2798. lapham, l. h. assassin or celebrity. 22 nov. 1975. pp . 16-18 harper's magazine 251.

2799. laqueur, w. terrorism makes a tremendous noise. jan. 1978. pp. 57-67 across the board 15.

2800. lasswell, h. d. world revolutionary propaganda. westport, conn. greenwood press, 1973.

2801. latham, a. the bravest journalist in the world. 9 may 1978. pp. 48-49, 51-54 esquire 89 freedom of expression can cost italian journalists their lives. arrigo levi, the editor of la stampa, braves the bullets.

2802. lavoinne, y. presse et cohesion sociale. le cas des prises d'otages!. 1979. pp. 35-41 revue francaise de communication.

2803. leibstone, m. terrorism and the media. paper prepared for the international association of chiefs of police: november 1978.

2804. leibstone, m. terrorism and the media. paper presented to the conference on moral implications of terrorism los angeles: ucla, march 1979.

2805. levere, j. guidelines for covering terrorists debated. 3 dec. 1977. p. 15, p. 35 editor and publisher.

2806. lewandowski, r. * lohr, s. buergerliche presse, gewalt gegen links. strategie der gegenreform. starnberg: raith, 1974. 187 pp.

2807. manchel, f. terrors of the screen. englewood cliffs: prentice-hall, 1970. 122 pp. on horror movies.

2808. mark, r. * et. al. price press pays for voluntary suppression. international press institute, june 1976. pp. 3-4 ipi report(monthly bulletin) 25:6 on media handling of terroristic incidents.

2809. mark, r. kidnapping, terrorism and the media in britain. in: ten years of terrorism. new york: crane, russak, 1979. pp. 76-86.

2810. mattelart, a. * mattelart, m. information et etat d' exception. in: de l'usage des media en temps de crise. paris: alain moreau, 1979.

2811. mccann, e. the british press and northern ireland. stanley cohen and jock young * (eds.). the manufacture of news. social problems, deviance and the mass media. london: constable, 1973. pp. 242-261.

2812. meeuwisse, e. th. f. * ploeg, h. m. van der. eens gegijzeld blijft gegijzeld? de invloeden van perspublicaties op de gevolgen van gijzeling. amsterdam: 27 juli 1979. pp. 1-7 intermediair 15:30 ' once a hostage always a hostage? the influences of presspublications on the consequences of having been a hostage'.

2813. mentzel, v. gijzelingen. films in beslag genomen, pers werken belemmerend. 7 july, 1977. pp. 28-29 de journalist 28:13/14.

2814. methvin, e. h. modern terrorism and the rise of megamedia in "the global village". unpublished paper: , march 1976.

2815. monaco, j. the mythologizing of citizen patty. in: james monaco * (ed.), celebrity. the media as image makers. new york: delta book, 1978. pp. 65-78.

2816. monday, m. what's wrong with our aim. 1977. pp. 19-20 quill.

2817. mosse, h. l. the media and terrorism. in: m. livingston et. al. * (ed.), international terrorism in the contemporary world. westport, conn. greenwood press, 1978. pp. 282-286.

2818. n. n. bericht aus bonn. die entfuehrung von peter lorenz - anfrage zu vorgaengen im wdr. march 1975. pp. 113-114 fernseh- informationen 6.

2819. n. n. cbs ignores silence request. 4 aug, 1974 the huntsville item 124:182.

2820. n. n. european terrorism and the media. report on the one-day conference organized by the international press institute on nov. 9, 1978, in-london. london: ipi, 1978. 18 pp.

2821. n. n. guatemalan cover-up. nov. 1978. pp. 52-54 index on censorship 7:6 on 28 may 1978 incident at panzo's and how reuters distributed the unbelievable government version of the incident.

2822. n. n. many stations enact guidelines on involvement with terrorists. 24 oct. * 1977. television/ radio 25:7.

2823. n. n. media misreport n. ireland. belfast: 1978. belfast workers research unit bulletin 6.

2824. n. n. objectivity and the tactics of terrorists. in: john c. merrill and ralph d. barney * (eds.), ethics and the press. readings in mass media morality. new york: hastings house publishers, 1975. pp. 199-205.

2825. n. n. reflections on terrorism and the media. june 1977. pp. 12-21 more 7 four articles on broadcasting coverage of ongoing crimes involving hostages.

2826. n. n. symposium media en gijzeling;. tekst van drie radio-uitzendingen. 's-gravenhage: stafbureau voorlichting van het ministerie van justitie, 1975. 18 pp.

2827. n. n. terrorism and the media. gaithersburg, md. iacp, 9 pp. update report 4:5.

2828. n. n. terrorism and the media. 1979. whole issue, 147 pp. terrorism 2:1-2 contains ed. proceedings of two conferences on the subject held in oklahoma, april 1976 and new york, nov. 1977.

2829. n. n. terrorismo e informazione. papers of international press institute conference on terrorism and the media in florence, june 16-18, 1978 roma: july 1978. pp. 411-508 affari esteri 10: 39 contains case studies on u. k. * italy, brd, usa, japan, spain and some general papers.

2830. n. n. the british media and ireland. london: the campaign for free speech on ireland, 1978. 50 pp.

2831. ncrv. drie radio-uitzendingen over symposium 'media en gijzeling'. den haag: stafbureau voorlichting van het ministerie van justitie, 1975. 18 pp. three radiobroadcasts on a symposium 'media and acts of hostage taking'.

2832. nelson, s. reporting ulster in the british press. august 1977. fortnight.

2833. nussbaum, h. von. das verhaeltnis politiker/journalist hat sich veraendert. ein interview mit horst schaettle(zdf) ueber die nachrichtensperre der letzten wochen. 5 nov. * 1977. pp. 1-4 epd/ kirche und rundfunk 86 brd: schleyer kidnapping and news management.

2834. paust, j. j. international law and control of the media: terror, repression and thealternatives. 1978. pp. 621-677 indiana law journal 53:4.

2835. pontello, c. * (ed.). terrorismo e informazione. 1978. pp. 411-508 affari esteri 10.

2836. redlick, a. s. the transnational flow of information as a cause of terrorism. in: y. alexander, d. carlton, and p. wilkinson * (eds.), terrorism: theory and practice. boulder: westview, 1979. pp. 73-95.

2837. said, e. w. covering islam. how the media and the experts determine how we seerest of the world. new york: 1981.

2838. salomone, f. terrorism and the mass media. in: m. cherif bassiouni * (ed.). international terrorism and political crimes. springfield, ill. charles c. thomas, 1975. pp. 43-47 author works as journalist for 'il tempo di roma'.

2839. saur, k. -o. die katerstimmung nach der nachrichtensperre. 17 dec. * 1977. pp. 2-4 epd/kirche und rundfunk 98 brd: schleyer case and press.

2840. schang, g. * rosenbaum, r. now the urban guerrillas have a real problem. they're trying to make it in the magazine business. nov. 1976. pp. 16-21 more 6 describes the efforts of the fugitive leaders of the weather underground to publish their magazine 'osawatomie'.

2841. schlesinger, ph. "terrorism", the media and the liberal democratic state. 1981. socialresearch 48 :1 to be republished in y. alexander and a. o'day*(eds.) terrorism in ulster and eire.

2842. schlesinger, ph. princes gate 1980 the media politics of siege management. 1980. pp. 29-54 screen education 37.

2843. schlesinger, ph. putting 'reality' together: bbc news. london: constable, 1978. 303 pp. pp. 205-243: the reporting of northern ireland.

2844. schlesinger, ph. the bbc and northern ireland. london: campaign for free speech on ireland, 1979. p. 10 the british media and ireland.

2845. schmid, a. p. * graaf, j. f. a. de. violence and communication. insurgent terrorism and the western news media. london and beverly hills: sage, 1982. 283 pp.

2846. schmid, a. p. terrorisme en de jacht op publiciteit. 4 dec. 1981. pp. 1-7, 13 intermediair 17:49 terrorism and the search for publicity.

2847. schneider, p. pressesfreiheit und staatssicherheit. mainz: hase & koehler, 1968. 211 pp.

2848. schultz, e. censorship is no solution to coverage of hostage situations. july 1977. pp. 6-7 rtnda communicator.

2849. schwartz, d. a. how fast does news travel. 1973. pp. 625-627 public opinion quarterly 37.

2850. sheatsley, p. b. * feldmand, j. j. assassination of president j. f. kennedy a preliminary report on public reactions and behavior. 1964. pp. 289-215 public opinion quarterly 28.

2851. siegal, a. canadian newspaper coverage of the flq crisis. a study of the impact of the press on politics. ph. d. dissertation: mcgill university, 1974.

2852. silj, a. brigate rosse - stato, lo scontro spettacolo nella regia della stampa italiana. firenze: vallecchi, 1978. 245pp.

2853. sincinski, a. dallas and warsaw. the impact of a major national political event on public opinion abroad. 1969. pp. 190-196 public opinion quarterly 33.

2854. smith, d. scenario reality: a new brand of terrorism. 30 march, 1974. pp. 392-394 the nation.

2855. smith, d. wounded knee: the media coup d'etat. 25 june, 1973. the nation.

2856. snider, m. * (ed.). media and terrorism. the psychological impact. a seminar sponsored by growth associates, a division of prairie view, inc. *3-4 march, 1978 newton, kansas: prarieview, 1978. 51 pp. 5 papers by f. m. ochberg, d. anable and h. siegel.

2857. sorrentino, r. m. * vidman, n. * goodslad, m. s. opinion change in a crisis; effects of the 1970 canadian kidnapping crisis on political and ethnic attitudes. 1974. pp. 199-218 canadian journal of behavioural science 6:3.

2858. stephen, a. a reporter's life in ulster. 29 febr. 1976. observer.

2859. stephen, a. mason wants ulster news black outs. 23 jan. 1977. observer.

2860. stern, j. ch. news media relations during a major incident. oct. 1976. pp. 256-260 the police journal 4.

2861. stoil, m. j. * brownell, j. r. research design for a study of threat communication and audience perception of domestic terrorism. new york: 1981. political communication and persuasion 1:2.

2862. stolte, d. das fernsehen als medium und faktor in krisenzeiten. 11 jan. * 1978. pp. 1-3 funk-korrespondenz 2 brd schleyer, mogadishu and media.

2863. taylor, p. reporting northern ireland. nov. 1978. pp . 3-11 index on censorship 7:6 author is reporter for the thames television 'this week' programme.

2864. terraine, j. * bell, m. * walsh, r. terrorism and the media. in ten years of terrorism. new york: crane, russak, 1979. pp. 87-108.

2865. terry, h. a. television and terrorism: professionalism not quite the answer. 1978. pp. 745-777 indiana law journal 53.

2866. turner, r. h. the public perception of protest. december 1969. pp. 815-831 american sociological review 34.

2867. uilenbroek, h. discussienota op komst over afspraken voor 'perspauze'. 16 febr. * 1978. p. 13 de journalist 29:4.

2868. walker, j. psychologist proposes terrorist news guides. 17 sept. 1977. pp. 12 editor and publisher.

2869. watson sr., f. m. terrorist propaganda. gaithersburg, md. iacp, 1975. 54 pp.

2870. weisman, j. when hostages' lives are at stake. should a tv reporter push on or pull back. 26 aug. 1978. pp. 4-6 tv- guide.

2871. werf, h. van der. 100 uur wereldnieuws op stoep haags nos-gebouw. 1 oct. * 1974. pp. 10-11 de journalist 25:19.

2872. wilkinson, p. relationship between freedom of press and information and publicity given by the mass media. paper presented at the council of europe conferenceon the defence of democracy against terrorism in europe, november, 1980. 1980.

2873. wilkinson, p. terrorism and the media. june 1978. pp . 2-6 journalism studies review 3.

2874. wilkinson, p. terrorism, the mass media and democracy. july 1981. pp. 35-44 contemporary review.

2875. wilson, j. v. police and the media. boston: 1975. 175 pp.

2876. woerdemann, f. was wird bei noch staerkerer belastung sein? aktuelle ueberlegungenzum thema "terrorismus und medien". pp. 1-3 funk-korrespondenz 47.

2877. wolf, j. b. terrorist manipulation of the democratic process. april 1975. pp. 102-112 police journal 48:2.

2878. zeman, z. a. b. nazi propaganda. london: oxford university press, 1973.

Q. THE ETIOLOGY OF TERRORISM

2879. abdel-malek, a. a critical survey of sociological literature of the causes of violence. mineo paris: unesco, 1975.

2880. adamo, h. vorgebliche und tatsaechliche ursachen des terrorismus. 1977. pp. 1436-1448 blaetter fuer deutsche und internationale politik 12.

2881. ahlberg, r. ursachen der revolte. analyse des studentischen protests. muenchen: urban,

2882. alexander, y. * gleason, j. m. * (eds.). behavioral and quantitative perspectives on terrorism. new york: pergamon press, 1981. 396 pp.

2883. baumann, m. bommi. wie alles anfing. munich: trikont, 1975. on the evolution of elements of the berlin student movement towards terrorism; by an insider.

2884. becker, h. outsiders. studies in the sociology of deviance. new york: 1963.

2885. benthem van den bergh, g. van. de staat van geweld. hedendaags terrorisme in lange-termijn-perspektief. . 1978. pp. 483- 499 de gids 140:8.

2886. bergedorfer gespraechskreis. terrorismus in der demokratischen gesellschaft. hamburg: 1978.

2887. berkowitz, l. studies of the contagion of violence. in: herbert hirsch, and david c. perry * (eds.), violence as politics. a series of original essays. new york: harper & row, 1973. pp. 41-51.

2888. blok, a. selbsthilfe and the monopoly of violence. 1977. pp. 179-189 in: human figurations, essays for norbert elias amsterdams sociologisch tijdschrift.

2889. bowen, d. * marotti, l. h. civil violence. a theoretical overview. cleveland, ohio: case western reserve civil violence research center, 1968.

2890. braunschweig, p. terrorismus als signal. ueber ursachen von terrorismus. bremen: 1973. pp. 190-200 junge kirche 34:4.

2891. buehl, w. l. * (ed.). konflikt und konfliktsoziologie. muenchen: 1973.

2892. burki, s. j. social and economic determinants of political violence: a case study of the punjab. 1971. pp. 465-480 middle east journal 25.

2893. burnham, j. roots of terrorism. 16 march, 1974. national review.

2894. cavalli, l. la citta divisa. sociologia des consenso e del conflitto in ambiente urbano. 2nd. edition: ivi, 1978.

2895. collins, r. three faces of cruelty: toward a comparative sociology of violence. 1974. theory and society 1.

2896. corning, p. a. * corning, c. h. toward a general theory of violent aggression. 1972. pp. 7-35 social science information 11:3-4.

2897. couzens, m. reflections on the study of violence. 1971. pp. 583-604 law and society review 5.

2898. crenshaw, m. the causes of terrorism. july, 1981. pp . 379-399 comparative politics 13:4.

2899. crick, b. * robson, w. a. * (eds.). protest and discontent. penguin: harmondsworth, 1970. 220 pp.

2900. davies, d. m. terrorism: motives and means. sept. 1962. pp. 19-21 foreign service journal.

2901. davies, j. c. when men revolt and why: a reader in political violence and revolution. new york: free press, 1971. 357 pp.

2902. dijk, j. j. m. van. dominantiegedrag en geweld. nijmegen: dekkers & van de vegt, 1977. 165 pp. multidisciplinary vision on etiology of violence.

2903. eckstein, h. * (ed.). internal war: problems and approaches. new york: free press, 1964. 339 pp. contains a. o. the theoretical study of internal war.

2904. eckstein, h. on the etiology of internal war. 1965. pp. 133-163 history and theory 4:2.

2905. feierabend, i. k. * feierabend, r. l. * gurr, t. r. * (eds.). anger, violence, and politics: theories and research. englewood cliffs, n. j. prentice-hall, 1972.

2906. feierabend, i. k. * feierabend, r. l. * nesvold, b. a. the comparative study of revolution and violence. . april 1973. pp. 393-424 comparative politics 5:3.

2907. ferrarotti, f. alle radici della violenza. ivi, 1979.

2908. field, w. s. * sweets w. h. * (eds.). neural bases of violence and aggression. st. louis: warren h. green inc., 1975.

2909. firestone, j. m. continuites in the theory of violence. 1974. pp. 117-133 journal of conflict resolution 18.

2910. flanigan, w. h. * fogelman, e. patterns of political violence in comparative historical perspective. , 1970. pp. 1-20 comparative politics 3:1.

2911. forster, r. * greenee, j. p. * (eds.). preconditions of revolution in early modern europe. baltimore: 1970. 214 pp.

2912. frank, r. s. the prediction of political violence from objective and subjective social indicators. paper presented to international psychoanalytical congress. edinburgh: 1976.

2913. friedlander, r. a. sowing the wind: rebellion and violence in theory and practice. 1976. pp. 83-93 denver journal of international law 6 analyzes background and causes of terrorism and discusses ways to control it.

2914. friedlander, r. a. the origins of international terrorism. a micro legal-historical perspective. 1978. israel yearbook on human rights 6.

2915. gagel, w. terrorismus: versuche zu seiner erklarung. 1978. gegenwartskunde 27:2.

2916. galtung, j. a structural theory of aggression. 1964. pp. 95-119 journal of peace research 2.

2917. geissler, h. * (ed.). der weg in der gewalt. geistige und gesellschaftliche ursachen des terrorismus und seine folgen. munich/vienna/: 1978. 224pp.

2918. geissler, h. * (ed.). der weg in die gewalt. geistige und gesellschaftliche ursachen desterrorismus und seine folgen. muenchen: olzog-verlag, 1978. 224 pp. wissenschaftliche fachtagung der cdu am 29 und 30 nov. 1977 in bonn.

2919. greig, i. subversion: propaganda, agitation and the spread of people's war. london: t. stacey, 1973. .

2920. gross, f. social causation of individual political violence. paper presented to the conference on terrorism in the contemporary world. glassboro state college: april 1976.

2921. grossarth-maticek, r. anfaenge anarchistischer gewaltbereitschaft in der bundesrepublik deutschland. bonn: hohwacht- verlag, 1975. 80 pp.

2922. gurr, t. r. * guttenberg, ch. r. the conditions of civil violence: first tests of a causal model. princeton, n. j. centerof international studies, 1970.

2923. gurr, t. r. a causal model of civil strife: a comparative analysis using new indices. 1968. p. 1104 american political science review 62:4.

2924. gurr, t. r. civil strife in the modern world: a comparative study of its extent and cau ses. princeton , n. j. 1969.

2925. gurr, t. r. new error-compensated measures for comparing nations: some correlates of civil violence. princeton, n. j. center for international studies, 1966.

2926. gurr, t. r. sources of rebellion in western societies: some quantitative evidence. 1970. pp. 128-144 annals of the american academy of political and social science 391.

2927. gurr, t. r. why men rebel. princeton, n. j. princeto university press, 1970. 421 pp.

2928. hacker, f. j. materialien zum thema aggression. vienna: 1972. on aggression.

2929. hamilton, l. c. ecology of terrorism: a historical and statistical study. unpubl. ph. d. boulder, co. university of colorado, 1978.

2930. hammes, n. ueberfaellig: die erforschung der ursachen des terrorismus. 1979. pp. 291-293 kriminalistik 6.

2931. hartup, w. w. * wit, j. de * (eds.). determinants and origins of aggressive behavior. 's-gravenhage: mouton, 1974.

2932. hewitt, chr. majorities and minorities. a comparative survey of ethnic violence. pp. 150-160 the annals 433.

2933. hibbs jr., d. a. mass political violence: a cross-national causal analysis. new york: wiley, 1973. investigation of psychological, socio-economic, and ideologicalhypothese on causation.

2934. hirsch, h. * perry, d. c. * (eds.). violence as politics. a series of original essays. new york: harper & row, 1973. 262 pp.

2935. jahn, e. das theorem der "strukturellen gewalt" als eine angebliche geistige ursache des terrorismus. . bonn: june 1979. pp. 23-29 dgfk-information 79/1 etiology of terrorism;reply to peter graf kielmansegg.

2936. jubelius, w. frauen und terror. erklaerungen, diffamierungen. june 1981. pp. 247-255 kriminalistik.

2937. karstedt-henke, s. soziale bewegung und terrorismus. alltagstheorien und sozialwissenschaft-liche ansaetze zur erklaerung des terrorismus. in: e. blankenburg * (ed.), politik der inneren sicherheit. frankfurt: 1980.

2938. kawa, r. strategien der verunsicherung. die demokratische linke im faden-kreuz der "suche nach den geistigen ursachen des terrorismus". jan. 1978. p. 107 das argument 20.

2939. kent, i. * nicolls, w. the psychodynamics of terrorism. 1977. pp. 1-8 mental health and society 1-2 sees etiology not in nature of terrorist but in legitimizing circumstances.

2940. kerr, l. youth gangs - a comparative historical analysis of their evolution from recreation to terror. . paper presented to the confer terrorism in the contemporary world. glassboro state college, april 1976.

2941. kerscher, i. sozial-wissenschaftliche kriminalitaets theorien. basel: beltzverlag, 1977.

2942. kielmansegg, p. politikwissenschaft und gewaltproblematik. ueber die gefahrender verlustes an wirklichkeit. bonn: june 1979.

2943. knauss, p. r. * strickland, d. a. political disintegration and latent terror. in: m. stohl * (ed.), the politics of terrorism. new york: dekker, 1979. pp. 77-117.

2944. leites, n. * wolf, jr., ch. rebellion and authority: an analytic essay on insurgent conflicts. chicago: markham, lieuwen,edwin, 1970.

2945. letman, s. t. some sociological aspects of terror-violence in a colonial setting. in: m. ch. bassiouni * (ed.), international terrorism and political crimes. springfield, ill. thomas, 1975. pp. 33-42.

2946. lupsha, p. a. explanation of political violence: some psychological theories versus indignation. nov. 1971. pp. 88-104 politics and society 2.

2947. lupsha, p. a. on theories of urban violence. march 1969. urban affairs quarterly 4 incomplete information.

2948. may, r. r. power and innocence. a search for the sources of violence. new york: norton, 1972. 283 pp.

2949. megargee, e. i. * hokanson, j. e. * (eds.). the dynamics of aggression. individual, group, and international analyses. new york: 1970. 271 pp.

2950. mehden, f. r. von der. comparative political violence. englewood cliffs, n. j. prentice-hall, 1973.

2951. mehnert, k. twilight of the young: the radical movements of the 1960s and their legacy. new york: holt, rinehart & winston, 1978. 480 pp. explores the subject world-wide.

2952. midlarsky, m. i. * crenshaw, m. * yoshida, f. why violence spreads: the contagion of international terrorism. june, 1980. pp. 262-298 international studies quarterly 24:2.

2953. moore, jr., b. injustice: the social bases of obedience and revolt. m. e. sharpe, inc., 1978. 540 pp.

2954. moscati, r. violenza politica e giovani. 1977. pp. 335-362 rassegna italiana di sociologia 18:3.

2955. muller, e. n. a test of a partial theory of potential for political violence. 1972. pp. 928-959 the american political science review 66:3.

2956. n. n. combats etudiants dans le monde. collection "combats" paris: editions du seuil, 1968. 310 pp. on the worldwide student revolt.

2957. n. n. internal war: the problem of anticipation. in: s. de sola pool * et. al. * (eds.), social science research and security: a report prepared by the research group in psychology and the social sciences. washington d. c. smithsonian institute, 1963.

2958. n. n. narren, traeumer und verzweifelte. westdeutsche vergangenheits-bewaeltigung: die suche nach den ursachen des terrorismus. 17 april 1978. pp. 113-129 der spiegel 16.

2959. n. n. ursachen der terrorismus in der brd. berlin: de gruyter, 1978. 174 pp.

2960. n. n. violence in america: the latest theories and research. jan. 1974. pp. 52-53 todays health 52.

2961. nardin, t. conflicting conceptions of political violence. 1973. pp. 75-126 political science annual 4.

2962. nesvold, b. a. a scalogram analysis of political violence. in: j. v. gillespie & b. nesvold * (eds.), macro-quantitative analysis conflict, development and democratization. beverly hills: sage, 1970.

2963. nieburg, h. l. the uses of violence. 1963. pp. 43-54 journal of conflict resolution 7:1.

2964. oestreicher, p. the roots of terrorism. west germany: a special case?. jan. 1978. p. 75 round table 269.

2965. pitcher, b. l. * hamblin, r. l. * miller, j. l. l. the diffusion of collective violence. febr. 1978. pp. 23-35 american sociological review 43:1.

2966. rock, m. anarchismus und terror. urspruenge und strategien. trier: spee-verlag, 1977. 105 pp.

2967. rose, t. how violence occurs: a theory and review of the literature. in: th. rose and p. jacobs * (eds.), violence in americ new york. vintage books, 1969.

2968. sabetta, a. r. transnational terror: causes and implications for response. 1977. pp. 147-156 stanford journal of international studies 12.

2969. sanford, n. * comstock, c. sanctions for evil. sources of social destructiveness. san francisco: 1971. 387 pp.

2970. schroers, r. der partisan. ein beitrag zur politischen antropologie. cologne: kiepenheuer und witsch, 1961.

2971. schwind, h. d. * (ed.). ursachen des terrorismus in der brd. berlin: walter de gruyter, 1978. 174 pp. roots of terrorism in the german federal republic.

2972. segre, d. * adler, j. h. the ecology of terrorism. 1973. pp. 17-24 encounter 40:2.

2973. short, j. f. * wolfgang, m. e. collective violence. chicago: aldine, 1972. readings in theory and research on violence as agroup phenomenon, with analysis of the forms, sources, and meanings of riotandrebellion.

2974. southwood, k. riot and revolt: sociological theories of political violence. 1967. pp. 1-75 peace research reviews 1:3.

2975. stone, l. recent academic views of revolution. in: l. kaplan * (eds.) revolutions. a comparative study from cromwell to castro. new york: 1973.

2976. storr, a. human destructiveness. london: sussex universitypress, 1972.

2977. strauss, f. j. die geistigen urheber des terrorismus. breitbrunn: 1977. pp. 22-24 deutschland-magazin 9:5.

2978. tanter, r. * midlarsky, m. i. a theory of revolution. 1967. p. 264 journal of conflict resolution 9.

2979. targ, h. r. societ. al. structure and revolutionary terrorism: a preliminary investigation. in: m. stohl * (ed.), the politics of terrorism. new york: dekker, 1979. pp. 119-143.

2980. united nations, general assembly. the origins and fundamental causes of international terrorism. doc. a/c. 6/418, 2 nov. * 1972 new york: u. n., 1972.

2981. venturi, f. roots of revolution. new york: grosset & dunlap, 1966.

2982. walzer, m. the revolution of the saints: a study in the origins of radical politics. cambridge, mass. : harvard university press, 1965.

2983. wassmund, h. die revolutionsforschung, ihr stand und ihre aspekte. 1976 universitas 31:4.

2984. weil, h. m. domestic and international violence: a forecasting approach. dec. 1974. p. 477 futures 6.

2985. weizsaecker, c. f. von. der heutige terrorismus ist ein krisensympton des heutigen bewusstseins. zuerich : 25 febr. * 1978. pp. 22-23, 28 tagesanzeiger magazin 8.

2986. werbik, h. theorie der gewalt. eine neue grundlage fuer die aggressionsforschung. muenchen: utb, 1974 . 206 pp.

2987. west, d. j. * wiles, p. * stanwood, c. research on violence. london: university of cambridge institute of criminology,

2988. wilber, ch. g. * (ed.). contemporary violence: a multi-disciplinary examination. springfield, ill. thomas, 1975.

2989. wilkinson, d. y. * (ed.). social structure and assassination. new brunswick, n. j. transaction books, 1976.

2990. wilkinson, p. social scientific theory and civil violence. in: y. alexander, d. carlton, and p. wilkinson * (eds.), terrorism: theory and practice. boulder: westview, 1979. pp. 45-72.

2991. wipfelder, h. -j. philosophie und ursachen des terrorismus. 1978. pp. 287-293 europaeische wehrkunde 32:6.

2992. wolfgang, m. e. youth and violence. washington, d. c. 1970. possible explanation for violent behavior in youth and discussion of society's responses to such behavior.

2993. zimmermann, e. soziologie der politischen gewalt. darstellung und kritik vergleichen der agregatdatenanalysen aus den usa. stuttgart: f. enke, 1977.

2994. zinam, o. terrorism and violence in the light of a theory of discontent and frustration. in: m. livingston * et. al. * (eds.), international terrorism in the contemporary world. westport, conn. greenwood press, 1978. pp. 240-268.

R. IDEOLOGIES AND DOCTRINES OF VIOLENCE AND VIOLENT LIBERATION

2995. adler, h. g. * voss, r. von * (eds.). von der legitimation der gewalt. widerstand und terrorismus. stuttgart: verlag bonn aktuell, 1977. ca. 128 pp.

2996. alexander, y. * (ed.). terrorism: moral aspects. boulder: westview, 1980.

2997. allemann, f. r. realitaet und utopie der guerillas. stuttgart: 1974. pp. 809-824 merkur 28:9.

2998. alvarez junco, j. la ideologia politica del anarquismo espanol(1868-1910). madrid: siglo xxi, 1976. 660 pp.

2999. apter, d. e. * joll, j. * (eds.). anarchism today. london: macmillan, 1971. 237 pp.

3000. apter, d. e. notes on the underground. left violence and the national state. 1979. pp. 155-172 daedalus 108:4.

3001. arendt, h. ideologie und terror. in: offener horizont: festschrift fuer karl jaspers. muenchen: r. piper, 1953.

3002. arendt, h. on violence. harmondsworth: penguin, 1970. 106 pp. major theoretical work distinguishing, defining, and classifying various forms of private and official political violence.

3003. arendt, h. reflections on violence. 1969. pp. 1-35 journal of international affairs 23:1.

3004. aron, r. history and the dialectic of violence: an analysis of sartre's "critique de la raison dialectique". cooper, g. (transl.). london: blackwell, 1975.

3005. bakunin, m. gesammelte werke. 3 vols. berlin: 1921.

3006. batalov, e. j. philosophie der rebellion. kritik der ideologie des linksradikalismus. berlin(east): verlag der wissenschaften, 1975. 290 pp.

3007. bell, j. b. on revolt: strategies of national liberation. cambridge: harvard university press, 1976.

3008. berki, r. n. marcuse and the crisis of the new radicalism: from politics to religion?. gainsville, florida: 1972. pp. 56-92 the journal of politics 34:1.

3009. berkman, a. now and after: the a. b. c. of communist anarchism. new york: vanguard, 1929.

3010. berkman, a. what is anarchist communism?. new york: 1972.

3011. berner, w. der evangelist des castroismus-guevarismus. regis debray und seine guerilla-doktrin. wieso "revolution in der revolution"? hrsg. in zusammenarbeit met dem bundesinstitut fuer ostwissenschaftliche und internationale studien. koeln: kappe, 1969. 82 pp.

3012. black, c. e. * thornton, t. p. * (eds.). communism and revolution. the strategic uses of political violence. princeton, n. j. princeton university press, 1964. 467 pp.

3013. blumenthal, m. d. * kahn, r. l. * et. al. justifying violence - attitudes of american men. ann arbor: university of michigan press, 1972. analyses particularly that violence employed on behalf of social change or social control.

3014. blumenthal, m. d. more about justifying violence: methodological studies of attitudes and behavior. ann harbor, mich. survey research center, institute for social research, university of michigan, 1975.

3015. bolaffi, a. ideologia e technica del nuovo terrorismo. march 1978. rinascita 35:12.

3016. boriies, a. * brandis, f. * (eds.). anarchismus: theorie, kritik, utopie. texte und kommentare. frankfurt a. m. melzer, 1970. 450 pp.

3017. bowles, r. * et. al. protest, violence and social change. toronto: prentice-hall, 1972.

3018. broekman, j. m. humanisme en terreur. nov. 1969. pp. 556-565 wending 24:9.

3019. brueckner, p. ueber die gewalt. sechs aufsaetze zur rolle der gewalt in derentstehung und zerstoerung sozialer systeme. berlin: 1978.

3020. brugman, j. zondaar of gelovige. de theologische achtergrond van het islamitische terrorism. march 1982. pp. 19-24 hollands maandblad 23:412 "sinner or believer, the theological background of islamic terrorism".

3021. buonarotti, f. conspiration pour l'egalite dite de babeuf. 2 vols. brussel: 1928. describes social consequences of reign of terror and backgroundto the conspiracy of 1796.

3022. burton, a. m. revolutionary violence: the theories. london: cooper, 1977. 147 pp.

3023. calvert, p. a study of revolution. oxford: clarendon press, 1970.

3024. camus, a. der mensch in der revolte. hamburg: 1953.

3025. carmichael, s. * hamilton, ch. v. black power. new york: random house, 1967.

3026. carmichael, s. stokeley speaks. new york: 1971.

3027. carr, e. h. michael bakunin. london: 1961.

3028. carre, o. l'ideologie palestinienne de resistance: analyse de textes 1964-1970. paris: colin, 1972.

3029. carter, a. the political theory of anarchism. london: 1971.

3030. caute, d. fanon. london: fontana/collins, 1970.

3031. cavalli, l. socialismo e violenza. 1977. pp. 134-199 citta e regione 3:4.

3032. chierici, m. mordwaerts. gewalt als credo. aschaffenburg: pattlock, 1976. 272 pp. orig. dopo caino.

3033. claussen, d. fetisch gewalt. zum historischen funktionswechsel des terrors. offenbach/m. 1977. pp. 14-19 links 93.

3034. cohan, a. s. theories of revolution: an introduction. london: nelson, 1975.

3035. cohn-bendit, g. d. linksradikalismus -gewaltkur gegen die alterskrankheit des kommunismus. reinbek: rowohlt, 1968. 277 pp.

3036. confino, m. il catechismo del revoluzionario. bakunin et l'affaire necaev. roma: adelphi, 1976. 266 pp.

3037. confino, m. violence dans la violence: le debat bakounine-necaev. paris: 1973.

3038. cranston, m. w. sartre and violence. july 1967. encounter.

3039. cranston, m. w. the new left: six critical essays on che guevara, jean-paul sartre, herbert marcuse, frantz fanon, black power, r. d. laing. new york: the library press, 1971. 208 pp.

3040. debray, r. la critique des armes. paris: le seuil, 1974.

3041. debray, r. prison writings. translated by rosemary sheed. new york: random house, 1973.

3042. debray, r. revolution in the revolution? armed struggle and political strugglein latin america. new york: grove press, 1967. a very influential analysis based on the "foco" idea.

3043. debray, r. strategy for revolution. blackburn, r. * (ed.). new york: monthly review press, 1970.

3044. derrienic, j. p. theory and ideologies of violence. 1972. pp. 361-374 journal of peace research 9 :4.

3045. dolgoff, s. la anarquia segun bakunin. barcelona: tusquets, 1976. 471 pp.

3046. draper, th. castroism, theory and practice. new york: praeger, 1965.

3047. elliott, j. d. writer-theologicians of urban guerrilla warfare. short essays in political science. washington d. c. american political science foundation, march 1975.

3048. engel-janosi, f. * et. al. * (eds.). gewalt und gewaltlosigkeit. probleme des 20. jahrhunderts. muenchen: oldenburg, 1977. 275pp.

3049. enthoven, f. b. studie over het anarchisme van de daad. amsterdam: 1901.

3050. fanon, f. the wretched of the earth. new york: 1968.

3051. fleming, m. the anarchist way to socialism. elisee reclus and nineteenth century european anarchism. ottawa: rowman and littlefield, 1979.

3052. freund, m. propheten der revolution. biografische essays und skizzen. bremen: schuenemann, 1970. 223 pp.

3053. friedrich, c. j. * (ed.). revolution. new york: atherton, 1966.

3054. friedrich, c. j. the anarchist controversy over violence. 1972. pp. 167-177 zeitschrift fuer politik 19:3.

3055. frignano, g. teoria della guerra di popolo. milano: librirossi, 1977.

3056. gendzier, i. l. frantz fanon: a critical study. london: wildwood house ltd., 1973. 300 pp.

3057. gerassi, j. * (ed.). venceremos: the speeches and writings of che guevara. london: panther, 1968. 606 pp.

3058. giesmar, p. fanon. new york: dial, 1971. 214 pp.

3059. green, g. terrorism: is it revolutionary?. new york: outlook publications, 1970.

3060. gregor, a. j. the fascist persuasion in radical politics. princeton, n. j. princeton university press, 1974. 472 pp.

3061. grundy, k. w. * weinstein, m. a. the ideologies of violence. columbus, ohio: charlese. merrill, 1974. 117 pp. describes types of ideologies woven into violence by groups, explores the arguments used to justify violence in each type, and illustrates the application of these justifications in concrete political processes.

3062. guerin, d. l'anarchisme. paris: 1965.

3063. guerin, d. ni dieu, ni maitre. anthologie de l'anarchisme. 4 vols. paris: maspero, 1976.

3064. guevara, e. (che). bolivianischer tagebuch. muenchen: trikont, 1968. 205 pp. el diario de che guevara. .

3065. guillen, a. desafio al pentagono. montevideo: ediciones andes, 1969.

3066. guillen, a. philosophy of the urban guerrilla. hodges, d. c. transl. new york: morrow, 1973. a seminal work, firstpublished as "estrategiade la guerrilla urbana". mont evideo, manuales del pueblo, 1966. 138 pp. .

3067. guillen, a. teoria de la violencia. buenos aires: 1965.

3068. gurr, t. r. the revolution - social-change nexus: some old theories and new hypotheses. 1973. pp. 359-392 comparative politics 5:3.

3069. haag, e. v. political violence and civil disobedience. new york: harper & row, 1972.

3070. hachey, t. * (ed.). voices of revolution; rebels and rhetoric. hinsdale, ill. dryden press, 1973.

3071. halliday, f. an interview with ghassan kannafani on the pflp and the septemberattack. may 1971. pp. 47-57 new left review 67.

3072. harich, w. zur kritik der revolutionaeren ungeduld. eine abrechnung mit dem alten und dem neuen anarchismus. basel: edition etcetera, 1971. 117 pp.

3073. harris, j. the marxist conception of violence. 1974. pp. 192-220 philosophy and public affairs 2 :3.

3074. haskins, j. revolutionaires: agents of change. philadelphia: lippincott, 1971.

3075. ho tschi minh. revolution und nationaler befreiungskampf. ausgew. reden undschriften, 1902-1968. fall, b. b. * (ed.). muenchen: piper, 1968. 398pp.

3076. hobe, k. zur ideologischen begruendung des terrorismus. ein beitrag auseinandersetzung mit der gesellschaftkritik und der revolutionstheorie des terrorismus. bonn: 1979. 48pp.

3077. hobsbawn, e. j. revolution und revolte. aufsaetze zum kommunismus, anarchismus undumsturz im 20. jahrhundert. frankfurt a. m. suhrkamp, 1977. 382 pp.

3078. hodges, d. c. * (ed.). philosophy of the urban guerilla. the revolutionary writings of abraham guillen. . new york: william morrow and co., 1973. 305 pp.

3079. hodges, d. c. the legacy of che guevara. a documentary study. london: thames & hudson, 1977.

3080. holz, h. h. hat der terrorismus eine theoretische basis?. 1978. pp. 317-329 blaetter fuer deutsche und internationale politik 3 "terrorismus ist die theorielosigkeit par excellence". - useful, marxist theoretical position.

3081. honderich, t. violence for equality. inquiries in political philosophy (incorporating three essays on politiccal violence). harmondsworth: penguin, 1980. 222 pp. the first, third and fourth essays were first published as "political violence" by cornell university press.

3082. hook, s. myth and fact in the marxist theory of revolution and violence. 1973. pp. 271-290 journal of the history of ideas 34:2.

3083. hook, s. the ideology of violence. april 1970. pp. 26-38 encounter.

3084. horowitz, i. l. * (ed.). the anarchists. new york: dell publishing, 1964.

3085. institut fuer marxismus-leninismus beim zk der sed * (ed.). * engels, f. ueber anarchismus. berlin: dietz, 1977. ca. 500 pp.

3086. ira, general headquarters. handbook for volunteers of the ira, notes on guerrilla warfare. reprint boulder, colo. paladin, 1956.

3087. james, d. * (ed.). the complete bolivian diaries of che guevara and other captured documents. new york : stein and day, 1968. 330 pp.

3088. joll, j. anarchism - a living tradition. in: david e. apter and james joll * (eds.), anarchism today. . london: macmillan, 1971.

3089. joll, j. the anarchists. new york: grossett & dunlap, 1964.

3090. kahn, l. r. the justification of violence: social problems and social solutions. 1972. pp. 155-175 the journal of social issues 28:1.

3091. kaminski, h. e. bakounine: la vie d'un revolutionnaire. paris: 1938.

3092. kaplan, l. * (ed.). revolutions. a comparative study from cromwell to castro. new york: 1973.

3093. karasek, h. propaganda und tat. drei abhandlungen ueber den militanten anarchismus. frankfurt: verlag freie gesellschaft,

3094. kravchinski, s. m. la russia sotteranea. new ed. milan: 1896. translated as underground russia. new york, 1883.

3095. krok, e. j. m. * (ed.). die gewalt in politik, religion und gesellschaft. stuttgart: kohlhammer, 1976. 248 pp.

3096. kropotkin, p. a. l'anarchie - sa philosophie, son ideal. paris: 1912.

3097. kropotkin, p. a. memoirs of a revolutionist. rogers, j. a. * (ed.). new york: doubleday-anchor books, 1962.

3098. kropotkin, p. a. selected writings on anarchism and revolution. london-cambridge, mass. 1973.

3099. **laqueur, w.** a reflection on violence. 1972. pp. 3-10 encounter 30.

3100. **laqueur, w.** the origins of guerrilla doctrine. 1975. pp. 341-382 journal of contemporary history 10:3.

3101. **lehning, a. * (ed.).** selected writings of michael bakunin. grove press. 1974. 288 pp.

3102. **lenin, w. i.** ueber den kleinbuergerlichen revolutionarismus. moskau: apn-verlag, 1974. 199 pp.

3103. **lenin, w. i.** was hat der oekonomismus mit dem terrorismus gemein?. in: ausgewaehlte werke, bd. 1. berlin: 1970.

3104. **lenk, k.** theorien der revolution. muenchen: fink, 1976. 208 pp.

3105. **lindner, c.** theorie der revolution. muenchen: wilhelmgoldman, 1972.

3106. **lussu, e.** theorie des aufstandes. wien: 1974.

3107. **lutz, w. * brent, h. * (eds.).** on revolution. eldridge cleaver discusses revolution: an interview from exile. cambridge, mass. winthrop, 1971.

3108. **mallin, j. * (ed.).** strategy for conquest. communist documents on guerrilla warfare. coral gables: university of miami press, 1970. 381 pp.

3109. **mandel, e.** revolutionaere strategien im 20. jahrhundert. politische essays. wien: 1978.

3110. **marcuse, h.** counterrevolution and revolt. boston: beacon press, 1972. 138 pp.

3111. **marcuse, h.** one-dimensional man: studies in the ideology of advanced industrial society. boston: beacon press, 1964.

3112. **marighella, c.** teoria y accion revolucionaria. cuernavaca, mexico: editorial diogenes, 1971.

3113. **martic, m.** insurrection: five schools of revolutionary thought. new york: dunellen, 1975.

3114. **maschke, g.** kritik der guerilla. fischer: 1973. 125 pp.

3115. **matz, u.** politik und gewalt. zur theorie des demokratischen verfassungsstaates und der revolution. freiburg-muenchen: verlag karl alber, 1975. 314 pp.

3116. **mcwilliams, w. c.** on violence and legitimacy. 1970. pp. 623-646 yale law journal 79.

3117. **miller, b. h. * russell, ch. a.** the evolution of revolutionary warfare: from mao to marighella and meinhof. in: r. h. kupperman and d. m. trent * (eds.), terrorism. stanford: hoover, 1979. pp. 185-199.

3118. **miller, m. a.** kropotkin. chicago: 1976.

3119. **moreno, f. j.** legitimacy and violence. 1974. pp. 93-103 sociologia internationalis 12:1-2.

3120. **morozov, n.** terroristicheskaya borba. london: 1880. " terrorist struggle". an important russian theoretical contribution; repr. in: feliks gross*(eds.) violence in politics. the hague, mouton, 1972. pp. 101-112.

3121. **morton, m. j.** terrors of ideological politics. cleveland: case western reserve university press, 1972. .

3122. **most, j.** memoiren. erlebtes, erforschtes und erdachtes. 4 vols. london: slienger, 1977. orig. new york, 1903-1907.

3123. **most, j.** the beast of property. new haven, conn. international workingsman'sassociation group, 1883. .

3124. **muehlmann, e.** chiliasmus und nativismus. berlin: 1961.

3125. **n. n.** anarcho-nihilism. 1970. pp. 2-33 economist 237-6635.

3126. **n. n.** materialien zur revolution in reden und aufsaetzen, briefen von f. castro, che guevara, r. debray. darmstadt: melzer, 1968. 264 pp.

3127. **n. n.** prairie fire: the politics of revolutionary antiimperialistic weather underground. san francisco: prairie fire distributing committee, 1974.

3128. **n. n.** sozialismus und terrorismus. offenbach: 1977. 78 pp.

3129. **n. n.** terrorism and marxism. nov. 1972. pp. 1-6 monthly review 24.

3130. **n. n.** terrorism in cyprus: the captured documents. transcribed extracts issued by authority of the secretary ofstate for the colonies. london: h. m. stationery office, 1956.

3131. **n. n.** textes des prisonniers de la fraction armee rouge et dernieres lettresd'ulrike meinhof. paris: maspero, 1977. 244 pp.

3132. **narr, w. d.** gewalt und legitimitaet. 1973. pp. 7-39 leviathan 1.

3133. **nechayev, s.** catechism of the revolutionist. in: m. confino * (ed.), daughter of a revolutionist. london: alcove, pp. 221-230.

3134. **nettlau, m.** der anarchismus von proudhon zu kropotkin. seine historische entwicklung in den jahren 1859-1880. berlin: 1927.

3135. **nettlau, m.** michael bakunin: eine biographie. 3 vols. london: 1896.

3136. **neuberg, a. (pseud.).** armed insurrection. new york: st. martin's press, 1970. first published in german in 1928; on comintern's insurrectionary theory.

3137. **nomad, m.** aspects of revolt: a study in revolutionary theories and techniques. new york: noonday, 1959.

3138. **nomad, m.** rebels and renegades. new york: 1932. on anarchist terrorism.

3139. **novak, d.** anarchism and individual terrorism. may 1954. pp. 176-184 canadian journal of economics 20.

3140. **oberlaender, e. * (ed.).** der anarchismus. olten-freiburg: walter, 1972. 479 pp. dokumente der weltrevolution. 4.

3141. **papcke, s.** progressive gewalt. studien zum sozialen widerstandsrecht. die rolle der gewalt am beispiel revolutionaerer und restaurativer ideen und bewegungen. frankfurt/m. fischer, 1973. 544 pp.

3142. **parkin, f.** middle class radicalism. manchester: manchesteruniversity press, 1968.

3143. **parrilli, r. e. f.** effects of castrismo and the guevarismo on leftish thought in latin america. 1972. p. 69 revista de derecho puertorriqueno 12.

3144. **perlin, t. m. * (ed.).** contemporary anarchism. new brunswick: 1978.

3145. **pirou, g.** george sorel. paris: 1927.

3146. **pomeroy, w. j. * (ed.).** guerrilla warfare and marxism. new york: international publishers, 1973. 336 pp.

3147. **radek, k.** proletarische diktatur und terrorismus. anti-kautsky. wien: 1920.

3148. **rammstedt, o. h. * (ed.).** anarchismus. grundtexte zur theorie und praxis der gewalt. koeln, opladen: westdeutsche verlag, 1969. 168 pp.

3149. **rendtorff, t.** politische ethik und christentum. munich: kaiser, 1978. 67 pp.

3150. **risaliti, r.** violenza e terrore nel marxismo. 1970. pp. 249-269 vita sociale.

3151. **robespierre, m.** textes choisis. poperen, j. * (ed.). 3 vols. 1956.

3152. **rocker, r.** johan most. berlin: 1924.

3153. **rocker, r.** the london years. london: 1956. johan most.

3154. **rojo, r.** my friend che. new york: dial, 1969.

3155. **rubin, j.** do it!: scenarios of the revolution. new york: simon and schuster, 1970. rubin, together with abbie hoffman "created" the yippiesas a fusion between the hippies and the new left.

3156. **said, a. a. * collier, d. m.** revolutionism. boston: allyn & bacon, 1971.

3157. **sarkesian, s. c. * (ed.).** revolutionary guerrilla warfare. chicago: precedent publishing, 1975. 623 pp. anthology containing work by both practitioners and scholars.

3158. **sartre, j. p.** der intellektuelle und die revolution. neuwied- berlin: luchterhand, 1971. 155 pp.

3159. **saxon, k.** the poor man's james bond. boulder, col. paladin press, 150 pp. guide to 'action'.

3160. **schack, h.** volksbefreiung. sozialrevolutionaere ideologien der gegenwart. frankfurt a. m. akademische verlagsgesellschaft athenion, 1971. 239 pp.

3161. **schickel, j. * (ed.).** guerilleros, partisanen. theorie und praxis. muenchen: carl hanser verlag, 1970. reihe hanser 42.

3162. **shigenobu, f.** my love, my revolution. 1974. by the leader of the japanese red army.

3163. **shulman, a. k.** red emma speaks. new york: rando, 1972.

3164. **silber, i. * (ed.).** voices of national liberation. the revolutionary ideology of the "third world" as expressed by intellectuals and artists at the cultural congress of havana, january 1968. brooklyn, n. y. central book comp., 1970. 326 pp.

3165. **sinclair, a.** guevara. london: william collins, 1970.

3166. **sorel, g.** reflexions sur la violence. paris: 1919. u. s. edition: reflections on violence. new york, macmillan, 1961.

3167. **spitzer, a. b.** the revolutionary theories of auguste blanqui. new york: columbia university press, 1957. 208 pp.

3168. **springer, ph. b. * truzzi, m. * (eds.).** revolutionaries on revolution. pacific palisades: goodyear, 1973.

3169. **stafford, d.** from anarchism to reformism. a study of the political activities ofpaul brousse, 1870-1890. london: 1971.

3170. **stanley, j. l. * (ed.).** from georges sorel. essays in socialism and philosophy. london: oxford university press, 1976. 398 pp.

3171. **stirner, m.** der einzige und sein eigentum. berlin: 1845.

3172. **stone, l.** theories of revolution. 1966. p. 159 world politics 18.

3173. **swomley, j. m.** liberation ethics. 1977.

3174. **tarnovski, v. (pseud. of g. romanenko).** terrorism i rutina. geneva: 1880.

3175. **terrorism research centre.** the morality of brutality. reflections on dedication in political violence. . expanded three-essaypaper cape town: trc, 1981.

3176. **trotsky, l.** against individual terrorism. new york: pathfinder press, 1974. 23pp. 4 articles.

3177. **trotsky, l.** terrorism and communism: reply to karl kautsky. ann arbor, mich. ann arbor paperbacks, 1961.

3178. **trotsky, l.** the defence of terrorism. london: georg allen and unwin, 1921.

3179. **trotsky, l.** the defense of terrorism - terrorism and communism. a reply to karlkautsky. london: george allen and unwin, 1935.

3180. **vizetelly, e. a.** the anarchists. new york: 1912.

3181. **waldmann, p.** strategien politischer gewalt. stuttgart: kohlhammer verlag, 1977. 140 pp.

3182. **wassmund, h.** revolutionstheorien. eine einfuehrung. muenchen: beck, 1978.

3183. **weiner, ph. p. * fisher, j. * (eds.).** violence and aggression in the history of ideas. rutgers university press: 1974.

3184. **wilkinson, p.** fascism has never believed in waiting for a democratic mandate. paper presented at the council of europe conferenceon the defence of democracy against terrorism in europe, november, 1980. 1980.

3185. **winston, h.** zur strategie des befreiungskampfes der afroamerikaner. ein kritische untersuchung neuer theorien des befreiungskampfes in den usa und in afrika. (east-)berlin: dietz, 1975. 302 pp. translation of: strategy for a black agenda.

3186. **wittkop, j. f.** bakunin in selbstzeugnissen und bilddokumenten. reinbek: rowohlt, 1974. 149 pp.

3187. **wolff, k. d. * (ed.).** tricontinental. eine auswahl, 1967-1970. frankfurt a. m. maerz verlag, 1970. 316 pp.

3188. **wolff, r. p. * moore, b. * marcuse, h.** kritik der reinen toleranz. frankfurt: 1966. includes marcuse's essay 'repressive tolerance'.

3189. **woodcock, g. * avakumovic, l.** the anarchist prince, peter kropotkin. schocken: 1971.

3190. **woodcock, g.** anarchism. a history of libertarian ideas and movements. harmondsworth: penguin, 1977.

3191. **woodcock, g.** anarchism: a history of libertarian ideas and movements. cleveland: meridian books(the world publishing company), 1962.

3192. **woods, j.** new theories of revolution: a commentary on the views of frantz fanon,regis debray, and herbert marcuse. new york: internationalpublish, 1972. 415 pp.

3193. **zahn, g. c.** terrorism for peace and justice. 23 oct, 1970. pp. 84-85 commonweal.

3194. **zenker, e. v.** anarchism. london: 1895.

3195. **zoccoli, h.** die anarchie und die anarchisten. leipzig: 1909.

S. COUNTERMEASURES AGAINST TERRORISM

S.1. General

3196. alexander, y. * browne, m. a. * nanes, a. s. * (eds.). control of terrorism: international documents. new york: crane, russak, 1979. 240 pp.

3197. aston, c. c. restrictions encountered in responding to terrorist sieges: an analysis. in: responding to the terrorist threat: security and crisis management ed byt. ed. by r. schultz and s. sloan. pergamon press, 1980.

3198. atwater, j. time to get tough with terrorists. april 1973. pp. 89-93 reader's digest 102.

3199. becker, l. g. * browne, m. a. * cavanaugh, s. * kaiser, f. m. terrorism: information as a tool for control. washington, d. c. library ofcongress: congressional research service, 28 july 1978. 237 pp.

3200. bell, j. b. a time of terror: how democratic societies respond to revolutionary violence. new york: basic books, 1978. 292 pp.

3201. bell, r. g. the u. s. response to terrorism against international civil aviation. 1976. pp. 1326-1343 orbis 19:4.

3202. ben rafael, e. * lissak, m. social aspects of guerrilla and anti-guerrilla warfare. jerusalem: the magnes press, 1979.

3203. billstein, h. * binder, s. innere sicherheit. hamburg: landeszentrale fuer politische bildung, 1976. .

3204. bishop jr., j. w. can democracy defend itself against terrorism?. may 1978. pp. 55-62 commentary 65 british and northern ireland experience.

3205. bobrow, d. b. preparing for unwanted events: instances of international political terrorism. paper. delivered at the international seminar on research strategies for the study of international politic terrorism, evian, france, 1977. government countermeasures.

3206. bodmer, d. terrorismus - bekaempfung. nov. 1977. p . 683-686 schweizerische monatshefte 57:8.

3207. bourne, r. terrorist incident management and jurisdictional issues. a canadian perspective. 1978. pp. 307-313 terrorism 1.

3208. brady, b. j. * faul, d. * murray, r. internment, 1971-1975. dungannon: st. patrich's academy, 1975. 15 pp. roman catholic viewpoints on internment of suspected terrorists in northern ireland.

3209. breit, j. m. * clark, d. k. * glover, j. h. * smith, b. j. a summary report of research requirements for sensing and averting critical insurgent actions in an urban environment. mclean, va. research analysis corp., 1966.

3210. browne, j. t. international terrorism: the american response. washington, d. c. school of internationalservice, the american university, december 1973.

3211. brueckner, j. a. * schmitt, h. th. verfassungsschutz und innere sicherheit. wupperthal: dt. consulting verlag, 1977. 383 pp.

3212. buchheim, h. der linksradikale terrorismus. voraussetzungen zu seiner ueberwindung. 1977. die politische meinung 22:170.

3213. burnham, j. the protracted conflict. 26 on countermeasures against terrorism.

3214. burton, j. deviance, terrorism and war. the process of solving unsolvedsocial and political problems. . oxford: martin robertson, 1979. 240 pp. contains almost nothing on terrorism.

3215. cederna, c. sparare a vista. como la polizia del regime dc mantiene l'ordine publico. ivi, 1975. on italian counter-measures.

3216. chapman, b. the police state. london: pall mall, 1970.

3217. clark, l. s. the struggle to cure hijacking. jan. 1973. pp. 47-51 international perspectives.

3218. clutterbuck, r. l. management of the kidnap risk. 1981. pp. 125-137 terrorism 5.

3219. cobler, s. law, order and politics in west germany. harmondsworth: penguin, 1978. deals with anti-terrorist measures.

3220. cole, r. b. executive security. a corporate study to effective response to abduction and terrorism. new york: john wiley andsons, 1980.

3221. conley, m. c. the strategy of communist-directed insurgency and the conduct of counter-insurgency.: 1969. pp. 73-93 naval war college review 21:9 central to achieve insurgent goals is theneed for revolutionary forces to displace existing civil authority. to counteract this effort the central thrust of counterinsurgency must be sociopolitical rather than military.

3222. cooper, h. h. a. terrorism and the intelligence function.: march 1976. p. 24 chitty's law journal 73:3.

3223. copeland, m. unmentionable uses of a c. i. a. counterterrorist activity.: 14 sept. 1973. pp. 990-997 national review 25.

3224. copeland, m. without cloak or dagger: the truth about the new espionage. new york: simon & schuster, 1970. contains information on the cia's computerized anti-terrorist system "octopus".

3225. corves, e. international cooperation in the field of international political terrorism.: 1978. pp. 199-210 terrorism 1:2.

3226. crozier, b. * **(ed.).** new dimensions of security in europe. london: instit, notes the new security threat posed by terrorists and suggests ways of combatting it.

3227. crozier, b. strategy of survival. london: temple smith, 1978.

3228. daniker, g. antiterror-strategie: fakten, folgerungen, forderungen, neue wege der terroristen-bekampfung. stuttgart: verlaghuber, 1978. 325 pp.

3229. davis, a. the industry response to terrorism. in: y. alexander and r. a. kilmarx * (eds.), political terrorism and business: the threat and response. new york: praeger, 1979.

3230. dean, b. organizational response to terrorist victimization: a case study of the hanafi hostage-takings. in: r. d. crelinsten * (ed.), dimensions of victimization inthe context of terroristic acts. montreal: international center for comparative criminology, 1977. pp. 119-127.

3231. ellenberg, e. s. international terrorism vs. democracy. cologne: 1972.

3232. epstein, d. g. combatting campus terrorism.: jan. 1971. pp. 46-47, 49 police chief 38:1.

3233. evans, e. h. calling a truce to terror. the american response to internationalterrori. westport, conn. : greenwoodpress, 1979. criticizes the depolitized u. s. approach which treats the matter in purely legal and humanitarian terms.

3234. evelegh, r. peacekeeping in a democratic society: the lessons of northern ireland. london: c. hurst, 1978. 174 pp.

3235. fisk, r. terrorism in the united kingdom and the resultant spread of political power to the army. paper presented at glassboro state college, new jersey, international symposium on terrorism in the contemporary world, april 26-28, 1976.

3236. flamigni, s. * **et. al.** sicurezza democratica e lotta alla criminalita. atti del convegnoorganizatto dal centro studi per la riforma dello stato 25-26 febr. 1975. roma: editori riuniti, 1975.

3237. fogel, l. j. predictive antiterrorism.: decision sciences, inc., april 1977.

3238. friedlander, r. a. coping with terrorism: what is to be done?. in y. alexander, d. carlton, and p. wilkinson * (eds.), terrorism: theory and practice. boulder, colo.: westvieew, 1979. pp. 231-245.

3239. friestad, d. e. a descriptive analysis of terrorist targets in a crime prevention through environmental design context. unpubl. doctoral dissertation(ph. d.) the florida state university school of criminology: 1978. .

3240. fuqua, p. q. terrorism. the executive guide to survival. houston: gulf publ., 1978. 158 pp. 1st ed. 1971.

3241. gaay fortman, w. f. de. rechtsstaat en terrorisme. alphen a/drijn: samson, 1979. 26 pp.

3242. gardiner, l. report of a committee to consider, in the context of civil libertiesand human rigths, measures to deal with terrorism in northern ireland. london: h. m. s. o., 1975. 78 pp.

3243. genscher, h. d. beitrag zur verbesserung der inneren sicherheit. ansprache am 13. 11. 1972.: 1972. pp. 1885-1886 bulletin . presse- und informationsamt der bundesregierung 158.

3244. genscher, h. d. erklaerung der bundesregierung zu fragen der inneren sicherheit abgegeben vor dem deutschen bundestag am 7. juni 1972.: 1972. pp. 1155-1161 bulletin. presse- und informationsamt der bundesregierung 84.

3245. genscher, h. d. interview mit dem saarlaend. rundfunk am 8. 10. 1972.: 1972. pp. 1705-1706 bulletin . presse- und informationsamt der bundesregierung 141.

3246. genscher, h. d. massnahmen zum schutz der inneren sicherheit. interview mit dem z. d. f. am 10. 9. 1972. : 1972. pp. 1533-1534 bulletin. presse- und informationsamt der bundesregierung 123.

3247. giehring, h. die reaktion des gesetzgebers auf den terrorismus. in: jugend und terrorismus. ein hearing des bundesjungend-kuratoriums. munich: 1979. pp. 61-83.

3248. glejdura, s. lucha contra el terrorismo internacional.: jan. 1978. revista de politica internacional 155.

3249. godfrey, d. the response of the banking community. in: y. alexander and r. a. kilmarx * (eds.), political terrorism and business: the threat and response. new york: praeger, 1979. pp. 244-264.

3250. graves, c. a. the u. s. government's response to terrorism. in y. alexander and r. a. kilmarx * (eds.) , political terrorism and business: the threat and response. new york: praeger, 1979. pp. 293-306.

3251. great britain. committee of privy counsellors on authorized procedures for interrogation of terrorist suspects. report. london: h. m. s. o., 1972.

3252. great britain. foreign office. report on procedures for the arrest, interrogation and detention of suspected terrorists in aden; 14 november 1966. london: h. m. s. o., 1966. 24 pp.

3253. greisman, h. c. terrorism and the closure of society: a social impact projection.: july 1979. pp. 135-146 technological forecasting and social change. 14.

3254. grondona, m. reconciling internal security and human rights.: 1978. pp. 3-16 international security 3.

3255. haakmat, a. r. de bestrijding van terreuracties. juridische en polemologische visies vergeleken.: 25 november 1977. pp. 9, 11, 13 intermediair 13:47.

3256. herold, h. perspektiven der internationalen fahnung nach terroristen.: april 1980. pp. 165-171 kriminalistik 4.

3257. heyman, e. s. * mickolus, e. f. * schlotter, j. responding to terrorism: basic and applied research. in: s. sloan and r. shultz * (eds.), responding to the terrorist threat: security and crisis management. new york: pergamon, 1980.

3258. hoffacker, l. the u. s. government response to terrorism: a global approach.: 18 march, 1974. pp. 274-278 department of state bulletin 70.

3259. horchem, h. j. die innere sicherheit der bundesrepublik deutschland. bedrohung und abwehr.: 1976. beitraegezur konfliktforschung 6:4.

3260. horchem, h. j. the german government response to terrorism. in y. alexander and r. a. kilmarx * (eds.) , political terrorism and business: the threat and response. new york: praeger, 1979. pp. 428-447.

3261. horowitz, i. l. political terrorism and state power.: 1973. pp. 147-157 journal of political and military sociology 1.

3262. hoveyda, f. the problem of international terrorism at the united nations.: 1977. pp. 71-83 terrorism 1.

3263. innenministerium rheinland-pfalz. (ed.). programm fuer die innere sicherheit in der bundesrepublik deutschland. staendige konferenz der innenminister/-senatoren des bundes undder laender, febr. 1974. mainz: krach, 1974. 28 pp.

3264. institute for the study of conflict. can israel contain the palestine revolution?. london: isc, 1971. 11 pp. conflict studies 13.

3265. international association of chiefs of police. threat analysis methodology. gaithersburg, md.: iacp, . 34 pp.

3266. jacobson, ph. terrorists at large: the trouble with arresting hijackers is that governments keep letting them go.: 6 nov. * 1977. pp. c1-c4; c4 washington post.

3267. janke, p. the response to terrorism. in: j. shaw, e. f. gueritz and a. e. younger * (eds.), tenyears of terrorism. new york: crane, russak, 1979. pp. 22-38.

3268. jenkins, b. m. * tanham, g. * wainstein, e. * sullivan, g. u. s. preparation for future low-level conflict. a report of a discussion, 19-20 oct. 1976

rand corporation, washington, d. c. santa monica: rand, july 1977. rand paper p. 5830.

3269. jenkins, b. m. a strategy for combatting terrorism. santa monica: rand, may 1981. rand paper series 6624.

3270. jenkins, b. m. upgrading the fight against terrorism.: 27 march, 1977. washington post.

3271. kaiser, k. * kreis, k. m. * (eds.). sicherheitspolitik vor neuen aufgaben. frankfurt/m.: alfredmetzner verlag, 1977. 447pp. also deals with fight against terrorism.

3272. kittrie, n. n. new look at political offenses and terrorism. in m. livingston * et. al. * (eds.), international terrorism in the contemporary world. westport, conn.: greenwood press, 1978. pp. 354-375.

3273. kittrie, n. n. reconciling the irreconcilable: the quest for international agreement over political crime and terrorism.: 1978. pp. 208-236 yearbook of world affairs.

3274. koch, k. enige opmerkingen over het terrorisme en de ontwikkeling naar een "sterke" staat.: march 1978. pp. 41-48 transaktie 7:1.

3275. kogon, e. * (ed.). terror und gewaltkriminatitaet. herausforderung fuer den rechtsstaat. diskussionsprotokoll reihe hessenforum. frankfurt/m.: aspekte verlag, 1975. 114 pp.

3276. kupperman, r. h. treating the symptoms of terrorism: some principles of good hygiene.: 1977. pp. 35-49 terrorism 1.

3277. lachica, e. japan using diplomacy to fight terrorists.: 10 march, 1975. washington star-news.

3278. legum, c. how to curb international terrorism.: jan. 1973. pp. 3-9 current history 147.

3279. lineberry, w. p. * (ed.). the struggle against terrorism. new york: h. w. wilson, 1977. 203 pp.

3280. mahoney, h. t. after a terrorist attack - business as usual.: march 1975. pp. 16, 18, 19 security management 19:1.

3281. maihofer, w. rechtsstaat gegen terrorismus.: 1976. tribuene 15:57.

3282. mcclure, b. corporate vulnerability and how to assess it. in: y. alexander and r. a. kilmarx * (eds.) , political terrorism and business: the threat and response. new york: praeger, 1979. pp. 138-169.

3283. mensing, w. zum "offensivkonzept zur bekaempfung des anarchistischen terrorismus" der cdu/csu.: 1976. aus politikund zeitgeschichte 25.

3284. **methvin, e. h.** domestic intelligence is our only curb on terrorism.: febr. 1976. pp. 10-12 human events 36.

3285. **mickolus, e. f. * heyman, e. s. * schlotter, j.** responding to terrorism: basic and applied research. in: s. sloan and r. schultz. * (eds.) responding to the terrorist threat security and crisis management. new york: pergamon, 1980. pp. 174-189.

3286. **mickolus, e. f.** combatting international terrorism: a quantitative analysis. ph. d. dissertation. new haven, connecticut: yale university, department of political science, 1981. 600 pp. book version forthcoming with greenwood press.

3287. **milte, k. l.** prevention of terrorism through development of supra-national criminology.: 1975. pp. 519-538 journal of international law and economics 10:2-3.

3288. **moore, k. c.** airport, aircraft and airline security. los angeles: security world publishing, 1976. 374 pp.

3289. **munck, l. de.** het internationale terrorisme en zijn bestrijding. leuven: katholieke universiteit, 1978. 154 pp. master thesis, dealing with u. n. approach to terrorism and its suppression.

3290. **n. n.** curbing terrorism.: jan. 1978. pp. 31-37 atlas world press review 25.

3291. **n. n.** deutsche massnahmen und initiativen zur terrorbekaempfung. hamburg: 1976. dpa-hintergrund.

3292. **n. n.** efforts continue to check arab terrorism. washington, d. c.: embassy of israel, 1973.

3293. **n. n.** erklaerung der bundesregierung zur inneren sicherheit. abgegeben von bundeskanzler schmidt vor dem deutschen bundestag am 13. maerz 1975.: 1975. pp. 341-348 bulletin. presse- und informationsamt der bundesregierung 35.

3294. **n. n.** kelley discounts fbi's link to a terrorist group.: 12 jan. 1976. p. 24 new york times.

3295. **n. n.** la lutte internationale contre le terrorisme.: 30 may 1975. pp. 3-67 problemes politiques et sociaux 259.

3296. **n. n.** la lutte internationale contre le terrorisme. paris: la documentation francaise, 1975. 68pp.

3297. **n. n.** political problems of terrorism and society. in: shaw, i. * e. f. gueritz, * a. e. younger * (eds .), ten years of terrorism. new york: crane, russak, 1979. pp. 39-55.

3298. **n. n.** president nixon establishes cabinet committee to combat terrorism.: 1972. pp. 475-480 department of state bulletin 67.

3299. **n. n.** reflexions sur la definition et la repression du terrorisme. actes du colloque, universite libre de bruxelles, 1973. centre de droit internationale et association belge de juristes democrates. bruxelles: ed. de l'universite, 1974. 292 pp.

3300. **n. n.** reports on a colloquium on "prophylaxie du terrorisme" held in dec. 1971 with international participants. revue trimestrielle dela societe internationale de prophylaxie criminelle. 20-23.

3301. **n. n.** sanctions against transnational terrorism. in: y. alexander, d. carlton, and p. wilkinson * (eds.), terrorism: theory and practice. boulder, colo.: westview, 1979.

3302. **n. n.** terrorisme. 's-gravenhage: ministerie van justitie, 1975. pp. 138-150 justitiele verkenningen 4 deals with various types of terrorism and provides a summary of antiterrorism measures.

3303. **n. n.** terrorism: growing and increasingly dangerous.: 29 sept. 1975. p. 79 u. s. news and world report interview with robert a. fearey, special assistant to the secretary of state and coordinator for combatting terrorism.

3304. **nollau, g.** wie sicher ist die bundesrepublik?. muenchen: 1976.

3305. **novogrod, j. c.** internal strife, self-determination and world order. in: m. c. bassiouni * (ed.), international terrorism and political crimes. springfield, ill.: thomas, 1975. pp. 98-119.

3306. **pedersen, f. c.** comment - controlling international terrorism: an analysis of unilateral forces and proposals for multilateral cooperation.: 1976. pp. 209-250 university of toledo law review 8:1.

3307. **peijster, c. n.** politiek terrorisme en de verdediging van de demokratische rechtsstaat. pp. 216-222 civis mundi 5.

3308. **pierre, a. j.** coping with international terrorism.: 1976. p. 61 survival 18:2.

3309. **pop, j. m. m.** enkele juridische aspecten bij de bestrijding van terreuracties.: 20 dec. * 1974. intermediair 51.

3310. **radliffe, j.** the insurance companies' response to terrorism. in y. alexander and r. a. kilmarx * (eds.), political terrorism and business: the threat and response. new york: praeger, 1979. pp. 265-276.

3311. **rose, r. n.** preventive measures against terrorists by the swedish police. washington, d. c,: law enforcement assistance administration, national criminal justice reference service, 1976. 7 pp.

3312. **rosenfield, s. b.** air piracy - is it time to relax our security?. in: j. s. schultz and j. p. thames * (eds.). criminal justice systems review. buffalo, n. y.: william s. hein, 1974. pp. 67-94.

3313. rosenthal, u. governmental decision-making in crises: cases of south moluccan terrorism. alphen a. d. rijn: samson, in dutch, forthcoming.

3314. rosenthal, u. terreurbestrijding in nederland: vijf thema's.: 1979. pp. 251-265 tijdschrift v. d. politie.

3315. roukis, s. * montana, p. j. * (eds.). managing terrorism: strategies for the corporate executive. westport, conn.: greenwood press, 1982.

3316. russell, ch. a. * banker jr., l. j. * miller, b. h. out-inventing the terrorist. in: y. alexander, d. carlton, and p. wilkinson * (eds.), terrorism: theory and practice. boulder, colo.: westview, 1979. pp. 3-42.

3317. russell, ch. a. * miller, b. h. terrorism, tactics and the corporate target. in: y. alexander and r. a. kilmarx * (eds.), political terrorism and business: the threat and response. new york: praeger, 1979. pp. 106-119.

3318. salewski, w. * lanz, p. die neue gewalt und wie ihr begegnet. locarno: droemer knaur verlag, 1978. 224 pp. salewski, a former police psychologist and adviser to the german govt. in matters of terrorism, describes 'the new violence and how to cope with it'.

3319. schmidt, h. erklaerung der bundesregierung zur inneren sicherheit und zur terrorismus bekaempfung.: , 22 april, 1977. pp. 361-365 bulletin des presse- und informationsamtes der bundesregierung 40.

3320. schutter, b. de. prospective study of the mechanisms to repress terrorism. in: reflections on the definition and repression of terrorism. brussels: institute of sociology of the free university of brussels, 1974. pp. 253-266.

3321. schwarz, h. die herausforderung des terrorismus. sicherheit nach innen und freiheitsrechte.: 1975. die politische meinung 20: 158.

3322. shaw, e. d. * et. al. analizing threats from terrorism. washington d. c.: caci, 29 april 1976.

3323. shaw, p. d. extortion threats: analytic techniques and resources.: 1975. pp. 5-16 assets protection 1:2.

3324. shultz jr., r. h. * sloan, s. responding to the terrorist threat. security and crisis management. new york: pergamon press, 1980.

3325. sirey, p. j. r. la repression internationale du terrorisme.: 1937. pp. 518-523 affaires etrangeres 7.

3326. sjaastad, a. c. deterrence of terrorism. norsk utenrikspolitisk institutt: 1975.

3327. sloan, s. * shultz jr., r. h. * (eds.). responding to the terrorist threat. security and crisis management. elmsford, n. y.: pergamon press, 1980.

3328. sloan, s. international terrorism: academic quest, operational art and policy implications.: 1978. pp. 1-6 journal of international affairs 32.

3329. sloan, s. simulating terrorism. norman: university of oklahoma press, 1981.

3330. sloan, s. simulating terrorism: from operational techniques to question of policy.: 1978. pp. 3-8 international studies notes 5.

3331. sulzberger, c. l. the antiterrorist league.: 14 apr. * 1976. p. 39 new york times.

3332. svensk polis. preventive measures against terrorists by the swedish police.: 1975. pp. 1-6 svensk polis 4 . s 1.

3333. tanham, g. * jenkins, b. m. * et. al. united states preparation for future low-level conflict.: 1978 . pp. 1-19 conflict:- an international journal for conflict and policy studies 1.

3334. tanter, r. * kaufman, l. terror and reprisal: process and choice. in: y. evron * (ed.), international violence: terrorism, surprise and control. jerusalem: hebrew university of jerusalem. leonard davis institute for international relations., pp. 203-230.

3335. terekhov, v. international terrorism and the fight against it.: 1974. pp. 20-22 new times 11.

3336. tomasevski, k. the united nations activities concerning the problem of terrorism.: 1980. pp. 61-76 archives of legal and social sciences 66:1-2 in croatian, with english summary.

3337. trent, d. m. a national policy to combat terrorism.: 197. pp. 1-13 policy review.

3338. tuckerman, a. u. n.: new look for 1972: debate on terrorism.: 2 oct. * 1972. p. 258 nation.

3339. u. s. congress, house. committee on the judiciary. federal capabilities in crisis management and terrorism. washington d. c.: gpo, 1978. 116 pp.

3340. u. s. congress, house. committee on the judiciary. federal capabilities in crisis management and terrorism. 95th cong. *2d sess.: 1979.

3341. u. s. congress, senate. committee on foreign relations. combatting international and domestic terrorism. . washington, d. c.: gpo, 1978. 119 pp.

3342. u. s. congress, senate. committee on the judiciary. west-germany's political response to terrorism. washington, d. c.: gpo, 1978. 23 pp.

3343. u. s. department of state. bureau of public affairs. office of media services. u. s. action to combat terrorism. washington, d. c.: gpo, 1973.

3344. u. s. department of transportation. federal aviation administration. u. s. efforts to deter hijacking. a presentation to foreign countries and airlines. washington, d. c.: f. a. a., 1970.

3345. u. s. private security advisory council. prevention of terroristic crimes. washington, d. c.: the administration, 1976.

3346. united nations. report of the ad hoc committee on international terrorism. new york: 1973.

3347. united nations. report of the ad hoc committee on international terrorism. new york: 1977.

3348. university of iowa. institute of public affairs. terrorism. part 1: the problem. part 2: the question of control. iowa city: .

3349. vinke, h. * witt, g. w. * (eds.). die anti-terror-debatten im parlament. protokolle 1974-1978. reinbek: rowohlt, 1978.

3350. vos, h. m. elementen voor een anti-terrorisme-ethiek.: febr. 1976. pp. 75-80 algemeen politieblad 125:4.

3351. wahl, j. responses to terrorism: self-defense or reprisal?.: 1973. pp. 28-33 international problems 5:1-2.

3352. waterman, d. a. * jenkins, b. m. heuristic modeling using rulebased computer systems. santa monica: rand, 1977. 53 pp. rand paper p- 5811.

3353. watson jr., f. m. political terrorism: how to combat it. new york: mckay, 1976.

3354. waugh, w. j. international terrorism: theories of response and national policies. ph. d. dissertation: university of mississippi,

3355. wermdalen, h. foeretagen och terrorismen. stockholm: foerfattares bokmaskin, 1977. 94 pp. on terrorism prevention for journalists.

3356. whitehead, d. attack on terror: the fbi against the ku klux klan in mississippi. new york: funk & wagnalls, 1970. 321 pp. written with the help of the fbi.

3357. wilferink, b. w. de internationale bestrijding van terrorisme. in: yearbook of volkenrechtelijk dispuut robert regout 1976/77. nijmegen: 1977.

3358. wilkinson, p. terrorism versus liberal democracy: the problems of response. london: institute for the study of powerand conflict, 1976. conflict studies 67.

3359. wilkinson, p. terrorism: the international response. london: chatham house, jan. 1978. pp. 5-13 the world today 34:1.

3360. wise, ch. * sloan, s. countering terrorism - united states and israeli approach.: 1977. pp. 55-59 middle east review 9:3.

3361. wolf, j. b. antiterrorism: objectives and operations. gaithersburg, md.: iacp, 1978.

3362. wolf, j. b. controlling political terrorism in a free society.: 1976. pp. 1289-1308 orbis: a journal of world affairs.

3363. wolf, j. b. strategic aspects of american anti-terrorist related intelligence activities. gaithersburg, md.: i. a. c. p., 1979. update report 5:6.

3364. wolf, j. b. target analysis. part ii: the essential component of anti-terrorist operations. gaithersburg, md.: iacp, 18 pp.

3365. young, r. * adams, j. case for detention. london: . 18pp. bow publications 19/4 argues for detentions of terrorists withouttrial in northern ireland.

S.1.1. Military and police

3366. ackroyd, c. * et. al. the technology of political control. harmondsworth: penguin, 1977. 320 pp. on british counter-insurgency techniques andtechnologies with special regard to northern ireland.

3367. adkins jr., e. h. protection of american industrial dignitaries and facilities overseas.: july 1974 . pp. 14, 16, 55 security management 18:3.

3368. alexander, y. * levine, h. m. prepare for the next entebbe. washington: . chitty's law journal 25:7.

3369. anderson, r. sidelights on the home rule movement. london: 1907. ireland and british police counter-measures against terrorists.

3370. applegate, r. * * (comp.). riot-control. material and techniques.: stackpole, 1969. widely used by the police around the world.

3371. applegate, r. * (comp.). kill or get killed. boulder, colo.: paladin press, 1976. a widely used book on suppression of unrest.

3372. barclay, c. n. countermeasures against the urban guerrilla.: jan. 1972. pp. 83-90 military review 52:1.

3373. beaumont, r. a. "military elite forces: surrogate war, terrorism, and the new battlefield".: march 1979. pp. 17-29 parameters, journal of the u. s. army war college 9.

3374. blechmann, b. m. the consequences of israeli reprisals. an assessment. ph. d. dissertation. washington d. c.: georgetown university, 1971.

3375. bourret, j. c. wie ein franzoesisches sonderkommando die in nov. 1979 besetzte moskee in mekka befreite. paris: editions france empire, 1981. cf. der spiegel, 22. 6. 81, pp. 144ff; on french nerve gasattack against the occupants of the holy shrine in mecca.

3376. bowden, t. men in the middle—the u. k. police. london: institute for the study of conflict, 1976.

3377. california office of emergency services. california - nuclear blackmail or nuclear threat: emergency response plan. sacramento, calif.: 1976. 40 pp. an officials' guide to emergency procedures.

3378. chase, l. j. * (ed.). bomb threats, bombings and civil disturbances: a guide for facility protection. corvallis, oregon: continuing education publications, 1971.

3379. clutterbuck, r. l. police and urban terrorism.: july 1975. pp. 204-214 police journal(england) 48.

3380. clutterbuck, r. l. the police and urban terrorism.: july 1975. outpost, magazine of b. s. a. police 53:7.

3381. cooper, h. h. a. evaluating the terrorist threat. principles of applied risk assessment. gaithersburg, md.: i. a. c. p., 22pp.

3382. dimitrijevic, v. nova konvencija za zastitu bezbednosti civilnog vazduhoplovstva.: 1971. pp. 551-562 anali pravnog fakulteta u beogradu.

3383. dodd, n. l. the corporal's war: internal security operations in northern ireland.: july 1976. pp. 58-68 military review 56.

3384. doss, s. r. defense planning for the 1980's and the changing international environment. washington, d. c.: 1975.

3385. dupuy, t. n. isolating the guerrilla. vol. iii: supporting case studies. washington, d. c.: hist. eval. and res. organization, 1 febr. 1966. distribution limitation now removed.

3386. elliott, j. d. contemporary terrorism and the police response.: febr. 1978. pp. 40-43 police chief 45.

3387. evans, r. d. brazil: the road back from terrorism. london: institute for the study of power and conflict, 1974. 18pp. conflict studies 47 concentrating on the 1969-72 government repression of urban guerrillas.

3388. fenello, m. j. technical prevention of air piracy.: 1971. pp. 28-41 international conciliation 585 .

3389. fraser, c. a. revolutionary warfare: basic principles of counterinsurgency. pretoria: 1968.

3390. galula, d. counterinsurgency warfare: theory and practice. new york: praeger, 1964.

3391. gennaro, g. de. la controguerriglia. fattori di successo.: 1966. pp. 1327-1334 rivista militar 22: 11.

3392. geraghty, t. who dares wins: the story of the special air services. london: arms and armour press, 1980. on british anti-terrorist unit s. a. s.

3393. greene, t. n. * (ed.). the guerrilla: and how to fight him. new york: praeger, 1962.

3394. gregory, f. protest and violence: the police response. a comparative analysis of democratic methods. london: institute for the study of conflict, 1976. 15 pp. conflict studies 75.

3395. haber, e. raid on entebbe. new york: delacorte press, 1977.

3396. ham, g. van. het moderne terrorisme en zijn bestrijdings-mogelijkheden. apeldoorn: nederlandse politie akademie, 1979. 101 pp.

3397. hermann, k. * koch, p. entscheidung in mogadishu. die 50 tage nach schleyers entfuehrung. dokumente, bilder, zeugen. hamburg: gruner und jahr, 1977. 248 pp.

3398. higham, r. * (ed.). bayonets in the streets; the use of troops in civil disturbances. lawrence: university of kansas press, 1969.

3399. hingley, r. die russische geheimpolizei 1565-1970. uebertr. aus dem engl. von r. schmitz. bayreuth : hestia, 1972. 399 pp. the russian secret police.

3400. hobsbawn, e. j. pentagon's dilemma: goliath and the guerrilla.: 10 july, 1975. pp. 20-21 nation.

3401. hoggart, s. the army pr men of northern ireland.: oct 1973. new society.

3402. hosmer, s. t. viet cong repression and its implications for the future. lexington: heath lexington books, 1970.

3403. illinois state police academy. anti-terrorism program. springfield, ill.: illlinois police academy, 1977.

3404. jenkins, b. m. soldiers versus gunmen. the challenge of urban guerilla warfare. santa monica, cal.: rand, 1974.

3405. kee, r. j. algiers - 1957. an approach to urban counter-insurgency.: 1974. pp. 73-84 military review 54:4.

3406. kitson, f. r. bunch of five. london: faber & faber, 1977. by counter-insurgency expert, describing his experience in kenya, malaya and cyprus.

3407. kitson, f. r. low intensity operations: subversion, insurgency, peacekeeping. london: faber, 1972. 208 pp. author is a counter-insurgency expert and reviews various experiences during the decolonization of the british empire.

3408. klare, m. t. supplying repression. new york: field foundation, 1977. on u. s. aid to 3rd world repressive regimes.

3409. kobetz, r. w. * cooper, h. h. a. target terrorism: providing protective services. gaithersburg, md.: international association of chiefs of police, 1978.

3410. koch, p. * hermann, k. assault at mogadishu. london: corgi books, 1977.

3411. krumm, k. h. probleme der organisation und koordination der terroristen-bekaempfung in der bundesrepublik.: 1977. aus politikund zeitgeschichte 41.

3412. kupperman, r. h. * et. al. an overview of counter-terrorism technology. washington, d. c.: acda, dec. 1977. classified report by the u. s. arms control and disarmament agency for the cabinet committee to combat terrorism and the national security council staff.

3413. laporte, m. histoire de l'okhrana. paris: 1935.

3414. leibstone, m. * evans, j. * shriver, r. countering terrorism on military installations. study prepared for the u. s. army: science applications, inc., july 1978.

3415. longuet, j. * zilber, g. les dessous de la police russe. paris: 1909.

3416. longuet, j. * zilber, g. terroristes et policiers. paris: 1909.

3417. lopez, v. c. what the u. s. army should do about urban guerrilla warfare. springfield, va.: national technical information service., 1975. 36 pp.

3418. mark, r. the office of constable.: 1978. on the london metropolitan police commissioner.

3419. mcdowell, ch. p. * harlan, j. p. police response to political crimes and acts of terrorism - some dimensions for consideration. toronto, canada: american society of criminology, 1975. 18 pp. annual meeting, 30 oct. -2 nov. * 1975.

3420. meulen, j. van der * (ed.). de bestrijding van terrorisme. in het bijzonder de rol van de krijgsmacht daarbij. stichting volk en verdediging: den haag, may 1979. 74 pp. kontaktbulletin 15:30 the fight against terrorism with particular emphasis on the role of the armed forces.

3421. meulen, j. van der. terrorisme en krijgsmacht.: sept. 1978. civis mundi.

3422. miller, a. h. implications from the police experience.: 1978. pp. 125-146 terrorism 1:2.

3423. moss, r. counter terrorism. london: 1972. economist brief books 29 claims that there is a need for specially trained police unit to respond to terrorists.

3424. moyer, f. a. police guide to bomb search techniques. boulder, colo.: paladin press, 200pp.

3425. n. n. aids to the detection of explosives. a brief review of equipment for searching out letter bombs and other explosie devices.: febr. 1975. pp. 48-49, 61 security gazette 17:2.

3426. n. n. fatal error: murder of a. bouchiki by israeli killers.: 6 aug. * 1973. pp. 31-32 time 102.

3427. n. n. the army line on northern ireland.: june 1979. pp. 97-98 state research bulletin 12.

3428. nikolajewski, b. asew. berlin: 1932. on the ochrana agent provocateur and russian terrorism before world war 1.

3429. o'ballance, e. israeli counter-guerrilla measures.: march 1972. journal of the united services institute for defence studies 117.

3430. ofer, y. operation thunder: the entebbe raid. the israeli's own story. harmondsworth: penguin, 1976. 141 pp.

3431. paget, j. counter-insurgency campaigning. london: faber & faber, 1967. 189 pp.

3432. paret, p. french revolutionary warfare from indo-china to algeria. london: pall mall, 1964.

3433. paust, j. j. entebbe and self-help : the israeli response to terrorism.: jan. 1978. the fletcher forum 2:1.

3434. perkus, c. cointelpro: the fbi's secret war on political freedom. new york: monad press, 1975.

3435. piekalkiewicz, j. israels langer arm. geschichte der israelischen geheimdienste und kommandounternehmen. frankfurt a. m.: goverts, 1975. 407 pp.

3436. price, d. l. ulster-consensus and coercion. part 2. security force attrition tactics.: oct. 1974. pp. 7-24 conflict studies 50.

3437. pustay, j. s. counterinsurgency warfare. new york: freepress, 1965.

3438. rabe, r. the police response to terrorism,. in: y. alexander and r. a. kilmarx * (eds.), political terrorism and business: the threat and response. new york: praeger, 1979. pp. 307-330.

3439. rapoport, d. c. the government is up in the air over combatting terrorism.: 26 nov. * 1977. pp. 1853-1856 national journal 9.

3440. roberts, k. e. terrorism and the military response. carlisle barracks, pa: army war college strategic studies institute, october, 1975.

3441. roberts, k. e. terrorism and the military response. military issues research memo: 14 oct. * 1975. 23 pp. this research memorandum discusses the terrorist threat to the u. s. * with emphasis on the fact that the u. s. military has increasingly been a target of terrorist activity.

3442. schiff, z. * haber, e. * ben-porat, y. entebbe rescue. new york: dell, 1977.

3443. schonborn, k. dealing with violence. the challenge faced by police and other peace-keepers. springfield, ill.: 1975.

3444. tanham, g. * et. al. united states preparation for future low-level conflict.: 1978. conflict 1:1.

3445. thompson, ch. r. defeating communist insurgency. london: chatto and windus, 1966. by a british counter-insurgency specialist in malaya.

3446. tophoven, r. der internationale terrorismus. herausforderung und abwehr.: 1977. pp. 28-38 aus politik und zeitgeschichte 6.

3447. tophoven, r. die israelischen konterguerillas. israels kampf gegen die fedayin.: 1974. pp. 33-44 wehrforschung 2.

3448. tophoven, r. gsg 9 - kommando gegen terrorismus. bonn: wehr & wissen, 1978. 96 pp.

3449. tophoven, r. gsg 9 - operation - mogadishu. feuertaufe der spezialeinheit.: 1977. pp. 13-17 wehrtechnik 11.

3450. tophoven, r. zahal in entebbe. anmerkungen zur psyche einer armee.: 1977. wehrwissenschaft-liche rundschau 1.

3451. u. s. army institute. department of defense guidance document on protection of maag/msn/mil personnel and installations against terrorism. fort bragg, n. c.: u. s. army institute for military assistance., april 1975. 116 pp.

3452. vasilyev, a. t. the okhrana. london: 1930.

3453. wilkinson, p. adaptation for the struggle against terrorism of international co-operation between the police and security services. paper presented at the council of europe conferenceon the defence of democracy against terrorism in europe, november, 1980.: 1980.

3454. williamson, t. counterstrike entebbe. london: collins, 1976. 184 pp.

3455. wolf, j. b. analytical framework for the study and control of agitational terrorism.: july 1976. pp . 165-171 police journal 49:3.

3456. wolf, j. b. anti-terrorism and west german police operations. gaithersburg, md.: i. a. c. p., 1978. update report 4:4.

3457. wolf, j. b. anti-terrorism: operations and controls in a free society. pp. 35-41 policestudies: the international review of police development 1:3.

3458. wolf, j. b. anti-terrorism: technological, corporate and personal considerations. gaithersburg, md.: i . a. c. p., 1980. update report 6:2.

3459. wolf, j. b. counter-terrorism and open societies. counterforce: the monthly newsmagazine on terrorism 11/1977-2/1978.

3460. wolf, j. b. enforcement terrorism.: 1981. pp. 45-54 police studies: the international review of police development 3:4.

3461. wolf, j. b. intelligence operations and terrorism. gaithersburg, md.: international association of chiefs of police, 1981. update report, 7:1.

3462. wolf, j. b. police intelligence - focus for counter-terr0rist operations.: january, 1976. pp. 19-27 the police journal 49:1.

3463. wolf, j. b. prison, courts and terrorism: the american and west german experience.: july, 1977. pp. 211-230 the police journal 51:3.

3464. wolf, j. b. urban terrorist operations.: october, 1976. pp. 227-284 the police journal 49:4.

S.1.2. Legal

3465. andrews, j. the eurpean convention on the suppression of terrorism.: 1977. pp. 323-326 european law review 2.

3466. aston, c. c. international legislation against politioal terrorism. in: political terrorism: a united nations association special report ed. by a. martin.: march, 1980.

3467. aston, c. c. the un convention against the taking of hostages: realistic or rhetoric?.: dec. 1980. terrorism: an international journal 5:1-2.

3468. barber, ch. t. sanctions against modern transnational crimes. bloomington, indiana: conference on new directions in international relations teaching and research., may, 1976. 28 pp.

3469. bassiouni, m. c. international extradition and world public order. dobbs ferry: oceana, 1974.

3470. bassiouni, m. c. the political offense exception in extradition law and practice. in: his international terrorism and political crimes. springfield, ill.: thomas, 1975. pp. 398-447.

3471. baudouin, j. l. * fortin, j. * szabo, d. terrorisme et justice;entre la liberte et l'ordre: le crime politique. môntreal: editions du jour, 1970. 175 pp.

3472. bekes, i. the legal problems of hijacking and taking of hostages. in: m. livingston * et. al. * (eds.) , international terrorism in the contemporary world. westport, conn.: greenwood press, 1978. pp. 346-353.

3473. bennet jr., w. t. u. s. initiatives in the united nations to combat international terrorism.: 1973. pp. 752-760 international lawyer 7:4.

3474. bennett, r. l. u. s. initiatives in the united nations to combat international terrorism.: 1973. pp . 753-759 international lawyer 7.

3475. bennett, w. t. u. s. outlines principles for work of ad hoc committee on terrorism.: 3 september 1973. pp. 337-339 department of state bulletin.

3476. bennett, w. t. u. s. votes against u. n. general assembly resolution calling for study of terrorism.: , 22 jan. 1973. pp. 81-94 department of state bulletin.

3477. bik, r. g. c. het europees verdrag tot bestrijding van terrorisme, 27 januari 1977. skriptie nederlandse politie akademie. apeldoorn: febr 1978. 47 pp.

3478. blishchenko, i. p. * zhdanov, n. v. combatting terrorism by international law.: 1976. pp. 81-96 soviet law and government 14:3.

3479. blum, y. z. state response to acts of terrorism.: 1976. pp. 223-237 german yearbook of international law.

3480. boyle, r. p. * pulsifer, r. the tokyo convention on offenses and certain other acts committed on board aircraft.: 1964. pp. 305-354 journal of air law and commerce 30.

3481. boyle, r. p. international action to combat aircraft hijacking.: 1972. pp. 460-473 lawyer of the americas 4.

3482. brach, r. s. the inter-american convention on the kidnapping of diplomats.: 1971. pp. 392-412 columbia journal of transnational law 10.

3483. brandt, w. internationale massnahme gegen terror und gewalt. feststellungen vor dem bundeskabinett, 31. 10. 1972.: 1972. pp. 1817-1818 bulletin. presse- und informationsamt der bundesregierung 153.

3484. caloyanni, m. a. le terrorisme et la creation d'une cour repressive internationale.: 1935. pp. 46 ff revue dedroit international 15.

3485. child, r. b. concepts of political prisonerhood.: 1974. pp. 1-33 new england journal on prison law 1.

3486. council of europe. european convention on the suppression of terrorism. strasbourg: council of europe , 27 jan 1977. 9 pp. european treaty series 90.

3487. council of europe. explanatory report on the european convention on the suppression of terrorism. strasbourg: council of europe, 1977. 30 pp.

3488. dershowitz, a. m. terrorism and preventive detention: the case of israel.: 1970. pp. 3-14 commentary 50:6.

3489. dewar, m. internal security weapons and equipment of the world. charles scriber's sons: 1979, on repression technology.

3490. diplock, l. report of the commission to consider legal procedures to deal withterrorist activities in northern ireland. london: h. m. s. o., 1972. 42 pp.

3491. donnedieu de vabres, h. la repression internationale du terrorisme. les conventions degeneve.: 1938. pp. 37-74 revue de droit international et de legislation comparee 19.

3492. dumas, j. de l'urgence d'un accord international contre les actes de terrorisme.: 1935. pp. 281-287, 343-348 la paix par le droit 45.

3493. dumas, j. du fondement juridique de l'entraide internationale pour la repression du terrorisme.: 1935. pp. 609-640 revue de droit international et de legislation comparee 16.

3494. elwin, g. swedish anti-terrorist legislation. amsterdam: july 1977. pp. 289-301 contemporary crises 1.

3495. emanuelli, c. les moyens de prevenion et de sanction en cas d'action illicite contre l'aviation civile internationale. paris: 1974. 160 pp.

3496. eustathiades, c. la cour penale internationale pour la repression du terrorisme et le probleme de la responsabilite internationale des etats.: 1936. pp. 385-415 revue generale de droit international public 43.

3497. evans, a. e. aircraft hijacking: its cause and cure.: 1969. pp. 695-710 american journal of international law 63.

3498. evans, a. e. aircraft hijacking: what is being done.: oct. 1973. pp. 641-671 american journal of international law 67.

3499. feraud, h. j. la convention de montreal du 23 septembre 1971 pour la repression d'actes illicites diriges contre la securite de l'aviation civile.: 1972. pp. 1-29 revue de science criminelle et de droit penalcompare 1.

3500. fitzgerald, g. f. offences and certain other acts committed on board aircraft: the tokyo convention of 1963.: 1964. pp. 191-204 canadian yearbook of international law 2.

3501. fitzgerald, g. f. toward legal suppression of acts against civil aviation.: 1971. pp. 42-78 international conciliation 585.

3502. franck, th. m. international legal action concerning terrorism.: 1978. pp. 187-197 terrorism 1.

3503. frank, t. m. * lockwood, b. b. preliminary thoughts towards an international convention on terrorism.: , 1974. pp. 69-90 american journal of international law 68:1.

3504. friedlander, r. a. coping with terrorism: what is to be done?.: 1978. pp. 432-443 ohio northern university law review 5.

3505. friedlander, r. a. terrorism: documents of international and local control, 1977-1978. oceana: 1978. .

3506. friedlander, r. a. terrorism: what's behind our passive acceptance of transnational mugging?.: 1975. pp. 10-71 barrister 2.

3507. gaynes, j. b. bringing the terrorist to justice. a domestic law approach.: 1978. pp. 71-84 cornell international law journal 11:1 on international extradiction ofpolitical offenders.

3508. ginzburg, n. la lutte contre le terrorisme. revue de droitpenal et de criminologie et archives internationales de medicine legale 15.

3509. golsong, h. la convention europeenne pour la repression du terrorisme; clarifications et precisions sur le droit d'asile.: jan. 1978. p. 3 le monde diplomatique.

3510. golsong, h. the european convention on the suppression of terrorism: provocation or instrument of peace?.: 1977. pp. 5-7 forward in europe 1.

3511. green, l. c. international law and the suppression of terrorism. g. w. bartholomew * (ed.).: 1975. malaya law review legal essays.

3512. green, l. c. the legalization of terrorism. in: y. alexander, d. carlton, p. wilkinson * (eds.), terrorism: theory and practice. boulder: westview, 1979. pp. 175-197.

3513. hirano, r. convention on offences and certain other acts committed on board aircraft of 1963.: 1964. pp. 44-52 japanese annual of international law 8.

3514. hirsch, a. i. * otis, d. aircraft piracy and extradition.: 1970. pp. 392-419 new york law forum 16 .

3515. holden, a. how much use is our anti-terrorist law?.: 2 nov. * 1975. p. 6 sunday times.

3516. hruska, r. l. aircraft piracy amendments of 1972; remarks in the senate.: 15 febr. * 1973. pp. s1183-a1186 congressional record(daily ed.) 119.

3517. ingraham, b. political crime in europe: a comparative study of france, germany,and england. berkeley: university of california press, 1979.

3518. inter-american judicial committee. draft protocol on terrorism.: 1970. p. 1177 international legal materials 9.

3519. jack, h. a. terrorism: another u. n. failure.: 20 oct. 1973. pp. 282-285 america.

3520. janke, p. international drive to curb terrorism. an enlarged reference book, 1976-77 london: 1977. the annual of power and conflict.

3521. kalmthout, a. van * fillet, h. uit franco's nalatenschap: decreto ley 10/1975. de agosto, sobre prevencion del terrorismo.: march 1976. pp. 121-135 ars aequi 25:3 spain.

3522. keijzer, n. het europees verdrag tot bestrijding van terrorisme. deventer: kluwer, 1979. 36 pp.

3523. kos-rabcewicz zubkowksi, l. the creation of an international criminal court. in: m. c. bassiouni * (ed .), international terrorism and political crimes. springfield, ill.: thomas, 1975. pp. 519-536.

3524. kos-rabcewicz zubkowski, l. essential features of an international criminal court. in: m. livingston * et. al. * (eds.), international terrorism in the contemporary world. westport, conn.: greenwood press, 1978. pp. 333-340.

3525. kutner, l. constructive notice: a proposal to end international terrorism.: 1973. pp. 325-350 new york law forum 19.

3526. league of nations. international conference on the repression of terrorism, geneva, 1937. proceedings of the international conference on the repression of terrorism, geneva, nov. 1st-16th, 1937. geneva: 1938. 218 pp.

3527. leaute, j. terrorist incidents and legislation in france. in r. d. crelinsten, d. laberge-altmejd, and d. szabo * (eds.), terrorism and criminal justice: an international perspective. lexington, mass.: lexington books, heath, 1978.

3528. lissitzyn, o. j. international control of aerial hijacking: the role of values and interests.: 1971 . pp. 80-86 proceedings of the american society of international law.

3529. litvin, m. aircraft security and the repression of terrorism.: oct. 1976. pp. 50-60 revue de droit penal et de criminologie 1.

3530. lopez gutierrez, j. j. should the tokyo convention of 1963 be ratified?.: 1965. pp. 1-21 journal of air law and commerce 31.

3531. loy, f. e. some international approaches to dealing with hijacking of aircraft.: 1970. pp. 444-452 international lawyer 4.

3532. mallison jr., w. t. * mallison, s. v. an international law appraisal of the juridical characteristics of the resistance of the people of palestine. the struggle for human rights. in: m. c. bassiouni(ed.), international terrorism and political crimes, mallison, s. v. springfield, ill.: thomas, pp. 173-190.

3533. mallison jr., w. t. * mallison, s. v. the concept of public purpose terror in international law: doctrines and sanctions to reduce the destruction of human and material values. in: m. c. bassiouni * (ed.), international terrorism and political crimes. springfield, ill.: thomas, 1975. pp. 67-85.

3534. malmborg, k. e. new developments in the law of international aviation: the controlof aerial hijacking. .: 1971. pp. 75-80 proceedings of the american society of international law.

3535. mankiewicz, r. h. the 1970 hague convention. journal ofair law and commerce 37.

3536. maul, h. gesetz gegen terrorismus und rechtsstaat.: 1977. deutsche richterzeitung 55:7.

3537. mckeithen-smith, r. l. prospects for the preventing of aircraft hijacking through law.: 1970. pp. 61-80 columbia journal of transnational law 9:1.

3538. mcmahon, j. p. air hijacking: extradition as a deterrent.: 1970. pp. 1135-1152 georgetown law journal 58.

3539. meyer, a. der begriff "terrorismus" im lichte der eroerterungen auf dem fuenften kongress der vereinigten nationen betr. die verhuetung von verbrechenund die behandlung von verbrechern in genf, 1, bis 12. 9. 1975.: 1976. pp. 223-233 zeitschrift fuer luftrecht und weltraumrechtsfragen 25:3.

3540. meyers, l. europees verdrag tot bestrijding van terrorisme.: july 1977. pp. 321-327 tijdschrift voor de politie 39:7-8.

3541. mickolus, e. f. multilateral legal efforts to combat terrorism: diagnosis and prognosis.: 1979. 13- 51 ohio northern university law review 6.

3542. migliorino, l. international terrorism in the united nations debates.: 1976. pp. 102-121 italian yearbook of international law 2.

3543. mok, m. r. de strijd tegen de luchtpiraterij.: 1973. pp. 837, 839 nederlands juristenblad.

3544. mok, m. r. het europees verdrag tot bestrijding van het terrorisme.: 16 july, 1977. pp. 665-671 nederlands juristenblad 22.

3545. moore, j. n. toward legal restraints on international terrorism.: 1973. pp. 88-94 american journal of international law 67:5.

3546. munck, l. de * (ed.). het internationaal politiek terrorisme.: 1979. 76 pp. kib vizier 2:2-3.

3547. murphy, j. united nations proposals on the control and repression of terrorism. in: m. c. bassiouni * (ed.), international terrorism and political crimes. (. springfield, ill.: thomas, 1975. pp. 493-506.

3548. murphy, j. f. prof. gross's comments on international terrorism and international criminal jurisdiction.: april 1974. pp. 306-308 american journal of international law 68:2.

3549. n. n. a study of the applicability of the laws of war to guerrillas and those individuals who advocate guerrilla warfare and subversion. washington, d. c.: u. s. army, office of the judgeadvocate general, 1972.

3550. n. n. american draft convention on terrorism.: 1973. survival 15:1.

3551. n. n. anti-terrordebatten, die, im parlament. protokolle- 1974-1978. reinbek: rowohlt, 1978.

3552. n. n. approaches to the problems of international terrorism. symposium, 10: 1976. p. 483 journal of international labor and economics 10.

3553. n. n. convention to prevent and punish acts of terrorism. note: 1971. p. 898 american journal of international law 65.

3554. n. n. der buerger ruft nach haerteren strafen. sondergesetze fuer terroristen - todesstrafe fuer geiselnehmer?.: 1977. pp. 26-33 spiegel 31:39.

3555. n. n. documenti: convenzione europea sulla repressione del terrorismo. strasburgo, 10 november 1976.: , april 1977. rivista di studi politici internazionali 44:2.

3556. n. n. la notion de terrorisme en droit compare. in: reflexions sur la definition et la repression du terrorisme. brussels: editions de l'universite de bruxelles, 1974. pp. 229-239.

3557. n. n. law enforcement faces the revolutionary-guerrilla criminal.: dec. 1970. pp. 20-22, 28 fbi law enforcement bulletin 39:12.

3558. n. n. measures for protecting public order. especially against terrorists.: nov. 1975. pp. 705-722 rivista di polizia 28:11 article, in italian, analysing the applicationof laws for combatting terrorism.

3559. n. n. regering over gijzeling; beklemmende vragen van recht en gerechtigheid.: 12 oct. * 1974. p. 1113 nederlands juristenblad 49:34.

3560. n. n. terrorism and political crimes in international law.: nov. 1973. pp. 87-111 american journal of international law 67.

3561. n. n. terrorism: the proposed u. s. draft convention.: 1973. p. 430 georgia journal of international and comparative law 3.

3562. n. n. the convention for the prevention and punishment of terrorism.: 1938. p. 214 british yearbook of international law 19.

3563. n. n. the i. c. a. o. and arab terrorist operations. a record of resolutions. jerusalem: ministry for foreign affairs, 1973.

3564. n. n. the role of international law in combatting terrorism.: january 1973. pp. 1-7 current foreign policy.

3565. n. n. the terrorism act of south africa.: june 1968. pp. 28-34 bulletin of the international commission of jurists.

3566. n. n. the united nations response to terrorism. in: y. alexander and r. a. kilmarx * (eds.), political terrorism and business: the threat and response. new york: praeger, 1979. pp. 428-490.

3567. n. n. wetgeving inzake terreur. beknopt rechtsvergelijkend onderzoek op het gebied van de wetgeving betreffende de preventie of bestrijding van terreur in een aantal westerse democratieen. nijmegen: katholieke universiteit, 1976. 53pp.

3568. nagel, w. h. het europees verdrag over de bestrijding van terrorisme van 27 januari 1977.: 24 sept. * 1977. nederlands juristenblad 32.

3569. panzera, a. f. postal terrorism and international law.: 1975. pp. 762-765 revista di diritto internazionale 48.

3570. paust, j. j. a survey of possible legal responses to international terrorism: prevention, punishment and cooperative action.: 1975. pp. 431-469 georgia journal of international and comparative law 5.

3571. paust, j. j. responses to terrorism: a prologue to decision concerning measuresof sanction.: 1977. pp. 79-130 stanford journal of international studies 12.

3572. pella, v. v. la repression du terrorisme et la creation d'une cour internationale., p. 120.: 1939. p. 785 5 -6.

3573. pella, v. v. les conventions de geneve pour la prevention et la repression du terrorisme et pour la creation de la cour penale internationale.: 1938. pp. 409-453 revue de droit penal et de criminologie et archives internationales de medicine legale 18.

3574. pels, m. europees verdrag en bestrijding van terrorisme. pp. 19-24 kriminologenkrant 28.

3575. philipp, o. m. internationale massnahmen zur bekaempfung von handlungen gegen diesicherheit der zivilluftfahrt. berlin: duncker und humbolt, 1977. 154 pp.

3576. poulantzas, n. m. the hague convention for the suppression of unlawful seizure of aircraft [16 dec. * 1970].: 1971. pp. 25-75 nederlands tijdschrift voor internationaal recht 18:1.

3577. pulsifer, r. * boyle, r. the tokyo convention on offences and certain other acts committed on board aircraft.: 1964. pp . 305-354 journal of air law and commerce 20.

3578. radvanyi, m. anti-terrorist legislation in the frg. washington, d. c.: library of congress lawlibrary, 1979. 140 pp.

3579. rafat, a. control of aircraft hijacking: the law of international civil aviation.: 1971. pp. 143-156 world affairs 134.

3580. rogers, w. p. u. s. and cuba reach agreement on hijacking.: 5 march 1973. pp. 260-262 department of state bulletin.

3581. roux, j. a. le projet de convention internationale pour la repression des crimes presentant un danger public.: 1935. pp. 99-130 revue internationale de droit penal 12.

3582. rovine, a. w. the contemporary international legal attack on terrorism.: 1973. pp. 3-38 israel yearbook on human rights 3.

3583. roxin, c. strafprozessordnung. gerichtsverfassungs-vorschriften. mit denneuen bestimmungen zur bekaempfung des terrorismus.: 1976. dtv - beck texte 580.

3584. rubin, a. p. terrorism and social control.: 1979. pp. 60-69 ohio northern university law review 6.

3585. russell, ch. a. * banker jr., l. j. * miller, b. h. out inventing the terrorist. in: u. s. congress, senate. committee on governmental affairs. an act to combat international terrorism. report to accompany s-2236. 95th cong. * 2nd sess. washington, d. c.: gpo, 1978. pp. 372-430(appendix f).

3586. samuels, a. crimes committed on board aircraft: tokyo convention act, 1967.: 1967. pp. 271-277 british yearbook of international law 42.

3587. schloesing, e. la repression internationale du terrorisme.: april 1973. p. 50 revue politique et parlementaire 841.

3588. shearer, i. a. extradition in international law. manchester: manchester university press, 1971. 283 pp.

3589. smith, c. l. probable necessity of an international prison in solving aircraft hijacking.: 1971. pp . 269-278 international lawyer 5.

3590. smith, m. prospects for the prevention of aircraft hijacking through law.: 1970. pp. 60-80 columbia journal of transnational law 9.

3591. stein, t. die europaeische konvention zur bekaempfung des terrorismus.: 1977. pp. 668-684 zeitschrift fuer auslaendisches oeffentliches recht und voelkerrecht. 37:3-4.

3592. stratton, j. g. the terrorist act of hostage-taking. considerations of lawenforcement.: june 1978. pp. 123-134 journalof police science and administration.

3593. street, h. the prevention of terrorism(temporary provisions) act 1974.: april 1975. pp. 192-199 criminal law review.

3594. sundberg, j. w. f. antiterrorist legislation in sweden. in: m. livingston * et. al. * (eds.), international terrorism in the contemporary world. westport, conn.: greenwood press, 1978. pp. 111-121.

3595. sundberg, j. w. f. the wisdom of treaty making: a glance at the machinery behind the production of law-making treaties and a case study of the hague hijacking conference of 970.: 1972. pp. 285-306 scandinavian studies in law.

3596. taulbee, j. l. ret. aliation and irregular warfare in contemporary international law. chicago: january 1973. international lawyer 7.

3597. tharp, p. s. the laws of war as a potential legal regime for the control of terrorist activities.: 1978. pp. 91-100 journal of international affairs 32.

3598. tiewul, s. a. terrorism: a step towards international control.: 1973. p. 585 harvard international law journal 14.

3599. u. s. congress, house. committee on foreign affairs. problems of protecting civilians under international law in the middle east conflict. washington, d. c.: gpo, 1974.

3600. u. s. congress, house. committee on the judiciary. implementing international conventions against terrorism. report together with dissenting views to accompany h. r. 15552. 94th congr. *2nd sess. washington, d. c. : gpo, 1976. 16 pp.

3601. u. s. congress, senate. committee on governmental affairs. an act to combat international terrorism. hearings 95th c washington d. c.: gpo, 1978. 1190 pp.

3602. u. s. congress, senate. committee on governmental affairs. an act to combat international terrorism. report to accompany s. 2236. 23 may, 1978. 95th cong. * 2nd sess. washington, d. c.: gpo, 1978. 430 pp. report no . 95-908.

3603. u. s. department of state. convention to prevent and punish the acts of terrorism taking the form of crimes against persons and related extortion that are of international significance.: 22 febr. * 1971. the department of state bulletin 64:1652.

3604. u. s. department of state. current foreign policy: role of international law in combatting terrorism. washington, d. c.: gpo, 1973.

3605. u. s. department of state. the role of international law in combatting terrorism. washington, d. c.: gpo ,

3606. united nations. causes and preventions of international terrorism. comments of member states on the question of the protection and inviolability of diplomaticagents and other persons entitled to special protection under international law.: united nations., november 1972. united nations study a/c 6/418, corr 1 add 1.

3607. united nations. convention for the suppression of the unlawful seizure of aircraft, the hague, 16 dec. 1970.: 2 nov. 1972. a/c 6/418 annex 3.

3608. united nations. convention for the suppression of unlawful acts against the safetyof civil aviation, montreal, 23 sept. 1971. a/c. 6/418 annex 4,.: 2 nov. 1972.

3609. united nations. convention on offenses and certain other acts committed on board aircraft, tokyo, 14 sept. 1963.: 2 nov. 1972. a/c. 6/418 annex 2.

3610. united nations. convention on the prevention and punishment of crimes against internationally protected persons, including diplomatic agents. ga res. 3166, 28 u. n. gaor supp. (no. 30), u. n. doc. a/9030 <1973>: 1973. pp. 91-95 department of state bulletin 70.

3611. united nations. general assembly resolution on terrorism: final text and member votes. u. n. a/res/3034(xxvii): 18 dec. 1972.

3612. united nations. league of nations convention for the prevention and punishment of terrorism, geneva, 16 nov. 1937.: 2 nov. 1972. a/c 6/418 annex 1.

3613. united nations. legal committee report on the terrorism issue.: 16 dec. 1972. a/8069.

3614. united nations. state responsibility to deter, prevent or suppress skyjacking activities in their territory, 1970. a/res/2645(xxv),.: 25 nov. 1970.

3615. united nations. the general assembly resolution on terrorism: the final text and member votes.: 18 dec. 1972. a/res/3034 (xxvii).

3616. united nations. u. n. draft resolution on terrorism submitted by the united states. un: a/c/ 6/1. * 850: 25 sept. 1972.

3617. united nations. u. n. general assembly. report of the ad hoc committee on internaional terrorism. gaor 28th sess. * supplement no. 28(a/9028): 1973.

3618. vabres, h. d. de. la repression internationale du terrorisme; les conventions degeneve.: 1938. pp. 37-74 revue de droit international et de legislation comparee 19.

3619. weis, p. asylum and terrorism.: december 1977. pp 37-43 international commission of jurists review.

3620. white, g. m. e. the hague convention for the suppression of unlawful seizure of aircraft.: 1971. pp. 38-45 international commiss of jurists review 6.

3621. wilkinson, p. problems of establishing a european judicial area. paper presented at the council of europe conferenceon the defence of democracy against terrorism in europe, november, 1980.: 1980.

3622. williams, m. * chatterjee, s. j. suggesting remedies for international terrorism. use of availableinternation. means. london: nov. 1976. pp. 1069-1093 international relations 5:4.

3623. wood, m. the convention on the prevention and punishment of crimes against internationally protected persons, including diplomatic agents.: 1974. p. 791 international and comparative law quarterly.

3624. yamamoto, s. the japanese enactment for the suppression of unlawful seizure of aircraft ad international law.: 1971. pp . 70-80 japanese annual of international law 15.

3625. zotiades, g. b. the international criminal prosecution of persons charged withan unlawful seizure of aircraft.: 1970. pp. 12-37 revue hellenique de droit international 23:1-4.

S.1.3. Hostage saving measures

3626. beall,(marshall) d. hostage negotations.: 1976. military police law enforcement journal 111.

3627. ben-porat, y. * haber, e. * schiff, z. entebbe rescue. new york: dell, 1976. 347 pp.

3628. bennett, j. p. * saaty, t. l. terrorism: patterns for negotiations. three case studies through hierarchies and holarchies.: the wharton school, university of pennsylvania, august 1977.

3629. bolz jr., f. a. detective bureau hostage negotiating team. new york,: n. y. city police department, 1975 .

3630. cooper, h. h. a. hostage negotiations. options and alternatives. gaithersburg, md.: international association of chiefs of police(i. a. c. p.), 65 pp.

3631. cooper, h. h. a. hostage rescue operations: denouement at algeria and mogadishu compared.: march 1978. pp. 91-103 chitty'slaw journal 26.

3632. cooper, h. h. a. kidnapping. how to avoid it, how to survive it. gaithersburg, md.: i. a. c. p., 19pp.

3633. crelinsten, r. d. * laberge-altmejd, d. * (eds.). hostage taking: problems of prevention and control. montreal: international centre for comparative criminology, 1976. final report on management training seminar.

3634. gelb, b. a cool-headed cop who saves hostages.: 17 april 1977. pp. 30-33, 39-91 new york times magazine.

3635. international association of chiefs of police. hostage negotiation - training key no. 235. gaithersburg, maryland: iacp, 1976. 5 pp.

3636. kobetz, r. w. * cooper, h. h. a. hostage rescue operations and teaching the unteachable.: june 1979. pp. 24-27 police chief.

3637. kobetz, r. w. * goldaber, i. checklist for tactics and negotiation techniques in hostage incident responses. gaithersburg, md.: iacp, 1975.

3638. kobetz, r. w. hostage incidents: the new police priority.: march 1975. police chief 45.

3639. kobetz, r. w. hostages: tactics and negotiation techniques. au of chiefs of police since 1968.

3640. maher, g. f. hostage. a police approach to a contemporary crisis. springfield, ill.: charles l. thomas, 1977.

3641. maher, g. f. organizing a team for hostage negotiation.: june 1976. pp. 61-62 police chief 43:6 discusses nassau county, n. j. * police training methods.

3642. mcclure, b. hostage survival.: 1978. pp. 21-48 conflict: an international journal for conflict and policy studies 1.

3643. mcclure, b. hostage survival. paper, glassboro. n. j. * international symposium on terrorism in the contemporary world, 26-28 apr. *1976: 1976. 11 pp.

3644. mickolus, e. f. negotiating for hostages: a policy dilemma.: 1976. pp. 1309-1325 orbis 19:4 reprinted in j. d. elliott and l. gibson, *(eds.) contemporary tdrrorism: selected readings, gaithersburg, maryland: international association of chiefs of police, 1978, pp. 207-221.

3645. mickolus, e. f. negotiating for hostages: a policy dilemma. philadelphia: 1970. pp. 1309-1325 orbis 19:4.

3646. n. n. hostage negotiations.: oct. 1974. pp 10-14 fbi law enforcement bulletin 43:10 on the new york city hostage negotiatingteam.

3647. n. n. patience sieges: dealing with hostage-takers.: 1976. pp. 21-27 assets protection 1:3 hostage - taking incidents in the netherlands, great britain, usa and ireland recounted; reviews methods used by governments in dealing with hostage situations.

3648. needham, j. p. neutralization of prison hostage situations. huntsville, texas: institute of contemporary corrections and the behavioral sciences, sam houston state university, 1977. 48 pp.

3649. new york city police department. technical manual for hostage situations. mimeo new york: .

3650. reber, j. r. * singer, l. w. * watson, f. m. hostage survival.: aug. 1978. pp. 46-50 security management.

3651. schlossberg, h. * freeman, l. psychologist with a gun. new york: 1974. on new york city police department's hostage negotiations team.

3652. silverstein, m. e. emergency medical preparedness.: 1977. pp. 51-69 terrorism 1:1 on terrorism victims.

3653. u. s. congress, senate. committee on the judiciary. hearings. terroristic activity. part 5: hostage defense measures. washington, d. c.: gpo, 1975. pp. 261-317 94thcong. * 1st sess. * july 25, 1975.

3654. wilkinson, p. admissiability of negotiations between organs of the democratic states and terrorists. paper presented at the councilof europe conference on the defence of democracy against terrorism in europe. november, 1980.: 1980.

3655. winkates, j. e. hostage rescue in hostile environments: lessons learned from the son tay, mayaguez and entebbe missions. in: y. alexander and r. a. kilmarx * (eds.), political terrorism and business, the threat and response. new york: praeger, 1979. pp. 357-427.

3656. wolf, j. b. hostage extraction: a comparative analysis of the options. gaithersburg, md.: iacp, 1980. .

3657. zartman, i. w. * (ed.). the 50 percent solution: how to bargain successfully with hijackers, striker, bosses, oil magnates, arabs, russians, and other worthy opponents in this modern world. garden city, n. y.: anchor press, 1975.

S.1.4. Protecting individuals against terrorism

3658. alexander, y. * kilmarx, r. a. * (eds.). political terrorism and business. the threat and response. new york: praeger, 1979. 345 pp.

3659. bassiouni, m. c. protection of diplomats under islamic law.: july 1980. pp. 609-633 the american journal of international law 74:3.

3660. bilek, a. j. prevention of terroristic crimes. security guidelines for business, industry and other organizations. washington d. c.: g. p. o., may 1976.

3661. burns international investigation bureau. executive protection handbook.: burns international security services, 1973.

3662. cunningham, w. c. * gross, ph. j. * (eds.). prevention of terorism: security guidelines for business and otherorganizations. mclean: hallcrest, june 1978. 98 pp.

3663. cunnliff, r. e. * mccoy, k. b. safeguards against terrorism. a handbook for u. s. military personnel and families.: air university, 1973. 52 pp.

3664. ellenberg, e. s. western democracies vs. terrorism. a study of ineffectiveness. n. p. *: 1974.

3665. grodsky, m. protection of dignitaries.: 4 oct. * 1972. pp. 1-6 international police academy review 6:4.

3666. hamer, j. protection of diplomats.: 3 oct. * 1973. pp. 759-776 editorial research reports 7.

3667. hoffmann, p. die sicherheit des diktators. muenchen: piper, 1977. 328 pp. on security precautions taken to protect hitler's life.

3668. juillard, p. les enlevements de diplomates. paris: centre national de la recherche scientifique, 1972 . pp. 205-231 annuaire francais de droitinternational. 17.

3669. leibstone, m. terror and its survival. discussions about manipulable operational conditions which have favored the political terrorist. gaithersburg, md.: iacp, 15 pp.

3670. mcguire, e. p. safeguarding executives against kidnapping and extortion. london: the conference board record, june 1974.

3671. monday, m. * profitt, j. protecting yourself from terrorism. phoenix: joseph davidson co., 1978.

3672. n. n. ——. counterforce. a monthly newsletter published by fred rayne, head of rayne international a protective agency for corporations.

3673. n. n. executive protection handbook. miami: burns international investigation bureau, 1974. 24 pp.

3674. rayne, f. executive protection and terrorism.: oct. 1975. pp. 220-225 top security 1.

3675. shaw, p. terrorism and executive protection.: 1976. pp. 8-13 assetprotection 1:4.

3676. siljander, r. p. terrorist attacks. a protective service guide for executives, bodyguards and policemen. . springfield: thomas, 1980. 328 pp.

3677. u. s. department of defence. department of the army. personnel security. precautions against acts of terrorism. washington d. c.: headquarter, dept. of the army, june 1978.

3678. u. s. department of justice. private security advisory council. prevention of terroristic crimes. boulder, colo.: paladin press, 30pp.

3679. u. s. department of justice. private security council. prevention of terroristic crimes: security guidelines for business, industry and other organizations. washington, d. c.: gpo, 1977. 29 pp.

3680. u. s. department of state. countermeasures to combat terrorism at major events. case study. washington, d. c.: 1976. 66 pp.

3681. wilson, j. v. * fuqua, p. terrorism - the executive's guide to survival. gulf publ.: nov. 1977.

S.1.5. Countermeasures against regime terrorism

3682. aleff, e. * reinter, j. * zipfel, f. * [idee, ausw. und bearb.]. terror und widerstand 1933-1945. dokumente aus deutschland und dem besetzten europa. berlin: colloquium verlag, 1966. - 234 pp.

3683. berman, h. j. the struggle of soviet jurists against a return to stalinist terror.: june 1963. pp. 314-320 slavic review 22.

3684. blankenburg, e. * (ed.). politik der inneren sicherheit. frankfurt a. m.: 1980. on anti-terrorism in the german federal republic.

3685. cowan, l. children of the resistance. the young ones who defied the naziterror. london: frewin, 1968. 191 pp.

3686. fogelson, m. r. violence as protest. new york: doubleday, 1971.

3687. foot, m. r. d. resistance. an analysis of european resistance to nazism, 1940-1945. london: eyre methuen, 1976. 346pp.

3688. hoffmann, p. problems of resistance. national socialist germany. in: wittell, f. h. and locke, h. * (eds.), the german church struggle and the holocaust.: maine state university, 1975.

3689. international commission of jurists. * swiss committee against torture. torture: how to make the international convention effective. adraft optional paper. geneva: international commission of jurists, 1980. 60 pp.

3690. mallison, s. v. * mallison jr., w. t. control of state terror through the application of the international humanitarian law of armed conflict. paper presented to the international symposium on terrorism in the contemporary world glassboro, n. j. *april 26-28, 1976. 16 pp.

S.1.6. Critiques of state countermeasures against insurgent terrorism

3691. amnesty international. report of an aid mission to northern ireland 28 november - 6 december 1977. london: amnesty international, 1978. 72 pp.

3692. bakker-schut, p. h. politieke justitie in de bondsrepubliek duitsland.: 15 febr. * 1975. pp. 203-212 nederlands juristenblad 50:7.

3693. balbus, i. d. the dialectics of legal repression: black rebels before the american criminal courts. new brunswick, n. j.: transaction books, 1976. 269 pp.

3694. berry, s. the prevention of terrorism act: legalized terror. cotton garden london: socialist workers, printers and publishers, 1977. 15 pp.

3695. blank, m. * et. al. wohin treibt der rechtsstaat?. koel: pahl rugenstein, 1977. on german anti-terrorist measures.

3696. boell, h. * wallraff, g. berichte zur gesinnungslage der nation/ bericht zur gesinnungslagedes staatsschutzes. reinbek: rowohlt, 1977.

3697. brady, b. j. * faul, d. * murray, r. british army terror. west belfast: september 1970,

3698. brueckner, p. * et. al. 1984 schon heute, oder wer hat angst vorm verfassungsschutz?. frankfurt a. m.: verlag neue kritik, 1976. 132 pp.

3699. brueckner, p. * krovoza, a. staatsfeinde. innerstaatliche feinderklaerung in der bdr. berlin: wagenbach, 1972. 115 pp.

3700. catholic commission for justice and peace in rhodesia. civil war in rhodesia. abduction, torture and death in the counterinsurgency campaign. salisbury: the commission, 1976.

3701. connell, d. u. k.: the prevention of terrorism act.: 1980. index on censorship 3.

3702. dachs, h. das "anti-terroristen-gesetz" - eine niederlage des rechtsstaates.: 1976. neue juridische wochenschrift 29:47.

3703. dupont, f. la securite contre les libertes. le modele ouest-allemand modele pour l'europe. paris: edi , 1970. 301 pp. on the growing state surveillance of citizens in the german federal republic and its implications for europe.

3704. enzensberger, h. m. * michel, k. m. folter in der brd. berlin: rotbuch verlag, 1973. kursbuch 32.

3705. faul, d. * et. al. h-block the care and welfare of prisoners in northern ireland.

3706. faul, d. * et. al. the castlereagh file. allegations of r. u. c. brutality 1976-1977.

3707. faul, d. * murray, r. * (comp.). british army and special branch ruc brutalities, dec. 1971-febr. 1972. dungannon: st. patrick's academy, 1972. 78 pp. roman catholic viewpoints on alleged brutality by royal ulster constabulary special branch 1971-1972.

3708. faul, d. * murray, r. the hooded man. british torture in ireland.: august 1971.

3709. faul, d. * murray, r. the ruc: the black and blue book. dungannon: st patrick's academy, 1975. 108 pp. roman catholic viewpoints on alleged brutality by royal ulster constabulary 1969-1975 against suspected terrorists.

3710. faul, d. * murray, r. violations of human rights. 1968-1978.

3711. faul, d. s. a. s. terrorism. dungannon: the author, 1976.

3712. fillet, h. uitsluiting van verdedigers in de bondsrepubliek duitsland. pp. 525-536 ars aequi.

3713. freund, w. s. am rande des terrors.: 1977. pp. 366-380 die dritte welt 4 west germany; effect of anti-terrorism measures on intellectual climate.

3714. frostmann, h. m. international political terrorism and the approaching emergence ofthe authoritarian state.: 1981. 146 pp.

3715. gollwitzer, h. * menne, a. les nouvelles restrictions aux libertes en allemagne de l'ouest.: march 1978. le monde diplomatique.

3716. haasbroek, n. * et. al. brochure naar aanleiding van de radioserie van nico haasbroek overde rote armee fraktion door de vpro-radio uitgezonden in 6 afleveringen van 5 augustus tot en met 23 september <1977>. hilversum: het gooi, 1977. 49 pp.

3717. hansen, k. h. gegen terror - fuer mehr demokratie. unpublished.: 1978. on german anti-terrorist legislation by spd member of parliament.

3718. heldmann, h. h. die neue ordnung unserer sicherheit oder: die gewoehnung an den polizeistaat. weinheim: , 1973. pp. 103-112 vorgaenge 12:2.

3719. hirsch, j. der sicherheitsstaat. das "modell deutschland", seine krise unddie neuen sozialen bewegungen.: eva, 186 pp.

3720. horowitz, i. l. civil liberties dangers in antiterrorist policies.: march 1977. pp. 25-32 civil liberties review.

3721. horowitz, i. l. transnational terrorism, civil liberties, and social science. in: s. m. finger and y. alexander * (eds.), terrorism:interdisciplinary perspectives. new york: john jay press, 1977. pp. 283-297.

3722. internationalen liga fuer menschenrechte(ed.) sektion w. berlin. * humanistischen union, landesverband berlin(ed.). * zabern, t. von * (eds.). dokumentation ueber die art der fahndungsmassnahmen im zusammenhang mit der lorentz-entfuehrung. berlin: 1975. 65 pp.

3723. internationales arbeiterarchiv. konterrevolution in der brd. ein handbuch zur entwicklung der inneren sicherheit. zuerich: eco-verlag, 1976. 119 pp.

3724. komitee voor de rechtsstaat * (ed.). europees verdrag tegen terrorisme. dokumentatie. amsterdam: kvdr , 1979. 63 pp.

3725. kommunistenbund. nach schleyer-sonderkommandos in der brd. zugiger ausbau der neuen gestapo. verlag arbeiterskampf: 1978. documents activities of state security organs. this book has been confiscated under p. 88a of the penal code.

3726. landelijk comite zuid-molukken. zwartboek assen, september 1977. rotterdam: ordeman, 1977. on the trial of the de punt train hijackers and a police weapon search in south moluccan communities.

3727. lehning, a. * wielek, h. * bakker-schut, p. h. duitsland: voorbeeld of waarschuwing. west-duitsland een politiestaat of de geschiedenis herhaalt zich. baarn: wereldvenster, 1976. 83 pp.

3728. lowry, d. r. draconian powers: the new british approach to pretrial detention of suspected terrorists. .: 1977. pp. 185-222 columbia human rights law review 9.

3729. lowry, d. r. ill-treatment, brutality and torture: some thoughts upon the "treatment" of irish political prisoners.: 1973. p. 553 depaul law review 22.

3730. mack, a. terrorism and the left. pp. 18-31 arena 51.

3731. mahler, h. wie westberliner staatsanwaelte den landfrieden wieder herstellen und das recht brechen. eine dokumentarische studie ueber die praktische verwirklichung des gleichheits-grundsatzes in westberlin. .

3732. mcguffin, j. internment.: april 1973. northern ireland.

3733. mcguffin, j. the guinea pigs. harmondsworth: penguin, 1974. on torture in northern ireland by the british.

3734. medisch-juridisch comite voor politieke gevangenen. * rood verzetsfront. ——. utrecht: mjc, 1977. informatie bulletin39=repressie. on european convention to fight terrorism.

3735. meulen, j. van der. anti-terrorisme wetten in de brd.: nov. 1977. pp. 54-57 wetenschap en samenleving 77:9-10 plus various other related articles, also on italy.

3736. n. n. "bommi" baumann. wie alles anfing. beslagnahmt. dokumentationueber die beschlagnahme von literatur. diskussion ueber das buch:.

3737. n. n. buback - ein nachruf. wer sich nicht wehrt, lebt verkehrt. dokumentation der auseinandersetzungen um die dokumentation "buback - ein nachruf". berlin: das politische buch, 1977.

3738. n. n. die antiterror-debatten im parlament. protokolle 1974-1978. reinbek: rowohlt, 1978.

3739. n. n. het europees verdrag ter bestrijding van het terrorisme: een kwestie van vertrouwen? bijzonder nummer van nederlands juristencomite voor de mensenrechten.: dec. 1977. 35 pp.

3740. n. n. terreur. utrecht: vredesopbouw, oct. 1977. 24 pp. on the european convention against terrorism and the dutch antiterrorist legislation(w. h. nagel) and the dutch commission nonviolent conflict resolution(h. tromp).

3741. n. n. zur verfassung unseres demokratie. reinbek: rowohlt, 1978. 92 pp.

3742. nicolas, e. * tongeren, p. van, * et. al. repressie in nederland. amsterdam: vangennep, 1980. 264 pp.

3743. o'boyle, m. torture and emergency power under the european convention on humanrights. ireland vs. the united kingdom.: oct. 1977. pp. 674-706 american journal of international law 71:4.

3744. rauch, e. the comptability of the detention of terrorists order (northern ireland) with the european convention for the protection of human rights.: 1973. p. 1 new yorkuniversity journalof international law and politics 6.

3745. rueter, c. f. een "lex baader-meinhof"?. delikt en delinkwent.

3746. ruthven, m. torture. the grand conspiracy. london: weidenfeld & nicolson, 1978. 342 pp.

3747. schlesinger, ph. on the shape and scope of counter-insurgency thought. in: g. littlejohn * et. al. * (eds.) power and the state. london: croom helm, 1978. pp. 98-127.

3748. scorer, c. * hewitt, p. the prevention of terrorism act. the case for repeal. london: national council for civil liberties, 1981.

3749. scorer, c. the prevention of terrorism's acts 1974-1976: a report on the operation of the law. london : nccl, 1976. 39pp.

3750. shackleton, e. a. a. review of the operation on the prevention of terrorism. temporary provision acts 1974 and 1976. london: hmso, 1978. 88 pp.

3751. sonnemann, u. * (ed.). der misshandelte rechtsstaat in erfahrung und urteil bundesdeutscher schriftsteller, rechtsanwaelte und richter. koeln: 1977.

3752. taylor, p. beating the terrorist? interrogation in omagh, gough and castlereagh. harmondsworth: penguin, 1980.

3753. u. s. congress, house. committee on the judiciary. hearings. fbi counterintelligence programs. 93 rd. cong. * 2nd sess. washington, d. c.: gpo, 1974. 47 pp. on cointelpro operations against "extremists".

3754. weiss, p. joe mccarthy is alive and well and living in west germany: terror and counter-terror in the federal republic.: 1976. pp. 61-88 newyork university journal of international law and politics 9.

3755. wright, s. an assessment of the new technologies of repression. in: mario hoefnagels * (ed.). repression and repressive violence. abridged. amsterdam: swets & zeitlinger, 1977. pp. 133-166.

T. SPECIAL FORMS OF TERRORISM

T.1.1. Assassination

3756. abrahamsen, d. the murdering mind. new york: harper colophon, 1973. 245 pp.

3757. agirre, j. operation ogro: the execution of admiral luis carrero blanco. new york: quadrangle, 1975. 196 pp. a journalist interviews the four eta members who killed the spanish chief of government, carrero blanco, on dec. 20, 1973. - the original edition: operacion ogro. como y por que ejecutamos a carrero blanco, was published in paris, ed. ruedo iberico, 1974.

3758. bebel, a. attentate und socialdemokratie. berlin: 1905.

3759. bell, j. b. assassin!. new york: st. martin's pres, 1979. 310 pp.

3760. bornstein, j. the politics of murder. new york: william sloine associates, 1950.

3761. bremer, a. h. an assassin's diary. new york: harpe 's magazine press, 1973.

3762. cassidy, w. l. planned political assassinations. an introductory overview. gaithersburg: i. a. c. p., 29 pp.

3763. cassidy, w. l. political kidnapping. boulder, colo.: sycamore island books, 1978. 47 pp.

3764. commission of inquiry into the conspiracy to murder mahatma gandhi. report. 6 vols. new delhi: 1970 .

3765. crotty, w. j. * (ed.). assassination and the political order. new york: harper & row, 1971. 562 pp.

3766. demaret, p. * plume, chr. target degaulle. new york: dial, 1975.

3767. donovan, r. j. the assassins. new york: harper, 1952.

3768. ellis, a. * gullo, j. murder and assassination. new york: stuart lyle, 1971.

3769. fine, s. anarchism and the assassination of mckinley.: july 1955. pp. 777-799 american historical review 60.

3770. gross, f. political assassination. in: m. livingston, et. al. * (eds.), international terrorism in the contemporary world. westport, conn.: greenwood press, 1978. pp. 307-315.

3771. havens, m. c. * et. al. assassination and terrorism: their modern dimensions. sterling swift: 1975.

3772. havens, m. c. * leiden, c. * schmitt, k. m. the politics of assassination. englewood cliffs, n. j.: prentice-hall, 1970.

3773. horowitz, i. l. assassination. harper and row: 1972.

3774. howard, d. r. political assassinations. towards an analysis of political crime.: 1977. series sss.

3775. hurwood, b. j. society and the assassin: a background book on political murder. new york: parent's magazine press, 1970.

3776. hyams, e. killing no murder: a study of assassination as a political means. london: 1970.

3777. joesten, j. de gaulle and his murders. isle of man: times press, 1964.

3778. kelly, j. b. assassination in wartime.: oct. 1965. p. 101 military law review 30.

3779. kirkham, j. f. * levy, s. * crotty, w. j. assassination and political violence. a staff report to the national commission on the causes and prevention of violence. washington, d. c.: gpo, 1969.

3780. lacasagne, a. l'assassinat du president carnot. paris lyon: 1894.

3781. laney, r. b. political assassination: the history of an idea. ann arbor: university microfilms, 1966. .

3782. lerner, m. assassination. in: encyclopedia of the social sciences. new york: 1933.

3783. levy, s. g. political assassination and the theory of reduced alternatives.: 1971. pp. 75-92 peace research society papers 17.

3784. liman, p. der politische mord im wandel der geschichte. eine historisch=psychologische studie. berlin : 1912.

3785. marshall, j. the twentieth century vehme: terror by assassination.: june 1945. pp. 421-425 blackwood's magazine 257.

3786. mcconnell, b. the history of assassination. london: frewin, 1969.

3787. mckinley, j. assassination in america. new york: harperand row, 1976.

3788. milicevic, v. der koenigsmord von marseille. bad godesberg: 1959.

3789. mindt, r. assassins and murderers: a comparison.: february 1976. pp. 2-17 monatsschrift fuer krimonologie und strafrechtsreform. 59.

3790. organization of arab students. the lost significance of shiran's case. los angeles: organization of arab students, 1969. on the murder of robert kennedy.

3791. **raper, a.** the tragedy of lynching. chapel hill: university of north carolina press, 1933.

3792. **remak, j.** sarajevo. london: 1959.

3793. **schorr, d.** the assassins.: 13 oct. * 1977. pp. 14-22 new york review of books 24:16.

3794. **sparrow, j. g.** the great assassins. new york: arco, 1969. 207 pp. sketches major assassinations in history.

3795. **trub, j. d.** how terrorists kill: the complete terrorist arsenal. boulder: paladin, 1978.

3796. **u. s. congress, senate. committee on** governmental operations for intelligenceactiviti. alleged assassination plots involving foreign leaders. an interim report. 94th. congress 1st session washington d. c.: gpo, 1975. 349 pp. 94-465 on congo, cuba, dominican republic, vietnam, chile, involvement of cia.

3797. **u. s. government. national commission on the** causes and prevention of violence. assassination and political violence. staff report new york: bantam, 1970.

3798. **whittier, ch. h.** assassination in theory and practice: a historical survey of the reli gion and philosophical background of the doctrine of tyrannicide. washington, d. c.: library of congress,congressional research service, government divi sion, specialist in humanities and religion., 12 april 1978.

3799. **wilde, h.** der politische mord. bayreuth: 1962.

3800. **wilkinson, d. y.** political assassins and status incongruence: a sociological interpretation.: 1970. pp. 400-412 british journal of sociology 21:4.

3801. **zentner, chr.** den dolch im gewande. politischer mord durch 2 jahrtausende. muenchen: suedwest verlag, 1968. 223 pp.

T.1.2. Bombing

3802. **ariel, d.** explosion!. telaviv: olive books, 1972.

3803. **bennett, r. k.** brotherhood of the bomb.: dec. 1970. pp. 102-106 reader's digest.

3804. **bomb research center.** ——. new york: 8 dec. * 1971. morning telegraph.

3805. **brodie, t. g.** bombs and bombings. a handbook to detection, disposal and investigation for police and fire departments. springfield, ill.: thomas, 1975.

3806. **fbi.** bomb summary: a comprehensive report on incidents involving explosive and incendiary devices in the nation - 1974. washington, d. c.: 1975. 32 pp.

3807. **gibson, b.** the birmingham bombs. chichester: rose, 1976. 164 pp.

3808. **harris, f.** the bomb. passos, j. dos(preface). reissue chicago: 1963. orig. new york, 1920.

3809. **ikle, f. c.** the social impact of bomb destruction. norman: university of oklahoma press, 1958.

3810. **lewald, ch. e.** fundamentals of incendiarism for raiders and saboteurs, and for planning measures. washington, d. c.: researchanalysis corporation, 1956.

3811. **macdonald, j. m.** bombers and firesetters. contrib. by r. b. shaughnessy, j. a. v. galvin. springfield, ill.: thomas, 1977.

3812. **n. n.** behind the terror bombings.: 30 march, 1970. p. 15 u. s. news & world report.

3813. **n. n.** bomb plots: warning on terror war.: 26 oct. * 1970. p. 36 u. s. news & world report.

3814. **n. n.** bomb threats.: oct. 1974. p. 21 ne-environment.

3815. **n. n.** bombing incidents - 1972.: april 1972. p. 21 fbi law enforcement bulletin.

3816. **n. n.** death comes in small parcels.: dec. 1971. p. 56 economist.

3817. **n. n.** how israelis started the terror by post. london: 24 sept. 1962. pp. 3-11 the sunday times.

3818. **n. n.** new arab terror - murder by mail.: 2 oct. * 1972. p. 31 newsweek.

3819. **n. n.** new way to war on innocents: swissair crash.: 9 march, 1970. p. 32 newsweek 75.

3820. **n. n.** terror through the mails: the bombs posted in amsterdam leave a trail that stretches back to the core of the palestine guerrilla movement. pp. 15-16 economist.

3821. **packe, m. st. j.** the bombs of orsini. london: 1957. french 19th century terrorism.

3822. **stoffel, j.** explosives and homemade bombs. springfield ill.: thomas, 1973. 324 pp.

3823. **u. s. civil aviation security service.** bomb threats against u. s. airports, 1974. washington, d. c.: u. s . department of transportation. federal aviation administration, 1975.

3824. **u. s. congress, senate. committee on the** judiciary. hearings. terroristic activity part 7: terrorist bombings and lawenforcement intelligence. 94th cong. * 1st sess. washington, d. c.: gpo, 1976.

pp. 497-605 mostly on weather underground, with many documents.

3825. u. s. department of justice. bomb summary. a comprehensive report of incidents involving explosive and incendiary- devices in the nation. washington, d. c.: 1972, fbi uniform crime reports, published annually.

3826. u. s. department of transportation. federal aviation administration. bomb threats against u. s. airports. washington, d. c.: 1974.

T.1.3. Hijacking and hostage taking

3827. aggarwala, n. political aspects of hijacking.: 1971. pp. 7-27 international conciliation 585.

3828. alix, e. k. ransom kidnapping in america, 1874-1974: the creation of a capitalcrime. carbondale: southern illinois university press, 1978.

3829. andel, w. m. van. gijzelingsdrama vraagt om politieke en principiele bezinning.: 19 oct. * 1974. nederlandse gedachten.

3830. arenberg, g. hostage. washington: american police academy, 1974.

3831. arey, j. a. the sky pirates. new york: scribner's, 1972. 418 pp. appendix a, pp. 314-414, includes inventory of skyjackings, 1930-1972.

3832. aston, c. c. governments to ransom: the emergence of political hostage-taking as a form of crisis. 1982 westport, connecticut.: greenwood press,

3833. aston, c. c. hostage-taking: an overview. in: the age of terror ed. by d. carlton and c. schaerf. london: macmillan press, 1980.

3834. aston, c. c. international law and political terrorism. forthcoming, 1982 westport, connecticut: greenwood press,

3835. aston, c. c. political hostage-taking; a statistical analysis. forthcoming: . terrorism: an international journal.

3836. atala, ch. le "hijacking" aerien ou la maitrise illicite d'aeronef hier, aujourdhui, demain. ottawa: , 1973. 119 pp.

3837. austria. federal chancellery. the events of september 28 and 29, 1973. a documentary report. vienna: , 1973. 92 pp. on the terrorist attack on a train carrying soviet jews.

3838. baccelli, g. r. pirateria aerea: realta effettiva e disciplina giuridica.: 1970. pp. 150-160 diretto aereo 9:35.

3839. baldwin, d. a. bargaining with airline hijackers. in: w. zartman * (ed.), the 50 percent solution. new york: doubleday, 1976. pp. 404-429.

3840. blacksten, r. * engler, r. hostage studies. arlington: ketron, 1974. offers theoretical models of political kidnappingsbased on game and decision-making theories.

3841. blair, e. odyssey of terror. nashville: broadman press, 1977. 316 pp. on hijacking.

3842. bolz jr., f. a. hostage confrontation and rescue. in: r. h. kupperman and d. m. trent: terrorism. stanford: hoover, 1979. pp. 393-404.

3843. bongert, y. * kellens, g. * leaute, j. * schaub, s. * grebing, g. * lafon, j. * taillanter, r. le. taking hostages. paris: neret, 1975. 84 pp.

3844. clyde, p. an anatomy of skyjacking. london: abelard shuman, 1973.

3845. clyne, p. anatomy of skyjacking. levittown, n. y.: transatlantic arts, 1973. categorizes six types of skyjackers.

3846. connolly, c. herrema. siege at monastervin. dublin: olympic press, 1977. 114 pp. on ira kidnapping of dutch industrialist.

3847. cooper, h. h. a. pacta sunt servanda: good faith negotiations with hostage takers. gaithersburg, md.: international association of chiefs of police training program, 1977.

3848. cooper, h. h. a. the hostage-takers. boulder, colo.: paladin press, 1981. 100 pp.

3849. crelinsten, r. d. * szabo, d. hostage taking. lexington mass.: lexington books, 1979. 160 pp.

3850. dimitrijevic, v. aircraft hijacking. typology and prospects for prevention.: 1971. pp. 93-102 medunarodni problemi 23:3.

3851. eisenkolb, g. das kommando "muenchen schalom". wien: molden, 1976. 316 pp. olympic games 1972 incident.

3852. elten, j. a. flugzeug entfuehrt. muenchen: goldman, 1972.

3853. evans, a. e. aerial hijacking. in: m. cherif bassiouni * (ed.). international terrorism and political crimes. springfield, ill.: charles c. thomas, 1974.

3854. fariello, a. the phenomenon of hostage-taking: the italian experience. in: r. d. crelinsten and d. szabo * (eds.): hostage-taking. lexington, mass.: lexington books, 1979. pp. 97-103.

3855. fitzgerald, b. d. the analytical foundations of extortionate terrorism.: 1978. pp. 347-362 terrorism 1.

3856. frackers, w. organizational aspects of hostage-taking prevention and control inthe netherlands. in: r. d. crelinsten and d. szabo * (eds.): hostage-taking. lexington, mass.: lexington books, 1979. pp. 105-118.

3857. french ministry of the interior. contribution a l'etude du phenomene de la prise d'otages. livre i.: ,

3858. hassel, c. v. * et. al. hostage-taking problems of prevention and control. montreal: international center for comparative criminology university of montreal, oct. 1976.

3859. hassel, c. v. the hostage situation: exploring the motivation and cause. the police chief.

3860. horvitz, j. arab terrorism and international aviation.: 1976. pp. 145-154 chitty's law journal 24 .

3861. hughes, e. terror on train 734; hostages taken by south moluccan guerrillas.: august 1976. pp. 64-69 reader's digest 109.

3862. jack, h. a. hostages, hijacking and the security council. new york: world conference on religion and peace, 1976.

3863. jacobson, p. m. from piracy on the high seas to piracy in the high skies: a study of aircraft hijacking. .: 1972. pp. 161-187 cornell international law journal 5.

3864. jenkins, b. m. * johnson, j. * ronfeldt, d. numbered lives: some statistical observations from seventy-seven international hostage episodes.: 1978. pp. 71-111 conflict 1.

3865. jenkins, b. m. hostage survival: some preliminary observations. santa monica, calif.: rand, april 1976 . 16 pp. rand paper p-5627.

3866. jenkins, b. m. hostages and their captors: friends and lovers. santa monica: rand corporation, october 1975. p-5519.

3867. kupperman, r. h. * wilcox, r. h. * smith, h. a. crisis management: some opportunities. in: r. h. kupperman and d. m. trent * (eds.), terrorism. stanford: hoover, 1979. pp. 224-243.

3868. kwok, m. l. * peterson, r. e. political kidnapping: 1968-1973.: 1974. journal of contemporary revolutions 6.

3869. landes, w. m. an economic study of the u. s. aircraft hijacking, 1961-1976.: april 1978. pp. 1-32 journal of law and economics 21.

3870. marks, j. m. hijacked. nashville: t. nelson, 1973. 167 pp.

3871. mcclure, b. hostage survival. in: m. livingston * et. al. * * (eds.), international terrorism in the contemporary world. westport, conn.: greenwood press, 1978. pp. 276-281.

3872. meyer, a. internationale luftfahrtabkommen. band iv: luftpiraterie -begriff, tatbestaende, bekaempfung. . koeln: carl heymanns verlag, 1972. 245pp.

3873. miller, a. h. negotiations for hostages: implications from the police experience.: 1978. pp. 125-146 terrorism. 1.

3874. miller, a. h. swat(special weapons and tactics) - the practical link in hostage negotiations. in: y. alexander and r. a. kilmarx * (eds.), political terrorism and business : the threat and response. new york: praeger , 1979. pp. 331-356.

3875. miron, m. s. * goldstein, a. p. hostage. kalamazoo: behaviordelia, 1978. 190 pp.

3876. montreuil, j. la prise d'otages.: jan. 1974. pp. 15-25 revue internationale de criminologie et de police technique 27:1.

3877. n. n. a practical guide to hostage survival. in: hostage situations: tactics and countermeasures. gaithersburg, md.: research division, technical research unit, internationalassocia of chiefs of police, pp. 9-14.

3878. n. n. extortion.: 1975. asset protection 1 entire issue.

3879. n. n. hostage-negotiation response. gaithersburg, md.: professional standards division of the international association of chiefs of police, 1976. training key number 235.

3880. n. n. patient sieges: dealing with hostage-takers.: 1976. pp. 21-27 assets protection 1.

3881. n. n. preliminary research on hostage situations.: march 1977. pp. 73-77 law and order 25:3.

3882. new york state special commission. official report. on attica. new york: bantam books, 1972. on sept. 1971 hostage taking incident in a new york prison.

3883. office of aviation medicine. master list of all hijacking attempts, worldwide, air carrier, andgeneral aviation. washington, d. c.: department of transportation, federal aviation administration(14(updated periodically ,

3884. oren, u. ninety-nine days in damascus: the story of professor shlomo samueloff and the hijack of twa flight 840 to damascus. london: weidenfeld and nicolson, 1970.

3885. pepper, c. b. kidnapped! seventeen days of terror. new york: harmony, 1978. 150 pp. on a 1977 kidnapping, milan, italy.

3886. phillips, d. skyjack. the story of air piracy. london: harrap, 1973.

3887. reitsma, o. * labeur, c. de gijzeling. honderd uren machtloze kracht. amsterdam: bonaventura, 1974. 160 pp. sept. 13, 1974 japanese red army action against french embassy in amsterdam.

3888. rich, e. flying scared: why we are being skyjacked and how to put a stop toit. new york: stein and day, 1972.

3889. salewski, w. luftpiraterie: verlauf, verhalten, hintergruende. muenchen: 1975.

3890. samuels, j. m. hostage situations. gaithersburg, md.: iacp, 18 pp.

3891. samuels, j. m. kidnap/hostage negotiation and parallel actions. in: hostage situations: tactics and countermeasures. gaithersburg, md.: research division, technical research unit. international associa- tion of chiefs of police., pp. 1-8.

3892. shepard, i. m. air piracy: the role of the international federation of airline pilots associations.: , 1970. pp. 79-91 cornell international law journal 3.

3893. simon, d. w. * rhone, r. s. * perillo, m. simulation of the seizure of heads of state. mimeographed madison, n. j.: drew university department of political science, january 1977.

3894. sloan, s. * kearney, r. * wise, ch. learning about terrorism: analysis, simulations, and future direc-tions.: 1978. pp. 315-329 terrorism 1.

3895. sloan, s. * kearney, r. an analysis ·of a simulated terrorist incident.: june 1977. pp. 57-59 police chief 44.

3896. snow, p. * phillips, d. leila's hijack war. london: pan, 1970.

3897. snow, p. * phillips, d. the arab hijack war. new york: ballantine, 1970. 176 pp. concentrates on the sept. 1970 dawson field incident and the jordanian civil war triggered off by it. - also published as: leila's hijack war. london, pan books, 1971.

3898. souchon, h. hostage-taking: its evolution and significance.: june 1976. pp. 168-173 international criminal police review no. 299.

3899. stech, f. j. terrorism and threat communication. mimeographed. bethesda: analytic support center, 31 may 1978.

3900. stephen, j. e. going south: air piracy and unlawful interference with air commerce.: 1970. pp. 433-443 international lawyer 4.

3901. stewart, m. j. hostage episodes. 1973-1977: chronology. unpubl. text.

3902. sundberg, j. w. f. lawful and unlawful seizure of aircraft.: 1978. pp. 423-440 terrorism 1.

3903. turi, r. t. * et al. descriptive study of aircraft hijacking. huntsville, texas: institute of contemporary corrections and the behavioral sciences, 1972. 171 pp.

3904. u. s. congress, house. committee on interstate and foreign commerce. aviation safety and aircraft piracy. washington, d. c.: gpo, 1970. 488 pp.

3905. u. s. congress, senate. committee on finance. skyjacking. hearing. 91st cong. * 2nd sess. * 6 oct, 1970 washington, d. c.: gpo, 1970. 26 pp.

3906. u. s. department of state. background documentation relating to the assassinations of ambassador cleo a. noel, jr. and george curtis moore. washington, d. c.: u. s. department of state, 1973.

3907. u. s. department of transportation. federal aviation administration. domestic and foreign aircraft hijackings, as of july 1, 1976. washington, d. c.: faa, 1976. 61 pp. updated version of jan 1, 1977, 63 pp.

3908. u. s. department of transportation. federal aviation administration. hijacking statistics. u. s. registered airport, 1961 - april 1975. washington, d. c.: faa, 1975. 18 pp.

3909. u. s. department of transportation. hijackings: selected readings. washington, d. c.: library services division, july 1971.

3910. whelton, ch. skyjack. new york: tower publication, 1970.

T.1.4. Kidnapping

3911. alves, m. m. kidnapped diplomats: greek tragedy on a latin stage.: 1970. pp. 311-314 commonweal 92 .

3912. arnau, f. menschenraub alexander p. katjepow, berthold jacob, jesusde galindez, ben bella, adolf eichmann, antoine argoud, mehdi ben barka, moise tschombe, komponist isang yun und andere. muenchen: 1968. 232 pp.

3913. baumann, c. e. the diplomatic kidnappings: a revolutionary tactic of urban terrorism. the hague: martinus nijhoff, 1973. 182 pp. 22 cases of diplomatic kidnappings from the period 1968-1971 are discussed.

3914. bewegung 2 juni, 1975. die entfuehrung aus unserer sicht. n. p. on kidnapping of peter lorenz.

3915. clutterbuck, r. l. kidnapping.: oct. 1974. pp. 529-534 army quarterly 104.

3916. cox, r. v. deadly pursuit. harrisburg, pa.: cameronhouse, 1977.

3917. fawcett, j. e. s. kidnappings versus government protection.: 1970. pp. 359-362.

3918. geyer, g. a. the blood of guatemala. the nation on kidnapping of archbishop mario casariego.

3919. hamilton, l. c. political kidnapping. unpubl. paper boulder: university of colorado, 1976.

3920. hunt, d. on the spot. london: peter davies, 1975. british ambassador to brazil on diplonappers.

3921. international association of chiefs of police. political kidnappings. gaithersburg, md.: iacp, 31 pp.

3922. jenkins, b. m. terrorism and kidnapping.: june 1974. 10pp.

3923. mangham, w. d. kidnapping for political ends.: 1971. seaford house papers.

3924. melo, a. l. le inviolabilidad diplomatica y el caso del embajador von spreti.: 1970. pp. 147-156 revista de derecho internacionaly ciencias diplomaticas 19:37-38.

3925. messick, h. * goldblatt, b. kidnapping: the illustrated history. new york: dial, 1974. 206 pp. journalistic treatment of major kidnappings.

3926. middendorff, w. menschenraub, flugzeug-entfuehrungen, geiselnahme, kidnapping historische und moderne erscheinungsformen. bielefeld: gieseking, 1972. 62 pp.

3927. miller, g. kidnapped at chowchilla. plainfield, n. j.: logos international, 1977. 181 pp.

3928. miller, g. 83 hours till dawn. garden city, n. y.: doubleday, 1971.

3929. n. n. kidnapping incidents.: dec. 1967. pp 24-33 bulletin of the international commission of jurists.

3930. najmuddin, d. kidnapping of diplomatic personnel.: febr. 1973. pp. 18, 20, 22, 23 police chief 40 :2.

3931. navarro olmedo, f. el secuestro de 60 milliones de dolares. el golpe maestro de los "montoneros" victoria guerrillera en argentina. mexico, d. f.: editorial posada, 1976. 151 pp. on the kidnapping of jorge and juan born, 19 sept. * 1974 in argentina.

3932. o'mara, r. new terror in latin america: snatching the diplomats.: 1970. pp. 518-519 nation 210:17 .

3933. rose, r. n. new developments in the taking of hostages and kidnapping - a summary. washington, d. c.: law inforcement assistance administration, national criminal justice reference service., 1975. 9 pp.

3934. sponsler, t. h. international kidnapping.: jan. 1971. pp. 25-52 international lawyer 5.

3935. stechel, i. terrorist kidnapping of diplomatic personnel.: 1972. pp. 189-217 cornell international law journal 5.

3936. u. s. congress, house. committee on internal security. political kidnappings, 1968-1973. 93rd cong. * 1st sess. * 1 aug. * 1973. washington, d. c.: gpo, 1973. 54 pp.

3937. vayrynen, r. some aspects of theory and strategy of kidnapping.: 1971. pp. 3-21 instant research on peace and violence 1:1.

3938. vidal, d. wave of abductions in columbia creates climate of insecurity.: 26 june, 1978. p. a-6 new york times.

3939. williams, d. a. bus-nappers; chowchilla, calif. * kidnapping.: 2 aug. * 1976. pp. 29-30 newsweek.

3940. wohlstetter, r. kidnapping to win friends and influence people.: 1974. pp. 1-40 survey 20:4.

T.1.5. Nuclear terrorism

3941. alexander, y. * ebinger, ch. political terrorism and energy. the threat and response. new york: 1982.

3942. bass, g. * jenkins, b. m. * keller, k. * reinstedt, r. motivations, capabilities and possible actions of potential criminal adversaries of u. s. nuclear programs. santa monica, cal.: rand, 1982.

3943. beres, l. r. apocalypse. chicago: university of chicagopress, 1980.

3944. beres, l. r. international terrorism and world order: the nuclear threat.: 1977. pp. 131-146 stanford journal of international studies 12.

3945. beres, l. r. terrorism and global security: the nuclear threat. boulder: westview, 1979. 225 pp.

3946. beres, l. r. terrorism and nuclear threat in middle-east.: jan. 1976. pp. 27-29 current history 70 :412.

3947. beres, l. r. the nuclear threat of terrorism.: 1976. pp. 53-66 international journal of group tensions 6:1-2.

3948. beres, l. r. the threat of palestinian nuclear terrorism in the middle east.: 1976. pp. 48-56 international problems 15.

3949. berkowitz, b. j. * et. al. superviolence: the civil threat of mass destruction weapons. santa barbara: adcon corporation, 1972.

3950. billington, g. r. nuclear terrorism. maxwell air force base, ala.: air warcollege, air university, 1975. 46 pp.

3951. blair, b. g. * brewer, g. d. the terrorist threat to world nuclear programs. pp. 379-403 the journal of conflict resolution 21:3.

3952. blair, b. g. a proposal for analyzing the terrorist threat to u. s. nuclear programs. unpublished manuscript: yale university, 1976.

3953. brenan, g. the spanish labyrinth. an account of the social and political background of the civil war. . cambridge: 1943.

3954. buchanan, j. r. * (ed.). safeguards against the theft or diversion of nuclear materials. pp. 513-619 nuclear safety 15.

3955. burkowitz, b. * et. al. superviolence: the civil threat of mass destruction weapons. santa barbara: adcon corporation, sept. 1972.

3956. burnham, s. the threat to licensed nuclear facilities. mclean, va.: mitre corporation, mitre technical report mtr- 7022 authorized distribution only.

3957. california office of emergency services. nuclear blackmail or nuclear threat. emergency response plan. . sacramento, cal.: california office of emergency services, 1976. 40 pp.

3958. chester, c. v. estimates of threats to the public from terrorist acts against nuclear facilities.: november 1976. pp. 659-665 nuclear safety 17.

3959. cohen, b. l. potentialities of terrorism.: june 1976. pp. 34-35 bulletin of the atomic scientists 32:6.

3960. coleman, j. p. international safeguards against non-government nuclear theft:a study of legal inadequacies.: 1976. pp. 493-513 international lawyer 10.

3961. comey, d. d. perfect trojan horse; threat of nuclear terrorism.: june 1976. pp. 33-34 bulletin of the atomic scientists 32:6.

3962. crenshaw, m. defining future threat: terrorists and nuclear proliferation. paper: . 26 pp. delivered to the conference on international terrorism: national, regional, and global ramifications, organized by the ralph bunche institute andcity university of new york, june 1976.

3963. denike, l. d. radioactive malevolence.: february 1974. pp. 16-20 science and public affairs.

3964. douglas, j. h. the great nuclear power debate.

3965. dunn, l. a. * bracken, p. * smernoff, b. j. routes to nuclear weapons: aspects of purchase or theft. croton-on- hudson, n. y.: hudson institute, april 1977.

3966. flood, m. * white, r. g. nuclear prospects. 1976: . pamphlet on possibilities of nuclear terrorism in the united kingdom.

3967. flood, m. nuclear sabotage.: october, 1976. pp. 29-36 bulletin of the atomic scientists 22.

3968. frank, f. nuclear terrorism and the escalation of international conflict.: 1976. pp. 12-27 naval war college review xxix.

3969. jenkins, b. m. * krofcheck, j. the potential nuclear non-state adversary. report prepared for the congress ofthe u. s.: office of technology assessment, may 1977.

3970. jenkins, b. m. * rubin, a. p. new vulnerabilities and the aquisition of new weapons by nongovernment groups. in: a. e. evans and j. f. murphy * (eds.), legal aspects of international terrorism. washington, d. c.: american society of international law, 1977.

3971. jenkins, b. m. new vulnerabilities and the acquisition of new weapons by non-govern- mental groups. ups.)paper presented at the 1976 conference on international terrorisme, u. s. department of state, at washington, d. c.

3972. jenkins, b. m. nuclear terrorism and its consequences.: july 1980. pp. 5-16 society.

3973. jenkins, b. m. terrorism and the nuclear safeguards issue. santa monica: rand, jan. 1975. rand paper p -5339.

3974. jenkins, b. m. the consequences of nuclear terrorism. santa monica: rand, 1979.

3975. jenkins, b. m. the impact of nuclear terrorism. santa monica: the rand corporation,

3976. jenkins, b. m. the potential for nuclear terrorism. santa monica: rand, may 1977. 9 pp. rand paper p- 5876.

3977. jungk, r. de atoomstaat. amsterdam: elsevier, 1978. 176 pp.

3978. karber, ph. a. * et al. draft working paper b: analysis of the terrorist threat to the commercial nuclear industry: summary of findings. vienna, va.: bdm corporation, 1975. bdm/w-15-176-tr.

3979. karber, ph. a. * et. al. draft working paper c: analysis of the terrorist threat to the commercial nuclear industry: supporting appendices. vienna, va.: bdm corporation, 1975. bdm/w-75-176-tr.

3980. karber, ph. a. * mengel, r. w. * greisman, h. c. * newman, g. s. * novotny, e. j. s. * whitley, a. g. analysis of the terrorist threat to the commercial nuclear industry. report submitted to the special safeguards study, nuclear regulatory commission, in response to contract no. at(49-24)-0131. vienna, va. 414 pp. bdm/75-176-tr.

3981. karber, ph. a. * mengel, r. w. * novotny, e. j. s. a behavioral analysis of the terrorist threat to nuclear installations. unpublished manuscript prepared for the u. s. atomic energy commission: sandia laboratories, july 1974.

3982. kinderman, e. m. * et. al. the unconventional nuclear threat. stanford: stanford research institute, menlo park, 1969.

3983. kinderman, e. m. plutonium: home made bombs?. in: u. s. senate committee on government operations, peaceful nuclear exports and weapons proliferation. paper presented to the conference on nuclear public information, information3, organized by the atomicindustrial forum, march 5-8, 1972. washington, d. c.: government printing office, 1975. pp. 25-26.

3984. krieger, d. m. nuclear power: a trojan horse for terrorists. in: b. jasani * (ed.), nuclear proliferation problems. cambridge: mit press for the stockholm international peace research institute., 1974. pp. 187-200.

3985. krieger, d. m. terrorists and nuclear technology: the danger is great; the question is not whether the worst will happen, but where and how.: june 1975. pp. 28-34 bulletin of the atomic scientists 31:6.

3986. krieger, d. m. what happens if. ? terrorists, revolutionaries, and nuclear weapons.: 1977. pp. 44-57 the annals of the american academy of political and social science. 430.

3987. kuipers, m. nucleair terrorisme. unpubl. paper groningen: polemologisch instituut, 28 pp.

3988. kupperman, r. h. * et. al. mass destruction terrorism study. washington, d. c.: acda, classified report by the u. s. arms control and disarmament agency for the cabinet committee to combat terrorism and the national security council staff.

3989. kupperman, r. h. nuclear terrorism: armchair pastime or genuine threat?.: 1978. pp. 19-26 jerusalem journal of international relations 3.

3990. leon, p. de * jenkins, b. * keller, k. * krofcheck, j. attributes of potential criminal adversaries to u. s. nuclear programs. santa monica, calif.: rand corporation, february 1978. r-2223- sl reprinted in: u. s. congress, senate, committee on governmental affairs. an actto combat international terrorism, hearings beforethe committee on s. 2236. 95th cong. * 2d sess. * 1978, 555-639.

3991. lovins, a. b. * lovins, l. h. energy policies for resilience and national security. 1982.

3992. mabry jr., r. c. nuclear theft: real and imagined dangers. master's thesis,: march 1976. 144 pp. the study investigates the availability of fissionable material, vulnerable portions of the nuclear fuel cycles, weapon construction, and the regulations regarding the protection of fissionable material.

3993. matson, e. k. terrorists armed with nuclear weapons. maxwell air force base, ala.: may 1976.

3994. mcphee, j. the curve of binding energy. new york: farrar, straus and giroux, 1974. 170 pp.

3995. meguire, p. g. * kramer, j. j. psychological deterrents to nuclear theft: a preliminary literature review and bibliography. gaithersburg: national bureau of standards, march 1976. nbsir 76-1007.

3996. mengel, r. * et. al. analysis of the terrorist threat to the commercial nuclear industry. vienna, va.: the bdm corporation, 1975.

3997. mengel, r. w. terrorism and new technologies of destruction: an overview of the potential risk. report prepared for the national advisory committee task force on disorder and terrorism. vienna, va.: bdm corporation, 25 may 1976. w-76-044-tr.

3998. mengel, r. w. the impact of nuclear terrorism on the military's role in society. in: m. livingston * et. al. * (eds.), international terrorism in the contem porary world. westport, conn.: greenwood press, 1978. pp. 402-414.

3999. meyer, w. * loyalka, s. k. * nelson, w. e. * williams, r. w. the homemade nuclear bomb syndrome.: july 1977. nuclear safety.

4000. mullen, r. k. mass destruction and terrorism.: 1978. pp. 63-89 journal of international affairs. 32.

4001. mullen, r. k. the international clandestine nuclear threat. santa barbara: mission research corporation, june 1975.

4002. n. n. austria seeks atom guerrilla.: 23 april, 1974. p. a-18 washington post.

4003. n. n. nuclear theft and terrorism. discussion group report. in: sixteenth strategy for peace conference report. muscatine, iowa: stanley foundation, october 1975. pp. 33-40.

4004. n. n. the threat of nuclear terrorism in the middle east.: jan. 1976. 15 pp. currenthistory 70:412.

4005. norman, 1. on nuclear weapon sites; next target of terrorists?.: june 1977. pp. 28-31 army 27.

4006. norton, a. r. * greenberg, m. h. * (eds.). studies in nuclear terrorism. boston: g. k. hall & co., 1979. .

4007. norton, a. r. terrorists, atoms and the future: understanding the threat.: may 1979. pp. 30-50 naval war college review.

4008. norton, a. r. understanding the nuclear terrorism problem. gaithersburg, md.: international association of chiefs of police, 1979.

4009. phillips, j. a. * michaelis, d. mushroom: the story of the a-bomb kid. new york: morrow, 1978. 287 pp. .

4010. phillips, j. a. the fundamentals of atomic bomb design. an assessment of the problems and possibilities confronting a terrorist group or non-nuclear nationsattempting to design a crude pu-239 fission bomb. junior thesis: princeton university, 1976.

4011. ponte, l. who is arming the new terrorists?.: april 1977. pp. 34-124 playgirl.

4012. rosenbaum, d. m. nuclear terror.: 1977. pp. 140-161 international security 1 reprinted in j. d. elliott and l. k. gibson*(eds.), contemporary terrorism : selected readings pp. 129-147. (gaithersburg: international association of chiefs of police, 1978).

4013. salmore, b. * simon, d. nuclear terrorism in perspective.: july 1980. pp. 21-23 society.

4014. schelling, th. c. who will have the bomb.: 1976. p . 77-91 international security i.

4015. scott, d. terrorism: the nuclear threat. washington d. c.: citizens energy project, 1981.

4016. shapley, d. plutonium: reactor proliferation threatens a nuclear black market.: 9 april 1971. pp. 143-146 science.

4017. taylor, th. b. * vancleave, w. r. * kinderman, e. m. preliminary survey of non-national nuclear threats. . stanford: stanford research institute, technical note ssc-tn-520 -83.

4018. u. s. congress, senate. committee on banking, housing, and urban affairs. exports of nuclear materials and technology. washington, d. c.: gpo,

4019. u. s. congress, senate. committee on government operations. peaceful nuclear exports and weapons proliferation: a compendium. washington, d. c.: gpo, 1975.

4020. watson jr., f. m. terrorists and the homemade 'a'bomb. gaithersburg, md.: iacp, 23 pp.

4021. willrich, m. * taylor, th. b. nuclear theft: risks and safeguards. cambridge, mass.: ballinger press, 1974. 252 pp.

4022. wohlstetter, r. terror on a grand scale.: may 1976. pp. 98-104 survival 18.

4023. woods, g. d. the possible criminal use of atomic or biological materials.: june 1975. pp. 113-123 australian and new zealand journal of criminology 8:2.

4024. zofka, z. denkbare motive und moegliche aktionsformen eines nuklear terrorismus. essen: auge, 1981. 107 pp. 'thinkable motives and possible forms of action of nuclear terrorism'.

4025. baron, d. p. the increasing vulnerability of computers to terrorist attack. london: foreign affairs research institute, 1978. 10pp.

4026. clark, r. c. technological terrorism. new york: devin- adair co., 1978.

4027. cobler, s. die gefahr geht von den menschen aus. der vorverlegte staatsschutz. berlin: 1976.

4028. hurwood, b. j. torture through the ages. paperback library: 1969.

4029. kupperman, r. h. * et. al. the near-term potential for serious acts of terrorism. washington, d. c.: acda, april 1976. classified report by the u. s. arms control and disarmament agency for the cabinet committee to combat terrorism and the national security councilstaff.

4030. lea, h. ch. a history of the inquisition of spain. new york: 1906.

4031. lea, h. ch. a history of the inquisition of the middle ages. new york: 1906.

4032. leibstone, m. corporation terror. violence and the business community. gaithersburg, md.: iacp, 21 pp.

4033. n. n. social prophylaxis as a form of terror. in: carl friedrich * (ed.), totalitarianism. new york: grosset & dunlap, 1963.

4034. newhouser, c. r. mail bombs. gaithersburg, md.: iacp, 32 pp.

4035. scott, g. r. history of torture. london: sphere books, 1971. 328 pp. 1st ed. 1967.

4036. shue, h. torture.: 1978. pp. 124-143 philosophy and public affairs 7:2.

4037. stephens, m. m. the oil and natural gas industries: a potential target of terrorists. in: r. h. kupperman and d. m. trent * (eds.), terrorism. stanford: hoover, 1979. pp. 200-223.

4038. trub, j. d. how terrorists kill: the complete terrorist arsonal. boulder, colo.: paladin press, 1978. .

4039. verin, j. torture and hostage-taking. new york: unitednations social defense research institute, 1971 . 8 pp.

T.1.6. Other forms of terrorism

U. VARIA AND RELATED STUDIES

4040. alcock, n. * quittner, j. the prediction of civil violence to the year 2001. unpubl. manuscript. ontario: canadian peace research institute, 1977.

4041. astorg, b. d. introduction au monde de la terreur. paris: editions du seuil, 1945.

4042. ben–dak, d. * (ed.). the future of collective violence. societ. al. and international perspectives. lund: studentlitteratur, 1974. 251 pp.

4043. berger, a. a. television as an instrument of terror. essays on media, popular culture and everyday life. . new brunswick, n. j.: transaction books, 1980. 214 pp.

4044. brown, l. a. diffusion patterns and location. a conceptual framework and bibliography. philadelphia: regional science research institute, 1968.

4045. buckley jr., w. f. dance of the terrorists. national review.: 1974. 26 on u. n. debate on terrorism .

4046. chapman, r. * chapman, m. l. the crimson web of terror. boulder, colo.: paladin press, 160 pp. by cia veteran.

4047. curle, a. mystics and militants. a study of awareness, identity and social action. london: tavistock, 1972.

4048. dimitrijevic, v. medjunarodni terorizam.: 1980. pp. 23-44 arhiv za pravne i drustvene nauke.

4049. dimitrijevic, v. sta je medjunarodni terorizam.: 1979. pp. 55-67 jugoslovenska revija za medjunarodno pravo.

4050. dimitrijevic, v. terorizam u unutrasnoj i medjunarodnoj politici. beograd: radnicka stampa.: 1981. 220 pp.

4051. eayrs, j. diplomacy and its discontents. toronto: university of toronto press, 1971.

4052. eckhardt, w. * koehler, g. structural and armed violence in the 20th century. magnitudes and trends. : 1980. pp. 347-375 international interactions 6:4.

4053. ellsburg, d. the theory and practice of blackmail. in: o. young, bargaining. urbana, ill.: university of illinois press, 1975.

4054. gusfield, j. r. mass society and extremist politics.: 1962. pp. 19-30 american social review 32.

4055. hamilton, c. m. p. terrorism. its ethical implications for the future.: dec. 1977. the futurist 11:6 .

4056. hamilton, m. p. terrorism: its ethical implications for the future.: dec. 1977. pp. 351-354 futurist 11.

4057. holmes, r. l. violence and non-violence. in: j. a. shaffer * (ed.), violence: award-winning essayes in the council for philosophical studies competition. new york: david mckay, 1971.

4058. hunter, e. l. huurmoordenaar carlos. de gevreesde terroristenleider. amsterdam: teleboek, 1976.

4059. israel, g. ou mene le terrorisme?.: 1968. les nouveauxchiers 13/14.

4060. kamp, a. * quittner, j. cycles foresee the future of international violence. unpubl. manuschript. ontario: canadian peace research institute, 1977.

4061. karagueuzian, d. blow it up!. boston: gambit, 1971.

4062. kwitny, j. the terrorists: thriving black market puts military weapons into amateurs' hands; small arms abound; legal export shipments can-and do go away.: 11 jan. 1977. wallstreet journal 189 :1.

4063. laqueur, w. diversities of violence and the current world system. in: civil violence and the international system. london,the international institute for strategic studies, 1971, adelphi papers 82-83. pp. 9-16.

4064. levitt, e. e. the psychology of anxiety. indianapolis: bobbs-merrill, 1967.

4065. lewis, f. the anatomy of terror.: 18 nov. 1956. p. 67 new york times.

4066. martin, j. politics of terror.: 1971. pp. 95-103 partisan review 38:1.

4067. mekden, f. r. von der. comparative political violence. englewoodcliffs, nj: prentice hall, 1973.

4068. melman, b. the terrorist in fiction.: july 1980. journalof contemporary history 15:3.

4069. morton, m. j. the terrors of ideological politics. cleveland: the press of case western reserve university, 1972.

4070. n. n. 't kan anders. amsterdam: . 't kan anders 2:6 -7 transcript of a symposium held in june 1979 by a workgroup for ecology, pacifism and socialism.

4071. n. n. getting away with murder.: 4 nov. 1972. pp. 15-16 economist.

4072. n. n. pvda en terrorisme. pp. 156-169 socialismeen democratie 30:3 reactions by p. j. kapteyn, a. van der leeuw, relus ter beek on alfred mozer: de gedesintegreerde internationale (socialisme en democratie 29:10, pp. 454-456. oct. 1972). with a reply by alfred mozer.

4073. n. n. terror und terrorismus.: 1976. tribune 15: 57.

4074. n. n. terrorist acts against united nations missions.: 1971. p. 61 united nationschronicle 8.

4075. n. n. when tradition comes to the aid of terrorism.: 17 march 1973. p. 23 economist.

4076. novotny, e. j. s. * karber, ph. a. organized terror and politics. in: american political science association. short essays in political science. washington, d. c.: 1973.

4077. o'brien, c. c. liberty and terrorism.: 1977. pp. 56-67 international security 2.

4078. reenen, p. van. overheidsgeweld. een sociologische studie van de dynamiek van het geweldsmonopolie. alphen a. d. rijn: samson, 1979.

4079. roeling, b. v. a. * et. al. politiek geweld. utrecht: vredesopbouw, 1978. 112 pp. 7 articles on different aspects of violence based on lectures given in fall 1977 at the rijksuniversiteit utrecht.

4080. russett, b. m. who are the terrorists?.: july 1980. p. 16 society.

4081. schelling, th. c. arms and influence. new haven: yale university press, 1966. discusses 'coercive bargaining' which is relevant in the context of terrorism.

4082. schwarz, u. die angst in der politik. dusseldorf-wien: 1967. 244 pp.

4083. simp, h. r. terror.: 1970. pp. 64-69 u. s. naval institute proceedings 96.

4084. strauss, h. revolutionary types.: 1973. p. 307 journal of conflict resolution 14.

4085. taylor, ch. l. * hudson, m. c. world handbook of political and social indicators. 2nd ed. new haven: yale university press, 1972.

4086. taylor, e. the terrorists.: 1973. pp. 58-64 horizon.

4087. troch, e. vier miljard gijzelaars. wereldpolitiek 1945 tot heden. antwerpen: standaard, 1977. 338 pp. .

4088. vestdijk, s. het wezen van de angst. amsterdam: de bezige bij, 1979. 700pp. the a.

4089. wallace, m. d. * varseveld, g. van. violence as a technique of social change. toward emperical measurement. paper presented at the annual meeting of the canadian research and education association.: university of manitoba, june 1970.

4090. wimmer, e. antimonopolistische demokratie und sozialismus. wien: globus verlag, 1974. 66 pp. pp. 49-56: uber denterrorismus.

4091. young, o. bargaining. urbana, ill.: university of illinois press, 1975.

---

barker, d., 2213.
barker, e., 1956.
barker, r., 1184.
barnett, d., 1693.
barnett, m., 2729.
baron, d.p., 4025.
barrie, g.n., 2622.
barritt, d.f., 913.
barron, j., 386. 387.
barrue, j., 2214.
barry, t.b., 914.
bartholomew, a.a., 2457.
bartoldi., 2215.
barton, a.h., 2328.
bartsch, g., 706.
basker, d., 1336.
bass, g., 3942.
bassiouni, m.c., 186. 1337. 1341. 2623. 2624.
  2730. 3469. 3470. 3659.
bastiaans, j., 2329. 2330. 2331. 2332. 2333.
bastos, r.r 1877.
batalov, e.j., 3006.
batigne, j., 2334.
batselier, s.de, 2416.
baudouin l.r., 1753.
baudouin, j.l., 2476. 3471.
bauer, e.f., 2625.
bauer, y., 1359.
baumann, c.e., 187. 3913.
baumann, m., 2883.
bauss, g., 707.
baxter, r.r., 82.
bayce, d.g., 915.
baylay, d.h., 1555.
bayo, a., 2523.
bayssade, p., 1648.
bazalgette, c., 2731.
beall,(marshall) d., 3626.
beasley, p.s., 916.
beaton, l., 1904.
beaufre, a., 2524.
beaumont, r.a., 3373.
bebel, a., 3758.
bechelloni, g., 2732. 2733.
becker, h., 2884.
becker, j., 708.
becker, l.g., 3199.
becker, p., 388.
beckett, j.c., 917.
begeleidings-commissie   voorbereiding   projekt
  sociaal-kultureel werk., 1185.
begin, m., 1360. 2216.
bejar, h., 1878.
bekes, i., 3472.
belack, c.n., 1408.
belcher, j., 1941.
bell, g., 918.
bell, j.b., 83. 170. 188. 189. 919. 920. 921.
  922. 923. 924. 1044. 1361. 1409. 1410. 1411. 1649.
  2073. 2074. 2217. 2218. 2219. 2734. 3007. 3200. 3759.
bell, m., 2864.
bell, r.g., 3201.
belloni, a., 1803.
beloff, m., 190.
belz, m., 2335.
bemmelen, j.m.van, 2626.
ben amon, s., 1412.
ben rafael, e., 3202.
ben-dak, d., 4042.

ben-dor, g., 1413. 1414.
ben-porat, y., 3442. 3627.
benewick, r., 191.
bennet jr., w.t., 3473.
bennett, j.p., 3628.
bennett, r.k., 192. 3803.
bennett, r.l., 925. 3474.
bennett, w.t., 3475. 3476.
benthem van den bergh, g.van, 2885.
beraud, b., 1623.
beres, l.r., 2075. 3943. 3944. 3945. 3946.   3947.
  3948.
bergedorfer gespraechskreis., 2886.
berger, a.a., 4043.
berger, p.l., 84. 565.
bergeron, l., 1905.
bergier, j., 2076.
bergquist, m., 2077.
beristain, a., 2477.
berki, r.n., 3008.
berkman, a., 2220. 3009. 3010.
berkowitz, b.j., 3949.
berkowitz, l., 2336. 2735. 2887.
berman, h.j., 3683.
berman, j.j., 389.
berner, w., 3011.
bernstein, l., 1278.
berry, s., 3694.
bertelsen, j.s., 566.
bertini, b., 1045.
bettelheim, b., 2337.
bewegung 2 juni, 1975., 3914.
bianchi, h., 2478.
bicudo, h., 390.
biedma, f., 1833.
bigney, r.e., 2525.
bijlsma, j., 2363.
bik, r.g.c., 3477.
bilek, a.j., 3660.
billington, g.r., 3950.
billstein, h., 3203.
bin der, s., 709.
binder, s., 3203.
biocca, e., 391.
bishop jr., j.w., 3204.
bishop, v.f., 436. 1415.
bite, v., 193.
black, c.e., 3012.
black, r.j., 2526.
blackburn, r., 1754.
blackey, r., 3.
blacksten, r., 3840.
blackstock, n., 392.
blackstock, p.w., 4.
blair, b.g., 3951. 3952.
blair, e., 3841.
blanco munoz, a., 1879.
blank, m., 3695.
blankenburg, e., 3684.
blaufarb, d.s., 2527.
blechmann, b.m., 3374.
blei, h., 710.
blishchenko, i.p., 3478.
bloch, h.a., 2338.
block, s., 393.
blok, a., 676. 2888.
bloomfield, l.m., 2627.
bluhm, h.o., 2339.
blum, r., 642.

falk, c., 2235.
falk, r.a., 2651. 2652.
fall, b.b., 1597. 1598.
fallaci, o., 2236.
fallah, s.m., 21.
faller, e.w., 2653.
fanon, f., 1661. 1662. 3050.
faraone, r., 1844.
farhi, d., 238.
fariello, a., 3854.
farrel, m., 955.
farren, m., 1956.
fattah, e.a., 100.
fatu, m., 1325.
faul, d., 3208. 3697. 3705. 3706. 3707. 3708. 3709. 3710. 3711.
favrod, c.h., 1663.
fawcett, j.e.s., 3917.
fbi academy., 22. 23. 24.
fbi., 1957. 1958. 1959. 3806.
fearey, r.a., 239. 2101.
federn, e., 419.
feierabend, i.k., 240. 2905. 2906.
feierabend, r.l., 240. 2905. 2906.
feld, e., 1728.
feldmand, j.j., 2850.
felgas, h.a.e., 1729.
feller, s.z., 2654.
felsenfeld, l., 25.
fenello, m.j., 3388.
fenwick, c.g., 2655.
fenyvesi, ch., 2353.
feraud, h.j., 3499.
ferguson, y.h., 615.
ferrarotti, f., 1065. 2907.
ferreira, j.c., 1818.
fest, j.c., 420.
fetscher, i., 732. 733.
fichter, t., 734.
field, w.s., 2908.
fields, r.m., 421. 2354. 2355. 2423.
figley, ch.r., 2356.
figner, v., 1290. 2237.
fillet, h., 3521. 3712.
findley, t., 2027.
fine, s., 3769.
finer, s.e., 101.
finger, s.m., 181.
fini, m., 1066. 1067.
fiorillo, e., 1068.
firestone, j.m., 2909.
firth, c.e., 1248.
fisher, e.m., 1337. 1341.
fisher, j., 3183.
fishman, g., 2488.
fishman, w.j., 241.
fisk, r., 956. 957. 3235.
fitzgerald, b.d., 3855.
fitzgerald, g.f., 2627. 2656. 3500. 3501.
fitzgibbon, c., 958. 959.
five sisters., 1291.
flamigni, s., 3236.
flanigan, w.h., 2910.
fleming, m., 2761. 3051.
fletcher-cooke, c., 689.
flood, m., 3966. 3967.
flores castro altomirano, e., 2657.
fly, c.l., 2357.
fogel, l.j., 3237.

fogelman, e., 2910.
fogelson, m.r., 3686.
foley, ch., 1528. 1529. 1530. 2238.
foner, p.s., 1960.
foot, m.r.d., 3687.
footman, d., 581.
forman, j., 1961.
forster, a., 582.
forster, r., 2911.
fortin, j., 2476. 3471.
fortuny, j.m., 661.
foster, j., 1962.
frackers, w., 3856.
frame, w.v., 422.
francis, r., 2762. 2763.
francis, s.t., 1764. 1963. 2102. 2103.
franck, th.m., 2764. 3502.
francke, h., 2658.
francos, a., 1435.
franda, m., 1589.
frangor, g.d., 523.
franjieh, s., 1436.
frank, f., 3968.
frank, g., 1367. 1368. 1369.
frank, j.a., 1155. 1911.
frank, r.s., 2912.
frank, t.m., 3503.
franzius, e., 1531.
fraser, c.a., 3389.
frazier, h., 423.
freed, d., 424.
freedman, l.z., 2424.
freeman, l., 3651.
french ministry of the interior., 3857.
freund, m., 3052.
freund, w.s., 3713.
frey, p., 1156.
freymond, j., 583.
friedlander, r.a., 242. 243. 2104. 2105. 2659. 2765. 2913. 2914. 3238. 3504. 3505. 3506.
friedmann, w., 584.
friedrich, c.j., 425. 426. 427. 3053. 3054.
friestad, d.e., 3239.
frignano, g., 3055.
fromkin, d., 585.
fromm-reichmann, f., 2358.
fromm, e., 2425.
frostmann, h.m., 3714.
fuchs, n.l., 2605.
fuentes mohr, s.a., 2359.
funke, m., 11. 428. 735. 736.
fuqua, p., 3681.
fuqua, p.q., 3240.
furmanski, l.s., 960.
gaay fortman, w.f.de, 3241.
gablonski, e., 2544.
gagel, w., 2915.
galeano, e., 429.
gall, n., 430. 431.
gall, s.n., 2239.
gallasch, p.f., 2766.
gallet, m., 244.
galli, g., 1069. 1070.
gallois, p., 2489.
galtung, j., 102. 2916.
galula, d., 3390.
galyean, t.e., 2660.
gambescia, p., 1119.
gamson, w.a., 586. 2767.

macbride, s., 2269.
macdonald, j.m., 2456. 3811.
mack, a., 1426. 3730.
madison, a., 667.
madruga, l., 1854.
maerker, r., 1272.
maestre alfonso, j., 479.
magner, j.w., 231.
magowan, v., 947. 948.
maher, g.f., 3640. 3641.
mahler, h., 771. 772. 773. 774. 775. 776. 777. 3731.
mahoney, h.t., 3280.
maier, f.x., 1713.
maihofer, w., 3281.
maisonneuve, h., 682.
maitron, j., 892. 893. 894.
majdalany, f., 1714.
malawer, s.s., 2681.
malik, s., 2682.
mallin, j., 613. 614. 1603. 2569. 2570. 3108.
mallison jr., w.t., 2683. 3532. 3533. 3690.
mallison, s.v., 2683. 3532. 3533. 3690.
malmborg, k.e., 3534.
manchel, f., 2807.
mandel, e., 3109.
mangham, w.d., 3923.
manhattan, a., 984.
manheim, j.b., 37.
mankiewicz, r.h., 3535.
mann, c., 2623.
manoranjan, m., 1571.
mansback, r.w., 615.
manusama, j.a., 1210.
manzer, r., 1917.
manzini, g., 2270.
mao tse-tung., 2571. 2572. 2573.
marcellin, r., 895.
marcuse, h., 2684. 3110. 3111. 3188.
mardor, m., 1381.
marenssin, e., 778. 779.
mariel, p., 1084.
marien, m.h., 1211. 1212.
marighella, c., 1820. 2574. 3112.
marine, g., 2000.
mark, c.f., 1474.
mark, r., 2808. 2809. 3418.
markides, k., 1540.
markoff, j., 903.
marks, j., 480.
marks, j.m., 3870.
marks, l., 1243.
marotti, l.h., 2889.
mars, p., 135.
marshall, j., 3785.
martic, m., 3113.
martigoni, g., 1085.
martin, d., 481.
martin, f.y., 993.
martin, j., 4066.
martin, j.j., 2001.
martinelli, a., 2002.
martines, l., 1086.
martinez anzorena, g., 1855.
martinez codo, e., 1788.
marucci, e., 1133.
maschke, g., 3114.
maser, w., 2271.
masotti, l.h., 2003.

massu, j., 1677.
matekolo, i., 1475. 2004. 2138.
materne, y., 482.
mathews, a.s., 1736.
mathiez, a., 896. 2272.
mathu, m., 616.
matson, e.k., 3993.
mattelart, a., 2810.
mattelart, m., 2810.
matz, u., 3115.
maul, h., 3536.
maullin, r., 1895.
maulnier, t., 483.
maura, r., 1163.
maurer, m., 2005.
max, a., 1789. 1856.
maximoff, g., 484.
may, r.r., 2948.
may, w.g., 298.
mayans, e., 1857.
mayer-tasch, p.c., 2685.
mazlish, b., 2273.
mccamant, j.f., 136. 1762.
mccann, e., 2811.
mccartney, j., 2006.
mcclung, l.a., 985.
mcclure, b., 299. 3282. 3642. 3643. 3871.
mcconnell, b., 3786.
mccoy, k.b., 3663.
mcdaniel, j.f., 1299.
mcdonald, l., 1790.
mcdonald, l.p., 2007. 2008.
mcdowell, ch.p., 3419.
mcfee, t., 986.
mcguffin, j., 3732. 3733.
mcguire, e.p., 3670.
mcguire, m., 2274.
mchale, v., 1087.
mckeithen-smith, r.l., 3537.
mckeown, m., 987.
mckinley, j., 3787.
mckinsey, l.s., 1918.
mcknight, g., 2275.
mclellan, v., 2009.
mcmahon, j.p., 3538.
mcnamara, ch.b., 897.
mcphee, j., 3994.
mcwhinney, e.w., 2686. 2687. 2688.
mcwilliams, w.c., 3116.
mea, l.della, 1140.
meaker, g.h., 1164.
mealing, e.t., 988.
meden, v., 300.
medina ruiz, f., 1896.
medisch-juridisch comite politieke gevangenen., 485. 3734.
mednick, s.a., 2498.
medvedev, r.a., 486.
medzini, r., 2139.
meeuwisse, e.th.f., 2812.
megargee, e.i., 2949.
meguire, p.g., 3995.
mehden, f.r.von der, 2950. 4067.
mehnert, k., 2951.
meinhof, u., 780. 781. 782.
melady, m., 487.
melady, t., 487.

salmore, b., 4013.
salomon, e.von, 840.
salomone, f., 2838.
salvemini, g., 521.
salvi, s., 696.
samuels, a., 3586.
samuels, j.m., 3890. 3891.
sanders, e., 2042.
sanford, n., 2969.
sarhan, a., 156.
sarkesian, s.c., 3157.
sarmiento, r.a., 1872.
sartre, j.p., 522. 1129. 3158.
sasho henshu committee., 1636.
sassano, m., 1109.
sater, w., 2299.
saur, k.-o., 2839.
savinkov, b., 1309. 1310.
savoie, c., 1262.
saxon, k., 3159.
sayegh, a., 1502.
sayigh, r., 1503.
saywell, j.t., 1928.
sburlati, c., 1329.
schack, h., 3160.
schaefer, g., 841.
schaerf, c., 209. 2081.
schaf, f., 4.
schafer, s., 2506.
schamis, g., 2596.
schang, g., 2043. 2840.
scharff, w.h., 2465. 2474.
schaub, s., 3843.
scheerer, s., 2507.
schelling, th.c., 4014. 4081.
schelsky, h., 842.
schenkel, j.f., 54.
scherer, j.l., 338.
schickel, j., 3161.
schiff, z., 1504. 3442. 3627.
schlesinger, ph., 2841. 2842. 2843. 2844. 3747.
schloesing, e., 3587.
schlossberg, h., 3651.
schlotter, j., 3257. 3285.
schlottman, r.s., 2465. 2474.
schmid, a.p., 57. 157. 158. 1237. 2845. 2846.
schmidt, d.a., 1354.
schmidt, h., 3319.
schmiedling, w., 1311.
schmitt, c., 2597.
schmitt, d., 1025.
schmitt, h.th., 3211.
schmitt, k.m., 292. 3772.
schneider, p., 2847.
schonborn, k., 3443.
schornhorst, f.th., 2707.
schorr, d., 3793.
schreiber, j., 2598.
schroers, r., 2970.
schubert, a., 843.
schultz d.o., 2302.
schultz, d.p., 2404.
schultz, e., 2848.
schultz, r., 1615.
schutter, b.de, 3320.
schuyt, c.j.m., 159.
schwab, p., 523.
schwartz, d.a., 2849.
schwarz, h., 3321.

schwarz, j.e., 1263.
schwarz, u., 4082.
schwarzenberger, g., 2708.
schwind, h.d., 2971.
schwinge, e., 844.
schwinghammer, t., 2507.
scianna, f., 1130.
sciascia, l., 1131. 1132.
scobie, w.i., 1528.
scorer, c., 3748. 3749.
scott, a.m., 2599.
scott, d., 4015.
scott, g.r., 4035.
scott, m., 1026.
scott, s., 2302.
scott, w., 902.
seale, b., 2044.
sebastian, r.j., 2405.
sederberg, p.c., 160. 672. 2045.
sedition committee., 1581.
segal, j., 2406.
segal, z., 2406.
segre, d., 2972.
seidl-hohenveldern, i., 2709.
seiffert, j.e., 1637.
selva, g., 1133.
selzer, m., 339.
selznick, p., 524.
sen, n., 1582.
sernicoli, e., 1134.
servier, j., 340.
sewell, a.f., 2466.
seymour, w.n., 1616.
shackleton, e.a.a., 3750.
shaffer, h.b., 341.
shanab, r.e.a., 596.
shapiro, g., 903.
shapley, d., 4016.
sharabi, h., 1505.
shaw, e.d., 3322.
shaw, j., 342.
shaw, p., 3675.
shaw, p.d., 3323.
shearer, i.a., 3588.
sheatsley, p.b., 2850.
shepard, i.m., 3892.
shepard, w.f., 904.
sherman, j., 58.
sherman, r., 1720.
shigenobu, f., 3162.
shipley, p., 1264.
shoham, s.g., 2498.
short jr., j.f., 343.
short, a., 1617.
short, j.f., 2973.
short, k., 2600.
shriver, r., 3414.
shubber, s., 2710. 2711.
shue, h., 4036.
shuja, s.m., 1618.
shulman, a.k., 3163.
shultz jr., r.h., 2170. 3324. 3327.
shultz, r., 344. 1619.
shy, j.w., 636.
siahaya, t., 1238.
sichtermann, b., 717.
siegal, a., 2851.
silber, i., 3164.
silbersky, l., 2303.

2190. 2191. 2192. 2193. 3342. 3653. 3824.

u.s.congress, senate. committee on the judiciary. subcommittee on criminal law and procedures., 2315.

u.s.department of defence. department of the army 3677.

u.s.department of justice., 64. 65. 3825.

u.s.department of justice. law enforcement assistance administration., 66. 67.

u.s.department of justice. private security advisory council., 3678.

u.s.department of justice. private security council., 3679.

u.s.department of state., 2194. 2195. 2196. 3603. 3604. 3605. 3680. 3906.

u.s.department of state. bureau of public affairs. office of media services., 3343.

u.s.department of state. library., 68.

u.s.department of state. office to combat terrorism., 2197.

u.s.department of transportation., 71. 3909.

u.s.department of transportation. federal aviation administration., 69. 70. 3344. 3826. 3907. 3908.

u.s.government. agency for international development. mission in vietnam., 1621.

u.s.government. national commission on the causes and prevention of violence., 3797.

u.s.national advisory committee on criminal justice standards and goals., 358.

u.s.national commission on the causes and prevention of violence., 2060.

u.s.national governors' association., 2061.

u.s.office of strategic services. research and analysis branch., 549.

u.s.office of the u.s.chief of counsel for the prosecution of axis criminality., 550.

u.s.private security advisory council., 3345.

uilenbroek, h., 2867.

ulam, a.b., 1319.

united nations., 72. 73. 1400. 2715. 3346. 3347. 3606. 3607. 3608. 3609. 3610. 3611. 3612. 3613. 3614. 3615. 3616. 3617.

united nations.fifth congress on prevention of crime and the treatment of offenders., 2517.

united nations, general assembly., 2980.

united nations, general assembly. ad hoc committee on international terrorism., 2198. 2199.

united nations, secretariat., 74.

university of iowa. institute of public affairs., 3348.

uschner, m., 1800.

utrecht, e., 1239.

vabres, h.d.de, 3618.

vaders, g., 2411.

vajpeyi, j.n., 1585.

valat-morio, p., 211.

valentini, c., 1056.

vallaud, p., 1547.

vallieres, p., 1932. 1933.

valsalice, l., 1901.

van voris, w.h., 2412.

vancleave, w.r., 4017.

varenne, h., 909.

varseveld, g.van, 4089.

vasilijeric, v.a., 2716.

vasilyev, a.t., 3452.

vayrynen, r., 3937.

veen, th.w.van, 647. 648.

vega, j.de 1858.

venohr, w., 699.

venter, a.j., 1748. 1749.

venturi, f., 2981.

verburg, j.j.i., 1225.

verhegge, g., 649.

verin, j., 4039.

verwey-jonker, h., 1240.

vestdijk, s., 4088.

vestermark, s.d., 2062.

viano, e., 2348.

vidal, d., 3938.

vidman, n., 2857.

vieille, p., 551.

villemarest, p.f.de, 359.

vinke, h., 3349.

vizetelly, e.a., 3180.

vocke, h., 1548.

volck, h., 853.

volk, s.s., 1320.

volker, b., 854.

vorwerck, e., 1873.

vos, h.m., 3350.

voss, r.von, 2995.

vucinic, m., 2717.

waciorski, j., 166.

wagenlehne, g., 855.

wagoner, f.e., 1723.

wahl, j., 3351.

wainstein, e., 3268.

waldmann, p., 167. 1179. 1817. 3181.

wales, g.e., 1691.

walker, j., 2868.

walker, w., 2200.

wallace, a.f.c., 2413.

wallace, m., 37. 202. 360. 1974.

wallace, m.d., 4089.

wallon, h., 910.

wallraff, g., 3696.

walsh, r., 552. 2864.

walter, e.v., 168. 169. 361. 553.

walter, g., 911.

walter, h., 2609.

walton, p., 2063. 2515.

walzer, m., 170. 650. 2982.

warth, h., 1801.

wassermann, r., 856. 857.

wassmund, h., 2983. 3182.

waterman, d.a., 3352.

waterworth, p., 1033.

watson jr., f.m., 3353. 4020.

watson sr., f.m., 2869.

watson, f.m., 75. 362. 3650.

waugh, w.j., 3354.

waxman, c.i., 1424.

weatlake, m., 642.

wechsler, h., 2361.

wedge, b., 1830.

weed, s., 2414.

wegener, u., 2605.

wehr, p., 554.

weil, c., 555.

weil, h.m., 2984.

weinberg, l., 1146.

weiner, m., 1586.

weiner, ph.p., 3183.

weinstein, e.a., 2472.

weinstein, m.a., 3061.

weis, p., 3619.

weisband, e., 2764.

weisl, w.von, 2610.

B I B L I O G R A P H Y: TABLE OF CONTENTS